LAND POLICIES OF UPPER CANADA

CANADIAN STUDIES IN HISTORY AND GOVERNMENT

A series of studies edited by Goldwin French, sponsored by the Social Science Research Council of Canada, and published with financial assistance from the Canada Council.

1. *Church and State in Canada West, 1841-1867.* By John S. Moir

2. *The French Shore Problem in Newfoundland: An Imperial Study.* By Frederic F. Thompson

3. *The Alignment of Political Groups in Canada, 1841-1867.* By Paul G. Cornell

4. *The Private Member of Parliament and the Formation of Public Policy: A New Zealand Case Study.* By Robert N. Kelson

5. *The San Juan Water Boundary Question.* By James O. McCabe

6. *The Mark of Honour.* By Hazel C. Mathews

7. *The Political History of Newfoundland, 1832-1864.* By Gertrude E. Gunn

8. *The Clergy Reserves of Upper Canada: A Canadian Mortmain.* By Alan Wilson

9. *Land Policies of Upper Canada.* By Lillian F. Gates

LAND POLICIES OF UPPER CANADA

by

Lillian F. Gates

UNIVERSITY OF TORONTO PRESS

To the memory of
my brother, Reginald,
and
my father, Edward Cowdell

PREFACE

"WHEN A MAN SITS DOWN to write a history," wrote the author of *Tristram Shandy,* "... he knows no more than his heels what lets and confounded hindrances he is to meet with in his way—or what a dance he may be led, by one excursion or another before all is over." That has been my experience in writing this book. It was my intention to give an account of the land policies of both Upper Canada and Lower Canada to 1841, but I soon found it advisable to confine myself to the upper province. By 1955 this study had been completed to 1841 and was submitted as a doctoral dissertation at that point. Since so many questions relating to the land policies of Upper Canada were in an indeterminate state at that date, it seemed unwise to stop here. It was some time before I decided that it would be possible to revise what had been written and to complete the Upper Canada part of the story without writing the Lower Canada part also. It has been my intention to relate the land policies of the province as closely as possible to its political history but it has not proved possible to discuss certain topics adequately without sacrificing a chronological arrangement of the material. There are certain "excursions"—into Indian lands, mineral lands, and timber lands —that I would like to have taken but this study had become so lengthy and had taken so much time that I was obliged to forego them.

It is with gratitude and affection that I recall the kindly guidance of Professor Frederick Merk of Harvard University, under whom the first part of this study was done. I have to thank Professor Edward Fox of Cornell for his expert advice on maps and Mr. Richard E. Rosenbaum for his skill in drawing them. Part of chapter four appeared as an article in the *Canadian Historical Review* in 1957 and I have to thank the University of Toronto Press for permission to use this material here. From the staffs of all the libraries and archives I have received much appreciated assistance, but I must make especial acknowledgment of the unfailingly courteous and efficient help given me by the staff of the Provincial Archives of Ontario and of the long continued favours allowed a mere faculty wife by the libraries of Cornell University. To the editors of this series, and to Mr. Donald G. Smith of the University of Toronto Press, my sincere thanks for numerous helpful suggestions. And finally I must state that the many conversations I have had with my husband Paul W. Gates on the subject of land policy have at times discouraged and exasperated me but also informed and inspired me. On his intellectual—and financial—resources I have made heavy drafts, and I acknowledge them with pride and gratitude.

New York

Ithaca

LILLIAN F. GATES

CONTENTS

PREFACE   vii

1. Great Britain's Plans for Canada   3

2. The Loyalists and the Crown Lands   11

3. Simcoe's Five-Year Plan   24

4. The Troubles of Peter Russell   39

5. Two Avaricious Administrators   62

6. Sir Francis Gore and the Radicals   75

7. The Surplus Poor in Upper Canada   85

8. Robert Gourlay and the Alien Question   98

9. Settlement Duties and U.E.L. "Rights"   123

10. Taxing the Speculators   142

11. The Failure of the Land-Granting System   152

12. The Crown Reserves and the Crown Revenues   160

13. Difficulties in the Middle of the Road   176

14. The Land Act of 1837   186

15. The Clergy Reserves   196

16. Lord Durham's Report and Its Aftermath   221

17. The Clergy Reserves Again   240

18. Debris and Debate under the Union   256

19. School Lands and Scrip   270

20. Settlers, Squatters, and Lumbermen   284

21. Conclusion   303

APPENDIX   309

NOTES   311

BIBLIOGRAPHY   355

INDEX   367

LAND POLICIES OF UPPER CANADA

GREAT BRITAIN'S PLANS FOR CANADA

THE TREATY OF PARIS of 1763, which left Great Britain in possession of Canada, left her also with the problem of fitting this and other newly acquired territories into an Imperial mercantilist structure. For four years, pamphlet warfare had been waged over Canada's prospective value to the Empire. Controversy still continues with respect to the motives of the British ministers in keeping the country. Did they really want the French colony on the St. Lawrence for itself, and did they intend to colonize it with British settlers?

"It is not flattering to modern Canadian susceptibilities to reflect that the whole of New France was weighed in the balance against the little French sugar island of Guadeloupe," wrote Chester Martin.[1] Apart from Pitt's bit of rhetoric, however, the question did not pose itself in this simple fashion to the ministers of George III; the fisheries were more important to Great Britain than both these territories. What Pitt, in December, 1760, considered returning in place of Guadeloupe and Goree was Canada north of the lakes, without Cape Breton and the present New Brunswick, minus the fisheries, stripped of much that made her valuable to the French, and confined within boundaries that would give the thirteen colonies protection.[2] By June, 1761, when negotiations with France had begun, the Cabinet had decided to retain all Canada, including Cape Breton, and to restore Guadeloupe and Belle-Isle in return for Minorca.[3] At that time, its members were debating not the Canada-Guadeloupe question but whether or not France should be permitted to retain a share in the Newfoundland fishery. After the victories of 1762, the Cabinet was sharply divided over the question of returning Guadeloupe, but the fate of Canada was regarded as settled.[4] As for the pamphlets, particularly the first one, *A letter addressed to Two great men*,[5] was it not the opening shot in a sham battle? Its anonymous author seemed more anxious that Guadeloupe be returned to France than that Canada be retained by Great Britain. One is tempted to conclude that the Canada-Guadeloupe controversy was originally raised to ensure the return of that unwanted sugar island to France and that the British ministry, though divided over Guadeloupe and the fisheries, never had any intention of relinquishing Canada once its conquest was complete.[6]

Great Britain, then, really wanted Canada. Why did she want it? Was it, as W. S. Wallace has suggested, merely to prevent others from making use of it,[7] or did she intend to colonize the province with British settlers, holding out to them the promise of a liberal land policy, an assembly, and the laws of England? The Board of Trade, in its report of June 8, 1763, considered the chief advantages for Great Britain to be the fishery of the Gulf and River St. Lawrence, from which British subjects had hitherto been excluded, and the fur trade.[8] Chester Martin has stated: "Among all the conquests of the Seven Years' War Canada was placed first among the 'Places where planting and perpetual Settlement and Cultivation ought to be encouraged. . . .'" [9] But Canada was merely named first, not placed first in the Board's report. It discussed the commercial advantages to be derived from the settlement and cultivation of other new acquisitions but said nothing about those to be derived from *settling* Canada.

Henry Ellis, whose "Hints Relative to the Division and Government of the Conquered and Newly Acquired Territories in America" was sent to the Board by Lord Egremont, Secretary of State for the Southern Department, suggested dividing Canada into two governments [10] and setting limits to the westward movement of the population of the thirteen colonies by a proclamation line. He thought that, as they increased in numbers, the people "would emigrate to Nova Scotia or to the provinces on the Southern Frontier. . . ." [11] Evidently, Canada was not expected to attract them. The Board approved of the idea of an Indian reserve but did not favour the division of Canada. Its Secretary, John Pownall, pointed out that such a scheme, in addition to being expensive, was "founded upon a supposed intention of settlement and jurisdiction as far as the Great Lakes, and does therefore militate against the general principles upon which all our system is founded." [12] British policy was to encourage seaboard colonies, not inland colonies that could not afford to purchase British manufactures. The Board did propose that the emigration of British and Protestant settlers to the former French colony on the St. Lawrence be encouraged as much as possible, although it acknowledged that the province would remain predominantly French for a "very long period of time." Egremont took no notice of this suggestion; he merely inquired by what methods the new governments in general could best be peopled.[13] In reply, the Board suggested issuing an immediate proclamation forbidding settlement in the Indian country (where Pontiac's uprising had by this time occurred) and encouraging settlement in East and West Florida and Nova Scotia. It did not mention Canada.[14]

Was this omission inadvertent or intentional, showing that Egremont and the Board of Trade had not yet agreed on the policy to be adopted with respect to Canada? They had already disagreed twice: on the division of the province and on placing the Indian country under the civil jurisdiction of the Governor of Canada.[15] Whatever the explanation of the omission, when the Proclamation of 1763 was actually issued, Canada was included among the new acquisitions to which its provisions were to apply.

Subsequently, the Board prepared a report which shows only a perfunctory interest in the settlement of Quebec. At its suggestion a notice was published in the *London Gazette* of November 22, 1763, that townships of 20,000 acres would be granted in East and West Florida to those who would undertake to settle them, within a limited time and at their own expense, with Protestant settlers from foreign countries or from other British colonies. Grenada was similarly advertised, although Nova Scotia was not, probably because it was not one of the "new" governments and also because there were already before the Board numerous requests for townships in Nova Scotia. "And as to your Majesty's government of Quebec," wrote the Board, "which has already upwards of eighty-thousand inhabitants, it does not appear to us to be particularly necessary to make any other provision for its further settlement, or to offer any other encouragement for the present than what are contained in the draft of the instructions." [16] Paragraph 45-52 of these instructions, containing the terms on which land was to be granted, were published by Governor Murray as directed on March 7, 1765, in the form of a proclamation which was circulated in the thirteen colonies. His proclamation did not, however, make any mention of an Assembly.[17] It may fairly be concluded, therefore, that the Canada of 1763 was not valued as an area for settlement, that "a large influx of population from the congested colonies to the south" [18] was not expected, and that the President of the Board of Trade, Lord Hillsborough, was disinclined to push the settlement of the province.

C. W. Alvord has argued that a "mistake was made when there was included in the proclamation the announcement of the boundaries of the province of Quebec with its eighty thousand French Canadians. By this inclusion, all those alluring promises to new settlers [an assembly and the laws of England] were put in force in the northern province." [19] No mistake was made. If the boundaries of Canada had not been included, the limits of the Indian country would have been very incompletely defined. Had the proclamation been completed while Shelburne still presided at the Board, the boundaries would certainly have been included because the report of his board of June 8 said, "the Limits of such Territory will be sufficiently ascertained by the Bounds to be given to the Governors of Canada and Florida . . ." and had discussed reducing the boundaries of Canada at some length.[20]

No mistake was made either when the Secretary of State, the Earl of Halifax, caused the Board of Trade to add to the proclamation the form of government which all the new colonies were to enjoy. Alvord has maintained that an assembly was impracticable because in Quebec there was only a handful of Protestants and therefore that province could never have been intended to have one. His opponents have contended that an assembly was deliberately promised to Quebec as one of the inducements to new settlers and proved impracticable only because the expected Protestant immigration did not occur.[21] There are good reasons for rejecting both these explanations. It seems clear that Halifax and Hillsborough fully intended the French and Catholic population not only of Quebec but also of Grenada to enjoy representative government.[22] Unfortunately, in both cases, the governors' commissions, which were copied from those usually given to colonial governors, required them to see that all members of the Assembly subscribed the Test, and it was here, as Hillsborough later admitted, and as C. S. Higham has pointed out,[23] that the "mistake" was made.

When the Board of Trade first reported on the form of government for the new colonies, it proposed government by a governor and council for them all.[24] Halifax, who had learned from his previous experience with Nova Scotia that infant settlements would not long be content under the rule of a governor and council,[25] disagreed and proposed that the proclamation make known the form of government to be established for the present and that intended for the future. The Board fell in with this suggestion, remarking that an open and public

promise that the new colonies should have assemblies would be an encouragement to settlers. Before writing this reply of October 4, the Board first reconsidered its report of June 8 in which it had clearly recognized that in Quebec
the number of French inhabitants "must greatly exceed, for a very long period
of time, that of Your Majesty's British and other Subjects who may attempt
Settlements. . . ." [26] With this consideration freshly in mind, the Board could
never have intended the constitutional settlement of Quebec to be dependent on
incoming British settlers. Furthermore, as has been shown, the Board was not
interested in promoting British settlement to that province as it ought to have
been if an assembly could not be established without it. Finally, we have Hillsborough's own statement of 1769, when he again presided at the Board of Trade,
and when that body was considering the difficulties which had arisen in Quebc
for lack of a "complete legislature" empowered to impose taxes:

The having a complete Legislature competent to those regulations, which a Colony under such
Circumstances necessarily require, appears to have been one of the first Objects; and there can
be no doubt, but that His Majesty's Commission and Proclamation in the provision they make
for this purpose, had in view to extend to his Majesty's new Subjects those Privileges, which
exist in the principles of a British Constitution. But the exercise and operation of this Legislative Power . . . [was] rendered impracticable by inserting in the Commission, without sufficiently adverting to the State of the Colony the restriction, that no person should sit in the
Assembly, who had not subscribed the Test. . . . [27]

Between 1765 and 1768 Hillsborough's successors at the Board of Trade had
made two unsuccessful attempts to secure for Canada the promised Assembly
but, limited by the wording of the Governor's commission as they pointed out,
it was a Protestant Assembly they then had in mind.[28] In July, 1769, when Hillsborough once more presided at the Board,[29] it produced its famous report which
stated emphatically that the proclamation had been intended to confer the
benefits of the British constitution upon the new subjects. He now urged that
an assembly be established in Canada in which Roman Catholics should have
thirteen seats out of the twenty-seven, and that the Catholic members be required to be seigneurs. Owing to Carleton's influence, the whole scheme was
rejected and Canada failed to receive an assembly of any kind until 1791.[30]

Sufficient has been said to make it plain that in 1763 the British government
had no expectation of colonizing Quebec rapidly with British settlers and that
the promise of an assembly was intended as much for the new French subjects
as for old subjects who might come to settle. The Proclamation of 1763 was
designed primarily to divert the swarming inhabitants of the thirteen colonies
from the Indian country to other areas for settlement, and to assure them that
representative institutions would be established and grants of land on liberal
terms would be made in the new territories. Canada was included in the document by design, not by accident, and its Governor received the same instructions
concerning land grants as the governors of Nova Scotia and East and West
Florida, areas in which the Board of Trade took a much more lively interest.

Paragraphs 45-59 of Murray's instructions of 1763 [31] were the first pronounce-
ments on land policy for the province of Quebec, and they remained in force
until 1771. The New England system of township planting was approved because it made possible mutual assistance and mutual protection. The townships
were to be 20,000 acres in size and were to contain reserves for military purposes

and for the growth of naval timber. A townsite was to be laid out with building lots and pasture lots for each family and lots for the church, minister, and schoolmaster. Compact little villages enjoying religious and educational advantages and surrounded by agricultural land and woodland—not lonely farmsteads—were what the framers of these regulations had in mind.

In order to prevent speculators from holding large tracts of land unimproved, grants were restricted to those who were in a position to cultivate them and the quantity was limited to 100 acres for each petitioner plus 50 for every member of his household, black or white. Additional land, not exceeding 1,000 acres, could be obtained if the applicant were able to cultivate it and pay, cash down, 5 s. for every 50 acres so granted. Detailed settlement duties were required and provision was made for registering proof that they had been performed. Unfortunately the filing of proof was not required before patent and, indeed, was not obligatory at all unless the grantee wished to apply for a second grant on the same terms as the first. All grants became subject to an annual quit rent of 2 s. per 100 acres after two years. These land regulations were first drawn up for Florida and were applied to Quebec with a few additions suggested by the reports of Murray, Gage, and Burton. They contain nothing really new, being practically the same as those laid down for Carolina and Georgia in 1755. Some of them had also been applied earlier to New York and New Hampshire.[32]

The Proclamation of 1763 had made known the rewards in land which were to be made to reduced officers of the army and navy and to disbanded men of the British forces who had served in North America during the Seven Years' War and were resident there. Five thousand acres were promised to field officers, 200 to non-commissioned officers, and 50 to privates.[33] These grants were to be exempt from quit rents for ten years but otherwise they were subject to all the foregoing regulations.

No great changes were expected to occur in the composition of the population of Canada immediately after it became British, and none did. Murray's proclamation making known the terms on which settlers could obtain land attracted those interested in the whale and cod fisheries to the shores of the Bay of Chaleur and the Peninsula of Gaspé—districts which both Murray and the home government were anxious to settle with British subjects,[34] but it did not bring settlers to the new colony. Some 100,000 acres were granted in England by order-in-council, chiefly to persons engaged in the fishing industry. The limitations and restrictions which were supposed to bind Murray were completely disregarded in these grants but other conditions respecting the raising of hemp, payment of quit rents, and the adequate settlement of the grants were imposed. Some town lots in Quebec were petitioned for and granted, but no action was taken on petitions from discharged soldiers for land at Chateaugay, nor on a number of petitions for land at the Bay of Chaleur.

The French Canadians do not seem to have been attracted by the terms of Murray's land proclamation, and the system of township planting so successfully used by this people later failed to appeal to them at this time. Maseres quotes a French Canadian as referring to the "high rates" at which land was granted before 1771,[35] and Murray found that the seigneurs would lease their lands for less than the Crown demanded.[36] Yet the quit rent of 2 s. per 100 acres amounted to only one-quarter of a penny an acre—less than was exacted in most seigneurial contracts.[37] Perhaps the explanation of the failure of the French Canadians to apply for lands is that which Carleton gave: the unfamiliar tenure. Perhaps it is simply that there was still plenty of room in the old seigneuries for the expanding population.

In 1771 the detailed land regulations were cancelled *in toto* and replaced by a single paragraph which directed that lands be granted in fief and seigneury, as before the conquest.[38] Various explanations of this *volte face* have been given,[39] but the most likely explanation seems to be that which A. L. Burt has emphasized—Carleton wished to restore the feudal system in Canada as a means of keeping the colony under control through its seigneurs, who would be bound to the Crown by the ties of self-interest.[40]

Shortt and Doughty, commenting upon Carleton's support of the loyalists' petition of 1787 for grants in free and common socage, observe that it was Carleton himself who had advised a return to the French system of land granting. But the documents to which they refer recommend only that French law and custom be made applicable to lands granted before the conquest and to lands granted by seigneurs since. These proposals were not to affect lands granted after the conquest by the Crown.[41] At the time, Carleton was not expecting many of the King's old subjects to seek homes in the province. For those who should come he did not propose the French tenure, as is clear from his letter to Shelburne of April 12, 1768:

For the foregoing reasons it has occurred to His Majesty's servants here that it might prove of Advantage if, whatever Lands remain Vacant in the Interior parts of the Province, bordering upon those, where the old Customs prevail, were henceforth granted on the like Conditions, *taking care that those at Gaspe and Chaleur Bay, where the King's old subjects ought chiefly to be encouraged to settle were granted on such Conditions only, as are specified in his Royal Instructions. . . .*[42]

However, there was at this time before the Board of Trade a petition to change a grant which had been made on the conditions laid down in Murray's instructions to one in fief and seigneury. The land in question lay in the very region where Carleton had thought tenure in free and common socage might be continued—the Bay of Chaleur. When he returned to England, his opinion was asked on this petition and he stated, without his previous qualifications, that "the granting of land in general in Quebec in seigneurie as under the French would be far more advantageous than in the manner prescribed in the Instructions." [43] Consequently, the additional instructions of 1771, which were then drawn up, revoked all previous instructions with respect to the granting of land and deprived Carleton of the power to grant land on anything but seigneurial tenure. Hillsborough presented these instructions to the Council with the added justification that two kinds of tenure in the same colony were confusing.[44]

The new land regulations met with a chorus of approval in which the old and the new subjects joined. Yet the new subjects, who are represented by Lieutenant-Governor Cramahe and the Board of Trade as being delighted with the change,[45] really stood to gain nothing from it. They perhaps regarded it as a sign that the old laws and customs governing the inheritance of their properties would be restored to them, but this favour did not require that all future grants should be in fief and seigneury, as the solution worked out in 1854 shows. It was the old subjects who stood to gain from the new land regulations and they knew it. New seigneuries were likely to be conceded chiefly to British merchants and traders who had come in since the conquest. They could thus acquire extensive tracts of land without the obligation of paying quit rents upon them and without being subject to the niggardly restrictions as to size imposed by the previous instructions. Moreover, the English-speaking inhabitants of Quebec were strangers to the laws and customs of the country and, as events proved, they sometimes preferred to remain in wilful—and profitable—ignorance of them. Even before the establishment of civil government, they had besieged Gage and Burton with requests for seigneuries,[46] and after 1771 their petitions poured in upon Cramahe. Twelve months after the receipt of the new land instructions, the Council had under consideration some forty-three petitions for seigneuries, most of them bearing English or Scotch names.[47] "One is tempted to speculate," says Burt, "upon what would have happened had not the outbreak of the American Revolution forestalled any action upon this swarm of appeals," and he adds that it was Cramahe who held up the decisions on these petitions.[48] Only one seigneury was granted between 1775 and 1792, the seigneury of Schoolbred on the Bay of Chaleur.[49] The instructions of 1771 were therefore of little practical importance except that they remained to plague the loyalists on their coming into the province of Quebec.

One is inclined to wonder whether it was these forty-three petitioners, and others who had bought seigneuries from the French,[50] who saw to it that the third draft of the Quebec Act contained a clause permitting those holding of the Crown in fief and seigneury to commute their tenure to free and common socage. This was a favourite project with the English-speaking inhabitants of Quebec because such a change in tenure would have given them control of the wild lands of their seigneuries and would have enabled them to sell those lands or to concede them at whatever rates they pleased; whereas, while they held under seigneurial tenure, they were forbidden to sell the unimproved land and were obliged to concede at the rates previously customary in the seigneury. The clause was deleted from the act before it was submitted to Parliament owing to the objections of Carleton and Hillsborough. English seigneurs had to wait until 1822 for the privilege they coveted, and, meanwhile, their interest in new seigneuries sharply declined.[51]

The second proviso to the fifth clause of the Quebec Act intimates that in future grants in free and common socage may be made. Hillsborough and Carleton objected to this proviso also; Carleton because he wished to make the seigneurial system the basis of the Crown's power in the province of Quebec,[52] Hillsborough because he was opposed to the settlement of the western territory by immigrants from any quarter. The fear of new Indian uprisings, the protection of the fur trade, and the cost of administering the area were only minor reasons for Hillsborough's stubbornness on this point. He and his mentor at the Board of Trade, William Knox, were convinced that inland colonies would not find it profitable to export their produce to Great Britain or the West Indies. Being unable to sell, they would be unable to buy, and therefore would begin to establish manufactures of their own to the detriment of their trade with the mother country. For this reason, "The inhabitants of America should be left along the sea coast according to England's ancient policy."[53] Even a hint that grants in free and common socage might be made in any part of the enlarged province of Quebec would, thought Hillsborough, tempt settlers into the forbidden area. In his opposition to such grants he was thinking primarily not of the old part of the province of Quebec but of keeping settlers from the thirteen colonies out of its new western annex.[54]

In addition, Hillsborough did not wish to make the western territory attractive to emigrants from Great Britain or Ireland.[55] As an Irish landlord, he was afraid that Catholic Quebec, like Protestant Nova Scotia, would draw too many Irish emigrants, and he and Knox were agreed that Ireland must not be depopulated. This possibility had long ago given British ministers concern. In 1762 the Board of Trade had become alarmed at the eager interest in emigration shown by the people of northern Ireland and had instructed the Governor of Nova Scotia not to grant land to these people nor to permit them to settle in the province unless they had been resident in a British colony for five years.[56] When it was proposed to include the Indian territory within the boundaries of Canada by the Quebec Act, Hillsborough at once took alarm for fear the guarantees given to Roman Catholics by that act should be an inducement to "the Roman Catholic subjects of Quebec and to *all other Roman Catholics*" to settle in the annexed territory. His inclusion of the phrase "all other Roman Catholics" is clearly a result of his fear that the Catholic peasants of Ireland might emigrate and explains his resolution to oppose this provision of the Quebec Act, as he had the Ohio grant, but "with tenfold strength. . . ."[57] Many who were not especially interested in Ireland shared Hillsborough's sentiments. In Great Britain, a reaction unfavourable to the promotion of colonies was already setting in as a result of the increasing friction with the thirteen colonies. The Solicitor General, Sir Alexander Wedderburn gave partial expression to these sentiments during the debates on the Quebec Act, and Knox developed them more fully after 1783.[58]

Carleton and Hillsborough did not succeed in deleting from the Quebec Act the intimation that grants in free and common socage might be made in future, but Lord Dartmouth assured Hillsborough that the Quebec Act by no means implied an intention of settling of the western territory annexed to Canada,[59] and Lord North remarked during the debate on the act "that all this uninhabited territory added to Canada should not be immediately considered as country which the government are to grant away."[60] It was probably owing to Hillsborough's influence that the new instructions issued to Carleton after the passing of the Quebec Act gave him no authority to make grants on anything but seigneurial tenure. Yet it remains a puzzle why the second proviso to the fifth clause was retained at all, unless its purpose was to leave the Crown free of statutory restrictions on its land-granting powers against the day when it might become advisable to permit settlement beyond the proclamation line.

CHAPTER TWO

THE LOYALISTS AND THE CROWN LANDS

THE PROCLAMATION of 1763 had included in the Indian Reserve the area subsequently known as Upper Canada. Although this territory was added to the old province of Quebec in 1774, the British ministry, as we have seen, had no intention of settling it and instructed Carleton to define the limits of the posts in the upper country and to permit no settlement beyond them.[1] These instructions were in effect throughout the American Revolution and partly explain the reluctance of Governor Haldimand to permit settlement in the vicinity of Detroit and Niagara, when Lieutenant-Governor Hamilton suggested it in 1778,[2] until he had received permission from home. Perhaps it was the difficulty of feeding the hungry refugees and the homeless Indian allies which made him think better of the idea. A few months later he wrote to Colonel Bolton, the commandant at Niagara, and to Lieutenant-Governor Hamilton at Detroit directing them to cultivate as much land as they could in the vicinity of the posts.[3] Bolton did not favour the project and remarked, "We must be cautious how we encroach on the lands of the Six Nations. . . ."[4] These Indians had ceded a tract on the east side of the Niagara River in 1764 to facilitate the transport of goods around the falls, but they had stipulated that the land should be reserved for the use of the Crown and they interpreted this to mean that no grants might be made nor improvements undertaken without their permission.[5] But Bolton changed his mind and later suggested allotting land to the refugees on the west or Canadian side of the river where these difficulties would not arise.[6]

By this time Governor Haldimand had become convinced that it would be useful to allow a few families to settle around the posts in the upper country to raise food for the garrisons. Having secured the home government's approval, he authorized the allotment of land to refugees at Carleton Island, Niagara, and Detroit in the summer of 1780.[7] At Niagara, a tract on the west side of the river was purchased from the Missisaugas and the Chippewas in May, 1781.[8] At Detroit, Hog Island was put under cultivation. The settlers were assisted with tools and provisions and were not required to pay rent, but they were subjected to restrictions which soon became irksome. They were required to sell the surplus of their harvests for the use of the troops, at prices fixed by the commandants of the posts, and they were not given title to their holdings but only the right of occupancy from year to year. By 1784 forty-four families had been settled at Niagara and a few at Carleton Island.[9]

When the terms of the Treaty of Paris became known to him, Haldimand saw that there were two classes of dispossessed for whom Great Britain would have to provide: her Indian allies and the loyalists. The obvious place to settle the

Six Nations was in what remained to Great Britain of the Indian Reserve, in other words, in what became Upper Canada. In his opinion, there was no room for the loyalists in the province of Quebec. In the lower part of the province the uncultivated lands would soon be required for the expanding French-Canadian population; in the upper country Indian territory ought not to be encroached upon. Cape Breton Island, the Gaspé Peninsula, and the shores of the Bay of Chaleur seemed to him the most suitable places to settle the loyalists and he urged these views upon the home government. Those loyalists who had already found refuge in the province he proposed to settle at Detroit, which he did not then know was to be given up; should they prefer it, he was ready to send them to the three localities mentioned above, and small settlements were eventually made at these three places.[10]

The loyalists, however, had ideas of their own. Some of them wished to settle in the district now known as the Eastern Townships,[11] but Haldimand was not disposed to countenance settlements so close to the American frontier. Loyalists and Americans, he informed Lord North, would not live peaceably together on opposite sides of the frontier, and since Canada, when the posts should have been given up, would hardly be worth fighting for, the sensible policy was to avoid a rupture by leaving the area east of the St. Lawrence unsettled as long as possible. He added, rather inconsistently, that when the area east of the St. Lawrence came to be settled, it might prove a good policy to place there a French-Canadian population, alien in religion, language, and customs to the restless New Englanders across the border.[12] One cannot but wonder whether concern for future generations of the expanding French-Canadian population or distrust of the future loyalty and politics of the refugees from the thirteen colonies was uppermost in his mind. Haldimand clinched his argument by asserting that the chief attraction which a settlement on the frontier had for some loyalists was the smuggling trade. Lord North accepted this line of reasoning, and the loyalists were refused permission to settle in those frontier areas for which they had asked.[13]

Some loyalists, anxious to end their wanderings, were inclined to take up land in the seigneuries. Without money, provisions, tools, or stock, they did not think themselves fitted to cope with the wilderness and they were willing to become the tenants of those who would provide these necessaries.[14] Several of the English seigneurs were eager to obtain loyalist settlers for their lands and held out inducements of one sort or another. But it was not Haldimand's policy to strengthen the English party in Lower Canada nor to permit the English to acquire land which future generations of French Canadians would need. While he could not forbid the loyalists to settle in the seigneuries, he did his best to dissuade them from doing so by refusing them the provisions and supplies which were normally issued to those who agreed to take up Crown lands.[15] After Haldimand's departure, in November, 1784, Lieutenant-Governor Hamilton, who was more sympathetic to the English party, drew attention to the treatment meted out to those loyalists who had settled in the seigneuries but he did not succeed in getting Haldimand's regulation set aside.[16]

In the spring of 1783 there were 30,000 loyalists in New York awaiting transportation to the new homes which the mother country had promised them. There was at first no thought of colonizing Upper Canada with these people. Prior to the conclusion of peace, the British ministry had thought the loyalists might be settled in those colonies of which England still retained control.[17] In March, 1783, Carleton wrote to the Governor of Florida recommending that he grant land free of quit rent to officers and soldiers wishing to settle there.[18] In addition, William Knox, Under-Secretary of State for the Colonies, had worked out a detailed plan for the founding of a new province between the Penobscot and tht St. Croix rivers for the reception of the loyalists. Knox's scheme had been approved and was ready to be acted upon as soon as hostilities ceased.[19] After the treaties of peace were signed there remained only Nova Scotia, bounded by the St. Croix, not the Penobscot, and Quebec, to which the loyalists might go.

It might have been expected that numbers of the immigrants would be settled in Quebec to provide a strong loyal element there. Carleton had long stressed the strategic importance of Canada, and, although the thirteen colonies had been lost, Great Britain still retained hopes of winning the west. The Revolution had shown the folly of relying on the masses of French Canadians for the defence of British interests in North America. If Canada was intended to become the "foundation" of a western commercial empire whose life-line would be the St. Lawrence, as G. S. Graham has suggested,[20] surely it would have been wise to strengthen the small British party in the province by the addition of loyalist immigrants. Yet only a small minority of the New York loyalists was sent there, about 1,500 persons, 1,050 of whom were listed as loyalists and the rest as disbanded troops and their families;[21] by contrast, some 28,000 persons went to Nova Scotia.[22]

The policy of discouraging loyalist settlement in Quebec also accorded with the views of Carleton and Knox, and particularly with the latter's plan for the creation of a new province "cherishing monarchical principles." In sending the loyalists to Nova Scotia, and in subsequently making their settlement the separate province of New Brunswick, the Imperial authorities were simply continuing unrevised, except for boundaries, a policy which had originally been devised to humble Massachusetts, which served to placate local discontents and rivalries in Nova Scotia, and which accorded with established Imperial policy of keeping the inhabitants of America along the sea coast.

Assuming no attempt was made to influence the loyalists in their choice of a new home, it is not surprising that the majority of them went to Nova Scotia. Since 1749 the British government had been promoting the settlement of that province,[23] and many New Englanders had responded to the invitation to settle there.[24] No doubt the majority of the loyalists preferred to follow them than to undertake the longer sea voyage to a more distant province whose laws and language were alien to them. William Dummer Powell states that those loyalists who had taken refuge in Canada before 1783 were anxious to settle in the upper province and to induce the main body of the loyalists to join them, but that they realized this could not be achieved unless certain alterations in the Quebec Act were first secured. A petition for this purpose was taken home by Powell but Parliament was busy and, before the ministry could consider it, "the Province of New Brunswick was organized and the Establishment of the Loyalists there too far effected to think of removal."[25]

It is not quite clear how it came about that some of the New York loyalists chose Canada. Canniff states that when the loyalists were undecided whether to embark for Nova Scotia or for Quebec, Carleton inquired of Michael Grass, who had been a prisoner of the French at Cataraqui, whether that district would be a suitable place for them and received an affirmative reply.[26] Ryerson states that Carleton "being unable to transport any more loyalists to Nova Scotia and New Brunswick" sent for Grass and asked him about Canada.[27] Whether Carleton suggested Canada to the loyalists or they suggested Canada to him is not known, but it would seem that the choice of a locality, Cataraqui, was made in New York by the loyalists. Fortunately, this choice coincided with some plans of Governor Haldimand's already under way.

Mindful of Pontiac's uprising which had followed the peace of 1763, Haldimand and the officers of the Indian Department had been apprehensive of the consequences when Great Britain's Indian allies should learn that their lands had been included within the boundaries of the United States by the Treaty of 1783.[28] When the news leaked out, despite Haldimand's efforts to conceal that part of the provisional treaty that related to the boundaries, the Indians were furious. To placate them, he assured them their losses would be made good and offered them new lands on the north shore of Lake Ontario. Finding that this idea appealed to them, Haldimand purchased from the Missisaugas a tract of land extending about forty-five miles up the lake and assigned the Six Nations a location on the Bay of Quinte. Subsequently, a majority of these Indians decided they preferred land on the Grand River (a situation Joseph Brant had wanted from the outset).[29] Another purchase was therefore made from the Missisaugas and within this area the Six Nations received a reserve six miles wide on either side of the river from its mouth to its source.[30]

The fear of an Indian uprising haunted Haldimand and led him to plan two strong posts, or rather military colonies, in the upper country to show the Indians that they had not been deserted by Great Britain.[31] One of them was to be established near Detroit for the purpose of holding the friendship of the western Indians and for raising grain and cattle for the upper posts.[32] In August, 1784, a military settlement opposite the Island of Bois Blanc on the Canadian side of the Detroit River was authorized. It was to be composed of reduced officers of the Indian Department and as many men of Butler's Rangers as wished to settle there. Long before Haldimand came to this decision, Lieutenant-Governor Hamilton had permitted the loyalists at Detroit to till land, although he made them no grants. He probably could not have prevented the impoverished refugees from squatting even though the Indian title had not been extinguished. The officers of the Indian Department themselves set a bad example by attempting to make purchases from the Indians for their own benefit, in defiance of the strict prohibitions of the Proclamation of 1763. As a result, it took years to untangle the conflicting claims of those who had been allotted land by the commandants at Detroit, those who had bought and sold these allotments, and those who had just squatted. On this turbulent and restless frontier the disciplined military colony planned by Haldimand was never established.[33]

The other military colony was to be at Cataraqui. Here Haldimand planned to lay out a township, to rebuild the fort, and to settle loyalists around it. The new post at Cataraqui was to replace that at Carleton Island which Haldimand feared would go to the United States when the boundaries prescribed by the Treaty of 1783 were drawn. Thus, early in June, when Carleton wrote that two hundred loyalist families wished to go to Canada and recommended that they be settled at Cataraqui, his letter simply made necessary an extension of Haldimand's original plan and forced no unwelcome decision upon him. Even after its receipt, he contemplated only a restricted settlement of loyalists in Upper Canada. His ultimate willingness to settle as many loyalists there as he could was occasioned, not by learning that the Indians desired white neighbours—he had been informed of this in May, not November—but by the fact that loyalist officers already in Canada had made it plain that they preferred a location on the upper St. Lawrence for themselves and their men. They wanted a farming, not a fishing, settlement, and Haldimand, who thought "humanity and justice" required that they have a choice, took pains to justify at some length to the home government the loyalists' preference for a settlement in the interior.[34]

The loyalists from New York, "incorporated" or "associated" into militia companies, had arrived in August, 1783, but most of them remained in the lower province until the spring of 1784 when unincorporated refugee loyalists, associated loyalists, disbanded loyalist regiments, and discharged soldiers all moved to the locations allotted to them. Nine townships running west from Point au Baudet, the western boundary of the last seigneury, had been surveyed for them at the request of Sir John Johnson, who preferred this location for himself and his battalion,[35] and, in addition, five townships running west from Cataraqui, as Haldimand planned. In June, 1784, Butler's Rangers were disbanded and a majority of them agreed to settle at Niagara, although it was with reluctance that they accepted their promised rewards of land on seigneurial tenure.[36]

Under the terms of the royal instructions of July 16, 1783, heads of loyalist families received 100 acres of land and 50 acres for every person then belonging to their families; single men received 50 acres. Discharged soldiers received 100 acres if privates, 200 if non-commissioned officers, and 50 acres for every person then belonging to their families. Family lands under these regulations were later restricted to men who came into the province before 1787. These grants were to be made only to persons ready to become actual settlers and were to be free of survey and patent fees.[37] A land policy which was a combination of homestead, head right, and military bounty grants was thus instituted.

Larger grants were made to reduced officers of provincial corps and of associated loyalists. Field officers received 1,000 acres, captains 700, subalterns, staff officers and warrant officers 500.[38] In addition, the following scale of grants for the 84th Regiment of Foot, which had been recruited under specific promises as to the amount of land it was to receive, was authorized: field officers, 5,000 acres, captains, 3,000, subalterns, 2,000, non-commissioned officers, 200, privates, 50. In 1788, the officers of Butler's Rangers and of the King's Royal Regiment of New York having petitioned for the same treatment as the 84th, Dorchester extended the above scale to "all reduced officers without distinction of corps . . ." who, prior to the date of his order, had actually obtained and improved the grants to which they were previously entitled.[39]

Only a single lot was assigned to officers at first, the balance of their land being later made up to them, and officers and men alike were to draw for their land. This impartial method of distributing the bounty of the Crown was determined upon by Haldimand who felt that it would be inequitable to allow the officers to monopolize the front lots and contrary to the royal instructions which required them to be interspersed among those of the men. The disgruntled Sir John Johnson protesting on behalf of himself and some other loyalist officers, was unable to move him on this point. But when the Surveyor General, Samuel Holland, complied with Johnson's wishes and assigned the lots in accordance with the plan the officers presented, the Governor was obliged to acquiesce.[40]

"Late loyalists," those arriving later than the families which Carleton had sent, were not entitled to all the foregoing privileges, but for some time the policy with respect to them was not clearly defined. To inquiries made in the spring of 1784 as to what encouragement would be given to persons from the colonies who wished to settle in Canada, Haldimand replied that those who could prove their loyalty would still be received and would be given land but that they could not expect provisions and other advantages like loyalists who had taken an early and active part in the war. The poverty and wretchedness of some of these latecomers moved him, however, to relax this regulation. Yet Haldimand was not anxious to see Lower Canada peopled by immigrants from the United States, whatever their degree of loyalty. With reluctance he had decided to settle the original loyalists in what he regarded as Indian territory though he had no wish to see further encroachments made on Indian lands by white settlers.[41] If he had remained in Canada, he would not have encouraged further emigration from the United States to any part of the old province of Quebec.

His successors did not know what policy to follow. Lieutenant-Governor Hay hesitated to make grants to loyalists arriving at Detroit in the spring of 1785, and Lieutenant-Governor Hamilton, who administered the province between Haldimand's departure and Dorchester's arrival in 1786, was uncertain whether to issue provisions to latecomers who had not made open demonstrations of their loyalty during the war.[42] The Colonial Office drew up a set of instructions which distinguished between those loyalists who had taken refuge in the province of Quebec previous to, or immediately after, the treaty of peace and the latecomers. The latter would have been refused provisions under its terms, but it is uncertain whether these instructions were ever sent.[43] Sir Guy Carleton also wished to know whether immigration from the United States was to be encouraged or connived at.[44] Chief Justice William Smith and Surveyor General Samuel Holland expected Carleton to come to Canada with "full instructions to improve the Province and encourage new settlers. . . ." Smith heartily approved such a policy in the belief that, on the whole, the Americans were well disposed towards Great Britain and inclined to return to their allegiance—a belief, remarked Adam Mabane, "for which there is not the least foundation but which may lead into Errors from which we will not awake till too late to prevent the evils arising from them."[45]

Carleton, who returned to Canada as Lord Dorchester, received the same land instructions as had Haldimand; loyalists in the United States were to be encouraged to settle in the province, although the character of the incoming "loyalists" had changed somewhat since Haldimand's day. There was, however, an additional paragraph the meaning of which is not clear. Section 43 permits land to be granted to "those only who may have withdrawn themselves from the said Provinces or Colonies *after* the signing of the definitive Treaty of Peace with the said United States and no other." [46] No restriction on land granting was imposed by these words and there seems to be no point in the sentence. Its probable meaning is, *immediately after* the signing of the treaty, and no doubt it was intended to draw the same distinction between early and late loyalists as that attempted in the tentative instruction referred to above.

Whatever official policy may have been intended, new settlers from the old colonies continued to swell the numbers of so-called loyalists in the new settlements, which, by the spring of 1787, were rife with discontent. John Collins, Deputy Surveyor General, and William Dummer Powell, at that time practising law in Montreal and who later became judge of the Court of Common Pleas for the District of Hesse, were appointed by Dorchester as a commission of inquiry to investigate and quiet the unrest. The Deputy Surveyor went on this mission armed with the authority to grant settlers who had already improved their land a bonus of 200 acres. This grant was known as Lord Dorchester's bounty. Dorchester's avowed object in making these grants was to encourage the cultivation of the soil, but, since the bounty lands were to be bestowed only upon "real loyalists" of "Peaceable decent deportment" and were to be withheld from persons of "doubtful principles and reputations," one suspects that his real object was to make it plain that the role of agitator would prove an unprofitable one. This promise of bounty lands was intended to hold good for a limited time only. In July, 1790, it was proposed in Council to receive no more applications for bounty lands since the "purpose" of the order had been achieved.[47] However, in this case, as in many others to come, it was found difficult to end the life of a bounty regulation once it had come into existence. The Executive Council of Upper Canada later set August 1, 1797, as the time limit for receiving and hearing claims for Lord Dorchester's bounty.[48]

Another task assigned the commissioners was to inquire into the character of all newcomers since the original settlement, "as many persons not entitled to the protection of the Crown were reported to have settled themselves among the loyalists." It turned out, however, that there were very few settlers of this class. One real cause of the trouble was that the only way in which newcomers could obtain land was by the slow adjudication of the Land Committee of Council on their claims and their pretensions to loyalty. This committee, with Hugh Finlay at its head, may not have been over meticulous in distinguishing the children of light from the children of darkness, but the delays and the expense attendant upon its decisions exasperated the impatient and impoverished immigrants. This is the beginning of the squatter problem in Upper Canada and the slow motions of the Land Department, both at this time and later, were never able to overtake it. Deputy Surveyor Collins gave the newcomers locations, settled disputes about boundaries and erroneous surveys, and straightened out other difficulties related to land. But one old grievance still rankled. When some of the loyalist officers had insisted on having the front lots and had refused to draw with the men, they had forfeited the confidence of the rank and file and it could not now be restored.[49]

Dorchester and his Council seem to have interpreted the vague words of the land instructions to mean that land was to be granted only to loyalists who before 1783 had given proof of their loyalty by joining the forces of the Crown.[50] What was to be done with "late" loyalists? Some of them were friends or relatives of the original settlers and many of them had plausible excuses for their failure to seek the protection of the Crown earlier. Sir John Johnson and many of the loyalist magistrates favoured the admission of such settlers provided they could prove their loyalty.[51] There were also the associations of so-called loyalists, who were primarily interested in speculation, whose leaders declared that all they needed to encourage them to place themselves once more under British rule was the grant of tracts of land ranging from one to forty townships, preferably situated on the New York frontier.[52]

The loyalist question was the subject of much debate in Council and occasioned sharp differences in opinion between the French and English parties. Four committees expressed their sentiments on this question. The Committee on the Courts of Justice, composed of Finlay, Mabane, and St. Ours, was not in favour of attracting immigrants from the United States. In the opinion of Mabane and St. Ours (Finlay dissenting), most of the loyalists who had stood forth on the King's side during the war had already sought refuge in Canada, New Brunswick, or Nova Scotia. Those Americans who now wished to come to Canada were not really loyalists: they were simply discontented with conditions in the United States. If it were policy to grant such people the protection of the Crown, they should be encouraged to go to the maritime provinces where they would not infect the loyal and contented French Canadians, the class of men "least likely to coalesce with the Neighbouring States of America." [53] The Committee on Population, Agriculture, and Settlement of the Crown Lands, composed of J. G. C. DeLery, Joseph de Longueil, Rene de Boucherville, Samuel Holland, and Sir John Johnson, opposed the loyalists' demand for grants in free and common socage and advised that lands continue to be granted on the unpopular seigneurial tenure. Sir John Johnson in a dissenting report argued that seigneurial tenure was unfair to the loyalists, adverse to agriculture, and would impede the growth of a populous English colony.[54] The Committee on Commerce and Police, composed of John Collins, Deputy Surveyor General, George Pownall, the Provincial Secretary, and William Grant and Edward Harrison, merchants, all members of the English party, made a brief and forthright report: "Commercial policy requires, that this great Country, should be peopled. Every encouragement therefore, should be held out to *all* who seek refuge, or fly from persecution, to its wild but friendly bosom. More especially to those who have suffered in support of His Majesty's ... Government." [55] The Land Committee, composed of Finlay, Collins, Grant, St. Ours, and de Lanaudiere, recommended not only that late loyalists be granted land but also that "industrious men ... be encouraged to come from all quarters to settle in this Province ... provided they will take the oaths prescribed and are well attached to the British government." [56] In Great Britain it was even proposed to send convicts to Canada and to put them to work in the interior of the country—a scheme which doubtless would have found favour with none of the French party and perhaps with few, if any, of the English.[57]

There seems to have been some difference of opinion among the English party as to what treatment should be accorded immigrants from the United States. The English merchants of Lower Canada naturally wanted to attract population to Canada. The loyalists of the upper province wanted the new settlements to become populous but they did not want newcomers to be treated like loyalists. Their sense of justice was outraged by such a proposal. Besides, as one of the loyalist officers asked, where was a labour force to be had if every immigrant could obtain land and be his own master?[58] By the spring of 1788 the Americans had begun to make settlements on the southern shores of Lakes Ontario and Erie and this finally convinced Dorchester that enterprise must not be lacking on the Canadian side. In the end, the policy adopted seems to have been to grant land to all whom the term loyalist could be stretched to cover and to encourage the "speedy settlement of the upper country with profitable subjects."[59] This decision is reflected in the new arrangements for settling loyalists worked out in 1788.

To prevent squatting and to expedite the allotment of land to acceptable settlers, Dorchester authorized the deputy surveyors in the new settlements to receive applications for land and to assign the settlers lots when these applications were *returned* approved by Council.[60] During his visit to the western settlements in the fall of 1788, the delays which loyalists encountered from the lack of a local authority to allot them land was brought home to him. After his return to Quebec, he appointed a land board for each of the four districts into which the new settlements had by this time been organized: Lunenburg, Mecklenburg, Nassau, and Hesse. These boards were permitted to assign incoming settlers who were ready to take the oath of allegiance a single lot of 200 acres and they were required to forward to Council with their recommendations whatever additional claims to land the settlers might have. The duty of allotting family lands to loyalists already settled in the upper districts was also entrusted to them but no power was given to allot family lands to newcomers.[61] The Land Committee of Council acted as a sort of court of appeal from the land boards and reported on the larger claims. The Committee's own recommendations were subject to the approval of the Council as a whole. Adam Mabane disliked the Committee's policies. He wrote pessimistically to Haldimand that it was evidently the intention to introduce as many immigrants from the United States as possible and that this could only result in the loss of the colony since the newcomers brought with them the same licentious and republican principles that had created the Revolution.[62]

There was one unfortunate decision come to during Dorchester's regime, although, if it had been rightly understood, perhaps no harm would have been done. Under the regulations of 1783, heads of loyalist families had received 100 acres and 50 acres for every member of their families, exactly the same grant as was given men who had joined loyalist regiments and fought as privates. Evidently the privates regarded this treatment as unfair, probably because loyalists who remained under arms until the end of the war had been promised 200 acres.[63] Moreover, newly arriving loyalists were receiving 200 acres, although not family lands, under the regulations of February 17, 1789.[64] The Land Board of Nassau dealth with these inequities by giving a twist of its own to Lord Dorchester's bounty. It decided that "as it appears to be the wish of government to distinguish their *active friends and adherents* by peculiar marks of attention *Those only* who had born arms, or in some other capacity had served government during the War . . ." should of right be entitled to Lord Dorchester's bounty in addition to their original grant of 100 acres. At the same time, the Board remarked that it would not grant family lands to newcomers (as indeed it had no power to do), but would leave "provision for their families to the Commander-in-Chief's future bounty, which will certainly follow their decent deportment. . . ."[65] Here is the origin of the U.E. policy instituted just one month later.

A report of the activities of the Land Board for Nassau of October, 1789, evidently came under Dorchester's eye, for in November he drew the attention of the Land Committee of Council to the fact that the local land boards had no authority to make locations to he sons of loyalists on their coming of age. He added that it was his wish to put a mark of honour, not upon loyalists in general, but "upon the families who had adhered to the Unity of the Empire and Joined the Royal Standard in America before the Treaty of Separation in the year 1783." Here Dorchester made the same distinction as the Land Board of Nassau had made. An order-in-council was then passed directing the land boards to compile lists of loyalists so defined, "to the end that their posterity may be discriminated from future settlers . . . as proper objects . . . for distinguished benefits and privileges." The same order-in-council authorized the boards "in every such case" to grant 200 acres of land to the children of "those loyalists," on the coming of age of sons and the marriage of daughters.[66] The unfortunate juxtaposition of these two statements cost the Crown 3,300,000 acres and £75,000 in land revenue, benefited speculators chiefly, and became one of the greatest obstacles to the settlement of the country. These U.E. grants were to be free of survey and patent fees, with the result that the land revenues of Upper Canada were for many years inadequate to sustain the burden of costs laid upon them. No list of U.E. loyalists seems to have been made at this time but those entitled to the letters were so distinguished on the militia rolls. The directions for enrolling them say, "Those Loyalists who have adhered to the Unity of the Empire and joined the Royal Standard before the Treaty of Peace in 1783, and all their children and their Descendants by either sex are to be distinguished by the following capitals affixed to their names: U.E., alluding to their great principle, the Unity of the Empire."[67]

In later years the text of Dorchester's order-in-council became the subject of much controversy. The loyalists were to claim that the order-in-council simply carried out the royal instructions as expressed to Dorchester, that they had been "promised" a grant of 200 acres for each of their children as part of their reward for their loyalty, that these grants of land were to be "free" gifts, that is, free from all conditions and all expenses, and that all loyalists, irrespective of the time of their arrival in the province, were entitled to land for themselves and their children.[68] These claims have no historical basis. The order-in-council originated with Dorchester, not with the home government. The loyalists had not been promised land for their children but only for themselves. The order-in-council granting land to their children expressly states that they shall comply with the general regulations,[69] and, by requiring the children of loyalists to show that "there has been no default in the due cultivation and improvement of the lands already assigned to the head of the family of which they are members," it limited the promise of land to the children of loyalists already resident in the province.

It is very unlikely that Dorchester intended this order-in-council to set up a permanent regulation under which children of loyalists could claim 200 acres of Crown land. The mark of honour was one thing, the promise of land another. Yet the loyalists seem to have assumed that since the two were granted by the same order-in-council they were necessarily to be interpreted in the same way. Dorchester could see that the original loyalists would soon be lost sight of in the swarms of newcomers unless they were distinguished in some way and he seems to have understood the quality of loyalist feeling—admirable from one point of view, narrow, obstructive, self-righteous, and selfish from another. The Land Board of Nassau had practically asked for some mark of distinction for original loyalists and had plainly hinted that Lord Dorchester's bounty should be that mark. What Dorchester did was to grant as the permanent mark of honour the letters U.E. to be borne by the original loyalists, their children, and *all* their descendants by either sex. That part of his order granting lands to the children — and he had had in mind originally only the sons [70]—was intended simply to meet the needs to which his attention had been drawn by the Nassau report: the rising generation had to be provided for.

There is definite evidence that the sons of other settlers were intended to be treated no differently from the children of loyalists. The Land Board of Nassau had already assumed that the children of other well-disposed settlers would receive grants. A few weeks after the U.E. regulation had been made, the Land Board of Mecklenburg inquired whether the sons of those who had been admitted to the district since 1784 were entitled to 200 acres when they applied for it, "seeing it is evidently the intention of government to give lands to all persons of good character who are able and willing to cultivate them and have not before received any," and received an affirmative reply.[71] This decision wiped out whatever restrictions the words "in every such case" and "those loyalists" of the original order-in-council had imposed. Certainly no one could regard 200 acres of land, obtainable at that time by every settler and the son of every settler on coming of age, as a distinguished benefit or privilege. Furthermore, the freedom from survey and patent fees was an indulgence to which every person settled under the instructions of 1786 [72] was entitled. There is nothing to show that this order-in-council, any more than many which were to follow, was intended to convey imprescriptible rights to which no time limit might be set and no conditions attached. Certainly the mother country put no such interpretation upon it, as later controversies show, but found herself obliged to accept the apocryphal interpretation of Dorchester's regulations which her ever so loyal, but expecting, children foisted upon her.

One interesting test of loyalty was imposed upon all applicants for land. In addition to taking the oath of allegiance, they were required to make and subscribe a declaration acknowledging the King in Parliament to be the supreme legislature of the province. The letter to Haldimand which laid down this regulation was accompanied by another explaining that in view of the statute 18 Geo. III, c. 12, the supremacy of Parliament was not to be understood as extending to taxation.[73] An order-in-council of January 12, 1790, required the land boards to see to it that all landholders in their districts subscribed the declaration if they had not already done so.[74]

By 1791 the population of the province of Quebec west of Point au Baudet had increased to about 10,000. It consisted of discharged soldiers of the regular army, the "original" loyalists, comprising under that term loyalist regiments and their families, the associated loyalists who had come from New York, and loyalists who were refugees from the rebellious colonies, and "late" loyalists, some of whom were suspected of being mere land seekers.[75] These people had been alloted lands by the Council sitting at Quebec, assisted, after 1788, by the four local land boards. Neither the size of their grants nor the conditions upon which they were made pleased them.

Among the complaints in the petition of April 15, 1787, was a demand for grants "according to English tenure." All the grants, whether to loyalists, soldiers, or simple settlers, had been made upon seigneurial tenure and were subject to a quit rent of one halfpenny an acre after the expiration of ten years.[76] One would expect the proviso of the Quebec Act, which had implied that grants in free and common socage might be made, to have been acted upon after the influx of loyalist refugees had begun, or at least after the peace of 1783 had closed the door to the return of the loyalists to their old homes. Yet Haldimand's instructions of that year and Dorchester's of 1786 specified the seigneurial tenure again.

William Knox seems to have had a good deal to do with the conditions on which the loyalists received their land. It was he who devised the declaration of loyalty to King and Parliament and it was he also who proposed that the lands should be subject to quit rents. These quit rents were intended to provide a fund for the support of the civil government of the colony until its legislature should have provided a permanent revenue for this purpose.[77] Knox, of course, simply suggested for Upper Canada the scheme which Shelburne had been developing for the thirteen colonies before its prospects were blighted by the Revolution.[78]

The dissatisfaction of the loyalists with their tenure was not slow in expressing itself. Almost as soon as the conditions were made known complaints began to reach Haldimand.[79] After his departure, the desire of the loyalists for a change of tenure was pressed upon the home government by Hugh Finlay, Sir John Johnson, and other loyalist officers.[80]

The unrest in the loyalist settlements and the petition of 1787 were sufficient to convince Dorchester that the loyalists' demands must be granted. It was, he wrote Sydney, a more urgent matter than the demand for a change in the form of government. He considered it essential to remove "the Smallest Cause of discord between the King's Government and His people . . .," and to make residence in the British provinces as attractive as in the rebel republic to the south.[81] Indeed, he went further than the loyalists themselves [82] by recommending not only that the lands be granted in free and common socage but also that they be granted free of quit rent.[83] The Imperial government was ready to take Dorchester's advice. On September 14, 1787, Sydney informed him that the loyalists would be granted the tenure for which they had petitioned.[84] A draft instruction was framed which omitted quit rents on all grants not exceeding 1,000 acres, and which empowered the Governor General to grant land in free and common socage. The draft further instructed him to propose to his Council a law enabling persons holding in seigneury or in roture to change their tenure to free and common socage with the consent of the seigneur. The proposed instruction, however, encountered the strong hostility of George Chalmers, Clerk of the Privy Council, who was convinced that colonists holding in free and common socage would soon seek independence. Its issue was never authorized.[85]

But the petitioners were soon to win their argument. Simcoe, the future Lieutenant-Governor of Upper Canada, added his voice to those from Canada demanding the change in tenures,[86] and Dorchester, after his visit to the western settlements in the fall of 1788, wrote home once more urging it. But already the decision had been made, and a dispatch was on its way informing him that grants in free and common socage would be made and that quit rents would be remitted for the first ten years.[87] The Constitutional Act which gave effect to the government's intentions makes no mention of quit rents. Clauses 43 and 44 simply provide that all future grants of land in Upper Canada should be made in free and common socage and that persons holding land on certificates of occupation might surrender the same and receive fresh grants on that tenure.[88] The loyalists had won. Other problems originating in the early years of settlement, notably the question of U.E. rights, were to plague Upper Canada for years to come.

... that the lands be granted in free and common socage but also that they be

CHAPTER THREE

SIMCOE'S FIVE-YEAR PLAN

THE CONSTITUTIONAL ACT of 1791 provided for the separation of loyalist and
English-speaking Upper Canada from the old province of Quebec and, by
promising grants in free and common socage, redressed the first of the long list
of grievances of which Upper Canada was to complain. The legislature with
which the new province was endowed found its power to frame a policy for the
disposal and settlement of the Crown lands restricted in several ways. First, and
most important, was the clause of the Constitutional Act which required that
land bearing a "due proportion" to the quantity already granted by the Crown
should be reserved for the support of a Protestant clergy and that, as future
grants were made, additional Clergy Reserves should be set aside equal to one-
seventh of their value.[1] Second, a separate instruction of September 16, 1791,
directed the Governor to set aside Crown Reserves equal in quantity to the
Clergy Reserves "for the purpose of raising, by sale or otherwise, a fund to be
hereafter applied to the support of Government."[2] Third, clause 42 of the act
required measures dealing with the Clergy Reserves or with the waste lands of
the Crown to be laid before both Houses of Parliament for thirty days, after
which the royal assent might be given to them provided neither House had
addressed the Crown to the contrary in the meantime.[3] Fourth, Dorchester's
instructions as Governor of Upper Canada, by which the Lieutenant-Governor
was also bound,[4] required him to refuse assent to all bills naturalizing aliens in
order to validate titles to land obtained from them, and the Trade and Navigation
instructions of the same date required him to notify the home government if
any persons should alienate land "other than to our natural born subjects of
Great Britain, Ireland or our Plantations in America" without first obtaining an
order-in-council approving the transaction.[5] An instruction similar to the first
had been issued to the governors of American colonies since 1773 and a provision
similar to the last had been included in the Trade and Navigation instructions
since 1697.[6] The alien question was one that was to cause much trouble in
Upper Canada. Finally, in the Governor's instructions the policy to be followed
with respect to the surveying, granting, and registering title to the Crown lands
was rather minutely set forth.

An unwritten restriction on the power of the legislature was the belief of
successive lieutenant-governors and of the Executive Council that the lands of
the Crown were not for the representatives of the people to meddle with. The
translator of La Rochefoucauld has made him say, "The leading articles of the
new constitution of Canada are as follows ... That the allotment of lands in
Upper Canada be, under certain restrictions, left to the authority of the local

legislature." [7] With this statement D. W. Smith disagreed. "The Legislature have nothing to do with the allotment of Lands, they belong to the Crown, and are granted by the Governor in Council," he wrote.[8] This represents the view held by the governing clique for many years. Clause 42 of the Constitutional Act, which clearly permits provincial legislation on this topic, subject to royal confirmation, was not taken advantage of, and it was not until 1837 that a measure was passed by the legislature touching the granting of Crown lands. By that time they had come to be thought of as public domain and the act referred to was entitled the Public Land Act.

The first Lieutenant-Governor of Upper Canada, John Graves Simcoe, could not bring himself to accept the American Revolution as an accomplished fact. In one of his unrestrained letters he wrote:

I would die by more than Indian torture to restore my King and his Family to their just Inheritance and to give my Country that fair and natural accession of Power which an Union with their Brethren could ... bestow.... Though a Soldier it is not by Arms that I hope for this Result, it is *volentes in populos* only that such a renewal of Empire can be desirable....

Simcoe cherished the notion of demonstrating to Great Britain's rebellious colonies, by means of the rapid and orderly development of his province, the advantages of the Imperial connection. He was convinced that the settlements west of the Alleghanies would soon realize that their interests were at variance with those of the Atlantic seaboard and that they would then become part of the commercial empire of Great Britain. He believed that the trade routes of the Great Lakes and the trans-Appalachian country could be made to converge in the peninsula between the lakes, and he therefore urged the rapid development of this area while the alternative trade route—the Mississippi—remained closed by Spain.[9] The capital of the new colony should be located in the heart of this peninsula and the site which he subsequently fixed upon was—inevitably —named London.

In common with most members of the governing class of his day,[10] Simcoe attributed the success of the American Revolution to the lack of a strong and loyal aristocracy in the colonies. In the new colony he hoped this defect would be made good by the introduction of "every establishment of Church and State that upholds the distinction of ranks, and lessens the undue weight of the democratic influence. . . ." Thus equipped, his province would be able to demonstrate the superiority of an aristocratic system of government over the wild and turbulent democracy which he so mistakenly imagined to be governing the United States.[11] With the happy history of Upper Canada before them, perhaps the western settlements could be "weaned away" from the United States and induced to throw in their lot with the British colonies situated on their natural outlet to the sea: the Great Lakes and the St. Lawrence River.[12] As the opening shot in a campaign of seduction, Simcoe sent a man named Collins to the Kentucky country to stimulate trade between the western settlements and Upper Canada and allowed him to carry several species of contraband to make his experiment profitable.[13] What Simcoe hoped for, Washington feared. "The touch of a feather would turn them away," he observed.[14]

To bring his schemes to success, Simcoe felt that it was essential for the mother country to give the new province adequate financial support in the beginning, rather than "trivial and procrastinated assistance" that might "starve into a petty Factory for the accommodation of the Fur Traders, what, if encouraged to attain its natural Dimensions, would dilate itself into an increasing and Majestic support of the British Empire."[15] Within five years he hoped to lay secure foundations for the development of such a colony in Upper Canada.

The most complete and most unrestrained account of Simcoe's hopes for Upper Canada is from the pen of Peter Russell. Russell was desperately anxious to receive confirmation of his appointment as Receiver General of Upper Canada and eager to assure Simcoe that he was in complete accord with his views for the new colony. Giving free reign to his fancy, Russell pictured the Indians of the Pacific coast, the Spanish inhabitants of California and New Mexico, the inhabitants of the trans-Appalachian country, all flocking to London, the "grand Mart and Imporium of the Western World," there to exchange their products for the excellent but cheap manufactured articles which Great Britain would provide. In short, by proper support of the colony of Upper Canada, Great Britain would be able "to ... secure ... to this country all those advantages which it once reasonably hoped to derive from the old Colonies without being loaded with the weight of their Government or Protection...."[16] Despite this fanciful vision of the future of Upper Canada, written to fall in with the mood of his prospective chief, Russell was a realist. "Our Chief is ... an excellent soldier," he wrote to his sister, "and a good natured man and in everything that is not an object of his Enthusiasm exceedingly sensible. But on such Subjects I must confess his Imagination seems to run away with him."[17]

In 1793 Captain Charles Stevenson had an interview with Secretary Dundas in which he outlined the following scheme as coming from Simcoe: Explain to Spain that America is hostile to her and that posts east of the Mississippi can never be advantageous to her. Get her to yield Pensacola to Great Britain and to concede also the right of navigating the river. Then Kentucky will "look up to you for Union or Alliance ...," and the American, "finding You in possession of both his flanks and on terms of friendship with all the Indian Nations at his back, would find it prudent to court your friendship."[18] Simcoe, who had certainly discussed plans of this kind, not excluding the possibility of war, with Sir Henry Clinton,[19] acknowledged that Stevenson had been much in his confidence but denied that he had been authorized to put forward these proposals. In response, Dundas merely remarked that discussions concerning the navigation of the Mississippi were "very premature" at the moment.[20] After all, Simcoe's plan for the winning of the west, whether in the exaggerated form in which Stevenson presented it or in the more moderate terms in which Simcoe himself outlined it, did not strike the Colonial Secretary with the force of a new revelation. Ideas similar to Simcoe's had been expressed by William Smith, later Chief Justice of Lower Canada, in a paper entitled by its editor "Observations on America."[21] Many of these notions had been brought forth during the peace negotiations of 1783, and in 1789 Grenville and Dorchester had discussed the possibilities of maintaining British influence in the back settlements.[22] So far as the Colonial Office was concerned, the scheme on which Simcoe's heart was set was a possible line of policy which future circumstances *might* make it worthwhile to pursue actively.

The first townships surveyed in Upper Canada were those on the St. Lawrence where Haldimand had placed the loyalists. He had received no specific instructions on the surveys except that he was required to reserve a glebe of 300 to 500 acres in each seigneury. He had directed that the new seigneuries (townships) should be six miles square "as the people to be settled there are most used to" that size.[23] They were divided into seven "concessions"[24] of twenty-five lots of 120 acres. For the loyalists at Niagara, two townships, Niagara and Stamford, were divided into small lots numbered consecutively, and there were no reserves. On the Detroit frontier, deep lots on a narrow frontage, such as the French settlers at Assumption were accustomed to, were laid out on the water boundary from East Sandwich to Gosfield.

Dorchester likewise had received no specific instructions on surveys. As a general rule, he had townships laid out nine miles by twelve if on a navigable river and ten miles square if inland. The river townships were divided into fourteen concessions of twenty-four 200-acre lots, the inland townships into ten concessions of thirty lots. A road allowance of sixty-six feet was left between concessions, and cross-roads were provided for at intervals of five lots. A town plot one mile square was laid out in the centre of the inland townships, and in the centre of the front of townships on navigable water. Within this area, a number of sites were reserved for public purposes and a reserve of half a mile around the town was left for the purposes of defence. The town lots were one acre in size and town parks of about 24 acres were laid out around the townsite for a distance of about on mile. Eight continuous farm lots in each corner of an inland township and ten in each corner of a river township were reserved. Since the townsite was also taken out of the front in the river townships, only two farm lots were left available for granting in the front concession, an arrangement which soon gave rise to complaint.[25]

Simcoe's instructions respecting the Crown lands became the basis of land policy in Upper Canada until 1826, although they were to be applied by successive administrators in a spirit very different from his. The instructions required townships, farm lots, town parks, and town lots to be of the size Dorchester had instituted but they did not prescribe the manner in which townships were to be divided or the reserves set aside.[26] As is related more fully in chapter IV, it was decided to scatter the reserves for the Crown and clergy throughout every concession instead of placing them in the corners of the townships. In practice, this system of scattered reserves was to be modified and the town plots were dispensed with except in special situations. The instructions specified that land was to be granted only to persons who could show they were in a position to improve it and their obligation to do so was to be expressed in the patents. But since the amount of improvement required was not precisely prescribed, it could not be expressed in the patents except as a general obligation, and for years the requirement seems to have troubled colonial secretaries and colonial administrators very little. In order to prevent a few favoured individuals receiving excessive grants, the maximum grant was prescribed in rather ambiguous language which was interpreted to mean 1,200 acres. All grants were to be issued free of expense except for fees payable to the officers of the Land Department according to a table to be established. Applicants for land were required to take the oath of allegiance and to subscribe the declaration to which reference has already been made.

Simcoe thought the land policy of Upper Canada was patent proof of the superiority of the British colony over the United States. At this time, the United States was disposing of its public land for cash in quantities no smaller than 640 acres,[27] a method which meant, said Simcoe quite correctly, that they became "the subject of unconditional sale to the Land Jobbers of America or Europe." In Upper Canada, on the contrary, the settler received his land free except for patent fees. Moreover, as the Whiskey Rebellion had shown, the citizens of the United States, particularly those in inland situations, were becoming restless under the growing burden of taxation, but the happy residents of Upper Canada had been relieved from all worries on this score. By reserving one-seventh of the land for the support of the civil government, the Crown had seen to it that "their present exemption from taxation will be the inheritance of their Posterity. . . ." It is ironic that Simcoe thought these reserves, which proved to be a grievance, would be a great inducement to immigrants. He realized of course that they would fail of their purpose unless there was a quick growth of population to make them valuable enough to yield an income.[28] Like every part of Simcoe's closely integrated policy, the success of this scheme depended upon rapid accomplishment.

The Queen's Rangers, a regiment raised at the instance of the Lieutenant-Governor primarily for use as a labour corps, afforded another proof of the mother country's solicitude for the infant colony. The Rangers were to receive only the usual soldiers' pay, but they were to be allowed to hire themselves out two days a week to private persons at stated prices set by the government. After five years service they were entitled to be discharged and to receive a grant of land. Through the services of this regiment, Simcoe expected that labour costs would be reduced, a capital and other towns would be founded, and roads, bridges, and mills would be constructed, thus insuring the rapid progress of Upper Canada along lines very different from "the slow unsystematic and unconnected Gradations by which the British Colonies in America have usually been formed. . . ." [29] Simcoe was very proud of the Queen's Rangers and of the elaborate scheme which he had worked out for their employment. The idea of a labour force was not, however, unique with him. It had been suggested by Colonel Henry Bouquet, by J. F. W. Des Barres, and by Governor Bellomont.[30]

It was Simcoe's firm belief that there were still thousands of the King's subjects in the United States who would gladly avail themselves of the opportunity to be once more under British rule, an opinion which La Rochefoucauld called "an empty dream." [31] On February 7, 1792, while still at Quebec, Simcoe issued a proclamation, identical with one issued at the same time for the lower province, making known the terms on which land could be obtained in Upper Canada, and he requested the Colonial Office to publish it in the English and the West Indian newspapers so that it might reach the people of the United States by that means.[32] He also opened an active correspondence with Phineas Bond, the British Consul at Philadelphia, who thought he could induce a considerable number of Quakers to make their home in Upper Canada. Further measures which he might have taken to secure settlers were probably dropped when he discovered that Dundas was by no means in favour of his going out of his way to "entice and allure them." Dundas was afraid that a too rapid influx of American settlers would not be conducive to the political stability of the new province and time was to prove him right. He warned Simcoe that an active immigration policy on the part of Upper Canada at the expense of the United States might lead that country to retaliate, and he expressed a doubt whether the province could hold its own in such a contest.[33]

Simcoe, however, had no notion of permitting Upper Canada to be overrun by unruly immigrants of unknown principles. He divided the province into nineteen counties,[34] and in October, 1792, appointed seven land board's to which he entrusted the allotment of land in thirteen counties, reserving to himself and the Council the hearing of all petitions for land in the Lake Erie counties eastward from Point aux Pins to the Grand River and in the Lake Ontario counties between York and the Bay of Quinte. Simcoe continued Dorchester's regulations, permitted the boards to give incoming settlers ready to take the oath of allegiance certificates for 200 acres, and advised them that "tho' His Majesty's bounty is not restricted solely to his own subjects, yet it is not meant to be extended to such as have wilfully resisted his Crown and Government, and who persist in principles and opinions which are hostile to the British Constitution." [35] Apparently the land boards closed their eyes to the loophole in Simcoe's statement which allowed repentant republicans to slip into the province. There are indications in the records of the time that the reluctance of these boards to admit new settlers from the United States did not please Simcoe.[36] At all events, in November, 1794, they were dissolved and their power of recommending immigrants for single lots was vested in the magistrates. At the same time the Council resolved that all persons professing the Christian religion whose past life was respectable and law-abiding and who were capable of manual labour should be admitted as settlers.[37] Loyalty as understood by the original loyalists was no longer to be the test of a settler's fitness to join the company of the elect in Upper Canada.

The change to the use of magistrates was part and parcel of Simcoe's plan for keeping the democracy of the new province in check by means of a loyal aristocracy. In 1792, he had appointed lieutenants of counties who were responsible for the supervision of the local magistrates. The magistrates in their turn were now to be held in some degree responsible for the conduct of those they admitted as settlers.[38] A loyal magistracy, Simcoe explained to Dundas, could be trusted to admit only such American settlers as would readily coalesce with the loyal inhabitants of Upper Canada. Unfortunately, this nicely detailed plan did not work out. Perhaps the lieutenants of counties were not sufficiently watchful of the "loyal magistracy," or perhaps the magistrates did not sufficiently inquire into the intentions of those to whom they allotted land. At any rate, the issuing of magistrates' certificates became one of the first scandals of Upper Canada.

It is odd that two persons well acquainted with the land regulations of Upper Canada—Richard Cartwright and D. W. Smith, the Acting Surveyor General—should have denied, the one by implication, the other outright, that the magistrates had this power. Smith rejected La Rochefoucauld's statement that "All the Justices of the Peace . . . possess the right . . . of assigning . . . every settler . . .

two hundred acres of land." [39] Yet the letter notifying the land boards that their functions were at an end and the public proclamation to that effect expressly state that in their individual capacities as magistrates they will still have this power.[40] On July 20, 1796, a public notice appeared over Smith's name announcing that the power of the magistrates to grant land had been suspended and that all persons holding magistrates' certificates must present them by August 20, otherwise they would not be honoured.[41] How could Smith have forgotten this notice and how could he also have forgotten the numerous letters about magistrates, certificates which his friend John Askin had written to him? [42]

From the outset Simcoe hoped to see Upper Canada settled not so much by individual effort as by the New England system of township planting.[43] He expected that petitions for townships in response to his proclamation would come chiefly from authorized representatives of associations of settlers already acquainted with one another, of the same religious persuasion, and more or less on a footing of equality. He knew that the people of Connecticut usually emigrated in this fashion, and he was anxious to encourage settlers from that "pure source of Emigration." [44] His original Queen's Rangers had been composed largely of Connecticut men,[45] and he believed there were still many persons in that state with loyalist leanings. The numerous petitions for land from associations of Connecticut settlers which the Council of Lower Canada had received before 1791 supported this belief.[46] In the early 1790's, too, the State of Connecticut was trying to dispose of its Western Reserve on the south shore of Lake Erie. Simcoe thought it would be desirable if a connection could be "formed between the Colony of Upper Canada and Connecticut and its offspring Vermont and the new Settlement on Lake Erie...." [47] He felt this could best be accomplished by peopling Upper Canada with Connecticut settlers whose prosperity would testify to the advantages of British rule.

The key figure in Simcoe's plans was the Reverend Samuel Peters of Connecticut. Simcoe was most anxious to have "a popular character" among the American loyalists sent out as Bishop of Upper Canada to establish the Church of England on a firm foundation.[48] Peters believed that true loyalists would follow him to the new province and that he could prevent religious feuds among them as "No stranger to their puritannical ideas of episcopacy" could.[49] Simcoe and Peters thought the matter settled before Simcoe left England and both men were bitterly disappointed by the government's refusal to provide a bishop for Upper Canada.

As soon as the first meeting of the legislature had taken place, Simcoe turned his attention to the hearing of petitions for townships. Between October 6, 1792, and July 24, 1793, some thirty-two townships were "granted," that is, assigned for settlement to the petitioners—the "nominees." [50] These townships included all the land readily accessible from the Lakes, the Rideau, the Trent, and the Thames, and that in the vicinity of existing or projected settlements. Incoming settlers had the choice of going beyond the Grand River to the far distant and unsurveyed townships on the shores of Lake Erie, which Simcoe was not yet willing to open to settlers,[51] or of making what terms they could with the nominees of townships. Fortunately for Upper Canada the nominees' monopoly did not last long.

Some of the original loyalists were greatly offended by this system of township granting and accused the government of having treated its enemies better than its friends.[52] The prominent loyalists would much have preferred to keep the power of recommending immigrants for land in the hands of the land boards, which they controlled, and they were sceptical of the value of an oath of allegiance in binding the newcomers to the Crown. Later writers have accused Simcoe's successor, Peter Russell, of admitting questionable characters[53] but contemporaries laid this fault at the door of the Lieutenant-Governor himself.[54] The inhospitable attitude on the part of the older residents towards newcomers professing loyalty was one of the difficulties in Simcoe's way—one which he discussed with his observant visitor, La Rochefaucauld-Liancourt.[55] While we may condemn their narrow jealousy, we can perhaps understand the bitter feelings of impoverished men towards those who during the war had allowed their prudence to get the better of their principles, as John Elmsley put it, and who now came "with property undiminished and persons unmolested" seeking a free grant of land from the sovereign whose cause they had not chosen to defend.[56]

Simcoe had no intention of permitting the nominees of townships to acquire extensive areas of land, and he rejected the offers of several groups of speculators to settle tracts of from nine to thirty townships.[57] The only advantage he intended to allow the nominees of townships was the privilege of surrounding themselves with settlers of their own choosing, and he did not feel himself precluded from placing settlers other than those recommended by the nominees in reserved townships if he should see fit to do so.[58] To *bona fide* leaders of associations of settlers he was willing to give the maximum grant of 1,200 acres but no more. It has to be admitted that the settling of townships on Simcoe's terms was not a business proposition. His scheme was suited only to co-operative associations of settlers, not to township promoters who were responsible for whatever expenses might be incurred in opening up new settlements.

As it turned out, petitions for townships did not come from *bona fide* leaders of associations but from speculators who did not understand that they had been assigned a trust and not a grant. Most of them expected to be allowed 1,200 acres for every settler they brought in and to receive from each of them a quit claim for 1,000 acres to recompense them for the expense incurred in promoting the settlement. As land in Upper Canada was granted under the identical proclamation as in Lower Canada, where this practice was countenanced, this mistake was a natural one. Other nominees planned to colonize their townships with settlers willing to pay an annual rent or a price for the land. As one group of Quaker speculators frankly told Simcoe, "Nothwithstanding whatever our Attachment to the British Government may be it doth not extend so far as to be at the expense of paying the passage of settlers, furnishing them with farming Utensils and Subsistence for 12 or 18 months without a prospect of some future Emolument to ourselves or posterity,"[59] and this sums up the attitude of all of them.

From the outset two members of Simcoe's Council opposed the township method of granting land, correctly fearing that it would lead to the selling of rights to townships and to endless confusion of claims.[60] Simcoe was soon warned that his trust had been misplaced and that some grantees were advertising their townships for sale.[61] After July, 1793, no more townships were granted, although large areas of land, chiefly on the Thames, were set aside for a limited time on the petitions of persons who undertook to settle them.[62] By the spring of 1794, Simcoe had come to the conclusion that it had been a mistake to entrust the settlement of the new province to self-styled "leaders" from the revolted colonies, most of whom had no prospect of leading forth loyal subjects of the Crown, or settlers of any kind, to the promised land of Upper Canada.[63] He decided to cancel several of the township "grants" he had made and in future to confer townships on "Old Country" men on whom he now thought it safer to rely. In August, 1795, two townships were thrown open to settlers because the nominees had taken no steps to settle them, and in May, 1796, a dozen others were declared forfeited because the grantees had failed to fulfil the conditions and had attempted to sell or rent to settlers.[64]

Just as Simcoe had no intention of encouraging unrestricted immigration into Upper Canada, so he had no intention of permitting unrestricted settlement within its boundaries. He was convinced that the best way to prevent the growth of a lawless class of backwoodsmen full of pernicious democratic ideas was to prevent the extension of the frontier of settlement while the townships already open to settlers were not yet fully peopled. He believed the formation of new settlements should be preceded by the establishment of military posts which would serve the double purpose of providing a local market for the settlers and of ensuring that the tone of the new communities would be one of loyal obedience to established authority.[65] Kingston, Niagara, and Detroit were not looked upon by Simcoe as suitable places for this purpose, not so much because considerable settlement had already taken place in their vicinity as because he believed Kingston and Niagara to be untenable military posts and Detroit likely to be handed over to the Americans. He wanted the arsenal for Lake Ontario to be established at York (the present Toronto) and that for Lake Erie at Long Point.[66] Two new internal routes to the west which he planned to open and settle would compensate for the loss of Detroit and the weakness of Niagara. One was to run from York to the headwaters of the Holland River by way of a new road to be called Yonge Street, and then via Lake Simcoe and the Severn River to Georgian Bay. This route was expected to provide a shorter and safer route for the fur trade. Its advantages had first been recognized by Pierre de Rocheblave who had tried to obtain from Dorchester a monopoly of the carrying trade over this portage.[67] The other route was from Burlington Bay to the forks of the Thames by way of a road to be called Dundas Street, then south down the Thames to Lake St. Clair, or north by way of the River aux Sables to Lake Huron. The post at Detroit he planned to replace by one at Chatham, eighteen miles from the mouth of the Thames. Most important of all, intended the new capital of Upper Canada—London—to be situated at the forks of the Thames in the heart of a fertile country and at the junction of the internal trade routes, where it would be protected by its distance from the lake shores against possible American attacks.[68]

If Simcoe's plans met with an unsympathetic response from Henry Dundas, they encountered outright obstruction from Lord Dorchester. The Lieutenant-Governor's mingled scheme of colonization and defence did not appeal to him in the least. Since he controlled the movement of troops, it was within his power to veto it. Dorchester was aware of the difficulties of keeping the expenses of distant posts within reasonable limits and was determined not to open the door to abuses of that sort. He did not think it wise to station troops in out-of-the-way places while there was danger of an Indian uprising and while a settlement had not yet been reached with the United States over the western posts. As soon as the dangers from these two sources had been averted, it was his intention to withdraw most of the troops from Upper Canada and station them in the lower province. Meanwhile he refused to allow his subordinate to occupy any of his carefully chosen objectives. Dundas agreed with Dorchester that troops could not be spared for inaccessible points like London, but he consoled Simcoe with the information that two provincial battalions of 750 men each were to be raised for the defence of the two Canadas and that these additional troops would make it possible for him to occupy London. His hopes for settlement were dashed, however, when he found that he could not recruit the necessary troops in Upper Canada.[69]

To add to his bitterness, Simcoe was not permitted to use the Queen's Rangers for the purpose for which they had been raised and which was so important a part of his cherished "system." In the summer of 1793, before Dorchester's arrival, he had moved the Queen's Rangers from Queenstown to York and had begun to fortify that post without first obtaining the approval of his military superior, Lieutenant-Governor Clarke. He wrote to Clarke asserting that it was impossible for him to distinguish between his military and his civil responsibilities and added that, as the approach of Wayne's army gave serious course for alarm, he considered it his civil duty to remove the whole body of the Queen's Rangers from the vicinity of Niagara to the uninhabited site of York[70] for the defence of the province. Clarke who was daily expecting the arrival of Lord Dorchester, did not attempt to prevent the carrying out of this peculiar bit of military strategy.[71]

If Simcoe was unable to distinguish between his military and his civil duties, Dorchester had no difficulty in making the distinction for him. He informed Simcoe that all establishments not ordered by the Commander-in-Chief were to be considered as done by him in his civil capacity and with the resources at his disposal in that capacity.[72] In the spring of 1794, the Queen's Rangers were withdrawn from York by Dorchester's orders and sent to Detroit and Niagara, and Simcoe was directed not to trouble himself further about the fortifications of York, which Dorchester regarded as too far away from the inhabited part of the country to be a suitable site for an arsenal.[73] Thus Simcoe's decision to occupy York prior to Dorchester's arrival, a decision probably based less on military strategy and more on a stubborn determination to have his own way, brought him nothing but humiliation.

He was further humiliated when, on October 7, 1794, Dorchester forbade him to use the Queen's Rangers for civil purposes. After the news of the signing of Jay's Treaty had reached Quebec, this restriction was lifted on condition that the transport of troops and stores and the existing military arrangements were not interfered with. Simcoe sulkily refused to take advantage of this partial permission in the expectation, as he informed his superior, that his system of

military defence and his plans for promoting the settlement of the province
would be adopted by the Imperial government now that the posts were to be
evacuated.[74] The Commander-in-Chief replied to this impertinent letter by
stating that he would withdraw all the troops from Upper Canada after the
posts should have been handed over, and that he would order one hundred of
the Queen's Rangers to military duty at Detroit and one hundred to Niagara.[75]
Unmoved by Simcoe's vehement protests, Dorchester issued him a last warning,
hinting that the duty of garrisoning Kingston might also be put upon the Queen's
Rangers.[76] This would have meant that practically the entire regiment would
have been assigned to purely military duties. Dorchester made good his threats
except the last. In June, 1796, all the troops were withdrawn from Upper
Canada except about forty of the Royal Artillery. Two companies of the Canadian Volunteers were sent up to man Kingston, but the duties of the other six
military posts were assigned to the Queen's Rangers.[77] Only 145 of them remained in the temporary capital of Upper Canada to console its Lieutenant-
Governor and even this number was later reduced by "great desertions." The
result was, as Simcoe's successor complained, that the work of raising the necessary buildings at York proceeded at a snail's pace.[78]

Throughout this controversy Simcoe wielded a doughty pen in defence of his
system, asserting that it had already received the blessing of the Imperial
authorities, as, indeed, his plans for London, York, and Long Point had.[79] In
opposing his military judgment to that of his Commander-in-Chief, he conjured
up the spectre of an Indian uprising swooping down upon his defenceless
province. To encourage settlers to come to Upper Canada and then to leave
them defenceless would, he declared, be "the most flagititious breach of National
honor and Public Faith . . .," and with exaggerated pessimism he predicted that
if the "limited ideas of Lord Dorchester" were adopted the province would
"moulder away into insignificance and Ruin." [80]

Dorchester was not the only one to disapprove of Simcoe's policies. The
merchants of Upper Canada realized quite as fully as Simcoe how much the
expenditures for the troops contributed to their prosperity and, quite apart from
considerations of defence, they were anxious to have the troops stationed in the
communities in which they were interested—Kingston, Niagara, and Detroit.
These were just the places that Simcoe intended to pass by in favour of Toronto,
London, and Chatham, virgin sites on which he could start *de novo* with nothing
to interfere with his detailed scheme of town planning.[81] Naturally there was
much opposition which Simcoe, intent on carrying out his policies, brushed
contemptuously aside.[82] While the site of Toronto was admitted by some to be
well chosen—Dorchester also had been planning a town there—[83] those persons
who had assumed that the government was to be continued at Niagara did not
look forward to the expense of removing to York and ultimately to London.
Those with vested interests at Kingston wished it to remain the naval station
for Lake Ontario and those at Detroit could hardly be expected to acquiesce
without a struggle in a policy designed to diminish the importance of the
Detroit settlements in the northwest trade.[84]

The unknown author of "Canadian Letters," who claimed to be unconnected
with the province, put up a strong argument in favour of placing the capital

at Kingston so as to attract population to an area which adjoined the lower province. Only as a result of a well-developed settlement along the shores of the St. Lawrence could the construction of canals be ensured and nothing, he was certain, would be more conducive to the prosperity of Upper Canada than the development of this export route for agricultural products. Various members of the Executive Council also expressed their disapproval of Simcoe's plans. The Secretary of the Land Board of Hesse, Thomas Smith, wrote, "A report prevails here that Governor Simcoe has quarrelled with his Council and is gone off to Toronto in a *pet*—representations have been made to the King and Parliament against him and the people are murmering very hard." [85] Even the cautious Peter Russell complained in a letter to Sir Henry Clinton of Simcoe's neglect of existing settlements and of his use of the labours of the Queen's Rangers to open a road towards "an *ideal* Capital in the Heart of a Wilderness which can scarcely be sufficiently peopled to feed it for fifty years to come." [86]

Lord Dorchester had learned that it was unwise to disregard the sentiments of the most articulate class in the community, the merchants. Before the quarrel between him and Simcoe had become too acrimonious, he tried to persuade his subordinate to reconsider, in the light of local advice and experience, the theoretical scheme he wished to impose upon the patterns of settlement already begun. The opinionated Simcoe disregarded this advice, and, obtaining no cooperation whatsoever from Dorchester, found reason to think that the merchants of Upper Canada carried more weight with him than the Lieutenant-Governor.[87]

There were other reasons for the strained relations existing between Simcoe and the merchants.[88] Simcoe's ideas of the prerogative powers of the Crown— and of its representative, the Lieutenant-Governor—were certainly high and his attitude towards those who did not share these views decidedly unfriendly, as W. D. Powell discovered.[89] Again, Simcoe's declared intention of freeing the slaves in his province by proclamation brought consternation to the merchants, who contended that, if he had his way, valuable rights of property (which the Imperial Parliament abolished by degrees elsewhere, and for which it was to pay £20,000,000) would be wiped out over night without a penny of compensation. The question was in the end dealt with, not by proclamation, but by an act, passed by a reluctant legislature under pressure from the Lieutenant-Governor, which prevented the perpetuation of slavery either from the natural increase of the slaves or by importation.[90]

Another bitter struggle took place between Simcoe and the merchants, three of whom were members of the Legislative Council, over the method of procuring provisions for the troops. For some years the garrisons at Niagara and Detroit had to be supplied from the neighbourhood of Kingston and this circumstance enabled a few merchants to buy up the flour and monopolize the business. Richard Cartwright became the supplier for Kingston, Robert Hamilton for Niagara, and John Askin and William Robertson for Detroit. When Upper Canada began to produce more than enough flour for her own needs and for the posts, the monopoly of the only cash market for flour which these merchants enjoyed enabled them to buy and sell at their own price. They were charged with favouring those already in debt to them and those who would take payment in goods or in merchants' notes, which were convertible into cash only at a discount.[91] When the Assembly met in May, 1793, it petitioned the Crown against the continuance of the monopoly.[92]

Simcoe disliked both the monopoly and the power over the struggling settlers which the merchants enjoyed, and he was eager to bring the provisioning of the posts under his own authority, seeing such control as means of bringing pressure to bear on the merchants in the Legislative Council who were opposed to some of his policies.[93] He proposed to buy flour direct from the settlers and to pay for it in specie, thus breaking the merchants' monopoly and putting specie into circulation.[94] The Treasury authorized the appointment of John McGill, Simcoe's Commissary, as agent for purchases and Simcoe began to put his new scheme into operation. A few months later he learned to his mortification that officials of the Treasury had changed their minds,[95] and that once again he had incurred the opposition of the Governor General, who objected to any civil appointee of Simcoe's interfering with the commissaries of the posts in Upper Canada.[96] A clumsy compromise was eventually worked out whereby Simcoe was permitted to name an agent for purchases who received his orders from Dorchester and his Commissary General but via the touchy Lieutenant-Governor.[97] The whole affair seems to have irritated the home government not a little and at one point in the argument it was ready to supply the troops from home instead.[98]

Simcoe's disappointment was bitter. He felt that he had been publicly humiliated and his influence with the Assembly of Upper Canada undermined.[99] He was eager for every bit of patronage, every mark of confidence, every inch of authority he could possibly lay claim to as Lieutenant-Governor,[100] but he was not motivated entirely by self-interest and vanity. What concerned him, almost from the hour of his appointment, was how to manage the Assembly. "The persons who shall compose the Assemblies," he told Russell, "must admittedly be dealt with as our Parliaments are & be purchased to their duty by the participation of the officers of government. Upright Intentions or a Government uprightly & wisely administered never did & never can stand in large and political societys upon the rectitude of its own measures." [101] After his arrival in the province, he lamented at length that his government was totally deficient of those means of forming an "influence" which the King's ministers at home enjoyed.[102]

Simcoe's plan of buying flour in small quantities direct from the settlers was a prelude to a much grander scheme he had in mind for making flour the staple of Upper Canada as tobacco had been the staple of Virginia. For every barrel of flour received into the storehouses, he proposed to issue notes redeemable in specie and made legal tender for the payment of taxes. The capital for their redemption was initially to be provided by Great Britain and repaid from the gradual sale of the lands bordering on Lake Erie, a district which he had withheld from settlement. By a scheme such as this, not only the posts, but before long the West Indies also, would receive cheap supplies, the province would enjoy a medium of exchange better regulated and more acceptable than merchants' notes, and the prosperity of the settlers and their attachment to the Crown would be secured. This ambitious and paternalistic project died on paper.[103]

Simcoe planned the colonization of his province with an eye to its future position in the British Empire rather than to what was practicable and feasible at the moment. He regarded the loyalist province of Upper Canada as a means of making good British losses in North America, applied the land regulations in a generous and confident spirit, and looked to the Imperial government to support him with the same generosity and confidence. But although the Colonial Office approved of some of the details that Simcoe submitted to them, it did not share his bold vision. Its commitment to the new province was a limited one.

In Canada, Simcoe's extensive and far-sighted plans met with the obstructive tactics of a more realistic and economical administrator, Lord Dorchester, who subjected him to the mockery of the hard-headed business men of his day, including his own Attorney-General,[104] and made even sympathetic observers think that "a man of plain common understanding would suit the Circumstances of this Country as well." [105] Some of the most prominent loyalists came to regard him with mistrust because he manifested "more joy over one republican professing repentance than over ninety and nine original loyalists." [106] Men such as Richard Cartwright thought him a little wild because he was trying to bring about in a few years' time changes which required a century for their accomplishment.[107] In the opinion of La Rochefoucauld, the five years which were all Simcoe had allowed himself for service in Upper Canada were hardly sufficient to lay the foundations of his plan whose branches were "so extensive and so numerous that a long series of years spent in the same spirit of unwearied exertion will be required to execute it in its whole extent." [108] But neither Cartwright nor La Rochefoucauld understood why Simcoe was pressing forward with such eager haste. His dream of reuniting the western settlements of the United States to a prosperous Upper Canada had to be realized while the Mississippi was kept closed by Spain. Once that river was opened to American trade and a right of deposit secured at New Orleans, the great opportunity would be lost.

To Simcoe everything depended on the success of his five-year plan, and it failed. Dundas disapproved of his policy of immigration promotion, Dorchester prevented his dream of loyal colonial cities springing up around well-chosen military posts from being realized, the services of his Queen's Rangers were taken from him, and those whom he had confidently expected to people townships for him turned out to be swindling speculators. "One by one his recommendations were disapproved of, gradually his troops were withdrawn, prop after prop vanished, until his schemes lay before him as confused and ineffectual as a flattened house of cards." [109] London remained an unrealized dream, Chatham only a paper town, and the "arsenal" of Lake Erie had not a soldier within miles of the few settlers at Long Point. York was a straggling settlement of about a dozen houses and had still to fight with Newark for the honour of being the seat of government, Yonge Street had been opened to Holland's Landing and Dundas Street had been cut through as far as Brant's settlement on the Thames and had also been extended from Burlington Bay to the Humber.[110] That was all. In 1796 Simcoe returned to England, fatigued, exasperated, defeated, but sustained by a sense of his own rightness and still burning with bumptious loyalty. A few months earlier, although he probably did not know it, the treaty of San Lorenzo opening the Mississippi to the United States had been signed.[111]

With his departure the concept of Upper Canada as a model province with its doors wide open to all repentant sinners from the United States seems to have disappeared. The new province fell under the control of less generous men bent on preserving distinctions between the original loyalists and later arrivals. With this narrow-minded group, whose loyalty became their profitable stock-in-trade, most of the officials sent out from England identified themselves.

Simcoe had remained in Canada four years, not five. On December 1, 1795, he applied for leave of absence on the ground of ill health and it was granted him.[112] He *was* ill, and had been since his expedition to the Maumee in 1794. In addition, he was dispirited and discouraged: as early as May, 1795, he had talked of resigning shortly "on account of his not being put upon the Staff." Peter Russell thought the real reason was Dorchester's "unexpected continuance in command,"[113] but it may well have been that Simcoe had come to admit to himself how unrealistic his hopes for Upper Canada had been—and perhaps how absurd his "enthusiasms," to use S. R. Mealing's term,[114] had made him seem to others. Simcoe was not recalled, but he was not returned either, although his commission as Lieutenant-Governor was not terminated until April 10, 1799. Perhaps he had no wish to return. Other employment was found for him and, in any event, his dream of utilizing Upper Canada as a magnet to attract the trans-Allegheny country back to British rule had gone glimmering. There is no evidence that the land speculators of Upper Canada prevented Simcoe's return, but it is certainly true that his policies had aroused much resentment and some of it, at least, was known at the Colonial Office.

CHAPTER FOUR

THE TROUBLES OF PETER RUSSELL

PETER RUSSELL, who became Administrator of Upper Canada on Simcoe's departure, was a man of very different temperament from his predecessor. Where Simcoe had been young, brash, and idealistic, Russell was old, cautious, and realistic. He wanted to do the thing nearest at hand that needed doing instead of embarking on extensive projects likely to be realized only at some distant day. For example, he thought it more sensible to settle compactly the area between York and the Bay of Quinte than to extend settlement north along Yonge Street or into the heart of the western peninsula.[1] He had not approved of Simcoe's grant of townships and was determined to limit the grants to ordinary settlers to 200 acres.[2] Russell, who was Receiver General before he succeeded Simcoe, seems to have had a bookkeeper's passion for order and exactness. He wanted to bring all the paper work relating to the Crown lands up to date, to hove all the proper forms complied with, and the fees, to which he and other officials were entitled, collected. He did not share Simcoe's illusion about the loyalty of immigrants who, after two decades of republicanism, came from the United States seeking free land from the Crown. He was cautious and somewhat timid, fearful of exceeding his temporary authority, and he had to withstand the pressures of two men more determined and more vigorous than he—Chief Justice Elmsley and Joseph Brant.

Russell inherited three tangled problems relating to the Crown lands from Simcoe. The first of these was the problem of the township grants. Before leaving, Simcoe had issued a proclamation of May 25, 1796, which declared certain townships forfeited and called upon the nominees of others to show cause by June 1, 1797, why their townships should not also be declared forfeited for failure to improve them.[3] Subsequently, the Surveyor General's Department reported that, out of the thirty-two townships granted by Simcoe, only six had received any considerable number of settlers, and in five of these many of the locations were later found to have been filled by fraud, the nominees having simply brought into the townships persons already in the province, and, in some instances, merely having borrowed their names. This was an old device which had been used successfully in New York, and Chief Justice William Smith ought to have been able to put both Simcoe and the Lieutenant-Governor of Lower Canada on guard against it.[4]

The threat of forfeiture brought forth protests from the nominees. Some of them asked for clarification of the terms upon which the townships had been granted and received the not very honest reply that the Proclamation of 1792 was itself sufficiently explanatory.[5] Although Simcoe had originally accepted the wording of the Lower Canada proclamation for his own, he later stated that it had not been satisfactory to him. The proclamation summarized the instructions but omitted the government's objections to making large grants and the statement that townships would be subdivided to suit the convenience of settlers.[6] Chief Justice William Smith of Lower Canada, who was believed by some of his contemporaries to be deliberately aiding American speculators,[7] considered 1,200 acres to be the usual grant contemplated by the instructions. The Council of Upper Canada, however, interpreted them to mean that the usual grants would be 200 acres, and 1,200 only in exceptional cases. Russell states that he had explained verbally in Council to "almost each" of the nominees of townships that all the Proclamation of 1792 promised them was the "Patronage of locasion" and the liberty to recommend settlers of property and education for grants larger than 200 acres, and that they themselves would receive no more than 1,200 acres.[8] Simcoe is accused of having given the nominees very different information. Ebenezer Allen, not a very trustworthy witness, declared that Simcoe himself had told him that he might sell to any good settlers. Thomas Ingersoll, who had opened a road into his township of Oxford at his own expense and brought in settlers, stated that Simcoe had informed him that forty families would be deemed an adequate settlement of the township. Aaron Greeley, who had built a saw mill and a grist mill for his settlers, claimed that Simcoe had promised him that if he would settle thirty families in the township of Haldimand and maintain them until they should be established on their farms, the rest of the township should be his own. William Berczy was another who claimed that townships had been granted on condition of settling thirty-eight families in each township, which would mean 1,200 acres to a settler.[9]

Berczy, relying on continued financial support from his American backers, the German Company or the New York Association, had brought to Upper Canada some sixty families of Germans from the Pulteney lands in the Genesee Country, where they had become dissatisfied with Pulteney's agent, Charles Williamson. Both Berczy and his backers expected that, after demonstrating their abilities as colonizing agents in the first township, Markam, additional townships amounting to one million acres would be made available to them.[10] Their settlers in Markam were supplied with teams and farm implements, provisions, mills, a schoolhouse, church, and clergyman.[11] But patents were not promptly forthcoming from the government of Upper Canada because the settlers were aliens not yet naturalized. Consequently, Berczy could not get mortgages on their farms to secure his loans to them. Neither could he get the additional land his American backers expected.[12] They soon withdrew leaving him to foot the bills for the opening up of the township of Markam.

One group of pertinacious speculators had asked for thirty townships and been refused. Five of them had been officers in loyalists regiments, but the sixth, Colin McGregor, was described by former Chief Justice Osgoode as "an other Character in New York the very Nest & Hotbed of Turbulence and Disaffection."[13] When they petitioned later, without naming McGregor, these loyalists received seven townships.[14] When Simcoe's proclamation of 1796 threatened forfeiture, their spokesman, Richard Duncan, appealed to D. W. Smith, hinting that a more intelligent system than that vaguely outlined in

Simcoe's proclamation of 1792 ought to be adopted. Duncan insisted that nominees of townships had been told they were simply required to settle forty families in four years, "with this encouragement from the Governor's own mouth, that the Terms of Upper Canada when ascertained, should not be on a worse footing than those adopted in Lower Canada." Duncan demanded to know why he and his colleagues could not have those terms. He also tried, unsuccessfully, to bribe Smith into helping him and his associates to secure secretly the townships with magistrates' certificates and warrants already issued for additional lands to loyalists. There is even a suggestion in his letter that such a proposal had been made to Simcoe himself and had not been rejected outright. Simcoe acknowledged that an attempt had been made to bribe him and Chief Justice Osgoode,[15] who was opposed to the granting of townships. As a means of settling the dispute, this group of speculators offered, if the Governor now thought he had made them grants in excess of what the royal instructions warranted, to relinquish their claims to townships in return for 10,000 acres apiece. Before the claims of Duncan and his associates could be considered, Simcoe had left Canada. When their proposal came before the Council, that body's response to its impertinent innuendoes was an order-in-council declaring their seven townships forfeited. Twelve months later, the same group petitioned again, humbly acknowledging that there had been just cause for throwing their townships open and asking for such an allowance as the nature of their intentions might entitle them to. Like other nominees, they received 1,200 acres apiece.[16]

To settle the disputes over townships, the Executive Council at first offered the six principal nominees of any township 1,200 acres apiece and expenses for surveys if they had actually begun to settle their township. Nominees who had done nothing were also offered the same quantity of land, provided they and their families became residents of the province. They all accepted this offer, except Berczy, who had learned that in Lower Canada the nominees of townships had obtained more generous treatment. Berczy somehow obtained an account of the discussions of the Executive Council of Lower Canada and of the instructions to Prescott of August 15, 1798, and published then in pamphlet form. The result was that all the nominees for townships in Upper Canada revived their claims and a "powerful combination" was formed under Berczy's leadership which Russell and his colleagues were unanimously determined to resist.[17]

Russell had at first been inclined to sympathize with Berczy, who had done more than anyone to settle his land and had been let down by his associates. But his attitude changed when he found that Berczy's backers had been a group of American speculators—Green, Hall and Company of New York—and when he was informed by Robert Liston, British Consul at Philadelphia, that they included Aaron Burr. Liston suspected these men intended to get hold of a large tract of land in Canada and colonize it with "persons of their own sentiments."[18]

In July, 1797, the Council decided to put an end to the claims of nominees of townships by granting the four principal nominees of any township 1,200 acres each, including former grants except military lands, provided they became residents of the province. Since this was the maximum allowed under the royal instructions, no larger grant could be made to those who were nominees for more than one township. Their settlers were to be confirmed in their locations provided they had not received land from the Crown elsewhere in the province.[19] No further locations were to be made by the nominees after July 3, 1797, and all the townships were thrown open to settlement. Some of the dissatisfied nominees attempted to block the government's policy by entering caveats against the granting of lots in townships which they claimed, but the Council met their manœuvre, which would have laid the whole province under an "interdict," simply by ordering its secretary not to receive caveats of this nature and by rescinding all orders-in-council in their favour.[20] These measures broke the speculator's monopoly of all the readily accessible townships. For three years there had been only one settler on the north shore of Lake Ontario from York to the Bay of Quinte, according to Russell. "In six Months after rescinding the Order-in-Council which locked up their Country to Land Jobbers—about 100 families sat down within that space. . . ." It is questionable, however, whether the settlement of the province was stimulated as much as Russell asserts. The patent records show that in several of the forfeited townships between York and the Bay of Quinte large blocks of land were subsequently located by officers of the government. In 1803, a traveller observed that the shores of Lake Ontario were not much settled and Lord Selkirk, who also visited the area in 1803, commented that the land had been granted away in large tracts to officials and that most of the valuable situations were gone.[21]

William Dummer Powell hints that the interpretation of the instructions by which the Council justified its policy of declaring the townships forfeit was not the one on which it had originally acted and that there had been "some juggle . . . some concealment." One thing which was certainly concealed from the Colonial Office was that some of those who had speculated in townships had been loyalists. The Council's report, summarizing the various interpretations that had been put on Simcoe's proclamation and justifying the forfeitures, said: "Nor is it likely that in thus laying the foundations for a future Aristocracy by the unequal distribution of Property which would naturally follow from even the most moderate of those systems . . ." the loyalists would have been forgotten. They had not been forgotten. They had participated in the land speculations, and the Council knew it.

Powell thought the Council ought to have admitted that it had erred in leading the nominees to believe that each of their settlers would receive 1,200 acres. It should then have informed them that if they could show they had settled forty families, each of whom belonged to the class entitled to the exceptional 1,200-acre grants, the townships would be confirmed to them and their associates, and they would then be free to carry out whatever arrangements they might have for reconveying parts of their grants to one another. Had the Council done this, argued Powell, "the most impudent tinker that ever hunted Gov. Simcoe to Castle Frank" would not have dared to murmur.[22] When General Peter Hunter took over the government of Upper Canada in 1799, Powell put these ideas before him, but the Lieutenant-Governor was evidently not disposed to reopen a matter which had been closed by his predecessors in office.

The nominees of townships were not without support. William Warren Baldwin was one who sympathized with them and never ceased to deplore the fact that the township method of colonization had not been given a fair trial. He thought it might have been "matured into the happiest system of land granting" and was a more practical method of settling the country than that of permitting individual locations to be scattered over millions of acres of wilderness.[23] Baldwin did not defend the fraudulent system of leaders and associates under which the leaders did nothing to develop the townships beyond paying the survey and patent fees. In many instances this is what occurred in Lower Canada and it might well have been common in some of the Upper Canada townships too.

On the other hand, the system of township planting could have allowed communities of friends to settle together and to pool their resources and their labour. It might have induced capitalists to invest their funds in the development of a compact settlement, as Berczy did, in the expectation of the double profit from land speculation and money lending. Grist and saw mills had to be provided and struggling settlers who possessed little but their labour had to obtain credit to tide them over until their farms became productive. Denied the benefits of township planting, the pioneers of Upper Canada, until 1815, tackled the wilderness single-handed and in scattered locations, obtaining what credit they could from merchants. The result was to bring into existence exactly what Simcoe had tried to prevent: a class of land speculators.

Under either the township system or the system of individual locations, the country would gradually have been settled, large proprietorships would have been created, and a class of mortgage-ridden farmers, or tenants, would have arisen. But the system based on individual locations was the more inefficient and costly of the two. Long distances had to be travelled to mill and market over trails that would have been proper roads in a well-planned settlement. The services of clergymen and schoolmasters were not to be had. Merchants gradually came into possession of thousands of acres by acquiring land in payment of debts from settlers who had failed in their struggle to make a living in the bush and by buying land rights at low rates from those who needed to cash in on them.[24]

Major Robert Mathews has described the process as it existed on the Detroit frontier in 1787:

Individuals procure immense tracts of land upon Indian Grants, sell it out in detail to poor wretches for £100 for three acres in front and 40 deep for which the Farm is at the same time mortgaged. The settler labours for a few years with only half his vigour, paying and starving all the time: and ultimately for debts on every hand is obliged to give up his Land. In Trade, the lowest of the profession resort to these obscure places. They are without education or sentiment and many of them without common honesty....

Much the same sort of thing continued even after settlers were able to acquire land, not by the purchase of illegal Indian titles, but by grant from the Crown. Their need of capital to develop it caused them to become hopelessly indebted to the frequently denounced "Shopkeeper Aristocracy" and eventually to lose their land.[25]

The new proprietors were not tempted to improve their land because it consisted of scattered locations. In time, the progress of settlement and the gradual change from a free grant to a cash sale policy made their holdings valuable and enabled them to garner an unearned increment. Those of Upper Canada's early merchants who were sufficiently clever augmented their wealth in this way, but it was a tricky business and many a merchant ended, like John Askin, land poor and unable to pay his Montreal creditors. The wealth acquired by the first generation from land speculation was reinvested in land by the second, so long as profitable opportunities were to be had. By the late eighteen thirties the wealthy were beginning to prefer town lots and town properties, and water lots and mill sites. Subsequently, they shifted to bank stocks and steamboat companies. By the third generation, fire insurance, boiler insurance, or life insurance companies and express companies attracted them. Eventually some of this wealth was reinvested in prairie lands and in the mortgage and finance companies in existence today.[26]

The defeated township promoters harboured bitter feelings towards those who had deprived them of their land, particularly towards D. W. Smith who had drawn up the reports concerning the activities of the land-jobbers on which Russell and the Executive Council had acted. Smith was not likely to be forgiven by these speculators for uncovering the real nature of their land jobbing. Possibly this is what John Elmsley had in mind when, commenting to Lieutenant-Governor Hunter on Smith's application for a seat in the Executive Council, he wrote:

The Memory of certain Events appears to me to be too recent, and the Opinion of the public, with respect to the share Mr. Smith had in producing them too undetermined to make it at present an advisable Step to promote him to a Situation which is generally considered a distinct mark of the favour of the governor, and which would in all probability be construed into a Declaration of Your Excellency's Sentiments on a point on which I believe it is your Intention not to declare any.[27]

It was some time before the parties and passions created by the forfeiture of the townships died down. In 1802, a wild rumour circulated that the malcontents were intriguing with a group of Americans to turn the province over to the United States. Congress was then expected to confirm their claims to the townships of which they had been deprived. Peter Russell, who did not live to hear about the fate of Texas, dismissed these rumours as "a Tissue of Absurdity & Improbability,"[28] but some of his colleagues in the government were more credulous. Among the members of the Assembly in opposition to the policies of the government were Mathew Elliott, Richard Beasley, Ralf Clench, and Angus McDonnell —none of whom represented districts in which the original loyalists predominated. Chief Justice Elmsley, applying a technique which has become all too familiar to us, intimated to Hunter that certain members of the Assembly were part of a conspiracy to seize the province for the United States. Powell, in a private memo apparently intended for his own use, identifies them. They were the four members of the opposition named above.[29]

Asa Danforth was another of the malcontents. With Aaron Greeley he had undertaken to settle the townships of Hope, Haldimand, Cramahe, and Percy and had also contracted to open a road from York to Kingston. The townships were declared forfeit, his claim that he had brought in 300 good farmers denied, and the road reported to be so imperfectly made that payment for it was delayed. Danforth states that "when the Executive Council saw that our Americans had made choice of the best lands in the province they laid a plan to recind & take away the Lands theretofore granted and placed their own locations on the land." Danforth had several interviews with Aaron Burr, who had been a member of the New York group backing Berczy. These raised his hopes that the province would be taken over. "How far distant you may conceive the time I cannot say," wrote Danforth,

... only observe that this is the fear of our [Upper Canada] officers of Government and that three fourths of the common people would be happy of a Change would they be sensible by Proclamation or otherwise, to them that His Majesty's Proclamation should be made good to them agreeable to the first & true intent and meaning when first signed ... not that this administration shall place such construction on their instructions from home as will rob and ruin the Subjects who have laboured under the greatest hardships, placing full dependence on the King's word.

Joseph Brant, who had disputes of his own about land with the government of Upper Canada, was expected to assist the invaders and their domestic supporters, and the plot was supposed to have been hatched during the summer of 1801 when Burr sent his daughter Theodosia and his son-in-law Alston to visit Brant at his home on the Grand River.[30] If the disgruntled speculators on both sides of the line ever concocted such a scheme, it never got beyond the stage of wild imaginings.[31]

The second problem Simcoe left to Russell was whether the Crown lands should be made to produce revenue and if so, by what methods. For many years the Imperial government regarded the Crown lands of Upper Canada as a convenient resource from which to satisfy the wants of the needy, the expectations of its old servants, the demands of the importunate. It began by rewarding loyalists, officers, and discharged soldiers with free grants of land on which the expenses of survey and patent were paid by the government, and it continued to make free grants, subject only to survey and patent fees, in the hope of attracting population to the province. Within a few years' time it was led to regret this liberality and to wish that the Crown lands could at least be made to pay their own expenses.

Although the Imperial government was veering towards a revenue policy, Simcoe favoured the continuance of the free grant system. Shortly before he left Upper Canada, the Colonial Secretary, the Duke of Portland, informed him that steps were being taken in the lower province to relieve the government of the expense of surveys and that he was expected to do the same thing in his province. He was also invited to give his opinion on the advisability of changing the land system from a free grant to a revenue basis.[32] A table of patent fees satisfactory to the Colonial Office had been adopted for Upper Canada on July 7, 1796, after several previous tables had been rejected.[33] The suggestion that the grantees of land should now be required to pay the expenses of survey was passed on to Simcoe already stamped with Dorchester's approval and, as such, it was not relished by him. In his ill-tempered reply to Portland, Simcoe charged that the expenses incurred in surveys in Upper Canada had been occasioned by the orders of Dorchester and the Council of Quebec before 1791, sneered at the "ostentatious pretext of this Quality [economy] on which His Lordship seems perpetually to dwell," and reiterated once more his own argument that an adequate support of the new province in the beginning would in the long run prove economy.[34] When this question was submitted to the Council of Upper Canada, however, Dorchester's suggestion was promptly approved and a survey fee imposed on every grant made after July 1, 1796, excepting grants to U.E. loyalists and military claimants. At the same time the Council revoked the power which magistrates had previously had of granting new settlers certificates for 200 acres. Thereafter, all applications for land had to be made to the lieutenant-governor-in-council.[35] The effect of these two measures was to decrease the facility and increase the expense of obtaining land in Upper Canada.

Portland's suggestion that the Crown lands be made to yield a revenue by the imposition of a fee, in addition to the expenses of survey and patent, did not appeal to either the Executive Council or the Lieutenant-Governor of Upper Canada. It was apparent to them that behind this proposal, which seems to have originated in Lower Canada, was the intention to grant townships on the system of leaders and associates, the system which Simcoe had already tried and found productive chiefly of fraud and chicanery. Moreover, as the system operated in Lower Canada, grants of 1,200 acres were made to all members of such groups, the leader paying the fees and expenses and the associates in return handing over to the leader all but 200 acres of their grants or selling out to him completely. Such arrangements were objectionable to the original loyalists of Upper Canada, as Simcoe pointed out to the Colonial Office. Five thousand acres of land was all that the highest ranking loyalist officers had received, and 200 all that a private had obtained. The leading loyalists, therefore, could hardly be expected to acquiesce in a system under which all newcomers could obtain 1,200 acres and strangers in the country, "of no figure in life," could become the possessors of whole townships.[36] John Elmsley feared that if grants of 1,200 acres were available, speculators from the States "using poor men's names ... would come to own a British province." He was, he admitted, "no enemy to speculation in lands" provided "the capital embarked in them belongs to the country and the profits arising from them are to remain in it."[37]

The Executive Council of Upper Canada, having turned down the plan of an additional fee, proposed selling some Crown land to raise funds for public purposes. This method, they hinted, would be "probably less offensive to the Loyalists who are the original Founders of this Colony."[38] But Simcoe felt that it would be unwise to bring the Crown lands on the market while there was still so much unimproved wild land in private hands, a factor which would prevent their bringing a decent price. It also meant either the sale of large tracts to land-jobbers or the sale of small lots to European immigrants. In view of the competition of American land-jobbers for settlers and, added Simcoe maliciously, the fact that Dorchester, by withdrawing the troops, had exposed the upper province to the dangers of an Indian war, this was impracticable. More impracticable still was Simcoe's own suggestion that future grants of land be burdened with quit rents which, if applied to public purposes would, he thought, be collected without difficulty, and "would form a distinction between the original Loyalist, and the future settler which would be most agreeable to the former and by no means unreasonable or unjust to the latter."[39] Happily, this proposal, so fraught with danger to the domestic peace of Upper Canada, was ignored by the Colonial Office.

Despite Simcoe's unfavourable report on the prospects of the land market, the Imperial government seriously considered disposing of the Crown lands of the Canadas by sale. In an effort to establish a uniform system, a protracted, three-cornered correspondence was carried on between Portland, Governor Prescott of Lower Canada, and, after Simcoe's departure, Peter Russell. Two detailed plans were finally worked out by Prescott. The first provided for grants subject to a fee of £25 per 1,000 acres, and the second for sales by auction and payment by instalments. Prescott came to prefer the latter plan, his Council the former, and both plans were eventually authorized by the Imperial government.[40]

In Upper Canada, Russell and the Executive Council were first asked to consider the additional fee of £25. They now welcomed the idea and were ready to put it into effect at once, provided it was clearly understood that the U.E. loyalists and the military claimants would still be entitled to free grants. They also insisted that the usual grants should continue to be 200 acres to ordinary applicants petitioning as individuals rather than 1,200 acres to each of a group of associates as in Lower Canada.[41] There were several reasons for this *volte face*. First, the province was sorely in need of revenue. Second, the members of the Council, now no longer under the influence of Simcoe, inclined more and more to the viewpoint of those loyalists who had deeply resented his liberality towards newcomers from the United States. Were the policy of making grants free of expense except for survey and patent fees continued, such newcomers would, in their opinion, receive their land on easier terms than the original loyalists who had first encountered the wilderness in Upper Canada. Even a fee of 6d. an acre would not equalize all the disadvantages with which the original loyalists had struggled.[42] Third, an increase in the land fees meant an increase in the value of the land and all those who had received large grants from the Crown were naturally interested in bringing this about.

John Elmsley was convinced that the land fees could safely be raised not merely to £25 per 1000 acres but to £45 without retarding the settlement of the country.[43] Like Gourlay and Wakefield later, he argued that labour would become more plentiful as land became dearer. Thus the means of employing capital to advantage would be increased. "While lands can be had as cheaply as at present that true proportion between capital and labor which is the only source of wealth in any country will never be attained in this," wrote Elmsley. "Instead of opulent farmers we will have miserable cottagers who cannot afford to cultivate their land properly, scraping a subsistence from an acre or two. . . . What is capital," he concludes, "but property unequally distributed?"[44] It was Elmsley's plan to make Upper Canada a country in which inequalities would be fostered instead of a land of opportunity in which the poor man might rise from the ranks of propertyless labourers.

While the Executive Council fell in line with the wishes of the Colonial Office and accepted the additional fee, it stood fast by its determination to make grants only to individual petitioners. In Lower Canada the Land Committee did not even take the trouble to work out the fees on anything less than 1,000 acres because it fully expected that they would be "discharged in the gross" by the leaders of townships.[45] In Upper Canada, the Proclamation of October 31, 1798, which announced the change in fees, stated that in future the fee would be 6d. an acre, exclusive of the expenses of survey. The survey money and half the patent fees were to be paid when the warrant of survey was taken out and the balance when the patent issued. The special regulation which applied to loyalists will be discussed in chapter V. No change was made in the size of grants to ordinary settlers, which remained 200 acres.[46] Portland, whose eyes had been opened by Prescott to the frauds perpetuated by the leaders of the townships, acquiesced and congratulated Russell on having avoided settlement by associated companies in Upper Canada.[47]

Under the old regulations, a patent for 200 acres cost a fee of £2 18s. 8d. sterling, which was divided among the officers of the Land Department. Under the new regulations, the same patent, exclusive of the survey fee, cost £5, of which £3 17s. 10d. went to the Crown and £1 2s. 2d. to the officers of the Land Department.[48] As the land officers were later to complain, their various shares on these small grants were trifling and inadequate.

Russell and his Council were subsequently authorized to dispose of the Crown lands by sale as well as by grant on a plan to be worked out in conjunction with Lower Canada.[49] Prescott's plan of sale appealed to the Council, and they resolved that as soon as the proper reservations could be made for the Crown, the clergy, and the claims of the U.E. loyalists, the whole of the Crown lands in Upper Canada should be offered at auction in limited quantities annually. The fees on sales of land in sizeable blocks would have compensated the land officers for the small fees on land disposed of in 200-acre lots by grant, a method then expected to be temporary.

Sale of public lands at auction was exactly the method being followed by the federal government of the United States at this time—one which Simcoe had condemned as conducive to speculation. It was also a policy which would have made Crown land harder to obtain and raised its value in the hands of those who already had it. Naturally enough, leading loyalists and Executive Councillors, who were well rewarded with Crown grants, and prosperous merchants, who had taken land in payment for debts, saw no harm in that. Russell's Council was made up of such persons and he, unlike Simcoe, was not the man to withstand them or to oppose policies which, originating in Lower Canada under very different circumstances, came to him already stamped with the approval of the home government.

Almost thirty years elapsed before a sales system was instituted. When the Council took stock it found that there were many land board certificates, loyalist and military claims still unlocated and that barely sufficient land remained to satisfy them. It therefore recommended that an extensive purchase be made from the Indians before the plan of raising a revenue from the Crown lands should become known. It also suggested that in the meantime land granting, which had been suspended in December, 1797, should be resumed at the new fees of £25 per 1,000 acres, in addition to the expenses of survey.[50] Russell acquiesced and agreed to ask Governor Prescott to purchase about twenty townships.[51]

Indian affairs for Upper Canada were managed by the Superintendent General of Indian affairs, who (after 1796) was directed by the Lieutenant-Governor or

Administrator, who in turn was subject to the general orders of the Governor General. In 1830 a separate Department of Indian affairs was created for Upper Canada and placed directly under the Lieutenant-Governor.[52] Until 1818, the Indians always received a lump sum for their lands paid in cash or in goods but subsequently the treaties provided for payment in annuities. Some lands were ceded in trust to be sold for the benefit of the Indians, the proceeds being invested for them.

The Indian lands of Upper Canada are too long a story to be included here. Briefly, the chief problems arose out of the efforts of Joseph Brant to obtain for the Six Nations an unrestricted title to their lands on the Grand River; the Indians' practice of making provision for half-breed families, or whites who had done the tribes a service, or of making leases to whites, which led to disputes about the rents; squatters' incursions on Indian lands; the failure of the Indian Department to collect on the sales of trust lands, or to invest the funds with proper care. Canadians have been wont to boast that in Canada the Indians have been treated more justly than they have south of the line. This may be true for the post-Confederation period but the earlier record is not exactly spotless.

Until 1798 the government experienced no difficulty in getting the Indians to surrender land for about 3d. an acre. After that date it encountered the obstructive tactics of Joseph Brant who was well aware of the potential value of the land and who realized that his people would not be able to support themselves from it in their traditional ways. Brant was none too eager to accommodate the government of Upper Canada, against which he had many grievances and which had begun to mistrust him. Moreover, the "loyal" Mohawk played a double role, keeping up his contacts with influential persons south of the border and giving them the impression that his influence in Upper Canada might be useful to the United States.[53]

Brant's principal complaint was that the Six Nations could not procure a patent for their land which would give them absolute title to it and leave them free to dispose of it as they saw fit.[54] The patent which Simcoe offered prevented them from alienating or leasing any of their land except among themselves or to the Crown.[55] This was so unsatisfactory to Brant that he hinted to the Americans that his people would like to have a tract of land in the United States "that we may call our own." [56] After negotiations with William Berczy for the sale of part of the Grand River lands fell through,[57] Brant made an agreement with a group of speculators with whom Israel Chapin, an American Indian agent, was connected.[58] Three hundred and eighty-one thousand acres of the Grand River tract were sold to them for prices ranging from 3s. to 6s. an acre, the payments to be extended over a number of years.[59] Since such prices could be obtained, the Indians were naturally reluctant to surrender their land to the government for 3d. an acre. They also felt that since the land was theirs, they should be free to dispose of it as they saw fit. After a bitter controversy, Brant succeeded in forcing Peter Russell, whose Council was unanimously in favour of yielding, to confirm this sale and to give the several purchasers their patents free of fees.[60] This dispute came at a time when the government of Upper Canada was troubled by domestic unrest,[61] uneasy about the activities of Spain in Louisiana, and anxious to retain the friendship of the Indians. But, nervous though he was, Russell would not be harried into giving the Indians a title that would leave them free to dispose of the rest of their lands when and to whom they pleased, perhaps even to Brant's American friends.[62]

Brant also tried to help the Missisaugas to resist the efforts to buy their land at a low price.[63] When the government attempted to purchase from them a much desired tract stretching along the shores of Lake Ontario from York to Burlington Bay, it discovered that Brant was dictating the terms. After remarking that it was too much like the Yankees to grasp the land too eagerly, Brant demanded on behalf of the Missisaugas at least 2s. an acre, unless the Indians were allowed to make such reservations within the tract as they pleased.[64] This was an unheard of price for Indian land. Russell allowed the matter to drop, hoping thereby to diminish Brant's influence and to bring the Missisaugas to more reasonable terms. In this he acted on the advice of Prescott who, believing that French emissaries were trying to arouse the western Indians to attack the British province, was most anxious to keep the Indian tribes of the two Canadas contented.[65] A litte later Brant proposed, on behalf of himself and the Missisaugas, to sell the government some 69,999 acres of land bordering on Lake Ontario at 1s. 3d. an acre on condition that it afterwards be given to the Comte de Puisaye, leader of the French émigré Royalists.[66] Russell declined the offer, both on account of the price and because it was not customary for Indian grants to the Crown to be fettered with conditions.[67] For seven years no Indian purchases were made, but in 1805, two years before Brant's death, the Missisauga tract was secured for approximately 5d. an acre.[68] In the interval, the Indians had learned from the experience of the Six Nations that it was one thing to sell land to private purchasers at high rates and another thing to collect from them.[69] By 1806, the War of 1812 had already begun to cast its shadow over the province and, for fear of upsetting the tribes, no further purchases of Indian land were attempted.

Failure to quiet the Indian title to additional land meant that the new sales policy, adopted in principle, could not be put into general effect until 1826. It was, however, given a trial on a small scale. Shortly after General Peter Hunter succeeded Russell, two townships were sold to pay for the road Asa Danforth was constructing between York and Kingston.[70] The results of this transaction were not altogether satisfactory. It was charged that the two townships, Dereham and Norwich, had been sold secretly in the Council room "amongst persons high in authority for one-third of their value. . . ."[71] These townships were offered for sale in blocks of 3,000 acres on the terms of half cash and the balance in two years in two equal instalments. Sealed bids were called for and the sale was advertised well in advance of the closing date. The method of sale was that which had been suggested by Portland[72] but it did not commend itself to the Executive Council whose members wanted the land sold at auction. In vain had John Elmsley tried to convince Hunter that auctions, while they might be regarded in Europe as not suited to the dignity of a monarch, were perfectly acceptable in America where people had "no such refined sensibilities."[73]

At this sale 81,000 acres were bought for £3062 5s. The largest purchasers were the Rev. Robert Addison, 9,000 acres; Robert Hamilton, a member of the

Legislative Council, 24,000 acres; William Willcocks and family (relatives of Russell), 15,000 acres; and H. Ball & Co., 12,000 acres.[74] In 1798, D. W. Smith had estimated the value of wild land at 6d. to 15d. an acre, but he expected the townships of Dereham and Norwich to sell at a higher price than other land as they were "more surrounded by Settlement." [75] The price obtained for them was certainly low, 9d. an acre, but not so low as one-third of their value, and perhaps if they had been sold at public auction public suspicion would not have been aroused. Although these townships sold for about one-third more than they would have produced under the fee system, the result was not considered satisfactory. In 1804, certain other land which had been reserved for sale was thrown open to location and all plans for the institution of a sales system were indefinitely deferred.[76]

The third piece of unfinished business which Simcoe left to Russell was exchanging the land certificates for the patents in free and common socage promised by the Constitutional Act. It took time to devise a method of survey and a form of patent which met the requirements of the act and the royal instructions and which also satisfied the people of Upper Canada. Simcoe had already incurred the hostility of the leading merchants of the province and in his handling of this question he incurred a great deal more.

One difficulty was that the Constitutional Act required Clergy Reserves proportionate to the size of each grant to be specified in the patents, to be nearly adjacent to the grants, and to be as nearly equal in value to one-seventh of the granted land as circumstances would permit.[77] In addition, Crown Reserves equal in extent to the Clergy Reserves had been required by a royal instruction.[78] These requirements delayed the adoption of a method of surveying new townships, particularly in Lower Canada where the method was not settled until 1797.[79] Meanwhile, the Land Committee of Upper Canada had adopted, on October 15, 1792, the famous chequered plan devised by D. W. Smith. The two-sevenths for the Crown and the clergy were provided by reserving seven lots in each concession, the reserves being staggered with respect to one another and to those in adjacent concessions.[80] Smith's plan aroused unfavourable comment in Upper Canada because it would prevent compact settlement. Petitions were sent to Simcoe asking for "the Lower Canada system" of reserves in the four corners of townships.[81] The petitions were rejected, and the chequered plan was approved by the Colonial Secretary as suitable for both Upper and Lower Canada.[82] In Upper Canada the chequered plan was not deviated from except for those townships, principally on the Niagara and Detroit frontiers, the St. Lawrence, and the lower Thames, which were fully or partially located before 1791. In such cases the reserves were set aside in other townships, or in blocks in the centre of the townships, or in the rear concessions.[83]

Under Smith's chequered plan no reserve lots were taken on the five road allowances running from front to rear of the townships, but on every concession line there were seven reserve lots. Since the early townships were laid out fronting on the lakes, it is obvious that the settlement and maintenance of the important early roads of Upper Canada, like Dundas Street, the Danforth Road, and later the Talbot Road, would be hindered by the reserves. In these and other instances the Council obtained permission to deviate from the approved system of reserves for roads.[84] Certainly the chequered plan did not facilitate the compact settlement of the country but, given the liberal land-granting system already in effect, such a development was not to be expected. The existence of the Crown and Clergy Reserves merely aggravated a problem which would have been serious without them.

Smith's chequered plan gave both Crown and clergy more than they were intended to receive, one-seventh of the townships being reserved for each of them instead of one-seventh of the land granted. Smith's error seems to have been derived from the Proclamation of 1792 which stated that only such parts of the townships would be granted as should remain after reserving one-seventh for the Crown and one-seventh for the clergy. When Attorney General White detected the mistake, no alteration in the chequered plan was made, but the method of specifying the reserve for each lot was corrected.[85]

The problems arising out of the Clergy Reserve clauses complicated and delayed the issuing of land patents, and there were additional problems still to be met. The failure of the government of Upper Canada to provide a satisfactory table of fees before July, 1796, was not the only, or the most important, factor in delaying patents. The amount of the fee due was not included in the wording of the patents themselves. Moreover, it is not the fact that "most of the settlers . . . when freehold tenure was established . . . were still in ignorance as to the nature or extent of fees liable by them when taking out their patents." [86] Those who had received land before 1791 were chiefly loyalists and military claimants and their grants were all "privileged," that is patent free. Even ordinary settlers allotted land under the instructions of 1786 were entitled to free patents. The absence of a firm table of fees does not seem to have hindered the settlement of the province. Speculators were not deterred from applying for townships nor individual settlers for 200-acre lots. But until a table of fees had been approved by the Colonial Office the land officers could not obtain even the half fees allowed them on privileged grants, and paid out of the provincial revenue supplemented by the Military Chest. Since their salaries were supplemented from this source, they felt the problem was an urgent one.

Simcoe seems to have wished to avoid all the trouble and expense that would be involved in exchanging certificates for patents. On the advice of Chief Justice William Smith of Lower Canada, he at first proposed that the legislature should pass an act giving the certificates the force of patents. He accepted this idea of Smith's shortly after his arrival in Canada, probably when he was under the impression that the certificates were still in the hands of the original nominees and before he had discovered the amount of land-jobbing that had gone on. Later, however, he abandoned this plan and issued a proclamation calling on all persons in the Home District to turn in the documents on which they based their claims to land in order that patents for grants in free and common socage might be prepared. More than two years elapsed before a second proclamation was published which applied to the other districts as well, and by November, 1795, only four patents had passed the Great Seal.[87]

The loyalists, despite their dislike of French tenure, responded to the proclamation very slowly. In a land where travel was both tedious and expensive, the

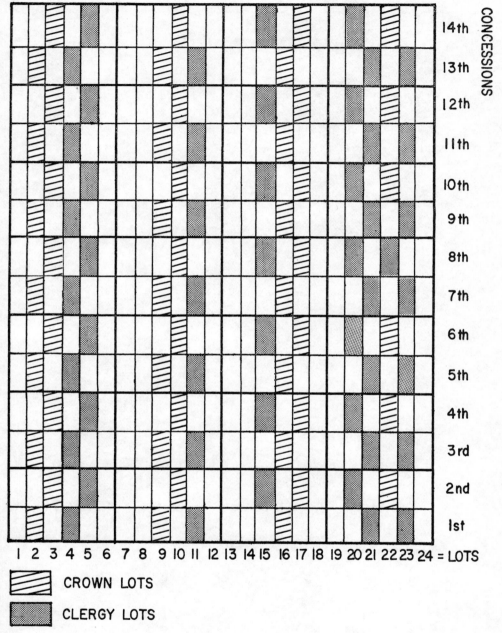

FIGURE 1. The Chequered Plan. Based on the illustration of the Plan accompanying D. W. Smyth's report on the reserved lands (P.A.O., Simcoe Papers, Env. 44).

CONCESSIONS — 1st 2nd 3rd 4th 5th 6th 7th 8th 9th 10th 11th 12th 13th 14th

LOTS — 1 2 3 4 5 6 7 8 9 10 11 12 13 14 15 16 17 18 19 20 21 22 23 24

CROWN LOTS

CLERGY LOTS

Figure 1. The Chequered Plan. Based on the distribution of the Plan accompanying D. W. Smith's report on the reserved lands. (P.A.O. Simcoe Papers, Env. 44).

pioneer farmer, once safely located on his land and secure in the promise of the Constitutional Act, put off from month to month the journey to the office of the Attorney General or Clerk of the Peace for his district. In the second proclamation Simcoe thought it advisable to make the threat—which was never carried out—that unless the certificates were turned in within six months' time the lands they covered might be deemed vacant and be granted to others.[88] William Dummer Powell opposed the issuing of this proclamation fearing it would create uneasiness and resentment. He did not think that Simcoe had the legal power to resume the grants and he "warmly and affectionately cautioned [him] not to commit himself in proclamations beyond his power to enforce obedience."[89] Several hundred of the certificates were sent in during 1795 and 1796, but as late as 1818 they were still being presented for patents.[90]

The greatest obstacle to the speedy exchange of certificates for patents was that by 1795 many of these certificates had passed out of the hands of the original holders and it was not an easy task to decide to whom the patents should now be made out.[91] In some cases the original nominees of the Crown had died intestate or after having devised their land by will. In other cases land held by certificates had been exchanged, sold, perhaps several times over, or mortgaged. In 1789, the consent of the local land board was made necessary to validate a transfer of land. This was intended to discourage those persons from applying for land who simply wished to turn their certificates into cash as soon as possible, and to prevent speculators taking advantage of the poor.[92] Unfortunately the land boards were not vigilant enough and by "tricks, contrivances, frauds and impositions" the certificates rapidly changed hands.[93] The wording of these certificates promised deeds only to the original nominees of the Crown, their heirs or devisees. Richard Cartwright observed of the certificates:

If they should now be delivered to the original holders of the certificates, the whole country will be thrown into confusion. In the technical precision of the law, the delivery of the patent completely overturns every prior sale or exchange—even those sanctioned by the Land Boards perhaps not excepted—invalidates every mortage, and gives a power to the party, his heirs or subsequent assigns, to eject the person who may have made a *bona fide* purchase and who may have expended in improvements twenty-five times the original value of the soil.[94]

No class of persons had more at stake in the solution of the foregoing difficulties than the merchants in whose hands many of the certificates had accumulated. Cartwright, a merchant of Kingston and a member of the Legislative Council, suggested to Simcoe a measure which would validate all *bona fide* sales or mortgages and make land held under certificates of occupation liable to claims under judgment of a court of law, or rights of inheritance, exactly as if held by patent in Great Britain. Cartwright also proposed that the patents should issue direct to present holders of certificates where they had been acquired as a result of a *bona fide* purchase or exchange, and that fees should be payable on such patents unless the original holder of the certificate had been exempt from them.[95] This proposal apparently failed to strike Simcoe as fair and reasonable. He was not at any time overly sympathetic to the merchants, and Cartwright had already incurred his displeasure.[96] Moreover, Cartwright's proposal was a reflection on the Executive Council, by whom certificates were confirmed before patents could issue for them. Suspicion and discontent had been aroused by the Council's decisions, which were regarded by the merchants as arbitrary, and dependent on political favour. In December, 1795, Simcoe forwarded Cartwright's bill to the Colonial Office without comment,[97] but by that time the merchants of Upper Canada had made another effort to protect their interests.

At the time of La Rochefoucauld's visit to Upper Canada the patent question was under discussion. It is obvious, from his confused account of the subject, that he received information on the question from disgruntled persons who had not got all of their transferred certificates passed by the Council. His comments on the patent question, made worse by Neumann's translation, can hardly have been good advertising for Upper Canada. La Rochefoucauld did not understand that the original nominees of the Crown, still in possession of their certificates, would not have had the difficulty in getting their patents which those who had bought certificates had experienced.[98]

Many persons in Upper Canada believed the certificates themselves were valid grants, and saw no need for patents. They thought that all that was necessary was an act of the provincial legislature giving the certificates the force of patents. Such an act would have confirmed the then holders of the certificates in their claims and would have saved those who were not loyalists, or who held certificates purchased from non-loyalists, the necessity of paying patent fees. To a speculator and non-loyalist like Robert Hamilton this was an important point. Hamilton was a merchant at Niagara, a partner of Cartwright, and a member of the Legislative Council. He is said to have boasted that he could carry through both Houses of the legislature a bill which would make the certificates valid grants and exempt present holders of land from patent fees.[99] Shortly after the Attorney General began to issue patents for certificates Hamilton attempted to stop him. On the advice of Powell,[100] Hamilton obtained from William Grant, at that time Solicitor General to the Queen, an opinion which raised doubts about the legality of omitting Clergy Reserve specifications from patents exchanged for certificates which had been issued before 1791 and about the legality of setting aside Clergy Reserves in solid blocks for townships which had been fully granted before that year. The only secure remedy, advised Grant, was an act of the provincial legislature validating those patents.[101] This opinion suited Hamilton to a nicety since it made necessary the interposition of the legislature and from it he felt confident of securing the sort of act the merchants wanted. He passed Grant's opinion on to Simcoe with the intimation that it was shared by some of the ministers of the Crown.[102] Simcoe was much annoyed. He believed Hamilton had created unnecessary problems and did not hesitate to give him a broad hint that these questions had been raised simply as a pretext for carrying on longer the "growing and mischievous evil of bartering the Certificates." [103]

Attorney General White regarded the patents about to be issued as simply confirming prior estates already granted by the certificates. Since these grants had been made prior to 1791, he thought it unnecessary to specify reserves for the clergy in the patent for each of them. He felt it sufficient merely to set aside from the Crown lands a quantity of reserves equal to one-seventh of these grants. This had already been done. Should the Solicitor General be right in his opinion that the certificates were not grants, then, said White, the patents issued in exchange for them would be the grants and would therefore have to contain Clergy Reserve specifications. But he believed it would be sufficient to specify those reserves in the blocks of Clergy Reserves already mentioned. The four patents previously issued without specifications would simply have to be recalled and issued in proper form. "We shall not then stand in need, Your Excellency may perceive of the interference of the Legislature to give these Grants validity," wrote White.[104] Apparently this was something Simcoe wished to avoid. The problem was referred to the Imperial authorities with the draft of a bill prepared by White, the first clause of which dealt with the Clergy Reserve specifications.[105]

This controversy over the Clergy Reserve specifications did not stop the exchange of certificates for patents. Simcoe decided to play safe and to include the clergy specifications in the patents thereafter.[106] Those persons who turned in certificates which had been transferred under the authority of the land boards or of the Executive Council were able to obtain their patents in their own names as a matter of course,[107] but those who turned in transferred certificates not authorized in either of these ways had to have them confirmed by the Executive Council before patents could issue in their names instead of in those of the original nominees. At this point the problem of the certificates was inherited by Russell.

Conflicting claims arose from both kinds of transfers. In order to prevent the issuing of patents for property in dispute, claimants would lodge caveats with the Attorney General. Merchants who held mortgages or claims of one kind or another against property held on certificates protected themselves in this way. The disputed cases came before the Council for decision. This practice proved to be a very inconvenient one for all concerned, especially when the caveat was not lodged until the patent was in its last stages. In October, 1796, the Provincial Secretary was instructed not to stop the delivery of patents after they had passed the Great Seal and the Registrar's and Auditor's offices "as the inconvenience attending the hearing of caveats at this stage are innumerable." Instead, the Attorney General was directed to publish a monthly list of the certificates turned in for patent. Unless caveats were lodged within a specified time after the publication of the lists, patents were to issue. Disputed claims were to be heard during the sittings of the legislature each year, an arrangement which put the distant settler to the expense either of employing an agent or of making the long journey to the capital.[108]

Attorney General White realized that the real issue at stake behind the controversy over the form of patents was the rights of purchasers of certificates and the unwillingness of the merchants to leave disputed claims to the decision of the Executive Council. He was well aware that once the legislature started discussing patents, some attempt would be made to regulate the terms on which they might be issued in exchange for certificates. He therefore included in his draft bill a clause giving the lieutenant-governor-in-council the right to decide disputed claims arising from the transferred certificates. He also asked the home government to consider the fundamental question whether the patents about to be issued were not simply confirmatory of prior estates already granted by the certificates. If so, asked White, would it not be simpler to issue the patents in the names of the original nominees, if deceased, rather than to make them out to their heirs or devisees? "For the mutations of property in this Province in ten years has been equally numerous and extraordinary. And if His Majesty's bounty is to be Confirmed in the representatives of the Grantees or Holders or agreeably to their dispositions, it is conceived from their endless variety that the Province cannot be settled in as many more." [109]

The law officers of the Crown avoided the difficult question of what was the precise nature of the right to land conveyed by the certificates, and did not return definite answers to the numerous questions raised by White. The first clause of his bill, legalizing the setting aside of Clergy Reserves in blocks for townships which had been settled before 1791, was acceptable to them. For the rest, they substituted a clause permitting persons holding land under certificates to petition for Letters of Declaration which were to name the original nominees of the Crown and were to have the same effect as if grants in free and common socage had originally been made to them. This meant that the heirs, devisees, assignees, mortgagees, or creditors of the original nominees of the Crown could prosecute their claims to land held under certificates in the courts according to the law of England as if the land had originally been granted in free and common socage.[110]

The government of Upper Canada refused to deal with the land certificates in the manner suggested by the law officers. By this time the province had a new Chief Justice, John Elmsley, whose views differed from those of White and the former Chief Justice, Osgoode, who had no objection to the proposed Letters of Declaration.[111] Elmsley insisted that the original holders of the certificates had not an equitable estate—they had an interest in the land unknown to the law. To give the certificates the effect of grants in free and common socage by issuing Letters of Declaration would be to burden the lands, which had in many cases been purchased and improved by others, with rights of dower and curtesy. On the inconvenience of these rights in a new country, where their chief value would be a nuisance value, Elmsley dwelt at length.[112] He drew up an entirely different measure which proved acceptable to the legislature and was passed in the session of 1797.

This act (U.C. Stat. 37 Geo. III, c. 3) created the first Heir and Devisee Commission and provided for the appointment of commissioners who were empowered to hear and determine claims to land brought forward by the original nominees of the Crown, their heirs, devisees, or assignees. In making their decisions, the commissioners were to be guided by "the best evidence they can procure, or that is laid before them, whether the same be such evidence as the law would require in other cases or not." Patents were to issue to those in whose favour the commissioners should decide unless the case was appealed to the Executive Council. The holder of a mortgage accepted by the commissioners as *bona fide* was to receive from them a certificate to that effect which, when registered, was to have the same effect as if the lands had been under patent at the time the mortgage was made. Similarly, all judgments which would have bound the lands if they had been under patent were to be binding under the certificates. This measure gave the merchants all that Cartwright had asked for and more.

All bills dealing with the Clergy Reserves or with the waste lands of the

Crown were required to be reserved for the royal assent. The bill which the law officers of the Crown had framed, based upon White's draft, had dealt not only with the exchange of certificates for patents but also with the Clergy Reserve specifications, and in transmitting it Portland had drawn particular attention to the necessity of reserving the bill if it should be passed.[113] The legislature of Upper Canada passed two bills, one dealing with the Clergy Reserves for grants in townships settled before 1791, which was reserved as required, and the other, Elmsley's bill, creating the Heir and Devisee Commission. As the provisions of this act differed so markedly from the measure which the home government had proposed, Russell wished to reserve it, but Elmsley and the Attorney General, arguing that such an act was urgently needed to put an end to the uncertain state of property in the province, persuaded him to give it the royal assent. The act became law before the Colonial Office became aware of its existence. Chief Justice Elmsley bullied Russell into assenting to this act, according to the latter, by threatening to introduce a bill to make certificates valid grants. Had this been accomplished, the land officers would have lost their fees.[114] The merchants and speculators of Upper Canada seem to have been determined to have a land act of their own devising and one suited to the pioneer state of the province. When Elmsley stated in his report on the act that five hundred claims in the Eastern District had been decided without an appeal the Colonial Office was naturally reluctant to disallow it.[115]

William Dummer Powell, puisne judge of the Court of King's Bench, had proposed a different solution of the land question. The chief difference between his ideas and those of Elmsley was that he wished to stick to the land laws of England while Elmsley wanted to avoid introducing their complications into a country to which they were not suited. Powell's measure made no provision for judgments obtained or mortgages entered into before patent, except where these had resulted in a change of possession. In these instances, the facts were to be ascertained by a jury. If the original nominee was still in possession of the land, his creditors would have been obliged to establish disputed claims on his property in the ordinary courts anew. Powell's view seems to have been that no judgments or mortgages properly binding on the land had been made, since the land had not yet been granted by the Crown. Yet the Constitutional Act intended to protect such rights, since it provided that the exchange of certificates for patents should not affect any interest in land already acquired by persons other than certificate holders. Naturally, Powell's bill did not recommend itself to the merchants, nor was Elmsley's measure likely to meet with Powell's approval. Elmsley had been appointed Chief Justice over his head and that was something he could not forgive. Powell at first refused to sit on the Heir and Devisee Commission. In his opinion, the commissioners had been invested with "a power greater than that of the Chancellor of England ... without a single principle for their Government or any known precedent to guide their Discretion." He added significantly that his refusal sprang from "a just veneration for the King's honour and the purity of the Channel through which Justice should be distributed to his subjects." [116]

The Heir and Devisee Act as originally passed was open to a serious objection. Men deeply interested in a lax interpretation of this law were appointed to administer it. Persons such as John Askin, Richard Cartwright, and Robert Hamilton, all speculators in certificates and all well acquainted with one another, were appointed commissioners and passed on one another's certificates.[117] True, the Chief Justice or a Justice of the Court of King's Bench had to be a member of each commission of three, but the act expressly permitted majority decisions and Powell's jury would have been a useful check on them.[118] As Powell had foreseen, a great deal depended on the composition of the commission. He himself was not a popular commissioner because, as John Askin complained, he was stricter regarding testimony and proof than the act required and demanded "proofs the collection of which at this late date is attended with expense." Justice Allcock was another who stuck so close to the law as to be "a very unfit man to act up to the Spirit of the Act." Allcock had his reasons. Repeatedly he found that "Speculators has [sic], generally speaking taken advantage of the indigent circumstances of the parties & contracted for the purchase of the Lands for considerations outrageously inadequate...."[119] Chief Justice Elmsley was more liberal in his decisions on land matters and Askin looked forward hopefully to his tour of the Western District.[120]

It was not long before the frauds which had occurred with respect to the land certificates began to come to light. In July, 1795, the Council had decided not to recognize the transfer of unlocated certificates, and shortly before the passing of the Heir and Devisee Act they had adopted the rule that in future unlocated certificates should not entitle even the original nominee to land until it had been shown that the applicant had not previously had land assigned to him in the province. Consequently, when unlocated certificates were presented to the commission they were rejected, whereupon their holders appealed to the Council to allow them to be located.

The Executive Council refused to consider for location any certificates which had not been brought forward prior to June 11, 1799, and adopted the rule that transfers of unlocated certificates would be recognized only if they were for loyalist or military claims. Even these were ruled out if the original holders of the certificates were residing in the United States.[121] Moreover, the holders of these unlocated transferred certificates could obtain patents in their own names only on paying the half fees which would have fallen on the Treasury, had the patents been taken out by the original grantees. The reason for the Council's refusal to recognize other kinds of transferred certificates presumably was that the loyalist, who had received family or bounty lands, and the military claimants, who also had received generous grants, had surplus lands to dispose of, but those who had received simply a 200-acre lot from the land boards or magistrates, if they had obtained their land legally as genuine settlers would have had no land to sell.[122]

Many of the transferred unlocated certificates proved to be certificates issued by magistrates when they had the right of recommending settlers for 200 acres of land. Those who had received the land had not held it long enough to receive a location from the Surveyor General but had disposed of it, sometimes to the very magistrate who had issued the certificate. This naturally gave rise to the suspicion that some of the magistrates had issued certificates for the purpose of re-purchasing them.[123] In other cases the grantees had sold their certificates to the deputy-surveyors to whom they had applied for a location.[124] Such buying and selling of magistrates' certificates was clearly contrary to the regulation. Land was assigned on these certificates on condition that the grantee had received no other land in the province and that he settle the land immediately and build a house within twelve months. Transfer of the location prior to patent without the consent of the Executive Council was forbidden.[125] "There has been ... much Imposition lately discovered regarding Majestrats Certificates and even Certificates from the different land Boards ...," wrote Alexander Grant to Askin. "The many frauds that has [sic] been Committed in keeping up Certificates and then brought forward by a second or third hand ... that the Council are indeed very nice in passing any wrighting or given any lands whatever...."[126] In the end, under the Heir and Devisee Act of 1802, the commission accepted for patent magistrates' certificates which had been located and transferred—and there were, according to Askin, "Hundreds & perhaps Thousands" of them—but those which were still unlocated were rejected by the Council.[127]

John Askin was one of those magistrates who had purchased unlocated certificates bearing his own authorization. He was unable to get them passed by the Council. Chief Justice John Elmsley informed him that he knew a house where there were five hundred of a similar nature only awaiting a favourable decision on Askin's claim to be brought forward.[128] But Askin did not give up hope, perhaps because he received an encouraging bit of advice from one cynical member of the Legislative Council, Robert Hamilton: "I still would maintain the Claim. Perseverance I know will do much when opposed to what they may affect to Call the public Good."[129]

In 1802, a new Heir and Devisee Act was passed to replace the original one, which was about to expire.[130] The old act had empowered the commissioners to hear only those claims to land which were based on land board certificates but many claims were based on other documents, such as Haldimand's certificates, magistrates' certificates, certificates of the Surveyor General's Department, Treasury tickets, and orders-in-council. These and other authorities for land were permitted by the new act to be presented to the commissioners. The Act of 1802 was even more liberal than its predecessor in the matter of proof. It authorized the commissioners to receive all such evidence as might be presented whether it was consistent or not with the rules of evidence laid down by the laws of England. This was an answer to the strictness of such commissioners as Allcock and Powell.

William Canniff remarks that in time the government discovered the abuses which had arisen out of allowing the certificates to be transferred and decided that "thenceforward" all patents should issue in the names of the persons who drew the land.[131] Lieutenant-Governor Hunter followed this procedure, as did his successors, but patents also issued as provided by the Heir and Devisee Acts. The Acts of 1797 and 1802 permitted patents to issue to the original nominees of the Crown, their heirs, devisees, and assignees, on the award of the commissioners. Under the Act of 1805, however, those of the original certificate holders who were still living and in possession of their certificates presented them direct to the Surveyor General's office for patents. The commissioners were restricted to hearing claims of the heirs or devisees of the original nominees, and their awards entitled these claimants to patents which, however, left the lands still subject to any liens or encumbrances with which they had been burdened. On the validity of such liens the commissioners were not by this act called upon to decide. Presumably, disputed cases were left to the ordinary courts. Nothing was said in the Act of 1805 respecting the rights of holders of transferred certificates. Canniff may have based his statement upon the restricted provisions of this act, which was amended three years later to permit the commissioners to decide upon the claims of assignees of the original nominees who had died or had left the province. It was in this amended form that the act was continued.[132]

The records of the Heir and Devisee Commission for the years 1797-1805, together with the Minutes of the Executive Council, which heard many of the larger claims, give some idea of the extent to which the land certificates had passed into the hands of speculators or merchants. The following table lists some of the larger holdings. Had the Council recognized all the transfers of unlocated certificates these figures would have been much larger.[133]

Name	Acreage
John Askin	9,600
The Baby Family	13,400
Hon. Richard Cartwright	9,790
William Dickson	5,350
Hon. Richard Duncan	5,100
Jacob Farrand	10,000
Joseph Forsyth	9,800
R. I. D. Gray	9,700
Robert Hamilton	40,645
John M'Kindlay	15,520
Robert M'Aulay	4,050
William Raddish	4,750
Livius P. Sherwood	3,900
Samuel Street	8,800
William Robertson	6,800

The Heir and Devisee Act was enacted primarily to protect those who had dealt in transferred certificates or who had accepted them, often no doubt reluctantly, in settlement of debts. Nevertheless, the majority of those who availed themselves of this act had only one or two claims to submit which they had acquired by inheritance, by legitimate purchase, or by exchange. To such people, the act was a great benefit since it provided them with a convenient way of validating their titles to land. From the administrative point of view, the act was not so satisfactory because many persons, once they had secured a report in their favour from the commission, failed to complete their titles by taking out their patents. Thus, much land remained on the Surveyor General's books as located but not patented. In some cases, the third generation of the original nominees of the Crown had to apply to the commission a second time. Furthermore, the Heir and Devisee Commission was at work just when the land officers were being pushed by Lieutenant-Governor Hunter to complete patents for land already granted. The result was that in many instances patents to the original nominees were completed, or nearly completed, when it would be discovered that the commission had allowed the land to some other claimants. The duplication of work which this occasioned naturally made the act unpopular with the officials of the Land Department.[134] The bulk of the commission's work was done by 1805, but it was not until 1896—a century after its creation—that its labours ended.[135]

CHAPTER FIVE

TWO AVARICIOUS ADMINISTRATORS

THE IMPOSITION OF THE NEW LAND FEES led to the clearing up of many questions that had been in dispute relative to the rights of U.E. loyalists and the claims of many persons to that distinction. Little interest was taken in the composition of the U.E. lists until 1796, when patents began to issue and patent fees were de-- manded.

Like other government officials who found it difficult to live within their incomes, Lieutenant-Governor Simcoe was anxious to claim his share of the land fees. On his arrival in Upper Canada he was annoyed to find that Dorchester and Haldimand had both set him an inconvenient precedent by renouncing their land fees. There is more than a touch of asperity in the letter in which he informed the Colonial Secretary that he would not feel it right to give up the fees he was entitled to "through any principle of personal popularity." [1] The table of fees he proposed for Upper Canada was too high and was not confirmed by the Colonial Secretary. [2] Although Simcoe was quite willing that the original loyalists should receive their grants free of fees, he thought it unfair that the expense of providing free patents should fall on the officers of the land-granting department, and he recommended that half fees be allowed these officials out of the provincial revenue, as had been the practice in Haldimand's and Dorchester's day. This proposal proved acceptable to the Colonial Office. [3]

Simcoe's proclamation of April 6, 1796, notified those entitled to the distinction U.E. to establish their claims before the Justices of the Peace in the Quarter Sessions between October 11 and November 15, 1796; otherwise, patents free of expense would not be allowed to them. [4] This method of deciding who was entitled to the distinction U.E. did not give general satisfaction. Powell advised Simcoe "to forego the Idea of administering by Proclamation . . .," and offered for his consideration a bill for ascertaining who were U.E. loyalists, the requirements of which were practically the same as those imposed by proclamation except that no time limit was mentioned. In this instance, as in others, Simcoe seems to have been disinclined to trust the provincial legislature and Powell was made to feel that his proposal was not welcome. [5]

The effect of Simcoe's proclamation was to restrict the right of receiving free patents to U.E. loyalists, although all who had settled in the province under any of the land regulations which preceded the Constitutional Act were equally entitled to this privilege. [6] Other steps towards limiting the number of free patents were taken. It was directed that if a grantee entitled to the remission of fees wanted more than one patent he was to be charged the full fee for every patent except that for the largest acreage, [7] and that the lands covered by any one patent must all lie in the same township.[8] In 1797, the Council decided to put an end to all the claims of loyalists and military settlers for additional land before the new regulations then under discussion should be adopted. It set August 1, 1797, and subsequently, November 1, 1797, as the date by which these claims were to be filed.[9] After this date military claimants were limited to the maximum grant of 1,200 acres. Ample opportunity was given the original loyalists to obtain free patents and all the land they were entitled to prior to the establishment of the new regulations. Under these circumstances, the old free grant policy might have been terminated in 1797 without any breach of promise on the part of the Crown.

There remains to be considered, however, the U.E. loyalists' "rights" arising out of Dorchester's order to the district land boards to grant land to the children of loyalists. The notion seems to have arisen that not only the children of U.E. loyalists but all their descendants were entitled to land free of expense. This erroneous interpretation perhaps arose from a confusion in the wording of the order concerning the registration of the U.E. loyalists and in the wording of the order which granted land to their children. The mark of honour was intended to be perpetual and to be borne by all their descendants; the order to grant lands, which was not a promise, was restricted to the children of the first generation of loyalists and there was nothing irrevocable about it.

Perhaps it was Simcoe himself who was responsible for this error. He tried to throw the responsibility for the heavy expenses of the Land Department of Upper Canada upon Dorchester. He sent Portland a copy of Dorchester's orders-in-council respecting the loyalists and placed the following interpretation upon them: "By the enclosed Resolutions . . . it will appear that the greater part of the Settlers of Upper Canada and their remotest Descendants from time to time were, in perpetuity, entitled to the Crown Lands, and to receive the Deeds and Surveys thereof, without *any expense whatsoever*." [10] This unwarranted interpretation of the resolutions raises the suspicion that Simcoe was animated by a desire to discredit Dorchester's proposals and to reveal inconsistencies in his policies. If so, his little spleen cost Upper Canada dear.

Governor Prescott of Lower Canada did not consider that Dorchester's regulations conferred upon the U.E. loyalists and all their succeeding generations a perpetual right to the Crown lands free of expense. His proposed regulation, providing for the additional fee, required half fees from loyalists and their children.[11] When Portland suggested that this regulation be applied to Upper Canada also, Russell pointed out, practically in Simcoe's words, that the loyalists and all their descendants appeared to be exempt from fees.[12] When he submitted Prescott's plan to the Council, he suggested that that part of it which required half fees from the U.E. loyalists and military claimants should not be put into effect. His Council agreed with him and also approved his suggestion that when the grantee was entitled to a free grant, the whole of the patent fee, and not merely a half fee, should be paid to the land officers out of the provincial Treasury. Elmsley even suggested that the land revenues of Upper Canada and Lower Canada should be regarded as one fund, remarking that just because the majority of the Loyalists had chosen Upper Canada was no reason why the land officers of that province should suffer.[13] In informing the Colonial Secretary of these ideas, Russell again urged that the promise to the U.E. loyalists should be kept and hinted, without committing himself, that some persons thought the promise extended even beyond the first generation. He proposed, however, that these benefits should be restricted to the U.E. loyalists already settled in the province.[14]

D. W. Smith realized that the problem facing the Executive Council was a triple one. First, something had to be done to reduce the expense the province was causing the mother country. The half fees were becoming a heavy burden upon the provincial Treasury, whose resources had to be supplemented by Great Britain out of the Military Chest. Second, the original loyalists, who were fully convinced that they and their children were entitled to patents free of expense, would become even more discontented when they discovered that they were now required to pay fees. Third, the land officers wanted the patent fees paid by the government, from which they were sure of collecting. Smith made several attempts to solve this triple problem while the claims of the U.E. loyalists were being considered by the Colonial Office. He was convinced that what the loyalists wanted was some sort of preference shown them "no matter in what way." In March, 1797, he proposed to set aside townships close to the loyalists' settlements. One-half of each of these townships was to be located by children of loyalists in 200-acre grants; the remaining land was to be sold to provide the province with revenue out of which the loyalists' half fees and other provincial expenses could be met. Smith pointed out that if half the land were sold for 2s. an acre in York currency, more revenue would be obtained than by charging the proposed additional fee of £25 per 1,000 acres.

In December, Smith produced a more elaborate proposal in which townships in each of the eight districts (into which the province was by this time divided) were to be surveyed into forty compact blocks of 1,200 acres, each block having 400 acres additional for reserves. Children of loyalists were to be allowed 1,200 acres and their choice of a location until half of each township had been located. They were to pay fees, full or half as might be decided, and the remainder of the land in the townships was to be sold. Those loyalists' children who did not choose to accept this offer were to be entitled to 200 acres patent free, while the remainder of their 1,200-acre block was to be sold. This scheme would also have yielded additional revenue but it required a radical departure from the established chequered plan. It could only have been taken advantage of by the wealthier loyalist families and might have led to speculation in 1,200-acre U.E. "rights," especially if they had been allowed at half fees.[15] Nothing came of either of these proposals. Smith's plan has been regarded as a device put forward in 1802 to secure for the land officers their old half fees; but it originated before their fees had been reduced and when the main problem before the Council was to increase the revenue of the province.[16]

The Colonial Secretary rejected the claims put forward on behalf of the descendants of U.E. loyalists by Russell and directed him to be guided by what the royal instructions themselves would warrant and not by any construction that had been put upon them. The instructions made no intention whatever of the children of the U.E. loyalists, to say nothing of more remote descendants. One concession was made by Portland: if the claimants had died, their wives and children might receive land in their stead. Furthermore, Portland directed that even the U.E. loyalists themselves were to be charged half fees on their grants. He wrote:

In so doing, the Principle of His Majesty's Instructions will be preserved for it cannot be supposed that the special favor thereby shown to a certain description of His Majesty's Subjects, was meant to be extended indefinitely, without reference either to time or Circumstances ... such a construction of His Majesty's Instructions would be contrary to every principle of common Sense ...[17]

In conformity with this decision, a fee of 6d. an acre, in addition to the expenses of survey, was imposed on all grants of land made subsequent to December 22, 1797. Half that fee, without the expenses of survey, was imposed on grants made to loyalists and their children of the first generation after October 6, 1798, the date on which Portland's dispatch was received.[18]

After sending this decisive refusal, Portland learned that the Executive Council was unanimously of the opinion that the "rights" of the U.E. loyalists to free land for themselves and their children should not be tampered with. Unfortunately for Upper Canada, Portland was induced to change his mind. He conceded that "from the construction which has been put upon his Majesty's Instructions ..." it had become necessary to make grants to loyalists free of all expense, but he would not agree to extend the royal bounty further than to the children of the first generation, nor would he allow the land officers full fees on these privileged grants.[19] Moreover, despite the various orders-in-council passed by Dorchester, under which loyalists became entitled to bounty lands and family lands free of expense, he ruled that no more than the quantity mentioned in the royal instructions—200 acres—would be granted on these terms. A second proclamation was therefore issued, on December 15, 1798, once more confirming the loyalists and, for the first time, their children in their claims to 200 acres of land free of expense, but restricting this right to those loyalists actually resident in the province before July 28, 1798, and enrolled on the U.E. list prior to the date of the proclamation.[20]

Peter Russell's administration of Upper Canada has usually been estimated in the light of the judgment which General Hunter passed upon him. "Russell," he wrote, "is avaricious to the last degree, and would certainly as far as depended upon him have granted land to the Devil and all his Family (as good Loyalists) provided they could have paid the fees." Portland, thus alerted, subsequently commented on the large amount of land granted by Russell, declaring the average size to be "459 acres for each grant. ..."[21] This judgment is not wholly borne out by the facts. Portland took the abstracts of the auditor's docket book of grants which had passed the Great Seal between July 3 and August 15, 1799, divided the total acreage shown by the number of grants, and got 459 for his answer. He incorrectly assumed this to be the average size of the grants made by Russell. His estimate is based on the return of patents completed, not of grants made, and 459 acres was the average amount of land covered by one patent. It proves nothing as to the size of grants because several grants, acquired perhaps by purchase of certificates, could be included in one patent, if they were for land in the same township. Although these patents issued in Russell's day, the grants might have been made by Simcoe, or even by Dorchester. If

459 did represent the size of the average grant, many of the loyalists were entitled to their original grant, bounty lands, family lands, and grants to loyalist officers, which tended to bring up the average. Finally, subsequent returns covering grants made prior to Hunter's administration give an average of about 257 acres.[22]

Russell successfully resisted the claims of promoters of townships, although it is true that the generous final settlement made with them benefited one of his relatives, William Willcocks, who had undertaken to settle Whitby. Russell also proved capable of writing a very firm—and very necessary—letter to D. W. Smith requiring him to see that the records of his office were so kept that it would be easy to ascertain whether an applicant for land had already received all he was entitled to. Likewise, he had the U.E. list carefully scrutinized so as to restrict that honour, and the privileges bestowed by it, to those who were strictly entitled to them.[23] This reduced the number of patents on which the government paid the half fees—a more certain and prompt source of income to the land officers than the full fees which settlers found it hard to accumulate.

Most of the orders-in-council for land passed in Russell's day were for small allotments to discharged soldiers, and loyalists and their children in accordance with established regulations.[24] The land-granting power of the magistrates having been revoked in 1796, new settlers had to apply directly to the Executive Council for land, and the Council, which was every day uncovering instances of speculation in magistrates' and land board certificates, was not very ready to allot land to supposed settlers coming from the United States. The rule required new settlers to reside twelve months in the province and to produce a certificate of good behaviour before land would be granted them, or else to prove that they had brought their families into the province.[25] On this score Russell's policy cannot be criticized, but his eagerness to have the fees on privileged grants paid by the government, the large size of the grants which he made to a few privileged individuals, and the invidious distinctions which he drew between one class of subjects and another place him in a very unfavourable light so far as modern historians are concerned.

Russell held the opinion, shared by Dorchester and Simcoe, that the possession of extensive property in land added to one's dignity and political influence, and that in this new province, where democratic and republican winds blew so strong from across the border, the bounty of the Crown could not be better exercised than in the creation of a class of landed gentry who would maintain those social gradations found in older and better established societies. With the ready help of the Executive Council,[26] he proceeded to exercise the discretion vested in him of making land grants up to 1,200 acres in accordance with these ideas. To magistrates and barristers the maximum grant was allowed. Grants of 1,200 acres were made to "old" merchants, 600 to young ones, and 400 to merchants' clerks. The wives of barristers and Members of Parliament received 600 acres of wild land to help sustain their dignity, and the children of loyalist officers, not content with the common portion of 200 acres, petitioned for, and received, several times this amount, according to their fathers' rank. The seven those social gradations found in older and better established societies. With the family has hitherto held in the society and which they with this aid will

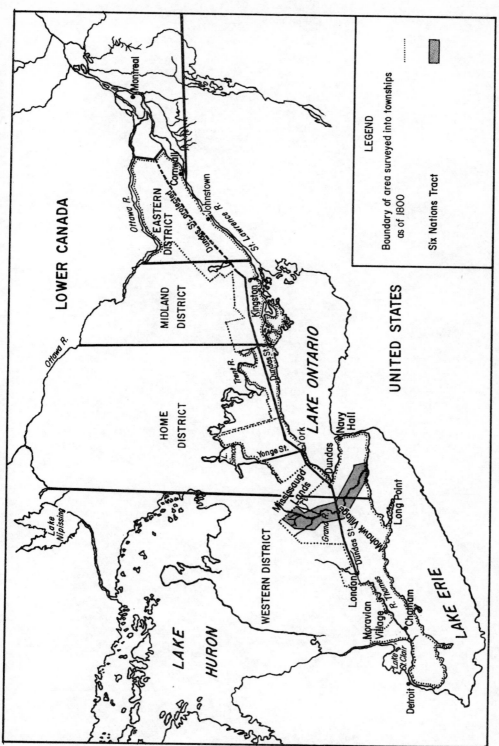

MAP I. Upper Canada in 1800. Based on D. W. Smyth's Map of Upper Canada published in London by W. Faden in 1800.

endeavour steadfastly to maintain," and they pointed out in support of the petition that they had educated themselves in Great Britain for the benefit of themselves and the country. A grant of 8,400 acres rewarded the patriotic intentions of these superior young gentlemen. A short time after this grant was made, an eighth son was born to Robert Hamilton and hardly had the child drawn breath before the father petitioned for an additional 1,200 acres of land on its account.[27] The wives and children of other legislative councillors also received 1,200 acres of land. The councillors, however, were not satisfied with the generous grants made to their wives and numerous children, and petitioned to be treated at least as liberally as the highest ranking loyalist officers, who had received 5,000 acres. "The Consideration which has induced us to join in this Request," wrote Russell to Portland, "... is the Propriety, if not the necessity, which we conceive to exist that all the Servants of the Crown in this Province should in their respective Stations support the Honor and dignity of His Majesty's Government, by adopting as large a plan in their domestic establishment & their manner of living as their Incomes will admit." This ridiculous argument moved the Colonial Secretary to allow them 6,000 acres, including all former grants made to them personally, but the grants were made not on the ground of their services in the Council, but to compensate them for the expense of removing from Newark to York where the seat of government had been established.[28]

It will be seen that in Russell's day the little clique in power, while observing the letter, if not the spirit of the regulations, freely helped themselves to the Crown lands. In fairness to Russell it ought to be pointed out that he simply continued a policy which had been begun by Simcoe.[29] As for the fees, there can be little doubt that Russell was eager for them. He fully expected that the fees allowed the Lieutenant-Governor would be his when he became Administrator, and was disappointed to find that he had to share them with the absent Simcoe.[30]

On August 16, 1799, General Peter Hunter arrived to take over the administration of Upper Canada. He had reached Quebec on July 13, and had spent a month there awaiting the departure of Prescott whom he succeeded as Commander of the Forces. In this interval the Executive Council of Upper Canada made haste to dispose of whatever land business the members and their friends were interested in before the arrival of the new Governor should complicate matters.[31] Hunter left York again on September 5, not to return until the spring of the following year, but this short period was sufficient for him to form the unfavourable opinion of his predecessor cited above. It is amusing that similar criticisms were levelled at Hunter himself by Justice Thorpe who said, "I find that Govr. Hunter has nearly ruined this province, his whole system was rapaciousness, to accumulate money by grants of land was all he thought of...." But Hunter was more fortunate than Russell in having a successor who defended him to the colonial authorities,[32] and he has since found historical friends in Chief Justice Macaulay,[33] D. B. Read, and Gilbert Patterson. W. R. Riddell has formed a less favourable opinion of him and, it would seem, with justice.[34]

The land measures which were determined upon in Hunter's day were designed to bring to a close the era of free grants with a view to the future sale of the Crown lands. They were also intended to prevent further extension of the surveyed areas so that the country might become more thickly settled, to enforce strictly the Proclamation of December 15, 1798, and to expedite the delivery of patents. Every one of these measures aroused opposition from one source or another.

To begin with, the Executive Council advised Hunter to grant no more land except to U.E. loyalists and their children, and to settlers who had already been promised land.[35] Russell and the members of the Council saw in the sale of the Crown lands the only method by which funds could be raised for roads, bridges, public buildings, and schools. Until government should "slacken its hand" in land granting, the value of the Crown lands would not rise much above the amount of the fees, nor would the value of the extensive grants which had been acquired by executive councillors, speculators, merchants, and leading loyalists increase, unless they happened to be in choice locations. Since few new grants were to be made except to the classes specified above, the Council suspended surveying activity in November, 1799.[36]

At this time there were warrants of survey outstanding for about 400,000 acres of land. The surveyed area available amounted to almost this quantity but three-quarters of it was in the less desirable Eastern District. Practically no land was to be had in the Western, Home, or Niagara Districts and, of the 96,000 acres available in the Midland District, two-thirds was reported to be unfit for cultivation.[37] Hunter's policy, which at first seemed a sensible one, meant that new settlers and children of loyalists wanting land were restricted in their choice of a location and had either to content themselves with whatever lots remained in the Eastern and Midland Districts, to lease Crown Reserves, or to purchase from large landowners. The shortage of good land open to location continued throughout Hunter's administration and was a potent cause of discontent. To make matters worse, in 1801, Hunter withdrew from location by "unworthy" and "common" applicants whatever lots remained ungranted in the Midland and Niagara Districts and reserved them for those petitioners whose "pretensions" warranted the favour.[38]

The Proclamation of December 15, 1798, which Russell had strictly enforced, aroused considerable resentment. The Executive Council was aware that the lists of loyalists sent in by the magistrates included the names of many persons who had no right to the distinction U.E. The list was revised and the names of those who had not joined the royal standard before 1783 were expunged. Secretary Jarvis, on his own responsibility, published in the *Gazette* of January 12, 1799, a list of the names which had been struck off, one of which was that of Samuel Jarvis. The Council apparently was not anxious to have its revision of the U.E. list to come to light right away and did its best to suppress the *Gazette*. It also hastened to issue a proclamation assuring the U.E. loyalists that "nothing will ever proceed from the Government that can in the slightest degree affect their interests. . . ."[39] This was quite a safe statement to make since the question at issue was who were U.E. loyalists.

After Hunter's arrival, the U.E. lists underwent a further strict revision.[40] An Inspector General of Public Accounts, John McGill, was appointed, whose duty it was to see that proper fees were paid on patents. Between May 9, 1802, and November 6, 1804, 904 names were struck off the list on his recommendation.[41]

This drastic purging of the lists aroused widespread discontent, which manifested itself after Hunter's death. McGill was accused of taking names off and putting them on the U.E. list as he saw fit. Many complained that their names had been removed before they had been given a chance of being heard in their own behalf.[42] Some members of the legislature proposed to declare the appointment of McGill illegal and others wished to call him before the Assembly to answer for his conduct.[43]

Loyalists and would-be loyalists had other grievances against Hunter. The Proclamation of 1798 limited the promise of free land to loyalists resident in Upper Canada on or before July 28, 1798. Settlers who came into the province from the Maritimes after this date found themselves excluded from its benefits. The Grand Jury of the London District complained to Hunter's successor that the loyalists had never been notified that they must present their claims within a specified time, that many of the new arrivals were not able to pay the fees demanded, and, consequently, that they could not get land on any terms unless they would take a Crown Reserve on lease or be content to labour on other people's land. "It ... is also the prevailing opinion," added the Grand Jury, "that this restriction was effected by the Executive Government of this Province, without the immediate direction of His Majesty...."[44]

The children of loyalists also had complaints to make. In June, 1803, the Council ruled that all future applicants for land must present themselves in person. This regulation, which was intended to prevent the frauds committed by persons claiming to be the agents of children of loyalists, also had the unhappy effect of depriving some persons of land because they could not afford the expense of a trip to York.[45] Furthermore, Hunter went back to Dorchester's original order and found that the promise of land was limited to children of those families which had duly cultivated the land already allotted them. Disregarding the previous custom of granting land to the children of all U.E. loyalists who had arrived in the province prior to July 28, 1798, and disregarding also the wording of the Proclamation of 1798, Hunter restricted the right to the children of loyalists who had been settled in the province by the date of Dorchester's order-in-council.[46] No wonder there was an outcry!

The military claimants also had grievances against Hunter. Those who had been soldiers in the regular army, seamen, or artificers had their names removed from the U.E. Lists by Russell and were thus deprived of land for their children. The right of military claimants to grants of land free of expense was now confined to British soldiers discharged in 1783; German troops and seamen were excluded.[47] Finally, those officers who had served in provincial regiments and who claimed the same quantity of land as had been alloted to officers of the 84th regiment under Dorchester's order of October 2, 1788, were refused it unless they had been resident in the province and had obtained land and had improved it by the date of that order.[48] These had been the conditions imposed by Dorchester but they were not enforced until Hunter's arrival in the province. Their revival at this late date added to the unpopularity of the Lieutenant-Governor. Officers of provincial regiments who had immigrated to Upper Canada from Nova Scotia found themselves refused not only the large grants which others of their rank had received but also a place on the U.E. list. They felt themselves to be very unfairly treated.[49]

Loyalists and non-loyalists alike also objected the increase in fees which took place in Hunter's day and to the efficiency with which they were collected. The table of fees adopted on July 9, 1796, had placed the fees on grants of 100 to 500 acres at £2 18s. 8d. sterling. Even these moderate fees deterred many persons not entitled to privileged grants from taking out their patents. When to these were added the survey fee of £1 7s. 6d. and the additional fee of 1798, the aggregate fee was so high that many completed patents accumulated in the Provincial Secretary's office unpaid and uncalled for. In July, 1799, the unpaid fees on these patents were estimated at £4,000.[50] In order to obtain relief for himself and the other officers who shared in the land fees, especially the Provincial Secretary, William Jarvis, Russell tried to devise some way whereby they could get their money. His efforts were thwarted by Elmsley, who dominated the Council and whose feelings towards the Administrator and "that absurd man, Jarvis," were far from cordial.[51]

The Proclamation of October, 1798, attempted to expedite the collection of fees for the future by requiring half the patent fee to be paid when the warrant of survey was presented for location. Owing to "the extreme scarcity of money in the Country," admitted Russell, more than half of those who received orders-in-council for land after this regulation went into effect were unable to pay their fees and to take out their warrants. Nevertheless, the Council ruled that the warrants of survey must be taken out and presented for location and the survey fees paid within one month of the date of the orders, or they would be rescinded and the petitions dismissed.[52]

In Hunter's day further steps were taken to ensure the prompt payment of fees. In 1800 the survey fee was required to be paid on all warrants issued between 1796 and 1798 before the land would be described for patent. In 1802 the whole of the survey and patent fees were demanded within three days after the order-in-council for land been issued. Holders of unlocated orders bearing a date prior to July 1, 1796, and who were not originally subject to patent fees, were required to pay those fees unless they were loyalists or military claimants. In 1803 the patent fees, which had been accepted in Halifax currency, were required to be paid in sterling or its equivalent, which meant that they became more burdensome by one-ninth. In 1804, because the land officers, particularly Secretary Jarvis, were complaining of their inadequate fees under the regulations of 1798, Hunter recommended that they be increased.[53] A second additional fee was then authorized which brought the cost of a 200-acre lot, inclusive of the expense of survey, to £8 4s. 1d., out of which sum the old patent fee of £2 18s. 8d. and the old half fee of £1 9s. 4d. were again allowed to the land officers.[54] Finally, the Council ruled that all orders-in-council for land, whether based on land board or magistrates' certificates, military claims, or U.E. rights, which were not located by June 26, 1804, would be considered void unless the holders would agree to pay the whole of the survey and patent fees within three days at the new rates.[55] As the Grand Jury of the London District pointed out, this last regulation bore with especial hardship on poor settlers who had gone to work to earn and save the amount of the land fees and had fancied themselves quite secure in the possession of an order-in-council for land.[56] The order also had the effect of putting half-pay officers and other privileged claimants with unlocated claims on the same footing "as any Settler from the States of America." [57]

The foregoing information is the foundation of fact behind the somewhat exaggerated strictures which Justice Thorpe passed on Hunter: "A Governor to enrich himself by the plunder of Eastern princes may be viciously grand, but the rapacity which would squeeze the pitiful dollars out of the Western poor was miserably mean and contemptibly wicked. . . ." [58] The new regulations explain, too, the more restrained comment which Chief Justice Macaulay felt compelled to make about Hunter: "Somewhat arbitrary in his measures he had contrived to provoke in some a bitter feeling of hostility and had rendered his government rather unpopular with the multitude." [59]

What justification is there for regarding Hunter as a rapacious administrator interested only in squeezing all he could out of Upper Canada? Hunter cannot be charged with making land grants left and right. All his regulations tended to restrict and not to increase the number of grants. But it was not the number of *grants made* which profited a governor, but the number of *patents completed*. Simcoe had tried in vain to secure the whole of the governor's fee on grants which had been made by him but which did not pass into patent until after he had left the province. His argument was that he had had the trouble of hearing the petitions and that all his successor had to do was to sign the patents when they were ready. Portland disallowed Simcoe's claim,[60] and Hunter no doubt knew that he could collect fees only on patents actually completed during his term of office. The successive regulations designed to secure prompt payment of fees and to expedite the passing of land into patent all tended to enrich the Governor, although they bore hard upon the poor settler.[61] Worse still, the settlement duty policy was sabotaged. Acting on the suggestion of Chief Justice Allcock (who seems to have been Hunter's evil councillor) the Council ruled that those who had received locations subject to settlement conditions might be relieved of these time-consuming duties provided they paid the fees of 1804 within the next twelve months and appointed an agent at York to take out their patents.[62]

Hunter tried to hustle the U.E. loyalist and military claimants into locating their orders-in-council for land and, to expedite their patents, he directed the Surveyor General not to locate such claimants on land subject to settlement duties.[63] He may have been anxious to clear away all the unsatisfied claims so that the Crown might know how much waste land it possessed before putting the new sales policy into effect, but William Dummer Powell has suggested that Justice Allcock pointed out to Hunter that since the half fees on privileged grants were paid by the government it would be to his advantage to get as many of them passed into patent as rapidly as possible.[64] There seems to be some basis for this charge. It was Allcock who proposed a regulation passed in 1804 directing the Clerk of the Council not to receive petitions from those claiming land as children of U.E. loyalists, unless they had empowered an agent resident at York to locate the land and take out the patent when completed.[65] By this means the unprofitable labour of hearing petitions and granting order-in-council for land which did not pass into patent during the Governor's term of office was held to a minimum. Though the Lieutenant-Governor benefited, the U.E.

loyalists did not, and it is more than probable that this new restriction reduced the value of the U.E. rights and made it easier for speculators to acquire them. These rights ware freely disposed of for anything from a gallon of whiskey to £5 or £6.[66] Hunter's regulations could only have served to stimulate this traffic and to direct it into a few hands.

Previous to Hunter's administration, patents had issued from the Provincial Secretary's office at a snail's pace. In Upper Canada obtaining a location was a complicated business and became more so when survey and patent fees were required to be paid in whole or in part on a grant before it could be located. Obtaining a patent after location involved a reference to six officials and the Lieutenant-Governor.[67] If the land was subject to settlement duties, it was necessary to file a certificate that the duties had been done. If a free grant had passed to an heir, been devised by will, or assigned, before patent, the claim had to be proved before the Heir and Devisee Commission before the patent could issue in the name of the claimant. The slowness with which patents issued under his procedure gave rise to complaints. Persons anxious for their patents employed attorneys to expedite them and sometimes offered to pay additional fees to have their titles put out of course. The American system, under which patents were obtained from district land offices, was commonly regarded as superior to the Canadian system, under which it was necessary to employ an agent or to go to York. In 1837, when the legislature of Upper Canada for the first time regulated the Crown lands by statute, one of the changes made required the Commissioner of Crown Lands to send patents to the district land agents to be given out without charge. Prior to 1837 patents were sometimes sent to the Clerks of the Peace or other local officials to be distributed, frequently on the eve of an election.

It was to Hunter's advantage to expedite the work of the Provincial Secretary's office, and William Jarvis, the Provincial Secretary, soon found himself an unhappy and much harrassed man.[68] Hunter set a weekly stint for the clerks to accomplish, had uncalled-for patents sent by the Secretary to his deputies in the various districts so that they might be issued, and the fees collected where they were due;[69] he succeeded in getting some 7,800 patents completed during his term of office.[70] The Lieutenant-Governor insisted on rushing the patents through to completion, despite the fact that at this time many land claims were pending before the Heir and Devisee Commission. Under such conditions it frequently happened that patents were issued to the original nominees of the Crown who had long ago transferred their land to others. When the Heir and Devisee Commission upheld the claims of the second parties, entitling them to receive patents in their own names, it was sometimes discovered that the Crown had already issued patents for the land in question and that the award of the commissioners was null and void.[71] Both privileged and unprivileged deeds were rushed through in this way, even though the patents were not being demanded by those entitled to receive them.[72] The result was that "the Shelves of the Office became loaded with Patents, the fees on which, the Executors of Lieutenant-Governor Hunter are daily receiving as the Patents are called for and the Emoluments of his successors unfairly anticipated."[73]

"This forced issue of patents," comments W. R. Riddell, "put into the purse of General Hunter a good deal of money, variously estimated at from ten to thirty thousand pounds, while the duty of supplying ... more effectual patents devolved on his successors to be performed gratuitously." [74] Hunter's income from fees has been greatly exaggerated—the amount was £4,393 15s. 11d., not quite all of it from fees on land.[75] The odium of this conduct should not fall on Hunter alone. The Attorney General had his share of the land fees, the Surveyor General his, and they evidently rejoiced in the prosperity Hunter was providing for them. "But alas the golden days are well nigh over," wrote Attorney General Thomas Scott to D. W. Smith in November, 1802. "You and I on sundry mornings have killed the goose that produced the golden eggs." [76] Never again, with the exception of the year 1824, were so many patents prepared as in the years 1798-1804.

One unfortunate official, the Provincial Secretary, William Jarvis, did not profit by the large number of patents completed during Hunter's administration. After supplying himself, at Hunter's direction, with a large number of printed blank forms, so that there would be no delay in issuing patents, he learned that the form previously in use had ceased to be acceptable to the judges and that his expenditures had been wasted. This happened twice. He was next directed to engross the patents on parchment instead of on paper and found that his share of the fees on small grants, particularly the half fee allowed under the regulations of 1798, did not cover the cost of the parchment and wax he had to provide. Consequently, the more patents Hunter hurried through the land offices, the more money he lost. His feelings towards the Governor were very bitter indeed. When Hunter died, Mrs. Jarvis wrote to her father, "Our trusty and well beloved governor is dead and if His Majesty can find another who can do more mischief, I am sure he had better clean the Kingdom ... as soon as possible. For my part, I think the Ministry must have scraped all the Fishing Towns of Scotland to have found so great a Devil." [77]

Matters came to a crisis when the land officers found that Hunter would not permit completed patents, on which the government paid the half fee, to be carried to the half fee account and paid by warrant on the Military Chest until such patents had actually been issued.[78] At this juncture, D. W. Smith proposed that revenue to pay the half fees on 200-acre grants to children of loyalists be obtained by selling half the Crown land in special townships in which they should be located.[79] This scheme was a revival of Smith's plan of March, 1797, but on this occasion he added two suggestions: that the government allow the land officers "the old reasonable half fee" of 1796, reduced in 1798 on 200-acre grants from £1 19s. 4d. to 11s. 1d., and that the loyalists' patents should not be made out until there was money in hand from the land sales. Thus the land officers would not have to wait for compensation for their labours or materials on free grants, and the province would not have to draw on the Military Chest to pay them. This scheme would have meant that the number of patents completed during Hunter's administration would have been sharply reduced and therewith the Lieutenant-Governor's fees. It is not surprising that Hunter preferred to recommend the increased fee of 1804 and the increased allowance to the land officers referred to above. The additional revenue made it unnecessary, for a time at least, for the province to call on the Military Chest.[80] But even the increased fee of 1804 left Secretary Jarvis little profit from his labours. Eventually, his fellow land officers agreed to share in the expense of providing parchment and wax and after many years of solicitation he was compensated for his earlier losses.[81]

On the face of things, Hunter's land measures were admirable. He strictly enforced the regulations, refused to approve what seemed to him unnecessary surveys, and tried to put some order and speed into the business of issuing land patents and collecting fees. Isaac Todd wrote of this Governor, "Gov. Hunter is very exact and wishes all under him to be so." The officials of the land-granting department found this out to their sorrow when Hunter, despite his eagerness to issue as many patents as possible, refused to sign 800 deeds because they had been carelessly drawn up.[82] Most important of all, Hunter attempted to clear the way for the sale of Crown lands by closing out all the old claims as rapidly as possible. In 1802 he issued a proclamation warning those who failed to follow up claims to land which they had filed with the Heir and Devisee Commission in 1797 or 1799 that the opportunity now offered them was positively the last and that the commissioners would "never more sit again. . . ."[83] Hunter's precise and military mind could not tolerate the tag ends of unfinished business which still cluttered the land offices and he made determined—and ruthless— efforts to dispose of them.

However desirable Hunter's land regulations may have been from the official point of view, they were most unwelcome to the people of Upper Canada. The new settler was disappointed in his hopes of receiving a free grant, the old settler found himself harried into paying his fees, and even the loyalist or military claimant found that his privileges had been restricted. "Tho my late good worthy predecessor was Sensible & Clever," wrote Alexander Grant, who administered Upper Canada in the interval between the death of Hunter and the arrival of Sir Francis Gore, "he latterly dealt very harse with most of the people that had any business with him."[84] Lieutenant-Governor Gore could not see any grounds for complaint against Hunter. "The most respectable persons, with whom I have conversed," he wrote, "do not complain of any."[85] However, it was not the most "respectable" persons who were likely to feel the oppressiveness of Hunter's measures, but the struggling settlers. As soon as his strong hand was removed, the gathering discontent burst forth. "There had hitherto been no political agitation in the newly settled province," writes Kingsford. "During the six years of his [Hunter's] government, the spirit which declared itself on his departure seems to have taken form."[86]

CHAPTER SIX

SIR FRANCIS GORE AND THE RADICALS

SIR FRANCIS GORE, who became Lieutenant-Governor of Upper Canada in 1806, inherited a troubled situation from his predecessor. During the year's interval between Hunter's death and his own arrival in Upper Canada, the malcontents grew bold and became an organized opposition.[1] The mild protests against the additional fees and the new regulations affecting loyalists and military claimants soon became demands for control of the Casual and Territorial Revenues of the Crown and for a voice in determining the regulations governing the Crown lands. The radicals tried to diminish the powers of the executive and to extend those of the Assembly by claiming for the latter the rights of nominating to office, of appropriating the revenues raised under the Imperial, as well as the provincial, statutes, and of supervising the expenditure of certain funds by commissioners of its choosing. Not until after the Rebellion were they able to make good these claims.

Alexander Grant, as Administrator of the province prior to the arrival of Gore,[2] was bewildered by the delivery at his door of the harvest of complaints which Hunter had sown. The labourer who had been most energetic in this unwelcome work was a newcomer to the province, Robert Thorpe, who had been appointed a Justice of the Court of the King's Bench in 1805. The new judge stepped willingly forth as both the champion of popular grievances and, as he hoped, the logical candidate to succeed Allcock as Chief Justice.[3]

"I opened the session on the 4th Inst.," wrote Alexander Grant to his friend John Askin, "and as yet the house of Commons do's nothing but vomiting grievance and Complaints Against the Administration of General Hunter and plaguing me, and his favoureds . . . our late puisne Judge [Thorpe] with that other Countryman of yours Mr. Weeks, are the fomenters of all the disorders amongst the Commons."[4] On February 10, Weekes moved that the assembly go into a committee on the state of the province. This committee, after protected debate, presented two addresses to Grant protesting against the regulations made by his predecessor. The first of these asked that those military claimants who since 1803 had been refused land because they were not British soldiers, and from whom full fees had been demanded on orders-in-council because they had not located their grants within the specified time, should be allowed land on the terms they had been entitled to earlier. The second address asked for the abolition of the additional fee of 1804 and requested that the loyalists who had been prevented from acquiring land because they had been unable to make the trip to York should be allowed to present their claims through an agent as before. To both these addresses Grant returned conciliatory and indefinite replies which proved unsatisfactory to the popular party led by Weekes. Three days later Weekes moved that the House consider an address to the Crown on the two topics on which Grant had given them no satisfaction.[5] These impatient tactics constituted the "plaguing" of which the poor Commodore—who was quite out of his element—complained.

Although Weekes's motion was defeated by the votes of the districts in which the first loyalists had settled, the Executive Council decided to make concessions. Two proclamations were issued. The one notified all military claimants who were actually resident in Upper Canada on July 28, 1798, that they would be entitled to land on the same terms as before. The other informed the children of U.E. loyalists that, except in the Home District, they might have their claims certified before the Justices of the Peace in Quarter Sessions and might then present them to the Council by means of an agent.[6] On the additional fee, Grant sheltered himself behind the usual defence, instructions from home,[7] although he was probably well aware that the increase had taken place at the instigation, not of the Colonial Office, but of the members of the Executive Council.[8]

Towards the close of his administration Hunter had attempted to coerce grantees of land into paying their fees and taking out their patents. Those who had received land under the regulations of 1798 and had not paid the second half of their fees were informed in January, 1805, that unless the entire fee was paid by June 1 they would become subject to the additional fee of 1804.[9] This measure, which many regarded as illegal,[10] caused wide-spread dissatisfaction and consequently was not enforced after Hunter's death, although it was not formally rescinded until 1809.[11] Certain expenses had been incurred in connection with these unpopular proceedings for printing of proclamations and for legal opinions. Such items were usually regarded as contingencies of the Lieutenant-Governor's office and were paid for out of that part of the provincial revenue which was not controlled by the Assembly. In this instance, however, according to W. D. Powell, Hunter's friends wished to keep the affair "out of view" of the home government, and advised Grant to pay the expenses by warrant on the provincial Treasury, although the Assembly had not authorized such expenditures.[12] Other warrants for the payment of the expenses of the commission of gaol delivery were also issued by the Administrator without a previous appropriation by the Assembly.

These unauthorized expenditures, amounting to £617 13s. 7d., were brought to the attention of the Assembly by the select committee appointed to examine the public accounts. An address was presented to Grant which termed the whole occurrence "extraordinary," characterized his act as unconstitutional, requested him to have the sum replaced in the provincial Treasury, and pointed out that no payments should be made from it in future without a previous appropriation by the Assembly.[13] Grant could say with truth that the occurence was not extraordinary. For two years Hunter had paid the judicial expenses referred to above out of the unappropriated residue of the provincial revenue without a previous appropriation by the legislature and no objection had been raised by the Assembly when the accounts were laid before it.[14] But this time the unauthorized expenditure included items of which the Assembly did not approve. "Had they not been blended," wrote W. D. Powell, "I apprehend, no exception would have been taken to the irregularity or want of a specific appropriation. . . ." [15] Grant's account of the affair to the home government gave no hint of this fact and his reply to the Assembly's address did not frankly admit that unauthorized payments had been made out of the provincial revenue; he simply promised an investigation.[16]

The Assembly was far from satisfied with this answer. When Black Rod came to summon the members to the Legislative Council chamber, where Grant was about to prorogue the legislature, he found the doors of the Assembly closed against him. Within, a sharply divided house considered in committee Grant's reply to their address. It would seem that the committee was prepared to report an address to the Crown, but the casting vote of the Speaker prevented the report from being received.[17] Black Rod was then admitted and the legislature was that day prorogued.

Within the Assembly, Justice Thorpe's supporters consisted of William Weekes, member for Durham, Simcoe, and East York, David McGregor Rogers, member for Hastings and Northumberland, Ralf Clench, member for the second, third, and fourth ridings of Lincoln, Ebenezer Washburn, member for Prince Edward, Thomas Dorland, member for Lennox and Addington, and Benajah Mallory, member for Norfolk, Oxford and Middlesex. In February, 1807, Justice Thorpe himself became a member of the Assembly, replacing Weekes, who had been killed in a duel, and he dominated the session of that year. In 1808 Thorpe returned to England and Joseph Willcocks, who sat for West York, Lincoln, and Haldimand, became the leader of the malcontents until the War of 1812 when he deserted to the enemy. Peter Howard, who had been elected for Leeds in 1805, also gave the group his support from time to time. Thorpe, Willcocks, and Weekes were Irishmen; the latter two have been represented as United Irishmen secretly engaged in an attempt to arouse discontent and perhaps insurrection in Upper Canada and financed by funds raised by the Irish of New York City. Weekes had spent some time there in the law offices of Aaron Burr, whose interest in Upper Canada has already been noted.[18]

However this may be, the grievances complained of were real enough, and had found expression before any of the Irish agitators came into the limelight. Rogers, Washburn, and Dorland had shown their dissatisfaction with the manner in which the provincial accounts were rendered,[19] and Mallory, Rogers, and Washburn had supported Weekes's motion "that it is expedient for this House to enter into a consideration of the disquietude which prevails in the Province by reason of the administration of Public Offices." [20] Clench, Washburn, Howard, and Dorland all belonged to U.E. loyalist families, although none of them represented constituencies settled by "original" loyalists. It is evidently not a new thing for indigenous left-wingers voicing native discontent to suffer from the support of some who attach themselves to their party and to be accused of furthering their cause with tainted funds.

When Lieutenant-Governor Gore arrived in Upper Canada, Justice Thorpe was completing his circuit of the Western, London, Home, and Niagara Districts. He received from the Grand Jury of each district flattering addresses which nonetheless hinted that the public tranquillity had been disturbed.[21] The address from the London District, which appeared in the *Upper Canada Gazette* of October 25, 1806,[22] specifically asked Thorpe to lay before the Lieutenant-

Governor the grievances of the people. The chief grievances were the exclusion of many persons from the U.E. list who believed themselves entitled to that distinction, the failure to pay the promised bounties to those who had raised hemp,[23] the imposition of the additional land fees, and the partiality with which the fees had been imposed.[24] Thorpe told Gore that the large tracts of land which had been bestowed upon officers of the government and their families had given offence. The people, he asserted, wanted the fees regulated by a provincial act and the land revenue as well as the customs revenue raised under Imperial acts to be accounted for to the people's representatives.[25]

In some respects Thorpe's complaints and arguments hark back to the controversies which preceded the American Revolution; in other ways they anticipate Mackenzie. "The government," wrote Thorpe, "continues the System which lost the States of America. . . ." Those features of the system he denounced were the appointment of governors "bred in the army, surrounded by a few half pay Captains," and the attention accorded the wishes of the merchants, "this Shopkeeper Aristocracy," which had grown rich "by the plunder of England, by the Indian Department . . . by a Monopoly of Trade and extortion of the people. . . ." The Crown land, he complained, "was to be heaped on a few and withheld from the many because it would be useless to the few if the many were not driven to purchase." Like Mackenzie, Thorpe complained that the province was supposed to have the blessings of the British constitution; yet the Assembly did not control the purse strings and its members were bribed to support the government by favours bestowed through the Land Department. Like Mackenzie, too, Thorpe warned that the population, "tho' lately poor and accustomed to subjection," had, in the frontier province of Upper Canada, become "independent and ready to turn on their oppressors. . . ." [26]

After the interview with Thorpe, Gore wrote to the foreman of the Grand Jury of the London District asking him what grievances the Jury had wished to call to his attention.[27] The Jury's reply reiterated the grievances of those who claimed to be U.E. loyalists and the complaints about the land fees. The Jury also pointed out the injustice of Hunter's regulation which declared void all orders-in-council not located by a certain date,[28] and asserted that favoured persons had been allowed to locate land in certain townships which had been withheld from other settlers.[29]

The author of *Letters from an American Loyalist,* an apologist for the Hunter administration, frankly admits that favouritism had occurred: "nor would an unprejudiced mind find anything very censurable in withholding from the casual settler admitted on grounds of favour, an advantageous location which might afterwards be granted to a person of superior pretensions. . . . Whatever dissatisfaction may have arisen [from this practice] can be ascribed only to that overweening self importance too prevalent in mankind. . . ." This pamphlet is usually attributed to W. D. Powell, although the author makes some statements about himself which Powell could not, with truth, have said. Powell was certainly helping Gore to prepare a defence of his administration, but one of Gore's letters makes it clear that the author of the *Letters* was Richard Cartwright, a prosperous merchant of Kingston, for whom Gore obtained 3,000 acres of land free of fees in return for his services.[29]

Justice Thorpe has accused Gore of attempting to force the Jury of the London District to sign a recantation of grievances and of threatening those who were officers with loss of their half pay if they refused.[30] This recantation, said to have been prepared by Gore himself but branded by him as a forgery,[31] re-stated the Jury's chief complaints and limited them to one topic: the exclusion from the U.E. lists of those loyalists which had come into the province after 1798, or who had failed to bring their claims forward before that date. The document also cleared Hunter of responsibility for the existing grievances and expressed concern "for what is past." None of the Jury, according to Thorpe, could be persuaded to sign it.

In an attempt to allay the prevailing discontent, Gore's first act was to accede to some of the demands put forward on behalf of the U.E. loyalists and military claimants. On October 31, 1806, he issued a proclamation opening the U.E. lists to additional names. Those who had hitherto neglected to establish their claims received another chance to do so and the children of those who had died without getting their names on the list were allowed to establish their parents' claims and thus to become entitled to the privileges allowed children of U.E. loyalists. Persons whose names had been suspended from the U.E. list without a hearing were now allowed to present their proofs and to have their names reinserted if found entitled.[32] These were the concessions, according to Thorpe, which Weekes had laboured to obtain.[33] They did not satisfy Thorpe because they did not benefit loyalists and military claimants who had come into the province since 1798. During the session of 1807, Thorpe brought forward a rather indefinitely worded address to the Lieutenant-Governor concerning the grievances of these people,[34] but his motion that the House go into committee on the subject was defeated, largely by the votes of the old loyalist districts.[35] Gore's proclamation had a pacifying effect. In the session of 1808 the Assembly voted him an address of thanks for his attention to the grievances of the military claimants and loyalists.[36]

One subsequent attempt to secure lands free of patent fees for "loyalists" and military claimants who arrived in the province after 1798 was to be made. On March 4, 1812, an address to the Prince Regent asking for free land for such claimants was carried by the votes of the newer districts. If this request were granted, argued the framers of this memorial, the effect would be "to induce many valuable people whose loyalty and attachment have been proved, to withdraw from the United States, and thus add to the strength and population of this fertile Province."[37] Three months later the War of 1812 broke out and it may be presumed, for we do not have the record, that no favourable reply was received.

Gore dealt with the Assembly's complaint about Hunter's unauthorized expenditure of provincial funds by ordering the disputed £617 13s. 7d. to be replaced in the provincial Treasury.[38] This satisfied the malcontents for the time being, and subsequently the Assembly voted to relinquish the money;[39] however, until the Rebellion, the Assembly continued to expand its claims until it finished by demanding, and receiving, complete control of the provincial revenue from whatever source derived.

In his report to the home government, Gore declared that the colony's one major grievance, the claims of the U.E. loyalists, had been dealt with by his proclamation of October 31.[40] All other complaints he attributed to the demagogic influence of Mr. Justice Thorpe and he attempted to rebut in detail the charges which Thorpe had brought against the administration of Upper Canada. He pointed out that an account of the revenue from Lower Canada had been annually inserted in the public accounts and that the land fees had been regularly accounted for to the Treasury. Gore did not believe that favoured persons had had their land fees remitted or reduced, although he admitted that, amidst the number of alterations which had taken place in the table of fees, the late Governor and Council might sometimes have "erred". He denied that land grants had been made otherwise than in accordance with established regulations except by special instructions from home, and he could not understand how the arrangements of the Land Department could have a tendency to enrich the few at the expense of the many, since all had received more land than they could reasonably claim.[41] Apparently it did not occur to him that the large grants made in desirable locations to a favoured few had forced other men to go further afield for their allotments or else to purchase land from speculators. He seems to have been blind to the fact that the difficulties of small landowners were increased by the existence of unimproved tracts in their neighbourhood held as a speculation by absentees.

Gore's defence obscured the real question at issue. The points in dispute during the sessions of 1806 and 1807 were the right of the Assembly to control the appropriation and expenditure of *all* the provincial revenue and to determine the regulations governing the Crown lands. By the Colonial Tax Repeal Act, the Imperial Parliament had deprived itself of the power to tax the colonies for the purpose of raising a revenue. It retained the right to regulate commerce by imposing customs duties and provided that the customs revenue should be disposed of by the colonial legislatures.[42] This act implied that in future all revenues raised in the colonies would be at the disposal of the colonial legislatures. Yet there was nothing in the act to prevent grants of Crown land being burdened with quit rents or fees for revenue purposes. Dorchester had earnestly advised the Imperial government to impose no quit rents in Canada except on large grants and to give up the proceeds of these to the provincial governments so "that all needs of discord between Great Britain and her colonies may be prevented." [43] Part of this advice was taken. After 1791 quit rents were not imposed but Crown Reserves were set aside in the expectation that they would yield a revenue which would make the civil government independent of legislative appropriations. Trouble was thus stored up for the future.

In 1798, when the additional fee was imposed on land patents, it was done for the express purpose of raising a revenue applicable to the expenses of the civil government. This of course was a prerogative act. The fee was not a tax imposed by the Imperial Parliament and therefore it did not come within the terms of the Colonial Tax Repeal Act. Nevertheless, its imposition violated the spirit, if not the letter, of that law. At 6*d.* an acre land fees amounted to £25 per 1,000 acres, £5 11*s.* of which went to the land granting officers and £19 9*s.* to the support of the civil government. The complaint concerning these fees was not that they had not been accounted for to the Imperial Treasury, as Gore pretended to think, but that they had not been accounted for to the Assembly.[44] The very fact that the multiplicity of regulations of various dates made it possible for officials to make "mistakes" which favoured certain persons was a telling argument in support of Thorpe's proposal to regulate the fees by a provincial statute instead of by instructions from home. Such an act would have had a twofold effect: one publicly enacted law would have replaced a confused set of regulations, and the revenue derived from that law would have been clearly at the disposal of the legislature since it would have been raised under a provincial statute.

During the session of 1807 the radicals in the Assembly attempted to subject the Crown lands to provincial legislation. Funds for roads had been appropriated by the provincial Parliament during the previous session,[45] and the Grand Jury of the London District had complained that the money had been spent more for the benefit of an individual, Colonel Talbot in this case, than for the common good.[46] A special committee, with Thorpe as chairman, was appointed to inquire into the state of the roads. Its report contained two proposals very unwelcome to the Executive Council. The first was that a road should be constructed from one end of the province to the other, that the line of it should be laid down in general by the legislature, in particular by commissioners appointed for each district, and the the legislature in appropriating the funds for the road should apportion it by districts. The second proposal was that a fund be raised from the sale of Crown land to be at the disposal of the legislature for roads. This report was accepted and it was resolved that a bill be drafted based upon it.[47] No further action was taken before the legislature was adjourned.

The manœuvres of Thorpe's party made Sir Francis Gore very indignant. "There is," he informed the Colonial Secretary, "a most insidious attempt to introduce the House of Assembly into the Management and disposal of the waste Lands of the Crown." In the Lieutenant-Governor's opinion, Thorpe had been urging the Assembly "to arrogate to themselves a Right to dispose of the Property of the Crown, which the British Parliament has never assumed," and he grandiloquently informed this troublesome judge that he considered himself the guardian of the King's property and that the Democratic part of the Constitution should never, while he administered the government, assume an unconstitutional power.[48] Gore overlooked the fact that the 42nd section of the Constitutional Act clearly permitted legislation affecting the Crown lands to be enacted by the legislature of Upper Canada and safeguarded that property by providing that such measures should be reviewed by the Imperial Parliament before the imposition of the royal assent.

Lieutenant-Governor Gore tried to give the Colonial Secretary the impression that the supporters of Justice Thorpe in the Assembly of 1807 were very few. He declared that only two persons supported him when he claimed for the Assembly the right of naming trustees for the public schools, and that no one shared his opinion that the customs dues imposed by the Imperial statutes were at the disposal of the legislature. He further asserted that Thorpe's address on the U.E. loyalists had been rejected, and that he had completely failed in his attempt to embarrass the administration.[49] The votes on the first two questions cannot be traced in the Journals. The address on the U.E. loyalists was rejected, but by only one vote.[50] Despite this failure, Thorpe's influence was far from negligible. He was a member of the two most important committees of the session, the committee on roads and the committee on public accounts. He was chairman of the first and his supporter, Rogers, was chairman of the other. That Gore himself feared Thorpe's influence is clear from his letter to his friend George Watson, in which he admits that "sedition is gaining ground faster than I apprehended . . ." and begs Watson to lose no time in exerting himself to "get me out of this province."[51]

Rogers' committee on public accounts questioned the right of the executive to dispose of any of the provincial revenue without a previous appropriation by the legislature. The revenue of Upper Canada was derived from one-eighth share of the customs duties imposed by the legislature of Lower Canada on goods imported into that province, from customs duties imposed by Upper Canada acts, customs duties imposed by the Imperial statute 14 Geo. III, c. 88, and from fines, forfeitures, and fees on Crown lands. The revenues raised under provincial acts and the share of the Lower Canada duties were at the disposal of the legislature but the revenue raised by the Imperial statute was paid out on warrants issued by the Imperial Treasury. The radicals of both Upper and Lower Canada thought that the Colonial Tax Repeal Act had made the Imperial duties subject to the provincial legislature.[52] In Upper Canada, Thorpe and his supporters charged that even funds raised under provincial authority were not wholly at the disposal of the legislature.[53] The *Letters from an American Loyalist* explain that the provincial act 41 Geo. III, c. 5, which applied the duties imposed by the Imperial act of 1774 to goods coming in at Upper Canada ports of entry, simply extended the Imperial statute without affecting the manner in which the money raised by it was to be appropriated. Consequently, the provincial legislature had no right to dispose of that revenue and, until Thorpe interposed, had laid no claim to it.[54] When the Colonial Secretary consulted the law officers of the Crown on this question, they upheld the claim of the Assembly to dispose of these duties in terms broad enough to include those from the Imperial act as well. Castlereagh sent this opinion to Gore on June 19, 1807,[55] but it was not acted upon for ten years.

Among the Scadding-McGill papers there is a brief note from Gore to McGill, dated 1807, stating that "Despatches of the utmost importance have arrived which require your immediate attention." It is possible that the dispatch which so disturbed Gore and prompted him to ask for McGill's advice was Castlereagh's letter of June 19. McGill's reports had resulted in the removal of many names from the U.E. list and this had made him very unpopular with the radicals. They also objected to his salary being paid out of provincial funds not under legislative control. His appointment was regarded as "illegal,"[56] and there could be little doubt that, should the legislature obtain control of all the provincial revenue, it would refuse to provide for his salary. We can only speculate on the nature of the disturbing dispatch. The one thing we do know is that Gore did not act on the opinion of the law officers for ten years and we may assume that its existence was generally unknown. (Indeed, the opinion was to be reversed in 1824.)[57] As chairman of the committee on public accounts, Rogers annually drew attention to the fact that the Imperial duties and the extension of those duties arising from the provincial act had not been accounted for to the Assembly.[58] But despite his efforts, Upper Canada's share of the Imperial duties did not finally come under the control of her own legislature until 1831.[59]

The attempt of the radicals to secure for the legislature control of the provincial revenue and of the Crown lands failed. Gore had Thorpe and C. P. Wyatt, the Surveyor General, who supported him, removed from office. He also dismissed Willcocks, who was Sheriff of the Home District, and Rogers, the Registrar of the counties of Northumberland and Durham,[60] and closed the columns of the *Upper Canada Gazette* to the radicals. By accusing their leaders of being in touch with United Irishmen in the United States, he smeared the party with the charge of disloyalty. Despite these successes, his troubles with the opposition were not yet over. During the next session, Joseph Willcocks was accused of having stated in the *Upper Canada Guardian* of October 1, 1807, that the members of the Assembly had been bribed by the Lieutenant-Governor.[61] He was found guilty of contempt by the Assembly and imprisoned by its order,[62] but this seems to have had little effect upon his popular support. In the elections of 1808, Willcocks and all the members of the radical party retained their seats, and a new adherent was gained in the person of John Willson, member for West York. Meanwhile, Thorpe and Wyatt sought redress in England.

John Mills Jackson published a pamphlet in support of Thorpe and Wyatt entitled *A View of the Political Situation in the Province of Upper Canada in North America.* Jackson, who had lived in Upper Canada during 1806 and 1807, was friendly with Thorpe and Wyatt and well acquainted with the views of the radical party. His pamphlet discusses the grievances respecting the U.E. loyalists, the land fees, and the large grants to favourites, and hints that the Indian Department was inefficient and corrupt. It also argues at some length the right of the legislature to control the entire provincial revenue. A copy was sent to the Lieutenant-Governor who wrote a lengthy—and on many points unconvincing —dispatch refuting its charges.[63] Gore also took much satisfaction in informing the Colonial Secretary that the Assembly had unanimously declared the pamphlet to be "a false scandalous and malicious libel."

Gore told the truth but not the whole truth. At Gore's instigation, and carefully coached by him, the leaders of the Assembly did obtain from that body a vote which unanimously declared the pamphlet a libel.[64] For a moment the courage of the radicals seems to have failed them. George Ridout, who was one of the Assembly's copying clerks, tells us: "When the question was put whether it was a libel or not, Willcocks and Rogers were the only two dissenting members, but when the ayes and nays were called for [i.e, a roll call vote] they thought proper to rise [with the ayes]." [65] Their courage soon returned, however. When it was moved that an address be presented to the Lieutenant-Governor approving of his administration and abhorring the pamphlet as false and libellous, they voted in the negative and were joined by John Willson and Peter Howard. On two subsequent motions relating to the pamphlet and address, these four voted the same way.[66] Two members who usually sided with the radicals, Dorland and Mallory, were both absent with leave.[67] Despite his negative vote, the reluctant Peter Howard was chosen by the Assembly as one of the two members who were to present the address to Gore. In trying to escape this unwelcome duty he had the support of his three colleagues who joined him in voting against the nomination.[68]

In 1811 Gore went home to England on leave, no doubt the better to defend his administration and to look around for some more comfortable berth. After his departure, William Warren Baldwin prophesied that many changes would be made without much noise or clamour, "which I am sure would not be the case was Mr. Gore here. His violent intemperence would have aroused the attention of the People and induced them to oppose the election of men to whom under a plain, unsuspicious administration they are not disposed to imagine an objection." If Gore should return to Upper Canada, he feared that it would mean "farewell to tranquillity and peace."[69] At the election, only six of the old members were returned. Among them, however, were Willcocks and Rogers. The War of 1812 helped to discredit the radical party and it was not until 1818 that the fight was resumed where Thorpe and his supporters had left off. The radicals succeeded in easing the regulations that affected the grants to loyalists and military claimants. They had raised the charge of favouritism. They had taught the Assembly to resist the executive's claim to manage the Crown lands without reference to public opinion. Most important, they had emphasized that these lands were a source of revenue. Thereafter, the Assembly's struggle to control the land policies of the province also became a struggle to control its land revenues and to make the executive financially dependent upon the legislature.

CHAPTER SEVEN

THE SURPLUS POOR IN UPPER CANADA

THE APATHY of settlers in the western peninsula of Upper Canada towards the aggressive prosecution of the War of 1812 and the overt hostility of some of the recent arrivals from the United States towards Great Britain caused the Imperial government to heed the warnings of the ultra-loyalists who had long been prophesying the dangers that would arise from allowing the province to be overrun by Americans. When the opinions of these colonial Cassandras were backed up by such men as Gore, Brock, Drummond, and Prevost,[1] the Imperial government resolved to close the province to would-be settlers from the United States. This decision was accompanied by another of equal importance. It had become obvious to the British government that even with Imperial assistance Upper Canada could not readily safeguard her frontiers against the expanding Americans while her population remained so scattered, so scanty, and, in certain strategic areas, so American in origin and sympathy. If, however, those bent on emigrating from the mother country could be induced to go to Canada instead of to the United States, and if, in addition, discharged soldiers and officers retiring on half pay could be persuaded by the offer of a grant of land to become settlers in the localities most open to attack, the population of the province might soon become adequate for defence and safely British in tone and sympathy.[2]

The portion of the province where it was essential to have loyal settlers was the stretch between Kingston and Cornwall. Unless this part of the St. Lawrence frontier was securely in British hands in time of war, Upper Canada was likely to be cut off from Lower Canada and from Imperial assistance as well. In the past, lawless characters of all sorts had found shelter in the numerous islands at the foot of Lake Ontario. American lumbermen had invaded the townships around the Bay of Quinte and had helped themselves to the Crown timber,[3] and many Americans had settled in the Johnstown and Midland Districts. Their presence was resented by the original loyalists of Stormont, Glengarry, and the Bay of Quinte townships who now found themselves separated by settlers whose sympathies were very different from their own. During the war nearly 300 of the Leeds militia had deserted to the enemy, according to Archdeacon Strachan,[4] and other settlers in the county had aided the invaders. Hostile American influences, diminished by the war, could not be allowed to regain strength in this strategic area so close to the American shore. The only effective means of resisting American infiltration was to settle the area compactly with British immigrants.

The newly projected Rideau Canal, which was intended to provide an alternative and less exposed route to the upper province, would also be easier to construct and defend if the adjacent townships were filled with military settlers and loyal immigrants. The security of the Rideau area was most pressing at the moment, and there the scheme of controlled colonization was to be given its first trial, but it was planned to apply it at a later date to other lines of internal communication.[5] It was with these ideas in mind that the Imperial government undertook a colonization project, the primary object of which was not to reward her veterans of the War of 1812 nor yet to provide her emigrating poor with good farmland, but to strengthen the physical and ideological defences of the province against the United States.

While the war was still in progress, various British regiments serving in the Canadas were promised that soldiers discharged in the province and recommended as suitable settlers would receive 100 acres of land free of fees in a military settlement, provisions for themselves and their families for one year, and necessary farm implements.[6] In order that the settlement might be compact, officers were at first to receive only 200 acres, but they were to be granted additional land in proportion to their rank.[7] Subsequently, officers of the army and navy who had not served in the Canadas also became entitled to grants of land on selling out and after they had declared their intention to reside in the colony. Half pay officers also obtained this privilege.[8]

The promises held out to immigrants from the British Isles were in the first instance very similar. Heads of families were to receive 100 acres of land patent free and their sons on coming of age were to receive a like allotment. Rations were to be issued free for six months and afterwards at less than cost until the settlers could harvest a crop. Tools were also to be sold to them at less than cost. The government undertook to settle the immigrants as a community, as far as was possible, to pay the salaries of a clergyman and schoolmaster, and to provide free transportation to the settlement. In order to prevent immigrants from settling in the United States after they had received the Imperial government's subsidies a deposit of £6 was required for every male and £2 for every female over sixteen years of age. This deposit money was to be returned in two years' time on proof that the immigrants were settled on their grants.[9] Only in Scotland was the government's scheme widely publicized, and those who took advantage of it were mainly farmers and labourers from the vicinity of Edinburgh and Glasgow.[10] In high hopes they and their families, numbering 700 persons in all, sailed for Canada in the summer of 1815, little expecting the cold reception that awaited them.

Lieutenant-Governor Gore was totally out of sympathy with the plans of the Colonial Office. His attitude reveals both personal pique and the narrow jealousy with which the U.E. loyalists viewed all newcomers. During the war it was of course impossible for the Scotch peasantry to continue emigrating to the United States, and Lord Bathurst, recognizing that some relief had to be found for these poverty-stricken people, sounded out the Lieutenant-Governor (who was than at home on leave) about the possibility of settling British emigrants in Upper Canada with free grants of land and rations for a time. Gore's reply was not encouraging. He thought that if the government's bounty were extended to immigrants in this way it might have the effect of lessening the favour shown the original loyalists and he reminded Henry Goulburn that when the French royalists had been granted assistance of this kind it had "occasioned in the Loyalist settlers and disbanded Officers and Soldiers great jealousy and discontent." [11] Subsequently, Bathurst put a similar query to Sir George Prevost, Governor of Lower Canada, and the latter consulted Colonel Edward Baynes and Sir Gordon Drummond about Upper Canada. Both Baynes and Drummond were heartily in favour of the plan of off-setting American influence by the importation of loyal settlers. By the time Gore returned to Upper Canada, plans for settling the disbanded troops and immigrants were already well matured and he was instructed to further them. [12]

During Gore's absence, it had become the practice to leave the actual business of locating and settling the soldiers and British immigrants to the Quarter-Master General, who was responsible to the Governor-in-Chief in his capacity as Commander of the Forces. Only the work of surveying the land and passing the patent was entrusted to the officials of Upper Canada. [13] Gore soon came to resent the interference in his province of the Governor-in-Chief and the Military Settling Department. He felt personally affronted by the Department's choice of agents, and was thoroughly annoyed by the limitations which its activities placed on his own land-granting powers. His annoyance manifested itself as concern for the welfare of the original loyalists and their children.

Prior to Gore's return the problem had arisen of finding suitable locations for the veterans and the immigrants. The government had undertaken to settle the immigrants as a community as far as possible. Bathurst seems to have expected that they would all be located in one township and that their "first huts" would be located, not on their individual lots, but in one central location. To facilitate the choice of a site for this purpose he authorized the use of a Crown Reserve, provided a similar reserve was set aside elsewhere in the township. [14] The discharged soldiers, too, were to be settled as compactly as possible on lots not exceeding 100 acres. To this end, where the land was good, the hitherto sacred Crown Reserves might be "subdivided into small lots" for their accomodation. [15] These very restricted provisions later served as Gore's excuse for granting Crown Reserves elsewhere in the province to favoured persons.

When the Governor-in-Chief, Sir Gordon Drummond, called upon the Surveyor General of Upper Canada, Thomas Ridout, for a report on the land available, he was informed that, except for the reserves, the Eastern, Johnstown, and Midland Districts were nearly all located. There was plenty of grantable land in the District of London, but this had all been placed under the exclusive supervision of Colonel Talbot [16] and, in any case, what the government wanted was to settle the most exposed frontier. Ridout pointed out also—and here was the root of the trouble—that there were many orders-in-council for grants of land to U.E. loyalists still unlocated, and he suggested that additional land should be purchased from the Indians, either on the St. Clair River frontier, north of Lake Ontario, or between Lake Simcoe and Georgian Bay. [17] This suggestion did not find favour with the Military Settling Department which had the safety of the proposed Rideau Canal in mind. Ridout was directed by the Colonial Secretary to report all land vacant and grantable, including the Crown Reserves, from the Eastern District to the Home District. These locations, composed almost entirely of scattered lots (about 300,000 acres, of which 200,000 acres were Crown Reserves), were placed at the disposal of the Military Settling Department by Gore shortly after his return to Upper Canada.[18]

Sir Gordon Drummond did not regard these scattered reserves as suitable for the immigrants who had been promised that they would be settled as a body. When he found that it was going to be difficult to make the desired compact settlement on the Rideau because much of the land was in private hands,[19] he proposed to Gore that the owners should be induced to exchange their holdings for land elsewhere. This suggestion, as might have been expected, fell on stony ground. Drummond's requests for the townships of Seymour, Plantagenet, and Alfred were likewise turned down.[20] While Gore and Drummond were debating where to put them, the immigrants, who had arrived in September and were scattered in various encampments from Kingston to Montreal, were being fed at government expense and becoming daily more disturbed over the fact that the six months' period of free rations which had been promised them was rapidly slipping by while they still did not know when—nor where—they could begin to raise food for themselves.[21] Unable to obtain from the Lieutenant-Governor and Council of Upper Canada a satisfactory site for a settlement, there was nothing Drummond could do except locate the settlers either in Glengarry or on the reserves in the Bay of Quinte townships, a location for which many of them were petitioning.[22] Alexander Macdonell was appointed agent for the Glengarry area, and David McGregor Rogers for the Bay of Quinte area.

Rogers' appointment was bitterly resented by the Lieutenant-Governor of Upper Canada and by his Executive Council. Rogers had sat in the Assembly of Upper Canada since 1797 and no member of that body had asserted its claim to dispose of the entire revenue of the province more pertinaciously than he. His long course of opposition to the colonial administration had made him *persona non grata* to Gore. Now Rogers was placing discharged soldiers and immigrants in choice locations which had long been withheld from the loyalists themselves.[23] He was not disposed to be very considerate of those whom he found squatting on the reserves,[24] and was suspected, justly or unjustly, of being anxious to put soldiers and settlers on these lots so that he might afterwards possess them himself. In any event, the Lieutenant-Governor could see no reason why "Mr. Goulburn's vagabonds" should be allowed "to pick the country" of valuable Crown Reserves which had been denied to all previous settlers, including the loyalists and their children, many of whom at that moment held land warrants which they were unable to locate.[25] Rogers' letter of February, 1816, asking for land in the township of Whitby for the use of the Military Settling Department and complaining of the dilatoriness of the Surveyor General's Department in supplying him with locations, infuriated Gore.[26] He moved swiftly to find another location which Drummond would have to accept. He ordered a range of townships to be surveyed west of the Rideau in a territory in which the Indian title had not yet been extinguished and offered them to Drummond for the compact settlement which, he reminded him, the home government desired.[27] Drummond accepted, remarking, however, that he presumed that settlers who had already been granted location tickets for Glengarry and the Bay of Quinte would not be disturbed.[28]

This solution gave the Lieutenant-Governor of Upper Canada much satisfaction for the moment. He took malicious pleasure in naming three of the five new townships, parts of which were of very poor quality, Bathurst, Drummond, and Beckwith, and he suggested McDonnell and Rogers as names for the other two.[29] He wrote Bathurst a rather vague account of his dispute with the Military Settling Department, making it appear that he had from the outset been most anxious to further the scheme of the Colonial Office for a compact settlement on the Rideau, but that Drummond's agents had been inclined to let the immigrants scatter themselves about, picking and choosing their locations.[30]

The long delay in settling the bulk of the immigrants of 1815 terminated when the new townships of Bathurst, Drummond, and Beckwith were allocated, and the new town of Perth in the southeast corner of Drummond was projected as the centre of operations. The work of settlement commenced April 18, 1816. A well-established road led from Brockville into the township of Kitley,[31] but the last twenty-one miles to the site of Perth had still to be cut. This work was done by the immigrants themselves, and Robert Gourlay commented wryly that their labours were "sweetened with the customary reflection of Canadian farmers that idle drones shared in its profits...."[32] Since the Perth settlers had lost much time waiting to be located, the government was obliged to issue them a year's extra rations.[33]

Despite this inauspicious beginning, the Imperial government continued the work of building up the military settlements until 1822.[34] The assistance given the civilian immigrants was, however, never again as generous as in 1815. After 1816 they were promised only land and some agricultural implements.[35] Nevertheless, lured by the accounts of the government's generosity which the immigrants of 1815 sent home, a steady stream of immigrants from Scotland (5,000 of them in 1817) continued to reach Quebec, hopeful that they too would receive the same assistance as had the immigrants of earlier years.[36] Sir John Sherbrooke, who succeeded Drummond as Governor-in-Chief in 1816, refused to permit immigrants to be located in the military settlements unless they could provision themselves for a year after their arrival there. Discharged soldiers entitled to government rations might manage to remain on their lots until they could harvest a crop but in Sherbrooke's opinion it was impractical for penniless settlers "not indulged with provisions to find means of subsistence in the heart of the wilderness." For the same reason he did not consider the Crown Reserves in unsettled townships suitable for needy immigrants. He directed that these settlers be placed on the Crown Reserves in settled townships,[37] but once again the jealous government of Upper Canada tried to prevent them from receiving these locations.

Contention between the administrations of Upper and Lower Canada had not been ended by the purchase from the Indians of the new townships west of the Rideau. Gore expected that the locations turned over to the Military Settling Department would be restored to the government of Upper Canada and that these locations would enable him to satisfy the land claims of the loyalists, a matter which he regarded as of much more importance than the Imperial government's scheme of colonization.[38] In this he was disappointed. The shortage of locations open to U.E. loyalists continued and did not dispose the members of the Executive Council of Upper Canada to see the province burdened with expensive surveys for British immigrants, particularly at a time when the mother country's decision to limit her financial assistance to the province threatened to cause the Council much political embarrassment.[39] When, under pressure from home to reduce expenses, Sherbrooke refused to permit Gore to draw on the Military Chest for the expenses of surveys, except as a short-term advance, the Council of Upper Canada recommended that in view of the state of the provincial Treasury no more land should be surveyed. It also suggested that if the Military Settling Department needed more lots, it should utilize the Crown Reserves already made available.[40] Nothing loath, Gore dismissed all Upper Canada's surveyors.

A few months later (June, 1817) Gore returned to England on leave, there to discover that his opinions no longer carried weight with the Colonial Office. When he found, too, that the interference of the Governor of the Lower Province in Upper Canada's affairs was likely to continue, he decided "that it is high time for a Person of my feeling and unfortunate irritability to make as good, and as honourable a retreat as possible. . . ."[41] Sherbrooke meanwhile had referred the whole quarrel home. The British government decided to continue meeting the expense of surveys for disbanded troops and immigrants from the Military Chest instead of from the resources of Upper Canada, but in other matters the Governor of Lower Canada was upheld.[42]

In the summer of 1817 the Military Settling Department began locating settlers on the Crown Reserves in the older townships and, as Upper Canada's surveyors had ceased laying off lots in the new townships, the Department was obliged to locate discharged soldiers on the reserves also. It now discovered that some of the reserves nominally at its disposal had been applied for on lease by persons who had recently put trifling improvements upon them, that a good many reserves were actually illegally occupied, and that the government of Upper Canada was not willing to confirm such locations to soldiers or immigrants. Captain George Fowler, Superintendent of Military Settlements, was indignant at what he regarded as a scheming attempt to keep the good reserves for favoured persons in Upper Canada and to leave only the inferior lots for his Department to assign.[43] An appeal to the Administrator of Upper Canada to turn over to the Military Settling Department additional Crown Reserves or grantable land in the settled townships to prevent disillusioned immigrants drifting off to the United States proved futile. Lieutenant-Colonel Samuel Smith and his Council took the position that as of July 31, 1817, there were still 132,623 acres of Crown Reserves at the disposal of that Department—however unsuitable some of this land might be—and that, in any event, Upper Canada had agreed to provide land only for such settlers as were to receive government rations. Further than this the Council was not disposed to delegate its own land-granting powers.[44]

A solution for all these petty troubles was not easy to find. Sir John Sherbrooke had a thorough appreciation of the view-point and the needs of the penniless immigrant. To sustain his flagging hopes and courage the immigrant needed prompt settlement on the land and absolute certainty of title to it. Settlers whose means were very limited and who were not entitled to government rations could not afford to put in any time upon a location which the government of Upper Canada might delay and, in the end, perhaps refuse to confirm.[45] In most cases, said Sherbrooke, immigrants would need eighteen months' rations before they would be self-supporting.[46]

Since the British Treasury was insisting on economy, the Colonial Office was obliged to reverse its policy and to restrain needy immigrants from leaving for Canada where their misery was likely to force upon the Governor of Lower Canada unauthorized expenditures.[47] The method devised was to publicize the fact that land would be granted only to "capitalists" who could associate ten or more adults with them in the venture of emigration and who could make a deposit of £10 per person repayable when they were settled on their land. To such capitalists a grant of 100 acres a head was promised and hope was held out of more. The supposed advantages of this arrangement were that the settlers would attack the problem of conquering the wilderness as a community, and not as isolated individuals, and that they would need no assistance from government.[48] Two groups of settlers emigrated under the £10 scheme but it soon lapsed so far as Upper Canada was concerned, perhaps, as Miss Cowan suggests, because of the inconveniences immigrants were subjected to in British North America.[49]

So far, the British government had denied any intention of encouraging people to emigrate from the British Isles. Its policy was to strengthen the defences of North America by inducing only such people to go there as would have emigrated in any event. By 1820 the government was feeling its way towards a policy of fostering emigration as one form of poor relief. In the spring of that year, certain Members of Parliament appealed to the government on behalf of the Scottish hand weavers of Lanark and Renfrewshire who wished to emigrate to Canada. The government agreed to grant every family 100 acres of land free of fees and, instead of providing them with rations, to lend them £10 per head. The government also agreed to pay the cost of transporting them from Quebec to the place of settlement but stipulated that the cost of the ocean voyage should be borne by the immigrants themselves.[50] All advances to the immigrants were to be repaid in ten years' time and title to the land was to be withheld until the loans had been paid off.

Upon these terms 167 families, consisting of about 840 persons, emigrated in 1820 and were settled in Lanark and Dalhousie townships; 1,875 more were settled in North Sherbrooke and Ramsay the following year. Some of them had been assisted to emigrate by public subscriptions. About 700 other immigrants from Scotland who came out on their own in 1820 and some discharged soldiers were also settled in these two townships. The four townships were known as the Lanark Settlement. The British government spent £3,090 18s. 8d. in surveys, and advanced the Lanark emigrants £22,724 17s. 10½d.[51] In addition, blankets, cooking utensils, and farming tools were supplied. Some assistance of this kind was also extended to those settlers who had come out on their own and who were not entitled to the government's provision money.[52]

After December, 1821, no new locations were made by the Military Settling Department. Twelve months later, its supervisory work at Richmond and Perth was brought to a close, although the Lanark agency was continued for one more year.[53] About one-third of the soldiers and immigrants located by the Perth office had been placed on scattered lots in the older townships there,[54] but by no means all the Crown Reserves and vacant lots in the Eastern, Johnstown, and Midland districts had been settled. No attempt had been made to settle the townships fronting on the Ottawa and those immediately in the rear of them because they were too far from the food depots.[55]

By December, 1822, the military and Lanark settlements contained a total population of 10,763 persons, of whom 3,570 were men; of these, 1,307 were discharged soldiers and 2,263 were immigrants.[56] All these people had been located by the Military Settling Department but not all of them had been sent to Canada by the British government. During 1817 and 1818, about 200 English and Irish families who had emigrated by way of New York City were forwarded to Upper Canada by James Buchanan, the British Consul at New York. The immigrants were of three sorts: British subjects direct from Great Britain and Ireland; British subjects who had lived in the United States for some time but who, dissatisfied with conditions there, wished to go to Upper Canada; and American citizens. Buchanan's active policy received the support of the home government so far as British emigrants arriving in New York were concerned. He was authorized to spend $10.00 a head in forwarding them to Upper Canada and Gore was instructed to put such settlers on the same footing as British settlers then being sent out under government auspices. Buchanan, however, exceeded his instructions. He was, so he said, receiving applications from "thousands" of disappointed emigrants who wished to leave the United States for Upper Canada, and he forwarded a few of them.[57] Gore objected strenuously to receiving people who had lived in the United States for a time, "as some of the very worst subjects in the province are people of this description." Since the war, such people had officially been regarded as aliens, and aliens could not hold land in Upper Canada. Gore also complained that there was not sufficient money to survey land for these people, or even for *bona fide* British immigrants, now that the mother country's assistance was to be limited to the annual Parliamentary grant. As a result of Gore's protests, Buchanan's instructions were countermanded.[58]

To what extent were the plans of the British government for the settlement and defence of the Rideau area successful? On paper at any rate, a compact settlement appeared to have been achieved in the Perth agency. Aside from the Clergy Reserves and the bad land, not more than 400 acres remained un-allotted in Drummond and the western half of Beckwith, and about 2,000 acres were still vacant in Bathurst township. The Crown Reserves in the military settlements were at first made available for location, but this permission was later rescinded. Lieutenant-Colonel Cockburn, the Deputy Quarter-Master General in charge, protested at this hindrance to compact settlement, and Lord Dalhousie, Governor-in-Chief, suggested that the Crown Reserves be abolished because they occasioned unnecessary expense for surveys; but Bathurst, after he had been tutored by Lieutenant-Governor Maitland, Gore's successor, refused to interfere with the usual method of making the reserves and required them to be respected.[59]

From the military point of view, it would seem that the whole scheme was not of much value. True, a population of about 11,000 had been brought in, but five-sixths of the newcomers were settled, not close to the frontier opposite the American shore, but thirty to fifty miles inland. This was true even of the discharged soldiers, the majority of whom were located in Bathurst, Drummond, Beckwith, Goulburn, Burgess, and Elmsley townships. Half of these soldiers were single men, or at least settled without their families, and it may well be doubted whether they became part of the permanent agricultural population of the province. The canal they were to help defend was not begun until 1826 nor finished until 1832. Meanwhile the rocks and swamps of Beckwith, Goulburn, Burgess, and Elmsley were enough to discourage the most persistent soldier settler.

Were the military settlements a success from the standpoint of the immigrants themselves? Did these people become independent farmers able to obtain from land of their own a better living than they had known in their old homes? It is hard to answer this question in an unqualified manner. Undoubtedly some of the settlers received good land, but it is equally certain that many were located in townships like North Burgess, Elmsley, Beckwith, and Goulburn in which there was a high proportion of rock and swamp. About one-fourth of the lots in Bathurst, Drummond, and East Beckwith were regarded by the Military Settling Department as unfit for cultivation and about one-fifth of the lots actually located were still unimproved in 1822. There is considerable contemporary evidence that many of the military settlers abandoned their land as soon as government rations ceased to be issued.[60] Crop failures in the early years obliged the government to issue rations even after the first harvest and to make loans for the purchase of seed wheat and potatoes. The burden of these debts induced many to leave the settlement. Those who remained, wrote Cockburn, "are struggling against the numerous difficulties which stand opposed to the speedy advance of indigent settlers howewer flattering may be their prospects of ultimate success." [61] About half of the locatees in the military settlement went promptly to work to complete their settlement duties, which consisted of residing on the lots three years, erecting a dwelling, and clearing four acres.[62] By 1830 roughly two-thirds of them had struggled through to patent.[63]

Much has been written of the subsequent prosperity of the Perth Settlement, but most of the supporting evidence consists of statements made altogether too soon after the settlement's foundation, and sometimes of statements by interested parties who wished it to be considered a success. Like many another pioneer community before and since, the Perth Settlement enjoyed good times while it served as a source of supply for a newer frontier, in this case, Lanark. Whatever the prosperity of the Perth Settlement may have become in twenty years' time, fully one-fourth of the original settlers did not wait for it but sold their land a year or two after patent.[64]

The Lanark Settlement, as is well known, was not a success. One cause was the original poverty of the settlers, particularly those of 1820, some of whom arrived in debt for their passage or in need of clothing, and who hoped that they might rely upon the provision money advanced to them to take care of their debts and needs.[65] The land on which they were located was, moreover, particularly unsuited to agriculture. Out of 570 lots granted the Lanark settlers, about 50 in east Ramsay were worth settling. With the exception of half a dozen lots in Lanark, Dalhousie, and North Sherbrooke, the rest "should never have been attempted to be settled," testified Charles Rankin in 1834. They were "a succession of rocky . . . ridges with scraps of good land in between . . . scarce exceeding an acre." [66] This condemnation was perhaps a bit sweeping, but as late as 1881 only 30 per cent of the area of these townships had been cleared and most of this was in pasture. Thirty-five per cent of Lanark, 60 per cent of Ramsay, and 75 per cent of Dalhousie and North Sherbrooke were reported as too rocky and stony for cultivation.[67]

The settlers on these hard-scrabble farms soon realized that they were engaged in an almost hopeless struggle with nature. Some 73 families out of 594 left the settlement almost at once, some of them without waiting for a location, others before all the instalments of government money had been paid them. Of those that remained, only 60 had succeeded in clearing 20 acres by 1828, while 186 had less than 10 acres cleared.[68] The process of clearing yielded the settlers potash but the cleared land itself proved of little use to them. Before long, the settlement began to decline. The young men drifted away to seek better opportunities elsewhere. Their fathers, believing that their sons were entitled to 100 acres of land on coming of age, like the Scotch settlers of 1815, petitioned on their behalf for "that same indulgence, that has been [shown] to many an adopted child of the British family." Their claims were rejected on the ground that no such promises had been made them.[89] After ten years in the country the Lanark settlers found themselves still burdened with debt, without title to their land and therefore without a vote. Moreover, they were unable to provide for their children, the sales system having been adopted for Crown land in 1826. In 1826, and again in 1831 and 1833, when the British Treasury began to press for payment, the settlers petitioned for relief, pleading the bad quality of the land, the lack of a market, and the loss of their children's assistance.[70] By this time, 73 of the original locatees had died and 93 additional families had moved away, making the task of those who remained in the settlement that much harder.[71]

In 1836 the British government finally relinquished its claim on the settlers, 364 of whom thought it worth their while to prove their settlement duties and to apply for free patents.[72] The Treasury wanted the £22,000 it had lent the settlers to be made good out of the land revenue of the province but the Colonial Secretary did not consider it politically expedient to charge the expense of this experiment in Imperial colonization—unpopular from the beginning—to the people of Upper Canada, particularly at a moment when the tide of their discontent ran high. In the Lanark Settlement very few of the lots were sold immediately after patent, perhaps because the settlers had lived on them for fifteen years and were not inclined to part with them for a song like soldier settlers in Richmond and Perth, who had obtained their titles early and had done nothing more than barely fulfill their settlement duties.

Shortly after the Lanark Settlement had been undertaken for the benefit of the Scotch weavers, the Imperial government again resorted to emigration as a form of poor relief—this time for the benefit of Southern Ireland where evictions, unemployment, and famine had resulted in serious political disturbances.[73] In 1823 the government offered to assist 600 persons to emigrate to Canada, promising them a free passage to the place of settlement, land, rations, and farming

utensils. Five hundred and sixty-eight persons availed themselves of this opportunity. In 1825 the offer was renewed and 2,069 more emigrants were accepted
from thousands of eager applicants. The immediate object was the relief of
distress and the pacifying of unrest in the most disturbed districts. The long-run
objective was to discover at what cost a married couple and three children could
be settled in Canada beyond the need of further assistance. The government
also wanted to know whether these "useless and miserable beings," as Basil Hall
called them, could be transformed into efficient farmers and peaceable subjects,
whether they would desert their lots and leave for the United States as soon as
rations ceased to be given them, and whether it would be cheaper for the owners
of large estates to assist their paupers to emigrate or to continue to support them
at home.[74] Wilmot-Horton, Under-Secretary of State for the Colonies, anxiously
watched the course of this experiment, hoping that it would prove the prac-
ticability of his proposal to allow parishes to mortgage their poor rates for the
purpose of raising funds to finance the emigration of their paupers. It was
Horton's contention that over a period of years the emigrants would be able to
repay the sums advanced them by their parishes [75] and the outcome of the Lanark
experiment was not yet sufficiently clear to be evidence against him.

The settlement of the Irish immigrants was entrusted, not to the Military
Settling Department, but to the civil administration of Upper Canada, the
Colonial Office evidently wishing to avoid the conflict of authority between the
Governors of the two provinces that had occurred before. Peter Robinson,
brother of the Attorney General of Upper Canada, was placed in charge of
selecting the immigrants in Ireland and of settling them in Canada. In fact,
the whole "conspiracy," as John Beverley Robinson called it, had been devised
by Wilmot-Horton with his assistance. "The benefits I contemplate," wrote
Robinson, whose mind was on Canada, not on Ireland, "are the great consump-
tion of provisions it will occasion for which government will pay in money." [76]

About half of the immigrants sent out in 1823 were settled in the township of
Ramsay and the rest in other townships that were either part of or adjacent to
the Lanark and military settlements.[77] Lord Dalhousie and Captain Marshall,
Superintendent of the Lanark Settlement, viewed with disfavour the intrusion
of the Catholic Irish into this district, fearing that the Irish and Scotch settlers
would never live peaceably side by side.[78] This time the home government
received criticisms of its colonization project from the authorities of the lower
province, who had not been entrusted with it, but the hitherto critical Lieutenant-
Governor of Upper Canada, Sir Peregrine Maitland, gave spirited support.
Dalhousie's fears proved to be well founded. In the spring of 1824 there were
riots involving the Scotch and the Irish in the township of Ramsay which cost
the life of one settler and caused injuries to others.[79] It may have been on this
account that the much larger group of Irish immigrants brought out in 1825 was
settled, with a few exceptions, in a different range of townships bordering on
the lakes which formed part of the Trent waterway. The townships most heavily
settled with Irish immigrants were Douro, Otonabee, Asphodel, Smith, Emily,
Ennismore, and Ops.

According to Maitland, the Irish received more government assistance than
any of the earlier settlers, thus causing them to be regarded with some jealousy

by less fortunate settlers.[80] They were undoubtedly settled on better land than the immigrants in the military or Lanark settlements, even those who were settled in the township of Ramsay. They were not required to pay their own passage, as had been required of all the earlier immigrants except those of 1815, nor were they expected to repay the cost of the rations issued to them, like the Lanark settlers. These privileged settlers had cabins erected for them and cows were supplied. But they were not, like the other settlers, promised a free 100-acre grant and a free patent when their settlement duties were completed, a fact which has been overlooked. What they received was a grant of 70 acres for every male between the ages of eighteen and forty-five and a promise of a patent "at cost." An additional 30 acres was reserved for a period of ten years for each grantee which he had the option of purchasing for £10. However, five years from the date of settlement, the 70-acre holding became subject to a quit rent of 2d. an acre, and this quit rent was payable also upon the 30-acre reserve when it was purchased. These quit rents were redeemable at twenty years' purchase.[81] Upon these terms, the immigrants would have paid 3s. 4d. an acre for the first 70 acres and 6s. 8d. an acre for the other 30, plus the patent fee for a 100-acre lot which other British subjects received free. However, the quit rent system which Wilmot-Horton introduced for these Irish settlers, and which he intended to make the basis of the Crown land system in all the colonies,[82] was abolished by Lord Goderich.[83] As a result, the Irish settlers subsequently received their land and their patents free.

If the emigration committee of the Imperial Parliament were to be convinced that the experiment of colonizing Upper Canada with Irish paupers had succeeded, and if it were to be persuaded to recommend its adoption on a wider scale, three things were essential: proof that the settlers remained on their grants and did not slip away to the United States; proof that the expense had not exceeded the estimated £60 for a family of five; and proof that the settlers could repay the amount spent on them, if so required. Peter Robinson, Dr. Strachan, and Lieutenant-Governor Maitland laboured hard, and not altogether succesfully, to provide this evidence,[84] and they took care to emphasize that the happy result which they claimed might be very different in future experiments differently conducted—a side glance, perhaps, at the Military Settling Department which had worked under less favourable conditions.[85]

Among the immigrants settled in 1823 there were 182 men, a third of whom were to abandon their locations during the first two years, although some of them were expected to return.[86] Fifteen more heads of families were located in the Bathurst district in 1825. Twelve years later, 83 of these Irish immigrants were recommended for their patents.[87] It would seem, then, that even in this poor district the Irish settlers clung to the land. In 1834 Peter Robinson reported that 271 of the 415 located in 1825 were entitled to receive their patents because their settlement duties (erecting a dwelling, clearing and fencing three and one-half acres) had been completed.[88] By 1846, 80 per cent of the land occupied by Robinson's settlers of 1825 had been patented,[89] and in 1862, the last of the 509 fiats for patents to Robinson's settlers issued.[90]

Did the Irish become permanent settlers? A detailed analysis of only one township, Emily, selected at random, has been made. Eighty-one of Robinson's settlers in this township were recommended for their patents in 1834. Many of them were obliged to mortgage their land and to struggle through successive mortgages to retain title. Sixty-one of them held their land at least until after 1841 and in many instances passed it on to their descendants. Five parted with 50 acres of their grant; three of the lots were patented to other persons (probably an evidence of error in the return of 1834); and in two instances the record is incomplete. Only three settlers sold their land shortly after patent.[91]

As for the expense, Robinson told a select committee of the House of Commons that the emigration of 1823 cost £22 1s. 6d. a head, and that of 1825 £21 5s. 4d.[92] Robinson died without settling his accounts with the Treasury. Years later, in 1841, his brother, John Beverley, complained at length to Sir George Arthur of the difficulty his brother had encountered in keeping his books in order and in producing vouchers for everything. John Beverley closed the account by paying £1,968 17s. into the Military Chest.[93]

The method used by Robinson and Strachan to prove the success of the settlers was to list and evaluate the livestock acquired by them during their first year, the quantities of products produced by them, and the value of the land they had cleared. They took no account of any debts the settlers might have contracted with local merchants and they assumed that their property could actually have been converted into cash. By this means they were able to show that in one year the immigrants had acquired property worth £11,000. They also assumed that the settlers could have spared part of this sum from their farming operations if they had been called upon to do so.

In 1848, Earl Grey, who was then considering methods of utilizing the Crown lands to promote emigration from the British Isles, asked Lord Elgin for the assessed valuation of the townships settled by Robinson's settlers. The return, dated 1846, showed an assessed valuation in the eight townships colonized in 1825 of £45,712 12s. 11 d. A second letter followed in which Grey pointed out that the emigration of 1825 had cost the British Government £43,145,[94] and asked, in evident surprise, whether the townships named in the return were those settled by Robinson. In reply, Elgin sent a second return, dated 1848, in which was shown an assessed valuation of £128,116 for seven of the townships. About 20 per cent of the land in these townships had been occupied by Robinson's settlers.[95] Presumably the earlier return gave the assessed value only of the land which was occupied by them. Obviously government promotion of pauper emigration was not a paying proposition figured on the ability of the settlers to create taxable property equal in twenty years' time to the amount that had been spent on them. It is impossible to calculate the indirect political and humanitarian benefits of the experiment. The settlement of these townships by Irish immigrants drew other settlers there also, many of them squatters.[96] Like the Perth settlers, they all benefited from the government's expenditures on settlers in more remote townships in the eighteen-thirties.

No conclusive results were obtained from this experiment in colonization which had been designed to show whether large-scale migration of poor emigrants was financially practicable and whether the emigrants themselves could repay the expense of settling them in Canada. One year after the emigration of 1825, the free grant policy was ended.

CHAPTER EIGHT

ROBERT GOURLAY AND THE
ALIEN QUESTION

THE EFFORTS OF THE ASSEMBLY to determine the land policies of Upper Canada were deflected into new channels by the War of 1812. In Thorpe's day the Assembly had been anxious to regulate the land fees by statute and to procure land for late loyalists. After 1815 the chief objectives were to prevent the government closing the province to American settlers, to subject the lands of absentees to taxation, and to secure free grants of land for militia men. An articulate minority which felt that the province's resources in land should not be frittered away in petty grants advocated the sale of the Crown Reserves and the Crown lands to secure funds for internal improvements.

The alien question became a political issue at the close of the war when Bathurst directed the Administrator of Upper Canada to grant no land to citizens of the United States and to prevent them from settling in the province until further notice.[1] The original loyalists, it will be remembered, had resented Simcoe's policy of encouraging immigrants from the United States. In their opinion the latecomers were mere land-seekers, and probably disloyal republicans. They were afraid of being swamped by these on-coming Americans and surpassed by them in political power and influence. To stem this republican tide, Upper Canada had passed an act in 1795 which made American immigrants ineligible for the Assembly unless they had been residents of the province since 1788.[2] The act also provided that natural born subjects coming into the province in future from places not under British rule would not be eligible until they had put in seven years' residence. This act, which Powell claims to have suggested,[3] was so badly worded that no provision was made for persons who had come into the province between 1788 and 1795. In 1800, a seven years' residence requirement and an oath of allegiance were also imposed on American immigrants before they could vote.[4] At the next session of the legislature, David McGregor Rogers tried to have this act repealed, terming it the "most unjust and impolitic act ever passed by any Assembly," but the majority was opposed to encouraging American immigrants, the Solicitor General remarking that the province "had already enough of them."[5]

These political disabilities had not deterred Americans from immigrating to Upper Canada. As one contemporary observer remarked:

... the prospect of an immediate advantage fires the wandering disposition of the American peasant, whilst that prospect subsists he has no other Inducement to make his pitch as he terms it; he has no real Attachment to any form of Government nor to any Country. The increase of taxes in the United States, the Monopoly of Lands in the hands of Government Agents, and of other Speculators, reasons, perhaps, less honorable, have driven an immense Number of them into Upper Canada; a pretence of loyalty whether well or ill founded pleads for their Admission, in point of Numbers they greatly surpass the King's old and faithful Subjects. The disposition is rapidly increasing. . . .[6]

Until the War of 1812 the population of the province continued to grow, chiefly from American sources. The newcomers, described as "atheists" and "prowling democrats,"[7] were not regarded with a friendly eye by the leading loyalists and officials and, naturally enough, they returned their hostility.

In the Upper Canada Sundries there is a copy of a petition to Congress, dated Kingston, December 3, 1807, in which the petitioners, professing themselves to be U.E. loyalists, complained that they had settled in "the Howling Wilderness of Canada Expecting to Injoy the Rights of free British Subjects" and now found themselves ruled by royal officials who failed to execute the laws and subjected them to tyranny and oppression. They asked that Upper Canada be admitted to the Union on the following terms: leased Crown Reserves were to become the property of the lessees, the Clergy Reserves in each township were to be granted for the uses of that township, all public lands in the province were to be used for provincial purposes, all private grants were to be held sacred, and the children of U.E. loyalists were to be entitled to grants of land as under the royal instructions. No threat to peace came from this movement but the loyalist districts became alarmed at the continued influx of American settlers and in 1811 petitioned Gore to check it, predicting that the British character of the province would otherwise be lost.[8]

During the pre-war period an attempt was made to increase the political influence of American settlers by securing for them the right to vote and the right to be elected to the legislature on easier terms than those prescribed by the Acts of 1795 and 1800. Those who supported this movement—which failed— were Mathew Elliot from Essex, Angus McDonnell from Durham, Simcoe, and East York, Richard Beasley from West York, Haldimand and the first riding of Lincoln, Ralf Clench from the other ridings of Lincoln, David McGregor Rogers from Hastings and Northumberland, Isaac Swayzie from Lincoln, Benajah Mallory from North Oxford and Middlesex, and William Weekes from Durham, Simcoe, and East York. On several occasions a majority in the Assembly voted with this group, but the Legislative Council prevented any concessions to American settlers. On the eve of the war the pro-American party succeeded in defeating an attempt to alter the electoral qualifications to the disadvantage of American settlers.[9] Among their supporters on this occasion were Henry Markle of Dundas, Willet Casey of Lennox and Addington, John Willson of West York, Philip Sovereign of Norfolk, and David Secord of Lincoln.[10]

The party which obstructed the attempt to limit the political power of American settlers was not scheming to bring about annexation to the United States. Most of the members were loyalists and actively demonstrated their loyalty during the War of 1812. This radical, rather than pro-American, party had become opposed to rule by a Lieutenant-Governor advised by a self-interested Executive Council, and they hoped to increase their own strength in the legislature by obtaining for recent immigrants from the United States the right to vote and to be elected to the Assembly without a seven-year delay. It is true that these critics of the government of Upper Canada were joined by some black sheep—Abraham Markle, Benajah Mallory, and Joseph Willcocks, all of whom went over to the enemy in 1812—but the radicals were essentially as loyal as their opponents.

It must be remembered that while Upper Canada was settled by loyalists, these loyalists were not all of one mind. From the very beginning, most of them wished to institute in the province the more democratic institutions they had been used to in colonial America. They were opposed by persons like Simcoe or D. W. Smith, whose background was military, not colonial, and who feared that the following of American precedents would lead ultimately to the breaking of the Imperial tie. "Our house of Assembly for the most part have violent levelling principles . . ." wrote D. W. Smith. "The Neighbouring States are to[o] often brought in as patterns & models. . . ." [11] This rift of opinion developed during the sittings of the first Parliament of Upper Canada over the passage of an act which organized the new townships on the pattern set by the democratic town meetings of New England. Township officials were to be elected by the inhabitants at annual meetings; the Justices of the Peace, however, were to be appointed.[12] One of the major causes of discontent in Upper Canada, almost down to the Rebellion, was the power of the Justices of the Peace in Quarter Sessions, power that the Reformers repeatedly attempted to reduce and to turn over to elected officials of the townships. In 1835, with the help of Sir John Colborne's remodelled Legislative Council, they succeeded in having the justices elected.

The radical party, which favoured the admission of American settlers and the extension of political privileges to them, received a temporary set-back as a result of the War of 1812. In 1814 they were unable to prevent the passage of an act requiring fourteen years' residence of American immigrants before they would be eligible for the Assembly.[13] This act, like the act of 1795, had a peculiar defect. No provision was made for persons who had come to the province between 1800 and 1814. As a result, some persons were deprived of the right of standing for the Assembly who had enjoyed it under the previous act.[14]

During the war some of the more recent immigrants from the United States deserted to the enemy, while many others waited passively for the American victory which they confidently expected. As a result of their disloyalty and at the suggestion of Sir Gordon Drummond,[15] Bathurst directed that no land be granted to Americans and that they be prevented from settling in the province. Persons who had continued to reside in the United States during the war, without a declaration that they remained British subjects, were now officially regarded as aliens, although formerly, when they emigrated to Upper Canada, they had been treated as natural born subjects or as their children.[16] Gore, who returned to Upper Canada in September, 1815, directed the commissioners for taking the oaths of allegiance not to administer the oath to any person who was not in office or the son of a U.E. loyalist without special permission.[17] Since no one could obtain a grant of land or safely acquire real estate by purchase in Upper Canada without taking the oath,[18] this regulation effectively discouraged immigrants from the United States. It also incensed those speculators who had large quantities of land for sale and who had looked hopefully forward to the close of the war, a rapid increase in population, and a rising land market. In their opinion the sort of immigrants who ought to be encouraged were American settlers with some capital or at least with some experience in settling wild lands, not bewildered paupers from the British Isles, helpless Highlanders, or artisans totally ignorant of bush farming.

The large landowners were anxious to find buyers for their land because they feared that heavier and more effective taxation would soon be imposed on wild land. Some of the commissioners for administering the oath of allegiance were themselves large landowners, and they were not in the least disposed to be bound by the new restrictions upon it. William Dickson, for example, had recently purchased 94,000 acres of Indian land on the Grand River in the township of Dumfries. This block of land had already passed through several hands and the title to it was quite tangled. Dickson had won his legal battles and had just begun to develop a settlement by bringing in forty families and spending £4,000 on opening roads and building mills, according to his own account,[19] when Gore's circular containing the regulation threatened to deprive him of all possibility of securing American settlers for his land. Because Dickson refused to obey Gore's instructions, all the commissioners were dismissed, new ones were appointed, and the circular was reissued by the Lieutenant-Governor.[20]

Among the commissioners dismissed were William Dickson and Robert Nichol. Nichol represented the County of Norfolk in the Assembly and was regarded as the leader of the opposition in the Assembly until 1821 when W. W. Baldwin stepped into this role.[21] On April 13, 1817, Nichol, seconded by Clench, moved that the House go into committee to consider the state of the province.[22] This was an opportunity for the members to unburden themselves of all their grievances. The exclusion of American immigrants, the inadequate and costly postal service, the detested Crown and Clergy Reserves, and the claims of the militia to grants of land were all discussed.[23]

Eight of the long list of resolutions which were drawn up and proposed for adoption concerned the alien question. The first three declared that the Act 13 Geo. II, c. 7, for naturalizing foreign Protestants, and the Act 30 Geo. III, c. 27, for encouraging new settlements in British North America were still in effect. The fourth asserted that subjects of the United States might lawfully settle in the province and hold lands. The fifth and sixth emphasized the need of the province for population. The seventh and eighth stated that American settlers had been deliberately discouraged from settling in the province and asked that the recent order-in-council prohibiting commissioners from administering the oath of allegiance be rescinded.[24] These resolutions make it clear that there was discontent in Upper Canada before Robert Gourlay arrived and that grievances were not limited to demands for grants of land for the militia or for payment of war losses, as Dr. John Strachan contended.[25] The first three resolutions were adopted after much debate. The fourth was lost by the casting vote of the chairman.[26] Gore forestalled any further discussion of his policies by proroguing the legislature.[27]

Those who were opposed to the exclusion of American settlers thought they had a sound legal weapon with which to defend their economic predilections. The Act 13 Geo. II, c. 7, provided that all aliens who had lived seven years in any of the colonies and had taken the prescribed oaths should be deemed natural born subjects. The Act 30, Geo. III, c. 27 declared that settlement of the British colonies in America, and the West Indies should be encouraged, that Americans who emigrated to these colonies should be entitled to bring with them a certain amount of property duty free, and that every white person so coming should be required immediately after his arrival to take the oath of allegiance and to swear it was his intention to reside or settle in the province. Gore's opponents argued that while these acts remained on the statute books Americans could not be refused admission to the province nor denied the opportunity to take the oaths. This party also declared that once the Americans had taken the oath they were entitled to all the privileges of natural born subjects and to hold land. The law officers of the Crown, however, took the view that while Americans could not be denied the opportunity to take the oaths, they should not be allowed to hold a grant of land until they had resided in the colony for seven years. They also contended that land which they acquired by purchase or inheritance during this period could be seized by the Crown.

The Crown's position enabled Bathurst to explain that his instructions which had excluded Americans had not been intended to contravene these statutes but to enforce them, particularly the seven years' residence requirement. This explanation seems like an attempt to cover up the error he had made in directing the government of Upper Canada "to prevent" Americans from settling in the province in contravention of the existing Act of 1790. Colonel Samuel Smith, who became Administrator of the province when Gore went home on leave in June, 1817, was now instructed to make it known that foreigners would not be permitted to hold land in Upper Canada until they had taken the oath and put in seven years' residence. He was also instructed to dispossess those persons not entitled to the privileges of natural born subjects who had acquired land in the province since the war. When an attempt was made to frame a proclamation in accordance with these directions, a number of new legal difficulties came to light which caused its publication to be suspended until they could be dealt with.[28] This was not accomplished for ten years.

In the midst of the controversy over the exclusion policy, the Assembly, which had shown marked hostility to both it and Gore, repealed the Acts of 1795 and 1814 and replaced them by one which required seven years' residence of candidates for the Assembly if they had taken an oath of allegiance to a foreign power or been stated residents of a foreign country.[29] Unfortunately the Journals of the Legislative Council for this exciting session are missing so that the extent of its opposition to this change is not known but, as amended, the bill became law. Since it applied only to persons then resident in Upper Canada and made no provision for future arrivals, Americans would have had to be in the province by 1811 and to have stayed during the war to have benefited from it.

The new Imperial policy of excluding American settlers was very unpopular with some members of the Legislative Council and Assembly. Indeed, Dr. Strachan was afraid that a majority of the councillors might be persuaded by Thomas Clark and William Dickson to oppose the policy, and he used this possibility as an argument to urge his own appointment to that body.[30] Before the arrival of Bathurst's instructions, Smith had been reluctantly obliged to summon the legislature. He had every reason to fear that the debate on the exclusion policy, which had been abruptly terminated by Gore on April 7, 1817, would be resumed.[31] Since the close of the previous session, Robert Gourlay had arrived in Upper Canada and was at this time actively supporting the malcontents.

Robert Gourlay was a Scotsman who arrived in the province at the end of May, 1817, to visit his wife's relatives, William Dickson and Thomas Clark. Dickson and Clark had visited the Gourlays at their home in Wiltshire and had interested them in Upper Canada.[32] Various explanations have been given by Gourlay of his trip to Canada, not all of them consistent.[33] Probably, he hoped to persuade his wife's cousin, Thomas Clark, to lend him a substantial sum—$20,000, according to Clark—to enable him to repay his debts and retain the lease of his farm in Wiltshire.[34]

Gourlay's decision to prepare and to publish a statistical account of Upper Canada was taken, he tells us, as a result of reading John Melish's *Travels Through the United States of America* while waiting for a ship at Liverpool.[35] This work describes the political condition of Upper Canada as follows: "The laws appear fair and equal, but there is a great deal of underhanded management and intrigue; and neither independence of sentiment nor freedom of speech or of the press are encouraged; indeed they are hardly tolerated. . . ."[36] A statement such as this was not likely to be forgotten by a man of Gourlay's temperament should anything occur to displease or frustrate him.

After visiting Montreal and the military settlements about Perth, Gourlay proceeded on foot as far as Queenston where he learned that Clark could not assist him and that he would lose the lease of his farm.[37] Gourlay explains that Clark's wealth was in land and that, while the latter wished to retire and go home to Scotland, he could not dispose of his property because of the depressed state of the land market. Gourlay, like the land speculators of Upper Canada, blamed this on the government's new policy of excluding American settlers.[38] Clark, in fact, did not want to lend Gourlay the money, "well knowing the visionary ideas and speculations of the man."[39]

Gourlay now began to think of becoming a land agent for Upper Canada. After some weeks spent in Buffalo and on a walking tour of the Genesee country, he returned to the upper province resolved to complete his statistical enquiries and to become a land agent for the province.[40] In his opinion, the Genesee country, whose settlement began ten years later than that of Upper Canada, was at this time ten years ahead, not because it had more natural advantages, nor because the art of clearing was any better understood, but because British capital had given it its initial stimulus. What Upper Canada needed was men of capital. If a flow of capital could once be directed to the province, immigrants would follow, independent of government assistance, and the exclusion of American settlers would then become of minor importance. While there were numerous general accounts of Upper Canada in print, none of them were sufficiently detailed or accurate to interest capitalists. The first thing to be done, then, was to compile and to publish an authentic statistical account of the province.

These ideas are to be found in Gourlay's first *Address to the Resident Landowners of Upper Canada,* published in October, 1817. To it he attached a list of thirty-one queries calling for a wide range of information concerning the population and natural resources of each township, the existence of mills, churches, and schools, the yield of crops, the price of land, wild and improved, the cost of clearing, and the amount of land for sale. He suggested that answers to his queries be drawn up at township meetings convened for the purpose, and he promised to publish the replies on his return to England.[41]

Gourlay's *Address* aroused widespread interest and general approval. A number of magistrates of the Niagara District, including Thomas Clark, promptly published a signed statement in the *Niagara Spectator* of November 8, 1817, recommending that township meetings be held to answer the queries. Some forty reports were subsequently received, chiefly from the Midland, London, Gore, Niagara, and Western Districts. The Ottawa, Johnstown, and Eastern Districts showed less interest. Not one reply was received from the Home District, which included the capital, York. A "monstrous little fool of a parson"—John Strachan —who alone found anything exceptionable in the proposed statistical inquiry, is responsible for having deprived posterity of the information about this district which otherwise Gourlay would have left.

Dr. John Strachan, at this time Rector of York and a member of the Executive Council, was the only person hostile to Gourlay from the outset, and was the main source of the opposition which was soon to overwhelm him.[42] Gourlay declared that he had never seen or met Strachan, had done him no injury, and could not account for his hostility to a project which everyone else approved. He thought, however, that the rumour that Strachan himself had been preparing to publish an account of the province might account for the latter's antagonism. Gourlay was not as innocent as all this. It would seem that he had early formed an unfavourable opinion of Strachan [43] and it may be that his incautious tongue gave the first offence. Certainly no respect for the cloth ever tempered his language towards his clerical opponent. He made, too, the tactical error of not showing his *Address* to Strachan before it was printed, and this slight was the more marked in that he had freely consulted other members of the Executive Council. The very fact that Gourlay's *Address* and the proposed statistical inquiry had met with Powell's approval was almost enough to ensure the disapproval of Strachan, who had little respect for the Chief Justice.[44]

Strachan's opposition was not based on personal considerations alone, as Gourlay seems to have realized after a time. Strachan was afraid that the proposed survey would ultimately lead to a demand for the sale of the Clergy Reserves and it was for this reason that he wished to stifle all discussion of the expediency of selling them before it got started. Gourlay made no mention of the Clergy Reserves in his first *Address*, but in the first draft of it he referred to "the able resolutions" brought forward at the close of the last session of the provincial Parliament. Two of these resolutions related to the Clergy Reserves; one stated that they were an insurmountable obstacle to the formation of a well-connected settlement, the other recommended that they be sold and criticized the endowment of the Church as "beyond all precedent lavish." [45] It is no wonder that these resolutions were held in abhorrence by the officials at York and, on the cautious advice of William Dickson, Gourlay deleted all reference to them.[46] Despite this revision, of which perhaps Strachan knew nothing, the *Address* still contained a sentence which may have alarmed him:

"What in your opinion retards the improvement of your township in particular, or the province in general. . . ." To this question diverse answers could be expected, but Strachan must have realized that one answer would be "the Clergy Reserves."

How could Strachan permit Gourlay's inquiries to go on and the results of them to be published in England? He might do the temporal interests of the Church untold harm. The man must be discredited, opposed, stopped. Strachan promptly warned Smith that in his opinion Gourlay was "a dangerous incendiary and his scheme of a topographical work a mere pretence to conceal his real views." "My opinions," records Strachan, "were treated with ridicule by the Chief Justice and therefore made no impression on the Administrator" [47]—a development not calculated to soften Strachan's feelings towards Gourlay.

Shortly after the publication of his *Address*, Gourlay set out on an eight weeks' tour of the western peninsula. He found that discontent increased as he travelled westwards. The chief grievances were that the claims for losses during the War of 1812 had not been paid and the militia had not received their promised grants of land. In September, 1815, Gore had reported that no application for militia grants had been made. He pointed out that only 50-acre grants had been promised at a time when ordinary settlers received 200, treatment "not very flattering" to the militia of Upper Canada. He suggested that the militia might be content with half the usual amount, provided the grants bore some mark of distinction, and he proposed that they be allotted out of the Crown Reserves.[48] In December, 1818, grants of 100 acres were authorized, free of fees, but not out of the Crown Reserves, and subject to the conditions of residence and cultivation.[49] Meanwhile, the long delay in determining the size and conditions of these grants had produced great discontent.[50]

Prior to the war, the western peninsula had received many settlers from the United States, and Gourlay found the policy of excluding Americans an unpopular one in that part of the province. On his return to Queenston he discussed this question with William Dickson and Thomas Clark, both of whom had become embittered by Gore's exclusion policy.[51] Gourlay now came to regard the exclusion of Americans as the main cause which retarded the progress of the province.

In February, 1818, Gourlay wrote his *Second Address to the Resident Land-owners* with this idea in mind. It proved to be a less temperate document than the first. It also had a very different emphasis and provided Strachan with ample ammunition to use against its author. Gourlay confessed that he had thought the chief obstacles to the prosperity of Upper Canada were "the errors of original institution," meaning the entire land-granting system and the reserves, but that he had come to the conclusion that the chief obstacles were "political." To remove them, he proposed that the provincial Parliament should undertake an inquiry into what hindered the prosperity of the province and should send the results home to England by commissioners empowered to solicit the co-operation of the Imperial Parliament.

Gourlay then launched into an attack on Gore's administration to show that the Governor had exceeded his powers in arbitrarily setting aside the provisions of the Act of 1790 for the encouragement of American settlers. Three-quarters of the population of Upper Canada was composed of American settlers, whose loyalty, asserted Gourlay, had been proved by the war. That conflict had brought to light unprincipled villains in Canada but the basest of all were not Americans but men of European birth. What could induce Americans to settle in Canada after the war, he inquired? Surely nothing but a prejudice in favour of the British government! This was a completely unrealistic reply which disregarded the fact that land was cheap in Upper Canada and that the reserves were a temptation to squatters. Despite his statement that he did not wish to cast contempt upon constituted authority, Gourlay declared that Gore had done irretrievable mischief, that he ought to have been impeached, and that, under his administration, the rights of property had been violated. "There must be something wrong," Gourlay hinted darkly, "with a government that cannot let Americans and others come in and go out as they please. I dwell on this subject not because it concerns the value of your property, which would have been double at this moment but for the narrow policy which has been pursued, but for the sake of the principle involved. You cannot expect a single British subject to come to Canada to purchase land, if security in property remains doubtful, and if the laws are to be at the mercy of every impetuous governor." [52]

Gourlay's *Second Address* was about to be printed when the administrator, Colonel Samuel Smith, informed the legislature that the Imperial government had decided to set aside the proceeds from the sale of the confiscated estates of traitors to pay the war losses, and he suggested that the immigrants whom the mother country was about to send to Upper Canada should receive their grants of land free of the provincial location and patent fees.[53] This speech angered Gourlay. He believed that the proceeds from the sale of the confiscated estates would not pay three pence in the pound on the war losses and he felt that the Assembly should have scorned this offer as an insult to those who had fought and suffered. He was exasperated also by the proposal that the assisted immigrants should have their fees paid for them while substantial farmers, who had come out at their own expense, were unable after weeks of waiting to get any satisfaction from the slothful officials of the land-granting department.[54] After reading Smith's speech, Gourlay dashed off an additional paragraph to his *Second Address* in which he reiterated the necessity of sending a commission to England. If substantial farmers in the mother country were made aware of the attractions of Canada, they would come without the help of private charity or the assistance of government. "I know," he concluded, "that you might draw every one of them here, if you would but clear the house of vermin and filth. It is quite natural for us to keep up our connexion with home but we cannot prefer a land of lice to a land of liberty."

Had Gourlay's *Second Address* been deliberately calculated to arouse the hostility of the official class of Upper Canada and of the most intolerant loyalists among its inhabitants, it could not have been better worded. It covered Gore with obloquy, and asserted that if Canada were united to "the land of liberty" south of the line her prosperity would be doubled. It upheld the doctrine that men are free to change their allegiance and quoted with approval Pope's lines:

For forms of government let fools contend
Whate'er is best administered is best.

In short, it challenged the whole loyalist position and tossed aside the fable so carefully fostered in Upper Canada that under the British Crown were to be had peculiar blessings unprocurable elsewhere.

This intemperate publication met with an unfavourable reception. One critic informed Gourlay through the columns of the *Niagara Spectator* that it had destroyed the fair prospects of his first *Address*. "The ... only grievance you seem to dwell on," said this writer, "is the non-admittance of settlers from the United States. This can be felt but ... by a part of the community ... the great landholders. ..." Another writer questioned the purity of his motives, pointing out that he was connected by family ties with some of the largest landholders in the province.[55] Strachan, who was making a tour of the lower part of the province, probably put the magistrates and clergy on their guard against Gourlay even before the *Second Address* appeared.[56] The result was that, with the exception of two townships, all the statistical information Gourlay obtained from the District of Johnstown came from a Presbyterian minister, only one township report was received from the Eastern District, and none at all from the Home District. No doubt the meeting of the township of Augusta is typical of others held in the older and more solidly loyalist districts. It resolved:

That however advantageous the information might be to Upper Canada resulting from proper answers to these queries and placed in *proper* hands, the present meeting cannot feel themselves justified in giving their support to the very injurious consequences which might result from such information placed at the disposal of a man of Mr. Gourlay's political principles.[57]

Gourlay denied that he was a mouthpiece of a party of landholders and that the exclusion of American settlers was Upper Canada's only grievance. The war losses had not been paid, the value of property had declined, the price of wheat was down, the province was practically devoid of specie, and the Land Board's neglect of its duties was every day driving valuable settlers from the country. Moreover, the ruinous patronage and favouritism which it exercised had the effect of so reducing the value of a grant of Crown land that it was but a paltry gift to the recipient and often ruined the unlucky settler in whose vicinity it was allowed to lie uncultivated and unimproved. To achieve redress of these grievances, three things were necessary: an act subjecting all wild land to taxation, prompt payment of the war losses, and the sale of the Crown Reserves. If the Imperial government would consent to the latter measure, ample funds could be secured to pay every claim for war losses, funds which would not be easily or quickly derived from the confiscated traitors' estates.[58]

Gourlay's attack on the Land Board was in part motivated by personal disappointment. He had applied for a grant of land, but, as it was known that he intended to return to England with the township reports, the Board informed him that when he returned as a permanent settler a grant of land would be made him in accordance with the regulations.[58] This reply did not suit Gourlay, who, in a letter to Colonel Smith, reviewed his correspondence with the Board, using his own case as an illustration of his complaint that its members were driving immigrants from the province.[59] He also charged that Strachan, as president of the Land Board, neglected his duties while he promoted activities to raise funds for the relief of poor immigrants or for schools which would be unnecessary were the resources of the province rightly administered. This turncoat Scotch dominie who had risen to power and office in Upper Canada might pose as a versatile scholar and open-handed churchman, intimated Gourlay, but essentially he was a mountebank and a vainglorious little man "whose charity blows a trumpet before it." The publication, in the *Niagara Spectator,* of Gourlay's letter of February 17 to Smith, coming as it did on top of the *Second Address,* aroused great indignation at York. "What could have induced you," wrote Thomas Clark from York, "to expose the President and others, and particularly yourself in the manner you have done I know not. Until this fatal error most folks here were inclined to befriend you: I can however now say, that it is my opinion that every man of respectability will be shy of you, should you come here...." [60]

Despite these evidences of disapprobation, Gourlay declares that his *Second Address* was an "unoffending production" save to Strachan.[61] He also claimed that it had inspired the Assembly to pass the "fourth" resolution.[62] This was the resolution which was about to be voted upon when the previous session of Parliament was suddenly prorogued by Gore and which stated that since the acts for naturalizing foreign Protestants and encouraging Americans to settle in Canada were still in force, citizens of the United States might lawfully settle in the province, hold land, and become naturalized subjects.[63] According to Gourlay, his proposed inquiry into the state of the province was also voted upon by the Assembly and carried. There is, however, no record in the Journals of a vote on the fourth resolution. The Assembly did, on several occasions, go into committee on the state of the province, at which times it may have discussed the alien question, although at the time it was prorogued it appears to have been considering chiefly revenue questions and the claims of the Upper House to amend money bills. Nothing was done to forward the proposed inquiry.[64]

The prorogation of the provincial Parliament for a second time in the midst of unfinished business and heated controversy stirred Gourlay to write his famous *Third Address to the Resident Landowners,* published on April 12, 1818. Nothing, said Gourlay, had been accomplished by the recent Parliament, nor was anything likely to be accomplished by the next one, presumably because it also would be prorogued if it showed an independent spirit. "It is not the men, it is the *system* which blasts every hope of good; and till the *system* is overturned, it is vain to expect anything of value from change of Representatives or of Governors." By the "system" he meant that the Legislative and Executive Councils were composed of practically the same persons who could thus prevent the legislature from taking any course which they disapproved of, and who, as the Governor's councillors, could advise him against adopting any policy unacceptable to them personally. The Assembly had complained of this situation in an address which it was about to request the Administrator to transmit to the Prince Regent when the Parliament was prorogued.[65] Under these circumstances, Gourlay advised the people to lay their grievances at the foot of the throne. He proposed that, through township and district meetings, a provincial convention should be elected to draw up a petition and choose commissioners to carry it to England. He suggested that those coming to the township meetings should each subscribe one dollar to defray the expenses of the commissioners and he hoped for 10,000 subscribers.[66]

Up to this point Thomas Clark and William Dickson, both members of the Legislative Council, had given Gourlay some support, although they had not approved all he had said or written. Gourlay states that it was Dickson and Clark, especially the former, who first drew him into political discussions by denouncing Gore's exclusion policy, but that they afterwards withdrew their support for fear of losing official favour and patronage. Clark, however, had been reluctant to see the *Second Address* published for fear he and Dickson would "be accounted the fathers of it," although he conceded that "it might contain a good deal of truth." Gourlay charged that it was Dickson who later persuaded Clark to raise the cry of sedition by publishing a handbill reminding Canadians that in Scotland those who had taken part in conventions such as Gourlay proposed had been convicted of sedition and transported.[67]

Clark's attempt to intimidate British subjects from exercising their undoubted right of petition failed. The first township meeting was held at Niagara on April 13. Other township meetings followed, and on May 4 the townships of the District of Niagara met, elected their district representatives, and set June 6 as the date for other township meetings, June 13 for district meetings, and July 6 as the date for the Convention.

A draft address to the Prince Regent was formulated at the Niagara District meeting and was turned over to a committee of four who were responsible for its wording and for its publication. This statement of grievances complained that commercial treaties neglectful of Canadian interests had been made;[68] that the grants of land promised militia men had not been made; that the war losses had not been paid although there were millions of acres of fertile land in Canada from which funds might be raised for this purpose; and that the Crown Reserves which were scattered throughout the province were being disposed of by the Executive Council to its favourites or by ministers at home who were ignorant of the circumstances. In the disposal of the Crown lands a system of patronage and favouritism existed, with the result that the management of public affairs had become corrupted, the value of the Crown lands had been reduced, poor immigrants derived little advantage from their grants, and U.E. loyalists could not realize the expected benefits from their rewards. These complaints were reiterated in the draft address of the Midland District.[69]

A small pamphlet was published by the Niagara committee which included all its proceedings to date and the text of the draft address.[70] Agents were sent out to distribute the pamphlet for sale and Gourlay, who undertook to do this work below Queenston, travelled as far as the Ottawa District. In the lower districts the pamphlets were not well received. An address read to the electors of the County of Stormont at the desire of the officers of the militia charged the proposed Convention and all who should support it with disloyalty.[71] It suggested that the changes in government which Gourlay advocated were unnecessary since Upper Canada governed itself and could petition the home government through its legislature. This argument overlooked the fact that the last legislature had been prorogued while trying to get the Administrator to forward an address which he disapproved of to the Prince Regent.

Despite opposition of this sort, over fifty township meetings were held,[72] the district representatives were duly chosen, and on July 6 a convention of fourteen delegates met at York. No representatives were present from the Ottawa, Eastern, and Home Districts, probably because in the former there were few settlers and no good roads, and in the two latter because military, official, and clerical influence had been used against Gourlay. The fourteen delegates included Nathan Hicok for the District of Johnstown; Richard Beasley and Captain Williamson from the Gore District; Roderick Drake from the Western District; Daniel Washburn, Thomas Coleman, Paul Peterson, Jacob W. Myers, and Davis Hawley from the Midland District; Robert Hamilton, Dr. Cyrus Sumner, John Clark, and Major William Robertson from the Niagara District; Calvin Martin from the London District; Robert J. Kerr represented the Newcastle District but was later replaced by T. D. Sanford. Six of these names are on the U.E. list and at least one other person belonged to a U.E. loyalist family.[73]

The chief business of the Convention was to draw up a petition to the Prince Regent and to arrange for commissioners to take it home. Some of the members were reluctant to go over the head of the provincial Parliament but Gourlay insisted that since the right of petitioning the throne directly had been called in question, it was necessary to assert that right. It was finally decided to send a deputation to wait on the new Lieutenant-Governor, Sir Peregrine Maitland, with two petitions, the one for the Prince Regent, the other for himself. The petition which was directed to Maitland asked him to order a new election and to recommend to the new Parliament an inquiry into the state of the province, the result of which should be sent to England. The address to the Prince Regent simply stated that if such an inquiry should be made, it would give the petitioners the fullest satisfaction. If not, the Prince Regent was asked to bear in mind the draft addresses from the Niagara and Midland Districts, and to lend a gracious ear if a commission should come home "from the body of His Majesty's loyal subjects in Upper Canada. . . ." Richard Beasley, who had been chosen chairman of the Convention, undertook to write to his friend, Lord Erskine, asking him to present the petition to the Prince Regent.[74] Whether Lord Erskine did so we do not know.

With the adoption of this roundabout procedure, the Convention brought its labours to a close. They do not seem to have been wholly satisfactory to Gourlay who complained that one annoyance succeeded another and that the delegates "though as good as the country could afford and perfectly loyal, were fit for nothing." "I gave up hope of my intended measures, and was glad to wind up matters in the best way I could . . . But for being bound to appear at your assizes . . . I should have turned my back on your convention the very second day of its sitting and left it to get out of the mud of Little York by its own shifts."[75]

Lieutenant-Governor Maitland refused to receive the address directed to him when Richard Beasley and the members of the Convention's permanent committee attempted to present it, claiming that it emanated from an unconstitutional body.[76] He ought to have known better. A few days previous to the meeting of the Convention, the Executive Council had been advised by both the Attorney General and the judges that the Convention would be neither seditious nor criminal since the British statute of 1795, commonly called the Riot Act, did not extend to Upper Canada.[77] This lack was soon to be remedied by the legislature, at Maitland's suggestion. After declaring that it was the only constitutional representative of the people, the Assembly, by a vote of 13 to 1, passed a bill which declared illegal all assemblies of delegates, whether appointed or elected, for debating matters of public concern. Willet Casey of Lennox and Addington, a constituency subsequently represented by Marshall Spring Bidwell and Peter Perry, was the only member present with courage enough to vote against this measure. Of the thirteen votes in favour, eleven came from counties east of York. The other eleven members, representing the western part of the province, failed to vote on this question.[78] Even Chief Justice Powell, who disapproved of the bill, took no open part against it.[79]

To a man like Gourlay, official opposition served only as a spur to further efforts. Although Maitland had refused to receive the Convention's address, he had expressed his willingness to receive petitions from townships or districts. Gourlay travelled from Kingston towards York, sending notices ahead of him, and held, in all, eleven township meetings at which petitions to the Prince Regent and the provincial Parliament were drawn up.[80] In the townships of Hamilton and Hope, which he visited on November 11 and 12, the magistrates collected a following, disrupted his meetings, and had addresses signed which negated the effect of his petitions.[81] This opposition seems to have brought his tour to an end.

Gourlay's opponents charged that the petitions he secured were not worded in full form at the time they were circulated for signatures and that the subscribers had been deceived.[82] Maitland subsequently wrote to the first signers of some of these asking them to state their grievances in detail. He received some very frank answers, lacking "the customary expressions of adulation," as one outspoken correspondent put it. Among the grievances touched upon were: the encroachments of the executive, particularly with respect to the disposal of the public revenue; the Road Act which required as much statutory labour from the small landowner as from the man "glutted" with landed property; the unequal assessment of land, all of it being rated alike despite its situation or value; the failure to tax large landholdings of absentee proprietors; and the unreasonable charges, the unnecessary delays, and the partiality of the land-granting department.[83]

Gourlay's triumphal progress from Kingston to York aroused the indignation of the authorities. They were itching to lay their hands on him and, at this very time, were consulting together as to how it could be done with success. They had already made two attempts and had failed. Prior to Maitland's arrival, and, at the urging of Strachan and Robinson,[84] Gourlay had been arrested at Kingston for libelling the government. He was released on bail and was subsequently acquitted at a trial which took place after the meeting of the Convention.[85] The jury's verdict, wrote Powell, who had disapproved from the outset, "was precisely the Desideratum of a Demagogue whose influence was subsiding. . . ."[86] A second charge of seditious libel led to another trial at Brockville, and once again the jury acquitted Gourlay. However, Strachan remained unshaken in his belief that Gourlay could still be convicted of libelling the government and that this was the proper way to destroy his influence.[87]

After the anti-Convention bill became law, Gourlay published an article in the *Niagara Spectator* of December 3, entitled "Gagged, Gagged, by Jingo," in which he reminded his readers that although the adjourned Convention could not legally meet again, township meetings could still be held to protest against the act and to consider what topics ought to occupy the next session of the legislature. Put these topics in the hands of your representatives as *instructions,* advised Gourlay, and if they do not follow your instructions and allow themselves to be overwhelmed by the "fascinations" of Little York, do not re-elect them. Above all things, instruct your representatives to keep hold of the purse strings.[88] This bit of advice must have angered Maitland, who had begun his administration of Upper Canada with the determination that the Assembly should *not* hold all the purse strings.[89] Gourlay called on all those who had been elected delegates from the townships of the Niagara District to meet with him on December 26, this time as individuals, not delegates, to consider what the next move should be.[90] However, on December 21, his career in Upper Canada was cut short by his arrest at Queenston under the provisions of the Alien and Sedition Act of 1804.

The Alien and Sedition Act of 1804 provided that any person suspected of promoting sedition who had not been an inhabitant of the province for six months, or who had not taken the oath of allegiance, might be arrested on the warrant of certain specified authorities. If the suspected person was unable to satisfy these officials of the innocence of his conduct, he could be ordered by them to leave the province. If he did not obey this order, he was to be arrested and held for trial without bail; if found guilty, he was to be required to depart from the province forthwith. Disobedience to this second order was punishable by death. The burden of proof was on the accused.[91] The two legislative councillors who issued the warrant for Gourlay's arrest were William Claus and William Dickson. When brought before them, Gourlay failed to show that the Alien and Sedition Act did not apply to him or to satisfy them of the innocent nature of his activities. Consequently he was ordered to leave the province by January 1, 1819.[92] On his failure to do so, he was imprisoned at Niagara.

Gourlay then applied for a writ of *Habeas Corpus.* He pointed out to Chief Justice Powell that the act did not apply to him because he had resided more than six months in the province prior to his arrest, because he was a British subject, and because he had taken the oath of allegiance.[93] This defence was weak. The Act of 1804 did not exempt British subjects from its operation. Indeed, as Riddell points out, it had been the definite intention of the legislature to bring certain classes of British subjects within its scope.[94] It was not enough for Gourlay to show that he had been six months in the province. He needed to show six month's residence *preceding the date of the warrant for his arrest.* Moreover, he did not state in his affidavit where er when he had taken the oath. Powell refused to discharge him, and he was sent back to jail at Niagara where he remained until the assizes in August. On this occasion, the only point at issue was whether he had refused to obey Claus' and Dickson's order to leave the province. There could be no doubt of this. In accordance with the court's order, Gourlay left the province within twenty-four hours after the conclusion of his trial,[95] and returned to England where for years he continually and unsuccessfully petitioned the House of Commons, sometimes urging an inquiry into his own affairs, sometimes into the affairs of the province.

W. R. Riddell has undertaken to defend the Chief Justice's course with respect to Gourlay. He contends that while Powell disliked the Alien and Sedition Act, he refused to release Gourlay on a writ of *Habeas Corpus* largely because of the weakness of his defence. "Gourlay nowhere in all his voluminous writings ... states when where or under what circumstances he did take the oath of allegiance," remarks Riddell.[96] This is not quite accurate. Gourlay mentions in his *Chronicles of Canada* and also in the *Neptunian* that he had been a commandant of Volunteers in Fifeshire and that as such he must have taken the oath of allegiance.[97] The records show that this information came to light during his Kingston trial. Riddell also contends that Gourlay did not exhaust all the legal resources open to him. He could have applied to the other judges of the Court of King's Bench for release on a writ of *Habeas Corpus* and shown proof then that he had taken the oath.[98]

The truth is that Gourlay's case was pre-judged before he was arrested. In November, 1818, Sir Peregrine Maitland asked all three judges their interpretation of the Alien and Sedition Act and their reply shows that Gourlay would have been unsuccessful in an appeal to any of them. Powell and his colleagues had decided that the act meant that the oath of allegiance must have been taken within the province, although the statute does not require this in so many words. This interpretation is not unreasonable because the statute was aimed at Americans and United Irishmen who might have taken the oath some time prior to 1776 or 1798 but from whom a pledge of future loyalty was desired. Even if he had been able to prove that he had taken the oath within the province, Gourlay would not have escaped from the operation of the act. "We are further of opinion," wrote the judges, "that Such an Inhabitant having resided six months and taken the oath of allegiance by an absence for some weeks in a foreign country within the six months immediately preceding the warrant of arrest leaving no fixed residence behind him becomes subject on his return to the full operation of the Statute."[99] Although Gourlay had been continuously an inhabitant of Upper Canada from October, 1817, to August 31, 1818, he had been absent from the province on his walking tour for more than a month within the six months immediately preceding his arrest, and he had no residence of his own. This fact was well known.[100] The little clique ruling Upper Canada had determined to drive him from the province and, if necessary, to strain the law, as Kingsford rightly says, in doing so.[101]

The government of Upper Canada vented its wrath not only on Gourlay but also on his supporters. The sheriff of the Niagara District and several justices of the peace and officers of militia who had supported him were dismissed.[102] The printer of the *Niagara Spectator*, a paper which had printed Gourlay's communications, was fined and imprisoned.[103] Militia men also discovered that they could not obtain land if they had been members of the Convention.[104] Official disapproval of the Convention was not lifted until 1826.[105]

After his return to England Gourlay became disillusioned with Upper Canada. For a time he believed a London newspaper report that the elections held in Upper Canada in the fall of 1820 had resulted in "the almost unanimous choice of his supporters." [106] This raised his hopes that an inquiry would at last be made into the state of the province, a commission sent home, and his actions vindicated. He was to be disappointed. The newspaper report, if correctly summarized by Gourlay, was quite inaccurate. It is true that out of the thirteen who had voted for the anti-Convention bill only three were re-elected, and that the four members for the County of Lincoln in the previous legislature were replaced by men who had supported him.[107] But, out of forty-one new members of the Assembly, no more than eight had associated themselves openly with him. This was a far cry from an Assembly almost unanimously composed of his supporters.

To Gourlay's disgust, no motion was made for an inquiry. Instead, the legislature busied itself with discussing the effects of the Corn Laws, the proposed alterations in the timber duties, and the desirability of improving the St. Lawrence waterway by the construction of canals. In this, the members showed that they had a better grasp of the realities of their situation than had Gourlay.

At the outset, Gourlay seems to have realized that the prosperity of a frontier agricultural economy depends upon its steady expansion, although he may not have put it to himself in those terms, and that in the western peninsula of Upper Canada the process had been halted by the decision to exclude Americans. But he had gone on to analyse the discontent as if Gore, the Executive Council, and the Land Department were responsible for it all. At times he wrote as if he thought a grand *exposé* by a commission of inquiry would cure all and he has over-emphasized the political grievances and the political discontent. To correct his picture and to give it depth, it is necessary to see the other forces at work behind the troubles of the political surface.

The troubles of Upper Canada in 1817 were fundamentally economic, not political. For the colony, as for the mother country, the post-war world was a changed world, to which her trade, her agriculture, and her price structure had painfully to adjust themselves. The artificial prosperity which the war had occasioned vanished with the return of peace. Wheat fell from $3.00 a bushel in 1815 to 40¢ and 50¢ in 1818.[108]. As a result of the fall in the price of agricultural commodities, the bottom dropped out of the land market and speculators in wild land, who had expected the previous steady rise in land values to continue, found the market stagnant and a period of depression before them which was to last for a good ten years.[109] Upper Canada now began to realize that Richard Cartwright's forecast of her economic future, written in 1792, had been correct:

As long as the British Government shall think proper to hire people to come over to eat our flour, we shall go on very well, and continue to make a figure, but when once we come to export our produce, the disadvantages of our remote inland situation will operate in full force, and the very large portion of the price of our produce that must be absorbed by the expense of transporting it to a place of exportation ... will give effectual check to the improvement of the country beyond a certain extent; ... and when we go beyond the banks of Lake Ontario, it will cost as much to bring our rude produce to market, as it will be worth....[110]

Factors other than "the stoppage of British gold" [111] contributed to the depression. All classes of society had lived more abundantly during the war than formerly. Large quantities of goods had been imported from England and sold on credit.[112] With the peace, the province was drained of specie to pay for them and farmers, country storekeepers, and Montreal merchants alike found themselves under a heavy burden of debt. If the merchants had attempted to collect through the courts it would have meant ruin for "two-thirds of the farmers in the Province." [113] "Why did you contract debts?" Gourlay inquired of them sternly. "It did not follow, because money was made more plenty and cheap by the immense issues of government during the war, that you were to become more and more extravagant." [114] To add to this distress, a considerable amount of destruction of private property had occurred in the western peninsula which had to be made good. Purchases of cattle, grain, and other supplies from the United States soon drained the province of its specie. [115] If the claims for war losses had been paid promptly, the distress would have been alleviated, but the impoverished and debt-ridden province had to wait nine years for the first payment of five shillings in the pound on claims which amounted to £400,000. These claims were originally allowed at £229,000, but were subsequently reduced to £182,130, and were not paid in full until 1833. [116]

The Imperial government did nothing to soothe the discontent and distress of a province whose woes were chiefly the result of her membership in the Empire. It added to them, in fact, by diminishing the preferences which her two chief exports, grain and timber, had hitherto enjoyed in the British market. From 1804 to 1815, Canadian wheat could be imported into England on the payment of duties varying from $7\frac{1}{2}d$. to $9\frac{1}{2}d$. a quarter, when the British price was 56s. a quarter. It also enjoyed a 10s. preference over foreign wheat. In 1815 colonial wheat was excluded from the British market until the home price was 67s. a quarter, when it was admitted duty free. [117] The raising of the colonial preference to 13s. did not reconcile Canadian exporters to this change. [118]

The Canadian timber trade was also threatened with duties from which it had long been exempt. From 1768 to 1795 all kinds of wood and timber except yards, masts, and bowsprits could be imported into Great Britain from British North America duty free, [119] and down to 1792 importers of such timber had received bounties. [120] In 1795 colonial timber became subject to the duties which had been imposed on wood in 1789 [121] but not to the additional duties with which wood imports were burdened in 1795, 1801, 1809, and 1813. [122] Furthermore, the duties on colonial timber were greatly reduced in 1809, and, from 1806 to 1812, naval timber from British North America could be imported duty free. [123] Under these favourable conditions the Canadian timber trade had been built up.

The complaints of British consumers over the high price of timber and their preference for Baltic timber led to a revision of the timber duties in 1821. A duty of 10s. a load then replaced the very low duties at which most sorts of colonial timber had previously been admitted; the duty on foreign timber was reduced from 65s. to 35s. a load. [124] When Gourlay was in Canada these alterations in the timber duties had not yet taken place, but Canadians knew they were in the offing, and they were one of the grievances listed at his Kingston meeting of October, 1818. [125]

The spirited controversy under way in Great Britain as to the wisdom of the commercial policy on which the timber duties had been based resulted in the general feeling that since the colonies were bound to throw in their lot with the United States, there was no sense in Great Britain's penalizing herself for their benefit. [126] This attitude, coming as it did on top of the war, caused many

Canadians to think that the mother country would cast the colony off or at least so neglect her economic interests that union with the United States would be necessary. These were the rumours "too shocking to be repeated in the Royal ear . . ." to which the draft address of the Niagara District had referred.[127] The growing indifference on the part of the mother country seemed apparent in her alterations in her tariff and in her failure to pay the war losses or to reward the militia by authorizing grants of land to all militia men—something which had been promised and repeatedly asked for in vain.[128] Moreover, the legislature of Upper Canada had been informed in March, 1817, that the Imperial Parliament would no longer make up the deficit incurred by the civil expenses of the province out of the Military Chest but would supplement the provincial revenues only by a fixed Parliamentary grant of £10,825 annually.[129] In such soil no wonder discontent flourished.

Despite his failure to relate the discontent of Upper Canada to the economic changes produced by the war, Gourlay was not blind to Upper Canada's more enduring economic problems, and he suggested remedies which were subsequently adopted. These remedies were not original with Gourlay. They had all been suggested in the township reports. He deserves the credit for bringing the reports into being, for developing the ideas they contained, and for calling attention to the economic problems with which Canadian settlers were struggling. An English traveller who visited Upper Canada in 1819 wrote:

I was surprised to find much discontent prevailing among the poorer settlers in Upper Canada. I could not always understand the grounds of their complaint, but they seemed to consider Mr. Gourlay as having wel explained them . . . his pamphlets . . . certainly appear to have spoken the sentiments of the poorer settlers, whose cause he had abetted against the more powerful land-holders, land-surveyors, and government agents.

Upper and Lower Canada, comments this author, were said to be agreed on only one thing: "a thorough detestation of their republican neighbours. In Upper Canada, however, . . . I did not find that this hostile feeling was much shared by the poorer settlers." [130]

Gourlay's *Statistical Account of Upper Canada* was published in London in 1822, three years after his return to England. The first volume contains the township reports. Sixteen townships followed the lead which Gourlay gave in his first *Address* in asserting that what the province needed was men of capital. As to what retarded the improvement of the province, twenty-eight reports, some of them applying to more than one township, replied with emphasis the unimproved land of absentees; twenty-two, 45 per cent of the total number of replies, answered the Crown and Clergy Reserves.[131] In many reports both the absentees' land and the reserves were alluded to and a number of them demanded that the reserves be sold. This sentiment was particularly strong in the London District. We have to thank Gourlay for clear evidence as to the complaints of the ordinary settler. These unsettled, untaxed, and unprocurable wild lands, privately owned or reserved, were the barrier that stood between him and decent roads, good neighbours, local schools, and rising land values in his township. They were constantly before his eyes, forever in his way, and foremost among his grievances. Only five of the township reports mentioned the exclusion of Americans, and three of these were signed by large landowners.

To remedy the evils complained of in the township reports, Gourlay proposed the imposition of a general land tax, the sale of the Crown Reserves, the use of the proceeds from them to pay the war losses, and the sale of the waste lands of the Crown to create a fund to assist emigration. The abolition of the Clergy Reserves he expected to result from the grand inquiry by the Imperial Parliament into the condition of the province which he felt the Canadians would eventually demand. The sale of the Crown Reserves to pay the war losses was an ingenious scheme. It is probable that it was first suggested to Gourlay by Robert Nichol and Thomas Clark who were anxious on their own account to get these claims paid. The report of the township of Nichol had pointed out that the reserves were not only an economic hindrance but a political danger. In the late war the Americans had promised them as bounty lands to their troops and they might again be made an inducement to invaders or rebels. For these reasons the report proposed that all the ungranted Crown lands in the surveyed townships be sold and the proceeds be used to pay the war losses and to improve the navigation of the St. Lawrence. In his reply to critics of his *Second Address*, and also in his letter to Administrator Samuel Smith of February 17, 1818, Gourlay supported this proposal. The draft addresses prepared by the Niagara and Midland Districts had also advocated the same idea. Before John Galt interested himself in Canadian affairs, Gourlay and his supporters in Canada had made the idea of selling the Crown lands to pay the war losses a thoroughly familiar one.

There had long been a widespread demand in Upper Canada for the taxation of absentees' lands. The statistical inquiries and the township and district meetings conducted by Gourlay simply gave popular sentiment a chance to express itself, and perhaps convinced Lieutenant-Governor Maitland that there was a genuine grievance to be redressed. Like Henry George at a later date, Gourlay advocated a single tax on land. He was convinced that land was the source of all wealth. Taxes on land stimulated its improvement, whereas taxes on houses, improvements, stock, mills, shops, and factories retarded the progress of industry and agriculture. He wanted to sweep away all existing provincial taxes and customs dues and substitute for them a tax which would be applicable to the land of residents and non-residents alike, and collectable by sale of the lands if they were allowed to become tax delinquent. Instead of rating all wild land in the province at 4s. an acre, as was then the practice, he proposed to assess both the wild and the cultivated land of each township at the same rate, on the ground that value was given to wild land by the labour bestowed on cultivated land in its vicinity. He finished off this simple scheme for the finances of Upper Canada by divising a formula—a theoretical and impractical one to be sure—for determining the value of land in any township in the province for tax purposes according to its population and the population of the neighbouring townships, but without regard to the terrain, quality of the soil, or timber.[132]

Gourlay believed that the proceeds of this land tax would pay for the civil expenses of the province and the construction of a system of provincial, district, and township roads, and would provide security for a loan to improve the navigation of the St. Lawrence and import contract labourers to work on the canals. With their savings these labourers would subsequently be able to buy land and, year by year, would be replaced by new labourers. In order to pay their taxes, speculators in wild land would be forced to improve their holdings or to sell to those who would; thus capital would be obtained for internal improvements, and a stimulus to emigration would be provided.[133] In all this Gourlay went much further than his supporters in Upper Canada. All they wanted was to subject the land of non-residents to statute labour for roads or to a small tax per acre in lieu of labour. These puny measures were shortly adopted and simply resulted in transferring the lands from one set of speculators to another set better able to carry them.

Although Gourlay was concerned with all sorts of problems, ranging from the profits of pasturing sheep on Boston Common to the proper route for the proposed Welland Canal, his fundamental interest was in bettering the condition of the poor. It is impossible to do justice to all his enlightened ideas here except so far as they relate to Canada. He realized that the beneficial effects of the reforms he advocated would be slow to appear, and he therefore proposed that emigration on a grand scale, under government supervision, and with government assistance, should be arranged for to provide a "vent" for the surplus poor of the British Isles.[134]

Gourlay has given us only a sketch of his ideas on emigration. The projected third volume of his work would have dealt with this subject more fully. His proposal was that the waste lands of the Crown in all the colonies should be sold to provide an emigration fund out of which the poor could be not merely transported from the British Isles but assisted to settle in the new world. This great task was to be entrusted to a grand national land board assisted in each colony by a local land board, half of whose members should be elected by the Assembly and half of whom should be "men of business" sent out from England. Haphazard settlement in the wilds of Upper Canada, with each settler fighting his battle with the wilderness single handed, was not what Gourlay had in mind, but orderly, controlled, systematic and compact colonization of the country.[135]

Gourlay was of the opinion that after ten years of careful nursing Upper Canada should have "independence"—not from the Crown, but from the ministers at home, who should withdraw from all interference in her domestic affairs. What he wanted for the province was not republican independence, as Maitland asserted, but self-government within the Empire. Nevertheless, like Durham, he thought this sort of independence quite compatible with the mother country's retaining control of the land of the colony and the revenues derived from it.[136] In 1826 Gourlay wrote to the members of the Assembly suggesting that they ask their constituents "if Canada is to be governed by blockheads after the rest of continental America chooses its own Governors." One of his letters was read in the Assembly during a debate on a resolution which stated that many loyal persons had sought redress of grievances through Gourlay's Convention. J. B. Robinson's attempt to get an amendment accepted which stated that "this House are satisfied that the Political Principles and plans of Mr. Gourlay are hostile to the Government of this Province and that no good and loyal subject can hesitate to declare his entire disapprobation of them ..." was decisively defeated (12 to 21).[137] Maitland accepted the Assembly's view of the Convention, and, with mental reservations, lifted the ban on grants of land to those militia men who had attended it.[138]

It will be obvious that Gourlay's ideas are very similar to those subsequently advanced by Edward Gibbon Wakefield and adopted by Lord Durham. Indeed, according to Gourlay, Wakefield admitted that he had taken his ideas on colonization from the latter's book.[139] Had the Colonial Office taken Gourlay's ideas seriously at the time and embarked on a programme of Imperial colonization beneficial both to the mother country and to the colony, it is possible that Imperial management of the lands would have aroused no popular resentment in Canada. By 1837 it was too late. The mother country had made the mistake of chartering the Canada Company and of using its payments for purposes which did not meet with popular approval.[140] As a result, between 1820 and 1837, the demand for popular control of all provincial revenue and all provincial resources became too insistent to be any longer withstood.

Together with his proposals concerning the settlement of Upper Canada, Gourlay recommended that an act be passed whereby Americans could become naturalized British subjects in Upper Canada.[141] It must be admitted that British policy towards alien settlers had all along been confused. Simcoe had early seen the necessity of defining the status of settlers from the United States and their children. He regarded resident Americans born before 1783, who had taken the oath of allegiance, as entitled to all the privileges of British subjects, but he defined their children born after 1783 as not so entitled, and enquired of Dundas how such children could be naturalized. Dundas thought the proper way to deal with the question was by a colonial bill reserved for the royal assent. Dundas' successor, Grenville, emphatically declared that the naturalization of aliens was an Imperial concern, not to be touched by a subordinate legislature.[142] There the matter rested for almost a generation. Meanwhile, Americans continued to emigrate to Upper Canada under the encouragement of the Act of 1790. Those who took the oath of allegiance were regarded as British subjects and many of them received grants of land from the Crown.

The exclusion policy adopted after 1815 forced the administration to decide whether Americans born before 1783 who had lived in the United States since that date were still natural born subjects, or whether they had been released from their allegiance by the Treaty of 1783. If they had not been released from their allegiance, then, despite their recent invasion of Upper Canada, they were entitled to settle in the province. Similarly, their children born after 1783 were entitled to the privileges of natural born subjects by the Act 7 Anne, c. 5. If they *had* been released from their allegiance, then the position of those whose sympathies had been with the mother country during the Revolution and who had emigrated to Upper Canada after 1783 had to be determined. Bathurst had directed that only those aliens who had come in since the war were to be dispossessed of their land; but the titles of those who had come in before 1812, many of whom regarded themselves as "loyalists," would also be invalidated if it should be decided that they had become aliens by the Treaty of 1783.

Although the immigrants who fell into this category had taken the oath of allegiance and had put in seven years' residence, they had not thereby become naturalized subjects, as John Beverley Robinson pointed out.[143] The Act 13

Geo. II, c. 7, which prescribed these two conditions for naturalization, applied only to persons born out of the King's allegiance and consequently did not apply to Americans born before 1783. Robinson might have added that even if Americans could become naturalized under this act, their titles to land would not be secure because titles acquired by aliens antecedent to naturalization were invalid. The instructions sent to Dorchester and Simcoe prohibited them from assenting to bills to validate such titles,[144] and this restriction was still in force. For fear of alarming half of the landowners of the province, the government of Upper Canada deferred the publication of Bathurst's instructions of 1817 to dispossess those Americans who had come in since the war until these legal problems should be settled.

No action was taken by the Colonial Office to clear up the alien question until 1824 when it was decided (in the case of *Thomas* v. *Acklam*) that British subjects who had continued to live in the United States after 1783 lost their citizenship.[145] This decision made it imperative that an act should be passed naturalizing the numerous inhabitants of Upper Canada whose rights of citizenship and titles to land would be affected adversely. After a long and bitter controversy over wording the act in such a way as to naturalize those who were not British subjects without stating that their existing status was that of aliens,[146] the Naturalization Act of 1828 passed. The act recognized as British subjects those who had received grants of land in the province from the Crown, who had held public office, who had taken the oath of allegiance, or who had resided in Upper Canada since before 1820. All these classes of persons were required to take the oath of allegiance if they had not already done so. Other residents were to be recognized as British subjects as soon as they had completed the seven years' residency requirement if they took the oath within three years from the passing of the act. The act also stated that titles to land derived through aliens were to be confirmed.[147]

This act did not end the controversy over the naturalization of aliens. It applied only to persons already resident in Upper Canada. Americans born after 1783 who immigrated there could be naturalized under the Act 13 Geo. II, c. 7, but not if they had been born before that date. The Imperial government refused to repeal this act, with its unsuitable definition of foreigners as persons born out of the King's allegiance, because it did not wish to raise with the United States the question of a subject's right to change his allegiance. It preferred that special acts should be passed naturalizing such persons as could not benefit by the existing statutes.[148]

The decision in the case of *Thomas* v. *Acklam*, first applied in Upper Canada to Barnabas Bidwell, at last made it clear that Americans were aliens and therefore could not legally acquire land. Since 1818 there had been no public agitation over the exclusion policy, largely because it had not been strictly enforced.[149] In 1826 the Assembly once more deplored this policy which depressed the land market and deprived the province of much needed population. A petition to the Crown was passed asking that Americans be permitted to settle in Upper Canada and to purchase land subject to the restrictions of the provincial statutes which excluded them from political privileges for seven years.[150] The votes on the various resolutions preliminary to the wording of this address show a decided majority opposed to the exclusion policy. John Beverley Robinson then moved an amendment that the Assembly would prefer to see the province filled up with immigrants from the British Isles than from the United States. This failed, but the voting was much closer, 14-16, with the affirmative votes coming entirely from the area east of York, except for one vote. The county of Lennox and Addington, as might be expected, was opposed to Robinson. The Assembly then voted, 19-11, that immigration from the United States would be a desirable addition to the assisted immigration being sent out from Great Britain.[151]

The members of the Executive Council were totally out of sympathy with this address. They admitted that it might not have been unreasonable when Upper Canada was first settled to give encouragement to settlers from the United States, but not after a generation of Americans had been brought up in republicanism. They pointed out, too, that the waste lands of the Crown were not as extensive as had been supposed and that they would be needed for immigrants from the mother country and by the children of the present inhabitants.[152] The Imperial government stuck to its policy of denying aliens the right to hold land in Upper Canada, and Bathurst replied to the Assembly that "His Majesty is convinced the Assembly would regret the success of any measure which would interfere with plans in contemplation for encouraging emigration from the United Kingdom."[153] No doubt this reply was pleasing to the newest settlements and to some of the loyalist districts whose influence in the province was on the wane, but it was not relished by other districts whose settlers were conscious of closer affinity to American backwoodsmen than to Irish peasants, Paisley weavers, or English paupers.

As the Rebellion of 1837 was to reveal, the policy of the British government towards American immigrants did not effectively isolate Upper Canada from American democratic ideas—it was much too late in the day for that—not did it completely bar Americans from the province. They continued to come in, either as squatters or as purchasers of land, in such numbers as to alarm Sir John Colborne. Goderich could only advise him to issue a proclamation stating that the law did not permit aliens to hold land in Upper Canada unless they obtained letters of denization or naturalization, and to seize for the Crown the property of one or two aliens as an example to the rest. The notoriety of this act might, he thought, check American immigration for the future and might even cause some of those already settled to withdraw without its being necessary to take other measures against them.[154]

Colborne did not attempt to put this advice into practice. There were several thousand Americans in the province who had come in since 1828 and who had no valid title to the land they occupied. Under existing laws, they had no prospect of acquiring one. The fact troubled them very little. Most of them were supporters of Mackenzie and, although they had no vote, it was inexpedient to add to their discontent.[155] The entire western peninsula of Upper Canada, where many of their fellow countrymen had settled, was in sympathy with them and totally opposed to the government's policy of discouraging settlers from the United States.

In the session of 1836-7 John Prince and William Hamilton Merritt, the representatives for Essex and Haldimand counties respectively, introduced a

bill to enable aliens to hold land in Upper Canada. These men professed
anxiety to amend the law so as to induce the European immigrants who daily
passed through the western peninsula on their way to Michigan and Illinois to
remain in Upper Canada. Their bill was also designed to regularize the land
titles of aliens who had acquired land in the past, provided they were living in
the province and settled on their land. In its original form it also conferred
citizenship upon aliens after they should have taken the oath of allegiance and
put in seven years' residence.[156] The opponents of the measure believed that
its real purpose was to attract, not European immigrants, but American settlers
and American capital to the lands of Upper Canada and they feared for the
future of British institutions in Canada and the fate of impoverished settlers
from the United Kingdom who were seeking land. "Who would wish to see
American land speculators getting into their possession large tracts of land of
this country?" enquired one opponent of the measure. Another reminded the
Assembly of "what happened in Texas," and a third warned that the bill meant
"opening the way for the advance guard of the enemy." [157] After a provision
was adopted requiring alien landholders to be actual residents and limiting the
amount of land they could hold at one time to 1,000 acres, the bill passed the
Assembly, but not the Council. With the exception of the towns of London,
Niagara, and Toronto, the votes of the entire peninsula of Upper Canada, from
the County of York west, were cast in favour of this bill. It was also supported
by some of the older settlements along the St. Lawrence, such as Stormont,
Glengarry, and Kingston, which were interested in drawing American capital
into the lumber industry.[158] The opposition came from the towns and from the
counties on the Ottawa, the Rideau, and Lake Simcoe, where immigrants from
Great Britain and Ireland had by this time been settled. It was not only the
Reformers who favoured the admission of American settlers but all who had
land to sell. At the next session of the legislature, Prince made another attempt
to get his bill through. Once again it passed the Assembly and again was not
returned by the Council.[159] As in 1812, so in 1837, the outbreak of the Rebellion
discredited the pro-American party and put an end to their demands. It was not
until 1849 that an act was passed permitting aliens to hold and transmit land
in the province of Canada.[160]

CHAPTER NINE

SETTLEMENT DUTIES
AND U.E.L. "RIGHTS"

SIR PEREGRINE MAITLAND, who became Lieutenant-Governor of Upper Canada in 1818, regarded himself as the sole channel through which the wants of the province should be passed on to the home government and he resented as a personal slight any suggestion for the improvement of the province which did not originate with him. Gourlay, Galt, and Dalhousie all suffered from his jealous temper.[1] Nevertheless, he was not a blind or a stupid man and, although he supported the persecution of Robert Gourlay, he learned something from his attempts at reform. The draft petitions from the Niagara and Midland Districts and the numerous township petitions which reached him, all emphasizing the inefficiency of the Land Department and all complaining that the wild lands of absentees were a burden on actual settlers, convinced him that there were genuine grievances that must be remedied. The alien question, too, was not ignored. The new Lieutenant-Governor put into practice some of the suggestions which James Buchanan had submitted to the Colonial Office in 1816, and which the Office had probably commended to Maitland's attention.

After Gore's departure, Buchanan again urged that British immigrants who had made a trial of the United States and been disillusioned should be made welcome in Upper Canada and be granted land, and that Americans ready to take the oath of allegiance should be permitted to purchase it. Buchanan thought there was no danger that the bulk of American settlers in Upper Canada would prove disloyal in case of another war. "National feeling or local attachment yield invariably with them to self interest," he observed. He pointed out that the preferences in the British market which Upper Canada enjoyed would make American immigrants as anxious as original loyalists for the maintenance of the British connection. In his opinion the exclusion policy was actually more dangerous to the province than an open door policy: the wealthy who could purchase land and take property were kept out while the bankrupt in property and character, the poor and worthless, could easily get in.[2]

Buchanan also advocated the imposition of a wild land tax, the gradual sale of the Crown and Clergy Reserves, the adoption of a system of settlement duties, the appointment of district agents to locate settlers, assistance to poor immigrants in the form of cash loans, and postponement of any demand for land fees until the settlement duties should have been performed. Finally he urged the government to promise all immigrants, alien or otherwise, that their children, like those of the U.E. loyalists, should be entitled to land, although not free of patent fees, on their coming of age or marrying.[3] Maitland was quite in sympathy with some of these suggestions.

In 1815, Bathurst had reduced the grant to common applicants to 100 acres.[4] In order to make it unneccessary for them to dance attendance at York, Maitland re-established the district land boards and gave them power to administer the oath of allegiance and to assign locations to immigrants from Great Britain or to immigrants coming from the United States who could produce certificates of British birth. The number of immigrants who sought the good offices of the British Consul in New York for this purpose hardly justified these special arrangements. In ten years' time they barely exceeded 500 heads of families, although Buchanan claims to have forwarded 7,000 persons to Upper Canada prior to 1821.[5] Subsequently, Maitland permitted the boards to assign pauper immigrants 50-acre grants free of fees and to locate militia and U.E. claims for residents of their districts to save them the trouble of a trip to York. As it turned out, most of the locations made by the land boards were to these classes. Very few fees-paying immigrants benefited from their services.[6] Magistrates who asked permisison to administer the oath of allegiance to well-recommended American settlers ready to purchase land were allowed to do so.[7] All othei applicants for land had to apply to the lieutenant-governor-in-council. Maitland found that Gourlay's strictures on the Land Department were not without foundation. He wrote to Bathurst, "The Land Council seems to have been sleeping over an Office choked with applications. I . . . intend keeping them to it, till the Office shall be cleared." He seems to have succeeded in making the Land Department more efficient. Gourlay himself testifies that "a goodly reform was brought about," although he took the credit himself.[8] The accumulated errors of the past were not to be disposed of so readily.

Lieutenant-Governor Maitland disliked the land-granting system of Upper Canada and, while he had to administer it, he was determined to counteract its evils as much as possible. In his opinion, too much land had been granted too readily and too little had been cultivated. He decided to correct the weakness in the land system by granting land to all classes of applicants strictly on condition of occupation and settlement. He also decided to subject all old grants which remained unimproved to a wild land tax. These twin policies involved him in endless controversies with the legislature and proved to be no solution for the land problems of the province.

From the beginning of Upper Canada's history land had been granted on condition of occupation and improvement but the requirement had neither been defined nor enforced. As Maitland informed Dalhousie, the terms of settlement originally imposed were simply "that the grantee should have a house in some part of the Colony."[9] This statement was not quite accurate as a summary of the regulations but unfortunately it was only too true an account of the interpretation which had been put upon them.

The Colonial Office had continually tried to prevent the evil of land speculation, which had beset the thirteen colonies, from arising in Canada. Murray's instructions,[10] adapted from instructions previously worked out for Georgia,[11] directed that grants be made only to persons who could show that they were able to improve them. The instructions also specified the settlement conditions in great detail and required them to be cited in the patents. Similar instructions were sent to Carleton in 1767.[12] After 1771 land was granted on seigneurial tenure which bound the grantee to reside on and cultivate his lot,[13] and this provision applied also to grants made prior to 1791 in Upper Canada. Dorchester's land regulations of 1789 required grantees to begin the improvement of their land within twelve months, on pain of forfeiting their locations.[14] Additional grants, whether military lands, bounty lands, or grants to the children of loyalists,[15] were all made subject to the general regulations and conditional upon the improvement of previous grants.

The trouble was not that these early regulations were inadequate but that the Land Committee of Council, headed by Hugh Finlay, was not anxious to enforce them. Disregarding the fact that grants to soldiers, as to other settlers, were subject to settlement conditions under the regulations of 1763 and 1783, the Council, whose members were probably speculating in land certificates, ruled that the lots assigned to disbanded soldiers had been granted as a reward for past services and therefore that they could not recommend that these lots be resumed by the Crown if they were not improved. When the Land Board of Mecklenburg expressed the opinion that some rule should be adopted relative to unimproved lots granted persons "not having the same pretensions," the Committee concurred but did not act,[16] and the buying and selling of certificates went on unchecked.

After 1791, land was granted in Upper Canada in free and common socage to those who could show they were in a position to improve it. Unfortunately, Simcoe's instructions did not specify the settlement conditions in detail and there were therefore no precise conditions to be inserted in the patents.[17] Nevertheless, it was generally understood that land was granted on condition of cultivation. The location tickets which preceded the patents contained this condition, and it was enforced by the early land boards.[18] It was also well understood that land would not be granted any applicant, whatever the nature of his claims might be, until he became a resident of the province;[19] but exemptions were sometimes made in favour of those who received an order for land from the Colonial Secretary.[20]

It was soon found that, despite the regulations which stipulated that grantees must cultivate their land, many persons allowed their lots to remain unimproved or sold them to speculators in wild land. If this evil were to be checked, more precisely stated and more carefully enforced settlement duties would have to be imposed. Before 1818 this problem was attacked in a piecemeal fashion. Simcoe made a beginning when he ruled that lots on Yonge Street would be granted only to actual settlers and on condition that within one year the grantee have a house built on his lot and be residing on it in person or by a "sufficient tenant."[21] In addition, Yonge Street settlers were made liable for statute labour on the road. Since every lot was to have its settler, the reserves having all been removed to the rear concessions,[22] there would be sufficient labour to keep this important road in repair. After June, 1798, the settlement duties were made more onerous, the settler being required not only to build a house 16 feet by 20 but also to clear half the roadway in front of his lot and to clear and fence 5 acres of land, all within twelve months.[23] Locations on Yonge Street were not confirmed until the Executive Council was satisfied that the promised improvements had actually been made.[24]

The foregoing conditions were known as "Yonge Street conditions" but they also applied to Dundas Street and were afterwards made applicable to other parts of the province.[25] Similar duties were imposed on some cross-roads.[26] The townships of Hope, Haldimand, Cramahe, and Percy, which had been forfeited by those to whom they had been granted, were put under Yonge Street conditions on being thrown open for location.[27] The ungranted part of the township of Markham, part of the township of Gwillimsbury, and the township of York were also put under settlement conditions (as were Scarboro, Pickering, Winchester, Whitechurch, Hope, Murray, Ancaster, Beverly, and North Oxford). After August, 1801, no lakeshore lot from the Etobicoke to the Trent could be obtained except on Yonge Street terms and by November, 1802, the greater part of the land then surveyed had been made subject to settlement duties.[28] When Dundas Street was extended from Burlington Bay to York, through the tract of land surrendered by the Missisaugas in 1806, not only the land along the road but the entire tract was put under Yonge Street conditions,[29] and no one was permitted to have more than 200 acres in that locality.[30]

No specific settlement duties were made generally applicable in Upper Canada before 1818 and even the partial system which had been gradually built up, although enforced for a time, was later sabotaged with the connivance of two lieutenant-governors. It took time to perform settlement duties and if settlers could not receive their patents until these duties were proved by the filing of a proper certificate, as Hunter at first required,[31] the land officers could not receive their fees until the patents were passed. This did not suit any of them from Lieutenant-Governor Hunter down, and it was not long before they began to seek a short-cut to the greatly desired fees. Smith put the matter up to Elmsley who "fluctuated" in coming to a decision. "On the one hand it is very desirable that the Secretary should be employed (engrossing patents)," wrote Elmsley. "On the other hand we depart from an established principle if we allow Deeds to issue for lands subject to Settling Duties, before those Duties are performed, to say nothing of the possibility that in the event those Duties are never performed, there may arise to the Secretary a claim for compensation of a very delicate nature." [32] Perhaps it was Elmsley's caution that restrained the land officers for a time, but eighteen months later, when he had left Upper Canada for the lower province and Allcock had replaced him as Chief Justice, the desired change was made.

On December 30, 1802, the Council passed a new regulation which required survey and patent fees to be paid in full within three days after the grant had been made and the patent to be taken out in three weeks' time, and this necessarily marks the abandonment of the settlement duty requirement.[33] It was replaced by an unenforceable proviso inserted in the patents, requiring grantees to reside on their lots for three years.[34] In 1804, at Allcock's suggestion, Hunter relieved those who had previously received land subject to settlement duties of these obligations, provided they paid the new fees of 1804 within the next twelve months and appointed an agent to take out their patents.[35] Locations on Yonge and Dundas Streets were excluded from Hunter's new regulations. Lieutenant-Governor Gore followed in Hunter's footsteps and continued to rescind settlement duties as a favour to individual applicants, except for special locations such as

the two streets and the Missisauga Tract.[36] However, Gore cannot be charged
with rushing land through to patent for the sake of the fees. He rescinded
Hunter's order requiring all fees in advance and arranged with the Colonial
Office to receive an annual allowance in lieu of fees, which he called "the most
unpleasant part of my Emolument." [37]

The results of this change of policy were as Elmsley had feared. Gourlay
relates that after Simcoe's departure the Council "broke faith" with the settlers
on Dundas Street and granted land to favoured persons from whom settlement
duties were not required.[38] E. A. Talbot reports that about thirty years after
the grants had been made they still remained "nearly an unbroken wilderness." [39]
Even settlers on Yonge Street had occasion to complain of grantees whose land
on the road was not cleared.[40]

The part of Upper Canada in which settlement duties were enforced was the
area controlled by Colonel Thomas Talbot. Talbot, at one time private secretary
and confidential aide to Simcoe, had received a grant of 5,000 acres and had
undertaken to settle it with foreign Protestants and to encourage the raising of
hemp. He was promised 200 acres for every settler he placed on 50 acres of his
own land and parts of the townships of Dunwich and Aldborough were reserved
on these terms for him.

In 1816, Dr. Strachan published in London *A Letter to the Right Honourable
Earl of Selkirk on his Settlement at the Red River near Hudson's Bay.* Selkirk
had received 1,200 acres in the township of Dover and, like Talbot, he had been
promised that for every settler he placed on 50 acres of land in that township
he should receive an additional 200 acres. In his letter Strachan commented
that 50-acre grants were too small and that the result would be that in a few
years the settler would sell his improved property for a trifle, or would be
compelled to purchase adjoining land from Selkirk at his price. "This is a way
of accumulating property not the most honourable to the peerage," observed
Strachan, "and attended with the most pernicious consequences to the colony,
and its administration. Such settlers consider themselves dupes: they become
discontented with their situation and with the government which permits such
transactions. It would be better for the king to grant at once any quantity he
chooses to a person he wished to serve than to grant it in this manner." Strachan's
words were directed at Selkirk, who was trying to get the time allowed him for
settling his reserved township extended, but they were equally applicable to
Talbot, some of whose settlers did indeed become resentful.

With 5,000 acres to settle, 20,000 acres seemed to be the maximum Talbot
could become entitled to. But he placed his settlers not on his own land but
on the reserved land, and successfully claimed 200 acres for settling each of
them. When the Executive Council of Upper Canada, which had at first acceded
to Talbot's demands for land, protested that he was not living up to the terms
of his agreement, claiming that he had forgotten all about hemp, was accepting
American settlers without their having been first approved at York, and that
the whole arrangement, as Talbot interpreted it, was capable of indefinite
extension and was by-passing the proper land granting authorities of the province, the Colonial Secretary limited the area in which Talbot could place
settlers and claim his 200-acre rewards to the vacant land in Dunwich and Ald-

borough. By January, 1820, Talbot had completed the location of these town-ships [41] and had "parlayed" his original grant of 5,000 acres into 65,570 acres.[42]

Talbot's influence was not limited to Dunwich and Aldborough. In 1809, at his own suggestion, Lieutenant-Governor Gore had entrusted him with continuing a road from the township of Burford to Dunwich and with locating settlers along it on Yonge Street conditions. The settlement duties were strictly enforced by Talbot who was naturally eager to make his own isolated townships more accessible by a good road. Gore, and subsequently Maitland, approved Talbot's suggestions for settling the area south of the Thames and gradually entrusted him with the location of settlers and the enforcement of settlement duties on other roads and in twenty-seven additional townships in the London and Western Districts.[43] In this "palatinate," to use Powell's term, the Colonel's word in land matters was law.[44]

Talbot's system was based on the conviction that settlers should have no title nor claim to their locations until their settlement duties were performed. He required each grantee to build a house, to reside on his lot, to clear half the road, and to clear and fence 10 acres next to the road. Every settler, said Talbot, needed that quantity of land for the support of his family. The work required a year or two and would attach the settler to the spot as his home.[45] Until the duties were done the location was not final, and Talbot states that he sometimes declared a lot forfeited and relocated it five or six times before he found a "faithful" settler.[46] Without Talbot's certificate the settlers could not apply for patents, nor could the government know from whom to demand fees or exactly how much land in the Talbot Settlement was vacant and grantable.

Relations between Talbot and the hard-pressed government of Upper Canada were not always harmonious. Settlers located by Talbot on the roads received 200 acres, although, in 1815, the grant to ordinary settlers was reduced to 100 acres. He also located Americans, who, after the war, were not supposed to be received as settlers unless they had been approved at York.[47] Talbot's settlement duties took time to perform and his poor settlers found it hard to accumulate the cash for fees in a community which still conducted most of its transactions by barter.[48] Meanwhile, the government had spent money on sur-veying townships from which there was little revenue and in which the unpaid patent fees accumulated. Such was Talbot's influence with the home govern-ment that in 1818 he was able to obtain a directive that fees should not be demanded until settlement duties were done and that he should not be restricted in accepting settlers except by Imperial statutes.[49] This meant that, under the Act 30 Geo. III, c. 27, he could continue to locate Americans. Although there were many settlers in the Talbot Settlement from Ireland and Scotland, most of them, reported Colborne in 1828, were from the United States. "They began in poverty and from my enquiries none of them cleared their land without assistance from Colonel Talbot or from their neighbours or without obtaining daily wages to enable them to occupy their land." [50]

Talbot was proud of his system and boasted that his settlement flourished as did no other area of the province, thanks to the enforcement of the settlement duties. One wonders how one man, unassisted by clerks or deputies, could possibly have supervised half a million acres of land. The testimony which Talbot himself gave against three of his settlers, when he was accused of dispossessing them for their political views, shows that his supervision was far from prompt, continuous, or close.[51] In all likelihood, his personal supervision was confined largely to the Talbot roads, and from the roads visitors and writers of travel accounts admired his work. Talbot put the population at 40,000 in 1831 and at 50,000 in 1837. The assessment returns of 1835 for the twenty-nine townships indicate that these figures were an over-estimate by about 20 per cent. In 1836, the amount of cultivated land totalled 101,184 acres, or about $2\frac{1}{2}$ acres per head of population. For the province as a whole, it was $3^1/_{10}$ acres.[52] At the same time, the five counties into which the Genesee Country was then divided had, on the average $4^7/_{10}$ acres of cultivated land per head of population.[53]

In return for locating settlers who had found their own way to him, for insisting on the performance of settlement duties sooner or later, and for super-intending the laying out of the Talbot roads, Talbot obtained a pension of £400 a year, which was paid from 1826 to 1853 and therefore totalled over £10,000. He is said to have spent £20,000 in the Talbot Settlement,[54] but it is not clear what proportion of this sum was invested in improving his own property and what proportion was spent in assisting distressed settlers or on mills or other improvements that did not yield him an adequate return. In addition to his pension, Talbot obtained 65,570 acres in Dunwich and Aldborough. For years this property remained unimproved and inconvenienced settlers. In the eighteen-forties, when wild land was being taxed $1\frac{1}{2}d.$ an acre by district councils which misunderstood their powers,[55] Talbot's land was gradually leased at an annual rental of £2 10s. for a 50-acre lot with an option to purchase at 30s. an acre on ten year's credit. In the eighteen-fifties, the land was being sold at $6.00 an acre.[56]

The gradual abandonment of the settlement duty requirement, except in the three special locations mentioned and in the Talbot Settlement, meant that the only restriction on grants of land was the provision inserted in patents since 1803 requiring three year's residence on every grant. Bathurst realized that this was a provision which could easily be evaded, and in 1816 he directed that in future every patent should contain a clause forbidding alienation of the land for three years on pain of forfeiture.[57] The new regulation was applied to grants already made although not patented, and was very unpopular.

When Maitland arrived in Upper Canada, complaints about the unimproved lands of absentees were coming in from Gourlay's township meetings. On October 14, 1818, public notice was given that grantees of land would be required to erect a habitable house and to clear and fence 5 acres in every 100.[58] Essentially, these were the old Yonge Street terms which were now extended and applied to all new grants. Previous to Maitland's new regulation, three years' enforced possession of a lot after patent was hopefully presumed to result in residence and improvement; in future, the performance of specific duties before patent was to be exacted of every grantee. Another regulation attempted to undo the errors of the past by providing that all locations subject to settlement duties made before August 1, 1819, would be rescinded unless a certificate showing the duties to have been performed was presented within twelve months' time and the patent sued out within one month thereafter.[59]

There was now no longer any need of the three-year restriction on sales after patent and it was abolished. The new regulations apparently gave Maitland much satisfaction. He announced to the legislature in 1821 that during the last two years "forty townships have been surveyed and in a great measure bestowed on conditions of actual settlement." [60]

The real problem, however, was not to devise regulations but to enforce them, and Maitland was but little more successful in this task than his predecessors. No patent could issue until a certificate from the district land board had been filed certifying that the settlement duties had been performed within the allotted time. When the land boards were abolished in December, 1825, settlers obtained their certificates from a magistrate of the district upon taking oath that the duties had been performed and bringing two disinterested persons to attest the fact.[61] Many settlement duty certificates were falsely sworn to because it was impossible for the members of the land boards or the magistrates to travel "thirty or forty miles into an uninhabited part of the country to ascertain if the parties had sworn truly or not." [62]

The new regulations were very unpopular, both with speculators and with genuine settlers. The latter complained that the duties could not be performed by poor settlers without capital in the time allowed. The result was that the regulations were forever being tampered with in an effort to devise some which would neither bear too hard upon poor settlers nor diminish the duties to such an extent that they would be no hindrance to speculators. These numerous changes were not likely to produce respect for the regulation; indeed, they were only productive of further complaints. Apart from the "habitable house"—an indefinite term—the amount of work required was finally reduced to clearing half the road and cutting down the timber for one chain in depth from the road. The time allowed was extended from eighteen months to thirty.[63] Colonel Talbot regarded these settlement duties as both inadequate and harmful. They could be performed in a day and left that part of the lot where the timber had been slashed but not cleared "an impenetrable jungle." In place of the regulations he recommended a five-year residence requirement.[64]

The manner in which the fees were to be collected also caused Maitland much trouble. Gore had rescinded Hunter's regulation requiring all fees within three days of the order-in-council for land, with the result that most settlers took their time about paying their fees, and one source of revenue on which the provincial government had relied rapidly dwindled away. This became a serious matter in 1817 when the mother country ceased to contribute to the civil expenses of Upper Canada from the Military Chest. After Gore's departure, the Executive Council tried to expedite the collection of long overdue fees by subjecting settlers who had received grants under the regulations of 1798 and who had not paid even the first half of their patent fees and the survey money to the increased fees of 1804.[65] They also ruled that fees on future grants must be paid within three months' time. Influenced by Talbot and Buchanan, Bathurst overruled the Council and directed that no demand be made for fees until the patent issued. The Council objected strenuously, stressed the colony's need of revenue, and pointed out that because of the lack of funds it had become necessary to pay the surveyors not in money but in a percentage of the land surveyed.[66]

Bathurst then suggested a compromise, and, after three tries, the Council devised a regulation on which its members could agree for more than a few days at a time. Except for the Talbot Settlement, fees were to be paid in three instalments: one-third on receipt of location, one-third when the certificate of settlement duty was filed, and one third when the patent issued.[67] The Council finally agreed to this proposal.

It is clear from several orders-in-council that some attempt was made to enforce the settlement duty regulations under Maitland's regime. For a time, those applying to be located on lots on which the settlement duties had not been done were required to pay for an inspection by a Deputy Provincial Surveyor, but eventually "so much imposition by applicants for forfeited lots" occurred that the Council ruled that in future no locations on forfeited lots would be granted.[68]

The attempt to enforce settlement duty regulations in Upper Canada once more brought to the fore the troublesome question of the U.E. loyalists' "rights." Grants to loyalists had hitherto been exempt from settlement duties unless they were located in the Talbot Settlement or on Yonge and Dundas Streets. They had always found a ready market and speculators had acquired extensive holdings by means of them. When Maitland revived the settlement duties in 1818, he applied them to all future grants without exception. He quite correctly held that the U.E. grants had always been made on condition of cultivation and that he was "merely enforcing old rules, not making new ones." [69] The effect of the new regulations can be traced clearly in the Surveyor General's record of locations. The big blocks of privileged locations stopped in October, 1818. Not half a dozen U.E. grants were located in the first half of 1819.[70]

Those entitled to land as U.E. claimants objected to the new restrictions, which tended to reduce the value of their "rights," and speculators who had already bought many of them did not wish to be put to the expense of clearing and fencing 5 acres and of building a house on every 200-acre lot. In the Assembly, on November 16, 1818, Alexander Martin and John Crysler, both representatives of loyalist constituencies, moved for a committee of the whole to consider the alterations and restrictions under which U.E. grants had been put, but the subject was not pursued. Some months later it was brought up again by the representatives of another loyalist constituency and again was dropped.[71] No further opposition to the new regulation, as applied to privileged grants, was voiced in the Assembly until 1828.

In the meantime, grants to militia men of 100 acres had been authorized on condition of residence and cultivation. At first, these grants were restricted as to location but in 1820 this limitation was removed on condition that settlement duties were performed and sworn to. Militia grants on which the duties were not performed were subject to forfeiture, to regrant, and, after 1829, to sale.[72] The new regulations tended to throw U.E. and militia rights on the market and to lower their value, since individuals who might have preferred to hold their land for a rise could not convert their right into patented land without expense.[73] On the other hand, the increase in the land fees which took place between 1819 and 1820, and the introduction, in 1826, of the auction system, under which Crown land was put up for sale at upset prices ranging from 4s. to 10s. an acre, added to the value of these rights in the hands of speculators and made it worthwhile to hold them unlocated or to pay for having settlement duties done on them. The tables given on p. 139 indicate that this is what happened.

Towards the close of Maitland's administration complaints about the settlement duties on privileged grants revived.[74] Why this controversy should have raised its head at this time, after slumbering for ten years, is not quite clear. It may be that in the interval speculators had purchased many privileged claims at prices depreciated by the regulations and were now organizing to fight for the removal of restrictions on these claims. Perhaps they realized there was no use in asking Maitland to lift the settlement duties but hoped that the new Lieutenant-Governor would be more complaisant.

When Sir John Colborne arrived, the newly elected Assembly of 1829 asked him, by a vote of 28-7, to abolish the settlement duties on the ground that they served no useful purpose.[75] There was some merit in this complaint. Many of the roads which settlers were required to open crossed high hills, swamps, or lakes and were impracticable for freight and passenger travel. "Many thousand pounds were consequently entirely and uselessly thrown away."[76] The members of Colborne's council informed him that there were two schools of thought within the province about the expediency of settlement duties, but they carefully refrained from committing themselves. They did, however, suggest a compromise, whereby a more perfect performance of lesser duties might be imposed.[77] The result was that in November, 1830, the settlement duties were revised once more. On this occasion the grantee was given his choice of thoroughly clearing half the roadway, sowing it with grass seed, and putting in two years' residence on his lot, or of making the road, and, in lieu of residence requirements, of clearing the timber from the front of his lot for one chain in depth from the road. Those who had received locations under earlier regulations were given the option of abiding by them or of complying with the new ones.[78] A party in the Assembly led by Peter Perry remained dissatisfied with these concessions but they were never again able to command their former support.[79]

It is difficult to understand how Sir John Colborne could have been persuaded to sanction this order-in-council which reduced the settlement duties to a level advantageous to speculators. Nothing was accomplished, except the destruction of a little timber, unless a genuine resident settler was established on the lot. The chief effect of the settlement duties, wrote Charles Buller, "was to occasion a certain outlay upon the land ... without ... diminishing in any degree the evils occasioned by the unsettled grants."[80]

Colborne seems to have realized after a time that the order-in-council of 1830 had simply favoured speculators. At his suggestion, a new set of regulations was adopted in May, 1832, which dispensed with specific settlement duties and simply stated that no patent would issue for land held on location tickets until it was proved that a resident settler had been established on some part of the grant.[81] This new regulation was more unpopular amongst speculators than the old. It was a simple matter to have a clearing made on a lot; it was a much more expensive business to establish a resident settler there.

The speculators, however, were anxious to get locations in the new townships being opened up at this time in order that they might profit by the labour of the immigrants. Agents were sent up and down the province to buy up U.E. rights, which were located in the names of the resident settlers whom the speculators placed on each lot. But these settlers were all under bond to retain for themselves only a small portion of the lot and to assign the rest to the person who had located them as soon as the patent issued. In this way speculative holdings of 10,000, 20,000 and even 30,000 acres were built up. Members of the Assembly engaged in this business; a son of former Chief Justice John Elmsley was one of the most notorious offenders and a member of the Executive Council.[82]

Colborne did his best to prevent this sabotaging of the government's policy. He allowed the *original* holders of U.E. and militia rights to locate in the townships being settled by immigrants and permitted individuals who had purchased rights to locate there provided they agreed to take up residence at once; but he refused speculators permission to locate their rights in these townships. Applications were forwarded to the Surveyor General by persons holding U.E. and militia rights to locate more than 100,000 acres in four townships recently opened in the Western District, and that official or his subordinate saw to it that some of those applying got the location they asked for. Colborne then directed that the issuing of location tickets cease and he suspended confirmation of those locations which had been permitted in contravention of his orders until some method could be found of checking the traffic in land rights.[83] In November, 1833, a new and more stringent order-in-council was issued. In future, no loyalist or militia rights were to be located except on condition that the *original* grantee was prepared to settle on the lot himself, and no patents were to issue for such grants until two years' residence had been completed.[84] At last a regulation had been devised which, it was hoped, would strike at the root of the evil—the transferability of U.E. and militia claims to land.

One concession was made to those entitled to U.E. and militia rights. If the original grantee did not wish to settle in person, he was to be allowed to locate his grant and to be entitled to the proceeds when the lot was sold by the Commissioner of Crown Lands at public sale like other government land. If this impracticable regulation had continued it would have meant an endless amount of detailed bookkeeping and the controversy over U.E. rights would have dragged on indefinitely. As it was, speculators tried to take advantage of its terms, arguing that they had powers of attorney from the original nominees to locate and dispose of their land rights.[85] Some purchased the rights without bothering about a power of attorney. Colborne was inclined to permit the speculators, at least the first class, to cash in on their rights in this way,[86] but Peter Robinson, the Commissioner of Crown Lands, objected to the additional work which this regulation would thrust upon his office.[87] The Executive Council, guided by the latter's brother, Chief Justice John Beverley Robinson, also opposed giving speculators the benefit of a provision intended to prevent the U.E. loyalists from "being driven by want of accommodation to sacrifice their rights to speculators," and he suggested that the regulation be suspended until a reference to the Colonial Secretary could be made.[88] Fortunately, Lord Aberdeen vetoed the proposed arrangement *in toto* but the principle of cash compensation to the holders of land rights was later written into law.

The new regulations of 1832 had greatly reduced the value of unlocated U.E.

and militia rights whether in the hands of speculators or of the original holders. The regulations of November, 1833, made unlocated rights acquired by speculators valueless,[89] and both sets of regulations aroused the Assembly to vehement protest It drew up a long-winded address to the Crown asking that U.E. and militia grants continue to be made on the same terms as previous to the year 1818—in other words, without restrictions. The address referred to the royal promise of land to children of U.E. loyalists, declared that this land had always been considered "in the light of a *debt* due" from the Crown, and maintained that it had originally been granted on no other condition than that the head of the family should cultivate his own grant. Militia men and children of loyalists sell their rights, explained the memorial, either because they are already settled on farms or because they are unwilling to take up land in refuse and back townships, the only areas in which their rights could be located. The address also complained that the restrictions had the effect of greatly reducing the price which could be obtained for their rights.[90] Opposition to the address came from all parts of the province, and efforts were made to weaken it by amendments. It finally passed, however, by a vote of 16–13.[91]

The arguments used by the Assembly in its address were far from sound, and the appeal to history was anything but accurate. During the course of the debate, the members in favour spoke of the land promised by the Crown as a debt due. Originally, there was no royal promise of land to the children of U.E. loyalists. The children's rights originated in Dorchester's order-in-council, which made no *promise* of land for the unlimited future and specifically subjected these grants to the general regulations.[92] Moreover, the form of the location ticket in use promised a grant of land so allotted "on such terms and conditions as it shall please His Majesty to ordain" when the grantee should have improved the same.[93]

The settlement duties had undoubtedly reduced the value of U.E. and militia rights. The Assembly maintained that higher prices would be obtained if the restrictions were removed and that, as a result, only those planning to cultivate land would purchase the rights. This was a specious argument. The history of the military bounty land warrants issued by the government of the United States, by the separate states of the Union, and by Upper Canada before 1818 shows that land rights, even when they are not restricted as to location or by settlement duties, tend to accumulate in the hand of speculators.[94] The request of the Assembly for the cancellation of all restrictions on these rights, while it might have benefited those U.E. loyalists and militia men who had not yet sold their rights, would have benefited far more the small group of speculators into whose hands many of the unlocated rights had already fallen. One member of the Assembly's committee, Allan MacNab, charged that the new regulations had been "cooked up" by one or two members of the Council and predicted that in a few months' time the order would be repealed. The *Niagara Gleaner* hinted that the order had been suggested by "certain harpies" near the seat of government watching for opportunities to enrich themselves.[95]

Sir John Colborne regarded the traffic in land rights as a great evil and did his best to check it, but he was unable to overcome the secret sabotaging of his policies in the Surveyor General's Department. Neither he nor his Council could withstand the pressure put upon them by the legislature, some of whose members championed the cause of the loyalists for its own sake while others did so to further the interest of speculators. The stringent regulations of November 8, 1833, were suspended until the Colonial Secretary should be heard from. Meanwhile, land rights were permitted to be located, subject to such future regulations as might be made, while those who had already located their grants were given a choice of abiding by the existing regulations or by those to come.[96] When in April, 1834, Colborne forwarded to the Colonial Secretary the Assembly's address on the subject of U.E. and militia rights, he had already begun to waiver. He hinted that he was fighting a losing battle, and that it would probably be expedient in the future to issue patents for land rights to the original nominees without requiring the performance of settlement duties, and to permit those speculators who had already acquired land rights at a depreciated price because of the restrictions to locate subject to the regulations of 1832. With this in mind he had already directed that a maximum of 10,000 acres to be set aside in each of several townships for the satisfaction of these claims.[97] For these modifications in the order-in-council of November, 1833, J. S. Cartwright, in an electoral speech in Lennox and Addington, claimed the credit.[98] The Surveyor General's Department disregarded the limitations and, a year later, Colborne realized that, with its connivance, speculators had obtained the most valuable lands in the new townships where the immigrants were settling.[99] Thereafter, by means of required weekly reports on all locations made with free grants, Colborne tried to keep the Surveyor General's Department under close supervision.

Barred from the new townships speculators turned back to the older townships. Vacant lots in the older townships had at one time been reserved for sale. In 1824 they had been re-opened to location. In 1833 they were again offered for sale at auction, and closed by Colborne's order to U.E. and militia locations.[100] In this instance also, the Surveyor General's Office disregarded Colborne's instructions to such an extent that the Lieutenant-Governor, in anger, informed Hurd that his whole Department should be re-organized and deprived him of the power to locate lots in older townships not open to general location, lots on lakes and rivers in any township, and all improved and forfeited lots.[101] Colborne was doing his best to prevent speculators from acquiring lands made valuable by other people's exertions. Had he remained in Upper Canada he would have learned that his efforts had been in vain.

Before a commission investigating the Crown lands and the Surveyor General's Department in 1839, Spragge, a junior clerk, testified that his superior, Radenhurst, had acted as a private land agent while still holding public office and that he had located the land rights of his clients on land in the older townships supposed to be disposed of by sale. Deputy Surveyor General William Chewett also testified that these irregularities had occurred and were still occurring but he did not name the guilty party.[102] Radenhurst also allowed privileged grants subject to settlement duties to pass to patent without proof that the duties had been done when the patent was claimed under the Heir and Devisee Act. He thus took it upon himself to act upon a doubtful interpretation of the act, and in contravention of the assignment provisions of the later Land Act of 1837, and to make "an alteration of great importance and questionable policy." [103] Sir Richard Bonnycastle, Commandant of the Royal Engineers, believed that if the quantities of land possessed by officers of the land-granting department were known, "wonder at the difficulties and disgusts of expectant settlers would vanish. . . ." [104]

When Hurd retired, Radenhurst applied for the post of Surveyor General. His petition was supported by some members of the Executive and Legislative Councils and by forty-five members of the Assembly, including Lount and Perry.[105] Spragge later testified that "the official favors" Radenhurst had done had got him "a numerous band of partisans." [106] Radenhurst was not appointed Surveyor General and was subsequently dismissed from the Land Department for other reasons. He may have been guilty of doing favours for the dozen or so members of the Assembly who had a few U.E. rights to locate, but the person who entered the largest number of U.E. rights in this period, chiefly for others, was Spragge. Between 1835 and 1837 he entered 52,600 acres of land.[107]

The Colonial Secretary, Lord Aberdeen, was reluctant to return a flat negative to the request of the Assembly for the removal of all restrictions on U.E. rights. He instructed Colborne to make his opinions known to the Assembly in the hope that it could be brought to see that no relaxations of the latest regulations could be made. Aberdeen pointed out that the U.E. loyalists had never been promised land free of all obligations, nor had they been exempted from future regulations. The rule against transferring certificates of location had never been lifted and therefore the sale of land rights was essentially illegal, although it had been permitted to continue for many years. The time had now come to put a stop to a traffic which depressed the value of Crown land, an important source of revenue since the institution of the sales system.[108] Aberdeen also refused to approve the cash compensation plan, arguing that the land grants which the loyalists had been promised "when they were newly banished from their native farms . . . were considered an almost indispensable allowance to those who were ejected from their homes than as a gratuitous gift which, if the grantees did not receive in kind, they might receive in value." He suggested also that a time limit should be set, beyond which no further claims for U.E. and militia rights would be received.[109]

A few months after this dispatch was written, Aberdeen was replaced at the Colonial Office by Glenelg. The latter disapproved of the auction sale and credit system under which the Crown lands were then being disposed of, planned a thorough revision of the regulations, and refused to give any directions about the U.E. rights until he should be ready to announce the details of a new land system. Meanwhile, no more claims were to be recognized, nor patents issued, for these rights until a policy with respect to them had been finally decided upon.[110]

The new instructions were a long time in coming. Meanwhile, the Lieutenant-Governor and Council would grant no more orders-in-council for land based on U.E. or militia claims. Previously granted rights were not allowed to be located, and located claims were not permitted to pass patent.[111] The land speculators in the Assembly grew impatient. During the session of 1835 four separate addresses were presented to the Lieutenant-Governor on the subject of the U.E. rights, one of which bluntly remarked that, ever since the first settlement of the province, unlocated land rights had been bought and sold and that previous members of the Executive Council had made large purchases of such rights and had them confirmed by their colleagues. Yet it was now pretended that the transfer of unlocated U.E. rights had never been authorized.

The Assembly, in which the Reformers had a slight majority, did not content itself with protests. It tried to take the solution of the question into its own hands by passing a bill to entitle purchasers of U.E. rights to receive patents in their own names. This was the first time in the history of the province that either branch of the legislature had made use of the power, granted it by the Constitutional Act, of legislating with respect to the ungranted lands of the Crown, and it is worth noting that when it was proposed to proceed by address instead of by bill the Assembly rejected this procedure by a vote of 19–29. The U.E. rights bill provided that in future no settlement duties should be required on any locations made with U.E. or militia claims. It passed the Assembly, 31–12, with as many Reformers voting for it as against it. Among the former were Peter Perry, who had introduced the bill, Gilbert McMicking, Alex MacDonnell, J. P. Roblin, and David Thorburn, all of whom were speculating in U.E. rights on a small scale. The Legislative Council took no action on this bill. The Assembly then tried to persuade the Council to concur in an address concerning the U.E. rights but the Council replied it had learned that the Executive Council advised the abolition of the settlement duty requirement and that it preferred to wait for the answer of the Colonial Office to this recommendation.[112]

On October 17, 1835, Colborne and the Executive Council, evidently alarmed at the boldness of the Assembly in attempting to bring under legislative control a matter hitherto reserved for the Executive, abolished the settlement duties on U.E. and militia claims already located.[113] In so doing, Colborne acted contrary to his instructions which had directed him to wait until the new land system should be devised. At the same time, the Lieutenant-Governor permitted the location of U.E. and militia claims to be resumed in certain specified townships, even though the terms on which patents would be granted were still unknown.

The remission of settlement duties led to a great rush to patent existing locations. During the seventeen years between November 14, 1818, when settlement duties went into effect, and October 17, 1835, when they were abolished on these privileged located claims, 2,078,489 acres of Crown land had been patented; in the three years between July 1, 1835, and October 4, 1838, 1,162,300 acres were patented.[114] The general attitude is well illustrated by a letter of Robert Stanton to John Macaulay in which the latter is advised to get out his patents as soon as possible, "for in these uncertain times when the movements of the very government have so little of stability in them there is no knowing whether the order of today may receive any attention tomorrow.... The view of the Home Government on the subject of U.E. rights changes with each Colonial Secretary. The question is certainly not settled." [115]

The result of the complete reversal of the regulations did not pass unnoticed in Upper Canada. As Donald M'Leod, a major-general in the Patriot Army, commented later:

Thousands of loyalists, finding their gifts of land impaired in value by oppressive and injurious imposts sold them to speculators for a trifle. After some years when the U.E. Lands had, under these circumstances, accumulated for an almost nominal value in the hands of speculators, the same irresponsible government, suddenly relieved all these lands from these settlement duties;

and thus, the property which those of these "endeared relations" had been coerced by official regulations to part with at a trifling value, were by the repeal of these regulations, at once raised to a high value, without encumbrance, in the hands of purchasers.[116]

M'Leod chose to forget that the regulations were repealed by the "Irresponsible executive" on the insistent demand of the Assembly.

Another result of the complete reversal of the regulations was that unlocated rights became more valuable. While it is true that the terms on which new locations could be patented had not been settled, it was not to be expected that the administration, which had yielded once and had abolished the duties on existing locations, would re-impose them. Consequently, there was a grand scramble to obtain rights and to locate land before all the worthwhile lots were gone. Between October, 1835, and the end of December, 1836, nearly 300,000 acres were located, and, in 1837, 122,500 acres were taken up with land rights.[117] Because of the press of business and the lack of surveyed land, the Land Department could not keep up with the demand. In September, 1838, it had on file unsatisfied orders for U.E. and militia claims totalling half a million acres. In April, 1835, Colborne had called for a report on U.E. and militia locations to date; when prepared, it showed that since the organization of the province 2,565,035 acres had been located by or patented to these classes of claimants and that they held unlocated orders for 455,650 acres more—a total of 3,020,685 acres.[118] A later report prepared for Lord Durham showed that by September 1838, 3,136,240 acres had been patented to these claimants, that 2,755,176 acres had been located by them but not yet patented, and that their unsatisfied orders for land amounted 526,282 acres, or a total of 3,937,113 acres in all. This meant that, in three years time, the U.E. and militia claims to land amounted to 917,013 acres. These statistics reveal the extent of the interest in U.E. and militia claims and make it plain why the settlement duty regulations which Colborne struggled so hard to enforce were so bitterly opposed.

The following table (Table I) of land granted to U.E. loyalists, militia men, and military claimants is tentative and has been compiled from the warrant and fiat books, special reports to Colborne, and the record of monthly returns of locations which he initiated in April, 1835, and which was continued until the close of 1838.[119]

There are gaps in the records from which the figures in the table have been taken which so far it has been impossible to fill. It is necessary to remember that the number of U.E. claimants would be increasing year by year as the children of loyalists attained their majority, but even so, the figures reveal the effect of Hunter's strictness in recognizing the claims of children of loyalists and the shortage of desirable locations open to them. The exceptionally large number of fiats issued in 1816, 1817, and 1818 testify to the back-log of land business which had accumulated during the war, as well as to the creation of the military settlements. The sharp decline in the number of fiats issued for privileged claims after 1818 marks the initiation of settlement duties. The growing quantity of unsatisfied orders-in-council for land shown in Table II testify both to the shortage of acceptable land and to the unwillingness, after 1818, to locate subject to settlement duties. Some of these orders were never located at all but were turned in for scrip.

TABLE I

GRANTS TO UNITED EMPIRE LOYALISTS, MILITIA MEN, AND MILITARY CLAIMANTS, 1798–1835

Year	Warrants and fiats issued	Orders-in-Council to serve as warrants
1798	400 acres	
1799	30800	
1800	26000	
1801	37200	
1802	16600	
1803	29000	
1804	13000	
1805	18400	
1806	52700	
1807	72600	
1808	79400	
1809	68400	
1810	63400	
1811	83800	
1812	40800	
1813	9800	
1814	200	
1815	37200	
1816	119400	
1817	88000	
1818	68400	16200 acres
1819	3000	72800
1820	2000	48800
1821	3800	38200
1822	—	27200
1823-35	21000	26600 (1823 only)

TABLE II

ORDERS-IN-COUNCIL ISSUED TO PRIVILEGED CLAIMANTS

Year	Described	Located	Unlocated	Total acres
1823–1833	203,715	211,480	207,030	622,225
1791–1835	2,565,035		455,650	3,020,685
1791–1838	3,136,240	275,176	526,282	3,937,698

Colborne's capitulation to the Assembly did not end the long controversy over U.E. rights. The order-in-council of October 17, 1835, affected only located rights and left the question of settlement duties on rights located subsequently, and on grants still to be made to the children of loyalists and to militia men, to be determined by the home government. Colborne, following the Council's advice, recommended that no further attempt should be made to exact settlement duties from the children of loyalist and militia men, and that certain townships should be set aside for the satisfaction of their claims.[121] Glenelg, still planning a revision of the land system, put this suggestion aside for the time being and once more directed the Lieutenant-Governor, now Francis Bond Head, to bring Aberdeen's dispatch to the attention of the Assembly. That body proved impervious to Aberdeen's well-reasoned arguments and continued to insist that U.E. and militia claims be freed of restrictions.

By this time, dissatisfaction with other aspects of the Crown land policy was increasing, and there was a growing conviction that the land regulations of the province ought to be determined by its own legislature. In 1835 the Assembly had unsuccessfully attempted to take these matters into its own hands. In 1837, with the blessing of the Colonial Office, it succeeded. An act was passed which was primarily designed to satisfy the holders of U.E. and militia rights.[122] The act provided that all persons entitled to free grants could locate their claims on any land open to location and not especially reserved. These claims were made assignable either before or after location and patents were permitted to issue in the names of the assignees. No settlement duties were to be required. Those who did not wish to take up land so open to location were to be entitled, either for themselves or for their assignees, to a credit of 4s. for every acre of their claims in the purchase of all classes of public land, whether ordinary Crown land, school land, or Crown and Clergy Reserves.[123]

This act was a triumph for the land speculators. By it they secured all their previous demands and more beside. Militia and U.E. rights were relieved of settlement conditions, they were made assignable, and although they were not made locatable at will, they were given a fixed valuation of 4s. an acre, a price which probably exceeded the cash value of the class of wild land that had been open to U.E. and militia locations. When the Land Act of 1837 was first introduced, it contained a clause which provided that only those U.E. and militia rights still in the hands of the original holders would be acceptable in the purchase of other lands. This restriction, which would have mitigated the worst effects of the measure while satisfying all who really had a claim on the government's bounty, disappeared before the bill reached its third reading.[124] When land rights were applied on Indian, school, or clergy land, the payments which the Indian, school, or clergy funds should have received had to be made up out of the Crown land revenues. This proved to be a serious drain. The return given below (which almost certainly should be dated January 1, 1843, since the practice of receiving land rights in payment for all classes of land ceased on that date) shows that between 1837 and 1843 over 200,000 acres of land rights were turned in, of which fully half were used in the purchase of special classes of land—principally Clergy Reserves.[125]

TABLE III

Acreage of rights applied	How applied	Value (£)		
		£	s.	d.
101,261 acres	Crown lands, 35,549 acres at average price of 10s.	20,252	4	10
	Interest on Crown lands	716	14	5
5,253	Town lots	1,050	15	
6,197	Park lots	1,239	7	11
4,167	Peterborough Mills	833	6	8
5,946	Military Reserve, Toronto	1,189	4	3
800	Indian Lands, 400 acres	160		
74,293	Clergy Land, 23,222 acres	15,770	19	4
9,665	Clergy interest	1,220	13	7
212,166		42,433	6	
Unapplied rights	Balance due in scrip	1,267	5	8

Classes of Claims: U.E., 84,958; Militia, 120,462; Army & Navy, 800; Dockyard, 5,946. Total 212,166 acres.

The Land Act of 1837, which had a life of only two years, was extended by an act of 1839,[126] and both acts were repealed in 1841. The new land act [127] passed by the legislature of the united province of Canada provided that the U.E. and militia claims in Upper Canada were to be converted into land scrip worth 4s. an acre receivable only in the purchase of Crown lands, the proceeds of which were not set aside for special purposes. Instalment payments on sales of public land already contracted for, as well as those yet to come, might also be made in scrip. This was a privilege which speculators had tried and failed to secure when the Act of 1839 was passed.[128] After January 1, 1843, no new claim for privileged grants was to be received unless on that date the claimant was a minor. Subsequent acts, however, extended the time for receiving scrip and it was not until January 1, 1862, that scrip ceased to be received in payment for land. Meanwhile, as will be related in a later chapter, the issuing of scrip gave rise to much criticism and turned in the end into a nasty scandal.

The effect of the land acts of 1837 and 1841 was that U.E. and militia claims were absorbed without the expenditure of as much land as would otherwise have been required for their satisfaction but the land revenue was, for many years, almost annihilated. Also, whereas the U.E. or militia claims had been receivable only for land open to general location, when used as land rights or land scrip, they were accepted in payment for land not open to general location, that is, scattered lots in the older townships, town lots in such communities as Toronto, Peterborough, Woodstock, and Cornwall, and the Crown Reserves in townships surveyed since 1824. As Spragge testified, the result was that "some of the most valuable lands in Canada West ... have been frittered away ... without the provincial revenue being any the better for it ... while all the lands of indifferent quality and little value remain...." [129]

CHAPTER TEN

TAXING THE SPECULATORS

LIEUTENANT-GOVERNOR Maitland's attempt to enforce and extend the settlement
duty regulations of the province to prevent unimproved lands from passing to
patent was paralleled by his efforts to force into cultivation land already in
private hands by subjecting it to taxation whether it was improved or not. The
impression sometimes prevails that a wild land tax was not imposed in Upper
Canada until 1819, but this notion is incorrect. An attempt to impose such a
tax was made very early in the history of the province. Peter Russell, when
first appointed Receiver General of Upper Canada, had seen the advantage of
such a tax and had suggested it in a letter to Pitt.[1] He reminded Pitt that in
some of the old colonies speculators had escaped the payment of quit rents by
not taking out their patents and had avoided the patenting of their land by the
repeated use of friendly caveats. To prevent these abuses in Upper Canada,
Russell proposed that grantees be required to take out their patents within six
months or lose their entries and that patented land be subjected to an annual
tax of about 2s. 6d. per 100 acres in addition to Crown quit rents.

Many difficulties unforeseen by Russell were to prevent lands from being
promptly located, carried to patent, and taxed. His proposal to tax all patented
land alike was presented in modified form by D. W. Smith to the first session
of the legislature of Upper Canada. Smith, who was a member of a committee
appointed to consider ways and means of raising a revenue, proposed that every
landowner should pay an annual tax of $\frac{1}{4}d.$ an acre on all his land except the
first 200 acres. Smith's proposal would have exempted the usual family allotment from taxation and thus have done rough justice to rich and poor. It would
also have imposed the same tax on wild land as on improved land, and, light
as it was, it would have tended to force the latter into cultivation. Smith
obtained Simcoe's support but not that of his colleagues in the Assembly.[2] As
landowners with more than the minimum holding, they knew that the tax would
fall chiefly on the class to which they belonged. Moreover, they believed that
taxes on real property would deter immigrants from coming into the province,
prevent a rapid increase in population and thus a rise in land values. They also
objected to the imposition of county rates for local purposes and preferred to
provide for all expenditures by the imposition of a duty of 6d. a gallon on wines
and spirits. They thus hoped to shift the burden of taxation to the merchants
engaged in the fur trade. As Simcoe complained to Dundas, "Three-fourths of
the Spirits passing thro' this Country is the property of the Merchants at Montreal, and what could justify a project which at the start must provoke Misunderstanding and perhaps vindictive measures between the two Provinces?"[3]

The impolitic tax failed to pass the Legislative Council, and no revenue measure was enacted during the first session of the first Parliament of Upper Canada.

In the next session, that of 1793, an act was passed which divided the population into eight classes according to the amount of real and personal property possessed and which imposed a graduated tax on each class, the proceeds of which were to be allocated for county purposes by the Justices of the Peace in the Quarter Sessions. The act also provided that future county rates should be imposed by the Justices and be similarly graduated.[4] This act affected only resident landowners. It is not clear whether it taxed wild land or not because no principles of assessment were laid down and each assessor was left to his own judgment. The result was that some counties—and some persons—were assessed much more lightly than others.[5] This defect in the law was remedied by the Act of 1803 which specified the kinds of property which should be rateable and gave each a fixed valuation, cultivated land being assessed at £1 per acre and wild land at 1s.[6]

The Act of 1803 was the outcome of six years of controversy about which we know very little. The Assembly was anxious to bring under taxation both the large quantity of wild land which residents of the lower province had acquired in Upper Canada and the lands of absentees in the United States.[7] In 1798 a bill for "the more specific laying of assessments," which subjected the wild land of residents and non-residents alike to taxation, had passed both the Council and the Assembly. Russell reserved this bill and sent it home with the comment that, in addition to a minor defect in the form, it was "contrary" to the fifteenth article of the instructions, and on this account it was disallowed.[8] On this point Russell was quite incorrect, and the Colonial Office does not seem to have noticed his error. The instruction did not forbid the enactment of measures which taxed the property of non-residents but simply required that they be reserved.[9] Indeed, there was already on the statute books an act taxing non-residents owning 200 acres or more 20s. a year for roads.[10] Yet somehow the impression prevailed that a bill for taxing the wild lands of non-residents would not receive the royal assent, and no further attempt was made to pass one until it was done under Maitland's direction in 1819. In 1800 a bill which imposed specific assessments, but which did not tax non-residents, was passed but reserved, and since notification of the royal assent was not received within two years' time, it did not become law.[11] In 1802 a third attempt was made to get a specific assessment act but the Assembly's bill, which was probably modelled on a recent New York act[12] and, like it, may have taxed non-residents, was not acceptable to the Council.[13] A fourth assessment bill, introduced in the session of 1803, was bitterly opposed at all stages. It finally passed the Assembly but was amended by the Council. Consequently, a new bill acceptable to the upper House had to be introduced. It passed the Assembly only by the casting vote of the Speaker. It was assented to by Lieutenant-Governor Hunter and not reserved, since it had become essentially the same as the Bill of 1800.[14]

Opposition to the Bill of 1803 came from the Niagara frontier and from the newer districts which one would naturally expect to have favoured a wild land tax.[15] This circumstance puzzled Lord Selkirk.[16] The reason for the opposition was that the original bill proposed to repeal that part of the Assessment Act of

1793 which required the Justices of the Peace to authorize a special assessment for the payment of wages to the members of the Assembly.[17] When the representatives of the newer districts succeeded in adding to the bill a clause directing the district treasurers to pay the members out of any funds arising from the Assessment Act, they were ready to vote for it and carried the bill over the opposition of the older districts, which had previously favoured it.[18] But this was the very clause the Council would not accept and it was dropped. "Nothing would tend more completely to ... a narrow and constricted Policy than the Idea of the members receiving Wages from their several constituents; an Idea which I trust will not be entertained by the Assembly for one moment," wrote the Colonial Secretary, evidently shocked by such a democratic arrangement. The representatives of the newer districts, however, were determined to have their wages but they were opposed to direct taxation of their poor constituents and wished to avoid burdening them with additional assessments.[19] In 1801 they had succeeded in attaching to a bill ratifying the agreement with Lower Canada for the division of the customs revenues an appropriating clause providing for the payment of members' wages out of this revenue. The Council expunged the clause and the Assembly, arguing that its rights had been infringed, threw out the agreement.[20] In 1803, after passing the Assessment Act without the provision for members' wages, the legislature passed a separate act providing that members should be paid by the district treasurers out of any funds in their hands, but special assessments had still to be imposed to cover these expenses.[21]

Representatives of the newer districts found other objectionable provisions in the Assessment Act of 1803. It allowed non-resident landowners to escape taxation and exempted the wild lands held by infants and married women. Owing to grants of family lands and special grants to the wives and children of influential people, much land was held by these classes of persons. Moreover, this provision of the law provided a convenient loophole for those who wished to escape taxation. Each householder was required to submit to the assessor of his parish or township a list of all the rateable property he possessed no matter in what township or district it lay. Failure to deliver a true list subjected the offender to a fine. Determination of the facts in such cases was left to the Magistrates in Quarter Sessions, although a minority in the Assembly had tried to require the use of a jury.[22]

Perhaps the most serious defect in the act was that it benefited the older districts at the expense of the newer ones. Although all unoccupied land belonging to residents of the province was theoretically brought under taxation (provided it was reported and did not belong to married women or infants), the taxes on such lands were assessed by, and paid to, the treasurer of the district in which the owner resided, not to the treasurer of the district in which the wild land lay. Thus the neediest and least populous townships were deprived of income which ought to have been theirs. The inhabitants of the London District stated the case for these districts in a petition to the Assembly. It asked that the lands of non-residents be taxed, that "land shall be rated and assessed in the District where it may be situated, and that the money raised thereon shall be paid to and for the use of such Districts." [23]

Despite the fact that the Act of 1803 was neither a fair nor even an effective piece of legislation, it was three times re-enacted at four-year intervals with only minor changes. The assessment value of wild land was raised to 2s. in 1807 and to 4s. in 1811. The clause exempting the wild land of infants and married women was removed, and "all rateable property" was more carefully defined as land held in fee simple, under promise of the same, under land Board certificates, orders-in-council, certificates of any governor, and leased Crown and Clergy Reserves.[24] Nothing was done to satisfy the complaints of the newer districts until 1815. Then an amendment to the Assessment Act was passed which was designed to transfer to the newer districts all taxes paid on land within their boundaries.[25] It proved to be unworkable and led to disputes between districts and, in the Act of 1819, was replaced by a clause which provided that taxes were to be paid only in the district where the land lay.[26]

Although various loopholes in the Assessment Act had been closed by 1817, it remained defective in three respects. It still applied only to residents of the province, it did not ensure that all land actually in private possession would be reported for taxation, and it contained no adequate penalties. The result was that much wild land was untaxed, either because the owners were non-residents or because they had not declared their ownership. Removal of the latter defect required more skilfully drawn legislation and a more active Land Department; removal of the clauses restricting the application of the act to residents of the province depended upon the home government.

From 1803 to 1817 the people of Upper Canada accepted the supposed refusal of the Imperial authorities to sanction an act taxing the land of non-residents. By 1817, even before Robert Gourlay had stirred them up, the people had become determined to subject the lands of absentees to taxation and to make them contribute to the upkeep of roads in lieu of the statute labour which their owners did not perform. The road act of 1793, which contained no penalties enforceable against non-residents, had been repealed in 1810. Lieutenant-Governor Maitland saw clearly that tranquility would not be restored to the province until many of the genuine grievances to which Gourlay had forcibly drawn attention had been remedied. The Assembly had twice attempted to bring the wild lands of both resident speculators and absentees under taxation, only to be blocked by the Legislative Council,[27] several of whose members had speculated in land on an extensive scale. Before the 1819 session of the legislature, Maitland induced Bathurst to approve in principle a wild land tax which should tax residents and non-residents alike. Thus he was able to open Parliament with the announcement that such a measure would receive the royal assent.[28] Any excuse the Council might have had for refusing to concur in a measure so clearly in the public interest and for which there was such a widespread demand was by this means removed.

The Assessment Act of 1819, passed unanimously by the Assembly and concurred in by a reluctant Council,[29] contained a long overdue change. It no longer accepted the word of the taxpayer as to the amount of real property he owned. Every rateable inhabitant had to give the assessor a list of all his personal property in the province, but he was asked to report only the real property he owned in the township of which he was a resident. The Surveyor General was required to furnish each district treasurer with a list of all the land granted or leased in his district and with subsequent annual lists of additional grants or leases. All land included in these lists was subject to taxation by this act, whether occupied or not, and the district treasurer was authorized to receive the taxes on unoccupied land from any persons offering to pay them. Wild land was assessed at 4s. an acre, cultivated land at 20s.[30] It is not quite correct to refer to this act as imposing a wild land tax of 1d. in the pound.[31] It was a general assessment act, subjecting all wild land, as well as improved land, to county rates which might not exceed 1d. in the pound. The rates were to be paid only in the district where the land lay, and the proceeds were to be paid over to the district treasurers for general county purposes, not simply for roads.

At the same time, another act was passed taxing all unoccupied granted land ⅛d. an acre for roads.[32] Previous to this act the unoccupied land of non-residents contributed nothing to the upkeep of the roads; the burden fell entirely on the resident settlers. Moreover, since all the property a taxpayer reported was assessed in the township of which he was a resident, all his statute labour was performed there and any commutation money he paid in lieu of statute labour was expended there. The effect of the new act was that a property owner was assessed for statute labour only on the real estate he owned in the district in which he resided. Property he possessed elsewhere, if unoccupied, paid ⅛d. an acre for roads. This tax could, with greater accuracy, be called a wild land tax, and it was the proceeds of this tax which the district treasurers were directed to pay over to the overseers of highways to be expended on roads. In addition, by reducing the amount of statute labour required of the lower assessment classes and increasing that of the wealthier classes, this act redressed another of the grievances of which Gourlay's township meetings had complained.

The great weakness of the Assessment and Road Acts of 1819 was that they did not contain adequate penalties. If the taxes were not paid within fourteen days after demands, the collectors were empowered to seize and sell the goods and chattels found on the property, but this was a totally inadequate remedy against non-residents and speculators on whose unimproved wild land there was nothing to seize. To be sure, taxes which were neither paid nor collected by distress were increased on the district treasurer's books by various percentages according to the length of time they were in arrears, but a book-keeping penalty of this kind did not disturb land speculators much nor lead them to pay their taxes. Perhaps it was the very ineffectiveness of the Assessment and Road Acts of 1819 which secured their passage. In 1824, when Maitland proposed to put teeth into these laws, there was a fight to the finish between the Governor and the Assembly on the one hand, representing the ordinary settler, and the Legislative Council on the other, defending the interests of the speculator in wild land.

Many owners of wild land neglected to pay their taxes because they hoped that the Assessment Act, which would expire in 1828 in any event, would be repealed, and, meanwhile, the only penalties which they incurred were book-keeping ones. The only remedy for this state of affairs was to make the act permanent and the land itself liable to sale for unpaid taxes, something which had been frequently proposed in the Assembly and in Gourlay's township reports.[33] With Maitland's approval, two bills were introduced into the Assembly in 1823. The first made the Road Act of 1819 permanent.[34] The second made the Assessment Act of 1819 permanent and subjected to sale by auction all land on which the taxes were eight years in arrears and on which no distress could be found.[35] Whoever would pay the taxes and costs and take the smallest number of acres of the land seized in compensation was to be declared the purchaser of them. No land was to be sold until it had been duly advertised and the original owner was to have twelve months in which to redeem his property on paying a premium of 20 per cent.[36] This bill encountered strenuous opposition in the Assembly, especially from such large landowners as Francis Leigh Walsh, William Warren Baldwin, Robert Nichol, and Alexander McDonnell,[37] but it finally passed, 19–12.[38]

In the Legislative Council, opposition to the bill was led by Thomas Clark and William Dickson, two of the largest landowners in the province. They received the secret support of the Chief Justice, William Dummer Powell, who thought that instead of selling land for unpaid taxes the province should wait for "the existence of proper distress on the lands"—in other words, he felt that the ineffectual assessment acts of the last thirty years should be continued. The Chief Justice argued that the districts did not require more revenue than they already had and he seems to have convinced himself that, because the bill imposed penalties upon married women and minors who could not themselves comply with the law, it was unconstitutional.[39] It is no wonder that his quibbling and persistent opposition to the Lieutenant-Governor's pet measure, despite the warnings of his friend, former Governor Gore, increased Maitland's growing dislike of him.[40]

Finding that there was a majority in the Council opposed to the bill and that it would undoubtedly be defeated, Maitland made it clear to those members who held office under the Crown that they would be wise to support it.[41] Powell and James Baby yielded; John Henry Dunn, the Receiver General, absented himself from the Council on the day of voting, as did John McGill, the Inspector General. Clark and Dickson, who had confidently expected the bill to be defeated, were furious when it passed. Dickson subsequently asserted that it had been passed in a most extraordinary and unconstitutional manner "by the exercise of undue influence from some secret quarter." The report of a special committee appointed by the Assembly in 1828 to consider the revision of the Assessment Act forced Maitland to defend himself to the Colonial Secretary.[42] James Kepler, to whom Maitland's dispatch was turned over, commented that although the bill itself was defensible, it was impossible to defend Maitland's clumsy indiscretion in openly employing the whole influence of government to carry it and that the best thing to do was to let his dispatch go unanswered.[43]

The first sales of land in arrears for taxes would, under the Act of 1824, have taken place in the spring of 1829. Before that time arrived, however, strenuous efforts were made to repeal the act and to amend the two assessment measures of 1819 which it implemented. Four speculators in wild land, the Rev. Robert Addison, William Warren Baldwin, the Hon. Thomas Clark, and the Hon. William Dickson, the chief witnesses examined by a committee of the Assembly, all made out a strong case for the relief of owners of wild land in arrears for taxes.[44] Some of their arguments were economically sound, but they aroused suspicion by making use of others which were worthless and insincere. For example, that favourite of the vested interests in all times and places, the widows and orphans argument, was trotted forth. Tender concern was expressed for them and for the U.E. loyalists and militia men who had received grants of land from their Sovereign as a reward for their services, without regard for the fact that most of it had long since passed out of their hands into those of speculators. The "worthy merchant" who had sunk the profits made in "laudable commerce" in land or who had been compelled to take payment in that commodity came in for his share of sympathy, despite the fact that it was well known that many a 200-acre grant had changed hands for a gallon of whiskey. In short, as a counter-petition from the County of Norfolk put it, "the great landholders ... wish to induce your Honourable House to repeal the present wild land assessment act under the plea of making it easier for the poor while they would exempt themselves from taxation and leave the poor to bear the burden of the Country. . . ." [45] The land speculators had the audacity to suggest that the wild land tax blighted the prospects of an aristocracy [46] and checked the growth of the propertied classes, "the guides, the patterns and the protectors of the people." [47] This crude appeal to the prejudices of the Colonial Office, which had always been thought anxious to prevent a wild democracy from ruling Upper Canada, proved to be in vain. Perhaps Lord Bathurst recognized it for what it was—a cold-blooded proposal on the part of the large landowners that they should be allowed to grow wealthy and "aristocratic" at the expense of poor settlers.

More honest objections to the forced sale of wild land in arrears for taxes were urged by those who contended that unproductive property ought not to be taxed, that a flat assessment rate of 4s. an acre on all wild land, irrespective of its situation, was inequitable, that the penalties exceeded the legal interest rate of 6 per cent and that the very existence of the Acts of 1819 and 1824 had depressed the land market and would prove the ruin of those who had invested in wild land.

The most sensible argument of all was put forward by those who insisted that the wild land tax would not cure the evils it was supposed to remedy. Maitland's great object was to force land into cultivation, not merely to bring about its sale, which would only transfer it from one set of owners to another. The landowners argued that in the existing state of Upper Canada's economic development it was not profitable for capitalists to lay out money in agriculture. The manual labour of the owner of the soil was, and would be for years, the only capital it was profitable to put into it, "Therefore it is in vain that the Legislature will attempt by the pressure of taxation to compel the owners of waste land to make it productive. . . ." [48] It was admitted that the pressure of the tax induced some owners to offer their land for sale at more reasonable prices than they might have done otherwise, but, it was objected, there was already more land for sale than could find purchasers and landowners, however willing, could neither sell nor pay these ruinous taxes. The result could only be that the land investments of many small men would be sacrificed for arrears and costs to the few capitalists able to carry unproductive investments in wild land over a long period. For example, John McGill informed Mrs. Simcoe that the price of land was less than it had been eight or ten years previously and that the granting of free land to immigrants and to the militia had made it practically impossible to sell except on long-term credit. D. W. Smith told her that it would not be worthwhile to hold the 5,000 acres Simcoe had received subject to tax and advised her to sell at a low price for cash.[49]

Unpopular as these arguments were, both with Maitland and with the public, they were sound. The previous lavish land-granting policy had already resulted in the dispersal of a thin population over an immense area and had established speculator control over the most fertile parts of Upper Canada. Just at the time when an attempt was being made to relieve the resident owner by forcing wild lands into sale and cultivation, some two and a half million acres of additional land were acquired from the Indians and surveyed, and portions of it were granted to privileged claimants and immigrants or, after 1826, offered for sale.[50] The Crown Reserves in the townships surveyed before 1825 were sold en bloc to the Canada Company which in turn retailed the land to settlers. The Huron Tract and the Clergy Reserves were also brought on the market. Moreover, American immigrants, who were able to purchase, were barred as aliens from acquiring land in Upper Canada. Thus the province was left to depend for settlers on the thin trickle of immigrants from Great Britain and Ireland, only a small proportion of whom brought sufficient capital with them to enable them to purchase land. Thus one mistaken policy was piled on another. The fundamental difficulty was that the damage had already been done. More land had been made available in Upper Canada than the resident population and the small number of immigrants annually reaching the province could use. As William Warren Baldwin put it, "Time alone could effect the due proportion of things."[51]

In 1828, the Assembly's Committee on the Assessment Acts brought in a report entirely favourable to the owners of tax-delinquent land. Four and a half million acres were thought to be in arrears for taxes and estimates of the amount of taxes and costs which would have to be raised by the sale of this land, ranging from £6,445 to £250,000, were presented. These figures were compared with the total amount of specie in circulation, which was estimated at £122,858. According to the committee, it was obviously impossible for the country to pay these taxes, and it therefore proposed that the sales of tax-delinquent land should be postponed and the penalties imposed by the Act of 1819 reduced. The legislature reduced the penalties on land more than four years in arrears for taxes from 100 per cent to 50 per cent, provided the assessments were paid by July 1, 1829, and it established that rate of penalty for the future. If the assessments were paid by July 1, 1828, the 50 per cent penalty was to be charged only on the arrears of the first five years, not for the whole period. Sales of land eight years in arrears were postponed for one year and then only the assessments and a penalty of 50 per cent and costs were to be charged.[52]

When sales of tax-delinquent land finally took place in the spring of 1830, it was found that the quantity of land eight years in arrears for taxes had been greatly exaggerated. Not four million acres but one million acres at most was put up at auction.[53] William Warren Baldwin had predicted that the greater part of a 200-acre lot would have to be sacrificed to meet the taxes and charges and that forced sales for cash, in the existing condition of the market, would bring very little more than 6*d.* an acre.[54] The percentage of each lot which was sold for taxes varied from 82.7 per cent in the Eastern District to 19 per cent in the District of Niagara and the price obtained from $4\frac{1}{2}d$. to 1*s.* 8*d.* an acre. Altogether, half a million acres changed hands for £13,612. The average price for all districts amounted to only $6\frac{1}{4}d$. an acre, as Baldwin had expected. Yet the average price at which the Canada Company was then offering the Crown Reserves was 10*s.* $3\frac{1}{2}d$.; the price of Crown land ranged from 4*s.* to 10*s.* an acre, depending upon the district, and the land sold at the tax sale had itself been assessed at 4*s.* an acre. There was no escaping the conclusion reached by an investigating committee of the Assembly after the sale that "there had been a sacrifice of property far exceeding the advantage to the public." [55] A subsequent revision of the Assessment Law gave some protection against such low prices by providing that tax-delinquent lands should be offered for sale at the upset price of 2*s.* 6*d.* an acre, that only so many acres were to be offered at that price as were necessary to cover the assessments, and that the quantity of land was to be reduced by bidding.[56]

The tax-delinquent land was bought not in small quantities for cultivation, as Maitland had planned, but for investment by men who already possessed thousands of acres. The Hon. Thomas Clark informed John Galt that he, in company with Samuel Street and William Dickson, was the principal purchaser and that together they had bought many thousands of acres spread over the different districts.[57] This fact does not appear from the published returns of the land sales but, no doubt, agents acted for these men in some districts. Instead of weakening the speculators' control of the land in Upper Canada, as it was intended to do, the wild land tax actually strengthened it and simply transferred the holdings of many small men to the ownership of a few who saw that the tax-delinquent lands were a good investment. As the *Quebec Mercury* pointed out, "The speculator who purchases at these sales knows that he may keep them for eight years without paying any tax, before they can be forfeited and sold for arrears, and he cannot employ his capital in any more profitable way than in buying for 4d. an acre land which he may hold up the next day at 5s an acre, and for which in the course of eight years he has every chance of getting 10s. . . ." [58] For example, in 1839 John Macaulay, informed his mother that he had an offer for one of her lots in Percy which had been bought at tax sale seven or eight years earlier for £5. He advised her not to sell for less than £150 and added that if times were prosperous the lot would bring £200.[59]

No reform was more strongly advocated by the supporters of Robert Gourlay than an effective wild land tax, and one would have expected Maitland's policies on this subject to have received the steady support of the Reformers in the Assembly. Yet the Act of 1824 was opposed not only by the speculators in the Assembly but by Reformers such as Samuel Casey and Daniel Hagerman, representatives of Lennox and Addington, and Robert Randal of the fourth riding of Lincoln. These men had not opposed the act on its first introduction, as the speculators did,[60] and it is probable that their opposition was directed not at the principle of the measure but at its provisions for the payment and expenditure of the taxes. By 1828 the Reformers seem to have become somewhat opposed to the wild land tax itself. They voted for the Assessment Act of that year which not only provided for the more convenient payment of taxes but also postponed the sales and reduced the penalties on tax-delinquent land. In 1835 the Committee on Grievances received one or two expressions of discontent with the wild land tax from witnesses,[61] and, subsequent to the Rebellion, Donald M'Leod pointed out that, although the wild lands of residents were taxed, the Clergy Reserves and the extensive holdings of the Canada Company were not, and he complained that the effect of the act had been to enable "a monied aristocracy" to purchase thousands of acres at nominal prices.[62] Mackenzie himself complained that during the years 1830-3 nearly 700,000 acres of excellent land, "chiefly in the old settlements and the property of individuals," had been sold for arrears of taxes at an average of 5d. an acre.[63]

What was especially galling to Mackenzie was the fact that the revenue resulting from the tax on wild lands was solely at the disposal of the Tory Justices of the Peace. The Road Act of 1819, which imposed $\frac{1}{8}d$. an acre on occupied lands for roads, had indeed directed that the proceeds of this tax should be paid over to the elected overseers of highways; but in 1824 these officials were abolished,[64] and the new road act of that year, which made the tax of $\frac{1}{8}d$. an acre pernament, directed that this money, like other assessments, should be paid to the district treasurers and paid out by them for roads as the Justices of the Peace should direct. The proceeds of the tax sales were also paid to the Justices.[65] In Mackenzie's opinion, these funds were "squandered" by Judge Robinson's irresponsible Justices who were not, like the elected overseers, "subject to any efficient accountability for their proceedings," [66] and were themselves made and unmade at will by the clique in power at York. In the *Colonial Advocate* of October 30, 1828, Mackenzie reported that a meeting of several townships held a short time previously at Markham had resolved, "That if the several townships of this province were entrusted with the power of choosing their local Magistrates, from time to time, and for a term of years, that arrangement would prove a remedy for many abuses which now disgrace our inferior courts of justice." Mackenzie had no respect for the ability or the impartiality of the average Tory Justice of the Peace, selected, as he believed him to be, "from a fraction of the population offensive to the mass of the inhabitants." [67]

Criticism of the manner in which the proceeds of the Assessment and Road Acts were to be expended was not merely a prejudice of the Reformers against Tory magistrates. More than one opponent of the Assessment Act of 1824 feared that the funds would be frittered away on temporary roads, frail bridges, and causeways and that the lion's share would go to the populous front of the townships at the expense of the wild land in the rear.[68] When Charles Buller came to write his report on the Crown lands for Lord Durham, he, too, expressed the opinion that the wild lands tax had not proved efficacious and that its proceeds had been badly expended. In its place, as we shall see, he proposed a much more radical scheme of taxation similar to that advocated by Robert Gourlay.[69]

Throughout the entire history of Upper Canada the question of what was the best policy to adopt for the Crown lands was debated over and over again with inconclusive results. Not until 1837, when it was too late, did the home government come to regard the Crown lands as Imperial capital to be carefully developed and expended for the benefit of the Empire.

CHAPTER ELEVEN

THE FAILURE OF THE LAND-GRANTING SYSTEM

Throughout the entire history of Upper Canada the question of what was the best policy to adopt for the Crown lands was debated over and over again with inconclusive results. Not until 1837, when it was too late, did the home government come to regard the Crown lands as Imperial capital to be carefully developed and expended for the benefit of the Empire. The unsatisfactory land-granting system was finally abolished in 1826, partly because it had defeated its own ends and partly because a revenue policy had been maturely decided upon. Three factors seem to have induced the Imperial government to make the change. One was the united chorus of disapproval of the existing system arising from various classes in Upper Canada, the second was the necessity of increasing the provincial revenue, and the third was the desire to administer the Crown lands of the various colonies of the Empire under a uniform system.

It will be remembered that as early as 1798 a sales policy had been decided upon but that it was not put into effect because sufficient land could not be secured from the Indians at reasonable rates. Between 1815 and 1825, nine Indian treaties were concluded which extinguished the Indian title to practically the entire peninsula between Lakes Ontario, Erie, and Huron.[1] There was now nothing to prevent the long contemplated change in land policy from taking effect. Indeed, it could have occurred at any time after 1815, but the anxiety of the Imperial and the provincial governments to offset American influences by colonizing the province with discharged soldiers and immigrants from Great Britain led, as we have seen, to a continuation of the land-granting system. Before it at length gave way to the revenue system in 1826, it had been condemned from every point of view and had been so whittled away that there was practically nothing of it left. The final change, when it did come, was not "born of scarcity" but of the provincial government's fear of becoming financially dependent upon the Assembly.

Lieutenant-Governor Gore considered the land system of Upper Canada a failure. It had not provided the Crown with either a revenue with which to govern and develop the province or a valuable commodity with which to reward those whose loyalty or services gave them a claim on its bounty. It had reduced the value of the grants of land made to loyalists and military claimants to the amount of the survey and patent fees, which other classes of settlers were obliged to pay, and it had prevented the Crown and Clergy Reserves from yielding much revenue.[2] He thought it would be a "blessing" if the practice of granting land were ended as soon as possible. If the land was sold for a fixed and moderate price, as in the United States, Gore believed that immigrants from that country, who previously had crossed the lakes solely because they could get land for 8*d.* an acre, the amount of the survey and patent fees, rather than from any preference for British rule, would cease to find Upper Canada attractive. This, in the Lieutenant-Governor's opinion, would be by no means the least of the blessings that might result from a change of policy.[3] W. D. Powell shared Gore's sentiments. He thought that *bona fide* immigrants from the United Kingdom might continue to receive free grants but that all others should be made to pay from $1.00 to $2.00 an acre for their land.[4]

Sir Peregrine Maitland criticized the Crown land policy from another angle— its ineffectiveness in settling the country. Under the existing system, tracts of country remained unimproved while settlement was unnecessarily dispersed. He advocated reducing the size of ordinary grants to 50 acres, which was all he thought poor persons capable of improving, and, in order to conserve the limited capital of such settlers, he proposed that their grants be made really free by not burdening them with survey or patent fees. On the other hand, he favoured raising the fees on larger grants very sharply so that this land would not be asked for except by those who really intended to make use of it. Eventually he came to the conclusion that the only wise policy was to dispose of the Crown land by sale instead of by grant.[5]

Maitland's policies had the effect of converting the land system of Upper Canada into a land-purchasing system even before 1826. The process was really begun in 1798 when the additional fee then imposed brought the cost of a 200-acre lot to 6*d.* an acre, plus the survey fee of £1 7*s.* 6*d.*[6] In 1804 the fee was raised to approximately 8*d.* an acre and the survey fee was set at £1 4*s.* 9*d.*[7] The fees remained at this level until 1819 when they were doubled, except for 100-acre grants.[8] In 1820 the fee was again practically doubled on 100-acre and 200-acre lots and more than doubled on larger grants. For a short time poor settlers unable to pay fees could obtain 50 acres free of all expenses but their acceptance of these grants made them ineligible for any additional quantities. When the Imperial government began to assist poor Irish and Scotch immigrants to settle in Upper Canada these 50-acre grants ceased to be made.[9]

Both of these new tables of fees were put into effect by Maitland before he had received the sanction of the home government,[10] and it was not until complaints reached him that the Colonial Secretary realized what had been done. He then inquired by what authority the table of fees had been changed.[11] Maitland explained that the change did not benefit any official in Upper Canada but added to the revenue of the Crown and that it had become necessary to increase the fees in order to raise a fund out of which to pay the patent fees on free grants to poor immigrants. This was the explanation publicly given at the time, coupled with the further excuse that the value of land in Upper Canada, and the cost of surveys, had practically doubled since 1804.[12]

No doubt there had been some increase in the value of land since Hunter's day but the increase in fees took place during the post-war depression when the value of land and of agricultural commodities was depressed. It was quite true that the land officers' share of the land fees was kept at the 1804 level, yet they benefited indirectly. The sharp increases in these fees tended to bolster the value of land in private hands, and many members of the official class, their relatives and friends, held large tracts. It was probably this group which urged the Executive Council to adopt a policy which would rig the market for their benefit. Maitland practically admitted as much when he explained to Bathurst that the large landowners had been complaining that they could not get an "adequate" price for their land while the Crown lands continued to be given away almost gratuitously. Since their holdings were now subject to a wild land tax, he thought their complaints not unreasonable. He added, however, that the fees established in 1819 and 1820 had been abolished and a new table had been adopted by an order-in-council of January 31, 1824.

The new regulations, which were eventually approved by Bathurst,[13] actually re-established the 1819 table, except for townships surveyed before that date,[14] but abolished the 50-acre free grants. This change also seems to have been made on the demand of the large landowners who found that the high fees of 1820 did not have the effect they expected. Land seekers, deterred by these fees from applying for Crown lands, had not turned to private owners but, representing themselves as destitute, asked for and obtained "the pauper's allowance of 50 acres."[15] The new regulations put an end to this possibility. Townships surveyed before 1819 remained subject to the 1820 table for a time but they were subsequently reduced to the fees of 1819.[16] In Upper Canada a 200-acre lot therefore cost 3s. an acre from 1820 to 1824 and at least 1s. 8½d. during the last two years of the so-called land-granting system.

The land-granting system was condemned not only by the Lieutenant-Governor and the land speculators but also by the loyalists and the recent immigrants, although for very different reasons. Many of the loyalists regarded Upper Canada as a preserve which the Crown had set aside exclusively for them to exploit. They had looked with disfavour on grants of land being made to "late" loyalists, the French royalists received no welcome from them, and they were no more ready to share the bounty of the Crown with the immigrants from Great Britain. When it came to paying for free surveys and free patents for them out of the provincial revenue, the inhabitants of Upper Canada could not see, according to Mahlon Burwell, why they should be taxed to "pay for the surveying and granting lands to induce others hereafter to reside in it."[17]

Those who regarded the newer immigrants from Great Britain and Ireland with a more hospitable eye gradually came to the conclusion that, after 1820 at any rate, the bounty of the Crown in land was not worth their acceptance. One hundred acres was all that the ordinary settler could obtain, and only 50 if he represented himself as a pauper unable to pay fees. In the opinion of experienced farmers, 200 acres was the least an industrious man with a family could accept.[18] After 1818 the Crown had practically no land to grant except in the townships recently acquired from the Indians. Except for some swampy and unsurveyed land in Prescott and Russell, Essex, and Kent, all the decent locations had been disposed of. It was the general opinion that good land could be had in the older settlements from private dealers for less than the 3s. an acre charged in fees, on a 200-acre grant in a remote township. Added to the dis- advantages of size, situation, and price was the fact that owing to the chronic shortage of surveyed land open for location[19] the would-be settler on Crown land was not free to choose his location and was subject to vexatious delays in getting a location at all. In newly surveyed townships, part of the land was made available for location by privileged claimants, part of it for fees-paying settlers, and part was used for 50-acre free grants for the poor.[20] Settlers were required to draw for their land and to accept whatever lot fell to them by chance. It is little wonder that disgruntled immigrants left for the United States and that others preferred to purchase land in the old settlements rather than to "go to the wilderness by lottery." [21]

In certain situations it was possible to get land at lower rates than the high fees established in 1819 and 1820. To induce settlers to locate on a new line of road from Kempenfeldt Bay on Lake Simcoe to Penetanguishine, 200-acre grants, double the usual quantity permitted since 1815, were offered for a brief period at the old fees of 1796 and on the same settlement duty conditions as were required in the Talbot Settlement.[22] In 1820, 100-acre lots on the north side of the road through the Mohawk Tract on the Bay of Quinte, and on the north side of the Long Woods Road (from Delaware Village to Moraviantown) were offered at the fee of 1804 to those who would do the settlement duties and make and maintain the whole width of the road.[23] In 1821 a road was planned from Lake Simcoe to the Ottawa through the rear townships of Peterborough, Hastings, and Frontenac Counties. Settlers were invited to take up land at the fee of 1819, subject to completing the usual settlement duties within two years from the date of location. "To have it in the power of the government to direct the population to any particular part by a partial reduction of the fees, was amongst the objects I had proposed to myself in increasing them . . .," Maitland explained.[24] However, by 1828, only two or three of the sixteen townships in this area had attracted settlers.[25] Dissatisfaction with the fee system was subsequently tersely expressed by William Lyon Mackenzie in a letter to Colborne: "The object hitherto has been *fees*—it ought to have been *settlers*." [26]

In 1823 the various defects in the land system were discussed by the Assembly. A number of resolutions were debated on which an address to the Crown was intended to be founded, but were finally shelved. The framers of these resolutions proposed to abolish the Crown and Clergy Reserves and to grant townships or other large tracts on reasonable terms to capitalists who would settle them, open roads, and build mills and forges.[27] This was the policy followed by the British government when it sold the Huron Tract to the Canada Company a few years later. The sale, however, failed to please the Assembly because by that time questions of land policy had become entangled with the efforts of that body to acquire control of the Casual and Territorial Revenue of the Crown.

At the conclusion of the Napoleonic Wars, Great Britain decided to limit her assistance to the civil expenses of Upper Canada to an annual Parliamentary grant of £10,825 for the salaries of the Lieutenant-Governor, the judges, and chief public officials, for certain pensions, and for a grant to the Society for the Propagation of the Gospel. Any expenditure beyond this amount was no longer to be paid out of the Military Chest but provided by the province itself.[28] Thereafter, the chief problem facing the Lieutenant-Governor and Executive Council was to raise the necessary funds without becoming dependent upon the Assembly. Under these circumstances, they naturally looked to the Crown lands for revenue. The Assembly, on its part, began to re-assert its old claim to control all revenue raised within the province, from whatever source derived.

When Lieutenant-Governor Gore informed the Assembly of the Imperial government's decision, he laid before it an estimate of civil expenses for 1817 not provided for by the Parliamentary grant. They amounted to £10,821. Income from the Imperial duties, fines, survey money, and rents applicable to these expenses was estimated at £2,000 and the legislature was asked to provide the balance, £8,281. However, when the House came to frame a supply bill, it voted unanimously to grant, not the excess, but the whole sum of £10,281, thereby reviving and asserting its old claim to appropriate the duties arising from the Imperial Act 14 Geo. III, c. 88. Lieutenant-Governor Gore appears to have raised no objection, having in mind, perhaps, that the Colonial Office had long ago informed him that the legislature was entitled to appropriate these duties.[29] The supply bill, as finally passed, provided only the £8,281 sterling for which Gore had asked, but the Assembly resolved that "the net amount of the duties and the fines and survey moneys, as appropriated and applicable to the Administration of Justice, do form part of the supply voted to His Majesty."[30]

The Assembly did not rest content with this victory. In 1816 a permanent appropriation act had been passed granting £2,500 annually towards the civil expenses of the province.[31] This sum was devoted by Lieutenant-Governor Gore in part to new expenses of which the Assembly had earlier disapproved.[32] Consequently, a bill to repeal the permanent Appropriation Act was introduced in 1818, although not proceeded in.[33] However, the report of the Committee on Public Accounts, which was adopted by the Assembly, closed with a strong demand that a complete statement of the provincial expenses as well as a detailed statement of the annual Imperial grant and of the Crown revenue from every provincial source be laid before the Assembly before it was again asked for an appropriation in aid of the civil expenses of the province.[34] Owing to a quarrel between the two Houses over the efforts of the Council to amend money bills, no supply was granted at this session.

When Sir Peregrine Maitland arrived in Upper Canada to succeed Gore he reported that "The Whole Revenue had ... been thrown into one mass, and made subject to the House of Assembly, so that there remained nothing at the disposal of the Crown."[35] The Lieutenant-Governor was thus brought face-to-face with the necessity of either submitting the policies of the executive to the financial veto of the Assembly or of redeeming the Crown revenues from its control and so developing them as to leave the Lieutenant-Governor free to bestow the patronage of the Crown in the manner he thought most likely to secure the Imperial connection and to counteract republican influences from across the border. What better mode of strengthening the Imperial tie was there than that of encouraging British immigrants, of developing an aristocracy of half-pay officers in Upper Canada, of supporting the established Church, and of ensuring that faithful servants of the Crown and their families were well maintained? Towards these objects the Assembly had already evinced a certain amount of hostility;[36] therefore the Crown lands and the Crown revenues could not be entrusted to it. Maitland was convinced that once the executive became financially dependent upon the provincial Assembly there would be an end to public peace and to all real resemblance to the institutions of the mother country.[37]

The small group of officials, churchmen, executive and legislative councillors, and ultra-loyalists who surrounded the Lieutenant-Governor—the Family Compact, to use a term Barnabas Bidwell had once applied to a group of office holders in Massachusetts [38]—were as anxious as he to preserve the executive's financial independence of the lower House. It had proved profitable to them in the past and would be in the future, as long as they could successfully restrict the interests of the Crown in Upper Canada to those policies which would preserve their political power and economic privileges. But their hold on power was slipping. Ever since Hunter's day there had been a party in Upper Canada demanding control of the provincial revenues and provincial resources. Since the war and the visit of Robert Gourlay, this group had won increasing support. Maitland's firm hand held them in check for a time, but, given the unwillingness of the Imperial government to continue subsidizing the province, all he could do was to postpone the inevitable struggle.

Early in the session of 1819, the Lieutenant-Governor informed the legislature that the Casual and Territorial Revenue was not at its disposal and that it was not applicable to the civil expenses of the province. He also made it plain that the Assembly would not be allowed to appropriate the funds arising from the Imperial duties. The Assembly acquiesced in Maitland's limitations upon its control of the revenue. Thereafter, the appropriation acts stated that certain sums were to be granted for the expenses of the civil government in aid of funds "already appropriated" to that purpose by the Imperial Statute 14 Geo. III, c. 88. The Assembly did not, however, always accept the estimates submitted to it. Payments to the clergy and pensions to militia officers remained a bone of contention between the executive and the lower House.

Since there was not much hope of inducing the Imperial Parliament to resume the financial burden for Upper Canada which it had so lately laid down, Maitland tackled the revenue problems of the province in three other ways. He attempted to make the Land Department self-supporting, tried to devise a satisfactory method of making the Crown Reserves productive, and suggested to Bathurst that to safeguard the Crown revenues in the future the Lieutenant-Governor should be definitely instructed not to relinquish the Casual and Territorial Revenues of the Crown nor permit the Assembly to appropriate the funds arising from the Imperial duties. His policy was approved and such an instruction was sent to him. Lord Bathurst seems not to have been aware that the law officers of the Crown had, in 1807, decided that the provincial legislature did have the right of appropriating the Imperial duties. In any case, when Lord Dalhousie raised this question, the law officers gave a different opinion, pointing out that the Imperial duties had been specifically imposed not to regulate trade and commerce but to raise a revenue and therefore were not affected by the Colonial Tax Repeal Act.[39]

Certain expenses connected with the Land Department of Upper Canada had, prior to 1818, always been defrayed from the Military Chest. These were the payments to the Indians for lands purchased for the Crown, the expense of surveys, and the half fees on privileged grants. After 1815 the expenditures for

these three items became especially heavy, owing to the large number of discharged soldiers, immigrants, and militia men for whom land had to be surveyed
and free patents provided. The Assembly made it clear that it was not prepared
to assume these expenses so long as the control of the natural resources of the
province remained a branch of the royal prerogative and while that prerogative
continued to be exercised primarily for the benefit of favoured individuals.
When all the revenue derived from the natural resources became part of the
provincial revenue and subject to provincial control, then the expenses of
developing and managing that revenue could properly be charged upon the
public—but not otherwise.[40]

Lieutenant-Governor Maitland was determined not to yield on this point.
When he submitted the estimates for 1820 he informed the Assembly that the
Casual and Territorial Revenue was "subject exclusively to the signification of
His Majesty's pleasure. . . . His Majesty," added Maitland, "grants land to whom
and on what condition he pleases, an unquestionable prerogative."[41] By taking
this firm stand the Lieutenant-Governor hoped to end, once and for all, any
claim of the Assembly to interfere with the management of the Crown lands or
the revenue derived from them. At the same time he realized that his government could not successfully maintain this stand without the resources of the
Military Chest to fall back upon unless the Land Department became self-
supporting. He therefore did not ask the Assembly to provide for new surveys,
although he felt justified in asking for the expenses of certain offices of public
reference connected with the Land Department. The Assembly agreed to these
requests.

Maitland overcame the lack of funds by paying the surveyors in land instead
of in cash. Bids were called for and the contracts were awarded to the surveyors
who would take the smallest percentage of the townships to be surveyed. Between
1819 and 1827, 3,623,657 acres of land were surveyed by contract at an average
rate of $4\frac{1}{2}$ per cent.[42] The surveyors were supposed to take their percentages
by lot after the reserves had been marked off, but when they drew inferior land
they were allowed to exchange it for land fit for cultivation.[43] The result was
that they usually obtained the best lots in the township and held them for sale
at about $1.00 an acre.[44] Since their land was the choicest and also free of
settlement duties,[45] it could command more than the Crown fees even though
located in an unsettled township. The system of paying for surveys in land was
later condemned as wasteful and inefficient. "Valuing the lands given at four
shillings an acre (which, as the contracts required the lands to be fit for cultivation, is a moderate valuation), the surveys paid in land cost more than twice as
much as those paid in cash, while it is notorious that the former were very
erroneous and defective," testified a later Commissioner of Crown Lands. "In
some cases concessions or parts of concessions shown on plans have no existence
on the ground, in others the lands have not been surveyed at all, but fictitious
plans and field notes prepared, which grossly misled those who referred to
them. . . ."[46]

Between 1818 and 1828 some 7,000,000 acres were acquired from the Indians
and added to the territory of Upper Canada. Until 1818 the Indians had always
received a lump sum for their lands, paid either in goods or in cash or in both,

but seven out of the nine land purchase treaties negotiated in Maitland's day provided for payment in annuities.[47] After 1818 the British Treasury expected the expense of additional purchaes of Indian lands to be borne by Upper Canada and Maitland proposed to raise the necessary money by selling a portion of the land at auction. The terms were to be one-tenth down with the balance secured by a mortgage. So long as the purchasers regularly paid the interest, the principal was not to be required of them. This plan was approved by the Treasury and Indian purchases to be paid for in annuities were authorized.[48] In 1820 some 98,000 acres of land were selected for sale which, on these terms, were expected to yield £3,500 annually, the amount of the annuities provisionally contracted for up to that time.[49] However, in a few months' time Maitland began to see that his scheme would not work. Even though the land was to be sold on a long-term credit basis, an adequate price could not be obtained in the current state of the land market. He was therefore obliged to ask the Treasury to permit a postponement of the proposed sales and to assume the expense of the Indian annuities for a time.[50]

Another attempt to make the Land Department self-supporting also failed. It will be remembered that one of the reasons given for doubling and redoubling the patent fees was the necessity of increasing the Crown land revenues so as to provide free patents for poor immigrants. The Crown's portion of the patent fees and the rent from leased lands proved unequal to this additional burden and recourse was had to the Military Chest once more to make up the deficiency.[51]

The unsolved revenue problems of Upper Canada pressed upon the provincial administration from two sides: the officials of the British Treasury insisted on economy while the provincial Assembly laboured to make good its control over both the financial resources of the province and the policies of its executive. In the hope of relieving the provincial government from this unwelcome pressure, John Beverley Robinson worked out a scheme for making productive the one valuable asset in the possession of the Crown—the Crown Reserves.

CHAPTER TWELVE

THE CROWN RESERVES AND THE CROWN REVENUES

THE CROWN RESERVES of Upper Canada had a double origin. A few were set aside by Lord Dorchester on his own initiative, the rest were authorized by the Imperial government after 1791. This trifling circumstance was unfortunate because Dorchester's motives were quite different from those of the Colonial Office and gave rise to a misunderstanding respecting the purpose of the Reserves. When advocating grants in free and common socage in Upper Canada, Dorchester suggested that in every township of 30,000 acres, 5,000 acres should be reserved "to reward . . . such . . . provincial Servants as may merit the Royal favour and [these reserves] will also enable the Crown to create and strengthen an Aristocracy, of which the best use may be made on this Continent, where all Governments are feeble and the general condition of things tends to a wild Democracy." [1] Indeed, in all the townships set out under his direction, he had already adopted this policy, and had set aside for the Crown one-eighth to one-seventh of the farm lots, in addition to reserves designed for public purposes in the townsites themselves. [2]

No mention is made of the Crown Reserves in the Constitutional Act or in the general instructions which accompanied it to Canada, perhaps because the policy of the Imperial government in making these reserves was one that could not be openly avowed. The home government was apparently unresponsive to Dorchester's suggestion, but two years later, when Lord Grenville became Secretary for the Home Department, he revived the question of the Crown Reserves with, however, an entirely different object in view. "There is one subject adverted to in the paper which I now enclose," he wrote,

of which no mention is made, either in the Bill transmitted [the first draught of the Constitutional Act] . . . or in the despatch which accompanies it. What I mean is, the suggestion relative to the possibility of making such reservations of Land adjacent to all future Grants as may secure to the Crown a certain and improving Revenue—A measure which, if it had been adopted when the Old Colonies were first settled, would have retained them to this hour in obedience and Loyalty. [3]

The paper to which Grenville referred, which is of unknown authorship, suggested that if reserves of land were made for the Crown like those the Penns were said to have set aside for themselves, "in the midst of every grant to individuals," it would obviate the necessity of the mother country's taxing herself for the support of the civil government of the colonies, and, since she had deprived herself of the power to tax her colonies, [4] of asking them to tax themselves. Thus the question which had been most in dispute between the thirteen colonies and Parliament would not arise. In Lord Durham's *Report* this proposal is attributed to the President of the Executive Council of the Province of Quebec, at that time Chief Justice William Smith, and is in consonance with Smith's ideas.[5]

It is hard to believe that this method of maintaining amicable relations between the mother country and her remaining colonies met with Dorchester's approval. Subsequent to the receipt of Grenville's dispatch, he sent home an account of his land regulations in which he referred to the reserves he had already made and merely remarked that they would become valuable when the population increased and that they might then assist in providing for the provincial expenditures.[6] It is unlikely that the man who had argued that even the trifling revenue from quit rents should be placed at the disposal of the colonial legislature would have approved of this new policy of providing a source of future revenue which was not to be at the disposal of those legislatures. At any rate, this scheme appealed to the Imperial authorities who, in a separate instruction of September 16, 1791, directed Dorchester to set aside in every township Crown Reserves at least equal in quantity to the Clergy Reserves for the purpose of raising a fund to be applied to the expenses of government.[7]

The notion that the Crown Reserves had been intended to reward deserving subjects prevailed in Upper Canada long after Dorchester's day. The Land Board of Hesse, for example, referred to a block of forty Crown and Clergy Reserves set aside in the vicinity of Chatham as "reserved for the friends of government and the clergy."[8] John Askin, too, "always thought the Crown Reserves were intended for particular friends of government."[9] D. W. Smith thought the Crown Reserves were "probably to reward Service and Merit as they occasionally occur," and shortly before the sale to the Canada Company he applied for a grant of this class of land.[10] This mistaken idea seems to have been so prevalent and so unpopular with the mass of settlers that Simcoe urged Portland to assure the province that the reserves would not be alienated from public purposes. Simcoe recognized that the average frontiersman seeking fertile land favourably located could not be restrained from squatting on desirable Crown or Clergy reserves, except by force, unless he could be made to feel a permanent interest in the advantages to be derived from them. For this reason he was anxious to supply the province with an efficient clergy at once and to set at rest all popular suspicions concerning the Crown Reserves.[11] He proposed that the reserves be leased and the revenues from the Crown Reserves be appropriated at once towards the expenses of the civil government and the defence of the province. However, the Colonial Secretary, while quite willing to have the reserves leased, was not ready to look so far into the future,[12] and the Crown Reserves remained unappropriated to any specific purpose.

On the whole, the Crown Reserves remained inviolate until about 1815. True, reserves were taken off certain lots and placed on others to facilitate the location and settlement of certain roads,[13] but the general rule was that the reserves were not to be changed in surveyed townships. No serious inroads were made on them until 1815.[14] In that year, at the direction of the Imperial government, the Crown Reserves in the counties of the Eastern District were placed at the disposal of the Military Settling Department in order that a compact settlement might be formed of the reduced troops and immigrants from the British Isles.

Lieutenant-Governor Gore seems to have regarded this order as giving him authority to confer Crown Reserves in other parts of Upper Canada upon persons of these classes when they were unwilling to accept land in the military settlement. The favoured few who were granted this privilege obtained much more valuable land in older, better settled, and more fertile townships than their fellows, who had to be content with whatever fell to their lot within the military settlement. Gore made forty-seven of these special grants, totalling about 7,400 acres, and his successor, Administrator Samuel Smith, ventured to make four more. A few prominent people obtained these grants but most of the recipients were merely disbanded soldiers.[15] One wonders whether they ever fulfilled the required settlement duties, or whether, like many other military grantees, they quickly disposed of their rights to others.

Lieutenant-Governor Gore's attack upon the hitherto sacred Crown Reserves had the effect of bringing the whole Crown and Clergy Reserve policy up for unfavourable discussion in the Assembly.[16] The question at issue was whether public property, made valuable by the labour of every settler in the province, would become the spoil of favourites. The Assembly, in the course of a vigorous debate on Gore's policies, framed a resolution calling for the sale of both the Crown and the Clergy Reserves.[17] The resolution was never put to a vote since Gore prorogued the Assembly to prevent any further discussion of his policies. This was the first of many subsequent resolutions relating to the disposition of the reserves and the Colonial Office may well have cursed the day that Gore meddled with them. He was later censured for his unauthorized interference with the property of the Crown.[18]

The Crown Reserves were safe in the hand of Gore's successor, Sir Peregrine Maitland. Maitland was a most zealous guardian of the Crown's rights, particularly of its Territorial Revenue, on which the executive's independence of the legislature turned. Using the reserves to reward individuals at the expense of the permanent revenue of the Crown seemed to him a short-sighted policy and, at his own request, he received a strictly worded instruction not to confer Crown Reserves on any settler, civil or military, without the authorization of the Colonial Secretary.[19] Schemes for utilizing the Crown Reserves to finance other objects, such as internal improvements, also met with his disapproval.[20] "In casting away the territorial revenue of the Crown," wrote Maitland, "you throw away ... the best source of future influence ... it has always been seen in this light by the Democratic party and it has always been a favourite object with them to get rid of the Crown Reserves." [21] Maitland was determined that they should not succeed.

Edward Allen Talbot was one of those urging the sale of the Crown Reserves. He was convinced that if, in addition to using the proceeds for the improvement of the internal navigation of the province, the government extended the privilege of purchasing the reserves to American immigrants willing to take the oath of allegiance, every acre would be bought up within three years—an argument not calculated to appeal to Maitland nor to quiet his suspicions of those who advanced it.[22]

The Crown Reserves had not lain wholly idle up to this time. As early as 1795, the Colonial Office, which was anxious to make the province self-supporting, had called for a report on the possibility of leasing both the Crown and Clergy Reserves.[23] Before his departure from Upper Canada, Simcoe had given some attention to the problem, and D. W. Smith had worked out for him the rough draft of a plan.[24] Subsequently, the Council, guided by Chief Justice Allcock, proposed to Peter Russell that the reserves be leased out at a rack rent (that is, a rent equal to the interest on the value of the land) for a term not exceeding twenty-one years.[25] Such terms, as Powell pointed out, were utterly unsuited to a new country where land had little value until labour had been spent upon it and where it was difficult to induce men to spend their labour on land not their own. Powell proposed instead that lessees be required simply to clear and fence one acre each year and to pay an annual rent of 1s. for every acre cleared. Provided they complied with these terms, they should have the privilege of renewing their leases every seventh year for the full term of twenty-one years on payment of a fine, fixed for the first fifty years at 20s. an acre for every acre cleared.[26]

D. W. Smith also favoured a twenty-one year lease, renewable every seventh year so as to assure the tenant a term of forty-two years on condition that he clear one acre of land annually and pay a fine on renewal of $1.00 per cleared acre. Smith estimated the value of wild land in Upper Canada at 50¢ an acre and he considered that the annual rent charged for a reserve, starting at $2.50 a lot, should be progressively increased so as to yield, over a period of twenty years, the present value of the land—$100—and during the entire period of forty-two years a little more than twice that sum. Smith thought that by that time the land would be worth $4.00 an acre and that the tenant should have the right to a further renewal of his lease at an annual rent of 6 per cent on the value of the land, on paying a fine of $40.00.[27] The Council, this time under the guidance of John Elmsley, then reconsidered the question and reported a leasing system based on Smith's plan, except that no mention was made of required improvements nor of fines on renewals. Elmsley saw no reason why the latter "abuse" should be instituted in a new country. The rent was set at 5s., 15s., and 25s. a lot for each of the three seven-year periods and thereafter was to increase 10s. every seven years.[28] This rent amounted to slightly less than Smith had proposed for the first twenty-one years but was considerably more for the second twenty-one years.

The Colonial Secretary approved the Council's plan with two exceptions. He thought a rent regulated by the price of wheat would be more just than a money rent—an idea already passed on to Russell by the Bishop of Quebec [29]—and he objected to the clause which permitted the leases to be renewed for the full term of twenty-one years at each of the three seven-year periods. After Hunter's arrival, the Council revised the proposed leasing system once more to meet Portland's wishes. It was decided that the leases should run for twenty-one years only and that the lessee should have only a verbal intimation that at the end of the first seven years the lease might be renewed for the full term of twenty-one years.[30] Since about two hundred applications for reserves had been received by this time, the Council thought it could safely demand higher rents than had originally been contemplated and set them at 10s., 20s., and 30s. for the three seven-year periods. This was a far cry from the 1s. per cleared acre which Powell had thought sufficient. Lessees were given the option of paying their rent in wheat, reckoned at three, six, and nine bushels, according to the period of the lease.[31] On May 28, 1801, public notice was given that applicants must come and declare their assent to the conditions on May 10, 1802, the date at which the leases were to become effective. A proclamation of October 14, 1803, called on them to pay their rents promptly to the sheriff of their district.[32]

More important than the actual terms on which the Crown Reserves were leased were the ideas expressed by the governing class of Upper Canada in the course of the discussion upon them. It was hoped that the leasing system would not only protect and develop the unpopular reserves but also reconcile the settlers to their existence. The patent fee on leases was £1 12s. 6d. but only 2s. 6d. was paid by the lessee, the rest being taken out of the rent. Thus the leasing system made it easier to acquire legal possession of a reserve than of a Crown grant, and it was fully expected that the lessees, realizing on which side their bread was buttered, would become a powerful body of supporters for the reserve system.[33] As John Elmsley put it, however important it might be to develop a revenue, "it is of much greater importance that the Established Constitution in Church and State should be so interwoven with the whole social system in Upper Canada as to engage men's interests as well as their feelings in its support and make it in popular and daily estimation no less essential to the security of property than to the preservation of religion and the maintenance of social order" [34]

Less worthy motives than these also were voiced. Smith, for example, told the Council that, "from strong political motives," Simcoe had planned to lease the reserves "progressively and not on any particular Day or even at a few particular periods." Perhaps Simcoe's object was to deal with the lessees of the reserves individually and to avoid having a body of delinquent or discontented tenants petitioning for time or changes in the leases all on the same date. He also may have been concerned that the tenants might gain an attentive hearing from the Council, and perhaps the sympathy of the Assembly. But if the lessees were to be prevented from bringing their influence to bear on the government, John Elmsley and his colleagues saw no reason why the government should not bring *its* influence to bear on the lessees. The Council considered the reserves not merely as a source of revenue "but as affording in the mean time [till they become valuable] in the mere conduct and management of them, the means of erecting and maintaining that influence which experience has shown to be essential to the strength and efficacity of the best constituted government." [35] In other words, what was wanted in the new province of Upper Canada was a few rotten boroughs. Elmsley went even further than this and hinted that if the lessee had, not a promise, but merely the hope of getting his lease renewed for the full term of twenty-one years at the end of the seventh year, it would give the government a degree of influence over him which would be highly desirable.[36] Such an attitude on the part of the little group of appointed officials augured ill for the domestic peace of Upper Canada.

The business of leasing the Crown and Clergy Reserves started out auspiciously but it soon became apparent that the reserves would be disposed of slowly and the rents collected more slowly still. It turned out that many of the early applications had come from speculators who had no intention of improving the land, much less of paying rent for it. They simply wanted to get hold of reserves valuable for their timber or their location in the hope of profiting from the expected rise in land values.[37] Since the leases were alienable this was possible.[38] These speculators did not content themselves with one lot, but petitioned, in some cases, for ten er twelve choice locations, and those who got in on the ground floor secured their leases before restrictions were placed on such applications.[39]

During the first twelve months the leasing system was in operation about 140 Crown Reserves were rented.[40] Twenty years later 706 Crown Reserves had been leased, or 10 per cent of the total. A larger percentage of the reserves in the Home and Newcastle Districts had been leased, but in the Western District only 1 per cent had as yet proved attractive to settlers.[41] Despite the fact that the reserves were being rented very slowly, the terms on new leases were twice revised upwards. In 1811 they were raised to 15s., 30s., and 45s. for the three successive seven-year periods and in 1819 to £1 15s., £3 10s., £5 15s.[42] The total quantiy of Crown Reserves in the townships surveyed before 1825 and not granted to the Military Settling Department was 1,564,350 acres. According to a report made to the Council in 1827, 1,232 reserves had been leased, or 225,944 acres.[43] However, only 883 leases had actually been made out, 220 of which had expired and had not been renewed.[44] If all 1,232 leases had been in force in 1827, the most that can be said for the leasing system is that after twenty-five years trial it had achieved 15 per cent results.

The rents from the leased reserves proved very difficult to collect. Warning after warning that the leases of those who continued delinquent would be cancelled went unregarded.[45] The arrears continued to mount until at the close of 1826 they totalled £7,000. The annual revenue from this property, which ought to have amounted to £4,000 in 1822,[46] hardly averaged £200 a year during the entire eighteen-twenties.

The problem of enforcing payment of the rents was never satisfactorily solved while the reserves remained under the management of the Executive Council. Delinquent lessees and their sureties were often found to be insolvent, or missing, and, if their lots had never been occupied, there was nothing on the property for the sheriff to seize. Where there were chattels, the sheriffs distrained for the rents, but before long doubts arose as to the legality of their doing so, especially as to their right to levy costs in addition to the arrears.[47] The legal difficulties were not solved until a Commissioner of Crown Lands was appointed in 1826 with the power to receive and distrain for the King's rents. Until this was done and a simpler legal process provided, the arrears did not defray the expense of recovery. It was this state of affairs which brought Sir Peregrine Maitland and John Beverley Robinson to the conclusion that the Crown Reserves could not be utilized to ease the revenue problems of Upper Canada until some more efficient method of exploiting them was devised.

In 1817 the financial assistance which Upper Canada received from Great Britain had been limited to the annual Parliamentary grant for the salaries of the chief officers of government. This in itself had caused the provincial executive headaches enough, but when the mother country intimated that she wished to terminate even this assistance and to make the province wholly responsible for the support of its civil government, Sir Peregrine Maitland and his advisers became gravely disturbed. John Beverley Robinson, who had been sent to England in 1822 to put forth Upper Canada's views respecting the project for uniting Upper and Lower Canada, undertook to explain to Wilmot-Horton, the Parliamentary Under-Secretary of State for the Colonies, how utterly unable the province was to assume this additional financial burden, what dire consequences would follow if the executive became completely dependent upon the provincial legislature for revenue, and how the Crown Reserves could be utilized to avert this evil fate.

Robinson took the view that the leasing system had been a great failure and that the only method of making the reserves contribute a substantial sum to the revenues of Upper Canada would be to sell them. He was averse to selling the Crown Reserves for less than 20s. an acre and he believed that in a few years this sum could be obtained. But Upper Canada's revenue problems could not wait for an upturn in the land market. Robinson therefore proposed to make a beginning by offering the Crown Reserves at a fixed minimum price of 20s. an acre and by crediting present lessees who became purchasers with the rent they had paid towards the purchase price, and future lessees who paid their rent regularly with half of it. When the entire two million acres of Crown Reserves should have been sold, the accumulated capital would yield an annual revenue of £80,000 which would provide not only for the expenses of civil government but for works of defence and internal improvements as well. Robinson thought that, with this relief in prospect, the Imperial Parliament probably could be persuaded to continue the annual grant until the provincial revenue should be equal to the burden.[48]

In 1823, after the plan for the union of the two Canadas had been temporarily dropped, Robinson's plan came in for serious discussion, An official of the Treasury thought it "too sanguine" respecting the prices at which the reserves would sell and concluded, "You will not, I am satisfied, by the sale of these lands be able to place the finances of the Colony upon any tolerable footing nor will the Colony be able to pay the Expense of their Civil Establishment . . . unless you can persuade the Legislature to impose some new taxes." [49]

With the exception of Powell, Robinson's colleagues on the Executive Council agreed that it was much more desirable to meet the revenue needs of the province by increasing the Territorial Revenues of the Crown than by appealing to the Assembly, but they did not entirely approve of his policy of disposing of the Crown Reserves. Strachan pointed out that the leasing system had failed in the past because free land in favourable locations was available. He argued that since this free land was rapidly disappearing, the system would be more productive in future. He was not very hopeful that the Crown Reserves would sell at 20s. an acre. "To fix upon this rate would be to lock up the reserves for a long time," argued Strachan, and he suggested instead a minimum price of 10s. Even at this price he thought the sale of the reserves would have to be assisted by restricting the free grants to the less favourable locations, and he favoured a continuation and combination of the leasing system with the proposed sales system.[50]

W. D. Powell's comments on Robinson's scheme show that the old notions of the Crown Reserves as a fund for rewarding the faithful servants of the Crown was still alive in Upper Canada. Robinson had stated that he did not know why these reserves had been set aside, but Powell, who had seen the inception of the system under Dorchester, believed that they had been intended "to support the splendour, liberality and munificence of the Crown without dependence on the people," that the Clergy Reserves were for the support of the Church, and that the province was to provide for the decent administration of government relieved of these other charges.[51] Powell seems to have had a poll tax, not a land tax, in mind, but Robinson thought such a tax would never be assented to by the legislature.[52]

Sir Peregrine Maitland gave his support to Robinson's plan for selling the reserves and suggested that it might even be applied to the Crown land in general. The experience of the United States, he thought, should dispel all fears that the adoption of such a land policy would check the flow of immigration into the province. In the past he had strongly advocated the retention of the reserves but this was only to prevent them from being frittered away in small grants to individuals. He was now of the opinion that it would be wise to safeguard the Crown property by converting it into cash and funding the proceeds. In that form it would be secure and no temptation to rebellion.

Maitland suggested that the reserves be classified and sold at minimum price to be established for each class. The Lieutenant-Governor admitted that the adoption of Robinson's plan would not provide an immediate or complete solution for Upper Canada's financial problems, but he thought that if the attention of British capitalists were drawn to the province, and if a sales office were opened in London, it would not be long before the interest on the fund accumulating from the sale of the reserves would make it possible to dispense with the financial assistance of the mother country.[53]

Meanwhile, proposals for the sale of the Crown Reserves were reaching the Colonial Office from a second source. Robert Gourlay's *Introduction* and his *Statistical Account of Upper Canada* were published in 1822. In them appeared his proposal that the Crown Reserves be sold to pay the war losses.[54] In July, 1822, Gourlay presented a petition to the House of Commons in which he suggested that both the Clergy Reserves and other public land in Canada should be sold under the management of a land board with headquarters in England.[55] In addition, although without money of his own or backing, he had been bombarding the Colonial Office with fantastic offers to buy one million acres of Crown land in Upper Canada at $1.00 an acre.[56] He proposed to settle the land with immigrants and to pay by instalments, receiving more land to settle as the process went on and as payments were made, somewhat as the Canada Company subsequently arranged to do.

A third source from which a proposal for the sale of the Crown Reserves reached the Colonial Office was John Galt. Galt had become an agent for the Canadian claimants for war losses and during 1822 had been discussing with the Treasury and the Colonial Office various schemes for the payment of these claims.[57] In December, 1823, he proposed to the Treasury that a commission be appointed to examine the state of the reserved lands with a view to selling them to meet the war claims as well as the civil expenses of the province. Subsequently, on February 17, 1824, he submitted to the Colonial Office a more specific plan for the sale of the Crown Reserves.[58]

By this time Robinson's plan for the sale of the reserves had been before the Colonial Office for a year and, when the founding of the Canada Company was announced, he believed that his plan was responsible for its creation. He states that during 1823 Galt was frequently in touch with the Colonial Office and that on some of these occasions he was shown by Wilmot-Horton Robinson's plan for the sale of the Crown Reserves. "Being a shrewd scheming man Mr. Galt immediately conceived the idea of getting up a Company and making a grand speculation of these Crown Reserves of which he knew as little as Mr. Horton did before I gave him my paper and that little I believe could not well have been less." [59] But the Treasury, Robinson's colleagues, and Lieutenant-Governor Maitland had all expressed the view that Robinson's plan would provide no immediate solution for the financial problems of Upper Canada. When Galt was asked whether it would be possible to form a company for the purchase of the reserves, he assured the Colonial Office that, on reasonable terms, the money would be forthcoming. The government then recommended the sale of the Crown Reserves to a company whose annual payments would immediately provide the necessary funds for the civil expenses of Upper Canada.[60] By the end of May, 1824, negotiations had progressed to the point at which a provisional committee for the new company was formed, and, by July 31, 1824, the Canada Company had been organized.[61] However, a long dispute over how much, if any, of the Clergy Reserves the Canada Company should also be permitted to buy delayed the issuance of its charter and the signing of its final contract with the government for another two years.

Gourlay, Galt, and Robinson were all entitled to a share of the credit for the formation of the Canada Company. Gourlay first gave publicity to the idea of selling the Crown Reserves, Robinson turned the thoughts of the Treasury and the Colonial Office in that direction, and Galt took up the idea and conducted the negotiations which resulted in the formation of the Company. But the terms of the contract and the charter pleased none of them. Galt objected because the funds were not to be devoted to the payment of the war losses, Robinson because the Crown Reserves were sold too cheaply, and Gourlay because he and his vague and grandiose schemes for the promotion of emigration were ignored.[62]

Lieutenant-Governor Maitland, who would have preferred Robinson's plan, was not pleased either. The interest on the funds from the sale of the lands would, he pointed out, have gradually diminished the Parliamentary vote and would have provided a permanent source of revenue, whereas the Canada Company's payments would end in fifteen years and then "the whole problem will have to be faced once more." The Lieutenant-Governor's final comment was, "There is in my mind something not very flattering to the respectability of the government in the circumstance of the Governor, Judges, and all the principal officers in such a province as this is, receiving their Salaries out of the Installments of a Joint Stock Company." [63] It is not surprising that the Canada Company, in the person of John Galt, the man who had done the most to organize it and had, indeed, hustled the Colonial Office along,[64] should have received a cool welcome from the government of Upper Canada. Thirty years later, commenting on the hasty and improvident sale to the Canada Company, John Beverley Robinson wrote:

What might have been done for the province by means of the Crown Reserves which could have been disposed of by Government by adding two or three clerks to one of the land Offices with little or no additional expense. We have now 380 townships in which the reserves would have amounted to more than three million acres if the system had been continued much of which would have sold by this time for 20/- an acre. What could not the government have done for the province with such a fund in promoting industries, public improvements, defences. But it has since been made evident enough that no system for procuring or dispensing such benefits through the agency of the government would ... have gone on long. The Assembly would have intervened and clutched all. Whether there is anything to regret in the turn which this and other things have taken no man can tell....[65]

The revenue problems of Upper Canada were solved at once by the annual payments which the Canada Company agreed to make during the period 1827 to 1842.[66] The Company's contract gave it the privilege of purchasing all the Crown Reserves not leased or applied for in the townships surveyed before March 1, 1824, at the rate of 3s. 6d. an acre. They amounted to 1,384,413 acres, and the Company exercised its option to the extent of 1,322,010 acres.[67] The leased Crown Reserves were granted to King's College as an endowment in 1827.[68] Townships surveyed after March 1, 1824, continued to be laid out according to the chequered plan; but their Crown Reserves were thrown open to sale like other government land when the sales system was adopted, although they were not thrown open to location as free grants.[69] The Imperial Clergy Reserve Act of 1840 repealed that part of the Constitutional Act which required Clergy Reserves to be set aside, the instructions sent the Governor of United Canada no longer required the making of Crown Reserves, and thus the chequered plan became unnecessary.[70]

The subsequent history of the Crown Reserves in the hands of the Canada Company shows that Robinson's estimate of their future value was too sanguine and that Strachan's belief that a price of 20s. an acre would "lock up the reserves for a long time" was correct. William Warren Baldwin put it more bluntly. The reserves, he said in reply to R. D. Hanson's queries for the Durham Commission, should have been sold or granted to individuals: "To shut them up in the Canada Company's hands had capped the pole of folly," a point of view amply justified by events.[71]

As a result of his visit to the office of the Holland Land Company,[72] Galt decided that expenditures for the improvement of the reserves should be confined to the blocks of reserves, of which the company had seventeen, comprising about 160,000 acres.[73] A down payment of one-fifth was required from purchasers, the balance being payable in five annual instalments at 6 per cent.[74] By April, 1829, about 50,000 acres of the reserves had been sold at an average price of 9s. 10d. an acre—land which three years earlier had been bought for 3s. 6d. on fifteen years' credit.[75] By 1835 the average price for the reserves had become 12s. 5d. and critics were contrasting unfavourably the Canada Company's high prices and credit policies with the low cash price policy which the Holland Land Company had come to adopt.[76]

About one-third of the Crown Reserves acquired by the Company had been disposed of before the Rebellion. Sales declined sharply during the period

1838-1842.[77] In the latter year, sales began to be supplemented by a leasing system under which the settler could lease land for ten years at a rent equal to the interest on the value of the land, with the option of purchasing at any time during the lease at a fixed advance upon the price at time of leasing.[78] By 1854 upwards of 531,000 acres were under lease, a large proportion of which had, by 1876, reverted to the Company.[79] By December 31, 1854, the Company still had about 400,000 acres of the Crown Reserves available, and it valued this property at roughly £300,000.[80] At this time its land was selling for 10s. to 25s. an acre in the Ottawa, Midland, Victoria and Colborne Districts, for 20s. to 50s. in the Western District, and for 20s. to 100s. in the London District.[81] On December 31, 1876, the Company had 200,000 acres of Crown Reserves, valued by this time at £291,611, almost as much as its 400,000 acres had been estimated at in 1854.[82]

This brief summary of the Canada Company's handling of the Crown Reserves which, with the exception of the blocks, it did practically nothing to develop, is itself enough to account for the hostility shown it by the legislature of Upper Canada and, after 1841, by that of United Canada. There were, in addition, other causes for Upper Canada's criticisms of the Canada Company; above all, the uses to which its payments were put by the British government whose penny-wise and pound-foolish policy had saddled the province with what Lord Sydenham is said to have called "a parcel of rapacious land jobbers." [83]

Patrick Shirreff, who in 1833 visited two of the Company's towns, condemned its policies. Settlers, he wrote, were tempted by the credit policy to purchase too much land, with the result that the interest on their debt was more than their farms would bear. Their uncleared land was too great a burden on what was cleared. At the time of Shirreff's visit to Goderich, Dunlop, the Company's agent, told him that all the original settlers except one had become so deeply in debt to it that they had left the district. Shirreff predicted that "The affairs of the Company are not likely to be soon wound up, as the lands of insolvent purchasers will, from time to time, return to its management, and the price of land will be raised beyond the demands of the population as well as let on lease. The political power of the Company will soon be felt and its minions thrust into the legislature.... The shareholders will ultimately occupy the position of absentee landlords and become the most avaricious of task masters." [84] The Company's affairs were not wound up until 1954. Whether it proved to be an avaricious taskmaster throughout the entire period only a detailed study of its operations can tell us.

The sale of the Crown Reserves to the Canada Company was followed up by the adoption of a sales policy for the rest of the Crown lands. When the new regulations went into effect on January 1, 1826, the lingering life of the old land-granting system was officially terminated. However, the change was more apparent than real. As has alrady been emphasized, he grants had been anything but free, and it was only in the newly surveyed townships that they could be obtained, all special locations having been closed in 1819 and made subject to public sale.[85] A special location was a term applied to "whatever land remains vacant and grantable in any townships which have been for some time settled." About 146,000 acres of land, including all vacant lots in the Midland, Gore,

Home, Niagara, and London Districts, were so classified.[86] The same rule applied to all broken lots, all town lots, and to certain other special locations. In addition to these restrictions, there were the Crown and Clergy Reserves, the School Reserves, the extensive area under the close control of Colonel Talbot, reserves for special purposes, and certain temporary restrictions on locations imposed from time to time. When these limitations, the chronic shortage of surveyed land, and the demands of the U.E. loyalists and militia men for locations are considered, it will be clear that after 1818 "free" government grants could be made within very narrow limits indeed.

Despite the attenuated condition to which the land-granting system had been reduced, its demise caused a commotion in Upper Canada. The Assembly of 1829 demanded to know why "so great a change was made by the Colonial Minister without addressing the Legislature of this Province," and down to the Rebellion there continued to be a group of dissatisfied members who agitated for a return to the old practice of making "free" grants of 100 acres to immigrants. In addition, this change of policy revived the Assembly's old demand for control of the Crown lands and the revenue derived from them.[87]

Colonel Talbot objected to the sales system being put into operation in any of the townships in which he was locating settlers because it did not ensure the improvement of the land and was not suited to poor settlers without capital. Accordingly, the sales system was not put into effect in areas under his control. But Talbot had little land left and his efforts to acquire additional townships failed. From an administrative point of view, the great weakness of his system was that it had caused expense without producing revenue. Talbot's settlers, once they had secured their settlement duty certificates from him, took their time about applying for their patents and he had neither the power nor the disposition to hurry them into paying their fees. When the Imperial government sent out an investigator, John Richards, to report on the land systems of the British North American provinces in 1830, he found that only 785 of Talbot's settlers had taken out their patents. If it was true, as Talbot claimed, that he had settled 6,000 families, then between £35,000 and £40,000 was due in fees from the others. This was a system that did not commend itself to extension, particularly at a time when Upper Canada's revenue problems were still pressing.[88]

It was, in effect, a despotically administered system which gave some of the benefits of the American pre-emption. It enabled settlers to get established on the land, provided they hit it off with Talbot and were willing to choose from the locations he offered, and it gave them a period of grace before they were called upon to pay for their land. The American system gave the right and the freedom to select a location on surveyed land before it was offered at auction. The government land sale, however, definitely ended their period of grace.

The new sales policy was based on the rules which had been worked out for New South Wales and Van Diemen's Land, modified, as Robinson had advised, to respect the rights of the U.E. loyalists and militia men.[89] The new regulations provided that after January 1, 1826, no more land was to be granted except to the U.E. loyalists, militia men, and military claimants entitled to grants under the existing regulations. Military claimants who were officers continued to be entitled to free grants until 1831 when they were allowed a remission on their purchases of Crown land. Before patent, they were required to prove that they had resided in the province for two years and that a resident settler had been established for two years upon some part of their land. Non-commissioned officers and discharged soldiers continued to be entitled to free grants on con- dition of residence and cultivation until 1834, when the privilege was limited to men discharged in the province. The Land Act of 1837 was to set January 1, 1843, as the terminal date for preferring claims under these regulations.[90]

Under the new sales system, land could be purchased from the Crown in quantities not less than 100 acres and not exceeding 1,000 acres. A ten per cent discount was to be allowed for cash. Payment might be extended over one year or five, but in the latter case legal interest would be charged. Settlers who had not the capital to buy land might obtain as much as 200 acres without purchasing, provided they would agree to reside on their land and improve it, and as much as 1,200 acres, if they could show that they had the capital to improve it. After seven years, a quit rent of 5 per cent of the value of the land at the time of the grant would become payable.[91]

No uniform sales price was established. Instead, valuations were made of the Crown land, based on soil, situation, and the price obtained for private land sold on several years' credit. The members of the legislature, the surveyors, the Grand Jurymen, the Magistrates in Quarter Sessions, and Colonel Talbot all were asked land values.[92] In June, 1826, the following prices were approved: in the Home District, townships south of Lake Simcoe were valued at 5s. and 6s. an acre, west of the lake at 5s., and north of it at 4s.; townships on the Trent waterway in the Newcastle District were valued at 5s., those in the rear of the Midland District at 4s. and 5s.; those on the Ottawa and Rideau Rivers at 5s.; the townships in the District of Bathurst, excluding those that formed part of the military settlement, and the marshy townships of the Western District were valued at 4s.; three townships in the London District were valued at 10s. and two or three in the Gore District at 7s. 6d.[93]

Peter Robinson, who had been in charge of the Irish immigration of 1823 and 1825, was appointed the first Commissioner of Crown Lands. His instructions, dated July 18, 1827, made two changes in the recently established sales system: the lots were to be offered at auction on the terms outlined above at an upset price sanctioned by the Lieutenant-Governor, and those who elected to take them on a quit rent of 5 per cent *per annum* of the price at which they were sold were to be required to pay rent from the outset and in advance. This privilege was to be restricted to purchasers of not more than 200 acres.[94]

The re-introduction of the quit rent system was the work of Wilmot-Horton, Parliamentary Under-Secretary of State for the Colonies, who regarded govern- ment assisted emigration of paupers as one means of improving the condition of the British poor. Under the new land regulations, indigent immigrants could no longer obtain free grants of land. Those with barely sufficient capital to tide them over the first year or two could not afford to purchase it. But the quit rent system offered such people a chance to establish themselves on the land without doing injustice to those in better circumstances who could afford to purchase it. "I am satisfied," wrote Wilmot-Horton to Strachan, "that we cannot begin too soon to adopt the quit rent system and to teach the people in those colonies not to be nervous at the sound of the name ... if we throw back the payment of that quit rent [to the Provincial Treasury] no sort of objection will exist to its imposition." [95] Others were less certain, including the Executive Council of Upper Canada.[96] In 1831, Goderich, perhaps with the previous unsatisfactory history of the quit rent system in all the North American colonies in mind, summarily abolished this method of granting land.[97]

The change from a free grant to a sales policy was not made at the request of the Canada Company. It was made because the old land-granting system had been condemned by those who had to administer it and because the Imperial government was anxious to develop all the sources of revenue which Upper Canada possessed. John Galt regarded the new land regulations as so prejudicial to the interests of the Canada Company as to make it questionable whether the Company should go on. What Galt objected to was government competition with private enterprise in the retail business of selling land. Had the Company been made the agent of the government in disposing of the Crown land, it would have been a more dignified arrangement, commented Galt, and one in harmony with the idea that the Company was to be the agency through which the land revenues of the province were to be developed and made available to the provincial government. Maitland met this complaint by pointing out that a policy of selling land at 4s. to 10s. an acre, instead of one of giving it away for a patent fee of £5 per 100 acres, could hardly be injurious to the Company: "All persons here, I believe, perceive very plainly another tendency in the new system." [98]

A second complaint of Galt's was that under the quit rent provisions of the new system any person could get 100 to 10,000 acres [99] of land on more favourable terms than those on which the Company had obtained its 2,200,000 acres. If the institution of the quit rent system was to be regarded as more important to the government than the payments promised by the Canada Company, said Galt, the directors should abandon the contract at once.[100] No doubt the wishes of the Canada Company had something to do with the decision of the Colonial Office first to narrow the benefits of the quit rent system and then to abolish it altogether.

Quite apart from the short-lived quit rent regulations, the new land system was ill devised. It did not satisfy many of the critics of the old land system and gave ground for many new criticisms. It did not produce the results that were expected from it and it failed to satisfy even the Colonial Office for long. It was, in a way, a sham. From January 1, 1826, to June 30, 1838, about 100,000 acres of Crown land were sold: in roughly the same period three times that quantity of land was granted to discharged soldiers and seamen alone.[101] In addition, of course, grants continued to be made to the U.E. loyalists and militia men and, as is obvious from Table II (see p. 139), more than ten times as much land was disposed of in this way as by sale. Above all, the new system was in marked contrast to the simple uniform plan of cash sales at a fixed price adopted in 1820 by the United States.

One of the worst features of the new system was that the exasperating delays and uncertainties of the old were not ended but continued to drive impatient immigrants over the border, where a more speedy and efficient land system was in operation.[102] There were no district agents to give information to bewildered immigrants, the business of valuing the lands went on very slowly, and the valuations, when announced, were regarded as much too high. Furthermore, a prospective purchaser could not be sure of getting the land he wanted since it lay with the Commissioner of Crown Lands to decide what land should be thrown on the market, and, even if the lot of his choice was put up for sale, he had still to wait for the auction to be held. At the sale he might be overbid by some speculator who next day would offer to resell the lot to him at $50 or $100 profit. Speculators frequently took land from immigrants in this fashion and, if unsuccessful in reselling it at once, simply ignored the "purchase" they had made, a practice made possible by the credit system and the fact that no deposit was required at the time of sale. Squatters also took advantage of this defect in the regulations. Real purchasers were overbid by squatters who never completed their purchases, in the expectation that by the time the next auction would be held those who had been interested in their lots would have departed.[103]

All these defects in the new land system were set forth by the legislature in an address to the Crown which asked for the appointment of district agents, the abolition of the auction sale system, and the establishment of fixed and more reasonable prices for the Crown land. In short, what the Assembly wanted, although it did not say so, was the American land system.[104] Oddly enough, the Reformers in the Assembly steadily voted against this address, paragraph by paragraph. An appeal to the Crown to direct the provincial executive to make changes, however desirable they might be, was not in their opinion the way to amend the land system of Upper Canada. They advocated a more forthright solution which would place the land once and for all under the control of the provincial legislature and regulate it by statute.[105]

Three years later, when their ranks had been strengthened by the election of 1834, the Reformers passed, 27-14, a strongly worded resolution in which they asserted the Assembly's claim not merely to determine the policies under which the natural resources of the province were to be administered but also to dispose of all the revenue derived from them. They swept away all distinctions between revenue raised by direct taxation and revenue raised from the sale of public property "which has been improved [in value] by the industry of the people in Peace and defended by their valor in ... War." For the Crown to take the increment in the value of the lands and to appropriate that revenue without the assent of the Assembly was, in effect, to tax and appropriate without consent, they argued. The Imperial government had long ago debarred itself from taxing its colonies by the Act 18 Geo. III, c. 22, and the Constitutional Act itself was clear evidence of the intention of the Crown to place the land revenues, except those derived from the Crown and Clergy Reserves, at the disposal of the province, "for it would have been needless for His Majesty to reserve to himself one-seventh had he intended to keep the whole," argued the Reformers ingeniously. As for the Canada Company, whose hated annual payments permitted the provincial executive to escape the financial control of the Assembly, its charter ought to be held invalid. The Company had been allowed to purchase, on improvident terms, land made valuable by the labour of the colony without the consent of the colonial legislature and in disregard of its rights. "The Charter and all the statutes connected with it," declared the Reformers, "are in violation of the 18th Geo. III, and the Constitutional Act." [106] It is obvious that no matter how well devised the land policies of the Colonial Office had been and no matter how well the provincial executive had administered them, the Reformers in the Assembly would not have been content. What they wanted was to take matters into their own hands and to devise a land policy based on the principle that the natural resources of the province were provincial, and not Imperial, capital.

CHAPTER THIRTEEN

DIFFICULTIES IN THE MIDDLE
OF THE ROAD

SIR JOHN COLBORNE and Lord Goderich, who jointly fell heirs to a land system devised by others, were far from satisfied with its working in Upper Canada, but unfortunately they could not agree on how it should be changed to promote the settlement of the province with British immigrants. For three years they debated the question back and forth to the accompaniment of a rising rumble of discontent in the Assembly. Colborne sympathized with the ideas of Wilmot-Horton but Goderich's views were close to those of the Wakefield school, whose adherents, like Gourlay, opposed the sale of land at low prices to poor men with litte capital but their labour. Wilmot-Horton proposed to allow parishes to raise funds to finance the emigration of able-bodied paupers and their families by mortgaging their poor rates, but neither Colborne as a colonial administrator, nor Wilmot-Horton as a humane reformer, was interested in the heartless business of "shovelling out" the surplus poor of the old land upon the new. The paupers, they thought, should be assisted not merely to emigrate but to settle in Canada. Neither of them was ready to assume that the demand for labourers would be sufficient to provide employment for these immigrants, and both favoured government assistance to them in the form of loans and government supervision in settling them on the land.

Prior to the establishment of the sales system, Wilmot-Horton's policies had been tried with inconclusive results. The Lanark and Irish experiments had, however, served to bring to light the decided hostility of a party in the Assembly to the introduction of pauper immigrants, one of its more outspoken members stating, with some justification, that the object of the Imperial government was to assist the provincial government in keeping down the older inhabitants.[1]

One reason for this hostility was that the management of pauper settlements gave the provincial executive too much political influence. It created for them something like the rotten boroughs of England. For example, money had been advanced to some of the settlers in the military settlements for the purchase of seed wheat and potatoes, advances which they were pledged to repay prior to receiving their patents. But, as Cockburn informed Dalhousie, "It having been found expedient for the interests of Government at the period of the Election in the Upper Province in 1820 that many of these Settlers should be legally empowered to vote, Deeds were accordingly issued unconditionally to Several Individuals of the Rideau Settlements while others ... remained excluded," and he suggested that the debt be forgiven all of them.[2]

Another method by which the provincial executive attempted to influence the elections was to allow those who held land merely on location tickets to vote.

If this practice had become established, the provincial government would always have had the power to sway the elections, a point to which Mackenzie drew attention in the *Colonial Advocate* of June 3, 1824. Voting on location tickets was allowed in the election of 1820 by the returning officer for the County of Durham, and this enabled him to declare George Strange Boulton elected over Samuel Street Wilmot. The location ticket-holders were new settlers in the township of Cavan, and the contest was as much between them and the "Yankie" settlers of the old lake shore townships as between the two candidates.[3] The upshot of the dispute was that the House of Assembly declared Wilmot elected and resolved, 25–10, "That location tickets confer no freehold and right to vote." [4]

The Attorney General, John Beverley Robinson, insisted that, because they were taxpayers and had an "equitable freehold," if not an actual one, the location ticket-holders were entitled to vote. The law officers of the Crown did not agree with Robinson. They met the equitable freehold argument by stating that where the holder of a location ticket had performed the conditions attached to it he would be entitled to vote, but not otherwise, because he would not be entitled to a patent and might never become entitled to one.[5] This was not the last of equitable freeholds. The topic was to come up again during the election of 1836.

The Assembly was eager to promote the settlement of the province, but not by pauper immigrants. Its favourite device—the encouragement of American settlers—was anathema to both Maitland and Colborne. The latter was convinced that the retention of Canada by the Crown depended upon the colonization of loyal British immigrants. "If we do not fill up the country our neighbours will," he wrote.[6] Colborne's attempts to "fill up the country with loyal British immigrants" only succeeded in incurring the hostility of the Assembly and the criticism of the Colonial Office. "The general opinion [is]," wrote Colborne, "that there is a faction in Upper Canada hostile to emigration, and endeavouring in conjunction with some of the leading political characters of the House of Assembly of the Lower Province, to check the tide of Emigration from the Mother Country to the Canadas." [7] Mackenzie, in his frank *Sketches of Canada and the United States,* declared that he was less interested in seeing the province filled up with immigrants from Great Britain, who did not understand the political issues at stake in Upper Canada and who could too easily be managed by the provincial government, than he was in obtaining "the blessings of self-government and freedom for those who now constitute the settled population." "Our objection to paupers," stated Mackenzie, "is that they are only fit to be slaves." Others who perhaps did not take the Reform position on all questions clearly resented the idea that a pauper population needed to be imported and maintained, at provincial expense, to confer British feeling on the province.[8]

Although the Imperial government did not continue to assist paupers to emigrate to Upper Canada after 1825, they continued to arrive with the help of private agencies or of their parishes. Sir John Colborne faced the difficult task of caring for an increasing number of such immigrants, who were now required to pay for their land and for whom financial assistance was not readily forthcoming either from Imperial or provincial sources. He sympathized with the immigrants' efforts to establish themselves as landowners as soon as possible, recognizing that this was the ardent hope that had led many of them to emigrate and, moreover, that this was the only practical solution for men with families.[9] Only the head of the family could as a rule hope for employment but on the land the services of the whole family could be utilized.

The Lieutenant-Governor did not propose to abolish the sales system but he did wish to lend the settler a hand in his struggle with the wilderness. Colborne had little confidence in the schemes of township promoters who financed the emigration of "followers" from Great Britain. The promoters were promised land for themselves in proportion to the number of persons they settled. Generally ill feeling resulted.[10] Moreover, the large grants made to them remained largely unimproved and were as great an inconvenience as the reserves.

What the government should do, argued Colborne, was to undertake the role of township promoter itself and "plant men in the room of trees." It should settle groups of immigrants in one township at a time, open roads, build temporary log huts, find employment for the immigrants, and issue them provisions for a time. After the Clergy Reserves had been set aside, half the remaining land in the township should be sold to poor immigrants on the instalment plan and the provincial government should be authorized to assist them with an amount equal to the instalment payments on their land. Once they were established in a township, the reserved alternate lots could be sold to settlers with capital at double the original price.[11] Colborne used an argument in support of this scheme very similar to that put forth by the advocates of federal land grants to American railroads: the alternate sections could be sold for the double minimum and thus the government would lose nothing. The catch in a scheme of this sort was that all depended on an equal quantity of government land being sold. Colborne was most indignant when he later discovered that the Surveyor General's Department had permitted U.E. loyalists and militia claims to be located in townships improved at government expense.[12] Without asking for the approval of the Colonial Office, Colborne began to try out his ideas in the township of Ops, but when the Colonial Secretary, Sir George Murray, voiced his disapproval, he discontinued the experiment. At the time, Murray expected that the Canada Company would be unable to fulfil its contract and that the various expenses which its payments had enabled the government to meet would fall on the Casual and Territorial Revenue. The large sums which Colborne required for subsidizing the pauper immigrants could not therefore be taken from this revenue, as had been planned. This financial uncertainty lasted only a few months, however.[13]

In 1830 a special investigator, John Richards, was sent out by Murray to report on the land system and to see whether some uniform and economical plan could be adopted for all the British North American colonies.[14] His report [15] might well have been written by Robert Gourlay or E. G. Wakefield but it was not out of sympathy with what Colborne had been trying to do in Ops. All four men thought that the Crown lands could provide the revenue for their own development, but whereas Gourlay, Wakefield, and Colborne proposed administration of the lands and settlement of the immigrants under government auspices, Richards favoured private associations of capitalists. He showed tenderness, to say the least, towards the Canada Company. He thought it would be desirable if large tracts of Crown land adjoining the Company's land could be sold to capitalists "who might act in union with them," and he pointed out that if government land in the vicinity should be sold at an average rate of 5s. per acre, it would injure the Company. On the other hand, if the government should sell at the Company's rates it would become unpopular. Two groups of promoters tried to obtain large tracts north of the Company's lands for colonization but their schemes did not meet with the approval of either Colborne or the Colonial Office.[16]

By the time Richards' report was presented, Lord Goderich had succeeded Murray as Colonial Secretary. He whole-heartedly agreed with his predecessors that in Upper Canada the abolition of the land-granting system was a reform long overdue. No more complete indictment of that system exists than his dispatch to Colborne of November 21, 1831.[17] His conclusion was that whatever disadvantages the sales system possessed, it could not entail as great evils as the land-granting system. "The example of the United States has shown that without any of the complicated regulations by which it has been attempted to guard against the misapplication of Land acquired gratuitously, . . . we may safely trust to the interest of purchasers as a sufficient Security that Land which has been paid for will be turned to good account," wrote Goderich, little realizing how the history of land speculation in the United States, under both the credit and the cash sale system, belied his words. Complete impartiality, he believed, could only be achieved by disposing of the land at public auction. For this reason he directed that the practice of making private sales at the upset price to recent immigrants should cease. He disliked, too, the sale of land on credit and in 1831 reduced the time allowed for the payment of instalments from five years to two.[18]

Goderich did not adopt policies altogether in harmony with Richards' report, but he did act on Richards' rather broad hint that it would be to the advantage of the Canada Company if the price of land were raised. He justified his action, no doubt sincerely, by Wakefieldian reasoning. To make the settler pay for his land did indeed deprive him of capital which he needed for the development of his farm, but the Colonial Secretary was convinced, from the number of emigrants flocking to the United States, that it was the lure of high wages and the general prosperity of a country which attracted settlers, not the promise of free land. If the land revenue could be made really productive, good roads and schools could be provided for the settlers at provincial expense instead of by inefficient statute labour and grudging local contributions. Under such a system, settlers would gain rather than lose by paying for their land. The average valuation that the Executive Council had placed on the Crown land was 5s. an acre, and Goderich was for a time content that this should be the upset price; but in 1833 he ruled that in future 10s. an acre should be the minimum price for Crown land and two years the maximum period of credit. After the receipt of this order the upset prices set by the Commissioner of Crown Lands ranged from 10s. to 20s. an acre.[19]

Goderich's ideas as to how poor immigrants should be treated, if not obtained from Richards' report, were in accord with it. The report was an able one that showed a grasp of both the economic and the social realities of backwoods farming. The gist of the matter was that, no matter whether land was cheap or even free, the capital costs of farm-making, even at this early date and in wooded country, were more than poor immigrants could provide. Without capital, a settler could not bring his land under cultivation unless he understood "wilderness farming" or how to exchange labour for labour, like the American settlers who "work their dealings without the interchange of money." [20] The best thing for an immigrant to do, said Richards, was to hire himself out for a year or two, learn the "rough farming business" and save. He concluded with a paragraph which Frederick Jackson Turner would have enjoyed but which no British Colonial Secretary could read without uneasiness.

But when we view a country to be redeemed from the wilderness to a state of agriculture lot by lot, without an original investment, or improved education or in fact controlling minds or superior classes to direct, lead or concentrate public feeling, it is to be feared that such a mode of procedure would be in hostility to the best interests of our institutions.... But with the Americans such a retail occupation of the wilderness is by no means objectionable.[21]

Fundamental to Goderich's colonial policy was his belief that in the colonies the political and social system of the mother country should be reproduced. He wrote:

Without some division of labour, without a class of persons willing to work for Wages, how can society be prevented from falling into a state of almost primitive rudeness, and how are the comforts and refinements of civilized life to be preserved?

These persons [indigent emigrants] at home have, almost invariably, been accustomed to earn their subsistence as Labourers, nor is there any reason why, upon arriving in the Colony, they should at once be raised to the situation of landholders: it is sufficient advantage to them to have the certainty of finding employment at wages infinitely higher than they had been accustomed to & of being able to acquire Land at a cheap rate out of the savings of their industry.

Indigent Emigrants should never, except as a measure of the last necessity, be settled on lands allowed them on more favorable terms than to any other class.... tempting into the class of Landowners those who would naturally remain labourers, appears to me a course opposed to the clearest interests of the Colony.... The only event in which I could sanction an exception in favor of indigent Emigrants, would be the case of there being no other possible means of providing for their subsistence than by their Settlement on land.[22]

Sir John Colborne continued to argue with Goderich that private employment would not absorb the indigent immigrants, that government would have to find work for them clearing land, that the rate of wages would not drop in the Canadas while it remained high in the United States, and that the supply of labour would not become more abundant while the existing disproportion between population and unsettled land continued.[23] He was convinced that the best way of correcting past errors was to condense the population by opening up new townships one at a time, directing poor immigrants to them, and settling them with government assistance.[24] Colborne had no fear that those who became the debtors of the Crown would make common cause with the political malcontents of the province. He thought they would soon appreciate their improved condition, and the events of 1837 were to prove him right.[25]

In 1831 Colborne tried a method of assisting poor immigrants which differed from that which he had begun to use in Ops. As before, they were to be sold land on credit, three years' credit this time instead of five, and at 5s. an acre instead of 4s. Those who could not afford the down payment of one-fourth were to be given an additional three years' credit before it was required. Those who could not provision themselves were to be advanced £3 for every acre they cleared up to four, the loan to be repaid with interest in five years' time.[26] This scheme, put into effect for the benefit of families from Wiltshire and Yorkshire, who had been sent to Oro, Douro, and Dummer townships, proved unacceptable to the Colonial Secretary. As he reminded Colborne, assistance schemes had not worked well in the past, and large sums were still due the Treasury from earlier groups of immigrants. Goderich directed that in future immigrants who needed assistance should be employed opening roads or in clearing land and building log houses when no other employment could be found for them. He grudgingly conceded that some of them, as a reward for good conduct, might be allowed to purchase land on credit.[27]

Sir John Colborne made full use of these limited powers in promoting the settlement of the province. In 1832, land in the townships of Ross, Pembroke, Westmeath, Medonte, Orillia, Oro, and Sunnidale was offered at 5s. an acre on six years' credit to such poor immigrants as could provide themselves with tools and provisions. Log houses were built for them and some assistance in opening roads was given. Destitute immigrants who did not find private employment were put to work on roads, particularly a new road from the township of Caradoc, through Adelaide and Warwick, to Lake Huron. About £31,000 was expended in these ways during 1832, a year in which the outbreak of cholera increased the sums that had to be spent on immigrants.[28]

When Colborne found that making roads with the labour of inexperienced immigrants was inefficient and costly, he proposed to put them to work on five-acre allotments making small clearings, building shanties, and planting crops, as the Colonial Secretary himself had suggested, until the townships which they were engaged in opening up had attracted sufficient settlers of the "better" sort to provide them with continuous private employment. Colborne believed that the cost of this programme could subsequently be recovered by the sale of the crops and of the land when it was put up for auction at an enhanced minimum valuation. In this way, a sort of revolving fund could be created which would enable the government to care for successive waves of indigent immigrants for whom private employment was not to be found. The Colonial Secretary, whose principal point was that relief should be given by employment, not by gratuitous grants of land or supplies, but who had been disturbed by the cost of Colborne's programme of 1832, sanctioned the experiment, which was already under way in the townships of Sunnidale and Nottawasaga.[29]

Colborne's plan, nicely figured out on paper, did not work smoothly in practice and involved him in a dispute with the Assembly which shortened his days in Upper Canada. In 1834 Samuel Lount, one of the leaders of the Reform party, brought up in the Assembly a petition from one of the Nottawasaga settlers complaining of the conduct of the government's settling agents and asking for an inquiry. The report of the select committee, to which the petition was referred, asserted that the whole settling project had been badly managed. The immigrants had received inadequate food of poor quality, yet £2,000 had been expended in settling 33 families of 144 persons, some of whom had already left the country. The committee ended by requesting the dismissal of the two agents of whom the settlers had complained, A. B. Hawke and H. Young. The whole quarrel was publicized in the Assembly's *Journals* and no doubt added to the growing conviction of the Whig government that Colborne was an incompetent and extravagant Administrator who was becoming a political liability.[30]

In the next session, the Assembly resumed its attack on the land policies of the executive. This was the session in which Mackenzie obtained the appointment of a select committee on grievances. Among the leading questions put to the witnesses were four which related to land. The responses elicited, except from such witnesses as Archdeacon Strachan, W. P. Markland, and Peter Robinson, accorded with the views of the Reformers. The witnesses agreed that the increased value of the Crown lands had been created by the resident settlers of the province, that the sale and disposal of the public lands, including natural resources of all descriptions, ought to be regulated by provincial statute, and that the land revenues of the province ought to be available for paying the claims for war losses.[31] The report itself, the "Seventh Report on Grievances," although printed and widely distributed, was not adopted until the next session of the legislature.

Sir John Colborne's comments on the report show that his views on land policy were widely at variance with those of the Reformers, who had won control of the Assembly in the elections of 1834. It was not so much a matter of details as of principles. Colborne ignored the Assembly's argument that whatever was paid to the clergy or to public officials, whether out of the Canada Company's payments, out of the Crown lands revenues, or out of income from fees, was really paid by the people, and he called those sums appropriated by the provincial parliament "the entire amount raised by the people." [32] The right of the Imperial government to control the land policies of the province as well as to dispose of its land revenues was to his mind beyond question. As he saw it, the mother country was not interested in raising a revenue from Upper Canada for her own benefit but she was interested in planting British immigrants there and in strengthening the political and commercial ties between the colony and herself. He hoped that all arrangements for disposing of the Crown lands in Upper Canada "would have in view chiefly the actual conditions in the Mother Country and the errors which were committed in first occupying and dividing the province.[33] But the Assembly was not interested in helping Colborne to remedy past errors by enforcing settlement duties on U.E. loyalist grants nor in colonizing the country with pauper immigrants from Great Britain, unless they could be taught to look to the legislature, and not to the executive, as the source of power. This was really what Lount had attempted to do in championing the Nottawasaga petition. The Assembly's catalogue of grievances, as outlined in the "Seventh Report," accused the Lieutenant-Governor of failing to show proper respect for the people's representatives, and his own comment reveals that he and the Assembly were far apart.

Colborne did not wish, however, to colonize Upper Canada with supposedly obedient pauper immigrants alone; he wanted to establish a respectable yeomanry and a class of gentlemen as well. He would have agreed with John Galt that "In Upper Canada the source of dissatisfaction lies in having given an English constitution without the materials necessary to work it ... Upper Canada ... wants a class of inhabitants whose circumstances and education would ... place them independent of the government and enable them to act as a check both on the popular and the official faction." "I hope," wrote Colborne in 1829, "that the House of Assembly will never again be constituted as it now is." [34]

In Colborne's day there were two political parties in Upper Canada. On the one hand, there were the Reformers who wanted to remodel the institutions and policies of the province along more democratic—and more American—lines, and who demanded equal treatment for all religious denominations. Above all, this party wished to shake off, if not the Imperial connection, at least the Imperial controls, which, in their opinion, had operated to the disadvantage of the common man. On the other hand, there were those who believed that safeguarding the Imperial connection and preserving British institutions in Upper Canada required the maintenance of the privileged position of the Church of England, the fostering of an upper class in colonial society, the establishment of a high degree of executive influence and executive freedom in the matter of appointments and disbursements, and suppression of all criticism of the *status quo*.

At the commencement of Sir John Colborne's term of government, Archibald McDonald warned him that the Reformers had so far been patient, waiting the opportunity to amend what they disliked. Their restraint, however, had only made Maitland's administration more obstinate and had given it the appearance of more support than it had. As McDonald wrote to Colborne:

Indeed the gradation with which matters declined from a state of confidence and courtesy to a state of mutual suspicion and recrimination is unaccountable on any rational grounds ... if mutual disgust proceeded for the next 10 years or even less at the same rate of increase as the last, allegiance would depend on a calculation of strength & owe itself to the maxims of prudence not the affection of British subjects.[35]

Nine years later, almost to the day on which this letter was written, the rebels marched on Toronto.

During his eight years as Lieutenant-Governor, Colborne tried to steer a middle course between the two parties, while at the same time attempting to bring into existence as rapidly as possible a third force composed of recent British immigrants upon whose loyalty he thought the Crown could safely rely.[36] He met the usual fate of those who walk in the middle of the road: he was assailed from both sides. The trouble was that before he arrived in Upper Canada, "the seeds of distrust," to use Mackenzie's phrase, had been sown.[37] During the years 1830-34, there was a marked increase in the number of British immigrants arriving in Canada via the St. Lawrence and the United States, but the political results seem to have been a disappointment to Colborne. After the elections of 1834, he explained to the Colonial Office that "of course" the newcomers, who had become landed proprietors and independent, were "inclined" to democratic elective institutions. William Allan, one of the commissioners of the Canada Company, put it more wrathfully: immigrants, he said, "may soon be corrupted & then they are the vilest of all the democrats." [38]

Early in his administration Sir John Colborne gave offence to the right-wing element in Upper Canada by his failure to put himself into the hands of Maitland's advisers from the start and by his coldness towards Strachan's young men, "merely because they are Strachan's. If they joined in denouncing his government," wrote his Solicitor General, "he would see that he had no supporters." [39] Colborne's first speech to the legislature, in which he advocated the repeal of the Alien Act, caused Robert Stanton to write, "A loyal Yankee is the first Commoner in this loyal British Province." [40] This Act was the one under which Gourlay had been expelled and which Gore had originally intended to use to put undesirable Americans over the border.[41] Colborne's nominations to the Legislative Council, his foundation of Upper Canada College, his permitting Mackenzie to take the oath required of members of the legislature after he had been four times expelled by the Assembly, and his conciliatory attitude towards the Assembly caused him to be regarded by the conservatives as a popularity seeker easily terrified at the first sign of popular dissatisfaction.[42]

Colborne's remodelled Legislative Council accepted the Parish Officers Act, of which Macaulay wrote that it would lay "the foundations of evil ... broad and deep. That Act will be the great schoolmaster to educate our population in the principles and practices of democracy. I can not endure the idea of elective dispensers of justice in each township. It is essentially opposed to the old English constitutional principle that the King is the Fountain of Justice.... It is the soil in which will be planted and nurtured the tree of republicanism...." [43]

Strachan accused Colborne of failing to consult his council, of being deaf to private remonstrance, and of being subject to no more check than the Emperor of Morocco.[44] "Sir John Colborne," wrote Strachan, "... has done more to destroy everything British in the Colony than all its enemies & these praises [referring to the conventional language of an address] may detain him longer among us than might otherwise be the case ... a deputation of one or two Resolute men should be sent home with these addresses—authorized to tell the Ministry that if they continue to attend to such persons as Ryerson and Mackenzie & to break down the Constitution the Conservative party will turn round upon them & first trample on the necks of those miscreants and then govern ourselves." [45] If sentiments like these had been expressed by Mackenzie, Strachan would have been the first to cry, "Treason!"

Some inkling of the dissatisfaction of the conservatives with Sir John Colborne must have reached the Colonial Office through Strachan. In 1835 it became plain that Colborne had not the support of the Reformers either. As will be seen, he was also to arouse the wrath of the Methodists and Presbyterians by his handling of the Clergy Reserves question, and he had proved a persistent and troublesome subordinate to the Colonial Office. He had to go, not because he had become more conservative, as Miss Dunham suggests,[46] but because he had no politically articulate support.[47] By this time, too, the home government had decided to give the colonial horse a slacker rein, and obviously Sir John Colborne could no longer be left in the saddle. In October, 1835, he was informed that his defence of his administration was not acceptable and that he would shortly be replaced.[48]

Politics and personalities aside, what can be said of Colborne's policies, particularly his colonization programme? As a piece of Imperial statesmanship it may be defended; as local administration it must be condemned. The testimony of the government agent, A. B. Hawke, before a select committee of the Assembly, was very damaging. Hawke admitted that there was no prospect of obtaining returns which would justify further expenditures from the lands which the immigrants had cleared or from the crops which they had planted. He testified that about £700 had been spent on the immigrants for transportation, medical care, shelter, and seed, for which they had made no return in labour.[49] He also later acknowledged to Lord Sydenham that the business of locating immigrants in remote townships was more expensive than locating them near towns, as the government had to find employment for them on roads. Opening roads increased the value of land, admitted Hawke, but they should only be undertaken at government expense where a large proportion of land in a township still belonged to the Crown, and this had not always been the case.

In answer to the complaint that money spent colonizing indigent immigrants was money wasted, Hawke testified that it was true that such immigrants, settled with government assistance, showed a constant tendency to drift off to the United States unless there was something, such as a grant of free land, to tie them to the country.[50] Sir George Arthur subsequently came to the same conclusion and urged that free grants of 50 acres should be made to immigrants.[51] The temporary use of five-acre plots, which was all Colborne could offer them after 1833, was not enough. The Sunnidale settlers complained of the size of these allotments and, after Colborne had left the country, demanded of the Executive Council—in vain—free patents for them, asserting that they had not understood that all they had been granted was a right of occupancy and a right to the value of their improvements until the land found purchasers.[52] To compete with the United States, Canada needed to offer high wages, ample employment, and free land. As for Colborne's earlier policy of allowing six years' credit to poor immigrants unable to pay cash for land but able to begin improving it with their own resources, Hawke acknowledged that he did not know of a single instance in which such persons had paid anything on account of principal or interest. The upshot of the matter was, as the hard-headed Charles Poulett Thomson later emphasized, that once free land was no longer available, what Canada needed was not a grandiose scheme for transferring the indigent population of the mother country to the colony but men of capital and a programme of public works to absorb such immigrants as voluntarily found their way there.[53]

CHAPTER FOURTEEN

THE LAND ACT OF 1837

COLBORNE'S SUCCESSOR, Francis Bond Head, arrived in Upper Canada on January 23, 1836, a few days after the opening of the session of the legislature. The new Lieutenant-Governor read the Assembly his instructions which constituted the government's answer to the "Seventh Report on Grievances." The new Colonial Secretary, Charles Grant, Baron Glenelg, considered that Goderich's instructions concerning the Crown lands, and particularly his dispatch of November 8, 1832, had in part removed the grievances complained of. Grants of land had been forbidden, an impartial system of sales by auction had been instituted, and full compliance with the requests of the Assembly for information about the collection and expenditure of the Casual and Territorial Revenue of the Crown had been ordered. Goderich had certainly remedied some of the land grievances voiced in the past, but the "Seventh Report" had raised the more fundamental problems of the right of the Assembly to dispose of the Territorial Revenues of the province and to regulate its land policies by law. These were questions which Glenelg's reply did not discuss.[1] Once again the Assembly discussed the land-granting system and referred the topic to a committee which prepared an address on the subject,[2] but before it could be adopted, the legislature was prorogued.

Lieutenant-Governor Head seems very early in the day to have come to the conclusion that the issue in Upper Canada was republicanism *versus* monarchy and that the republican party, as he chose to style the Reformers, was determined to "possess themselves of the government of the province for the sake of lucre and emolument."[3] So far as the land system was concerned, he believed that the policies of the Reformers were designed to further the interests of the land speculators in the province and would result in complete disregard of the interests of poor immigrants from the mother country. He was determined to thwart them, despite the fact that members who were not Reformers had joined in criticizing the Land Department. Head was to discover that even an Assembly from which the so-called republicans had been excluded would want the very policies of which he disapproved.

Head opened a vigorous offensive by dissolving the provincial Parliament and by using all the influence at his disposal to secure the election of "loyal" members. "It was stated, but I believe without any sufficient foundation," wrote Lord Durham, "that the Government made grants of land to persons who had no title to them, in order to secure their votes. This report originated in the fact that patents for persons who were entitled to grants, but had not taken them out, were sent down to the polling places to be given to individuals entitled to them, if they were disposed to vote for the Government candidate."[4]

Two of the constituencies in which the government was accused of manu-
facturing votes were Simcoe, where Samuel Lount, subsequently hanged for his
share in the Rebellion, was a candidate, and the second riding of York, where
Mackenzie was a candidate. A committee of the Assembly which investigated
the election reported that, of the 1,478 patents issued by Head, only 233 were
on orders-in-council issued during his administration, and that only 150 of these
patents had issued in the period between the end of the session and the elections.
The report acknowledged that Provincial Secretary Jarvis had sent 303 patents
to the County of Simcoe, but "on his own initiative" because, as he had testified,
his office was "daily thronged with persons from a distance" asking about the
state of their patents. It was also asserted that only 18 of the patents delivered
had been voted upon.[5]

There are definite holes and suspicious weak spots in this defence. If Jarvis'
office had really been "daily thronged" by people clamouring for their patents,
one wonders why there was such apathy at the election. It is highly probable
that he did not act on his own initiative. At a meeting of the Council, at which
William Allen, Augustus Baldwin, and John Elmsley were present, it was decided
that Wellesley Richey should make a report on the names of persons in Simcoe
who were entitled to patents, particularly in the townships of Medonte, Oro,
and Orillia, where half-pay officers, discharged soldiers, and pensioners had
been settled.[6] It is hard to believe that no use was made of Richey's report in a
county that had in the past elected a Reformer like Samuel Lount.

The township of Adelaide in the county of Middlesex was another area in
which commuted pensioners and old soldiers had been settled. In addition to
settlement duties, these settlers were required to put in three years' residence
on their grants before they could get their patents. J. H. Askin, however,
pointed out to Head's secretary, John Joseph, that their votes "would be of
infinite consequence in the present struggle" and that he understood that most
of them had performed their settlement duties and "only wait for the time to
elapse which is required of them."[7] Lord Durham, in stating that patents were
issued on the eve of the election to persons "who were entitled to grants but
had not taken them out," overlooked the possibility that patents may have been
issued to persons not entitled to them *at the time they received them.* There is
more than a hint in the records that this is what happened.

Clearer evidence comes from the Council records of April 28, 1836. On this
occasion the Council considered a suggestion, emanating from Head, that patents
be issued on location tickets to those settlers who had not yet paid the whole
purchase money or complied with the existing regulations. The justification
advanced for Head's suggestion was that such settlers had an equitable interest
in their land beyond the property qualification for the franchise required by law.
"Would it not be expedient," the Council was asked, "to let them have their
patents so as to enable them to vote—the title to be void if the purchase money
not be paid up or the regulations not fulfilled?"[8] The Council unanimously
approved this corrupt scheme as "most beneficial to the province" and referred
to the law officers of the Crown for a method by which it could be carried out.

It is impossible to say to what extent Head's scheme was put into effect, but
certainly the fact that it was planned was known in the province at the time

and was approved by those who saw in it "the means of returning to the House of Assembly a very different class of men to the present. . . ." [9] Mackenzie asserted that 51 patents distributed in the township of Brock were "got out in such haste that they were without any proper designation of chains or boundaries." [10] Charles Duncombe accused the Land Department of having issued patents for the whole of a lot when only a part had been paid for, and of issuing patents for parts of lots without describing the parts when only a portion of the purchase money had been paid but when the original intention had been to buy the whole lot.[11] There is *something* that needs explaining. Why should blank descriptions have issued from the Surveyor General's office in 1836, descriptions which, J. B. Spragge testified, would have to be recalled to have the metes and bounds filled up? [12]

The most telling argument advanced by the Tories was the fact that the Reformers had been defeated in seventeen other contests in addition to Simcoe and the second riding of York. The Tories contended that in view of the fact that their margin of victory was 100 votes on the average, it could not be pretended that they owed their success in all these contests to Head's misuse of the Land Department. This argument is not conclusive. There were other devices than the making of freeholders available to the executive. William Kirby suggested that returning officers at the polls be required to demand of all voters born in the United States whether they had met the qualifications of the Naturalization Act [13] by taking the oath of allegiance within the province. Attorney General Jameson, commenting on this "loyal" suggestion, doubted the propriety of Head's issuing such a circular of instructions, but remarked it was the right of every candidate to insist on proof that the oath had been taken within the province by such would-be voters, "an essential which will puzzle a vast number of the worst characters in the province to prove." [14] Mackenzie charged that such a circular of instructions had been issued and that, at the Oxford and Middlesex elections, persons who had voted in half a dozen previous elections were barred from the polls as aliens, even when they had offered to take the oath of allegiance on the spot. Their votes were excluded, he declared, on the ground that they had not brought with them a certificate of having taken the oath within the province.[15] William Warren Baldwin made the same charge.[16] In other constituencies, according to Mackenzie, the Reform candidates abandoned the contest either because their supporters were intimidated by violence or because they knew that patents were ready to be issued to qualify voters for the government party if needed.[17]

A number of prominent Reformers were defeated in the elections: Bidwell, Perry, Lount, and Mackenzie himself, as well as less important men, so that in the new Assembly Head's supporters had a majority of 26. Mackenzie's surprise and bitterness at his defeat are well known. He was "frantic with choler" [18] and, from an active, lively and genial person, characteristics which even his enemies conceded,[19] he became bitter, moody, and excitable. It is not surprising that the leading Reformers, believing that the election had been stolen from them by the Lieutenant-Governor's corrupt use of the Land Department, took the steps during the next eighteen months that led to the Rebellion. What trust could be placed in constitutional opposition? What was there to prevent the

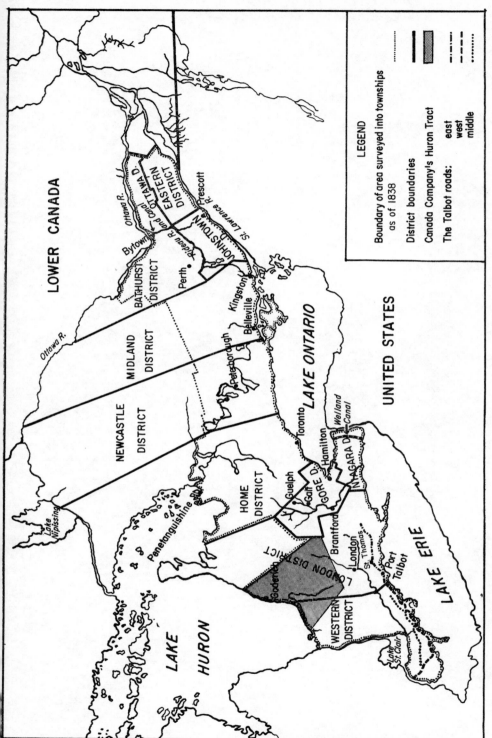

MAP II. Upper Canada in 1838. Based on James Wyld's map published by him in London in 1838.

Tories winning another victory by the use of corrupt practices in the land-granting department? Indeed, they soon showed their hand.

Shortly after the new legislature met, R. G. Dunlop, member for Huron, introduced a bill "to amend the representation of the people and give property its due weight." [20] This measure provided that those who held land on location tickets from the government, from the Canada Company, or on twenty-year lease from either source should be entitled to the franchise if, at the time of voting, they had five acres cleared. The bill also raised the property qualification for eligibility to the Assembly and gave representation to all towns with a population of 1,000. "Dunlop and the Canada Company have given birth to this monster," commented Mackenzie.[21] William Warren Baldwin was sufficiently disturbed by the rumour that such a bill would be introduced that he protested to Glenelg in advance. If the Tory party actually should dare to use location tickets as the basis for the franchise, predicted Baldwin, "it will hasten on rapidly the conviction of the people that they must separate from England." The use of location tickets would mean that the representatives in the Assembly would be the representatives of the tenants-at-will of the Crown, not of the freeholders, and, added Baldwin, "You know the people will not long bear this."[22] Dunlop's measure passed its second reading 47–8 but was not carried further. Later in the session the Tories consolidated their victory by a different means. They extended the life expectancy of the Assembly by an act which provided that the legislature should not be dissolved on the death of William IV, an event which was imminent.

The victory of Head and his supporters in 1836 is not to be explained wholly by their use of corrupt practices. The tactics of the British Constitutional Society and of the Lieutenant-Governor, who made loyalty to the mother country and her institutions the chief issue, Bidwell's unwise action in laying before the Assembly Papineau's letter which lauded republican institutions,[23] and the resentment aroused by the Assembly's failure to vote supplies would probably have given the government party additional seats, if not a majority.[24]

Flushed with confidence as a result of his victory at the polls, the Lieutenant-Governor tried to obtain from the Colonial Secretary a free hand in administering the land policy of the province. He wanted to be able to show "by facts instead of by arguments that a triumph of Constitutional over Republican principles in a British Colony is productive of good to the country." [25] His object, he explained, was to check speculators who, by keeping up the price of land, drove immigrants from the country. Such a broad grant of powers, had Head received it, would have covered his extraordinary conduct prior to the elections. Glenelg, while approving Head's motives, declined to grant his request. The land business of the province, he replied, must be managed on settled principles in all parts of British North America. These principles were: no more free grants; sales at public auction; surrender of the net proceeds of the Casual and Territorial Revenue of the Crown to the provincial legislature, provided permanent provision for the support of the civil government was established by law; participation of the provincial legislature in the formulation of rules for administering the Land Department. To these principles, the government was already committed.[26]

In fact, Glenelg had carefully seen to it that the government was publicly committed on the two last controversial issues by directing the Governor of New Brunswick to make public certain dispatches which contained these concessions. He had further authorized him to assent to acts relating to the Crown lands provided they did not go into effect for four months so as to allow time for them to be considered by the Imperial Parliament and disallowed if necessary. Glenelg arranged that the legislature of New Brunswick should meet some weeks before the legislature of Upper Canada and that the latter in turn should precede the meeting of the legislature of Lower Canada. He directed that his views should receive "general publicity" and that they "should be fully and clearly developed to the legislative bodies of New Brunswick, and through them, to the legislatures of the other British North American provinces." [27]

The Colonial Secretary hoped for a settlement on what he called "Constitutional Principles." [28] What he feared was that Head and the victorious Tories of Upper Canada would go to extremes.[29] By publicly committing the government in his New Brunswick dispatches, he hoped to steer them away from reactionary and unwise policies. He had begun to feel uneasy about Head's policies and warned him that "The principle that the land granting system is to be made the subject of local legislation is beyond the reach of debate." [30] In addition to asking for a free hand in land matters,[31] Head had begun to talk about introducing "Acts of a stern and decisive Nature." He had also objected to the policy of surrendering the Casual and Territorial Revenue to the legislature. He asked to be permitted to tell the Assembly that the conduct of the late House had caused the intended concession to be withdrawn, and he proposed that the question of whether the Assembly or the Lieutenant-Governor should dispose of these revenues be reconsidered.[32] In this instance also Glenelg replied that a pledge had been publicly given [33] and could not now be retracted.[34] In the early weeks of the session the new Assembly referred consideration of the land-granting system to a select committee [35] and Head informed the chairman that under certain circumstances he was authorized to surrender to the legislature the regulation and disposal of the Crown lands.

Prior to the meeting of the legislature Head had been collecting opinions about the Crown lands system. A. B. Hawke, the provincial government's chief emigrant agent, emphasized that Canada had to compete with the United States for immigrants. Therefore he favoured a uniform, single-price, cash sales policy similar to that in effect in the United States but without its auction sale provisions. When the Crown had raised its minimum price to 10s. an acre in 1833, the Canada Company and private landowners had increased the price of their land also. Hawke recognized that under these circumstances it would be impossible to reduce the price of Crown land to a uniform low rate in all townships because persons who had bought on instalments at the higher rates would demand a revision of their contracts if their land were devalued. He proposed therefore that in new townships a fixed price of 4s. an acre should be charged and, to prevent speculators turning their attention there, that this price should be coupled with a restriction on the quantity of land to be sold any one settler.

Hawke was opposed to the credit system because it enabled speculators to outbid actual settlers and prevented immigrants from settling together. He pointed out that a system which gave purchasers three years to pay the balance due on Crown lands, nine years if the land was a clergy reserve, which did not strictly enforce payment of the annual instalments, and which permitted payment to be made in current bank paper, really afforded greater facilities for speculators than the system in force in the United States since the issue of the specie circular. "Land ought to be disposed of by Government," advised Hawke, "not so much for the purpose of raising revenue ... [as] to induce the emigrant to purchase land on such terms as will secure his permanent residence. . . ." As for the policy of increasing the supply of labour by preventing immigrants from becoming landowners too soon, Hawke said bluntly, "The price of labour is regulated by its value in the United States and cannot be materially affected by anything this government can do." [36]

Robert Baldwin Sullivan, Head's Commissioner of Crown Lands, wanted to administer the lands, not like a statesman with the larger aspects of the question in mind, but like a careful business man concerned with accumulating all the revenue he could. Later, he was to advocate more enlarged views of land policy. Sullivan favoured a flexible system which allowed for a high degree of executive discretion. He proposed putting the land up to auction and selling on the instalment plan in well settled areas but selling at a fixed price and for cash in remote townships where auctions were of no advantage and instalments a poor risk. [37]

The nature of the report which the Assembly's committee on the land-granting system drew up became known to Head before it was submitted to the legislature. Apparently it was quite a blow to him. He seems to have expected that the new legislature would have complete confidence in his discretion and would trustingly resign the future of Upper Canada into his hands. In an indignant letter to Glenelg he denounced the committee's stand.

The leading recommendation contained in the report, I regret to say is, that the whole of the Crown lands shall at once be offered to the public, (in other words to the People) at the low price of 5/- an acre. Now this is the evil I anticipated ... This is why I asked in despatch 69 to be freed of restrictions relating to the Crown lands so as to be able to deal with speculators.

Ignoring Glenelg's previous warning that the question was beyond debate, Head criticized the policy of entrusting the Crown lands to the provincial legislature instead of to the Lieutenant-Governor. Under such a system, he argued, there would be no one to protect the immigrants from the

instinctive rapacity of the existing inhabitants ... the best House of Assembly we can ever hope to get have framed this report advocating sale at 5/- an acre. . . . The members naturally are and always have been Land Jobbers. It is their interest and that of the Legislative Council that the lands should be divided among the people at a low price not with a view to improving them but to sell them at exhorbitant rates to the poor immigrants. . . . Against this project there is not one dissentient voice. . . . [38]

To bolster his position, the anti-American and anti-democratic Head did not scruple to quote with approval from Jackson's message to Congress of December 1836, and to refer to "the veteran president of the United States" as "the highest practical authority." Land speculators, Jackson had said, tend to monopolize the best of the public lands, to oblige immigrants to purchase at two or three times the government price, and to establish a non-resident proprietorship which hinders the progress of the country. "Much good, in my judgment would be produced," he added, "by prohibiting sales of the public lands except to actual settlers at a reasonable reduction of price and to limit the quantity which shall be sold them." [39]

Glenelg wrote the excited Head a soothing reply in which he denied that it had been his intention to deliver the property of the Crown in Upper Canada "to the Rapacity of Interested Men." He reminded him that acts relating to the Crown lands were required to be reserved and that this practice adequately safeguarded the interests of the Crown and all classes of its subjects.[40] Glenelg also sent Head a new instruction abolishing the credit system and requiring that, after June 15, 1837, the full purchase price be paid within fourteen days of sale.[41] Meanwhile, Head evidently succeeded in bringing some influence to bear upon the land committee of the Assembly. Their report, first submitted to the legislature on January 6, differed from the plan Head had condemned in his dispatch written a week earlier. Gone was the obnoxious recommendation that all Crown lands be offered at a fixed upset price of 5s. an acre. Determination of the upset price and of the regulations governing sales was to be left to the lieutenant-governor-in-council and, in other respects, the field for executive discretion was to be widened.

Head subsequently gave a very different account of the passage of this bill in his *Narrative*.[42] He states that the Assembly,

entirely of its own accord, deemed it advisable to invest in the representative of their sovereign that amount of honourable confidence which dignifies the character of monarchical institutions, and which most particularly facilitates colonial government . . . nothing could be of more vital importance to the Crown than this proof . . . of [the Canadians'] sensible repugnance to that levelling insatiable desire of the adjoining Republic always to be restlessly transferring, from the executive branch of their legislature to an ungovernable mob, the patronage which, in monarchical institutions, is confidently reposed in the Crown.

The Public Lands Disposal Act of 1837,[43] as finally passed by a vote of 22–14, provided that: no public land was to be sold at private sale unless it had first been offered at auction; the upset price and the terms and conditions of sale were to be determined by the lieutenant-governor-in-council; lessees or occupants of the Crown lands, or individuals who might be injured if they were unable to purchase a particular tract, were to be permitted to purchase at a valuation fixed by the lieutenant-governor-in-council; district agents were to be appointed for the sale of the land; the lieutenant-governor was authorized to spend up to £1,000 out of the Crown lands revenues in the establishment of a grist or saw mill in each township;[44] settlers who purchased 50 acres of land were to be entitled to have the adjoining 50 acres reserved for them and to receive it as a free grant if they resided on their purchase and improved it. It will be seen that Sullivan's flexible system rather than the uniform cash sales policy advocated by Hawke was adopted.

The new Act differed from the draft bill for disposing of the Crown lands in New Brunswick, a copy of which Glenelg had sent to Head. Those clauses which related to the surrender of the Casual and Territorial Revenue in return for a civil list were not followed. Head had asked Glenelg for detailed instructions as to what these terms would be. He also intimated that the legislature had not shown much interest in the topic because it feared it would be making a losing bargain, since the land revenues, apart from the Canada Company's payments, were trifling.[45]

The important difference between the two measures related to free grants. These had been absolutely prohibited by the New Brunswick bill, but the Assembly of Upper Canada insisted on safeguarding the rights of those entitled to these grants under existing regulations—the U.E. loyalists, the militia men, and military claimants. The act made some concessions to the Lieutenant-Governor; it conceded a great deal more to the speculators in land rights. Militia and U.E. loyalist claims were freed from settlement duties, and holders of these rights were permitted to use them, at the rate of 4s. an acre, in the purchase of Crown, school, clergy, and Indian Trust lands. The *Correspondent and Advocate* of February 1, 1837, reported that during the debate on the bill it was intimated that the committee which drafted it had had a private caucus with the Lieutenant-Governor and had prepared its report under his influence and direction. A. N. MacNab stated that the fourth clause of the report was the one above all others that Head insisted on retaining. This was the clause that provided for the redemption of U.E. loyalist and militia rights. In its original form, it required that the rights offered for redemption be in the possession of the original claimants [46] and it fixed a value of 6s. 3d. an acre upon them. Solicitor General Hagerman opposed the fourth clause and the rate of 6s. 3d. an acre which, he argued, would have the effect of raising the minimum value of all land to that high figure and, "in impassioned language" he denied that Head had helped prepare the committee's report.[47] The Assembly adopted the report, 37–9, but before the bill based on it was passed the rate had been reduced to 4s. and the restriction that rights should be in the hands of the original claimants had disappeared.

The extent to which this act furthered speculation has already been shown in chapter IX. It is amazing that a Lieutenant-Governor really anxious to protect the interests of immigrants, as Head, tutored by Sullivan and Hawke, undoubtedly was, should have found any satisfaction in it, unless he was blinded by the concessions to his vanity and to his demand for executive freedom of action. The probable tendency of the act, and the interests behind it, were apparent to Head's contemporaries, if not to him. William Warren Baldwin wrote a trenchant criticism of it for the Durham Commission [48] and the Chief Clerk of the Crown Lands Office testified, "The principal object of the act appears to have been to benefit speculators." [49] But Head so little understood the true nature of the measure that he urged that the royal assent be given to it immediately so that its benefits might be felt before the season for immigration closed.[50]

From the scanty records in the Assembly's Journals it is not easy to say what motives were uppermost with the opponents and supporters of this measure. Men like W. H. Merritt and W. H. Draper objected to government enterprise in the milling business. Some regarded the cash-sale-at-auction system as a stimulus to speculation and as no guarantee that the land would be improved.[51] The opposition of others may have been owing to the fact that the existing regulations under which free grants were permitted did not include certain classes of the provincial militia and seamen. Before it was known what the

Crown's action on the Land Act of 1837 would be, the Assembly passed an address asking for grants to these militia men. Several other resolutions were also introduced for free grants to other categories of soldiers and seamen.[52] But an address which asked for free grants to settlers and immigrants was defeated.[53]

A minority of about a dozen members, most of them Reformers, opposed the bill in the form in which it was first introduced, favoured a free grant system for the benefit of immigrants, and coupled with this a demand for a clause requiring all Crown lands to be offered for sale at the upset price of 5s. an acre. This would have left the lieutenant-governor-in-council no freedom of action.[54] The effect of such a system might well have been to leave only the less desirable lots as free grants for immigrants, but the uniform and reduced price would have been to the advantage of those of them who could purchase their land.

As for the 50-acre purchase 50-acre free grant clause of the act, it perhaps indicates not so much real concern for the immigrant on the part of the majority, as a belief that a remnant at least of the free grant system should be kept for its propaganda value. At the last moment, some members of the minority proposed to reverse this clause and to give any settler who had not previously received free land the right to a 50-acre free grant and the option of purchasing the adjoining 50 acres at 5s. an acre within three years. They were unsuccessful.[55] Head called the members of the legislature land jobbers and E. B. O'Callaghan wrote of the combination of Anglo-Canadian Tories and Yankee speculators who were governing Upper Canada.[56] Certainly the divisions during the debate justify these epithets and reveal, moreover, that in the Assembly it was the small group of Reformers, who had been accused of hostility to British immigrants, who steadily supported the free grant proposals provided they were regulated by law.

The Land Act of 1837 received the royal assent after about a year's delay owing to the dissolution of the Imperial Parliament and did not come into force until 1838. Since it is confusing to give this act a post-Rebellion date, it has been referred to throughout by the year in which is was passed, which corresponds to its legal citation, 7 Will. IV, c. 118. Glenelg approved this act although he disliked two of its clauses because they enabled the Lieutenant-Governor to deal "with . . . the public property in such a manner as to gratify individuals. . . ." Sir George Arthur was directed not to exercise the power which the act gave him of making private sales at a valuation and 50-acre reserves for free grants, and he was asked to secure the omission of the clauses when the act came up for renewal. These were two of the provisions which had given Head satisfaction. He felt that the Colonial Office had given the "republican members" of the Assembly an opportunity to gloat over this public admission of lack of confidence in the lieutenant-governor-and-council and he described Glenelg's dispatch as "sickening."[57]

The Land Act of 1837 was not a constructive piece of legislation. The main grievances of which the province had complained had been the existence of the Crown and Clergy Reserves, the favour shown by the Land Department to insiders, the uncertainties and delays of the system, and the regulation of the land system by orders-in-council instead of by provincial statute. Not one of these grievances was remedied by the new act. Yet here was a chance, as Baldwin remarked, "to remodel anew by legislation."[58] Here was a moment when, according to John Macaulay, "beautiful harmony" prevailed between the three branches of the legislature.[59] What use did the Assembly make of its opportunities? The private interests of the holders of land rights were well served but public interests were grievously injured. And this by an Assembly forty-four of whose members proudly classed themselves as British Constitutionalists, and by a Lieutenant-Governor who had denounced the reformers as out to capture the government of the province for the sake of "lucre and emolument."

CHAPTER FIFTEEN

THE CLERGY RESERVES

No PART of the Imperial government's policies in Upper Canada drew more criticism from contemporaries than the practice of setting aside reserves of land for the support of a Protestant clergy. The policy was disliked for the means adopted and for the ends sought. Provision for the clergy was made by the Constitutional Act which required that one-seventh of every township be set apart as Clergy Reserves according to the unpopular chequered plan.[1]

The intentions of the British government in creating the Clergy Reserves later became a matter for dispute among the various Protestant denominations. The policy was adopted, in principle at any rate, long before there was any expectation that loyalists would occupy the upper province. Murray's instructions stated that "to the end that the Church of England may be established . . . and that the said inhabitants may . . . be induced to embrace the Protestant religion . . . land would be set aside for the support of Protestant ministers and school masters."[2] Subsequently, other motives were added to the original one of converting a Roman Catholic colony into a Protestant one. When loyalists began to settle in what was to be Upper Canada, the Society for the Propagation of the Gospel suggested that their religious welfare be provided for by setting aside land for the support of the Church of England.[3] In 1828, Viscount Sandon testified before the Canada Committee that Grenville had told him that the Clergy Reserves plan "was a good deal derived from information they had collected from an officer that had been much in Pennsylvania of the system with regard to land appropriated to religion and education in that state."[4] There is obviously an error here. In the Quaker colony of Pennsylvania land was not appropriated for the support of a clergy. The *Crown* Reserves may have been modelled on those which Penn was said to have made for himself and his heirs.[5] It is more likely that William Knox and the Society for the Propagation of the Gospel were the sources from which the plan for Clergy Reserves emanated.[6] Simcoe approved of the reserves for political as well as religious motives. "But in regard to a colony in Upper Canada which . . . is peculiarly situated among a variety of republics," wrote its future Lieutenant-Governor, "every establishment of Church and State that upholds the distinction of ranks, and lessens the undue weight of the democratic influence, ought to be introduced. . . ."[7]

The debates on the Constitutional Act make it clear that at the time the Imperial government intended to provide only the Church of England with an endowment of land, although it was disposed to make monetary grants to other Protestant denominations.[8] Pitt, in explaining the provisions for the clergy, drew attention first to the thirty-fifth clause which provided for the distribution of sums for the support of a Protestant clergy out of tithes for lands or possessions occupied by Protestants. Here, no use was made of the term "established church." The thirty-sixth clause, went on Pitt, provided reserves of land for the permanent support of a Protestant clergy. All or part of these reserves might be used to endow rectories to which clergy of the *established* church would be presented. That by the established church he meant the Church of England is clear from the fact that he went on to say this was done to encourage the established church and that possibly a bishop of the established church might be sent to sit in the Legislative Council. Dundas's statement that the reserves for the church and the Crown had been "fixed at a larger proportion than was originally intended, with a view to enabling the King to make from those Reservations such an allowance to Presbyterian ministers, Teachers and Schools, as His Majesty should from time to time think proper" also supports this view.[9] There was no mention of an endowment of land. All that can be said is that the framers of the Constitutional Act intended to make it possible for the Crown to exercise the royal bounty in favour of other Protestant sects from time to time.[10]

It was not the government's intention to provide the Church of England with a lavish endowment. When Fox objected that one-seventh was too much, Pitt remarked that one-seventh "had almost grown into an established custom where land had been given in commutation for tithes." He explained that, in addition to reserves of one-seventh of the land already granted, it was planned to make reserves of one-seventh in connection with all future grants "in proportion to such increase as may happen in the population and cultivation of the said province," and that if one-seventh proved to be too much, the amount could be revised.[11] The difficulty proved to be not the one-seventh policy, but the fact that grants—and, as a legal consequence, reserves—were made out of all proportion to the actual settlement of the province. By 1824 the Clergy Reserves amounted to 1,658,860 acres, exclusive of leased reserves and reserves which had been occupied by squatters for ten years, and these reserves cannot have been as great a hindrance to the settlement of the country as the 5 million acres in the hands of speculators at that time.[12]

It also was not expected that the Clergy Reserves would remain uncultivated for a long period of time. The government's intention was that proprietors of land should be induced to provide for the clearing of the reserved lands and the building of parsonages. By this means, explained Dundas, landowners could relieve themselves from tithes, "a burthen which is naturally irksome to them." [13] This scheme was never put into effect. It would have been practical only if the Crown land had been settled, as in New England, by organized town proprietors instead of by individuals, lot by lot.

No provision for the collection of tithes from Protestants had been made by the Constitutional Act, and both Dorchester and Simcoe advised against the introduction of "this most grievous of all burdens." [14] Tithes were never demanded in Upper Canada, but public uneasiness as to the rights of the clergy in this respect continued. In 1816 Gore advised Bathurst that it would be inexpedient to organize parishes and induct clergymen until these fears were allayed.[15]

Until 1819, the Clergy Reserves were managed by the Executive Council of Upper Canada on the same principles as the Crown Reserves; that is, they were leased for twenty-one years at rents which were increased at seven-year intervals.[16] This system proved no more satisfactory for the Clergy Reserves than it did for the Crown Reserves. By 1818 only 620 leases were in effect, approximately one-fourth of the land specified in patents as Clergy Reserves, but of course, a considerably smaller proportion of the amount reserved for the clergy in every township under the chequered plan.

By 1818, dissatisfaction with the whole system of reserves had been aroused by Lieutenant-Governor Gore's conferring Crown Reserves on favourites, and by the activities of Robert Gourlay. In 1817 the Assembly had debated a series of grievances relating to the Crown land policies, the ninth of which declared that the Crown and Clergy Reserves were "unsurmountable objects to the forming of well connected settlements. But in a political point of view, the measure is still more objectionable from the holding out of great inducements to future wars with the United States by affording the means of partially indemnifying themselves to reward their followers in the Event of conquest." The eleventh resolution declared the reservation of one-seventh for the Protestant clergy "an appropriation beyond all precedent lavish"; it proposed that part of the reserves be sold and churches be created and endowed from the proceeds, and that a smaller proportion of land in each township be reserved for the clergy.[17]

This attack upon the endowment of the Church aroused Upper Canada's leading Anglican churchman, Dr. John Strachan, to action. The session of 1817 had been prematurely prorogued by Gore to prevent these extraordinary and pernicious resolutions, as Strachan called them, from being voted upon, but Strachan was fearful that those opposed to the reserves would return to the attack now that Gore had returned to England.[18] Strachan bestirred himself not only to discredit Robert Gourlay and to draw the attention of the Imperial government to the unfriendly attitude of a party in the Assembly but also to get the reserves out of the hands of the government, safely into the possession of the church, and put to some use as soon as possible. "The attack on the seventh," admitted Strachan to Bishop Mountain, "arises in great degree from nothing appearing to have been done with them." [19]

Administration of the reserves by the Land Committee of the Executive Council was not satisfactory to Strachan, who pointed out to Maitland that only 620 leases were in effect but that there were applications for almost as many more which had not been completed, that the rents on existing leases had not been strictly collected, and that the arrears of rent amounted to £2,477 12s. 8½d. He proposed that the Clergy Reserves be managed by a special committee or Clergy Corporation, as they were in Lower Canada.[20] The members would serve without pay and could be expected to take more interest in the endowment than ordinary laymen.[21]

The Clergy Reserve Corporation of Upper Canada was duly created in 1819.[22] Until 1834, it managed the leasing of the reserves on principles already established by the Executive Council and changes desired by it required the Council's approval. One of its earliest requests was for permission to lease lots on roads passing through Clergy Reserve blocks at lower rates than usual to attract settlers, a commendable effort to meet criticism of the reserves. The clergy were requested to report on the condition of the reserves in their districts and they were authorized to receive applications for leases to save petitioners the trouble of going to York. Many of the desirable reserves were now found to have been occupied by squatters, sometimes two to a lot. To discourage this practice, the Council decided that in such cases the reserve should be divided between the occupants and leased to them, each paying as much for his part as he would have for the whole.[23] Those who wanted only one half a reserve could obtain it, after 1822, at an annual rent of $5.00, $10, and $15 for three successive seven-year periods.[24]

The Clergy Corporation succeeded markedly in increasing the number of leases, a task which, of course, became progressively easier with the development of the province and the abolition of the free grant system in 1826. In 1823, rents on renewals of leases made prior to 1811 were set at 65s., 100s., and 135s. for the next three seven-year periods, and rents on renewals of leases made under the regulations of 1811 were to be 80s., 115s., and 150s.[25] In February, 1825, the Corporation was directed to cease making leases on account of the expected sale of Clergy Reserves to the Canada Company.[26] It resumed leasing in April, 1829, after other arrangements had been made with the Canada Company.

The Corporation did not succeed in making the reserves more productive than the Land Committee of Council had. Rents continued to be in arrears, the sheriffs proved to be unsuccessful as collectors and were themselves sometimes in arrears.[27] Receipts averaged only £200 a year until 1830 and this sum was wholly absorbed in the expenses of collection.[28] Between 1820 and 1834 some £11,000 was collected, almost one-third of which was paid over to the President of the Clergy Corporation for stipend and travelling expenses.[29] In addition, the Corporation suffered from the defalcation of its secretary. In February, 1832, the Imperial government, which was expecting Upper Canada to pass an act to re-invest the reserves in the Crown, once again directed the Clergy Corporation to suspend leasing.[30] Its powers were never restored. In 1834 the leasing system was discontinued and the collection of rents on existing leases became the duty of the Receiver General's office [31] which, for a year or two, brought the revenue up to about £4,000.

After the passage of the Clergy Reserve Sales Act of 1827 it was possible for lessees to buy their holdings at private sale and this privilege continued even after 1834 when the auction system was instituted for clergy land. Approximately 700 lessees had applied to purchase their leaseholds by 1840.[32] Some of them, perhaps many, may have been unable to carry out their intentions promptly since the quantity of land for sale under the Act of 1827 was limited and since, after 1837, cash payment was required.[33] In 1837 there were 361,000 acres, or 1805 clergy lots, under lease.[34] In 1842 there were still 1,147 Clergy Reserves leased which should have yielded about £4,000 in rent annually but by this time collections had once again slumped to one-fourth of what they should have been.[35] These old leases and arrears were to provide troublesome questions for the government of United Canada after 1841. In 1849 there were still 140,000 acres of Clergy Reserves under lease on which the annual rent payable was

£2,450.[36] Rents on leased Clergy Reserves continued to be shown in the annual returns of the Commissioner of Crown Lands until 1861 and rents on unleased clergy land was being paid as late as 1869.[37]

It was the creation of the Clergy Corporation that revealed the widespread opposition to endowing one denomination of Protestants with property made valuable by the labours of all classes of settlers and caused the claim of the Church of England to exclusive right to the Clergy Reserves to be challenged.[38] Maitland referred the touchy question to the Colonial Office, which was advised by the law officers of the Crown that the term "a Protestant clergy" used in the Constitutional Act might be extended to include the clergy of the Church of Scotland, although not ministers of other dissenting sects, but that clause 38 of the act permitted the Crown to authorize the endowment of Church of England rectories in every township with so much of the Clergy Reserves as the lieutenant-governor in council saw fit to give and that there was no legal obligation to retain any of the reserves in any township for the benefit of the clergy of the Church of Scotland. The question was one of political expediency, as Bathurst pointed out to Maitland, and as James Stephen pointed out to Wilmot-Horton four years later.[39] In 1823, William Morris, member for Carleton County, brought the claims of this church before the Assembly which, by a vote of 20–6, passed an address to the Crown asking that the Church of Scotland be provided for out of the reserves or from some other source.[40]

When the Imperial government decided to end its annual grant for the support of the government of Upper Canada, questions related to land policies became acute and led John Beverley Robinson to place his plan for the sale of the Crown Reserves before the Colonial Office. Up to this point Crown and Clergy Reserves had been managed on the same lines and condemned on the same grounds. If the sale of the former were to be decided upon, it was certain to strengthen the growing demand for the sale of the latter.[41] In fact, in 1823, the Colonial Office asked Dalhousie to consult the Bishop of Quebec about methods for making the reserves immediately productive so that the support of the colonial clergy could be transferred from the British Treasury to the Clergy Reserve Fund and that sums already advanced for their support could be repaid from that source.[42] Strachan promptly worked out a plan of his own for the sale of the reserves in Upper Canada, secured Maitland's approval of it, and went to England in February, 1824, to present it to the Colonial Office.[43]

Strachan proposed that the Clergy Corporation should have the power to sell the reserves by auction with the exception of sufficient land in each township to endow three or four parsonages. He considered the leasing system a failure. He believed that it might work better in the future than in the past, but that the church could not safely wait. She needed greatly to increase the number of her clergy without delay lest she be left far behind in the competition with other denominations in Upper Canada. Already, the Presbyterians were beginning to assert themselves and had asked that their clergy be provided for out of the reserves or by some other means. The first possibility must be forestalled. Strachan felt that this was the moment to put the church's endowment beyond the reach of her competitors and to remove it as a temptation to rebellion. He wanted the sale of the reserves to be entrusted to the Clergy

Corporation, and the proceeds to be invested in British funds for the benefit of the Episcopal clergy. To make doubly sure he proposed that the forty-first clause of the Constitutional Act, which empowered the provincial legislature to vary or to repeal the Clergy Reserves provisions of the act, be repealed. If Strachan's scheme had gone through, other Protestant churches would have been shut out completely.

By the time Strachan's proposal reached the Colonial Office, the negotiations with John Galt which led to the formation of the Canada Company were under way. From the beginning, Galt had stressed the hindrance which both classes of reserves were to the settlement of the country. By the time he had begun to try to organize a company, his project definitely included both the Crown and the Clergy Reserves,[44] and, a few weeks later, he was suggesting that the proposed company should buy all the reserves of both kinds in the townships surveyed before March 1, 1824.[45]

At the outset, Strachan did not appear openly hostile to the proposed sale to the Canada Company. He may have calculated that it would safeguard the endowment of the church and secure money for an expansion of her activities without delay, but it is possible that he was more calculating than this. If part of the reserves were sold to the Canada Company, the remainder would certainly rise in value as a result of its activities. The clergy could, so to speak, ride along on the Company's coat-tails. Before the negotiations were concluded, an attempt was to be made to whittle down the portion to be sold to one-third.

The Colonial Secretary now began to doubt whether he could get a bill for the sale of all the Clergy Reserves through Parliament, whereupon Galt and his backers suggested that the proposed company should take two-thirds of the reserves and that the other third "should be considered on a broader principle, it being evidently liable to be called an excessive endowment."[46] What Galt, who was anxious to get rid of the reserves, had in mind here is not clear. Bathurst intended to fund the proceeds from the portion to be sold for the benefit of the established church, but, like Strachan, he thought a proportion should be retained for glebes.

It was not to the Company's advantage to let any other group profit by its labours in colonizing Upper Canada. Therefore, in return for giving up one-third of the reserves, the promoters asked that they be allowed to buy other land to facilitate making roads, that they have the refusal of forfeited locations, and that the business of settling poor immigrants in undeveloped townships on the same terms as the Irish immigrants of 1823 be entrusted to them.[47] This last request was opposed by Strachan who feared that "the Grace of the Crown" would not reach the immigrants.[48]

Pari-passu with discussions about what proportion of the Clergy Reserves the proposed company should be allowed to buy, went discussions about what price it should pay for them and how that price should be determined. The promoters were not friendly to the idea of a valuation nor could they agree upon the basis on which it was to be made. The quantity of Clergy Reserves to be sold was still undetermined at the end of June when Galt, on behalf of the promoters, offered to buy all the Crown Reserves and half the Clergy Reserves in the townships surveyed before 1824 at 2s. 6d. an acre in preference to all the Crown

Reserves and two-thirds of the Clergy Reserves at a valuation.[49] This was just half the price Galt had originally thought a company might give.[50] As one of the promoters, Simon McGillivray, subsequently explained, the continued existence of unsold Clergy Reserves would be a drag upon the Company's operations and therefore would make the whole transaction less profitable.[51] Strachan and Peter Robinson advised Bathurst that it would be better to sell the Crown Reserves through the Executive Council and the Clergy Reserves through the Corporation than to accept Galt's offer. They submitted a long calculation on the probable value of the reserves and suggested a price of 6s. 8d. an acre.[52] In reply, Galt poked fun at "the arithmetical riches of their prospective revenues" and hinted that if the Clergy Reserves were not sold the Company might not be inclined to pay even 2s. 6d.[53]

After numerous misunderstandings, it was agreed that the Company would buy the Crown Reserves and half the Clergy Reserves in the townships surveyed before 1824, that the price would be determined by a valuation to be made by five commissioners by a method not very precisely stated, that the Company's payments should extend over fifteen years, and that each year it should take possession of so much land as was equivalent to its annual payment of £20,000.[54] On behalf of the clergy of Upper Canada, Strachan strenuously and successfully fought this sale. His opposition, which both surprised and annoyed Bathurst,[55] began before the award of the commissioners was made known and was not based on the price alone.

On the eve of Strachan's departure from England at the end of September, 1824, he received a copy of the agreement with the Canada Company.[56] Strachan states that the moment he received it he saw the "pernicious effects" of the third article [57] which allowed the Company to make deferred payments extending over fifteen years. It was Strachan's contention that if the Company paid cash, the clergy fund would obtain a greater return in interest alone over fifteen years than the capital and interest together would give under the deferred payment plan. Strachan, who was still hoping that a valuation of at least 5s. an acre would be placed on the land, pointed out also that if the Company took up land equal to £20,000 a year, it would be able to purchase only 26,667 acres of Clergy Reserves a year and would probably chose the choicest, leaving the balance "locked up" by the government's agreement to sell to the Company.[58] In addition he objected to valuing the reserves on the basis of the cash sales that had been made "if confined to large tracts...."[59] What Strachan wanted for the church was a substantial capital sum, the interest on which would allow an immediate expansion of her activities. To secure immediate and substantial aid it would be worthwhile to make some sacrifice of future financial gains; but if all that could be obtained was a sale at a low valuation with the purchase money paid in instalments over fifteen years, it would be far better to let the Clergy Corporation manage the property.[60]

Strachan did not tell his Bishop on his return all the objections to the sale which he had in mind.[61] He waited until he had reached Upper Canada and had secured Maitland's support. His first move was to suggest that, at the very least, the Clergy Corporation should be allowed to name one of the commissioners who were to value the land.[62] This suggestion came too late. In December,

1824, John Davidson had been appointed fifth commissioner. Strachan's hopes of an acceptable result now vanished.[63] The commissioners, he thought, would be wax in the hands of a man like Galt. Backed by Maitland, he began his fight to withdraw the reserves from the sale to the Canada Company.

Before Strachan learned of Davidson's appointment, he had written to Bishop Mountain proposing two clauses which he thought ought to be introduced into the Canada Company bill to prevent injustice being done the church.[64] An extract of this letter, the original of which has not yet been found, shows that the first clause would have provided for two commissioners from the Canada Company, two from the Clergy Corporation and for a fifth if they could not agree. The second clause, which is not part of the extract, probably provided for appropriating other land for the clergy in lieu of the reserves to be sold. Maitland also wrote to the Bishop endorsing the plan for a land company which Strachan had devised.[65]

Strachan had drawn up a substitute plan for a land company under which the Canada Company was to be offered one million acres of land recently purchased from the Indians at 4s. an acre cash in lieu of the Clergy Reserves.[66] One million acres was the figure tentatively used by Strachan, but this figure was later changed by Maitland to three million acres,[67] part of which was to be in substitution for the Clergy Reserves.[68] This land was not to be laid out on the chequered plan, but 2,500 acres in each township were to be reserved for religion and education. The Company was to support a clergyman in each township and to build a church, school, and house for the schoolmaster. The purchase money from the sale was to be funded and out of the proceeds the government of Upper Canada was to receive £8,000 a year for the support of the civil government. Strachan stressed the advantages to the Company of one continuous tract of land, as opposed to the scattered lots of their existing agreement which was based on reserves. He proposed that in the new tract houses should be built and 5-acre clearings made on each lot before sales were made to British immigrants, and he thought such improved properties could be sold at 30s. an acre.[69]

This scheme, which called for a much greater outlay of capital than, judging by their subsequent conduct, the Canada Company had any intention of making, is interesting for what it reveals of the political ideas of Maitland and Strachan. Strachan pointed out that in the new area the Company and its people would be "in a manner insulated and kept within themselves—are not therefore involved in the prejudices, difficulties and mismanagement that sometimes prevails in the older Districts." In other words, they would not be contaminated by the Yankee prejudices of some of the older settlements. The Justices of the Peace, went on Strachan, would virtually be nominated by the Company and would consist chiefly of its confidential servants. In a few years time the district would be entitled to thirteen members in Parliament and would have its full proportion of political influence, which, it is clear, he assumed would be thrown on the conservative side. A nice scheme for a gigantic rotten borough![70]

Strachan now had three strings to his bow. If the valuation turned out decently, he could withdraw his opposition to the sale. If it proved to be too low he could urge that other land be substituted for the Crown and Clergy

Reserves along the lines of his plan. If the Canada Company refused the land offered in substitution, he could suggest that the Episcopal clergy should receive a block of land in lieu of the reserves sold against their wishes.

In May, 1825, the commissioners of evaluation made their award. Strachan vehemently protested against the sacrifice of half the church's "property" at the low figure of 3s. 6d. an acre which they had set instead of the 8s. 6d. an acre he now considered reasonable.[71] Under his guidance, the Clergy Corporation of Upper Canada drew up a petition to Parliament asking that the Clergy Reserves be withdrawn from the sale to the Canada Company. Strachan was most eager to be chosen to take this petition to England, but he was thwarted by his Bishop who wanted his son, the Rev. G. J. Mountain, to go instead. In Strachan's opinion, the younger Mr. Mountain was not capable of conducting the complex moves and counter-moves by which he had planned to defend the interests of the church. The Clergy Corporation of Upper Canada remedied the matter by making Mountain its agent to act jointly with a skilful negotiator, John Beverley Robinson.[72] The two agents found it expedient to yield to Bathurst's wish that the petition not be presented to Parliament,[73] but they both continued to oppose the sale. Robinson argued that the evidence before the commissioners justified a price of 7s. an acre rather than 3s. 6d. payable in fifteen instalments and, like Maitland and Strachan, he suggested that it would be desirable to exchange both Crown and Clergy Reserves for a tract of land.[74]

By the time Mountain and Robinson reached England, the bill for the sale of the Clergy Reserves to the Canada Company had passed the Commons and been introduced into the Lords. Robinson suggested that this bill be amended to permit other lands to be substituted for the Clergy Reserves.[75] The Company was impatient for the bill and for its charter, which had not yet been issued. It was late in the day to make changes. The Society for the Propagation of the Gospel wanted the bill amended so as to make it plain that the proceeds of the sale were to be for the benefit of the Episcopal clergy exclusively. The Colonial Office, which had already been advised by the law officers of the Crown that the Church of England did not have an exclusive right to the reserves, could not consent. The Society next proposed a second reference to the law officers on the ground that they had not had before them all the pertinent material.[76] Here was a state of affairs which threatened to prevent the passage of the Canada Company's bill through the Lords. The substitution plan offered a way out. Two weeks later, Bathurst had agreed to amend the Canada Company bill to permit the substitution, but he insisted that the option of accepting or rejecting the exchange lay with the Company.[77] Mountain succeeded in persuading the Company to put off a decision "until communication could be had with Upper Canada." That gave Robinson an opportunity to urge that Strachan be sent home to negotiate on behalf of the clergy.[78]

In the end, John Galt, representing the Canada Company, and Strachan, the champion of the Clergy Reserves, came to an agreement which the Imperial government was willing to implement.[79] The Company consented to relinquish the 829,430 acres of the reserves for which they had been willing to pay 3s. 6d. an acre, or £145,150 5s., and to take from the Crown for the same sum one million acres of the Huron Tract.[80] Strachan favoured this settlement in the expectation that the province woud benefit from the rapid development of a district which might have remained "a wilderness" for years, although he had earlier been very sceptical of the Company's real usefulness.[81] Under the terms of this settlement, less than 3s. 6d. an acre was obtained, and all that remained of Strachan's land company plan was the agreement to substitute other land for the Clergy Reserves.

By this arrangement, remarks Galt, the clergy gained rather than lost, since they received back the 829,430 acres of reserves which the Canada Company had proposed to buy and, in addition, the government granted them 750,000 acres more. This statement is not accurate. An additional block of Clergy Reserves amounting to 157,142 acres, not 750,000 acres, was created to take care of the fact that patents for land within the Huron Tract would not be valid without a Clergy Reserve specification, and since the land was not surveyed on the chequered plan, it had to be set aside elsewhere.[82]

There was at one point a possibility that out of the Canada Company negotiations the clergy of the established church would obtain an endowment, if not larger than that they already claimed under the Constitutional Act, at any rate one that would be exclusively theirs. The new clause, which was added to the Canada Company's bill at the last minute, was not worded so as to permit the Crown to sell lands in the Huron Tract to the Company in lieu of half the Clergy Reserves. It enabled the Crown to appropriate other land for the clergy if part of the Clergy Reserves should be sold. The wording of this act gave the impression that the substituted land was to be appropriated as Clergy Reserves and that the clergy would still be entitled to the unsold half of the reserves and also to the proceeds from the portion sold to the Canada Company.

Charles Lindsey was of the opinion that the allotment to the clergy of land in lieu would not have been a direct increase in the quantity of the reserves, but that it was intended to have that effect. Out of the Canada Company's payments, the Presbyterians and Catholics were to get a financial grant; this would have silenced the Scotch and left the Church of England to enjoy a monopoly of the reserves in peace.[83] How correct is this interpretation which Lindsey left unsupported by any evidence?

Before it was known whether the Canada Company would choose the Clergy Reserves or the Huron Tract, the Assembly of Upper Canada protested against any increase of the Clergy Reserves under the terms of the Canada Company Act. The Assembly had the notion that additional land, equal to one-fourteenth of the land in townships surveyed before 1824, was to be reserved to replace that half of the reserves which was to be sold.[84] Bathurst explained that the Assembly had misunderstood the act. Its object, he asserted, was not to increase the amount of the reserves specially allotted by Parliament for the established church. Bathurst's statement was perfectly correct. If the Episcopal clergy had obtained a grant specifically to them in lieu of the reserves sold, they would have lost all claim to any share in the payments from the Canada Company, as the Rev. G. J. Mountain, acting for the Clergy Corporation, had been informed.[85] The result would have been to leave the Canada Company's payments for the Clergy Reserves, which by the second clause of the Canada Company's

Act were to be used solely for the support of a Protestant Clergy, completely at the disposal of the Crown. As Lindsay said, a fund would have been created out of which the Crown could assist other Protestant denominations without burdening the Treasury or detracting from the size of the endowment which the Church of England regarded as rightfully hers.

John Galt was as disturbed as the Assembly by the proposal to substitute land for half the Clergy Reserves. He wrote to Wilmot-Horton:

> The construction which you put on the 3rd clause of the Act of Parliament differs from that of the Assembly of Upper Canada. It was of *their* construction that I complained and yet yours seems no less objectionable, for if the new lands which you propose to give the clergy are to enable Dr. Strachan's company to be formed, the Canada Company ought to be dissolved. There is not room in the province for two companies.[86]

A few weeks later, the negotiations between Galt and Strachan were well under way and, in the end, it was not the clergy who received a tract in lieu, but the Canada Company. Perhaps both sides were the more readily brought into agreement because the one had come to fear the competition of Strachan's proposed land company and the other the opposition of the Assembly. Subsequently, the Crown made annual grants to Anglicans, Presbyterians, Methodists, and Catholics out of the Canada Company's payments—a use of the funds which did not make the sale to the Company any more popular in Upper Canada.

Strachan and Robinson both fought hard against the Canada Company, the one to rescue the Crown Reserves, the other not only to rescue the Clergy Reserves from its clutches, but also to secure for the Church of England an endowment which would be undeniably hers. They both met defeat, the one completely, the other partly, and this could not have been a pleasant experience for men who had become accustomed to having their advice on the affairs of Upper Canada taken. Robinson "mourned over [the Crown Reserves] as dead and gone...."[87] Strachan failed in his efforts to put the endowment beyond peril, but he had fought a successful delaying action. He had prevented the endowment from being sold for a song and had kept it intact. He had won a battle which it would have been better if he had lost because, in the end, he was to lose the war.

Both Robinson and Strachan predicted that the Canada Company would turn out to be a mere land speculation. Strachan, moreover, believed that Upper Canada's economic troubles were passing. In a memo to Maitland he said:

> Whatever impulse such a company might have given the province twenty years ago when it was little known & the population insignificant it can have little effect now when the causes of depression are rapidly disappearing, when Colonial restrictions are giving way to a more enlightened policy, when the population ... is already occupied in the most magnificent internal improvements.... Under circumstances so favourable it is rather to be feared that the Canada Company would encumber the Colony with help than assist its progress by monopolizing a large portion of its most convenient & fertile land.[88]

After the plan to sell half of the Clergy Reserves to the Canada Company had been abandoned, Bathurst returned to the proposals previously urged upon him by Strachan: endowment of rectories and sale of part of the reserves by the Clergy Corporation.

Preliminary steps for creating rectories had previously been ordered[89] but all that had been done was to pass the Tithe Declaratory Act of 1822 to remove

the public's fear that rectors would have the right to tithes, and to enable such
glebes as had been selected to be leased on the same terms as Clergy Reserves
instead of being held on licences of occupation from year to year.[90] Both the
creation and the endowment of rectories were authorized by the Colonial
Secretary in July, 1825.[91] Bathurst advised Maitland that in parishes where the
members of the Church of Scotland predominated "a proportionate allotment
should be reserved for the provision for a minister of that Church." [92] However,
the method proposed by the Executive Council made no provision for the
Scottish clergy, and ardent Anglicans like Robert Stanton rejoiced in the fact.[93]
The Council's scheme was inexpedient and Maitland realized it. The rectories
were not established and endowed. By 1825 it was too late to be endowing
rectories. The problem of utilizing the Clergy Reserves had ceased to be merely
a question of land policy. It had given rise to pamphlet warfare and to a bitter
sectarian conflict between the various Protestant denominations in Upper
Canada [94] which was to drag on until 1854.

During the first session of the ninth Parliament in 1825, the Assembly had
received a number of petitions asking that the income from the Clergy Reserve
Fund might be shared by all denominations of Protestants. Action was deferred
to the next session when an address to the Crown was passed which complained
of the Canada Company's Act and also asked that the injurious Clergy Reserves
be sold for education and internal improvements.[95] Bathurst's answer merely
referred to the Assembly's mistaken interpretation of the Canada Company Act
and was silent, the Assembly complained, on "the material part of the address." [96]
The Assembly then passed a series of resolutions which asserted the right of
the provincial Parliament to legislate on the reserves question, denied both the
legality and the justice of the Church of England's claim to exclusive right to
the reserves, and declared that a large proportion of the inhabitants thought that
the reserves should be used for education and for erecting churches for all
denominations. All these resolutions passed by large majorities which included
the votes of members later classed by Strachan as members of the Church of
England.[97] The one on education was passed by the largest majority of all,
31–2.[98] As Maitland later wrote Huskisson, the proposal to divert the Clergy
Reserves to education had brought the "sects" to the hearty support of the
church's Presbyterian opponents.[99] A bill for the sale of the Clergy Reserves
was carried in this Assembly but failed to pass the Council.[100]

The boldness of the Assembly in asserting its right to legislate on the Clergy
Reserves stirred Strachan and the home government to action. In February,
1827, Wilmot-Horton introduced a bill to authorize the Clergy Corporations of
both Upper and Lower Canada to sell one-fourth of the Clergy Reserves in
each province at a rate of not more than 100,000 acres in any one year. The act
would have benefited only the Church of England; Wilmot-Horton stated flatly
in the debate that the lands in question were the "property" of the Church of
England.[101] Opposition on the part of those who, like Hume and Baring, objected
to the revenues benefiting only that church, and who wanted an inquiry into
the state of the various denominations in Canada, led Wilmot-Horton to withdraw the bill and to promise such an inquiry.[102] Strachan, however, urged that
part of the reserves be sold without waiting for an investigation and agreed

that in view of the opposition the Clergy Corporation should not be mentioned.[103] A new bill was introduced in May which became the Clergy Reserve Sales Act of 1827. It entrusted the sale of the land to the lieutenant-governor-and-council, provided that the proceeds should be invested in British government securities and the income appropriated by the Crown for the improvement of the balance of the reserves or for the support of a Protestant clergy.[104] This act left the Constitutional Act still open to amendment and the question of what denominations were to benefit from the reserves unresolved.[105]

The debate in the Imperial Parliament during the spring of 1827 and the resolutions of Upper Canada's Assembly during the session of 1826, which had asserted that only a small proportion of the inhabitants of the province belonged to the Church of England, brought Archdeacon Strachan, pen in hand, to her defence. "When contrasted with other denominations the Church of England needs not to be ashamed of the progress she has made," he informed Wilmot-Horton. In proof, Strachan enclosed an ecclesiastical chart of Upper Canada, compiled by him, which was later published in a Parliamentary paper and which contained inaccurate statistics unfavourable to other denominations. The Methodist preachers were referred to as itinerant "teachers," most of them from the United States "where they gather their knowledge and form their sentiments ... the tendency of the population is towards the Church of England, and nothing but the want of moderate support prevents her from spreading over the whole province," wrote Strachan.[106] He supported the Clergy Reserve Sales Bill then pending in the Imperial Parliament, arguing that the popular objection to the reserves as an obstacle to settlement would be removed and that more Church of England clergy could be supported in Upper Canada where their influence would strengthen the Imperial bond if the bill were enacted.

The passage of the Clergy Reserves Sales Act of 1827 did not still the clamour over the reserves because it provided for the sale of only one-quarter of them, because the revenue from sales was not placed at the disposal of the provincial legislature, and because inter-denominational rivalries and prejudices had been exacerbated by Strachan's chart and by the prospect that the Clergy Reserves were at last going to produce some revenue. "The Dissenters will be on the look out for a share of the Clergy Reserves and our Legislature must expect that its next session will be very much occupied in attending to the claims of Ranters, Jumpers, Mennonites, Tunkers, Davidites, & Co, & Co. ... Our Parliament will be converted into a theological seminary," wrote Robert Stanton scornfully.[107] Mackenzie's *Colonial Advocate* urged that the reserves be used for education or that all denominations should share in them, attacked the accuracy of Strachan's chart, and published accounts of various meetings of protest.[108] The Church of Scotland began to gather information about its membership and Mackenzie urged the Secession Church to do likewise. A recent grant to King's College was an additional cause of discontent. This institution had been given a charter which required the members of its governing body to be members of the Church of England, and it had been granted 200,000 acres of leased Crown Reserves as an endowment. Its Church of England supporters regarded this gift as a timely demonstration of the home government's support of the church in Upper Canada.[109]

The next session of the provincial legislature saw another struggle over the Clergy Reserves. The address to the Crown, passed by a vote of 21–9, was no modest proposal for the division of reserve monies among all denominations of Protestants, but a forthright request that the Clergy Reserve fund be placed at the disposal of the provincial legislature for education or internal improvements and that the charter of King's College be revised "on more comprehensive principles." It denied that the tendency of the population was towards the Church of England, declared "that there is in the minds of the people generally a strong and settled aversion to anything like an established church," and deplored the disparaging references to the Methodist preachers. Strachan explained to the Legislative Council, and years later to Egerton Ryerson, that he had never represented nor supposed that the body of the Methodist people were disloyal, that his statement referred not to the native born Methodist preachers but only to those Methodist preachers who came from the United States.[110]

Archdeacon Strachan made a fundamental mistake in sending his ecclesiastical chart to the Colonial Office, as even his fellow churchmen recognized.[111] George Ryerson predicted that it would have an effect on the elections of 1828 unfavourable to the Anglicans and believed that it had dealt the Anglican Church in Canada a mortal blow.[112] Strachan had made statements that he could not substantiate and his enemies took prompt advantage of his mistaken zeal. A select committee of the House of Assembly put him through a searching examination in which he had to admit that his statistics were compiled from memory. Probably aware that the Presbyterians were gathering statistics township by township to bolster their case and that the Methodists could present detailed statistics of membership in their circuits, he began to circularize the Anglican clergy of Upper Canada, inquiring about their activities. His Bishop suggested that the Anglicans of the province should demonstrate their strength to the home government by petitioning congregation by congregation, but Strachan preferred that the Bishop himself should petition to be heard on behalf of the church. "This will sustain the dignity of our Establishment," wrote Strachan "and not descend to a measure which would induce every man to think that our retaining the reserves depended on his signature—references to the people at large smells too much of Democracy for me." [113]

In 1828, the crisis in Lower Canada led to the appointment of a committee of the House of Commons to inquire into the grievances of that province. It also took testimony from both Presbyterians and Methodists respecting the inaccuracies in Strachan's chart. On the method by which the Clergy Reserves should be made income producing, the committee heard from Wilmot-Horton and James Stephen. The former conceded that the recent Clergy Reserves Sales Act would not remedy the grievances caused by the reserves and that it was desirable to sell them as soon as possible, although with safeguards to prevent the land being sold for next to nothing in a glutted market.[114] Stephen objected to the reserves in strong terms. They were, he said, precisely the most inconvenient provision for the clergy that could have been imagined; both clergy and colonists would, he thought, benefit from disposing of them entirely and at once. As for price, he thought that the 3s. 6d. an acre offered by the Canada Company not too low but too high. The Canada Committee concluded that "the adherents of the Church of England constitute but a small minority in the Province of Upper Canada," but they made no definite suggestion as to how the Clergy Reserve fund should be allotted except to say that an adjustment satisfactory to the province should be made. In the end, the Colonial Office answered the Assembly's address of 1828 merely by saying that much information would be needed before a revision of the recent Clergy Reserves Sales Act could be made.[115]

To the Anglican party in Upper Canada, the report of the Canada Committee was a bitter disappointment. Sir John Colborne, a few months after his arrival in the province, asserted that the report, plus Stephen's absurd opinions, were being quoted by all the mischievous papers and had done untold harm.[116] John Beverley Robinson wrote Wilmot-Horton that the report had brought "mortification and disappointment unspeakable to many who are just as *liberal* disinterested and patriotic as those gentlemen who feel entitled to sneer at our attachment to the King and Church as antiquated prejudices." As for the reserves, in his opinion, the committee had been "gulled" and had accepted statements about their current value, the impossibility of disposing of them, and the obstacles they presented to settlement which were absolutely silly. He denied that the Clergy Reserves were generally held to be a great obstacle to the settlement of the country. No complaints of this kind had ever been voiced until within the last five years, said Robinson, quite overlooking the protests of the Assembly in 1817. As for the recent complaints, they were chiefly the work of sectarians and speculators who did not scruple about letting their own tracts of land lie waste. "The truth is," wrote the Attorney General, "while a township is but little settled the reserves are no more a bar to improvement than other unoccupied lands—when that township begins to be tolerably well settled the reserves are eagerly taken up by tenants and are occupied like other lots, and then the grievance ceases. No greater imposition has been practised in this age of humbug, than in the statements which have been made respecting these reserves." As for the supposed impossibility of disposing of the reserves except at a very low price or on deferred quit rent, the Commissioner of Crown Lands was at the moment, said Robinson, actually disposing of "hundreds on hundreds of these worthless lots for 10-15-20/- per acre by instalments commencing immediately." [117]

While this debate over the Clergy Reserves continued and grew more bitter, the Clergy Reserves Sales Act remained in force. The general instructions which Huskisson sent with this act stated that revenue was to be regarded as less important than disposing of those reserves which were a hindrance to settlement. However, in every township a glebe of 300 or 400 acres was to be preserved.[118] Peter Robinson was appointed to manage the sales, and it was left to him to recommend what lots should be sold at private sale and at what prices. More than the limit of 100,000 acres a year was promptly applied for during the first year, and inspections and valuations continued to lag behind the demand.[119] In 1830, the Council directed Robinson not to sell more than one-fourth of the reserves in any township and established a minimum price of 10s. an acre in new townships.[120] In 1834, when the auction system replaced that of private sale, the upset prices ranged from 10s. to 15s., and the terms were one-tenth cash with the balance in nine equal annual instalments.[121] In 1837, cash payment was required for the reserves as for other land, actual settlement was demanded, and lessees were required to pay up all arrears of rent before being allowed to purchase.[122]

The Clergy Reserves Sales Act seems to have been regarded in Canada as a general invitation to the land hungry to occupy the reserves, and the manner in which the act was administered encouraged them to help themselves. Persons wishing to purchase put in an application which was regarded as giving them a right of pre-emption at whatever valuation was fixed after the reserve had been inspected. Without further formality, many persons then took possession of the reserve of their choice. When the auction system was adopted, lessees and their assignees and those whose titles had not progressed beyond the application-to-purchase stage were regarded as still being entitled to purchase at a valuation based on the value of unimproved land. Squatters also claimed this privilege and were allowed it until 1836, when Robert Baldwin Sullivan became Commissioner of Crown Lands He restricted the privilege to squatters whose occupancy antedated the adoption of the auction system. So numerous were the applications to purchase under pre-emption privileges that Sullivan was finally forced to discontinue sales at auction so as to reserve for the pre-emption claimants the balance of the acreage permitted to be sold under the Act of 1827. Many of those who applied to purchase were already on the land and had not obtained regular sales contracts when sales under the act ceased. Others, who were outright squatters and who had never troubled themselves about an application to purchase, were subsequently to claim that their repeated efforts to regularize their position failed. Thus the limitations of the Act of 1827 were to create a difficult squatter problem for the future.[123]

The results of the Clergy Reserves Sales Act fully justified the reluctance of Strachan to see the reserves sold to the Canada Company and the strictures of Robinson on the report of the Canada Committee of 1828. Within three years of its passage, the reserves were selling at an average price of 15s. an acre and, during the life of the act, 530,913 acres were sold at an average price of 13s. $4\frac{1}{2}d$.[124] To be sure, the land was sold on ten years' credit and some of it, particularly in the Johnstown District, was stripped of its timber and abandoned. However, these results compare favourably with the 3s. 6d. which the Canada Company had proposed to pay on fifteen years' credit without interest—terms which Robinson considered equivalent to a cash price of 2s. 1d. an acre.[125] Not more than seven or eight persons purchased clergy land in quantities exceeding 1,000 acres—at least in their own names—and, considering the relatively high prices for which the reserves sold, one is tempted to conclude that nine-tenths of them passed into the hands of owner-occupants. Four-fifths of the acreage was sold prior to the Rebellion, and the surprising thing is that the instalment payments were quite regularly paid. By the close of 1837, the arrears did not exceed 20 per cent of the amount then due. There was a serious slump in collections in 1838, but in 1839 and 1840 recovery was prompt.[126] The purchasers were either established farmers in the older districts buying land for their sons or new immigrants with capital.[127]

After 1827, then, Upper Canada could no longer legitimately complain that the Clergy Reserves were a hindrance to settlement. They could be leased from the Clergy Corporation whose activities, suspended during the negotiations with the Canada Company, were resumed in 1829 and continued until 1832; they could also be purchased from the Commissioner of Crown Lands on much easier terms of credit than Crown land or than the Canada Company would grant for the Crown Reserves it had bought. Yet the Reformers in the Assembly continued to regard the Clergy Reserves as a grievance because only a part of the reserves could be purchased and because the revenue from them was not being used for the benefit of the province as a whole, nor was it at the disposal of its legislature.

Meanwhile, Sir John Colborne had become Lieutenant-Governor of Upper Canada and was actively promoting the settlement of the province by British immigrants. Colborne was somewhat critical of the work of the Clergy Corporation. He acknowledged that the Clergy leases enabled poor immigrants to get established on the land, but he thought that $\frac{1}{2}d.$ an acre for twenty-one years would be a rate that would cause the reserves to be taken up quickly and would enable settlers to accumulate the capital with which to purchase at the end of that time. The rate Colborne suggested was much lower than the $5.00, $10.00, $15.00 rate for a lease of three seven-year periods established in 1822 for half reserves.[128] Although no admirer of Strachan, Colborne yet wished to protect what he regarded as the endowment of the Church of England against a day when, as a result of colonization, her adherents would be the most numerous religious denomination in the province. Early in his administration, he came to the conclusion that in view of sectarian jealousies the best thing to do was to lift the whole question out of provincial politics. He therefore suggested to Goderich that the Imperial Parliament be asked to re-invest the reserves in the Crown for the support of a Protestant Episcopal clergy and such other Protestant clergy as the Imperial government should choose to assist.[129] The continued opposition of the Council to the Assembly's various proposals for using the reserves for education and the general improvement of the province confirmed him in this opinion.

The Colonial Secretary contrived a nice solution of the Clergy Reserves question which made it unnecessary for a number of delicate questions relating to them to be decided. The law officers of the Crown were of the opinion that the clergy of the Church of Scotland were a Protestant clergy within the meaning of the Constitutional Act. If so, was not the charter of the Clergy Corporation illegal? Were not all Protestant sects entitled to a share of the reserves? Would it then not be wiser to divert the revenue to the support of education or some other purpose of general benefit? These and other problems Goderich chose to put aside and to deal with the reserves in a pragmatic fashion. The plain fact was that the Clergy Reserve system was a costly failure. During the forty years the system had been in existence, the total amount of income the reserves had yielded had not equalled the expense of managing them. In addition, they had been an obstacle to the settlement of the province, a recurring topic of complaint, and had created sectarian animosities. Therefore, wrote the Colonial Secretary, "His Majesty's Government have advised the abandonment of the Reserves ... for the simple reason that after an experience of forty years they have been found not to answer ... expectations. ..." [130] Instructions that no more reserves be leased or sold followed this statement of policy. [131] A royal message inviting the legislature to amend the Clergy Reserves provisions of the Constitutional Act accompanied this dispatch. [132]

Goderich also supplied a bill which provided for the repeal of the Clergy Reserves provisions of the Constitutional Act, vested existing reserves in the Crown, declared existing contracts of sale or lease valid, and required lessees to pay their rents to the Crown. Goderich's dispatch arrived on the very day the legislature was due to be prorogued The bill was introduced without delay, a motion for a second reading, seconded by Bidwell, received a majority of 29–7, but the members of the Assembly, anxious to go home, showed no disposition, according to Colborne, to take the bill into consideration, and the *Journals* bear him out. Resumption of sales was then authorized. [133]

Charles Lindsey, in his *History of the Present Position of the Clergy Reserves*, accuses Colborne of taking "effectual measures" to make the passage of this re-investment bill impossible. He states that in the session of 1831, Colborne killed it "by a premature prorogation three days after its introduction," and that in the next session, when there was ample time to consider it, the bill was not even carried beyond its first reading. "All the evidence goes to prove that the Canadian oligarchy wished to defeat a measure which the Imperial authorities had recommended and of which the great majority of the people anxiously desired the success." [134]

Lindsay is unfair to Colborne but his suspicion that the church party was working against the bill was well founded. Of course Colborne did not like the re-investment bill. He had suggested a bill re-investing the reserves in the Crown for religious purposes; what he got was a bill that would have merged the Clergy Reserves in the mass of Crown lands and freed them of all restrictions. Strachan prepared to fight the re-investment bill to the end. His plan was to defeat it in the Council if possible. If he did not succeed, he intended to incorporate the message with the bill and to send it back to the Assembly "where," he predicted, "it will be defeated." As a last resort, he planned to send an agent to England to lobby against its confirmation. [135] The sentences of the royal message which Strachan felt that some members of the Assembly would never accept were those references to the just claims of the established churches of England and Scotland and the intimation that the clergy would be otherwise provided for. Goderich's re-investment bill was introduced a second time by the Attorney General in the session of 1832-3 and again allowed to die. Strachan's supporters did not want it and neither did the Reformers. What they wanted was not re-investment but the sale of the Clergy Reserves, as their support of Perry's sale bill at this session shows. [136]

Had this re-investment bill passed—and been confirmed—it would have settled the Clergy Reserve question and removed it from Canadian politics a full twenty years before that happy result was finally achieved; but its passage at this time would probably have intensified the struggle over control of the Casual and Territorial Revenue of the Crown in Upper Canada. To have abolished the Clergy Reserves by merging them into the Crown lands and then to have provided for a Protestant clergy by grants out of the Territorial Revenue, with preferential treatment for the Church of England, would merely have strengthened the determination of the Reformers to win for the province complete control of all sources of provincial revenue.

In the session of 1833-4, the conservative minority in the Assembly was prepared to support a bill which would have ended the practice of creating Clergy Reserves for the future, but the reforming majority led by Perry and Howard was not to be satisfied with a measure which would have left the existing reserves untouched.[137] Instead, they put through, by a vote of 22–12, a bill to repeal the Clergy Reserve provisions of the Constitutional Act and to provide for the sale of all the existing reserves for the support of education. This bill took the management of the reserves entirely out of the hands of the provincial executive and entrusted their sale to twelve district commissioners assisted by the clerks and collectors of the townships in their districts. Such clergy land as was not sold at private sale nor under lease was to be offered at auction by the commissioners. One-fourth of it in each township annually, and after the fourth year, all that remained, was to be sold at an upset price to be determined by the board of the township. The terms were one-tenth down and the balance in nine annual instalments. Actual settlement of the land was not required of purchasers by this bill as it was under the Crown's instructions for the sale of Clergy Reserves.[138]

The loosely worded provisions in this bill respecting private sales would have enabled the Assembly's commissioners to reward their friends and to make it easy for lessees, squatters, and collusive speculators to acquire the reserves at a low rate. No greater degree of impartiality in the land system would have resulted from the Assembly's taking the management of the reserves out of the hands of the provincial executive and certainly no substantial endowment would have been obtained for the cause of education. Six of the commissioners named in the bill were members of the Assembly, five were former members, and none were members of the Legislative Council or of the provincial executive. By pointing out that for three years the Assembly had had the management of the school lands voluntarily surrendered to it by the Crown and that in the course of that time it had not taken a single step towards turning the endowment to account, the Legislative Council cast doubt upon the sincerity of the Assembly's concern for education and implied that the members merely wanted to get their hands on the reserves.[139] In the Assembly, William Morris made that point even plainer by moving that the authority for sales be placed in the hands of the sheriffs. This amendment was decisively defeated, 9–23, the majority being determined to bring about the rapid sale of the reserves by placing the management of them in the hands of the Assembly's nominees, assisted by popularly elected officials, rather than in the hands of appointees of the Lieutenant-Governor.[140]

A year later, after the election of 1834 had increased the strength of the Reformers, Perry introduced another bill for the sale of the reserves for education, the provisions of which were very similar to those of the previous bill, and it passed the Assembly, 39–7.[141] The Council rejected Perry's bill and tried to get the Assembly to concur in a vaguely worded address asking the Imperial Parliament to take over the problem and to settle it "with a due regard to

religion, the principles of our constitution and the tranquillity of the province."
The Assembly's answer was a strongly worded resolution which deprecated
Imperial interference on a subject which was legally under provincial jurisdiction. The Assembly also intimated that the composition of the Legislative
Council should be changed to prevent it blocking the people's will.[142] In 1836,
Peter Perry again introduced a bill for the sale of the reserves for education
which passed the Assembly, 35–5. The Council returned the Assembly's bill so
amended as to provide for the re-investment of the reserves in the Crown for
religious purposes only. Nothing was left of the Assembly's bill but the word
"whereas." It indignantly amended the bill back again to its original form.[143]

It was at this point in the history of the Clergy Reserves dispute that Sir John
Colborne made the mistake of creating and endowing rectories in Upper Canada
with portions of the Clergy Reserves. This step was taken with the advice of
his Council and, according to Strachan, "after much deliberation." "It was,"
says Lindsey, "almost the last act of his government performed under peculiar
circumstances of embarrassment, when his mind was perplexed by the intelli-
gence of his recall." [144] On January 15, 1836, the Council recommended the
endowment of 57 rectories, and the patents for 44 of them had been completed
by January 25, when Colborne was succeeded by Head.

The existence of the rectory patents did not become known until after Colborne had left the country and then the news aroused widespread dissatisfaction. The Assembly, by a vote of 38–5, resolved that the endowment of the
rectories called for "immediate remedy," and throughout the province the rectories were condemned in public meetings and newspapers.[145] Colborne and
his Council were charged with acting secretly and with rushing the patents
through to completion before the Lieutenant-Governor's successor should arrive.
The very language of the Council's recommendation, which advised that "no
time be lost" in preparing the patents, has been quoted in proof of this charge.
The Imperial government itself was accused of having broken faith with the
people of Upper Canada by authorizing the endowment of rectories after publicly
declaring only a few months previously that the future appropriation of the
Clergy Reserves was a question for the local legislature to decide. A newly
organized society, the Friends of Civil and Religious Liberty, put the whole
dispute in a nutshell when it said, "The state has no wealth but the people's
wealth and therefore that wealth cannot be bestowed partially." [146]

Colborne's successor, Francis Bond Head, expressed his regret at the action
of his predecessor and declared that the rectory patents constituted one of his
most serious embarrassments in the administration of his government.[147] However, he did not choose to inform the Colonial Office of their existence until
December 7, 1836, although throughout the year they had occasioned much
public discussion and discontent. During the notorious election campaign of
1836, Head and his supporters, in their strenuous efforts to defeat the Reformers,
found the rectory patents a nasty obstacle on the road to victory. In this election,
the basic issue was not the Clergy Reserves but the subject of the rectories kept
arising. William Ryerson wrote to his brother:

We are on the eve of a new election; the excitement throughout the country at large, & especially the parts where I am best acquainted, exceeds anything I have ever known. I feel very

fearful of the results. There would be very little cause for doubt or fear as to the results was it not for one of the last acts of Sir John Colborne's administration in establish [ing] & endowing . . . 57 rectories . . . if the election should turn out most disastrous to the best interests of the country, it can only, or chiefly, be attributed to that unjust & most impolitic act . . . everywhere the rectory question meets us. . . .[148]

In the new Parliament, the rectories question was the subject of a lengthy and violent debate which lasted from four in the afternoon until two the following morning. The House was in a disgraceful uproar, reported Mackenzie, with some members stamping their feet, beating on the stovepipe with a piece of iron and one of them, MacNab, grunting like a hog in derision of the Reformers. The latter were in a minority, 32-21, and unable to defeat a resolution which stated, "This House regards as inviolable the rights acquired under the Patents by which rectories have been endowed and cannot therefore either invite or sanction any interference with the rights thus established." [149]

Matters were not improved when Glenelg directed Head to inform the protesting Presbyterians that the Imperial government had not authorized the creation and endowment of the rectories and that the law officers of the Crown were of the opinion that the patents were invalid. This information was sent to the Synod of the Church of Scotland in Canada in September, 1837. At the same time Head informed the Synod that Strachan had been invited to amend the case for the church if he could and that in the meantime proceedings on the rectory question would be suspended. A few months later, the law officers reversed their opinion,[150] but since they had stated that the rectors would have the same ecclesiastical jurisdiction as the rectors of an English parish, the legislature of Upper Canada, in the session of 1839, passed the act 3 Vic., c. 74, which denied them this jurisdiction.

Why were the law officers so uncertain regarding Colborne's actions with respect to the rectories? After the passage of the Clergy Reserves Sales Act of 1827, the Colonial Office had directed that 300–400 acres of reserves be kept in every township for a glebe. In February, 1832, Colborne had suggested that a surplus of £4,000 derived from the Casual and Territorial Revenues, and not needed for the payment of salaries and allowances to clergymen, as the Clergy Reserve Fund was now able to provide those sums, might be used to build rectories and churches. Goderich had approved of this idea and had suggested in addition that some of the money might be spent in preparing "for profitable occupation that moderate portion of Land which *you* propose to assign in each Township for increasing the future Comfort, if not the complete maintenance of the Rectors. With this view it appears to me that it would be most desirable to make a beginning in this salutary work by *assigning it a portion at least of the £4,000. . . .*" Colborne's subsequent specific suggestions for the expenditure of this money having been approved, he felt himself authorized to build rectories and churches and to prepare glebe lots for cultivation.[151]

After Colborne had made his decision, the Council began to have the glebe lots selected in townships where this had not already been done, to see that the selections did not occasion disputes with lessees or pre-emption claimants, and to devise the form of paten to be used. In September, 1834, Mackenzie reported, as a result of what he called his "Tour of the West Riding," that Strachan was selecting all the best reserves for glebes, and later he quoted R. B. Sullivan as having told the Assembly that Strachan had applied for 235,206 acres of Clergy Reserves for glebes and that the Council had recommended 85,000 acres for this purpose.[152] The work of selection took some time but by January 16, 1836, the specific endowments for fifty-seven rectories, 27,069 acres, had been chosen. As a final step, the Council recommended that "no time be lost" in preparing the patents. Their report to Colborne misquoted Goderich as follows: "Pursuant to the view of Lord Goderich, shown by his despatch of the 5th of April, 1832, in which he concurs with your Excellency, and expresses *his* desire 'that a moderate portion of *land* should be assigned in each Township or Parish, for ensuring the future comfort, if not the complete maintenance of the Rectors, . . .,'"[153] and had used this misquotation to justify their recommendation that the endowments be patented. On the basis of the above facts it was decided that Colborne had not been specifically authorized to create and endow rectories.

This embarrassing opinion was reversed when Strachan reminded the Colonial Office that on two earlier occasions the Lieutenant-Governor of Upper Canada had been specifically authorized to constitute rectories or parishes in every township and, on the second of these occasions, he had also been instructed to endow them with so much of the Clergy Reserves in each township as his Council should advise and to appoint incumbents.[154] Although Maitland had not used his power, this instruction had not been revoked. On the basis of these facts it was decided on the second occasion that the rectory patents were valid.

This decision overlooked the fact that since 1825 the Imperial government had twice changed its policy respecting the Clergy Reserves and that therefore Maitland's instructions had become obsolete. After 1831, a policy of re-investment was favoured and Colborne was told that an endowment out of the reserves to a proposed suffragan bishop was inconsistent with that policy.[155] By 1835 the government had decided to leave the disposition of the Clergy Reserves to the provincial legislature.[156] Colborne had been informed of this on three occasions during that year.[157] In endowing the rectories he was acting contrary to Imperial policy and he ought to have known it.

While the excitement over the rectory patents prevailed during the years 1836–9, the larger issue of the Clergy Reserves continued to be debated. In the thirteenth Parliament of Upper Canada, elected in 1836, the strength of the Reformers had been sharply reduced; but to John Macaulay's disappointment,[158] the newly elected Assembly, which contained so many of the "professed sons" of the church, favoured selling 100,000 acres of the reserves annually, funding the proceeds, and dividing the income among the denominations. One cannot be certain what scheme of distribution the Assembly would in the end have agreed upon nor how the Council would have wished to amend it, but we do know that Head was determined to add to his laurels by settling the Clergy Reserve question. He recommended that the income from the reserves be divided among the Churches of England, Scotland, Rome, and the Wesleyan Methodists in the proportion which these religious groups bore to one another *in the mother country*. Had the Council urged such a scheme upon the Assembly, agreement would certainly have been unlikely. The Solicitor General, C. A. Hagerman, balked at the inclusion of the Roman Catholics and the Canadian Methodists may well have wondered whether they would get a penny.

In the end, Head gave up the attempt. He directed Hagerman to introduce a re-investment bill, after the date set for prorogation and after many of the members had left for home, and reported inaccurately that Hagerman had failed in carrying it by only one vote. The truth was that he had only secured permission to introduce it on condition that consideration of it be postponed until the next session.[159]

During the summer of 1837 the Colonial Office suggested the creation of a fund from the sale of the reserves out of which the various denominations should receive assistance, either in proportion to their numbers or to the efforts they made to help themselves.[160] The latter plan had recently been put into effect in New South Wales. Glenelg sent Head a copy of the New South Wales Act, with the suggestion that a similar measure might restore harmony to his troubled province.[161] In Upper Canada the problem was really four-fold: to compose the conflicting claims of the various denominations; to satisfy those who were determined the reserves should not be diverted from religious purposes; to reconcile those who believed that churches should be supported on the voluntary principle; and to meet the argument that the reserves, made valuable by the labour of all, should benefit the province as a whole. The New South Wales system seemed to Glenelg likely to satisfy both the conscientious supporters of the Clergy Reserves and the supporters of the voluntary system, and, at the same time, to offer at least a rough measure of justice to all parties.

The second session of the thirteenth Parliament of Upper Canada was concerned primarily with the financial crisis and with finding a means of liquidating the £138,650 worth of new provincial debentures which had been issued.[162] In this connection the Reformers proposed that the existing Clergy Reserve Sales Fund should be used and, when this idea was rejected, advocated that the remaining reserves should be sold under the terms of a provincial act, the revenues being used to redeem the debentures. R. B. Sullivan had for some time been urging this policy for both political and economic reasons. If the reserves were sold and the revenues invested in the development of the province, they would not become "a reward for disaffection"; if they were reduced to cash, it would become obvious that they were not as magnificent as one-seventh of the wealth of the province, as those who detested them had explained. "The great mountain dwindles into comparative insignificance ... the illusion is dissipated." [163]

Before the third session of the thirteenth Parliament of Upper Canada met, the Clergy Reserves and the supporters of the voluntary system, and, at the harmony that prevailed was beautiful," [164] but it was not sufficient to settle the reserves question. A re-investment bill introduced by J. S. Cartwright angered Egerton Ryerson who regarded the proposal as "a base and cowardly betrayal of a vital principle of constitutional and free government." [165]

Almost a year elapsed before the legislature met again, and in the meantime the new Lieutenant-Governor, Sir George Arthur, had been busy with negotiations. At first he had hoped that the legislature would settle the question by adopting the system which he had helped to institute in Van Diemen's Land. Under this system, assistance was given to congregations which were prepared to build a church and a residence for their minister, but stipends were paid by the government only to the Episcopal, Presbyterian, and Roman Catholic clergy.[166] Strachan thought the Van Diemen's Land system unsuited to Upper Canada where there were many more sects and he was also strongly opposed to the New South Wales system because it was based on the voluntary system and treated all denominations alike.[167] Strachan's plan was to secure re-investment of the reserves in the Crown for religious purposes, then to persuade the home government to adopt a scheme of distribution more favourable to the Church of England, and to give each denomination "its share once and for ever." [168] This was the goal that Strachan never lost sight of throughout his tortuous negotiations—an endowment for the Church of England that would be indubitably hers.

Because the Assembly was divided into small factions, majority support for any course of action proved difficult to secure. The bill which finally passed the Assembly after a protracted debate of three weeks provided for the sale of the reserves like Crown lands, prevented the creation of Clergy Reserves in future, made possible the reservation of glebes for the various denominations, and required the investment of past and prospective revenues in provincial securities. It also granted out of Clergy Reserve funds salaries of £100 annually to resident ministers of all Christian denominations recognized by law, and provided that the surplus of the fund should be spent in erecting places of worship. Finally, it entrusted the administration of the act to a board of three commissioners to be named by both Houses of the legislature.

This bill was amended by the Council to provide salaries for an Anglican and a Roman Catholic Bishop and financial assistance to clergymen and ministers in proportion to the sums paid them by their congregations. However, permanent assistance of this kind was to be limited to the Churches of England, Scotland, Rome, and to British Wesleyan Methodists. Even in this form the bill was unacceptable to Strachan and John Macaulay who entered on the Council's *Journals* a long protest which concluded by saying that the bill "degraded the clergy of the Church of England to an equality with unauthorized Teachers and sanctions, so far as Human Enactment can sanction, the impious conduct of the wicked Jereboam who made Priests of the lowest of the People." [169] The important word in this protest is equality. The church's staunchest sons had by this time become reconciled to losing part of the reserves. The Council's amendments could not secure majority support in the Assembly and, in the end, the bill was dropped.

The Assembly then turned to a discussion of another Clergy Reserve bill. This bill repealed the Clergy Reserve clauses of the Constitutional Act and provided for the sale of the existing reserves and the appropriation of the prospective revenues by the legislature for religion and education. During the debate a new method of defending the church from her despoilers was resorted to by Burwell and Cartwright who offered a resolution to the effect that the forty-first and forty-second clauses of the Constitutional Act empowered the provincial legislature to make laws concerning only clergy lands taken in specifications. Land simply marked "reserves" on surveys and not specified was waste land of the Crown, the property of the British nation, and therefore was beyond the interference of the provincial legislature. Here was a proposition which brought the much divided Assembly together; it was decisively defeated, 5–39.[170]

The Assembly's second Clergy Reserve bill, which dealt only with prospective revenues and settled nothing as to the manner of distribution, finally passed by the casting vote of the Speaker. Two brief but drastic amendments were made by the Council. The revenue was devoted to religion, not to religion and education, and Imperial appropriation was substituted for provincial. Thus, control was reinvested in the Imperial Parliament. These amendments were accepted by one vote and, as Arthur himself acknowledged, at a late hour on the night preceding prorogation.[171]

Passage of this re-investment bill brought forth a spate of protest channelled to the Colonial Office by the able pen of Egerton Ryerson. Full and free discussion of the reserves question, complained Ryerson, had been officially frowned upon during the disturbed years 1837-9. Those who had persisted had been persecuted as agitators. The 22–21 vote itself was not a true indication of the opinion of the majority but a snap vote secured when many of the members had returned home.[172] This was hardly fair. The debate on the bill had dragged on for weeks and at no time had more than 45 members out of a total of 66 voted on the question. There had already been several late sessions and both sides well knew they were almost evenly matched; but the supporters of the bill as amended by the Council were, apparently, the more determined to stay the course.[173] The Assembly itself, argued Ryerson more justly, was not truly representative of the people of the province. It was still "Head's Assembly," elected in 1836 under what some regarded as peculiar circumstances in support of measures entirely distinct from the Clergy Reserves question.[174] This Assembly was still sitting despite the death of William IV in 1837. Previous Assemblies had voted by large majorities to use the reserves for education and general improvements but the present House favoured a solution of the reserves question utterly at variance with the wishes expressed by all former Houses.

The re-investment bill, which contained no restriction other than that the reserves were to be sold for religious purposes, would have put this land beyond the reach of the "rude and unprincipled assailants" of the Church of England and would have made it possible for the Imperial Parliament to appropriate the reserves among the denominations as inalienable endowments. Archdeacon Strachan promptly prepared to go to England to lobby for "not less than one-half or more than three-fifths" for his denomination. As for the dissenters, he thought the Presbyterians of all kinds might together receive one-fifth, the British Wesleyan Methodists should get an annual monetary grant, and, out of what was left, the Colonial government should assist "other respectable and deserving denominations at its discretion."[175] Strachan was still hoping that the share of his church would come in the form of land. In the end, the bill was not confirmed by the Imperial government. It was not the simple, unconditional re-investment bill that Goderich had originally suggested; the reserves were to be sold and the revenue used for religious purposes. It was a bill by which an inferior legislature would return to a superior legislature a delegated power which it did not choose to use—with a string attached. For this reason, the bill was rejected and the whole weary business had to be gone through again by Arthur's successor, Sydenham.[176]

CHAPTER SIXTEEN

LORD DURHAM'S REPORT AND
ITS AFTERMATH

"LAND POLICY," writes Chester Martin, "lay near the root of the whole fight for responsible government in Canada and provincial control of the public lands was the first fruit of that achievement." [1] What were the grievances of Upper Canada on this subject prior to the Rebellion and what part did they play in precipitating that struggle? With what accuracy did Lord Durham's report portray these grievances, how practical were the remedies it proposed, and to what extent were they put into effect? Did Lord Sydenham have a better grasp of the realities of Upper Canada than his predecessor? What had been accomplished by 1841 and what lessons had been learned—or might have been learned —for the future and what changes in land policy were made?

In the introductory paragraphs of his report Lord Durham lays it down as axiomatic that the resources of the colonies ought to be regarded as Imperial capital. "The country which has founded and maintained these Colonies at a vast expense of blood and treasure, may justly expect its compensation in turning their unappropriated resources to the account of its own redundant population...." [2] Durham's commission to Charles Buller empowered him to investigate the way in which the land system had worked with a view to throwing light not on the causes of the Rebellion but on the extent to which the system had promoted the settlement of the country and, particularly, emigration from the mother country. [3] The whole of Buller's report was slanted to that end. The result was an imperfect picture of the land grievances of the province and of the problems which had been stored up for the future.

Charles Buller, or rather Edward Gibbon Wakefield, who wrote Buller's report on Public Lands and Emigration, [4] pointed out that in the past the complaint of the colonies had been that the Imperial Parliament had not exercised its powers but had delegated them to a Lieutenant-Governor advised by an irresponsible and self-interested Executive Council. [5] Several of the questions put to John Radenhurst, Chief Clerk of the Surveyor General's Office, were tendencious and designed to establish this view of the matter. [6] The colonial legislatures, advised Wakefield, were the proper repositories of these powers if they were to be delegated at all; but the legislatures would, he thought, accept Imperial administration exercised for the mutual good of the colonies and the mother country. [7]

Wakefield's summary statement of the way in which land policy had been made in the past ignores the role of the Assembly. The Colonial Office had laid down the main lines of policy, the Council had worked out the all-important administrative details, and its advice had influenced, although not wholly occasioned, changes from one system to another. However, the Assembly had also petitioned the Crown for changes and its complaints had not been ignored. One by one the grievances of which Upper Canada complained during the years preceding the Rebellion had been remedied, but unfortunately each well-meant remedy had either failed to remove the evil complained of or had created a new evil in place of, sometimes in addition to, the old.

The first complaint had been that land was granted upon seigneurial tenure. The Constitutional Act redressed it by providing for the exchange of land certificates for patents in free and common socage. The exchange proved to be a complicated and lengthy business which delayed the issuing of patents, prolonged speculation in land certificates, and aroused bitterness and suspicion.

The second grievance arose out of the attempts of the Imperial government to change over from a free grant to a revenue system by increasing the patent fees and by imposing half fees on U.E. loyalist and military claimants. This grievance also had been remedied—too amply remedied. The regulations finally adopted confirmed the U.E. loyalists in their right to 200 acres patent free and also extended Imperial recognition to the claims of their children to the same privileges. The result was that the great number of U.E. loyalists' rights thus created fastened on the province the evil of land speculation from which the Imperial government had planned to protect it.

The third set of grievances grew out of the policies of Lieutenant-Governor Hunter, who had tried to keep the numbers of loyalists entitled to free patents to a minimum and who also, from motives not wholly disinterested, had attempted to expedite the passing of land to patent. These grievances were redressed only in part and could not have been more fully removed without making the term U.E. loyalists meaningless. The result was the development in Upper Canada of a discontented minority whom no tinkering with the land regulations would satisfy. They were bent on regulation of the Crown lands by statute, complete provincial control of the land revenues and, as a result, limitation of the executive's freedom of action. With this group, immigrants from the United States found political kinship.

The fourth grievance related to land policy grew out of the stagnation which appeared to threaten Upper Canada after 1815. How should population be attracted to the province and where should it be drawn from, the United States or Great Britain? Here was a problem which could not be solved without leaving one part of Upper Canada's society discontented. Here was a dispute which, originating in Simcoe's day, continued right up to the Rebellion and passed through several phases leaving first one side and then the other dissatisfied.

Until the War of 1812 American immigration was chiefly responsible for the rapid growth of the province. Many of those who wished American immigration to continue after the war did so from motives of self-interest. Then, as now, the steady growth of the economy was necessary to prosperity and, for Upper Canada, that meant primarily the expansion of the area under cultivation. Immigrants with capital, or at least with the ability to establish themselves on the land without it, were needed, and the United States was the source from which they were most likely to come. The Tory Party, unable to exclude Americans, did its best to minimize their political influence. They were handicapped, however, by the fact that the alien question (who, among immigrants of various dates, were aliens and who were not) had not been settled.

One would have expected the Tory loyalists of Upper Canada to have given hearty support to the British government's post-war policy of colonizing discharged soldiers and British immigrants in the province. At first, under the leadership of Gore, they were hostile—or at least unco-operative. Later, under the guidance of Robinson and Maitland, their attitude changed and they began to see both the economic and the political advantages of this immigration. As C. A. Hagerman put it, "The only thing that can save us from the Lower Canada French on the one hand or the United States on the other is by encouraging British immigrants and a Union of the provinces. . . . Every attention should be paid the immigrants." [8]

The Reformers also became aware of the political influence which these immigration and settlement schemes placed in the hands of the Tory government of Upper Canada and, while not opposed to the admission of British immigrants as such, they were not disposed to acquiesce in the use of the Crown lands and the Crown revenues to strengthen the hands of their political opponents. They assisted in driving from the province a Lieutenant-Governor who did not use this power corruptly and got in his place one who did. At times their opposition to the government's policies was so vituperatively expressed as to enable their opponents to accuse them of hostility to all classes of British immigrants, whether politically influential half-pay officers, assisted paupers "encroaching upon the political rights of the 'Children of the Soil'," or discharged soldiers "bribed and demoralized ruffians by whose assistance the cause of freedom is to be controlled." [9] By the eighteen-thirties both parties were anxious to promote the development of Upper Canada. The whole question was under whose auspices—the Tory executive or the Reform legislature—it was to be done, and what political party should be strengthened as a result. After the alien question had been decided in 1828, Americans, even though legally unable to hold land in Upper Canada, continued to come in as Buchanan had predicted they would,[10] to purchase land, to squat, to steal timber, and to settle as mechanics in the towns. Alien landholders and alien squatters, who looked to the Reformers to protect and regularize their position, voted for township offices, took control in some townships, monopolized the road money, and made things hard for British immigrants.[11] Under such circumstances it is not surprising that in 1836, when the Assembly voted on the question of permitting Americans to hold land in Upper Canada, representatives from the counties newly colonized with British immigrants voted solidly against it. Nor is it surprising that Head's appeal to their British traditions should have been so successful.

The most publicized of Upper Canada's grievances was the Clergy Reserves. This grievance, too, had been remedied in part before the Rebellion by the sale of one-fourth of the reserves, but the revenue arising from these sales had intensified the struggle for the equality of all religious sects in Upper Canada. In addition, the limitations on the amount to be sold, together with the slow process of inspection and valuation, had given squatters an opportunity to establish claims that were to complicate the sale of the balance of these lands during the years 1840–67. To these numerous squatters Mackenzie made a direct appeal, promising free gifts of the Clergy Reserve and glebe lots to those who were settled upon them.[12] Wakefield's report gave ample attention to the Clergy Reserves. Witnesses repeatedly deplored the harm they had done to the settlement of the country and the political turmoil they had created. Strachan and G. S. Boulton were exceptions.

Lord Durham dealt with the Clergy Reserves in vigorous language which proved misleading. The question of greatest practical importance on which the various political parties had differed, said Durham, had been the Clergy Reserves, and the bitterness of the dispute had become intensified by the endowment of the rectories. "In the opinion of many persons this [the rectories] was the chief predisposing cause of the recent insurrection. . . ." In addition, he quoted and accepted without modification the opinion of the select committee of the House of Commons of 1828 that these reserves had retarded the improvement of the colony more than any other circumstance.[14]

Durham's successor, Charles Poulett Thomson, later Lord Sydenham, took up this language and referred to the Clergy Reserves as "the one great overwhelming grievance—the root of all the troubles of the Province—the cause of the Rebellion. . . ."[15] This statement ignores other political and economic grievances, particularly the dispute over the control of the Casual and Territorial Revenue, a matter which Sydenham did not fully appreciate. It ignores, too, all the bitterness created by the "Family Compact." Mackenzie said, in a letter listing the various grievances of Upper Canada for Colborne's benefit, "The longer it be before the financial concerns of the colony are placed upon a system of strict accountability to the commons, the worse for British interests," and Marshall Spring Bidwell wrote:

It [the Clergy Reserve question] is not, however, by any means the Sole evil or the cause of the troubles in that country [Canada]. The System in which the Government has been administered—that of disregarding the opinions and wishes of the people generally and of advancing and sustaining and rewarding those only who adopted that Course, is at the foundation of all the troubles,—and while that System Continues it is of Comparatively little importance what is done with the Clergy Reserves.[16]

As for the rectories, they were one of the grievances mentioned in the "Declaration of the Reformers of Toronto." The resolutions of the eighteen township or district meetings reported in the *Constitution* all upheld this "Declaration" in general words, and mentioned specific grievances in their own words, but only one of them mentioned the rectories.[17] It is far more likely that the precipitating causes of the Rebellion were Head's misuse of the Land Department, coupled with the act of the newly elected legislature in extending its own life.[18]

Durham's recommendations that all the provisions in Imperial acts relating to the Clergy Reserves and the use of the Clergy Reserve Fund should be repealed, and that the problem should be left to the local legislature, were not followed. Had his advice been taken, Sydenham's political intrigues would have been unnecessary, the legislature of Upper Canada would have been free to frame a Clergy Reserve bill without regard to the bishops in the House of Lords, and the legal obstacles to provincial action—an uncharted rock on which Sydenham's bill was to founder—would not have existed.

If the Clergy Reserves received adequate attention from Lord Durham, the Crown Reserves did not. Durham, no doubt, regarded the deposition of these reserves as settled. By 1837, the leased Crown Reserves had been given to King's College; the unleased ones, in townships surveyed by March 1, 1824, had been sold to the Canada Company; in townships surveyed subsequently they were open to purchase. But the sale to the Canada Company had given general dissatisfaction and was still a lively issue. The Tories regarded the sale as an improvident one and a hindrance to the settlement of the country by British immigrants who might have taken up the Crown Reserves as they did the Clergy Reserves.[19] The Reformers denounced the sale because it permitted a group of favoured absentee speculators to profit at the expense of all whose labour had given value to the country and because the payments made by the Company were spent without the concurrence of the Assembly and in ways which they did not consider to be "for the public use and general benefit." [20]

Another complaint against the Canada Company was that it enjoyed special favours not open to other holders of wild land. Mackenzie's followers believed that the Company had the ear of the Colonial Office and that alterations in the regulations for the sale of Crown lands had been made to further its interests.[21] The Company was also thought to be escaping the wild land taxes to which other landholders were subject by not calling for patents for all the land its annual instalment payments entitled it to, but only for patents for land sold to settlers. Since unpatented and unoccupied land was not subject to taxation, this practice, it was believed, enabled the Company to hold its land for high prices without running into the tax costs that other land speculators had to meet.[22] In 1835, a select committee of the Assembly reported in favour of having the Company's charter abolished, or else of taxing all the lands placed at its disposal so as to force them to sale.[23] The charge of tax evasion had no validity after 1838. The Company was able to show by that time that its contract was two-thirds fulfilled and the land two-thirds patented. Of the 1,403,787 acres under patent, 692,282 acres were in the possession of settlers paying taxes on them; on the remaining 711,505 acres the Company paid the taxes.[24]

A major grievance against the Canada Company was that it had obtained a most favourable bargain at the expense of the province without the consent of its legislature, and that it had failed to abide by the conditions of the agreement. In making the contract, the Imperial government had entrusted the settlement of an undeveloped area of Upper Canada to a group of capitalists who were expected, by their expenditures for roads, bridges, and other public improvements, to give employment and to introduce capital into the province. While the main object of the sale had been to relieve the Treasury of the expense of supporting the civil government of Upper Canada, the Imperial government also planned to use part of the revenue for internal improvements. Instead of making this revenue available to the legislature, or even entrusting it to the governor-in-council, the Imperial government had agreed to allow the Company to retain one-third of the purchase price for the Huron Tract to be spent on approved public works. A similar arrangement had been made with respect to settlement duties on Crown Reserves not sold to settlers within the year they were patented to the Company. The Company preferred the option of spending

$35.00 a lot on approved public works in lieu of the settlement duties, rather than of paying out $25.00 a lot to the government of Upper Canada for the same purpose.[25]

What the Company did was to employ settlers to open roads and to pay them in land. One witness testified that for the first five years the Company paid for such labour one-third in cash and two-thirds in land at the rate of 7s. 6d. an acre.[26] Another testified that in some contracts for road-making the entire payment was in land at 15s. an acre— land which the Company had received from the government for 2s. 9d. It was also claimed that these fictitious expenditures were allowed them by the government of Upper Canada as part of the purchase price of their contract.[27]

Down to the Rebellion, the Canada Company was believed to have introduced very little capital into the province beyond the purchase price for the land, which was being spent on salaries and pensions; but as the Select Committee of 1835 complained, the Company actually took money out of the province. Mackenzie drew attention to the profits of the Company as reported to its annual meetings and complained that these sums were "lost" to the country and that farmers' sons had to pay dear for land.[28] On July 30, 1835, the *Correspondent and Advocate* noted with satisfaction a sharp decline in the value of the Canada Company's shares, a fall which the *London Examiner* had attributed to the resolutions of the Assembly calling for cancellation of the Company's charter.

W. W. Baldwin discussed the sale to the Canada Company at length for the benefit of the Durham Commission and denounced it in passionate terms, of which the brief and restrained words of his printed evidence give no hint. "It has been a miserable bargain" wrote Baldwin, "ruinous to the best interests of the province and will continue to be so to the end of time." [29] He recommended that the Company's contract be examined and, if it could be shown that the terms had not been rigidly lived up to, it should be abrogated, leaving to the Company only those lands actually paid for and patented.

Durham and Wakefield had before them all the evidence of Sullivan and Baldwin respecting the Canada Company, as well as the legislative history of Upper Canada. The sessions of 1835, 1836, and 1837 clearly show how much Upper Canada resented the sale. It was clear, too, that Mackenzie had counted on making use of the hostile attitude towards the Canada Company. His hand-bill calling for volunteers had promised free deeds to all settlers who lived on the Company's lands.[30] In the report Buller contended himself with saying that the sale to the Canada Company was intended to be a delegation of the government's power of disposing of the Crown lands and that settlement appeared to have proceeded somewhat more rapidly and regularly upon the Canada Company's land than on that retained by the Crown.[31] Lord Durham ignored the whole question.

A sixth grievance of which Upper Canada had complained was the patronage and favouritism, secrecy and inefficiency in the administration of the Crown lands. Gourlay's district and township meetings had stressed this complaint. The Assembly had, by repeated requests for information on surveys, grants, locations, authorities, fees, sales, valuation, and prices, shown its distrust of the executive,[32] and the Durham Commission took additional testimony on these points. These grievances had been remedied. The free grant system had given way to the sales system, valuations to a fixed upset price, and favouritism to the impartial system of sales by auction. Again, the result had been to create new grievances. Immigrants, complained the Assembly, were deterred from settling in Upper Canada because their choice of land was restricted, the upset price was too high—10s. for all qualities of land—and speculators, by fictitious purchases, prevented immigrants from obtaining desirable land at auction.[33] A final remedy ordered by the Colonial Office, cash payment within fourteen days, had not, it was admitted, been put into effect. The Commission received ample admission of the truth of these complaints from the Commissioner and the Chief Clerk of the Crown Lands Office. Only 300,000 acres of Crown land had been offered for sale in the decade 1827–37, and immigrants had in practice been thus restricted in their choice of land.[34] No wonder some of the government's critics saw in this fact a design to favour large landowners and the Canada Company.

On the eve of the Rebellion, the manner in which the Colonial Office was utilizing the Crown land revenues of Upper Canada constituted as great a grievance as the Clergy Reserves.[35] The Crown lands were regarded as provincial, not Imperial, capital because their value had been created by the settlers, not with the assistance of the mother country, but under the handicaps imposed by her policies: extensive reserves for the Crown and clergy and extensive grants by way of rewards to both civil and military persons, not all of whom had served in Canada. As one group of Mackenzie's supporters put it, "We are sensible, moreover, that the worth of the country is the work of our own hands." [36] When this wealth was realized by the sale of the land, the community which had created it was not permitted to dispose of it. True, the revenue was applied to provincial uses under the direction of the Colonial Office but not in ways that the Reformers regarded as of general benefit.

Until 1824, the revenues from the Crown lands did not cover the cost of acquiring and administering them, and the deficits had been made up out of the Military Chest.[37] By 1828 the Canada Company's annual payments had begun and the next year the Crown lands began to yield a steadily increasing revenue from sales and from timber licences. From this time on the Territorial Revenues of the Crown were worth fighting for. After 1827, when the Imperial Parliament ceased to make its annual grant for Upper Canada, the expenses of the civil government were paid out of the Casual and Territorial Revenues as were certain supplementary items which the Parliamentary grant had not covered since 1817. The Reformers in the Assembly resented this use of the land revenues, and in 1829 that body resolved that the possession of revenue by the executive, independent of the legislature, was inconsistent with public liberty.[38] Moreover, as Peter Perry pointed out at a later date, use of the land revenues meant that the financial needs of the province were really being met out of the land payments of struggling settlers, who were deprived of funds they needed to develop their farms, instead of by a tax levied by the legislature on the owners of improved property who had already made themselves comfortable and were in a better position to contribute to the necessities of society.[39]

In 1831, when the revenue from the Imperial customs duties was surrendered, the legislature granted a civil list, not, however, as large or as inclusive as the

Imperial government had requested. The Casual and Territorial Revenues were then used to supplement the civil list, for grants to King's College and Upper Canada College, for compensatory payments to officials in lieu of fees, for increased grants to the clergy, for pensions, and for assistance to immigrants.[40] Meanwhile, the province financed the construction of public works by borrowing. In 1834 it was proposed to raise money for the Welland Canal by taxing cultivated lands in the London, Niagara, and Western Districts 3d. an acre, uncultivated land 2d., and all land in other parts of the province 1d. This proposal to "tax the sweat of the farmer's brow" elicited from the *Correspondent* another diatribe on the manner in which the public revenues were being spent.[41] "The command over the wastelands ... and the civil and military expenditure derived from [Great Britain]," wrote Mackenzie, "have left all power in the hands of the executive government and rendered the apparent constitutional check derived from ... electing a legislature ... rather mischievous than otherwise, it serving as a cloak to legislative acts for promoting ... individual ... interests at the sacrifice of the public good, and that, too, with an apparent sanction from the people...." [42]

Not only were the Casual and Territorial Revenues appropriated without the consent of the province from which they were raised, they were also most inadequately accounted for to the Imperial government as well as to the provincial legislature. In 1830, the Assembly unanimously supported Mackenzie's motion for complete information about these revenues, and Goderich agreed to the request.[43] The Colonial Secretary himself was not much better informed, and he complained to Colborne of the complete lack of accounts, both receipts and expenditures.[44] A comparison of the estimated yield of the revenues from the Crown lands and Crown timber for 1831-3, on which Goderich was obliged to base his directions for expenditures, with the figures for these years subsequently supplied by Robert Baldwin Sullivan to Durham, shows that the revenue was about twice what he believed it to be. A comparison, too, of the amounts collected by the Commissioner of Crown Lands with the amount which the Receiver General reported having received from him reveals a marked discrepancy.[45] It is obvious the revenues were not paid over promptly. The unbusinesslike Peter Robinson, whose accounts for the Irish immigration of 1823-5 were not yet settled, died in 1837. His accounts with the government were then found to be more than £10,000 in arrears, but the trustees of his estate expected to be able to make this amount good from the sale of his property.[46]

Robert Baldwin Sullivan succeeded Robinson as Commissioner of Crown Lands and on the resignation of John Macaulay was appointed Surveyor General as well. No securities were received from Sullivan until the day after the question of securities had been raised in the Assembly.[47] An effort to find out what securities the former Commissioner of Crown Lands had given and a resolution that all monies received by the Commissioner should be placed at the disposal of the legislature and in future be paid to the Receiver General were blocked by the government's supporters in this conservative legislature.[48] Under the administration of R. B. Sullivan, the accounts of the Crown Land Department continued to be confused and unreliable. In 1839 the committee which Sir George Arthur appointed to investigate the Department uncovered various lax practices and large deficiencies for which Sullivan's subordinates were to blame.[49] Although the Commissioner made the sums good, the public once again suffered because Sullivan was later reimbursed out of the Crown land revenues by way of salary. He had had other responsibilities thrust upon him which, the Lieutenant-Governor believed, had made it impossible for him to supervise his own departments closely.[50]

For these successive grievances with respect to the Crown land policies and for this incompetent, if not dishonest, administration, the Reformers of Upper Canada had proposed a general remedy: regulation of the Crown lands by provincial statute and appropriation of the revenues by the provincial legislature. Three times during the life of the eleventh Parliament they attempted to get the Assembly to accept this principle and were out-voted about 2–1.[51] The election of 1834 gave them a triumph. Repeatedly, witnesses before the Grievance Committee favoured surrender of the revenues to provincial appropriation and regulation of the Crown lands by statute. When Head's Assembly was attempting to agree on the method of financing the debentures about to be issued, the Reformers, now in a minority, fought hard to bar the imposition of taxes for their redemption and to amend the bill so as to charge the debentures upon the revenues from the sale of Crown lands, Crown timber, and the Canada Company's payments.[52]

With the foregoing facts before us it is difficult to see what grounds Wakefield had for his belief that either the Tories or the Reformers of Upper Canada would acquiesce in Imperial administration of the Crown lands. Indeed, the Tory land jobbers had never acquiesced in it. They had got what they wanted through their influence in the Executive Council and when they met resistance in Colborne's day, they were ready to proceed by bill in the Assembly. When Glenelg finally agreed that the Crown lands should be regulated by statute, speculators in both camps promptly passed the Land Act of 1837 and secured for themselves advantages in the use of U.E. rights which the Colonial Office had refused to give. In future, they were likely to hold the Imperial government to its word and to insist that the land legislation, although still subject to Imperial confirmation, should be framed by the provincial legislature.

The Reformers had long agitated for provincial control on principle. Their point of view is well expressed by a petition to Head from the township of Albion which asserted the ability of the people to manage the wealth of the country which they had the wit to create. These petitioners had succeeded in establishing themselves as freeholders after what they described as an arduous struggle with frontier conditions during which they had been sustained only by "their God-given qualities of heart and mind." In the process, their intellectual abilities had been "awakened and improved by necessity." Could it be supposed that the qualities which had brought them so far would "fail then now in choosing good from evil . . . when the well being of their children is concerned?"[53] This skilfully worded petition, drawn up though it may have been for, rather than by, the English and Irish settlers in Albion, is a clear statement of the democratic faith of the Reformers.

Durham and Wakefield failed to do the Colonial Office justice; they did not make it plain that numerous grievances relating to land had been remedied.

Both men overlooked the role of the Assembly in bringing these changes about, ignored the hostility of the Reformers to the Canada Company, and failed to appreciate the strength of Upper Canada's conviction that the waste lands of the Crown had become public domain, the revenue from which ought to be administered by its own legislature. Their reports stressed, rather, the strains imposed by the Clergy Reserves, the partiality and favouritism shown under the free grant system, the inconveniences suffered by immigrants under the auction system, and the ill effects on the prosperity of the country of the extensive areas of unimproved land in the hands of speculators and absentees.

Before considering Wakefield's proposed reforms, it is as well to note that his report contained a number of errors into which he was led by the evidence of John Radenhurst, Chief Clerk of the Surveyor General's Office. Wakefield states that no settlement duties had been imposed in Upper Canada until 1818,[54] an error from which even a brief review of the controversy over U.E. rights should have saved him. The practice of charging an additional fee over and above the patent fees began not in 1804, but in 1798. The quantity of land patented on payment of fees prior to 1804 was not given nor were all the subsequent land regulations mentioned. It is unsafe to base any conclusions on the statistics given in Wakefield's report, resting as they do on the incomplete returns supplied by the unreliable Radenhurst. The report of the Surveyor General's Department showed 17,653,544 acres of surveyed land in Upper Canada of which 1,597,019 were vacant, including 450,000 allowed for roads. A total of 16,056,525 acres had been granted or appropriated. Of this quantity, Radenhurst accounted for 11,397,758 acres, leaving the disposition of 4,658,767 acres unexplained.[55] In 1839 a committee appointed by Sir George Arthur to investigate the Crown Lands and the Surveyor General's Departments accompanied its strictures on the lax manner in which the land business had been conducted with a more complete set of returns which showed a smaller quantity of surveyed land and accounted for most of the missing acreage.[56]

The report of Sir George Arthur's committee amply justified the public's complaints of inefficiency and favouritism in the administration of the public lands. The committee found that, contrary to the regulations, Radenhurst had acted as a private land agent while holding public office and, as the Lieutenant-Governor noted, he had not limited his favours to the members of one political party. He had allowed U.E. and militia claims to be located on land supposedly reserved for sale and had permitted patents to issue for land on which required settlement duties had not been done. Without authority, he had removed names from official maps showing locations granted, had prepared reports on claims which had misled the Lieutenant-Governor and his Council, and had taken it upon himself to interpret doubtful points in the law in ways which favoured speculators in land claims. The Lieutenant-Governor characterized the "delays and jobbing" which had occurred in the land offices as "quite shocking" and remarked that he was not surprised that the public had become impatient with the system that had existed.[57]

Lord Durham's recommendations for reforming the land system of Upper Canada were designed to meet the recurring complaint that the province was not "getting on like the States." Upper Canada needed to be made capable of attracting and holding British immigrants and, for that, something like the land system of the United States, "which," wrote Durham, "appears to combine all the chief requisites of the greatest efficiency," seemed to him necessary. But Durham does not appear to have been properly informed at first about the American system. He wrote Glenelg that the practice of allowing different methods in the different states had long ago been superseded by a uniform system under the control of the general government. Subsequently, in his report, this statement was rephrased and corrected.[58] The figures which Durham quoted on federal land revenues, £20,000,000 in the period 1797–1837, while off only about £2,000,000, gave an exaggerated impression of what could be obtained from the public domain. "Under the American system," observed Durham, "revenue from the public lands has amounted in one twelve month to ... more than the whole expenses of the federal government." Of the $90,000,000 which the federal government collected from the sale of land during this period, $40,000,000 was obtained during the years 1836 and 1837; the average annual amount for the entire period was $2,250,000. This was the gross revenue. Durham said nothing about the costs of administering the land or about the $26,000,000 spent in acquiring land from the Indians.[59] Nor does he seem to have been aware that the cash sale system gave less than universal satisfaction and that a vigorous land reform movement was under way.

In 1837 only a relatively small quantity of surveyed land remained to the Crown in Upper Canada—1,147,019 acres.[60] It was therefore more important, as Wakefield emphasized, to correct the evils of the past than to devise a new system for the future. To achieve this end, Durham recommended the integrated three-fold programme of reform presented in the report of the Commissioner of Crown Lands and Emigration, signed by Buller but written by Wakefield.

Wakefield suggested taxation of wild land at 2d. an acre to force large landowners into selling or improving their holdings, the promotion of emigration from the British Isles so that there would be buyers for the land, and a programme of public works that would improve the means of transportation and provide employment for emigrants who needed it. In future, advised Wakefield, Crown lands should be sold in unlimited quantities at a uniform cash price of 10s. an acre. All classes of reserved land, as well as all Crown lands, should be thrown open to purchase since it would be unjust to allow the Crown, the clergy, the colleges, and schools to withhold their land from settlement when private landowners were to be taxed to discourage them from following this policy. The revenues derived from the wild land tax and the sale of Crown lands and timber should be devoted primarily to public works and secondarily to paying the passages of selected poor immigrants and the expense of settling them, not on the land, but in employment. The fact that the labour supply of the colony had been increased by these means would induce men of capital to invest in and improve wild land. Prompt application of these remedies was desirable, but since the land revenues would for some years be small, a loan should be raised in England for public works and emigration. The Territorial Revenues would be sufficient security for the payment of the interest on the loan to begin with and would ultimately be ample to pay off the principal. In order to give permanence and security to the whole scheme, the Imperial

Parliament should regulate the sale of Crown lands, impose the wild land tax, create an Imperial commission to work out the administrative regulations, raise the loan, and appropriate the revenues. A subordinate colonial commission should be charged with the actual sale of the land, collection of taxes, superintendence of the public works, and reception and placement of immigrants.

As Charles Buller later pointed out to Parliament, it was Wakefield's minor recommendation that attracted a disproportionate amount of attention and criticism.[61] The suggestion that any portion of the land revenues should be used to pay the passage of immigrants was not welcomed in Canada. In his report on immigration, John Macaulay reminded Sir George Arthur that, during the preceding twelve years, £48,000 of Upper Canada's revenues had been spent on immigrants, many of whom had not remained in the province. Her Casual and Territorial Revenues, he thought, could be more wisely expended than in aiding the emigration of mechanics and labourers who, "hanging loose on the community," would move from place to place and eventually find their way to the United States. Nor could Upper Canada be expected to submit to a land tax or burden herself with a loan to enable immigrants to use her as a corridor to the United States.[62]

It is obvious that Wakefield's scheme was very similar to that proposed earlier by Robert Gourlay. In addition, Gourlay had urged that Americans should be admitted as settlers and Wakefield made the same suggestion. Upper Canada, he insisted, needed American backwoodsmen with their special "know-how" to make the first attack upon the forest and to ease the way for British immigrants with some capital who would buy out their improvements. In the past, however, American backwoodsmen had entered Upper Canada as timber thieves and squatters, not to buy land at 10s. an acre cash. There does not seem to have been a place for them under the proposed system except as purchasers of private or Canada Company land on credit.

Wakefield's proposals required Imperial taxation, Imperial legislation, and, to a degree, Imperial administration for their implementation. No reference was made in the report to the Colonial Tax Repeal Act which was a barrier to the imposition of a wild land tax by the Imperial Parliament. In practice, the legislature of Upper Canada had already been permitted to legislate for the Crown lands, and even John Beverley Robinson admitted it would be difficult to withdraw the concession that had been made.[63] It is difficult to see how Buller could feel justified in stating to Parliament without qualification: "We have not parted with our control over the lands but only with the proceeds of sales. The Crown still retains the entire management of the lands."[64] All the Imperial Parliament retained was a veto, not the best device for getting a positive programme into legislation.

Imperial administration was achieved for other colonies by the creation of the Colonial Land and Emigration Commisison but the powers of this body did not extend to the lands of the British North American colonies. It did, however, examine and report on colonial land legislation.[65] The Commission, like the Colonial Office, was dependent on official information from the colonies or private information supplied by interested persons. In the past, as Mackenzie complained, these sources had concealed the truth from the Colonial Office.

Wakefield's proposals would merely have complicated the machinery without improving it. The history of the Clergy Reserves after 1841 illustrates on a small scale the dissatisfaction which would have been created had the Province of United Canada been saddled with an Imperial land commission working through a subordinate colonial body.

In developing a programme of reform, Wakefield was struggling with three things not easily reconciled: his theories, particularly his belief that a sufficient cash price should be charged for land to prevent labourers from becoming landed proprietors for some years; the desirability of obliging speculators in wild land either to sell their lots to those who would improve them or to bear a greater burden of taxation for roads; and the attractions of the neighbouring republic where land could be had for $1.25 an acre. If stiff taxation should force speculators to sell, the price of land would be driven down. Since speculators held a great deal more land than the 1,147,019 acres which the Crown had vacant, it was clear that a plentiful supply of labour could not be maintained if the speculators were forced to sell their land at prices which immigrants could afford. On the other hand, if the price of Crown land was set in accordance with Wakefield's principles, the effect would be to rig the market for the benefit of speculators and to increase the attractions of the United States. As he himself confessed: "In the immediate neighbourhood of the United States ... it would be idle to seek, by means of a price for new land, the more important end of securing an ample and a constant supply of labour for hire. In respect to the price of public land, legislation for the North American Colonies must necessarily be governed by the course of the United States." [66]

The compromise finally recommended was a cash price of 10s. an acre and a wild land tax of 2d. At 10s., argued Wakefield, "there had been no deficiency of purchasers from the government and the Canada Company...." [67] This conclusion was not altogether justified by the evidence. It had been admitted that many of the sales made by the government had been fictitious purchases that were never intended to be completed. About one-third of the land offered for sale had been taken but only one-sixth had been patented. Furthermore, the sales had been made on credit and many of them had been special locations, not wild land in general. Wakefield justified 10s. an acre, rather than the American 6s. 3d. ($1.25), on the ground that much of the land revenue was to be spent on an extensive programme of public works. He admitted that a cash price of 10s. might cause land in private hands to be sold first but this he regarded as altogether desirable, as indeed it would have been since it would have meant more compact settlement of the country. But what happened in the end was that private landowners and the Canada Company got the protection of a 10s. tariff on Crown lands and did not become subject to the 2d. an acre tax which Wakefield proposed.

Robert Gourlay had proposed that both wild and improved land should be taxed at the same rate and that each township should be assessed in proportion to its population and situation. Wakefield proposed to equalize the tax burden on residents and non-residents by imposing a uniform land tax throughout the province of 2d. an acre on unimproved lots. Under the existing laws all land was taxed 1d. in the £, cultivated land was rated at 20s., and wild land at 4s.

In addition, settlers were subject to statute labour for roads, services which Wakefield valued at 15s. a 100-acre lot, but non-residents paid only one-eighth of a penny an acre in lieu of this service. A wild land tax of 2d. an acre would have equalized the burden on 100-acre lots, assuming that 30 per cent of an occupied lot was under cultivation. At this rate, the cost of holding a 100-acre lot unimproved would have jumped from 2s. 8½d. to 16s. 8d., a six-fold increase. Although witnesses before the Commission disagreed on the proper amount of the tax, "every witness examined on the subject concurred in the opinion that the imposition of such a tax was absolutely necessary." [68] This statement was untrue. Every witness whose evidence on this subject was published concurred, but William Warren Baldwin had given evidence on this subject and had denounced both the tax and the expediency of increasing it.

One of Baldwin's strongest criticisms of the wild land tax was that it had brought about the sacrifice of land at tax sale for as little as 6d. an acre. Such a result was not desired by Wakefield. His report met this difficulty by proposing that the tax could be paid in land in 100-acre lots at the rate of 4s. an acre. Land forfeited for non-payment of taxes should not be put up to tax sale but sold on the same terms as other Crown land and, when a sale was effected, the original owner should be entitled to a payment of 4s. an acre less the back taxes. The administration of such a provision would have been long drawn out, complicated, and expensive. In addition, it would have reduced the cash proceeds from the wild land tax, one source of revenue from which the interest, and ultimately the principal, on the proposed British loan was to be paid.

Wakefield believed that a wild land tax such as he proposed would result in the recovery of a large domain for the Crown but that, as Charles Buller realized, would have been neither certain nor prompt. [69] Four acres at 4s. would have paid the tax of 2d. an acre on a 100-acre lot but since it was proposed to accept surrenders only in 100-acre units it is obvious the provision could not have been utilized by men with a few bits of unimproved property here and there. Such persons, if threatened with forfeiture, would surely have preferred to sell to anyone who would pay cash, even less than 4s. an acre cash, than to wait indefinitely for their money from the Crown Land Department. Thus, the price of land would have been driven down and an opportunity would have been created for the Canada Company or speculators like William Dickson or T. C. Street, better able to carry their tax costs for a time, to add to their holdings.

Revenue from the sale of the Crown lands at 10s. an acre was to be the other source from which the proposed loan for internal improvements and the promotion of immigration was to be repaid. Since the Act of 1837 provided for use of U.E. and militia rights in the purchase of all classes of land, little revenue could be expected from land sales for some time. Two witnesses, R. S. Thornhill, Chief Clerk of the Crown Land Department, and W. W. Baldwin discussed the terms of the Act of 1837 and pointed out the advantages it gave to speculators in these rights; but in Wakefield's own summary of the land regulations of Upper Canada, the Act of 1837 received only incidental mention and nowhere did he discuss what could be done about these land rights.

Lord Durham ignored the Act of 1837 and brushed aside the activities of the Assembly, both as petitioner and legislator, with the statement, "The Provincial

Assemblies except quite recently in New Brunswick and Upper Canada have never had any role in this matter, nor is the popular control in those two cases much more than nominal." [70] To be sure, the Act of 1837 had only a life of two years and Wakefield and Durham may have expected that a bill to extend it would not prove acceptable to the Imperial Parliament. The way would then have been clear for an Imperial act embracing all parts of their comprehensive plan of reform. As matters worked out, the Act of 1837 *was* extended.[71]

In his report, Wakefield modified to some extent what he regarded as sound colonization practices to suit conditions in Upper Canada; but he also ignored certain political and economic facts that would have precluded the success of his ideas if they had been tried. In addition, his scheme was defeated by its own logic. The fundamental reform needed, as Wakefield himself emphasized, was the imposition of an adequate wild land tax. Such a tax could only have been secured by bringing pressure to bear upon the legislature of Upper Canada or by repealing the Colonial Tax Repeal Act—a course which seems never to have been contemplated. In Russell's opinion, the political difficulties in the way of securing a provincial act, and also of withdrawing from the province that share in framing land legislation which Glenelg had conceded, were too great and the quantity of Crown land still undisposed of too small to leave much hope of raising an emigration fund by the methods Wakefield advocated.[72]

Lord Sydenham had a better grasp of the economic realities of the situation in Upper Canada than either Durham or Wakefield, though he did not appreciate all the political realities. He actually wrote to Russell, "You must take a large Civil List. Government in this country depends on your not being obliged to go to the Assembly for what you want.... I am very much inclined to Stuart's advice about the Civil List ... not to take one but to keep the Crown Revenues and the 14 Geo. 3. It was a great mistake ever asking for a Civil List in these Colonies, when you have a sufficient revenue from Crown Property." [73] However, Sydenham could see that Wakefield's proposals were not suited to Upper Canada. From the land revenues, state-assisted emigration could be financed to an extent quite insignificant when compared with the amount of emigration taking place voluntarily.[74] He did not think that the farmers of Upper Canada would be able to hire immigrant labourers as Wakefield expected except for a few weeks in harvest time because they had little cash income. "Money. That is a thing never to be mentioned. Pigs, pork, flour, potatoes ... milk ... you must eat all you produce for devil a purchaser is to be found." [75] What was lacking in Upper Canada was not labour but a market. Sydenham wrote in a period of depression and one, moreover, when the British government was not assisting Upper Canada as it had in the past by expenditures for military or colonization purposes. The ability of the province to employ immigrant labourers, then, would depend not on the farmers of Upper Canada but on a continuing programme of public works.

How was such a programme to be financed? The major items—the canals—by the British loan; the subsidiary items—roads—by a wild land tax. Sydenham was convinced that Canada would not relish Imperial taxation for this purpose and he was wise enough to foresee that no effective wild land tax would be imposed by a legislature containing a large number of land jobbers. There was one other means of bringing wild land under heavier taxation and that was through the imposition of rates by local government bodies. Lord Durham had suggested that the Act of Union should provide for the creation of municipal authorities in order that the spheres of the central government and the local authorities should be clearly defined by the Imperial Parliament, and he had proposed that these elected bodies should have the power of imposing rates for local purposes.[76] But neither he nor Wakefield expected that they would be the agencies through which the all important wild land tax would be imposed, as did Sydenham. "Give the inhabitants in their district councils the power of levying a rate for roads, bridges, etc.," advised Sydenham. "The moment they get the power they will use it; and then goodbye to the jobbers; for the *inhabitants* feel the cause of their suffering; and by making the tax equally heavy on uncultivated as on cultivated land, they will very shortly bring these gentlemen to book."[77]

The district councils provisions of Sydenham's Union Bill were based on a special report made by J. W. Pringle[78] who drew a sharper distinction than even Wakefield had between the taxes paid by speculators and those paid by resident settlers. Pringle pointed out that the latter were taxed not only on their land but also on their personal property and did statute labour in proportion to their total assessment. The result was that they paid twenty times the taxes paid by non-residents who did nothing to improve the district. To correct these inequities he had recommended the creation of elected district councils with power to tax all lands, cultivated and uncultivated, to the extent of 3*d*. an acre.[79]

Both the Union Bill considered by the Imperial Parliament in 1839 and Sydenham's Union Bill were obnoxious to the Tories of Upper Canada,[80] and their local government clauses made them doubly so. John Macaulay called these clauses "an un-English innovation in our constitution which I could hardly have endured . . ." and Strachan wrote, "The whole country will be . . . afflicted with Democracy in its vilest form. . . ."[81] It was probably John Beverley Robinson, who was in England opposing the Union, and Edward Ellice who convinced Peel and Stanley that no desire had been expressed in Canada for local government institutions possessing the power of taxation. Ellice presented that argument to the House of Commons and, after disparaging the Pringle report and making an unpleasant allusion to the methods Sydenham was using to get results in Upper Canada, he inaccurately summarized the nature and effects of previous wild land taxes to show that a tax of 3*d*. would be confiscatory, charging that it was "the open and direct intention" to effect the confiscation of property through the proposed district councils. John Russell's reply to Ellice was weak and confused. He mixed up his facts also, attributed to the Assembly of Lower Canada a request for a system of municipal government so that a system of local taxation might be established which it had not made, but which the Assembly of Upper Canada had made for it, and he ended by withdrawing the clauses.[82]

Ellice had concluded his attack on the district councils by suggesting that if Canada really wanted these institutions her own legislature should be trusted to supply them. Russell passed this suggestion on to the indignant Sydenham.[83]

It was a shrewd move on the part of those opposed to district councils. The chances were that speculators' interests would be as well represented in the legislature as they had been in the past and that any bill creating district councils would also closely restrict their taxing powers. Sydenham secured municipal institutions for Lower Canada by means of an ordinance passed by the Special Council, and district councils were created for Upper Canada by an act passed after the Union.[84]

According to Sydenham, this act for Upper Canada was "word for word after my own ordinance for the Lower Province; thereby ... setting up my own particular legislation by the sanction of the United Parliament."[85] This statement gives the erroneous impression that Sydenham had got the kind of district councils he wanted in Upper Canada after all. As introduced, the bill was "similar in all essential features" to the Lower Canada ordinance[86] but, as finally enacted, it was a different measure. The ordinance had provided for elective councils[87] but the principal officials of the councils, namely, the wardens and treasurers, were to be appointed by the Governor and the minor ones were to be chosen by the warden and council with his concurrence. These provisions, which the Reformers of Upper Canada did not want applied to their province, were intended to give the government some influence in the localities. Indeed, Sydenham's whole system in Canada was one of "management" through government influence. The ordinance did not prescribe the rate at which land was to be assessed and it placed no restricton on the taxing power of the councils except with respect to the unconceded lands of the seigneuries. However, the by-laws of the councils could be quashed. The district councils were unpopular in Lower Canada because of the manner in which they had been created, and, except in the Eastern Townships, they made no use of their powers.

In Upper Canada the councils were constituted like those of Lower Canada but received taxing powers much more limited than those Pringle and Sydenham had intended them to have. The Tories opposed Sydenham's District Councils Bill and the Reformers were divided. W. H. Merritt supported it because it would mean heavier taxation of unimproved land. In Francis Hincks's view, once the councils were in operation, the magistrates could no longer "amuse themselves with the people's cash" and the defective provisions of the act could later be improved.[88] Robert Baldwin, A. N. Morin, and many Reformers opposed the bill on the ground that the advantages it conferred were not sufficiently great, that it gave the government too much power and the people too little, and that all municipal officers ought to be made elective. On this point they fought stubbornly to minimize the power of appointed officials and to obtain a more liberal bill applicable to both sections of the province. They succeeded in having the repeal of the Lower Canada ordinance considered in the committee of the whole; they tried to amend the bill so that the wardens should be appointed for only three years and afterwards be elected, but the amendment was lost by the casting vote of the Speaker. After this defeat they tried to have the other appointed officers chosen by the elected council and failed again.

The advantages conferred by the District Councils Act were limited indeed compared with the sacrifice of the elective principle in local government for which the Reformers had long fought. The original bill permitted the councils to assess wild land at a different rate than other land and to tax it up to 3d. per acre. As finally passed, it required the councils to accept the valuations already established by law, £1 per acre for cultivated land and 4s. for wild land, and to tax all land at the same rate on the assessed value. The maximum tax they could impose was 2d. in the £ on the assessed value, which meant a tax of two-fifths of a penny an acre on wild land. But the law also stated that the maximum tax that could be imposed on land alone was $1\frac{1}{2}d.$ an acre. If cultivated land, assessed at £1 an acre, were to pay a maximum tax of $1\frac{1}{2}d.$ an acre, the wild land assessed at 4s., if taxed at the same rate, would pay only three-tenths of a penny. This rate was a far cry from the 3d. an acre on uncultivated land which Pringle and Sydenham had proposed, or even the 2d. which Wakefield had recommended.

The change was made on the initiative of the government to make the bill more acceptable to anxious members of the Legislative Council.[89] Even the prospect of appointed wardens did not calm their fears. "Landless men," moaned John Macaulay, "will have no mercy on other folks acres," [90] and the *Western Herald* accused the Governor General of "laying the foundations of a Canadian republic" by giving the "sovereign people" the right to levy direct taxes and spend their own money without the intervention of appointed magistrates or commissioners.[91] The final vote in the Assembly, as analysed by this newspaper, was as follows. In favour: Upper Canada Ministerialists, 9; Lower Canada Ministerialists, 13; Upper Canada Reformers, 15; Lower Canada Reformers, 5; total, 42. Opposed: Upper Canada Tories, 11; Upper Canada Reformers, 6; Lower Canada Tories, 2; Lower Canada Reformers, 12; total, 31.[92]

The Act of 1841 not only restricted the taxing powers of the district councils but it also failed to make clear what taxing powers it did convey.[93] The result was that, in their eagerness to tax speculators and non-residents, half the councils passed by-laws which were quashed. The councils assumed that they could tax wild land up to $1\frac{1}{2}d.$ an acre, they added penalties to delinquent taxes, and finally they sold the land of those who refused to pay, although it was not clear that the law gave them the power to impose penalties or to direct the sale of land for unpaid taxes which had been imposed, not by the old and still existing Upper Canada assessments acts, but by their new by-laws. Complicated tax title problems arose and the legislature had to provide for the recovery by the owners of improperly sold land and for compensation to those who had bought and improved it.[94]

Charles Buller does not seem to have realized that the powers which the district councils of Upper Canada had received were limited, and that the Lower Canada ordinance would prove ineffective. In 1843 he was still expecting either the provincial legislature or the district councils to impose a tax on wild land so heavy as to be confiscatory in its effect. The District Council of the Eastern Townships had already enacted a by-law imposing on the British-American Land Company a tax "of so enormous an amount as by itself to be equivalent to direct confiscation." This by-law had been disallowed, but Buller regarded it as an indication of what was to be expected. Buller now admitted that it would take years before the tax of 2d. an acre suggested in his report would result in the resumption of extensive areas of wild land by the Crown. He wanted this result to be achieved quickly but without injustice to the proprietors. As an alternative to confiscation by taxation, he proposed something like a modern programme of land nationalization for Canada, under which the owners of wild land would have been compensated for their land by non-interest-bearing debentures to be gradually paid off out of the land revenues.[95] William Warren Baldwin thought Buller must be "out of his mind to propose such a diabolical plan." "Will the government and Parliament of England," he demanded of his son, "never let us alone to manage our local affairs?"[96] Of Buller's proposal, nothing more was to be heard.

The failure of the Imperial Parliament to enact Sydenham's municipal clauses gave the speculators in the wild lands of Upper Canada another triumph, one by which they continued to enjoy the assessment rate of 4s. an acre, established in 1819, until 1851,[97] despite many petitions to the legislature from frustrated district councils. The Cartwrights and Macaulays, the Hamiltons, Colonel Talbot, the heirs of Thomas Clark, T. C. Street, William Dickson, and the Canada Company, to name only the most prominent of the speculators, found it possible to hold their scattered lots, acquired as grants, by the use of U.E. loyalists and militia rights, at sheriff's sales, at tax sales, or by purchase, for many years. In some instances they were ultimately to sell them at greatly increased prices.

The drastic remedy for the existing evils of the land system prescribed by the Durham Report—stiff taxation of wild land—was not applied. So long as the Assessment Act of 1819 remained in force, the district councils could not bring about the results Sydenham had hoped for. While Durham's Report, particularly Wakefield's share in it, was not without influence on the course of land policy after 1837, the main recommendation, Imperial administration of the Crown lands, came too late in the day.

CHAPTER SEVENTEEN

THE CLERGY RESERVES AGAIN

WHEN CHARLES POULETT THOMSON, later Lord Sydenham, came out to compose the troubles of the two Canadas and effect the Union, he brought with him a bribe in the form of a promise of an Imperial loan which he was authorized to dangle temptingly before the legislature should it balk at doing as the Imperial government desired. Lord Howick wanted to make the settlement of the Clergy Reserves question by the legislature of Upper Canada a *sine qua non* to the promise of a loan, but Sydenham regarded this suggestion as utterly absurd. "Even Head's Assembly could never agree with the Council on the terms of distribution and there is not the smallest chance of the two bodies being ever brought to concur upon it. But it will be done easily enough in the United Legislature...," he wrote. By the time Sydenham reached Toronto he had changed his mind and had become convinced of the necessity of settling the question before the Union so as to prevent the religious disputes of the Upper Province coming before the united legislature, which would have troubles enough of its own.[1]

The Governor General recognized clearly that popular sentiment favoured using the Clergy Reserves for the support of education and schemes of internal improvements but he knew, too, that a bill with such provisions would meet stiff opposition in the House of Lords. The bill which he devised provided for the sale of the reserves for religious purposes and limited the quantity to 100,000 acres in any one year. The proceeds of both past and future sales were to be invested in provincial securities, and the income was to comprise a Clergy Reserve Fund for the support of all denominations of Christians. Those sums already being paid by order of the Imperial government to any religious denomination, and to which the faith of the Crown was pledged, were made a first charge upon the fund for the lives of those then receiving them, and any deficiency was to be made up out of the Casual and Territorial Revenues. When the Clergy Reserve Fund should yield a surplus above these charges half of it was to be allotted to the Church of England and the Church of Scotland jointly, numbering with the latter the Presbyterians of the United Synod of Upper Canada, and half to the other denominations recognized by law. The share of the Anglicans and the Scots was to be divided between them in proportion to their numbers and the share of the other denominations was to be similarly apportioned.[2]

In the course of the debate on Sydenham's bill, a number of significant amendments were rejected. These were: an amendment to distribute the Clergy Reserves Fund among all denominations according to their numbers; an amendment which provided for sale of the reserves by a method similar to that used for Crown lands and for provincial appropriation of the proceeds; an amendment which would have prevented the Casual and Territorial Revenues from being used to bolster the fund until it could bear the charges laid upon it. After these amendments were rejected, the Assembly passed the bill.[3] How did Sydenham get the Assembly to vote 28-20 in favour of a measure which devoted the reserves wholly to religious purposes when the same body under Arthur's management had, after weeks of debate, passed by only one vote a bill which likewise restricted them to religious uses but left the whole question of distribution to the Imperial Parliament?

Sydenham has given us the explanation himself, although in euphemistic terms: "I told you I would work my popularity to some purpose and I have done it," he informed Russell.[4] This popularity was acquired, according to John Richardson, by "condescending to the little arts ... playing with men's vanity ... their passions and their prejudices ... and enlisting ... personal and sectional interests." [5] Sydenham's opponents put it more bluntly: the legislature and the press had been corrupted by the Governor's use of his powers of patronage and appointment.[6] The Attorney General, C. A. Hagerman, who once described himself as a staunch Church and King's man, was persuaded to accept an appointment to the bench and thus the "great gun" of the Tories, as Sydenham called him, was silenced.[7] John Beverley Robinson, outraged by the turn of events after 1840 and the rise to power of new men, not of those "regularly bred," wrote bitterly of the degraded state to which the government of Canada had been reduced by the despicable Poulett Thomson and his shameful transactions of 1838-40. "I wish I could go to sleep and forget all that has happened since Sir John Colborne left Canada," wrote the Chief Justice, adding, "and indeed there were some ... things [which] ... had happened before ... that had better be forgotten." [8] Maitland's years in office were the good old days for men like Strachan and Robinson.

Not all the supporters of the Governor General's Clergy Reserves bill were venal. Many adherents of the two national churches recognized that the hour for a settlement had struck and agreed with Sydenham that probably never again could as good terms be got from a Canadian legislature.[9] The opposition comprised those radicals who still advocated the voluntary system or who preferred the cause of education or internal improvements, and eight die-hard Anglicans.[10]

In the Legislative Council, Sydenham's bill was passed by a vote of 13-5, but it was a chastened and humbled Council that took this action. Several members of the Council were office holders and members of the Executive Council. When, at the beginning of the session, they learned from the publication of Russell's dispatch of October 16, 1839,[11] in the *Upper Canada Gazette* of December 5, 1839, that opposition to the government's policies would cost them their appointments, most of them yielded. John Macaulay, for example, who held the office of Surveyor General, and who had joined Strachan in dissenting from Arthur's bill, now found that it was his duty to forward the views of the government whose servant he was.[12] This decision subjected him to a stern rebuke from Strachan who pointed out that the same principle by which he sought to justify his conduct would have justified the servants of Queen Mary in their condemnation of Ridley, Latimer, and Cranmer to the stake.[13]

Strachan, of course, could not be silenced. He circulated an address to his clergy in which he protested that the church was about to be robbed of her "acknowledged property," deplored the "defection and treachery" of her sons, and declared that Thomson's bill "degraded" the clergy of the Church of England by making them stipendiaries of the colonial government and by putting them on a par with the dissenting clergy.[14] A petition against confirmation of the bill was also industriously circulated for signatures. Sydenham who, like Durham, regarded the Clergy Reserves as "the one great outstanding grievance —the root of all the troubles of the province—the cause of the Rebellion,"[15] hoped it would be "all over" and confirmation a fact before the petition arrived. In this he was to be disappointed.

Sydenham's bill encountered the opposition of the bishops in the House of Lords. At their instance, it was submitted to the judges who found that the provincial Parliament had exceeded its authority in two ways. First, the Clergy Reserves Sales Act of 1827, which provided for the investment of the proceeds in British securities, contained no provision reserving to the provincial Parliament the power to alter its provisions in future. Therefore no provincial law could require the re-investment of the funds in provincial securities. Second, the powers granted to the province of Upper Canada by the forty-first clause of the Constitutional Act were prospective only and did not entitle its legislature to interfere with Clergy Reserves already brought into existence in accordance with the provisions of that act. Sydenham's bill providing for the sale of existing reserves and for the distribution of the revenue from sales was, therefore, beyond its powers. This, as Lindsey remarks, was an amazing ruling. Repeatedly, the Colonial Office had invited the legislature of Upper Canada to exercise powers which it evidently did not possess.[16]

There were two ways out of the difficulty. The Imperial Parliament could legalize the provincial act as the Canada Tenures Act of Lower Canada had been legalized or it could re-enact it as an Imperial statute. Sydenham himself preferred the first course, fearing that the House of Lords would "cut and carve" at the provisions of his bill should it be submitted for re-enactment. "Remember one thing," he warned Russell, "that if there be any attempt to give the Church of England a superiority in point of station, or title, or tenure of property, five-sixths of the province will never submit to it. . . ."[17]

Russell's government met the difficulty by passing a Clergy Reserve bill of its own. In its original form, this bill met with Sydenham's approval but he commented adversely on the distribution clauses finally adopted.[18] In an effort at compromise, the Archbishop of Canterbury had suggested that income from the one-fourth of the reserves sold under the Act of 1827 should be shared by the Churches of England and Scotland in the proportion of two to one; income from the reserves still to be sold should go one-third to the Church of England, one-sixth to the Church of Scotland, and one-half to the other denominations of Christians.[19] These distribution proposals were acceptable to Russell and became part of the Imperial Act 3 & 4 Vic., c. 78.

What exactly were Clergy Reserves? Were they all the land actually reserved for the benefit of a Protestant clergy, only that quantity which ought to have been reserved, or merely the land actually specified as Clergy Reserves in patents? This question came up for decision in 1842. The Executive Council of United Canada then ruled that the Clergy Reserve Sales Act of 1840 provided for the sale of lands *called* Clergy Reserves and that therefore all lands marked as Clergy Reserves on the chequered township plans, or set apart in blocks, or taken in specification in patents, even in excess, should be regarded as Clergy Reserves. When did the reserved lands become the property of the Church of England? Obviously the reserves did not become the property of the church until patented to her but the church's protagonists always thought and spoke of the Clergy Reserves and of the Clergy Reserve Fund as her "property." Gladstone considered that the Imperial Parliament had no right to appropriate the proceeds of the reserves among all Protestant denominations by the Act of 1840 but that it should have procured the surrender of the desired portion of the revenues from the *two* established Churches of England and Scotland. On the other hand, some of the Reformers of Upper Canada, when the Act of 1854 was being debated, refused to admit that "secularization" was the right term to use of land which had never been the "property" of any church.[20]

The Imperial Act of 1840 for the sale of the Clergy Reserves was, says Mac-Donald, "regarded, both in Canada and Great Britain, as a final settlement of a most difficult question.... From 1840-1849 no discontent was manifested in any quarter on account of the provisions of the Act."[21] It is true that official policy was to regard the question as closed, but it is hard to see how anyone conversant with the history of the Clergy Reserves question could have expected the Settlement of 1840 to prove final. Dissatisfaction with it was manifested almost immediately.

The provincial Act of 1839 and the Imperial Act of 1840 both provided for the transformation of a landed endowment into a monetary one and opened that endowment to Christians of all denominations, but there were important differences between the two measures. Although Sydenham had warned Russell that no superiority should be shown the Church of England, the tottering Whig government accepted a settlement practically dictated by the bishops which increased the joint share of the two established churches at the expense of the other denominations and also increased the share of the Church of England at the expense of the Church of Scotland. Russell had carefully explained to Parliament that no superiority was claimed for the Church of England and that the proportion of two to one rested on the number of adherents of the two denominations;[22] but the Scots felt that the census returns had been misused and were, according to Sydenham, "furious at having been jockeyed out of their fair share."[23] A committee of the General Assembly of the Church of Scotland protested against the act but Russell refused to consider reopening the question.[24] The Methodist Conference of 1841 also condemned the "unequal and unjust" provisions of the act "so different from every expression of opinion and feeling which has ever been made by the inhabitants of Upper Canada—so opposed to the recorded opinions of both branches of the Provincial Legislature...."[25]

One major defect of the Imperial act was that no hard and fast rule was laid down for the distribution of that portion of the funds not assigned to the two established churches. Sydenham's bill, however, had specified that the share of the other denominations was to be distributed in proportion to their numbers. As Egerton Ryerson foresaw, a good deal would depend on the impartiality of the Governor and his Council. This was the bill that was supposed to remove the Clergy Reserve question from politics, the "definite" settlement prepared by the Imperial Parliament for a province that had repeatedly expressed itself in favour of secularization of the reserves and whose legislature had been brought to consent to keeping them for religious purposes only by the shrewdest political management and in connection with a scheme of distribution far more just than that which the Imperial act contained. Not even the Anglicans were content and, behind the scenes, they were scheming to better their position.

In one respect the Imperial act was an improvement upon Sydenham's bill. It repealed those parts of the Constitutional Act that related to the creation of Clergy Reserves and thus ended the practice. In fact, the creation of additional reserves in Upper Canada had ceased, and their total acreage remained at the figure that had been reported to Durham—2,395,687 acres. The reason for this was that Durham had requested that the alienation of Crown land should cease so far as practicable.[26] In Upper Canada no new surveys were made until after the Union and consequently no additional Clergy Reserves were set aside after 1836.

For a time after 1840 the Clergy Reserves dispute slumbered, at least so far as the Assembly was concerned, probably because there was little to quarrel about and more pressing matters were to the fore. The Clergy Reserve Fund was not growing at a rapid rate because sales had been suspended, not because British capital had been diverted elsewhere by the Rebellion. With the resumption of sales in 1845, public interest in the Clergy Reserves question revived and, before long, the hitherto latent dissatisfactions with the Act of 1840 led the legislature of United Canada to demand its repeal.

The blame for upsetting the Settlement of 1840 is sometimes laid at the door of the Anglicans. Henry Sherwood, says Hincks in his *Reminiscences*, was "ill-advised enough to attempt in 1846 to improve the position of the Church of England."[27] He introduced into the Assembly an address to the Crown asking that the Society for the Propagation of the Gospel be entrusted with the management of a portion of the reserves equal to the Anglicans' share under the Act of 1840. The result, says Hincks, was that the radicals began to clamour for complete secularization. Lindsey puts it the other way around, asserting that by 1844 the Reform Party had once again begun to agitate for secularization and that the Anglicans, alarmed, tried to secure title to their share of the reserves before further spoliation of their church could take place.[28] Who, then, was to blame?

There was an important provision of the unconfirmed Clergy Reserves bill, which passed in Sir George Arthur's regime in 1839, which was not included in either Sydenham's bill or in the Imperial act. That was a clause requiring the Clergy Reserves to be sold in future like Crown lands. The Imperial Act of 1840 provided that the reserves were to be sold under regulations laid down by the governor-in-council and approved by the Crown. The result was that a body of land fully as extensive as the surveyed and unsold Crown land escaped the control of the provincial legislature. Yet the Assembly of Upper Canada had asked that the Clergy Reserves be sold like Crown land, and, in 1837, Glenelg had publicly stated it to be the government's policy to allow the provincial legislature to determine the land policies of the province, subject, of course, to Imperial review. For this defect, then, if for no other, the Act of 1840 would not have satisfied the Reformers for long. They became more and more dissatisfied when they found that Strachan was attempting from behind the scenes to influence the policies of the governor-in-council with respect to the reserves.

Lord Sydenham drew up new regulations for the sale of the Clergy Reserves without calling upon Bishop Strachan for advice, much to the latter's chagrin. The Governor General felt that the Bishop had no more right to be consulted than spokesmen for other denominations and, since the denominations were unlikely to agree, it would be unwise to call for their opinions.[29] In the past, Clergy Reserves had been sold on ten years' credit and at auction, except to lessees and some squatters who had been allowed pre-emption privileges. Those whose instalments were in arrears were not being pressed for payment owing to the disturbed state of the province.[30] Important changes in this system were planned by Sydenham.

The Governor General thought that the Clergy Reserves ought to be sold on the same system as the Crown lands as far as possible. This meant a cash instead of a credit policy. Sydenham was strongly of the opinion that it was politically unwise to create a large class of debtors to the government, even for Crown land, and more unwise when these debts would relate to the unpopular Clergy Reserves. He did not favour placing a uniform price on the Clergy Reserves, which varied greatly in value from the older, settled townships to the newer townships, because they were in effect a trust and it was the government's duty to get as much for them as possible. Nor did he favour sales at auction. His Commissioner of Crown Lands, R. B. Sullivan, convinced him that the uncertainties, delays, and expenses of the auction system were not offset by worthwhile results. "Combinations among purchasers and particularly squatters are not peculiar to this part of America," wrote Sullivan, "and my experience leads me to think that in very few cases little more than the upset price can ever be obtained at aution."[31]

What Sydenham preferred was to have the reserves valued—land and improvements separately—by inspectors, and then sold for cash to the first comer at prices established by the governor-in-council and based on these valuations, including the value of the improvements. This system, which turned out to be expensive and time-consuming, was established by the regulations of July 13, 1841, and approved by Russell.[32] Persons whose leases had not expired, or who were entitled to a renewal, were allowed the right of purchasing at the valuation upon payment of all arrears of rent. Squatters of five years' standing and those whose leases had expired were given pre-emption privileges entitling them to buy at the valuation less an allowance for improvements not to exceed 25 per cent of the purchase price. These inequitable regulations bore more heavily upon old lessees than upon more recent squatters. They obliged all occupants of Clergy Reserves, within twelve months after their land was offered for sale, to find the cash with which to buy their holding, not at their original value, but at 75 per cent of the current value of the improved property. Few pioneer farmers in Upper Canada could have complied with these conditions without assuming a heavy burden of debt and, as the Commissioner of Crown Lands pointed out, the more diligently they had improved their land the worse their condition would have been. Fortunately Sydenham's harsh rules were never put into effect.

Bishop Strachan vigorously criticized Sydenham's system not because it bore hardly upon occupants of clergy land but because it did not serve the interests of the church. What Strachan objected to was, that he had not been consulted, that the reserves were to be sold for cash, which could only mean at much lower prices than could be obtained from sales on credit, that lessees and squatters were not required to pay the full value of the property they themselves had brought under cultivation, that new leases were not provided for and existing lessees were being encouraged to purchase instead of to renew their leases, and that "instead of continuing to reserve the reserves with a view to future Territorial Endowment . . ." it was planned to bring the reserves on the market without delay. In short, the Bishop was still fighting the Imperial Act of 1840. One other objection made by Strachan is amusing. He disliked the fact that reports of appraisers of the reserves required confirmation by the governor-in-council. Wide discretionary powers in the hands of a Governor, advised by his Executive Council, had been exactly what Strachan approved of in the days when he had been a member of the inner circle, but now that he had become an outsider he mistrusted the Council's wisdom and impartiality.[33]

Sir Charles Bagot reconsidered the system which his predecessor had established and modified it, but not altogether in harmony with Strachan's wishes. With some misgivings, he instituted a credit system, advocated by Sullivan from the start but rejected by Sydenham, and granted more liberal pre-emption terms. Lessees whose leases had expired and squatters who had improved clergy land for five years prior to July 1, 1841, could now purchase at a valuation which no longer included the improvements, but they were charged 6 per cent on the purchase money from the date the lease had expired or from the date of occupancy.[34] These more liberal terms of December 10, 1842, brought a protest from the Society for the Propagation of the Gospel which argued that they set aside "the very principle of a lease of uncultivated land, namely that in consideration of low rent such land be brought into cultivation for the benefit of the owner, the tenant paying himself by crops he may raise during the continuance of his lease."[35] Such a principle was utterly unsuited to Canadian conditions where the clearing of forested land was such arduous work, as successive colonial secretaries had been repeatedly informed, and Bagot's new rules were confirmed.[36]

Before any sales could take place under the amended regulations, the reserves had to be inspected and valued. This work was begun in the summer of 1843 and halted on October 1, 1844, after the Church Society of the Diocese of Toronto had protested against the expense and the loss to the Clergy Reserve fund.[37] By that time two-thirds of the reserves had been inspected at a cost of £6,000. The Council received this complaint with sympathy, well aware that costs of administration already absorbed more than one-fourth of the income from the sale of the Clergy Reserves.[38] Inspections were later resumed and were continued in some districts until 1853, but the costs of inspection were charged to the purchasers.[39]

The returns of inspection show that the inhabitants of Upper Canada had not permitted the paper classification, Clergy Reserve, to stand between them and good land. In all the easily accessible townships on the St. Lawrence, the Lakes, the Rideau, Thames, and Trent waterways, the reserves, if not sold or leased, had become well-occupied by squatters, and sometimes there were several occupants to a lot. Good land in the new Huron District had not yet been seized by the squatters and they had avoided swampy townships in the Victoria District. The sandy lots in the Lake Erie townships, however, had been stripped of their valuable timber and then deserted.[40] The inspectors took as their guide the value of Crown land in the vicinity which was then being sold at auction for cash. It is hardly surprising that Strachan and his supporters complained that the resulting valuations were much too low, particularly as clergy land was being sold on four years' credit.

The inspector for the London District took it upon himself to comment upon the revised regulations which he regarded as still too harsh. Requiring one-third cash down would, he thought, result in driving off "a vast number" of the squatters and in depriving them of the fruits of their labour. Requiring them to pay interest on the purchase price from the date of their unauthorized occupation was also an injustice, since their land was valued not at what it was worth at the time they took possession but at its current value in the generally improved state of the province. In some instances the interest alone amounted to as much as the current value of the lot. How should squatters on clergy, Indian, Crown, or private land be dealt with? This was a knotty problem which repeatedly troubled the Executive Council and legislature of United Canada.

Sale of the Clergy Reserves was resumed in March, 1845,[41] under Bagot's rules. The business was entrusted to the Crown land agents, who were instructed to sell at the valuations, provided the price was not less than the upset price for Crown land in their district and provided that all arrears of rent and interest were collected along with the down-payment. From various parts of the province complaints against the new system poured in, and numerous petitions asked for the remission of rent or back interest The petitioners argued that when the Clergy Reserves were first thrown open to sale they had occupied the land expecting to be allowed to buy, but, owing to the fact that only one-fourth of the reserves could be sold and no more than 100,000 acres annually, their repeated applications to purchase had proved useless, and they now found the terms of purchase altered greatly to their disadvantage. Some of these squatters had a real grievance but those who occupied the land after the adoption of the auction system had no just complaint, as Sullivan had repeatedly pointed out ever since 1836.

As a result of these petitions, the Clergy Reserves sales system was again amended by the Council on November 18, 1845,[42] and the new rules were published in the *Gazette* of March 14, 1846, before they were confirmed by the Imperial government. The period of credit was now extended to ten years.

Instead of interest on the purchase money, those whose leases had expired were to be charged rent for the period of unleased occupancy at the rate of 35s. a year for the first seven years for a 200-acre lot, 70s. the second seven years, and 105s. the third seven years. These were the rents which had been in force at the time the leasing system was discontinued. The privilege of purchasing at a valuation which did not include the improvements was granted to lessees whose leases had expired prior to January 1, 1841, and to squatters who had been in occupation before that date, provided they paid up all back rent by January 1, 1847, and applied to purchase by that date. Where the accumulated arrears were large, arrangements could be made for paying them off in instalments as part of the purchase price. A solemn warning was given that persons occupying clergy land without authority after the publication of this notice would have no claim to pre-emption.[43] It seemed that a system had finally been devised which should speedily cause the Clergy Reserves to pass from the guardianship of the Crown and to become at last the property of the various classes of settlers—squatters, lessees, and new purchasers.

The new regulations of March 14, 1846, had hardly been in force a month before the sale of Clergy Reserves was halted and a new dispute concerning their management arose which was to end in the use of the endowment for secular purposes. Bishop Strachan would not admit defeat. He was still trying to secure for the Church of England a territorial endowment by having the management of the church's share of the reserves vested in the Society for the Propagation of the Gospel. He hoped that the Society might not be required to sell the reserves—at least not all of them—and that the leasing system might be revived. Under the Society's management the reserves would not be sacrificed at the low prices which the inspectors had recommended, nor burdened with the ruinously expensive administrative costs which Sydenham had imposed upon them. In 1844 a committee of the Assembly reported in favour of endowing the Church of England with her share of the reserves. Sir Charles Metcalfe, too, lent a sympathetic ear to the complaints of the Bishop, sending home the report of the committee, which had not been acted on by the Assembly, and recommending to the Colonial Secretary that each religious denomination in the colony should receive its share in land and should be allowed to manage it at its own discretion.[44]

So far as the Church of England was concerned, this scheme was similar to a proposition made by the Archbishop of Canterbury when the Act of 1840 was under discussion. It had been rejected by Russell who had pointed out that one of the essential points in settling the dangerous Clergy Reserves question was to provide that the reserves be *sold*. If it would have been unwise in 1840 to have given the Church of England power to manage her portion of the reserves and to lease them if she chose, by 1846 it had become ten times more dangerous to do so. Since 1837, with the exception noted earlier, the sale of Clergy Reserves had been suspended, the squatter problem had become more serious, and harsh regulations, although subsequently modified, had aroused widespread dissatisfaction. Was the Church of England party, which had fought the sale of the reserves every step of the way, to succeed now, at the last minute, in withholding any portion of the Clergy Reserves from the people of Upper Canada? No wonder the Reform party, well aware of the influences behind the scenes which the church had exercised, began to press for the secularization of the reserves and the right of the legislature of United Canada to do with them as it saw fit.

That staunch High Churchman, William Ewart Gladstone, who at this time was President of the Board of Trade, asked Metcalfe's successor, Lord Cathcart, for his opinion on his predecessor's recommendation of Strachan's proposals. He inquired, too, whether the Clergy Reserves had been valued as they should have been. Cathcart admitted that the expense of administering the reserves through the Crown Land Department was exhorbitant but cautioned that a strong feeling existed in the province against transferring the management of any share of the reserves from the government to a religious corporation or to any other body or individual whose main object would be to get as much out of the speculation as possible, both for the Clergy Reserve Fund and for themselves.[45] Proof of this statement came when Henry Sherwood, member for Toronto, presented a petition from the Church Society of the Diocese of York asking that the church's share of the reserves be managed through the Society for the Propagation of the Gospel.

In the debate which followed, Sherwood insisted that he wanted a careful inquiry by a committee representative of the whole House, "not the abominable U.S. system of majority and minority reports." Malcom Cameron, member for Lanark, declared that if the government knew the feelings of Canada West it would never propose "to hand over the settlers to different soulless corporations" and Ogle R. Gowan, member for Leeds, argued that what the country should create was an independent yeomanry, not a system of leasing to tenants who would "take the life blood out of the land." [46] The motion failed of adoption by a vote of 37–14 in an Assembly in which the Tories predominated, even though Sherwood had stated that the Society was willing to give up its desire to lease the lands and would undertake to sell them within a given term of years.[47] This motion of Sherwood's, it should now be clear, was by no means the first step taken to upset the Settlement of 1840.

Cathcart turned over to the Executive Council the question of the valuation set on clergy lands. That body concluded that in many districts the reserves had been valued at less than what private land in the vicinity was selling for and recommended the suspension of sales.[48] This recommendation was put into force on April 13, 1846. Unfortunately for the political peace of Upper Canada, the circular sent out by the Commissioner of Crown Lands gave the impression that sales were to be suspended as the result of a dispatch from the Colonial Secretary. Immediately the Assembly was aroused and asked for a copy of the documents. Cathcart replied, of course, that no such communication had been received. Baldwin and Roblin then introduced a motion regretting the suspension and expressing the hope that sales would be speedily resumed.[49] On May 4, 1846, the Council permitted sales to be resumed but at prices increased from 25 per cent to 125 per cent and based on the value of private land, not Crown land, in the vicinity.[50] The increase in prices led to additional protests being made to the legislature.

The Reformers were not content with bringing about a reversal of policy with respect to the reserves and they succeeded in making political capital out of the incident. In the session of 1847, Baldwin introduced a series of motions which charged that the sale of Clergy Reserves had been suspended by order of the provincial government, not the Imperial government, that the Assembly had "a just distrust of the influences by which such a measure might have been dictated . . ." and that the provincial ministers had worded the circular of instructions to the Crown land agents in such a manner as to throw on the Imperial ministers the odium which this change in policy was likely to bring on themselves. These motions failed, 26–32,[51] but the whole incident had aroused the determination of the radical Reformers to gain for the Canadian Parliament jurisdiction over the reserves and to secularize them once and for all. This determination was compounded partly out of hostility to the Church of England and the political influence she was still able to exert, and partly out of the conviction that, instead of treating the Clergy Reserves as a long-term speculation, the government ought to facilitate their acquisition by the people.

Robert Baldwin has been accused of being opposed to reviving agitation on the Clergy Reserves question and of being averse to secularization. He maintained, says McMullen "that things ought to be left as they were."[52] As the situation stood in March, 1846, the reserves were being sold on ten years' credit, and squatters and lessees were being allowed pre-emption on liberal terms. If this state of things could have continued, Baldwin, who was averse to touching vested interests, as his father had been in the days of the township promoters, would have been content. But, as he pointed out in an election speech in 1847, the question had become whether ecclesiastical corporations should be allowed to manage the reserves "and in their hands afford the means of creating an extensive tenantry to swell the influence of these bodies, or whether the reserves should be sold at a reasonable price to the people and thus add to the numbers and the influence of the independent farmers of the country."[53] In other words, what kind of society should the public land be used to create? This, as Baldwin said, was not a question of narrow interest but one of the most vital importance for the peace and prosperity of the province. Already there was another corporation at work, the Canada Company, which in 1842 had begun to dispose of its lands by lease. Of its terms, one critic wrote, "Never was so rapacious a a system of disposing of land carried out in America before."[54] Frederick Widder, one of the commissioners of the Canada Company, had suggested that the lands of the ecclesiastical corporations, if created, should be placed under the Company's management on a percentage basis.[55] Knowledge of the Canada Company's interest in the Clergy Reserves must have strengthened the determination of the radicals to prevent the Church Society of the Diocese of York from getting its way and must have brought Baldwin to the conclusion that the peaceful extinction of the reserves under the existing system was not to be expected and that, however reluctantly, he must give his vote for secularization.

"The Clergy Reserves," says Francis Hincks in his *Reminiscences*, "were the chief cause of the disruption of the Reform Party."[56] To go into all the political events connected with the passing of the Secularization Act of 1854 would take us deep into political history and away from the subject of land policy. Suffice it to say that some of the Upper Canadian Reformers felt that the safest course was to ask for an Imperial Act which would repeal the Clergy Reserves Act of

1840 and, in accordance with the constitutional principles enunciated by Glenelg to Head in 1835, give United Canada power to legislate on this much disputed domestic question. Others thought to expedite matters by asking the Imperial Parliament to legalize a Canadian act diverting the proceeds of the reserves to secular purposes. Apart from this dispute, which involved an important constitutional principle as well as a question of strategy, there was disagreement on two other points: whether it should be made plain to the Imperial Parliament, and particularly to the House of Lords, that the objective of Canadian legislation would be secularization, and whether the Canadian Parliament should pledge itself to continue out of the Clergy Reserve funds the payment of those stipends and allowances to which the faith of the Crown was pledged.

An added complication was the racial and Roman Catholic issue. The French-Canadian supporters of the Baldwin-LaFontaine ministry were reluctant to commit themselves to secularization as were the two leaders themselves. This angered the Clear Grits, the radicals of Canada West. On the other hand, the die-hard Anglicans asserted that those who wished to upset the Settlement of 1840 and to secularize the reserves were largely Roman Catholics. "If the property of the Church of England and of Protestants generally in this Province," said an Anglican petition of 1851, "is to be confiscated for public and secular purposes, it will never be borne that the lands and endowments held for a Romish priesthood should be inviolable and untouched".[57] Sydenham's hope of avoiding racial and religious bitterness in Canada by "settling" the reserves question in Upper Canada before the Union thus proved illusory.

The result of these political complications was that in the session of 1850, J. H. Price, Commissioner of Crown Lands in the Baldwin-LaFontaine government, introduced on his own responsibility a series of resolutions which led to the adoption, by a vote of 46–23, of an address asking the Imperial Parliament to repeal the Act of 1840 and to give the Canadian legislature power to deal with the reserves. The dissidents included those who wished to proceed by bill instead of address, those who opposed upsetting the "settlement," and those who were opposed to continuing the payment of the promised stipends.[58] Russell's government promised the necessary legislation, the Aberdeen government provided it, and then the Canadian Parliament enacted the Clergy Reserves Secularization Act of 1854.

The Secularization Act provided that the proceeds of the Clergy Reserves, past and future, were to form two funds, one for Upper and one for Lower Canada, and that these funds were to be divided among the municipalities of each section according to population, subject to the payment of the stipends and allowances charged on the Clergy Reserve Fund by the Act of 1840.[59] The Act passed the Assembly by a vote of 62–39, after much discussion over how the existing stipends were to be provided for, whether the reserves should be used for municipal purposes or for education, whether each section of the united province should have its own fund or should share one fund, and whether the fund should be appropriated among the municipalities on the basis of population or with some regard to need.[60] The size of the opposition is to be explained by the fact that the Clear Grits, who favoured secularization but opposed the continuation of the allowances, voted in the negative. Hume's prediction that the Act of 1840 would prove "to the last hour . . . a source of discord," was more than fulfilled.[61]

Canadian opposition to the Clergy Reserves was not consistently the same throughout the long history of the dispute concerning them. First, the reserves were disliked because they were in effect a speculation conducted by the government for the benefit of the church at the expense of the settler and they were obtainable only on a disagreeable form of tenure—leasehold. Opposition to the reserves was at first economic, not sectarian. The complaints of the Assembly and the township reports of Robert Gourlay asked that the reserves be *sold,* not that the Church of England be deprived of the endowment and put on a basis of equality with other churches. Second, those whom the reserves were intended to benefit turned out to be a minority assisted at the expense of the many. Strachan's vigorous defence of the landed endowment created hostility towards the Church of England and deep resentment at the political influence she was able to exert. Opposition to the reserves, which had been largely economic, became more and more sectarian. Third, when the reserves were at length put up for sale, the quantity annually available was limited, the price high, the terms stiff—and stiffer under the Act of 1840 than under the Act of 1827. The government's policy continued to be a grievance for economic as well as sectarian reasons. Among the radical Reformers of Upper Canada the conviction was strong that instead of treating the reserves as a long-term speculation the government ought to facilitate their acquisition by the people. Strachan and the Church of England party were thought to be influencing the government's policy in the opposite direction. The legislature therefore prevented Anglican meddling by secularizing the reserves once and for all. A fourth objection to the reserves developed when the dispute was nearing its final stages. Through the reserves the Canadian people were denied control of all the natural resources of their province, of revenue they had helped to create, and of jurisdiction over an important domestic question.[62]

The Imperial Act of 1853 and the Clergy Reserve Secularization Act of 1854 removed these complaints almost completely.[63] By 1854, however, about three-quarters of the reserves had already been sold, although more than £500,000 was still due on them in principal and interest.[64] After 1854, whatever regulations were applied to the Crown lands in a township were applied also to the Clergy Reserves of the township. By 1854 the Crown lands were no longer being sold under the cash sales system but on five years' credit. Settlement duty requirements did not apply to townships surveyed before the Union and consequently did not apply to the Clergy Reserves.[65]

As the following tables show, by 1865, only a remnant of the Clergy Reserves remained unsold.[66]

TABLE I

DISPOSITION OF THE CLERGY RESERVES

Sold under Act of 1827	530,713¼ acres
Sold under Act of 1840	1,126,880¾
Sold under Act of 1854	602,509¾
Rectory patents	15,048
Under lease in 1859	34,957¼
Unsold in 1865	30,559
TOTAL	2,340,668¼ acres *

* The total acreage of Clergy Reserves in Upper Canada was, in fact, 2,395,687 acres. The discrepancy between the total acreage of the Clergy Reserves and the acreage accounted for may be explained in part by the fact that some Clergy Reserve lots, which were not under lease, were being rented, and, as permitted by the Act of 1827, some Clergy Reserves had been granted in exchange for other property.

TABLE II

ANNUAL SALES OF CLERGY RESERVES

Year	Acres	Year	Acres	Year	Acres	Year	Acres
1829	18,014	1839	24,949	1849	70,726	1858	25,812
1830	24,705	1840	23,586	1850	93,245	1859	75,698
1831	28,563	1841	2,665	1851	91,706	1860	62,522
1832	48,484	1842	1,486	1852	94,942	1861	74,366
1833	62,282	1843	613	1853	150,809	1862	29,771
1834	59,326	1844	569	1854	127,638	1863	11,912
1835	59,003	1845	40,602	1855	129,037	1864a	22,265
1836	63,440	1846	179,271	1856	81,086	1864-5	19,160
1837	81,549	1847	196,568	1857	59,937	1865a	10,941
1838	21475	1848	81,373				

The superscript a = half year. Fractional quantities have been omitted.

In the pre-Rebellion period, 1837 was the peak year. The decline in sales in the immediate post-Rebellion period occurred not because British capital had been diverted elsewhere—American investments were not particularly attractive after the panic of 1837—but because sales at auction had been suspended in September, 1839, in order to save the limited acreage available under the Act of 1827 for pre-emption claimants.[67] Sales were completely suspended on July 1, 1841. The few sales shown for the years 1842-4 had been made prior to that date and were subsequently confirmed.[68] Sales were resumed in March, 1845, under the Imperial Act of 1840. The large sales of 1846 and 1847 were the result of the demand for land which had accumulated during the years of suspension, the adoption of the ten-year credit system in March, 1846, and the desire of squatters to take advantage of their pre-emption privileges before the deadline, January 1, 1847.

During the years 1845 and 1854, Clergy Reserves sold for an average price of 11s. 8d. an acre. They brought an average price of 14s. 6d. during the years 1855-7 but from then on the price of the picked-over reserves fell steadily until at the end they were selling for $1.50 or 7s. 6d. an acre. The squatter problem remained throughout. As late as 1860, in such early-settled counties as Stormont, Dundas, and Glengarry, the Crown Land Department was authorizing the sale of reserves at a valuation to the occupants, some of whom were newcomers while others had been in occupation thirty years and had made extensive improvements.[69] By 1859 the acreage of Clergy Reserves under lease had shrunk to 34,957½ acres.[70] Evidently these leaseholds were either purchased or not renewed since, after 1861, rents on leased lots no longer formed part of the collections from Clergy Reserves. Rent from unleased clergy land is shown in the returns from 1847 on, but by 1865 the amount collected had become insignificant.

By the close of 1865, 2,260,104 acres of Clergy Reserves had been sold for £1,210,745 5s. 11d. or 10s. 8d. an acre on the average. At $5.00 to the pound, the principal sum was $6,053,725, of which, on December 31, 1868, only $131,023 was still owing, plus $103,842 in interest. The lots not fully paid for included about 19,000 acres, on which only one instalment had ever been paid.[71] Disregarding the small fragment of 30,000 acres still unsold and the small sum still due, we can say that by Confederation the Clergy Reserves had been sold to the people and paid for.

What had happened to the Crown Reserves in the meantime? Of the 1,322,010 Crown Reserves acquired by the Canada Company, 33 per cent had been sold by 1837, 40 per cent (531,000 acres) was under lease in 1854, and, by 1876 15 per cent (200,000 acres) was still in the possession of the Company.[72] What burden of debt still hung over the lots that had been sold is not generally known. The larger quantity of Clergy Reserves managed by the government passed into private hands much more rapidly than the Crown Reserves of the Canada Company which were located, on the whole, in older townships. The rapid sale of the Clergy Reserves was the process Robert Baldwin supported in 1847 when he had insisted on the government's retaining control of them. However, it cannot be assumed that the government's policies, in contrast to those of the Canada Company, led to the establishment of independent farmers on land which they had succeeded in paying for. Wherever a credit policy for government land existed, it could both help and hinder actual settlers. What proportion of the Clergy Reserves passed to land speculators and were resold by them at a profit to individuals on mortgage?[73] What proportion of Clergy Reserve contracts were not completed by those who began the back-breaking work of subduing the forest but were disposed of as assignments to creditors or to those able to purchase an improved lot? These are some of the questions to which we still need answers.

After the passage of the Imperial Act of 1853 it was within the power of United Canada to utilize wisely the income from these natural resources of which it had insisted on taking control. In view of the history of the Clergy Reserves question, one would expect the fund to have been used for education, but common schools already had an endowment and to have proposed to use the fund for the support of institutions of higher education would have been to reopen the Clergy Reserves question in another form and might have further embittered the university question in Upper Canada. The method adopted, that of dividing the fund among the municipalities, was one readily applicable to both sections of United Canada and did not involve using a Protestant endowment for the benefit of Catholic schools. Moreover, as Hincks pointed out, since the municipalities could use their shares for general purposes, there was nothing to prevent them using the money for education if they saw fit.[74]

The existence of the fund tempted the municipalities to borrow recklessly on the strength of their expectations for public works.[75] They each received, from time to time, little dribbles of capital from a fund which, if kept intact, could have provided a handsome endowment for a university. In the end, the Clergy Reserves, which had originally been intended to support an educated clergy, through whose labours the colony was to be taught to "Fear God and Honour the King," provided a bridge here, an improved highway there, public services which in the years 1854-65 the municipalities could, at a more cautious rate, have provided for themselves.

Of recent years general condemnation of the Clergy Reserves has moderated and the interest of historians has shifted from the Clergy Reserves as the cause of the Rebellion to the validity of the policy upon which they were based and the manner in which they were administered. It has been argued that the reserves were genuinely made in the public interest, narrowly and mistakenly concieved to be sure and liberalized all too slowly, but sound in principle; that the policy was capable of producing the financial results expected of it and, if it did not do so, it was only because it was not persevered in long enough; that the reserves were not as great a handicap to settlement or to good roads as were the more extensive holding of land speculators.

The chequered plan did not retard the settlement of the country as much as has been claimed for three reasons: it was ignored by squatters; it never applied to many of the early settled townships; and it was modified in many other townships to facilitate the making of roads But reserves that were removed from one township or concession added to the evil in another. It is true, too, that clergy land could be acquired more readily than the land of speculators. Down to 1834 it could always be leased; after 1827 it could be purchased on easier terms than the Canada Company or private landowners would give. The weakness of this defence is that prior to 1827 freeholds, not leaseholds, were wanted and afterwards only a restricted and insufficient quantity of Clergy Reserves was offered for sale. In holding the reserves for the rise in value which the development of the country was expected to bring, the government acted the part of a land speculator—in the public interest to be sure—but it thereby resorted to a method of developing a source of income for the clergy which it had condemned as injurious to the public and had tried to discourage in its subjects by regulations and taxation. The reserves, remarks G. Riddell, were "in accord with principles the successful application of which was possible."[76] The principle on which the reserves were based is that earlier generations take thought for the needs of later generations, conserving public assets to provide for them. The question is, should this have been done chiefly at the expense of that element in the community least able to bear the tax upon its energy and resources: in Upper Canada, under the chequered plan, the backwoods farmer?

CHAPTER EIGHTEEN

DEBRIS AND DEBATE UNDER
THE UNION

AFTER THE UNION of the two Canadas, the lands of Upper Canada, now Canada West, were administered under the provisions of the Act of Union, the royal instructions, and provincial legislation. Control of the land revenues was surrendered to the provincial legislature by the Act of Union. These revenues became part of the consolidated fund on which, by the fifty-second clause of the act, a permanent civil list of £45,000 was charged and a supplementary one of £30,000 was established for the life of the Crown. Sir Robert Peel objected to the surrender of these revenues lest the Colonial legislature, by speedily selling the land, should dry up one of the sources of revenue on which the civil list was based and should then refuse to provide for it and revive the acrimonious disputes which had preceded the Rebellion. In reply, Lord John Russell pointed out that although the land revenues were surrendered, control of land policy was retained by the forty-second clause, which required acts relating to the Crown lands to be reserved for the royal assent.[1]

In 1835, however, Glenelg had pledged that the land system should be made subject to local legislation. The Imperial government's assent to the Land Act of 1837 was the first payment on this promise. Its assent to the Act of 1841, despite the very different recommendations of the Durham Report and of the Colonial Land and Emigration Commission, was the second. An attempt of the Commisison to burden the first Governor of United Canada with instructions requiring him to administer the land according to provincial law and also according to their detailed directions, failed. Russell accepted the draft instructions which his friend Lord Sydenham had drawn up for himself. They merely required the Governor to comply with the land laws of the province and, where no law applied, to abide by such instructions as he might receive.[2] Subsequently the Imperial government did not delay nor fail to assent to land legislation enacted by United Canada and the only bill reserved was Merritt's Common School Lands Bill of 1849. The details of the land system were not, however, prescribed in the provincial statutes. They were left to the governor-in-council with his colonial advisers. The Imperial Act of 1854, which modified the Act of Union, finally fulfilled Glenelg's pledge by removing the requirement that laws relating to the Crown lands be reserved. If ever the need for safeguarding the land revenues in this way existed, Canada had outgrown it by this time. She had resented the permanent civil list imposed on her revenues without her consent by the Act of Union and had, in 1847, secured the repeal of that part of the act in return for an adequate, although reduced, civil list approved by her own legislature.[3]

When the Act of Union went into effect, the Crown lands of Upper Canada were regulated by the Act of 1837. This act, it will be remembered, forbade free grants except to those entitled under existing regulations, provided for sales at auction, private sales of once publicly-offered land, private sales in certain cases at a valuation, the use of U.E. and militia claims at 4s. an acre in purchase of all classes of land, and the keeping by the Commissioner of Crown Lands of a register of assignments of claims to unpatented land, located or un-located. The life of this act, which had been limited to two years, had been extended to five by an act of 1839,[4] and the only change made was the addition of a clause making it easier to register an assignment to which the witnesses were dead or absent.

In his opening speech to the Parliament of United Canada, Sydenham hinted that Imperial assistance to immigrants arriving at Quebec was conditioned on the acceptance by the province of a bill about to be introduced for the disposal of the public lands.[5] At first glance this act appears to be essentially a re-enact-ment of the Upper Canada Act of 1837 and an extension of it to Lower Canada; but combined with it were certain provisions Sydenham wanted and some minor changes which had been suggested by the Colonial Land and Emigration Com-mission. The one major change of policy was the inclusion in the new act, 4 & 5 Vic., c. 100, of a clause once again permitting the governor-in-council to make free grants to actual settlers on what were later to be known as coloniza-tion roads.

Hugh Morrison has called attention to the fact that the free grant provision of the new act was contrary to its own opening clause, the principles of land policy laid down by Glenelg, the Act of 1837, the recommendations of the Durham Report, and the teachings of the Wakefield school. He has pointed out that these free grants were made available while the Land Act of 1837, which forbade them, was still in force and before the Act of 1841, which permitted them, had been introduced into the legislature. Faced with an unexpectedly large number of immigrants and inadequate employment for them, and anxious not to lose this population to the United States, Sydenham was obliged, says Morrison, "to fit his Wakefield theories into practical moulds."[6] Accordingly, he placed those immigrants for whom employment had to be found on 50-acre free grants adjacent to a new road which was about to be constructed to Owen Sound.

The practical Sydenham would have denied—and probably with vehemence—that he belonged to the school of "that scamp, Mr. E. G. Wakefield." It is true that he recognized the "impolicy of tempting the Immigrant Labourer to become a Landowner whilst he has no capital beyond his labour to offer, and that therefore the system of free grants of land is impolitic as a general principle . . ." but that was the extent of his agreement with Wakefield.[7] Sydenham did not condemn the free grant policy with regard to other classes of immigrants, and he declared, "So far from a high price being essential, as Wakefield has it, I would willingly *give* land to settlers who come *bona fide* to establish themselves and would engage to make roads, & c." As for the rest of Wakefield's "utterly impracticable" ideas—forcing concentration of population when "no man will go far into the woods if he can help it," charging a "sufficient price," enabling labourers to emigrate by raising a fund from the sale of Crown lands to pay for their passage—Sydenham would have none of them.

What was to become of the class of immigrants who could not provide their own passage money after they had arrived in Canada? Sydenham wrote indignantly:

To throw starving and diseased paupers under the rock at Quebec ought to be punishable as *murder*.... Land they cannot purchase; and if it is given to them it is no use, for they must starve for a twelvemonth till it yields a crop. Besides which, Irish and English labourers know no more of clearing and settling a forest than they do of longitude. It would take them a day to cut down a tree, which a backwoodsman will do in three minutes. Well, then, they may labour for wages. But few people can afford to pay for labour.... It is true there is a great outcry for labourers ... but when it comes to the point of hiring them, unless it be during harvest, every farmer in Upper Canada will tell you he cannot pay them.[8]

The only solution to the problem the Governor could see was to find employment for the immigrants on public works.

What concerned Sydenham was not Wakefield's theories but the Union. To him, the Union was a device for overcoming the obstructive tactics of the legislature of Lower Canada and the ability of the French Canadians to hamper British commercial interests in the St. Lawrence Valley. Upper and Lower Canada were to be linked together in an equal partnership in the new legislature, even though the latter exceeded the former in population by 300,000. Obviously it would not do to let this discrepancy grow even more marked by the loss of population from Upper Canada on the one hand and by the fecundity of the French on the other. Sydenham's problem was similar to the one which had faced Colborne ten years earlier. Colborne had been anxious to retain British immigrants in Upper Canada because he feared the Americans would fill up the province if the British did not. Sydenham was anxious to retain them to ensure British predominance in United Canada.

When the Governor first faced the problem of devising a policy to prevent British immigrants from straying across the border, Colborne's methods were explained to him by A. B. Hawke, Chief Emigrant Agent for Upper Canada.[9] Like Colborne, Sydenham concluded that if immigrants were already settled on small allotments of land they would not be so ready to leave the country when employment gave out. In May, 1840, when it seemed probable that the immigrants of that year would be too numerous to be absorbed by private employment, Sydenham decided to disregard the Land Act of 1837, to make small grants of unspecified size to immigrants, and to find employment for them on public works "such as a road that may be wanted. . ."[10] There was considerable debate when this proposal was put to the Executive Council of Upper Canada.

There were two schools of thought in the province on questions of land policy, and the differences between them had been brought to light by the report of the Assembly's committee on land granting of 1839. There were those who advocated changes in the land legislation; there were others who argued that the day had gone by for establishing any other system because the land still disposable was "trifling in amount and indifferent in quality." The latter group included the speculators in U.E. and militia rights who were anxious for a re-enactment of the Act of 1837, which had removed restrictions on these rights.

It also included the large landowners who had everything to gain from a continuance of the strict cash sales policy. The proponents of change included the Surveyor General, R. B. Sullivan, and his subordinates, Spragge and Chewett. They were of the opinion that the million odd acres of unlocated land in surveyed townships, plus the explored but unsurveyed land adjoining the Huron Tract, afforded an "ample field for the introduction of a better system." They were opposed to the admision of American settlers, and they favoured restricting the location of U.E. and militia rights to certain townships, imposing strict settlement duties, and making free grants to immigrants or reducing the price of inferior land in the older townships.[11]

In April, 1840, Lieutenant-Governor Sir George Arthur had asked the Executive Council what could be done for the expected immigrants. R. B. Sullivan, who was President of the Council, Surveyor General, and Commissioner of Crown Lands, had reported on the question, but the Council had twice failed to take action on his report. When Sydenham's proposal was laid before them on May 29, the problem was discussed once more. The minutes of the meeting reveal that the Council also was deeply divided, not over mere questions of administration, but over fundamental questions of policy.

R. G. Tucker, the Provincial Secretary, and William Allan, a Commissioner of the Canada Company, were the spokesmen for the large landholders whose object was to preserve their market by preventing additional areas of Crown land from being opened up to settlement at low prices or by free grants. They wanted "a fructifying stream" composed of immigrants with capital and of able-bodied poor whose presence would lower the rate of wages. They did not want "a desolating torrent" of pauper immigrants tempted to the province by the lure of free grants. Land granted to such persons, they argued, would in the end be transferred to others, perhaps before it was patented or the settlement duties performed, and in the process endless difficulties would be created for the Crown Lands Department and very little accomplished for the country. W. H. Draper, the Attorney General, shared their views. He pointed out also that the grants would not be valid and that if a free grant policy was desired the safest course would be to get the Act of 1839 disallowed.

Augustus Baldwin and R. B. Sullivan were opposed to creating in the new world a society of "masters and servants." The poor and under-privileged of the old world should be welcomed and given their chance in the new because "They come to increase our resources." The important thing was to put the poor man on his own land as soon as possible, thus giving him "an object . . . to work for." To prevent the immigrant's labour from being exploited for the benefit of others, they should be settled in a wholly vacant tract of country, "unimpeded by lands in the hands of non-residents," and, in order that they might learn the ways of the country and get roads opened, "old residents" would need to be settled along with them.[12]

The wholly vacant tract of country which Sullivan and Arthur favoured opening was the recently acquired Sauking cession on the eastern shore of Lake Huron. Across the water the Americans had already pushed into the Michigan peninsula and it was not desirable that Canada's territory should remain empty. But farmers could not be expected to purchase land cut off from the settled townships as this land was by large blocks of reserves. The sensible policy therefore was to open a road from the settled townships through the new townships and to establish a permanent population on the road to keep it from growing up again to brush. This end might be achieved, Sullivan thought, by offering 50-acre free grants and, since the first settlers would have the benefit of employment on the road but latecomers would not, none should be granted locations except those who were able to maintain themselves for twelve months. It was on this projected road from the northwest angle of Garrafraxa township to Owen Sound, the line for which had been surveyed in 1837 and which was subsequently extended south through the township of Peel, that Baldwin and Sullivan suggested settling immigrants.[13]

Before Sydenham's scheme was put into operation it became a policy of a broader character. Sullivan and Arthur were interested not only in immigrants but also in retaining well-established families of Upper Canada who were accustomed to the bush and had growing sons to place upon the land. These families were complaining that they could not get land on which to settle from their government.[14] They were either unable or unwilling to give 10s. or more an acre cash at the auction sales of Crown land and they were disinclined to pay the Canada Company's or speculators' prices for land on credit. The American prairies had already begun to attract settlers from the timbered lands of Upper Canada. The Rebellion had given an impetus to this movement, and a land policy based strictly on Wakefield's principles was likely to stimulate it more. Some outlet for the rising generation needed to be provided in Canada. Her resources needed to be opened up and developed for their benefit, a recurring problem it would seem. Free grants on roads designed to open up new townships, and low cash prices in those townships, would enable experienced pioneer families to provide for their children, leaving their improved farms, the dear land of the Canada Company, or the Clergy Reserves to be bought by British immigrants with capital.

A majority of the Executive Council could not at first be got to favour the admittedly illegal free grant policy, but Lieutenant-Governor Arthur persuaded them to recommend an appropriation for the road to Owen Sound without committing themselves on the question of land policy connected with it.[15] Sydenham, who had been won over by the common sense of Sullivan's views from his earlier notion of temporary five-acre grants such as Colborne had made, intimated that without the scheme for settling immigrants he was not prepared to approve the road.[16] The Council did not budge, preferring to postpone the opening of the road to running the risk of instituting an illegal policy which they did not want and which, after all, it seemed the number of immigrants needing assistance did not justify.[17] They yielded, however, after Hawke had reported that the immigrants were labourers, not trained farm servants, and that British immigrants were daily leaving the province for the United States. Sydenham also made it known that the British government approved of a policy which in fact had been outlined to it in only the vaguest manner.[18]

When the Colonial Office became aware that grants of 50, not five, acres were intended, Sydenham was called upon to justify that quantity. With the help of Hawke and S. B. Harrison, Arthur's private secretary, he did so, and

Sullivan hinted that even 50 acres would not induce experienced Canadian backwoodsmen to open up new land, however generous such a grant might seem to the theorists of the Colonial Office.[19]

The policy of 50-acre free grants for immigrants was accepted by the Council in September, 1840, but before the end of November Sydenham was tellling his friends in England that land was of "no use" to penniless immigrants and that, although a policy of combining settlement with employment on public works might be worked out for their benefit, immigrants were, as Colborne had discovered before him, practically useless for opening up new country. What he had done for them, he explained glibly, was not to settle them on free grants but to transplant experienced woodsmen there and thus make a place in the older townships for the immigrants' labour.[20] Sydenham soon became aware that even after the road had been opened up by more experienced labour, the free grant policy would benefit only a few of the immigrants. Out of 12,000 immigrants who reached Upper Canada in 1840, Hawke found only 150 heads of families able to maintain themselves for one year and therefore entitled to locations on the Owen Sound Road.[21]

At the outset, then, the 50-acre free grant policy was a policy that benefited not the immigrants but the existing population of Upper Canada. Moreover, it was at once modified to suit their needs. Without authorization, but probably aware of Sullivan's views, the agents for the Owen Sound Road scattered the settlers, leaving intervening reserves of 50 acres so that those who had the means of purchasing adjoining land might do so. After the Land Act of 1841 became law, the settlers were given 90 days in which to purchase these lots.[22] In 1843 some of them claimed that they had located on the road under the impression that the government would reserve the intervening lots for them to purchase when they could. The Council yielded to their pleas and reserved the lots for five years at 10s. an acre, or at 8s. per acre if bought and paid for within a year.[23] Thus, the 50-acre purchase and the 50-acre free grant provision of the Act of 1837 to which Glenelg had objected became the 50-acre free grant and the 50-acre reserve policy for which a minority in the Assembly had contended in vain.

The Colonial Office accepted Sydenham's justification of the 50-acre free grants still believing that they were intended primarily to benefit immigrants. Russell stated, however, that without the concurrence of the legislature the Crown could not promise the grants.[24] The legislature agreed with Sydenham's proposals and the 50-acre free grant policy was included in the Land Act of 1841 in a clause which confined the grants to new settlements and limited them to British subjects, not immigrants, who had not previously received land from the Crown. By this time, Sydenham, who was pretty confident of his ability to manage the legislature, had already put the free grants into operation on the Owen Sound Road.

It is perhaps noteworthy that the free grant clause of the Land Act of 1841 was contrary to the ideas of the Wakefield school which were so much in vogue at the time. It is more striking that the legislature should have accepted this clause because it marks a complete reversal of policy on its part. After the sales system was instituted there was always a minority in the legislature in favour of free grants to immigrants, but it was a small minority. Indeed, during the debate on the Land Act of 1837, the policy of making free grants to immigrants had been decisively defeated 8-32.[25] Why was it accepted in 1841?

"Many forces," writes Morrison, "contributed ... to the one result The desire of the landed proprietors to increase the value of his land, the patriotism of the United Empire Loyalist, the political desire of the British element, the fears of the militarists, the land hunger of the frontiersman and the desire to develop new country—all these led to the adoption of a modified policy of free grants. But the underlying factor that contributed to their success was the competition with the United States for the immigrant."[26] The chief cause was anxiety in Upper Canada over the effects of the Union. These other forces cannot be disregarded but they had not proved effective earlier. The eagerness of the landed proprietors to increase the value of their land had in the past led them to oppose the free grant policy. The U.E. loyalist had hid the light of his "burning patriotism" under the bushel of self-interest and had voted down the free grant policy repeatedly. In 1836-7 the Tories had become concerned about the decline in the volume of immigration to Canada. A select committee appointed at this session reported that all that was necessary to restore it was to institute a well-directed campaign of publicity, similar to that undertaken by the Canada Company, but at government expense and under government auspices.[27] The competition of the United States for immigrants was nothing new. Hawke had been drawing attention to it for years and urging, in vain, the adoption of a land policy similar to that of the United States.

By 1839 the situation was different. The union of the provinces was in the offing and the Tories of Upper Canada had become anxious to retain the existing population and to attract British immigrants as rapidly as possible. Sir George Arthur shared this anxiety and in his case it was heightened by the old bogey —fear of the Americans.[28] In the session of 1839-40 the members of the Assembly had urged that the ties of Empire be strengthened and had asked the assistance of the mother country in promoting immigration "to make the United Province British in fact, as well as name." They suggested the methods of 1824 and 1825, and declared that they were willing to assist by concurring in the disposal of the public lands in a way that would encourage immigration.[29] They kept this promise by voting for the free grant provisions of the Act of 1841.

Sydenham's views on land policy for Canada seem to have been a combination of those of Sullivan and Hawke. Hawke had repeatedly urged on his superiors a land system that was simple and cheap, and one which would compare favourably with the American system. Sullivan wanted price left to the discretion of the executive, urged that credit be allowed only for higher priced land, and condemned the auction system because it neither prevented the evils of the free grant system—delays, uncertainties, and large unimproved holdings— nor produced more revenue than was obtainable by sales at fixed prices. Sydenham favoured low, fixed, but not uniform prices and condemned both the auction system and sales on credit.

The Colonial Land and Emigration Commissioners preferred uniform prices, proposed that in future townships be laid out six miles square and be divided into tracts of 320 acres, suggested that the reservation of minerals to the Crown be omitted from patents in future, and advocated allowing squatters the right of pre-emption. They were concerned primarily about the large number of long-established squatters in the Eastern Townships of Lower Canada. The position of these squatters, who had come in from the United States, needed to be regularized, and the Commissioners recommended that they should be allowed to become naturalized and to acquire titles to their land.[30] However, their general remarks on the usefulness of squatters suggest that they had in mind a sort of double standard: the application of Wakefield's doctrines to prevent inexperienced British immigrants from wasting their needed labour in a struggle with the bush and, at the same time, the granting of pre-emption privileges to secure the labour of American backwoodsmen for the initial improvements on lots which would afterwards be purchased by British immigrants with some capital. Sydenham regarded the Commissioners' proposals on pre-emption as likely to encourage immigration from the United States and therefore opposed them. "There is a spirit of propagandism among American citizens," he wrote, "which makes it necessary to observe great caution in the matter." [31]

Sydenham did secure a naturalization act which, like the Upper Canada Act of 1828, was limited to aliens already resident in United Canada, enabled them to become subjects after seven years' residence, and protected titles to land derived through aliens. An act of this sort was needed for Upper Canada as well as Lower Canada because many persons who had refused to concede that their status was not already that of British subjects had failed to take advantage of the naturalization act of Upper Canada and had found themselves excluded from the polls during the hard-fought election of 1836.[32] The Tories of Upper Canada were angered by Sydenham's act because it offered a second chance to such persons.[33]

Certain harmless little suggestions which the Colonial Land and Emigration Commissioners had made respecting the appointment of district agents for the convenience of immigrants, the prompt delivery of patents, and the making of small reservations for public purposes were attended to in the new act, but the suggested changes in the methods of survey did not find favour with the Surveyor General's Department, which did not want to alter the standard size (200 acres) of the lots. Sydenham, who was planning his municipal councils policy and did not wish to reduce the size of their units, the townships, to six miles square, also found the suggested change unacceptable. The only part of the American system adopted at this time was that the astronomical system of survey was substituted for the magnetic system. But, beginning in 1854, the townships north of Lake Superior were surveyed on the American plan.[34] The proposed changes in the wording of patents were acceptable to Sydenham. The reservation to the Crown of base metals and coal, to be found in the early patents, had been dropped in 1798. After the Union, the Governor's instructions no longer required the reservation of precious metals. Since Simcoe's day, patents had contained a statement that land was not to be granted if it was found to be within a reserve of masting timber. At Sydenham's suggestion, this proviso also was dropped. It had been greatly disliked by the early settlers and had caused some confusion and uncertainty until Peter Russell suggested that it meant that either the whole lot in question was to be classified as a reserve of masting timber or none of it was.[35]

The uniform price desired by Wakefield was not established by the new land

law; instead, all terms and conditions of sale were left to the discretion of the
Governor and his Council. Since sales at public auction were not prescribed,
there could not be once publicly offered land available for purchase at the upset
price at private sale. The new land system was, therefore, less like the American
system than that which the legislature of Upper Canada had approved in 1837.
Squatters were not granted a *right* of pre-emption by the act but the clause
permitting the Governor to authorize private sales to occupants at a valuation
made it possible to protect them. The policy of allowing U.E. and militia rights
to be used at the rate of 4s. an acre in the purchase of land was continued with
those changes which have been discussed in chapter IX. A determined minority
evidently found parts of Sydenham's bill objectionable. The debate on the
second reading was twice put off, perhaps to enable Sydenham to work his
"popularity," and when it finally took place it was prolonged until a late hour.[36]

The Colonial Land and Emigration Commissioners did not like the free grant
provisions of the new act because they were not in harmony with "sound"
principles of colonization and because they might have the effect of depriving
the land companies of customers. They feared, too, that the settlement conditions imposed on these grants—four years' residence and the putting of one-third
of the grant under crops in that time—would prove unenforceable. The Colonial
Secretary, Stanley, who concurred in these criticisms, with reluctance advised
that the bill be confirmed and cautioned Sydenham's successor, Sir Charles Bagot,
in most emphatic terms against using the discretionary powers which the bill
gave him, particularly the power of making 50-acre free grants. Bagot tried to
calm the fears of the Colonial Office by pointing out that so far there had been
no great rush for these grants because they were too small and of insufficient
value to attract men with capital away from the land companies. The pressure
on Governors which made it difficult for them to manage the Crown lands never
came from the immigrant or settler class "whose influence must at any time be
unimportant" but from wealthier people who had made land speculation a trade.
"But it may be truly said," remarked the Governor General, "that in Canada
much has heretofore been done to promote Immigration—nothing to promote
settlement." [37]

Prior to the Rebellion, the Reformers had criticized the land regulations of
Upper Canada devised by the Imperial government and the provincial executive
on various grounds, not all consistent with one another, and had demanded that
the lands be disposed of according to a provincial act instead of under a be-
wildering series of orders-in-council. This criticism was not met by the new
land act. Only the skeleton of a policy was established and all details were left
to the governor-in-council.

There were really two tasks before the Executive Council: to devise wise
policies for the alienation of the Crown lands in future, and to clear away all
the tag-ends of unfinished business arising from policies in force before the
Union. In the interval between the Rebellion and the Union, Sir George Arthur
and the Executive Council of Upper Canada, under the guidance of R. B.
Sullivan, had begun to attack these problems. Despite the anxiety of Lieutenant-
Governor Arthur to increase the British population of Upper Canada, immigrant
settlers who held unlocated orders for land were denied permission to locate

them. These orders-in-council must have been issued prior to 1826 when the old land-granting system was abolished, and they amounted to 86,050 acres.[38] The Council's refusal to allow these orders to be located without special permission suggests that speculators were attempting to use this class of land right.

Sir George Arthur's Council also began the work of investigating the status of the large quantity of land which had been located but remained unpatented. This land was effectively closed to settlement, except by squatters, and, equally important, it paid no taxes if unoccupied. On April 4, 1839, a list of all unpatented Crown lands located prior to January 1, 1832, was published in the *Upper Canada Gazette*, and notice given that all unpatented free grants and locations subject to fees and which were unclaimed within a year would be forfeited. In addition, an inspection was to be ordered and those locations which had been granted subject to settlement duties and which were found to be unoccupied and unimproved were to be declared forfeited.[39] The quantity of land in this list was approximately 604,000 acres, two-thirds of it in four of the eighteen districts—Colborne, Newcastle, Simcoe, and Bathurst.[40] About one-fourth of the lots were patented within the year allowed. Against the remainder, the threat of forfeiture was not promptly carried out.

The inspection, which was ordered in the spring of 1840,[41] throws much light on the workings of the old settlement duty system. Half of the unpatented lots were found to be unimproved, unoccupied, and unclaimed, and they were declared forfeit, whether they had been subject to settlement duties or not.[42] The inspectors found many lots on which false settlement duty certificates had been filed and these, too, were declared forfeit. There were also many unoccupied and unclaimed lots on which settlement duties had been performed by persons who had subsequently never thought it worthwhile, or had been unable, to pay the patent fees. These were reserved for further consideration. In 1854, a proclamation debarred such grantees from taking out their patents if the fees were not paid up by January 1, 1855—almost thirty years after the free grant and patent fee system had ended.[43] Even then they were privileged to buy the land so forfeited at 2s. an acre.[44] Claimed lots, both unimproved and improved, were given individual consideration. These amounted to 82,000 acres. Ninety per cent of the unpatented but improved lots in the list were not claimed even by their occupants, who were probably squatters.[45] An additional six months was allowed occupants for filing pre-emption claims to these lots, which amounted to 92,400 acres.[46] When this land was put up for sale, the occupants were expected to pay cash for it. The total amount forfeited under these regulations amounted to 163,524 acres which were distributed as follows: [47]

DISTRICT	ACRES
Colborne	11,430
Ottawa	48,662
Dalhousie	15,672
Bathurst	13,607
Simcoe	32,295
Johnstown	8,485
Wellington	8,200
Brock	2,500
Eastern	1,600
Home	7,490

Victoria	5,650
Newcastle	4,623
Gore	2,550
Talbot	750

On March 10, 1846, a new warning was given, this time to all persons who held unpatented land located since January 1, 1832, to establish their claims and take out their patents within two years' time; otherwise their land would be resumed and resold.[48] There were 331,553 acres of land in this list, 136,092 of which were free grants and 195,461 were subject to the payment of fees. Four-fifths of it was in the Bathurst, Colborne, Simcoe, London and Western Districts. Much of the land in the Colborne and Simcoe Districts had been located to indigent immigrants at least by 1832, not as grants subject to fees, but as sales on the instalment plan at 5s. an acre. In the course of fourteen years on their 50-acre lots, the immigrants had not been able to accumulate the £12 10s. in cash to secure their titles. In the Western District some indigent settlers had been located in Warwick, Adelaide, and Plympton Townships but most of the land had been under the superintendence of Colonel Talbot. Free grants to a total of 31,850 acres were held by locatees who had not patented their land and had thus kept it off the tax roll, unless it had become occupied. The locatees of an additional 47,600 acres, which were subject to settlement duties and fees, may have done the duties under the eye of Colonel Talbot but they had not paid the fees.[49]

One objective of the framers of the Land Act of 1841 was to close out all claims to land under the old regulations as soon as possible. The act required new claims to be filed by January 1, 1843, unless on that date the claimant was a minor. New claims came principally from U.E. loyalists and militia men. The Council did not succeed in closing out their claims to scrip until May 30, 1850, and the right to use scrip until January 1, 1862. It refused to recognize other claims under the old regulations which had not been brought forward in good season, such as those of immigrant settlers, discharged soldiers, and dockyard personnel.[50] The rigour of the Council in rejecting claims based on old regulations and in refusing extensions of time for the completion of settlement duties brought complaints and interference from the legislature.

Much unfinished business remained from the old sales system in force in Upper Canada prior to 1841. On many of the sales made between 1828 and 1837 the purchasers had made only the initial payment, had stripped the land of its timber, and then abandoned it. Other delinquents had been deterred from completing their payments by the state of political and economic uncertainty in Upper Canada after 1837. In October, 1840, the Council cautiously began to put pressure on delinquents, calling first on those who had paid only one instalment and threatening them with the loss of their land if payment was not brought up to date in three months' time.[51] The collections on old accounts showed a marked increase after 1840 but it has to be remembered that these payments could now be made in scrip.

The Land Act of 1841 left it to the governor-in-council to establish the prices and conditions on which Crown land would be sold, and no act passed prior to 1854 limited their discretion on this point. Perhaps for this reason, no act relating to Crown lands was refused the royal assent. But Wakefield's ideas had taken firm hold of the Colonial Office and successive Governors were urged to secure a land system that would make possible the systematic colonization of a steady stream of British immigrants to Canada.[52] There was a general expectation in Great Britain that something great would be done for immigration from the Crown lands,[53] and this notion was fostered by some British travellers who visited Canada.[54] The result was that in the Executive Council a system had to be devised that would diminish the evils created by the old land-granting system, offset the attractions of the United States, take into account the expectations of the British government, and satisfy practical Canadians, who were by no means all agreed.

Realizing that if Canada were to attract immigrants the price of land would have to be close to the American price, Sydenham suggested 4s. and 6s. an acre for land in Lower Canada. The Colonial Land and Emigration Commissioners strongly urged the establishment of one fixed and somewhat higher price. They innocently believed that the "advantages" of Canada, where they expected the land revenues to be spent on public works and the promotion of immigration, justified a somewhat higher price for Canada's forested lands than the United States was charging for prairie soil, but they were willing to have the low price of 6s. an acre established for Lower Canada as an experiment.

Sydenham was a man of few illusions. He realized that British immigrants coming to Canada were only too likely to succumb to the temptation to belong to another nation if that temptation were strong. Therefore, the price of land in Canada had to be kept competitive. "It is not from acquisition of land by *poor* men, but from the speculations of the rich, that the country has suffered and continues to suffer," he reminded the Commissioners.[55] The Governor died the day after the Land Act of 1841 was passed, and, when it came into operation in 1842, his recommendations were adopted for Lower Canada, but in Upper Canada a uniform and higher price was established.[56]

In Upper Canada there were some special circumstances to be considered. Whatever price was established for Crown land would effect the price that could be set for Clergy Reserves and asked by the Canada Company. The scattered Crown Reserves were being sold by the Company for 12s. 6d. to 25s. on five years' credit, and land in the Huron Tract was being sold at a minimum of 7s. 6d. In addition, there were thousands of acres of land scrip to be absorbed at 4s. an acre. The higher the price of Crown land, the less land it would take to satisfy the scrip. These considerations, plus a desire to concentrate the population and to prevent British immigrants from attempting backwoods farming in the more remote townships, offset the wish to meet American competition. A cash sale policy and one price, 8s. an acre, was established for Upper Canada by Sir Charles Bagot and his Council, but this price did not apply to forfeited lands which were subject to special valuations.[57] A small quantity of land was sold on instalments, probably to squatters, between 1842 and 1845, at which time this leniency ended.

Dissatisfaction with the Crown Lands Department led the Assembly in August, 1845, to appoint a commission of inquiry. The extravagant costs of the Department, the inefficiency of its administration, and the patronage available to the government had given rise to much criticism and it was probably intensified by the Department's refusal to sell any more land on credit after July 1, 1845. Certainly, the witnesses did not limit themselves to the administration of the Act of 1841 but also attacked its principle—cash sales.

Most of those who testified favoured the credit system. They argued that the cash sales system was not really a cash sales system at all so far as the actual settler was concerned. What happened was that the desired land was purchased for the settler by a money-lender who resold it to him on credit at an increased price and who thus obtained a higher rate of interest for the use of his money than the usury laws allowed.[58] The land became security for the loan and, with the improvements made by the settler, was in many instances ultimately forfeited to the loan shark. "Trade in the lands owned by the needy . . . has been carried on to a most unknown extent by speculators of all kinds, from the Councillor to the member of the Lower House and the adventurer from the States . . .," wrote Bonnycastle in 1852.[59] "The prompt payment system," observed Ogle R. Gowan, "would in a few years create a landed aristocracy over the poor." [60]

Since poor settlers were obliged to obtain credit from some source, critics of the existing system proposed that the government provide it. They believed that the settlers would be able to meet the government's more reasonable terms and to retain possession of their land and improvements. Some realistic witnesses, doubtful even of this, urged that the land be sold on credit at a reduced price, at least as low as the American price; otherwise settlers would never remain in Canada to pay their debts, or succeed if they did remain. John Prince put it bluntly. Wild land was "dear at nothing, be it never so good and rich." It was the labour of the settler that gave value to the land, and the great objective of any land system must therefore be not revenue but population.[61]

In their report, the Assembly's commission strongly recommended sale of the Crown lands on credit, with the proviso that payments on credit sales should be required to be in money, not scrip, and that a down-payment of one-third or one-fourth be required. Various changes to provide for more economical administration of the Crown Lands Department were also recommended.[62] No major changes in land policy resulted from this inquiry. The Draper and Sherwood ministries of Lord Metcalfe and the Assembly were absorbed by the struggle over constitutional questions and, until they were settled, practical questions of economic policy had to wait. The price of Crown land continued to be 8s. per acre until February 14, 1848, when those lots which had been open to general location prior to 1841 were reduced to 4s., just a few days before the ministry went out of office.[63] The land in fifteen of the more remote townships was also reduced to 4s. by the new government in December, 1848.

After being written into the Land Act of 1841, the free grant policy was continued by the Draper and Sherwood ministries, of which Sullivan was not a member, in a rather half-hearted fashion. No more money was granted to make the Owen Sound Road as good a road as had been planned, but without this employment the settlers managed by haying and harvesting in other townships and on credit supplied by storekeepers. By 1845, all the lots on the road were taken, some of them having been purchased to extend the original allotments. The settlers were prospering and newcomers were clamouring for land in the rear of the road and squatting when they were told it was not open to settlement.[64] In consequence, in 1846, two new lines of road were run, one east, one west of the original road. The reserved 50-acre lots on the Owen Sound Road had prevented close settlement and good maintenance of the road. On the new roads this mistake was not repeated. Ranges of 100-acre lots were laid off; the front 50 acres was granted free; the rear 50 was reserved for nine years for purchase at 8s. to 10s. an acre, the price depending upon how soon the settler availed himself of the privilege of buying. However, the land was granted on less liberal terms than the settlers on the Owen Sound Road had obtained. In addition to putting one-third of his free grant under cultivation, the settler was bound to clear the whole width of the road and to keep it cleared until the lot on the opposite side should be sold. He also paid fees to the (now) unsalaried agent for the road for locating him and for certifying to his settlement duties. Thus, at no expense save for surveys, the Draper–Viger government, whose head was really unfriendly to the free grant policy, expected to make marketable the 150 acres it retained for every 50 it granted free. So great was the demand for land in Upper Canada by the mid-forties that all the free grants fit for settlement were promptly occupied.[65]

The following year, D. B. Papineau, Commissioner of Crown Lands in the Draper and Sherwood ministries, argued that enough had been done to develop the area north of the Huron Tract, and that it would now be in the interest of the province to stimulate the settlement of other areas, namely, the Colborne, Victoria, and Midland Districts. He suggested that a 120-mile line of road be laid out from the township of Mara on Lake Simcoe, in the rear of the Home District, to the lumbering stations on the Madawaska River in the District of Bathurst, with connecting north-south roads to the rear of the settlements in the Colborne and Midland Districts.[66] This policy, which later led to many settlers being located in areas not permanently suited to agriculture, was not put into practice at this time although surveys were begun.[67] A month later the Draper ministry was out of office and the Sherwood ministry which followed had a short uneasy life. The one accomplishment of the latter towards settling the country was to authorize the immediate laying out of a road on the Owen Sound principle from the township of Kingston to the Ottawa River. For this road, the influential member for Kingston, John A. Macdonald, had been pressing for some time.[68]

CHAPTER NINETEEN

SCHOOL LANDS AND SCRIP

THE LAND ACT OF 1841 remained in force in amended form until 1853 and, in the interval, dissatisfaction with it and with the Land Department increased. Some members of the Assembly vigorously opposed the forfeiture of claimed but unpatented lots on which settlement duties had not been done. However, the bills which were passed in 1844 and 1847 granting extensions of time for the performance of these duties on lots located prior to 1839 were not returned by the Council. As Draper pointed out, the changes in the law being demanded would have benefited speculators chiefly and would have undone much of the work that had been accomplished.[1]

There were other critics whose fundamental objection to the Act of 1841 was that it failed to apply the land revenues to some important provincial object. At the time of its passage, Francis Hincks and David Thompson had attempted without success to attach a rider which would have required the land revenues to be invested in provincial or municipal securities and would have permitted only the annual interest to be expended as part of the general revenue.[2] W. H. Merritt was another who regarded the Crown lands as capital—"the only real capital the country possesses"—that ought neither to be frittered away in free grants nor sold under an expensive administrative system to add a trifle to each year's general revenue.[3] There was still a third group, led by Baldwin, who criticized the extravagant cost of administration, resented the patronage which the appointment of district agents gave to the government, and who questioned the wisdom of entrusting the public revenues to them.[4]

Decisive changes in land policy might have been expected when the Baldwin—LaFontaine government took office in March, 1848. Sales of land had fallen markedly after 1846, as a result of the repeal of the Corn laws and the cholera epidemic of 1847, and were to be further affected by the annexation crisis of 1849. The tide of emigration from the British Isles had definitely turned away from Canada,[5] trade and commerce were depressed, the St. Lawrence navigation system on which the British loan of 1841 had been spent was still uncompleted, and Canada could not borrow the money to finish it. The country seemed to stagnate. What Canadian critics of the existing land system wanted was a policy liberal enough to attract settlers and to keep the economy expanding without encouraging speculators. What the British government wanted was to satisfy the expectations that had been aroused by Wakefield without going to any expense. The desire to promote emigration was "the reigning fancy of the day," but unfortunately the economical fever was "very strong upon John Bull" at the same time.[6] No fundamental change in land policy could be made while the Colonial Secretary was trying "to do something on a great scale for the encouragement of immigration" from the Crown lands of Canada.[7]

For six years, Sir George Grey did his best to convince the government of Canada that it was not by lowering the price of land that the settlement of the province would be promoted but by raising it and spending the proceeds upon improvements. He condemned the existing individualist system, even for immigrants with capital, because it was wasteful from the social and economic point of view, and wanted to substitute for it organized township planting "by Societies carrying with them as they advance all the means and appliances of civilization." Adequate funds for such ventures could be obtained, Grey thought, by raising the price of land and imposing a wild land tax.[8]

But it was the colonization of poor English and particularly Irish labourers without capital that gave Grey the most concern. His first proposal was that villages should be established in the vicinity of public works on which immigrants should be employed. Out of their savings they should be encouraged to purchase the freehold of their log houses and gardens and subsequently farm land in the vicinity, but they should continue living in the villages where they would have a more civilized existence. Grey proposed that the funds for communities of this mediaeval type should be provided by the British government and lent to land companies or private landowners who would administer the scheme and repay the government.[9] No co-operation whatever was forthcoming from the Canada Company, the British-American Land Company, or the North American Colonial Association when the plan was put up to them.[10] The impracticality of his proposals was then explained to Grey, whose notions of distances, climate, terrain and state of communications in Canada were evidently vague, by a dispatch from Elgin enclosing reports from Draper and Buchanan.[11]

The second proposal from the now somewhat discouraged Grey was that Canada should be made to realize that there was no hope of an Imperial guarantee for the construction of the Great Western Railway from Hamilton to Windsor, but that Canada's own revenues could enable her to guarantee interest on the bonds if she would adopt two of Grey's suggestions: an increase in the price of Crown land and a 6d. an acre tax on all lands whether improved or unimproved. With the construction of the road, immigration to Canada would be stimulated, land values would rise, and work could be provided for poor immigrants.[12] In Canada West, land taxes were imposed by the district councils within the limits and at the valuations set by the legislature. Cultivated land paid a maximum of $1\frac{1}{2}d.$ an acre and wild land three-tenths of a penny. Grey's proposals would have increased the former tax four-fold and the latter tax twenty-fold. Much as some interests in Canada West wanted the Great Western Railway there was not the remotest chance of persuading the legislature to burden the landowners to this extent.

J. R. Godley's scheme for removing two million persons from Ireland and providing one-third of the cost of passage out of a 1 per cent property and income tax on Ireland was urged on the Treasury at this time and supported by Chief Justice J. B. Robinson. Godley proposed to organize an Irish Canada Company which should buy the land, settle the immigrants, make loans to district councils for public works, and receive, in addition to profits from resale of the land, £5 for every immigrant it settled.[13] But no one in Canada wanted another land company, and Godley's scheme was condemned by all parties, including Grey.[14] The Colonial Secretary preferred to rely on the immigrants' own initiative to get him across the Atlantic, but he wanted Canada to stimulate that initiative by spending money on public works and railways.

By this time the Irish famine had occurred and thousands of diseased and destitute persons had emigrated to the United States, which had begun to protect itself by restrictive legislation. Under the circumstances, a large increase in the number of Irish immigrants to British North America was to be expected and Grey became increasingly anxious to provide employment for them. He now proposed enlisting 24,000 men "from the semi-barbarians of Mayo and Donegal," utilizing one-twelfth of them for a month at a time in military duties and employing the rest on public works, particularly in the construction of the Quebec to Halifax Railway for which Major Robinson had recently completed his survey. Grey thought the expense of transporting the immigrants should be borne by the mother country and the expense of employing them by the colony. He also suggested that part of the immigrants' wages should be held back to pay for the cottage and the lot of land assigned them on arrival. In this way a cheap labour force under military discipline could be provided. From the sale of ungranted Crown land within ten miles of the road, and from a tax on land already granted within the area, the Assemblies could give financial aid to the railway.

In the Baldwin–LaFontaine ministry, R. B. Sullivan was back in office as President of the Council. Elgin reported that all his ministers were well disposed towards fostering immigration from the British Isles but that Sullivan, who was an Irishman, was the most interested.[15] Sullivan's attitude toward the Irish immigration problem was sympathetic, but, unlike Grey's, realistic. He pointed out that it was impossible for the province, whose resources were already strained, to give a guarantee to the proposed railway, and that, in any event, a railway from Toronto to Lake Huron would do the province more good than the proposed Quebec to Halifax Railway. As for the increased value to be given land by the construction of this or any other railway, poor immigrants would not be able to buy such land and those with capital would already find abundant moderately priced land with access to roads and markets. On the whole, Sullivan showed very little enthusiasm for Grey's plan of importing thousands of ignorant, ill-disciplined Irish contract labourers held in "comparative thralldom . . . to work at low wages. . . ." What Grey was offering Canada, Sullivan made plain, was what she had—labour. What she most needed was capital.[16]

Neither Sullivan nor his colleagues thought Wakefield's ideas and the elaborate schemes of Sir George Grey based upon them were practical, and it is clear that Elgin agreed with his ministers. To adopt them in a country bordering upon the United States was to run the risk of diverting the stream of immigration there almost completely, as J. R. McCulloch had already warned.[17] Price, instead of being the pivot on which the entire land and colonization policy turned, as it was for the Wakefield school, was regarded by Sullivan as incidental—a device to discourage people from obtaining land they did not intend to use. Population and the actual settlement of the country were more important to him than revenue from Crown lands, the Clergy Reserves, school lands, or any other special endowment.[18]

In Sullivan's opinion, the best method of getting immigrants established on the land was to place them there at once on 50-acre grants.[19] "I do not think employment on public works advances the education of the immigrant in the way of settlement a step," wrote Sullivan. "He wants to clear land, to plow, to sow and to reap.... There can be no education in the way of clearing and cultivation unless through the means of working on the land ... the new immigrant is ... inefficient but his deficiencies are far less felt when he works upon his own lands...." On public works entrusted to private contractors, argued Sullivan, immigrants would be in competition with experienced "canallers" from the American side. The conditions of life and employment were likely to be demoralizing, and they would save little money.

The free grant policy had up to this time been limited in its effectiveness by the fact that settlers on colonization roads were required to show that they could maintain themselves until they had raised a crop. Sullivan recognized that destitute immigrants could not take advantage of the free grants and in his report he made it clear that it was at this point that the assistance of the British government could most usefully be given.[20] Sullivan appears to have been interested in the immigrants for their own sake, not merely because their coming would stimulate the economy and increase the value of land in Canada, and he seems to have thought that an effective immigration policy would be one intended to assist them to realize *their* dreams—land and independence in the new world.[21]

The government did not plan, while Sullivan was a member of it, to recoup the value of land given away as free grants by placing a higher price on the remaining land. Such a policy, said Sullivan, discouraged the first settlers and prolonged their isolation and helplessness. However, in order to prevent speculators from profiting where the government refrained from doing so—the crux of the matter as Godley pointed out [22]—Sullivan wanted actual residence to be required of all purchasers of land in new districts. Subsequently, as the settlers became more numerous and more prosperous, they could tax themselves for such improvements as roads and public works, as time had shown to be desirable. "Here no champion of the bold debt building entrepreneur is speaking but rather the honest conservative anxious to pay off old debts before incurring new one ...," remarks J. E. Hodgetts. He sees in Wakefield's very different schemes "a bold policy ... like modern pumppriming" that was expected to "set up a chain reaction which would populate and enrich the colony." [23] Hodgett's estimate of Sullivan is rather harsh. Sullivan was genuinely concerned about the immigrant. The policies of the Colonial Office called for high-priced land to provide money for public works in advance of settlement to ease the path for those who could pay, and to provide employment for the poor with the hope that they would ultimately save enough to buy high-priced land. Sullivan's policies were just the reverse: low-priced land, even some free land, to give the poor their opportunity by putting them on their own land as soon as possible, and public works when the community felt able to afford them.

In August, 1848, the Baldwin–LaFontaine government decided on a further development of the colonization road policy. Two new roads in the Wellington and Simcoe Districts were begun—the Toronto and Sydenham, and the Durham Road [24]—and parallel roads on either side of the two main roads were projected. Settlers on these roads were required to clear twelve acres of their 50-acre free grant in four years and they were given the privilege of purchasing an additional 150 acres at 8s. an acre.[25] The Baldwin–LaFontaine government planned to build the two main roads at provincial expense but it had taken office under difficult financial circumstances and was unable to carry out these projects fully.[26] In October, 1848, Sullivan, the chief proponent of the 50-acre free grants, accepted a judgeship and his place in the government was taken by William Hamilton Merritt.

Sir George Grey did not respond sympathetically to Sullivan's suggestion that immigrants should be assisted to settle directly on the land. This kind of assistance had been tried and found much too expensive. However, he was reluctant to abandon his cherished plan for a colonial railway or other great public work constructed by immigrant labour. He therefore suggested that the preference on colonial timber over Baltic be reduced by raising the colonial duty from 1s. to 7s. 6d. a load, in order that from the additional revenue the Imperial government might guarantee the interest on the entire capital to be raised for the construction of the railway. As an alternative, he suggested that British North America should guarantee one-third of the annual interest and great Britain two-thirds.

Francis Hincks, the Inspector General of Finances, drew up for his colleagues a memo which, while it expressed little enthusiasm for the Quebec to Halifax Railway as a partnership enterprise, advocated the change in the timber duties for the purpose of financing it solely as an Imperial concern. The financial uncertainty and commercial distress created by the Revolutions of 1848, plus the indifference of men like Peel and Gladstone to the colonies, made Russell's government reluctant to propose the railway to Parliament.[27]

The Baldwin–LaFontaine government then showed more readiness to assist this railway by including in the Hincks Guarantee Act of 1849 a clause offering not only a ten-mile strip of all ungranted Crown land on either side of the proposed route and all lands needed for a right of way but also £20,000 annually, if needed, towards paying the interest on the guaranteed bonds.[28] Hincks, when in London in 1849, unsuccessfully urged the adoption of the colonial offer upon Grey. However, the annexation crisis ended all hopes of getting Imperial aid for public works in Canada for the time being,[29] and, when the project was revived in 1851, Russell's government went out of office before Canada, Nova Scotia, and New Brunswick had reached an agreement on the railway.

The devising of the commercial and economic policies of the Baldwin–LaFontaine government was largely in the hands of the Inspector General, Francis Hincks, who was interested primarily in attracting British capital to Canada.[30] Hincks had drawn up a programme of his own to enable Canada to put her financial house in order and to lift herself by her own boot-straps. This programme—local government reform, taxation, and pledging the land revenues as security for a loan—was definitely a business man's programme. Nowhere does

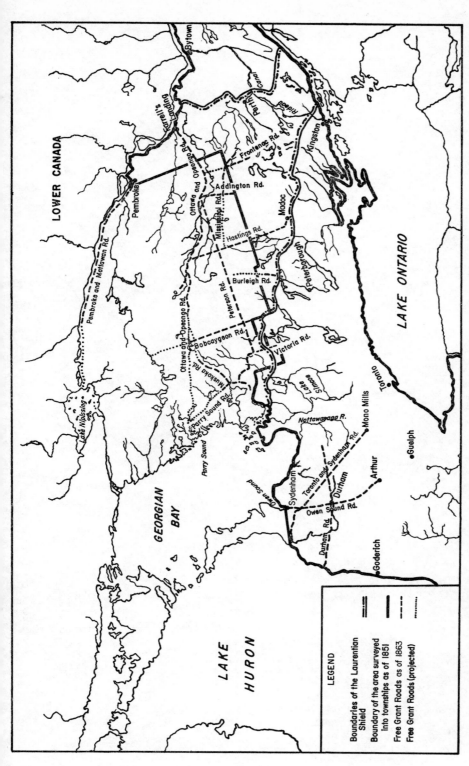

MAP III. Canada West in 1852, with later free grant roads. Based on map in W. H. Smith's *Canada, Past, Present, and Future.* Routes of the free grant roads laid out before 1850 are taken from Smith. Routes of the later free grant roads are taken from Canada, Sessional Papers, 1861, no. 15, and modified from information in the Report of the Commissioner of Crown Lands, Canada, Sessional Papers, 1863, no. 6. Boundaries of the Laurentian Shield are taken from the Report of the Geological Survey of Ontario, 1946.

it reveal that concern for the immigrant which Sullivan had shown. With Hincks, the immigrant was merely a pawn in a larger game.

Hincks regarded the public lands as provincial capital which ought to become available for investment in public works, particularly railways. Canada needed her railways at once as a supplement to her canals, and therefore Hincks was not content with the slow process of building up a fund from this source. Since 1837, the Crown Lands Department had been a deficit-producing department that was expensive to administer and took in much scrip and little money. The receiving of scrip needed to be terminated promptly, the business of the department simplified, and the revenues increased before the Crown land revenues could be seriously considered as the basis for a loan. "During the last four years, claims to the extent of £220,000 have been settled by Means of this Scrip. This Amount would of course have been available for investment but for the existence of these claims," wrote Hincks—a statement that was completely misleading about these book-keeping transactions.[31] Hinks believed the scrip had been nearly all paid in and that the outstanding claims were "of no great magnitude" and would be very speedily extinguished.

Despite his emphasis on revenue, Hincks approved of a limited free grant policy as a supplement to a cash sales policy and he justified it on the ground that the value of the remaining Crown land woud be increased. He was opposed to the credit system, even though it might make possible higher prices for land, because, like Wakefield, he thought it tempted labourers to become landed proprietors too soon. But he did not think Wakefield's notions of a "sufficient price" suitable for a country subject to American competition for settlers. What he advocated was the American plan of first offering land at auction at an upset price of $1.25 and then opening once-offered land to entry at the minimum price. He professed to think that the power of the district councils to tax was an adequate safeguard against the evils of speculation inherent in the American system.

In the United States, where the ability of counties to tax was not nearly so restricted as it was in Upper Canada, the cash entry system described above had had the positive effect of driving the settler to the loan shark and the negative effect of not preventing speculation, as Hincks ought to have known. What Hincks might have said was that the taxing powers of the district councils might be *made* an adequate safeguard. Sydenham's District Councils Act had received his hearty support, imperfect as that measure was, and the Baldwin–LaFontaine government now prepared, for the second time, to improve it. Robert Baldwin had long been anxious to secure for Upper Canada a democratic system of local self-government and a more equitable system of taxation. Hincks's main object was not to correct the evils of past land policies through taxation but to enlarge the taxing powers of the municipalities so that they would be able to undertake public works of a local character and assist in the financing of railways.[32]

The first Baldwin–LaFontaine ministry had attempted to amend the assessment laws of Upper Canada so as to assess land at its real value instead of at the arbitrary value fixed in 1819. It had also proposed to exempt from taxation personal property such as household furniture, farm implements, and mechanics' tools to the value of £250, and to subject other forms of personal property—book debts, merchants' goods, promissory notes, bonds, and mortgages—to taxation. This effort to make all forms of capital pay their share was denounced as "odious and inquisitorial," and unfair to the merchants of the upper province. All the country demanded, argued the Tories, was a revision of the existing inequitable method of assessing landed property.[33] They attributed the defeat of the Baldwin–LaFontaine government in the elections of 1844 to its assessment bill.[34]

In 1846, the Draper government amended the District Councils Act so as to make the district officials elective and attempted to amend the assessment law of Upper Canada so as to have land assessed at its actual value; but it also proposed to abolish the township assessors, who were elected, and to replace them by assessors for assessment districts appointed by the district councils. No additions to the categories of personal property to be taxed were to be made. This bill proved to be unpopular with the representatives of the rural constituencies and did not go beyond the committee stage.[35]

When Baldwin and LaFontaine returned to power a second time, they reorganized the local government councils on a township and county basis, with elective officers, and passed a new assessment law for Upper Canada.[36] Again there was a great debate over the personal property clauses. The government proposed to allow a basic personal property exemption, which would have covered the average farmer's or mechanic's household goods and working equipment, and to tax those forms of wealth likely to be accumulated by the business and professional classes. In the end, they accepted a rather narrow definition of personal property for tax purposes and failed to obtain a personal property exemption, but they got rid of the out-of-date and arbitrary land valuations of the old assessment act and the limitation upon the rate of taxation established in 1841, which had for so long protected land speculators. Despite this act, absentee speculators continued to hold large quantities of wild land. In 1860, 3,500,000 acres were still so held, two-thirds of it in Grey, Simcoe, Lambton, Huron and Bruce, Peterboro and Victoria, Frontenac, and Lennox and Addington Counties.[37] In the Assembly there continued to be pressure for an even more effective assessment act, one that would allow annual sales of land in arrears for taxes and taxation of unpatented land bought on credit.

William Hamilton Merritt, who became President of the Council in Sullivan's place, had ideas similar to those of Hincks. Both men regarded the land as provincial capital. Hincks wanted to build railways but Merritt wanted to create a permanent endowment for schools as well. Merritt complained that the transfer of the Territorial Revenues to provincial control had not resulted in any improvement. The public domain, instead of being devoted to some useful purpose, was still being regarded as so much plunder. Approximately 2,000,000 acres had been set aside for Clergy Reserves and 500,000 for the universities and the grammar schools. Public attention had been fixed on these reservations and little attention had been paid to the process by which 34,000,000 acres of public domain, taking Upper and Lower Canada together, had passed into private hands.

Merritt thought that the best method of utilizing the public domain for the general benefit was as an endowment for common schools. In the United States, the federal government had reserved the sixteenth section of every township of the public domain for common schools. In New York State, a permanent common school fund had been created in 1805 out of the sale of 500,000 acres of state land. In 1816 this fund had been increased from the same source, and by 1823 the revenue from the sale of such state lands as remained had been appropriated to common schools.

In Upper Canada no endowment for common schools had been obtained. At an early date, the legislature had petitioned the Crown for an endowment for free grammar schools and a university, but it had left elementary education to be provided by the family. With the tacit approval, but not the formal consent, of the home government, some 550,000 acres had been set aside for higher education, and Peter Russell's Executive Council had recommended that at least half of this reserve should be for the university.[38] These school reserves, which were subsequently found to amount to only 467,675 acres, were not distributed among other land open to grant. They consisted originally of ten townships plus parts of two others, six of the townships being east of York, six west; but many changes in the location of the school reserves were subsequently made.[39] Nothing was done with these reserves for years. Formal approval of the action of Russell's Council was not received and, since the reserves consisted of completely undeveloped and unsurveyed townships, no rents could have been obtained from them nor could they have been sold at a worthwhile price while the free grant system existed.[40]

The existence of these large blocks of unutilized school reserves became a subject of complaint about 1812. The most influential voice was that of Thomas Talbot who told Gore that the development of "the most delightful and valuable part of the province" was being obstructed.[41] In 1809 Talbot had persuaded the Lieutenant-Governor to entrust him with making a road (the Talbot Road East) through the school townships of Yarmouth, Southwold, and Houghton and with placing settlers there on Yonge St. terms. In 1819 a number of lots in these townships were sold at auction under his supervision at a minimum upset price of 10s.[42] Except in Houghton, very little of the land brought more than a penny or two over the minimum, and the sales were discontinued.[43]

The greatest grievance arising out of the school reserves was that when they became productive they would, like the Clergy Reserves, benefit only that minority of the population which could afford to send its children away from home for advanced schooling. What the province needed was a well-supported system of common schools. Prior to the Rebellion, members of the Assembly had repeatedly asked for it. In 1807, the legislature had made a temporary grant for the support of district schools, as there was as yet no income from the school reserves for free grammar schools, and in 1808 it had made this grant permanent.[44]

Meanwhile, the demand for common schools had become more insistent.[45] In 1816 the legislature made an appropriation in aid of common or township schools and petitioned for a landed endowment for them. The township schools which came into existence were dependent partly upon the small legislative appropriation, partly upon pupils' fees. These schools did not meet with the approval of

Sir Peregrine Maitland, who complained that some of them employed American school-masters and American textbooks.[46] To counteract their influence, he proposed to establish central schools in each township upon the model of the National Schools of the Church of England and to keep the school system under close executive control through appointed boards of education for each district and a General Board of Education with Dr. Strachan as president.

With the approval of the home government, this system was established in 1823.[47] The General Board was entrusted with the superintendence of both the new schools and the district schools. It was also given the task of selling the school reserves in eight of the townships (six of them in the London District) for their support. Fixed prices were established for the various townships, and the school reserves, like the Clergy Reserves, were sold on ten years' credit. In the London District, sale of the school reserves was entrusted to Colonel Talbot, who had been pressing for this privilege for some time.[48]

These new arrangements for the support of education did not satisfy Upper Canada. The legislative appropriation for common schools had been halved in 1820 and, in consequence, a number of the schools had been closed.[49] Moreover, the school system had been placed under the superintendence of a determined Anglican, Dr. Strachan, and, by 1832, the school reserves had become reduced in quantity and quality. In 1830, Strachan had suggested that where the school reserves constituted whole townships, one-half should be exchanged for a like quantity of land in other unsettled townships "so that a moiety in each may be at the disposal of gov't for actual settlement in order to make the remaining half sooner available." The Executive Council supported this proposal, pointing out that it would enable the government to disperse immigrants more generally throughout the country, but it added the proviso that the substitution should not diminish the value of the school reserves. However, the result was that by December, 1832, some 105,000 acres of land, formerly school reserves, in valuable townships in the London District were acquired by individuals—and probably with U.E. or militia rights. It may well be doubted that they were sold as Crown land to immigrants, or even to residents of the province, since the total sales of Crown land up to 1832 amounted to only 24,737 acres. Nor could they have been sold still classified as school land since the total sales of school land up to 1832 were reported to be 12,000 acres. The alienated land, and some 65,000 acres of school land in Alfred and Plantagenet townships previously thrown open to location by Lieutenant-Governor Gore were replaced by a larger quantity of land, 272,600 acres, but in inferior townships. The surveyors who had surveyed the school townships received 19,282 acres, Upper Canada College got 66,000 acres, and, when, in 1827, King's College, York, had been granted 225,273 acres of leased Crown Reserves, the Crown resumed an equal quantity of school reserves. Thus, by 1832, only half of the quantity originally reserved for schools remained.[50]

In 1831, the Assembly tactfully and successfully requested that the revenue from the school reserves be paid to the Receiver General and be placed at the disposal of the legislature.[51] Subsequently, the Crown agreed to make good any losses in land suffered by the school endowment, not including what had been granted to King's College and Upper Canada College, and to exchange Crown land in settled townships for unsaleable school reserves.[52] The powers of the General Board for Education were terminated in 1832, but the school reserves continued to be sold by the agents it had appointed, as well as by the Commissioner of Crown Lands, without any over-all supervision or system. The resulting confusion had to be straightened out by a special committee appointed by Sir George Arthur and headed by John Macaulay. After the Union, Sydenham placed the school reserves, hereinafter called grammar school lands, under the control of the Commissioner of Crown Lands to be sold on the same terms as Clergy Reserves.[53]

On the eve of the Rebellion there was still no endowment for common schools. After the Union, the legislature provided that a permanent fund should be created for common schools out of the selling or leasing of any lands which might be granted and that the annual provincial appropriation for common schools should eventually come entirely out of this fund.[54] But by mid-century no landed endowment had been created. Meanwhile, a group in the legislature continued to press the case for common schools and to hold up the example of New York State to Canada.

No one was more persistent in pressing the case for common schools than Merritt. At the same time, he was eager to promote the rapid settlement of the country and the construction of public works. He was therefore critical of all policies that reduced the cash revenues of the Crown Lands Department. He was opposed in particular to the free grants and the scrip provisions of the Land Acts of 1837 and 1841.[55]

When the Draper ministry was in office, Merritt had reproached the government with maintaining a Crown Lands Department that did not earn enough to pay for its own stationery. In 1845 he had procured a committee of inquiry which revealed that the expenses of the Department were on the average 26 per cent of its total receipts, both in cash and in scrip, and were growing.[56] Merritt presented to this committee the draft of a bill which would have appropriated the Territorial Revenues for common schools, prevented the issue of any more scrip, set a terminal date for the use of that already issued, consolidated the Crown Lands Department with the Surveyor General's Department, and permitted the government to contract with any company or person to dispose of the Crown lands to the best advantage and for a fixed percentage of the sales receipts.

Merritt favoured turning over the administration of the entire public domain, including the Clergy Reserves, to the Canada Company on such a contract basis and was privy to Fred Widder's attempts to secure the approval of the various ecclesiastical bodies for this policy.[57] At this time, Merritt made no mention of the Canada Company, probably wisely, but, to demonstrate the practical and economical nature of his proposals, he submitted along with his bill an offer from Absolom Shade to sell and settle the block of clergy lands in the County of Waterloo and the Crown lands north of the Canada Company's lands in the Huron Tract for 6 per cent on the sales.[58] Shade offered to sell the choicest block of land still remaining, one that was compact and without reserves. His operation would have been free from many of the time-consuming administrative duties growing out of past transactions that fell upon the Crown

Lands Department. Nevertheless, thereafter, 6 per cent became the magic figure which critics of the Land Department thought its expenses ought not to exceed.

When Merritt entered the Baldwin–LaFontaine government as Commissioner of Public Works and President of the Council he did so in the expectation that his ideas about developing the resources of the province and utilizing its land revenues would be adopted.[59] At the time he was popularly regarded as a sort of provincial wizard about to do wonders for the finances of the province.[60] One of his main criticisms of the land legislation was directed at the scrip provisions of the Act of 1841. Under the law, no new claims were admissible after January 1, 1843, unless the claimant was a minor on that date, but, as Merritt complained, the government continued to acknowledge claims and to issue scrip in satisfaction of them.[61]

What Merritt and the Upper Canada Reformers regarded as the most flagrant violation of the law had been occasioned by Lord Metcalfe's proclamation of February 20, 1844. Some Lower Canada militia men who had served during the War of 1812 claimed that they had been deprived of their right to land as a result of the Quebec *Gazette*'s misprinting of a proclamation notifying applicants to file their claims before August 1, 1830, instead of August 1, 1831. During the ministerial crisis that followed the resignation of the first Baldwin–LaFontaine government, the supporters of Lord Metcalfe obtained from him a proclamation allowing these militia men one year, from March 1, 1844, to file their claims and permitting them to be validated if necessary by a statement made under oath without the production of certificates of service or discharge. A large number of these belated claims, now no longer worthless, had already been acquired by speculators.[62] Since the Land Act of 1841 did not expressly restrict Lower Canada' scrip (worth 3s. 6d. an acre) to that province, it was received after the Union for Upper Canada land too, and, the Crown Lands Department allowed the Upper Canada rate of 4s. for it.[63] By December 31, 1846, £111,400 worth of this scrip had been issued[64] and, according to Merritt, most of it was being applied on Upper Canada land. At 8s. an acre for land, the scrip was equivalent to approximately 280,000 acres. Representatives of Upper Canada were indignant at what they regarded as an illegal concession to Lower Canada at their expense. Metcalfe's opponents from both sections charged that the whole thing had been a "job" perpetrated to favour the candidacy in Lower Canada of one of Metcalfe's supporters, D. B. Viger, who was then without a seat.[65]

The use or misuse of its scrip-issuing powers by the Crown Lands Department continued to arouse the suspicions of Reformers. The committee appointed in 1846 to investigate the Department recommended that all scrip issued prior to 1846 be made payable by January 1, 1848, and that all issued thereafter be made payable in one year's time. Merritt, who regarded all claims to scrip filed after January 1, 1843, as illegal, asked for a statement of the amount of scrip issued since that date. The return showed that £185,781 worth of scrip had been issued for Upper and Lower Canada in the years 1843-6, and that approximately £ 76,500 was still to be issued on already admitted claims.[66] At 8s. an acre this figure was the equivalent of 655,782 acres of Upper Canada land. Obviously the land revenues would continue to be insignificant as an endowment for schools and useless as a security for a loan while this state of things continued. Merritt was determined to end it.

Shortly after Merritt became a member of the government, his colleagues agreed to the creation of an endowment for common schools and to the restriction on the use of scrip which he desired. "The most important measure was decided upon, that has ever occupied their attention, or that of any preceding Council, since the discovery of Canada," wrote Merritt triumphantly in his journal. He continued,

The land claims are to be cancelled in one year, all public lands to be appropriated, and the proceeds applied for the creation of a Common School fund until the sum reached £1,000,000 and 1,000,000 of acres of the best land in Huron Tract, or elsewhere to be reserved for this express object, (not to be exchanged for scrip.) . . . If possible, limit the land claims, hereafter to be allowed, and name a special commission to investigate them, of which I should like to be the Chairman.[67]

Only part of this programme was enacted into law.

The Baldwin–LaFontaine administration made various amendments to the Land Act of 1841 in 1849. Its basic provisions, cash sale and satisfaction of the land claims in scrip, were not touched, but some criticisms of the administration of the act were met by the new law.[68] The amendments did not restore locations made prior to January 1, 1832, which had already been declared forfeit, despite numerous petitions on this point, but they gave later locatees of land still unpatented two years to pay any overdue fees and to perform settlement duties to which they might be subject. The terminal date, May 30, 1851, was subsequently extended three times.[69] The extreme tenderness of the legislature thus allowed those who had promised to clear the roadway and a few acres across the end of a 200-acre lot almost two decades to complete what they had undertaken to do in two years.

No special commission to investigate the claims for scrip was created. The date for the establishment of all claims, including those of minors, was set at May 30, 1850, and an act passed in 1850 made void all scrip not utilized within one year's time.[70] At last it seemed that the drain on the land revenues caused by scrip would shortly cease.

Merritt's Act to Raise an Income for Common Schools[71] was also passed in 1849. It set aside not ten million acres, as Merritt had earlier proposed,[72] but one million acres out of the unsold lands in the Huron Tract for common schools and appropriated the Crown land revenues for their support until an endowment should have been built up which would produce an annual revenue at 6 per cent of £100,000. The capital of the school fund was to be invested in provincial debentures, or in the debentures of companies incorporated by the legislature for the construction of public works, but on a much more conservative basis than had been suggested by Merritt's railway committee of 1847.[73] Merritt succeeded in protecting the school lands from being picked over by speculators using scrip by a clause which provided that no more land in the Huron Tract should be sold until the school endowment had been selected. Land once classed as school land could not be purchased with scrip.[74] Thus, late in the day, one of the principles for which the Reformers had contended was written into law: the land revenues were to be devoted to an important provincial object. Nevertheless, in 1856, a committee of the Assembly, of which Merritt was chairman, had to remind the government of the day of its obligations under the law to the common school fund.[75]

The terms on which the school lands were to be sold were not prescribed by the act but left to the discretion of the governor-in-council. Ten years' credit was allowed, as for the purchase of Clergy Reserves, and settlement duties of building a house and clearing five acres annually for five years were imposed, although, later, the amount of clearing was reduced to two acres annually.[76] An upset price of 12s. 6d. an acre was at first set for common school lands, later 10s., and, after 1857, $2.00 an acre, although some land was sold for less. By 1865 the 1,000,000 acres of common school lands had been sold. The grammar school lands were sold after 1841 on the same terms as Clergy Reserves and after 1854 like common school lands. About 45,000 acres remained unsold in 1865.[77]

Merritt did not long remain a member of the Baldwin–LaFontaine government. Both Grits and Tories charged the government with extravagance, and he sympathized with the demand for retrenchment. Merritt argued that the government's expenses could be halved. Among other changes, he proposed to reorganize the Crown Lands Department so as to make it a source of revenue instead of expense. He contrasted the American system with that of Canada to the detriment of the latter, ignoring the fact that in the United States the satisfaction of the soldiers' land bounties, like the redemption of Canada's scrip issues, had so burdened the land revenues as to lead President Fillmore to warn the nation that little revenue could be expected from the public lands for some time. After making provision for terminating the issue and receipt of scrip and the practice of making free grants, Merritt proposed to contract out the management of the Crown lands for a fixed percentage of the land revenue, and to raise on its security a loan of £2,500,000 at 4 per cent which was to be relent to railway companies at 6 per cent. His colleagues would not agree to this method of managing the Land Department by contract, nor did they think that economies could safely be made by cutting salaries or reducing surveys at a time when settlers were clamouring for land. Merritt left the government in December, 1850.[78]

An attempt was soon made to undo Merritt's scrip legislation and to extend the time for receiving scrip beyond the date set by the Act of 1850. A return of all persons to whom scrip had been issued since 1841, the nature of their claims, and the names of persons who actually received the scrip was then called for by suspicious members of the Assembly in 1851. The return was presented, but, on the motion of Sir Allan MacNab and John A. Macdonald, it was not printed.[79] Subsequently, when it began to appear that many fraudulent claims had been entered and that extensive forgeries had been committed by persons claiming scrip on assignments, they changed their minds and the return was ordered to be printed, not in the appendix to the *Journals*, but privately for the use of members.[80] Also, the Assembly voted by a large majority against extending the time for receiving scrip.[81] However, the new Land Act of 1853, passed by the next administration, permitted scrip to be redeemed in land and extended the time for receiving it in payment on existing land contracts until July 1, 1854; but it forbade consideration of any claim for land not already located. Thus no more scrip could issue for U.E. loyalist and militia claims.[82]

The quantity of land scrip issued in accordance with the Acts of 1841 and 1849 may be seen from the following list which shows the amounts issued up to April 30, 1851.

U.E. Claims	£ 76,590
U.C. Militia	33,717
Emigrant	5,697
Military	31,566
Compensatory	11,812
L.C. Militia	116,583 16s.
TOTAL	£275,964 16s.

Most of this scrip soon found its way into the hands of land dealers. Much of it was issued to them in their own names as assignees of the claimants, more of it passed through their hands as attorneys, and still more was purchased by them from the original holders.[83] Since the scrip would only bring its face-value if exchanged for government land, those who wished to convert it into cash were obliged to sell to land and scrip dealers at a discount ranging from 15 to 50 per cent. "At present [1854] it may be got in Toronto at about £33 for £40," wrote Christmas.[84]

The effect of this issue of £275,000 worth of scrip receivable in the purchase of Crown land and in the payment of instalments and interest on old land contracts was that for many years the land revenue was almost annihilated. For example, for the years 1841-4 inclusive, £74,767 was received in scrip, £6,731 in cash. This was by no means sufficient to pay the expenses of the Land Department.[85] But this was not all. For many years, the issuing, redemption, and cancelling of scrip was carelessly managed, and this laxity made it possible for forged scrip to get into circulation. John Langton, the newly appointed Auditor General, stated that he believed the forgery had been committed "by a person intimately acquainted with the Crown Lands Department." "It is notorious," wrote Langton, "that some of the Agents are said to have been in the habit of receiving payment in money and paying the Department in Scrip. They dealt in scrip—and maybe in forged Scrip it would seem to me." [86] Three-quarters of the forged scrip examined by Langton had been turned in by three agents, Alexander, Baines, and Geddes, and half of this by Baines alone. The person actually responsible for the issue of the forged scrip was never named. "I know who did it pretty well," wrote Langton to his brother, "but I cannot find any clue to his confederates and if I could bring it home to him, which is perhaps doubtful, he cleared out to the States two years ago and is beyond my reach." [87] Apparently these hasty crossings of the border have not been all from one side! Further than this Langton did not go. Joseph Cauchon, then Commissioner of Crown Lands, directed him to drop his examination of the scrip accounts. At this time, Langton had examined half of what was supposed to be all the cancelled scrip. Among it he had found £10,000 worth of forged scrip, and, among the other half, which was destroyed without further examination, there may well have been another £10,000 worth of forged paper. The long story of the U.E. rights thus comes to its sordid end.

CHAPTER TWENTY

SETTLERS, SQUATTERS, AND LUMBERMEN

MAJOR CHANGES in the land policies of Upper Canada were made under the Hincks-Morin administration which took office on October 28, 1851, and remained in power until September 8, 1854. Although the Act of Union had not yet been shorn of its forty-second clause, the new Land Act of 1853, 16 Vic, c. 159, passed by this administration, was assented to by the Governor and not reserved for the royal assent as the Act of 1841, which it repealed, had been. The Act of 1953, like its predecessor, provided for the keeping of a register of assignments extended the time for receiving scrip, but left changes in the price and conditions of sale of Crown land to be made by the governor-in-council.

One unfortunate change written into the act was a provision permitting claims for compensation for deficiencies in surveys to be made if submitted within five years from the date of discovery; whereas the previous act required claims to be filed within five years from the date of patent. When the Crown Lands Department decided that this statute applied retrospectively, the door was opened to old claims which had been rejected. Land or scrip was given in compensation at the discretion of the commissioner, and, since the deficiencies were estimated at their current value, exhorbitant quantities of land could be obtained for insignificant deficiencies in old grants. In two notorious instances, land with substantial improvements was occupied by squatters who found they were expected to buy, not from the government, but from the new owner, at a valuation of $6.42 an acre.[1]

A "proper" credit system accompanied by safeguards against abuse by speculators had been strongly advocated by the committee which had investigated the Crown Lands Department in 1846 but no changes had been made by the Draper government. During the Baldwin–LaFontaine administration, both Hincks and Merritt had opposed the credit system. It was favoured, however, by A. N. Morin, the leader of the French-Canadian Liberals, and by the Clear Grits of Upper Canada. Morin thought of the Crown lands as an instrument of social policy. He had in mind primarily the needs of French Canada where the young people were showing a distressing tendency to emigrate to the United States; but his views were equally applicable to Upper Canada if farmers' sons and poor immigrants were to be provided with land there.

Morin believed in a democratic land policy. He thought its object should be not revenue but the speedy settlement of the country with small proprietors, without the intervention of profit-taking land jobbers as middle men between the cultivators of the soil and their government. A nation of independent landed proprietors, not burdened with heavy debts or rents, was in his opinion the best guarantee of peace and order for the future. An unrestricted cash sale policy, he argued, might increase the land revenue, but it would not limit the amount of land speculators could obtain and it would not ensure the improvement of the land. He recognized, however, that a policy of cash sale at nominal prices, restricted to actual settlers, could not be adopted. The hard fact was that the Crown land in certain areas was in competition with the Clergy Reserves, school lands, and Indian lands, and its price could not be reduced to a nominal sum without "annihilating" these trusts. The alternative was the credit system.

The French-Canadian leader had his way. In 1849 the credit system was restored, although only in Lower Canada. In 1852 it was extended to Upper Canada, ten years being allowed in those counties where the price of Crown land was 7s. 6d., four years where it was 4s. Some of the safeguards against speculation which had been suggested in 1846 were adopted. A down-payment of the first instalment, rather than one-third or one-quarter of the price of the lot, was required, sales were limited to 200 acres to one person, and stringent settlement duties were imposed which required the building of a house. Continuous residence and the clearing of five acres annually for five years were also insisted upon.[2] Lots in townships surveyed before 1841 were subsequently exempted from these requirements because they were inferior land that had been on the market for some time and could best be utilized by being added as a wood lot or pasture land to an existing farm. One important suggestion— that only cash be received on credit sales—was ignored. Changes in the price of land in Upper Canada were made in 1854 when certain townships, chiefly those undesirable from an agricultural point of view, were reduced in price to 2s. an acre.[3]

The new credit system and the new low prices were adopted for Upper Canada at what seemed to be an appropriate moment for small farmers trying to establish themselves on the land. A sharp falling off in the demand for land in Upper Canada had been caused by the repeal of the Corn laws and had not been offset by the reductions in the price of Crown land in 1848. But by 1850 the annexation crisis was safely over, reciprocity was in the air, railways were being constructed, the Crimean War had created a demand for wheat and animal products, and the timber trade was flourishing. The population was growing rapidly, although only to a small extent from immigration, and the price of land was rising. The farmer could be sure of a market for all he had to sell, and at good prices. In other respects, 1852 was not a propitious moment to institute the credit system in Upper Canada. This was a period when it might have been expected that a runaway land boom would occur and, despite Morin's regulation, it did, as may be seen from the following table.[4]

CROWN LAND SOLD IN UPPER CANADA, 1848–1857

Year	Acres	Year	Acres
1848	6,583	1853	235,228
1849	14,265	1854	529,180
1850	36,536	1855	461,368
1851	81,949	1856	140,520
1852	50,837	1857	122,119

The creation of a class of small landed proprietors was not facilitated by the supposedly safeguarded credit system. Speculators, as Morin later admitted, were likely to find their way around any restrictions no matter how well enforced.[5] The 200-acre restriction on the amount of land that could be purchased on credit was evaded by means of assignments, a device that had been extensively used in the past by leaders and associates. Likewise, U.E. loyalist and militia grants, full fee grants, and clergy and Crown sales, a few of which had been made on credit between 1841 and 1845, all had been assigned before patent. All this should have been a warning to Morin. In Lower Canada, the bulk of the credit sales made between 1848 and 1854 were in the County of Ottawa where timber men found it cheaper to make use of the new credit system to purchase timber land than to pay stumpage. In Upper Canada most of the sales during the years 1852-4 were in the counties of Huron, Grey, and Bruce where speculators made use of the system to acquire land fit for cultivation and were able to hold it for years on credit without paying taxes. Some county councils thought they had the power to sell such unpatented land for overdue taxes, but a case brought by T. C. Street, who had kept his instalments up to date but who was remiss in his payment of taxes, revealed a loophole in the assessment law which deprived them of this power. "The amount of friction that arose in the early 'sixties from the sales of wild land for taxes was enormous and the ownership of many farms came into question about that time in this harrassing way. Much anxiety and unnecessary expense was caused to unoffending settlers," comments the historian of Simcoe County. The defect in the law was remedied the year Street's case was decided in his favour by a new assessment act which specifically subjected to taxation unpatented land sold or leased, or for which a license of occupation had been granted. The new act also provided that such land might be sold for unpaid taxes, the tax title giving the purchaser only such rights as the original purchaser had acquired.[6]

Morin seems to have realized after a time that the new credit system was being utilized by speculators. The Crown Lands Department found that it was called upon to register assignments and to issue patents to the assignees for land on which the required settlement duties had not been performed. It also found that land was being sold and resold on assignments when the original purchaser was still in arrears to the Crown. As a result the Department refused to register assignments for land on which the required settlement duties had not been performed and on which instalment payments were not up-to-date. Provided this regulation could be enforced, the activities of speculators would be hampered. But assignments that could not be registered under the regulations continued to accumulate in the Crown Lands Department and eventually Commissioner L. V. Sicotte ordered that all should be registered on receipt, whether or not arrears had been paid or settlement duties performed.[7] The registers for Upper Canada show that from May 17, 1840, to March 3, 1864, 16,320 assignments were registered, some for whole, some for parts of lots. If one assumes that no lot was assigned more than once before patent and that the average assignment was for a half lot of 100 acres, this figure would mean that 1,632,000 acres of land, a quantity approximately equal to half the Crown land sold or granted in Upper Canada from 1845 to 1865, was assigned by the original purchasers or grantees before patent, much of it soon after it was acquired.[8] But these are assumptions that cannot safely be made. A detailed study of the assignments would probably throw much light on speculation in Upper Canada and on the financing of new settlements.

The Hincks–Morin government found it as difficult to enforce a settlement duty policy as Sir John Colborne had, and before long was hearing complaints that the duties were too onerous. Morin appreciated best the problems of Lower Canada where young men, leaving the seigneuries to work a few weeks making a clearing on their new government lot and then returning to their parents' homes until the next season, found five acres a year more than they could manage. He therefore favoured reducing the quantity to two acres annually and was not disposed to declare land forfeit for want of residence if improvements were made yearly.[9] In Upper Canada, land which had been sold subject to settlement conditions at the reduced price of 7s. 6d. was relieved of these conditions, provided the purchasers would pay the former price of 8s.

The Land Act of 1853 authorized the government to open up new areas to settlement and to make free grants not exceeding 100 acres on the colonization roads. Strictly speaking, colonization roads were roads opened through unoccupied Crown lands, on which free grant lots were laid out for settlers on both sides. However, the term was also applied to other roads than free grant roads. The new routes were intended to be made passable for wagons loaded with half a ton of freight and drawn by two horses or oxen. They were to be opened at government expense, and subsequently to be maintained by the settlers. This obligation proved to be too heavy. Some of the roads became impassable and year after year the government was obliged to make additional grants for their repair.[10] The Baldwin–LaFontaine administration had been unable to obtain adequate appropriations for surveys and roads for new settlements, but their successors obtained the funds in part from colonization grants made by the legislature and in part by encroaching on Merritt's sacred school endowment. The land act empowered the governor-in-council to reserve as an improvement fund one-fourth of the proceeds from the sale of common school lands in any county, and one-fifth of the proceeds from the sale of unappropriated Crown lands. With funds from these two sources, the Hincks–Morin administration decided to open two new main routes through the western peninsula, the Elora and Southampton roads, a road from the township of Woolwich to Lake Huron, and to continue the Durham Road through the township of Greenock to Lake Huron. In addition, several roads connecting the main ones were authorized.[11]

The Hincks–Morin government also undertook to open roads in the Ottawa–Huron region. D. B. Papineau had earlier suggested that this be done[12] and, in 1849, James H. Burke, Crown Timber Agent at Bytown, had made a similar proposal. Burke had presented the plan to the Commissioner of Crown Lands as a means of relieving the shortage of land for settlement; but it is clear that he had in mind also the benefits the lumber industry would obtain from having supplies close to hand. Burke acknowledged that the shanty market would not be a permanent market for the settlers' surplus crops and that it was only while the timber trade was at its peak that the land in the rear of the Colborne, Victoria, and Midland Districts could be peopled. He therefore suggested that the land should be sold at low prices and that mills should be constructed at government expense. After the shanty market had moved on, Burke thought the settlers could find a market on the Ottawa or the Bay of Quinte, but he does not seem to have asked himself whether they could survive in competition with farmers in more fertile sections of the province nearer their market.[13] Time was to show that they could not.

Four colonization roads in the Ottawa–Huron region, two east-west and two north-south, were projected by the Hincks–Morin administration. They were the Pembroke–Mattawan, the Ottawa and Opeongo, the Hastings and Mattawan, and the Addington Road.[14] The Ottawa and Opeongo was begun, and a road south from Pembroke to Arnprior was constructed. Subsequent administrations opened part of the two east-west roads and additional north-south roads, as well as those already planned.[15]

While the 50-acre free grant and colonization road policy had been more or less in abeyance and the credit system had been stimulating speculation, the growing shortage of land open to settlement created for the Crown Lands Department a serious squatter problem. This, of course, was nothing new. From the outset, the government of Upper Canada had been plagued by squatters. It had tried to prevent the practice by requiring surveyors to report the presence of squatters and by ordering the latter to vacate their improvements, warning them that disobedience would disqualify them from receiving regular grants from the Crown.[16] These threats had not been effective and, for several reasons, the squatter problem continued to grow more serious.

First, before the establishment of the land boards, land could be obtained only by petitioning the governor-in-council and this was too slow a method for impatient refugees and land seekers who joined the original loyalists in the new settlements beyond the Ottawa or opposite Detroit. Second, owing to the numerous grants made to "privileged" claimants, a constant shortage of surveyed land open to settlers soon developed. Third, after the establishment of the sales system there were no local agents from whom prospective settlers could obtain reliable information and a location without delay. Fourth, land desirable for its location, its timber, or its quality lay idle, a constant temptation to the poor and landless. Such was the land of speculators, the unimproved grants of U.E. loyalists, militia men or pensioners, the Indian land on the Grand River, the special locations closed to ordinary applicants, the Crown and Clergy Reserves, and the land of the Canada Company. Finally, after both 1783 and 1812, a class of backwoodsmen was attracted to Upper Canada from across the border. They were accustomed to make a living from the land by "pitching" and "shifting" and were not disposed to pay attention to the regulations of a monarchical government which they did not expect to last and which, in any event, could not grant titles to aliens.

When the Canada Company was negotiating for the purchase of the Crown and Clergy Reserves, it at first proposed that squatters on these lands, if removed, should receive a fair compensation for their improvements, a proposal to which Lord Bathurst initially raised no objection.[17] Subsequently, it was proposed that the Company's purchase should not include Crown Reserves occupied by squatters of ten years' standing. To this the Company objected, preferring to have the option of taking the land, and it suggested waiting until the report of the commissioners evaluating the Company's proposed purchase should reveal what the number of squatters might be. Then the Company could discuss whether it would be "worth consideration to make any provision for dispossessing them." [18] The agreement finally arrived at exempted lands occupied by squatters for ten years from purchase and gave the Company the option of declining to take lots occupied for less than ten years or of accepting them and ejecting squatters at its own expense. Nothing was said about compensation for these unlucky settlers,[19] whom G. H. Markland regarded as "wholly unworthy that an enactment should be passed in the Imperial Parliament to shield them." [20]

Many Crown Reserves were returned as vacant, and were therefore included in the Company's purchase, although they were occupied legally or occupied by squatters of ten years' standing. There were other reserves returned as occupied which ought to have been included in its purchase. An arrangement was made between the government and the Canada Company whereby, in lieu of land mistakenly included in its purchase, the Company received an equal quantity of the land incorrectly excluded, it being understood that the Company was to sell to squatters at the price of wild land, to be settled by arbitration, and to allow them all the benefits of their improvements.[21]

The Canada Company's treatment of squatters was not exactly in accord with this arrangement and was one of the many complaints against its conduct in Upper Canada. William Hamilton Merritt attributed the political influence Mackenzie acquired to his opposition to the Canada Company and remarked that the elections of 1828 were in progress just at the time the Company was notifying squatters to vacate its lands.[22] Unless squatters could prove ten years' occupancy, they were obliged to purchase the land at the Company's price or become its lessees.[23] The Company's officials testified that there was scarcely a district in the province in which they had not been under heavy expense in prosecuting actions of ejectment against squatters, that squatters made the worst of purchasers, never paying more than the first instalment, and that the Company never recognized squatters in any way unless they became purchasers or lessees. "If they do neither, the Company sells the land to the first applicant at the usual price of wild land in the neighbourhood without reference to the improvements made by the squatters which improvements the purchaser or lessee either purchase from the squatter or take as a matter of course as remuneration for the legal expenses they may be put to in repelling the squatter from their land." The witness stated that the parties purchasing usually preferred paying to incurring the squatter's enmity, that the latter's demands became more reasonable once the land was definitely sold, and that "satisfactory adjustment is usually effected without the Company's interference" [24] How equitable this satisfactory adjustment would be for squatters whose occupancy rights were not protected by law may be questioned.

The usefulness of squatters in opening up new country was generally admitted, and, from an early date, the squatter was popularly regarded as equitably entitled to compensation for his improvements if he were dispossessed.[25] Charles Buller's report admitted that the government's complicated and inconvenient land regulations had helped to create the serious squatter problem and conceded the usefulness of these backwoodsmen. Buller recommended that squatters on public land should be granted a right of pre-emption which would entitle them to purchase at the upset price, on time if necessary, and that those on private land should by law become entitled to compensation for their improvements.[26] The Colonial Land and Emigration Commissioners accepted Buller's views— views which had previously been expressed by the Lower Canada Commissioners of 1836—and recommended that squatters be allowed pre-emption privileges.[27]

In Lower Canada the Crown lands had not been regulated by statute before the suspension of the constitution. Consequently, Durham could issue his proclamation of October 31, 1838, granting all squatters in occupation of Crown land prior to September 10, 1838, a right of pre-emption at a price subsequently set by Glenelg at the upset price for Crown land.[28] Nine hundred and eleven persons promptly filed claims to pre-emption on Crown land, and others took advantage of the proclamation to commence squatting.[29] The Colonial Secretary, on the mistaken assumption that the decline in the land revenues of Lower Canada was to be attributed to Durham's proclamation instead of to the suspension of sales, directed that the proclamation be revoked and the right of pre-emption limited to claims filed by September 30, 1840.[30]

Lord Durham could not deal with the squatter problem in Upper Canada by proclamation since the Crown lands were regulated by statute and the legislature was in existence. The Land Act of 1837 permitted, at the discretion of the governor-in-council, private sales of Crown land at a valuation to lessees and occupants who would be injured if they were unable to purchase a particular lot. This provision, under which squatters could be protected from the risks of an auction sale, was not acceptable to Glenelg, who asked that it be omitted from the act when renewed. This was attempted but not accomplished, there being a large majority for the act as it stood.[31] Nor was this clause omitted from the Act of 1841 which applied to both sections of United Canada. It was thus possible for squatters to purchase their land at private sale but they never obtained in United Canada the *right* of pre-emption which Durham's *Report* had recommended. John Beverley Robinson was always careful to use quotes when referring to the squatter's so-called "right" of pre-emption.

The land regulations in force in Upper Canada from 1841 to 1852 required cash sales, but a small quantity of land was sold on the instalment plan between 1842 and July 1, 1845, at which time this leniency ended. Many of the applicants to the Crown Lands Department were squatters on forfeited land or on Clergy Reserves [32] and when cash became the rule, dissatisfaction with the policies of the Department promptly expressed itself and led the legislature to set up the commission of investigation of 1846, before which numerous witnesses demanded the credit system. The high cash prices being demanded for land and the growing shortage of land tempted men to squat on both surveyed and unsurveyed land not yet open to location. The government continued to frown on settlers on such locations and to refuse them permission to purchase.[33]

Squatters on Crown land were treated with leniency by the Crown Lands Department even though they must have exhausted its patience by passive resistance and indifference to the regulations. Under the Land Act of 1841, land was sold at public sale, thirty days after notice had been given, to the first applicant with the cash and was not put up at auction unless two or more applicants wanted the same lot and could not agree to divide it. Occupants of Crown land could apply to purchase at private sale, and the local agents of the Department were instructed not to sell lots occupied and improved by squatters to others without informing the former of their pre-emption privilege and urging them to apply for it by a certain date. But after getting an order-in-council for pre-emption, squatters often remained contented with this protection and made no move to pay. The Crown Lands Department found it necessary to stir them to action by charging interest from the date of the order and giving them three months in which to purchase. Even after the expiration of this period of grace, squatters were for years protected by the Department's reluctance to sell them out and by the rule that no lot with valuable improvements could be sold to another without an express reference to the Department.[34] In areas opened by colonization roads, the government did its best to persuade squatters to move to free grants on the road or else allowed them to purchase 50 acres of the lot on which they had squatted on four years' credit.[35]

By the close of the 'forties the demand for land in Upper Canada had become pressing. From various Crown land agents came complaints of conflicts between squatters and purchasers. The purchasers were often determined not to allow a neighbourhood to be "spoiled" by the presence of squatters, particularly if the latter came from a different religious and social milieu. The Crown Lands Department itself was being criticized for not making more land available for settlement. "If government so far neglects its duty to public interests as to keep large blocks of land out of the market and in a state of nature that man is to be praised and not blamed who enters upon it, makes a clearance, builds a house and constructs roads," declared the *Elora Backwoodsman*.[36] In Wellington County, squatters moved into the township of Minto, which had not been opened to settlement, and from Huron County the Crown land agent reported that he was incessantly being applied to for land and urged the opening of several new townships.[37] In 1851 the government opened Minto to sale and in 1854 three recently surveyed townships in Huron County. They were to be sold at 10s. an acre on a credit of ten years, payable in ten annual instalments and limited to 200 acres to a buyer. The settlement conditions were actual occupation, "immediate and continuous," the clearing of two acres annually for five years, and the erection of a house.[38] The result was a mad scramble for lands in this area, and fraud and violence were common, both on the part of those who claimed pre-emption privileges and those who tried to get possession of good lots improved by others.

The trouble, according to John Clarke, Crown land agent for Huron County, was caused by "professional" squatters who were not actual settlers. Such men slashed a little timber and then rolled a few logs together as the ground work for a shanty on as many lots as they could and then sold these "improvements" to others who made use of them to claim pre-emption privileges from the government. In some instances, actual settlers resorted to this practice in order to raise the money for the first instalment on the one lot they intended to keep —all they could buy under the regulations of 1852.[39] The innocent purchasers of such improvements found, however, that the Crown land agents, who had been instructed not to allow pre-emption on "trivial pretences," would not recognize the squatter's right to sell these improvements, nor allow the purchasers to base a claim for pre-emption upon them. The squatters complained that the Crown land agent and his son had sold to Toronto speculators land on which *bona fide* settlers had made extensive improvements, disregarding the latter's pre-emption privileges. The numerous complaints of those who had been cheated out of their improvements, their money, and a location in a province where government land fit for cultivation was rapidly disappearing made it necessary for a special squatter commission to be appointed to untangle the conflicting claims.

The two commissioners appointed by the Governor were Ogle R. Gowan and Morgan Hamilton. Their report, dated February 4, 1857, and limited to the County of Huron, acknowledged the truth of the complaints. Nearly one-half of the land had been sold to non-resident speculators, the 200-acre limit on purchases ignored, claims to pre-emption disregarded, and the improved lots of actual settlers deliberately sold to speculators who afterwards demanded of the settler a price of $4.00 to $12.00 an acre in excess of the government's sale price.[40]

A new agent was appointed for the County of Huron. He was Charles Widder, who had himself purchased 8,000 acres, resold them to J. Luke Robinson at $8.00, and assured him he could sell on time to actual settlers at $10.00 an acre —five times the government price for land that was intended for actual settlers in 200-acre lots.[41] No action was taken by the Taché—Macdonald government, which had taken office in May, 1856, to give relief to the settlers in Huron because the commissioners' report was regarded as "incomplete." Meanwhile, the bitterness of the dispute was intensified by the delay. In addition, the conduct of the new agent gave rise to the suspicion that he was working in the interests of the land speculators. One indignant resident of Howick complained in December, 1857:

The Settlers lands are sold over their heads and their hard labour and toils openly trafficed [*sic*] away by the agents of the Speculators.... Things are coming to a fearful crisis, men that came in before the sale and suffered the hardships of a new country and spent their all in securing a home are now determined to spill their blood on the lands before they suffer those who should have no claim to drive them off.... The general opinion of the People is that our Governor and Council are highly censurable for the delay in the settlement of the difficulties and if lives are lost fearful charges will be laid to their account for allowing such sores to fester so long.[42]

The second report, on the County of Bruce, was completed in January, 1858, and was a much milder document. The agent was found to have shown favouritism and to have disregarded the 200-acre limitation; but, on the whole, he was let off much more easily—if not actually whitewashed—than the agent for Huron, and the evidence against him was not printed.[43]

In their first report, the commissioners had recommended that many of the sales be cancelled. The report of the Commissioner of Crown Lands for 1857 also recommended that these sales to "men of wealth and ... influence" who evidently expected "... that they would ultimately be able to induce the government to yield to their solicitations and confirm the sales ..." be cancelled and that innocent third parties who had purchased from them at an advance of

100 per cent to 1,000 per cent be given the right to recover at law what they had paid the speculators and also be granted pre-emption rights to land. Whether this recommendation was intended to be limited to innocent settlers who had bought no more than 200 acres is not clear. The Macdonald-Cartier government, when it finally acted, simply directed the Crown land agents to adjudicate the disputes according to the law and the regulations, assisted by one of the commissioners.[44]

The disputes in the County of Wellington, particularly in the township of Minto, which had been opened to sale in 1854 subject to prompt occupation and settlement, were not investigated until 1859, when the task was entrusted to William Spragge, Chief Clerk of the Crown Lands Department. Spragge found that the elderly Crown land agent, Andrew Geddes, assisted by his son, had told would-be settlers that there was no land left for sale in Minto when in reality many lots were held by his son on fictitious sales. These lots were subsequently resold to settlers who paid the son a sum in excess of the government price and received from the agent a receipt for their first instalment as original purchasers from the Crown at the government price of 7s. 6d. The agent had also permitted friends to evade the 200-acre limitation on purchases by the use of fictitious names and he had charged settlers a fee to which he was not entitled. Spragge recommended that Geddes should be required to make restitution and that no further instalments should be received on the 20,000 acres of land in Minto reported to be still unoccupied by the purchasers. The land should be inspected, resumed if found unimproved, and again offered for sale.

For some time, the Commissioner of Crown Lands, P. M. Vankoughnet, took no action on Spragge's report which, to be of value, required prompt action. Eventually, he decided that there was "no need" to send the report to the Executive Council and that, on account of his age and long services, Geddes should not be dismissed but merely reprimanded and required to make good losses to individuals. Whether these losses were to include not only the illegal fees but also the illegal profits made by his son with his connivance is not clear. The reprimand was not sent until March 3, 1862, almost three years after the date of Spragge's report. In 1863 the Assistant Commissioner of Crown Lands was not able to tell an investigating committee whether the settlers had been informed of the Department's decision or whether Geddes had made restitution.[45]

The disputed claims to land in Huron, Bruce, Grey, Perth, and Wellington counties did, however, come before the Executive Council. It directed, by an order-in-council of November 4, 1861, that settlers were to be favoured as against speculators when they were resident on the lot and had five acres under crop. That a good deal of the land in these counties remained in the hands of non-residents, unimproved and not fully paid for, is clear from the efforts of the Crown Lands Department to bring the land to patent. In November, 1861, the settlement duties were dispensed with for those purchasers who would pay an additional charge of 1s. 3d. an acre and who would complete their payments by February 1, 1862. When William McDougall (a Clear Grit) became Commissioner of Crown Land in the J. S. Macdonald–Sicotte ministry in 1862, this policy, which favoured speculators, was reversed and proof of settlement duties was again required before land in these counties could pass to patent.[46]

Not all the guilt for these land scandals rested on the shoulders of the Crown land agents or the speculators whom they had obliged. The squatters also had violated the regulations, abused the pre-emption privilege, and, in some instances, connived with speculators. Public opinion was now turning against the squatters. The attitude of Upper Canada society towards them had hardened since the early days when men squatted "almost through self defence," as the Land Board of Hesse had put it.[47] Squatters opened up new land to be sure, but, in the opinion of some, their presence depreciated the value of a township.[48] Their conflicts with one another in the new settlements and with their neighbours in the older townships, where they had seized on vacant and abandoned lots, were coming to be regarded as a disgrace to a now more settled community. The disputes were only part of the evil. The squatters' activities were not benefiting the land. Uncertain of his tenure and title, the squatter tended to "exhaust" the soil by his methods of cultivation and took no pains to erect decent buildings or fences or to maintain roads.[49] In timbered country he was likely to choose a lot bearing a good stand of pine, strip it of its timber, and then abandon it, after helping himself also from adjacent land.

The Land Act of 1853, unlike the Act of 1841, did not distinctly state that private sales to occupants might be made at the discretion of the governor-in-council, and squatters began to fear for their pre-emption privilege The omission was remedied by an order-in-council of August 9, 1853,[50] but the privilege of pre-emption was soon to be ended. An editorial in Francis Hincks's *Examiner* denounced squatting and pre-emption because they had produced a class of professional squatters who were a nuisance to lumbermen, to actual settlers, and to the Crown Lands Department which now began to accumulate testimony unfavourable to squatters. A. J. Russell, the Assistant Commissioner of Crown Lands, told a committee of the Assembly in 1854: [51]

Squatting is injurious to the future character of the settlement. The land is taken up by a poorer and inferior class of settlers. The best lands are picked out by them before the survey takes place, to the exclusion of settlers with more means who cannot be expected to join in the squatting or settle on the inferior lots afterwards; and they do not with us supersede the squatters, by buying them out as in the United States, but on the contrary avoid such settlements as unsuitable to live in, squatter settlements are thereby deprived in a very considerable degree of the advantages of having settlers of means and education, and of the benefits of the expenditure of their money, and of their example in improved cultivation, as well as other services and assistance in municipal affairs and in educational and other social matters of the greatest importance to their future prosperity.

In January, 1859, public notice was given that no claim to pre-emption would be entertained after September 1.[52] Squatters who did not purchase by that date were charged an annual rent of $5,00 for a 200-acre lot in addition to the purchase price. In 1861, after ample warning, the Crown Lands Department began to close out all its scattered lots in the older townships at auction for cash as rapidly as possible so as to end the evil of squatting.[53]

In Upper Canada, the squatter problem was less serious than in the townships of Lower Canada where there were many squatters of long standing on private land, the owners of which had not come forward to claim their property until it had been improved by others. Determined efforts were made by representatives from Lower Canada to secure for these squatters a legal right to adequate compensation for their improvements. An act of 1853 [54] allowed Lower Canada squatters compensation for improvements but did not specify how the amount was to be determined or the payment enforced. It also permitted the title-holder compensation for the use of his land and damages. In 1854, J. S. Sanborn of Compton introduced a bill to improve the law of betterments which passed the Assembly 52–25, with all the negative votes coming from Upper Canada except for two cast by the representatives of Three Rivers and Montreal.[55] In 1856 J. B. E. Dorion, of Drummond and Arthabaska, introduced another bill for the same purpose, which specified that the improvements and the land were to be valued by a jury of experts and gave the title-holder the choice of paying the occupant compensation or allowing the latter to buy the land at the valuation in three instalments. The preamble stated bluntly that squatters were being deprived of the fruits of their labour without compensation and that no man was justified in enriching himself by the labour of another.[56] This bill, as well as the squatter bills of 1854, 1857, 1858, 1859, 1860, 1863, 1864, and 1865, all passed the Assembly but were not returned by the Council.

The members recorded in open opposition to these measures came entirely from Upper Canada. Three or four Upper Canada members supported Dorion's Bill of 1856, and, in 1863 and 1864, representatives from counties where there was a squatter problem, such as Huron and Bruce, Leeds and Grenville, Wellington, Waterloo and Peel, voted for the bill. Twice, these squatter bills were amended so as to apply to Upper Canada but this manoeuvre was the work of those hostile to the bills and the amendments failed. No adequate act was passed to protect occupants of private land in Lower Canada in their improvements and no act at all existed for Upper Canada. Moreover, an act of 1865, which applied to Upper Canada alone, enabled one who had never occupied his Crown grant to recover his land from a squatter unless it could be shown that for twenty years he had been aware of the squatter's presence and provided forty years had not elapsed since the squatter entered the land.[57]

One member of the Legislative Council, John Macaulay, would like to have secured for the squatters in Upper Canada some degree of protection. He consulted John Beverley Robinson on the subject, who replied,

I have no sympathy with the genus squatter.... If I were like Louis Napoleon legislating for a country I would [allow] no preemption right to be [given those?] who have gone upon land to which they well knew they had no ... claim ... but would give them plainly to understand that so far from the impudent act of trespass giving them a claim they might be satisfied that whatever other persons might get a grant of land—they certainly never should—on any terms.

I think the favour that has always been shown to squatters has a democratizing tendency and leads to confusion in the notions of *meum* and *teum*.

Robinson admitted that in many new countries, including some British colonies, "they have gone much farther in protecting mere possession against legal right than we have chosen to do." He expressed his willingness to give advice on drafting a bill such as Macaulay wanted but effectively discouraged him from introducing one, warning him that his measure might go into the legislative hopper in one form and emerge so altered that he would not care to be known as its sponsor.[58]

In October, 1854, after the Hincks–Morin government had given place to the

MacNab–Morin government, a committee of the legislature, with A. T. Galt as chairman and four one-time Commissioners of Crown Lands among the members, made an extensive enquiry into the system of managing the Crown lands.[59] To satisfy the demand for land in the western peninsula, the previous government had decided to bring the remaining Crown and school land in Wellington, Perth, Huron, Bruce, and Grey counties on the market and to open about 370 miles of new roads (not free grant roads) in these counties.[60] The committee had to consider whether the land made available should be thrown open to cash sale, as in the state of Michigan, or continue to be sold on credit in restricted quantities and subject to settlement duties. The committee's hearings took place while sales were in progress in the western counties and while the land disputes already referred to were developing there.

A. N. Morin, the current Commissioner of Crown Lands, continued to defend the credit system on the grounds of broad social policy. He pointed out that cash sale would benefit speculators and was therefore incompatible with a policy of appropriating public monies for opening roads into new districts. Morin regarded squatting as one of the inevitable evils of a new and rapidly developing country. He favoured giving squatters a right of pre-emption and a right to compensation for their improvements.

A. T. Galt and Fred Widder, the one connected with the British American Land Company, the other with the Canada Company, vigorously denounced settlement duties and the credit system and favoured unrestricted cash sale at the existing prices. But Galt advocated limiting the application of this system to the surveyed area, allowing squatters the right of pre-emption on unsurveyed land and adopting a fixed uniform price for land subsequently to be surveyed and offered for sale. Where land had been sold subject to settlement duties and had not been occupied, Galt proposed the imposition of an additional money payment or penalty. To prevent speculators holding lots bought on credit, unpatented and therefore untaxable if unoccupied, he proposed to give the municipalities power to sell such unpatented lots subject to the claim of the Crown.

William Spragge, at the time chief clerk of the Executive Council, was averse to a liberal credit policy which encouraged poor settlers to go on the land too soon with insufficient capital and burdened with a long-term debt. Too often, said Spragge, the result was that they were obliged to sell their improvements and interest in the land for an inadequate sum "to persons who can command capital and who, it is well known, acquire free holds upon a large scale. . . ." While expressing "a paternal solicitude for the humbler class of settlers," he still proposed an increase in the price of Crown land, a reduction in the period of credit to five years, and a down-payment of two-fifths. He proposed to encourage compact settlement by imposing a 25 per cent penalty for squatting, by requiring immediate occupation and settlement duties, and by devoting half of the revenue from down payments to township roads.

Most of the witnesses were opposed to cash sale although they admitted that the credit system needed safeguards. David Roblin, representative from Lennox and Addington, argued that the only result of cash sale would be that the speculator would sell land on credit at an advanced price, "in fact pursue the very course the government are asked to give up and which only makes this difference that it will retard the settlement of the country to put money into the pockets of the rich at the expense of the hard working man." David Gibson made a telling point in favour of the credit system: not only did it enable new and poor settlers to get on the land earlier than they could otherwise have done but it put them on a par with capitalists by enabling them to share in the rise in land values. Andrew Russell dealt effectively with the argument that the American example of cash sale at a uniform price should be followed. Cash sale favoured speculation. This was an evil much more serious in Canada, where nature had narrowly limited the area fit for agriculture, than in the United States, where the tide of settlement, blocked by speculation in one area, could find an outlet elsewhere. "Opinion in the Province," wrote Lord Elgin, summing up the debate, "runs strongly in favour of facilitating its [wild land] acquisition in small lots by actual settlers, and of putting all possible obstacles in the way of its falling into the hands of speculators." [61]

The inquiry of 1854, in addition to making plain the popular preference for the credit system, revealed also that broader questions of land policy were attracting attention. By mid-century the square timber trade of the Ottawa Valley was being supplemented by the sawn lumber industry, which was eventually to replace it. With this development, the interests of settlers and lumbermen began to conflict. Lower and Innis remark:

For a generation or more lumberer and settler upon the Ottawa had been on the best of terms, then quite suddenly a discordant note began to make itself heard ... by mid-century the lumberman was finding that the settler in the course of his clearing was burning up pine that could very well have been used, the settler that the lumberman was anxious to keep him out of certain areas of the woods.[62]

In the past it had not been the practice for lumbermen to buy timber land from the Crown but to obtain the right to cut timber on a timber berth in return for ground rent and timber dues on the quantity cut. By mid-century, the Crown Lands Department, which had been criticized for contributing to squatting by keeping large blocks of land off the market when men were in search of homes, began to permit settlement on land included in timber licences. Sometimes, the so-called settlers were interested only in the timber and abandoned the land after stripping it. Such settlers did not pay for the timber at the rate the lumberman did. They took possession of the land as squatters, or on credit, with no down-payment if in Lower Canada, or with only one down-payment if in Upper Canada. In the past, the lumberman had not been averse to settlers who followed on his heels, brought supplies of hay and grain nearer to him, and reduced his costs. But he now objected to losing pine from land on which he had paid ground rent and he thought a land policy that permitted the destruction of pine forests in areas that never could support agriculture a senseless one. The lumbermen were accused of wishing to retard the settlement of the country and the development of a permanent industry—agriculture. The settlers were accused of cheating the government out of revenue it would have had from timber dues, cheating the lumbermen within whose limits their lot of land lay, and endangering by fire a valuable natural resource.

This growing controversy between settlers and lumbermen caused a few people to realize that a land classification programme should be undertaken without delay. James H. Burke, who in 1849 had advocated placing settlers on roads leading to lumber camps on the Madawaska, regarded that river as the northern boundary for settlement and did not favour the survey and settlement of the Ottawa and Opeongo Road.

Let us not be understood to encourage the wanton, foolish and insane policy of the Crown Lands Department in surveying a township where nothing but pine and rock exist, or where, to get a thousand acres of habitable land, settlers may be thrown in to spread fire and havoc through the pine forests; we go for keeping a fair line of demarcation between the lumbering and the agricultural regions as nature has laid it down.

A. J. Russell advised that settlement should be confined not to the scraps of good land in the timbered country but to such tracts of good land as would support communities large enough to provide the minimum social services such as roads and schools.

Most of those who spoke for the lumber industry were just as strongly opposed to cash sale as were those who were interested in agricultural land and for the same reason. They feared that if a change were made from the licencing system to cash sale, small operators would be ruined and the timber lands would pass into the hands of speculators. T. C. Keefer, however, who was anxious to see the country between the Ottawa and Georgian Bay opened by a railway and given access to the Chicago market, favoured cash sale. He could see no reason why the timber trade could not be carried on there, as it was in the western peninsula, as part of the operations of a permanent settled population which supplied saw logs to the mills instead of by migratory bands of lumber men who provided a market for the farmers' surplus. He regarded the former system as more conducive to the settlement of the country but he limited his suggestions to this area which he believed to be fit for permanent settlement.

Cash sale of timber land was advocated before the committee by a Mr. Jonathan R. White, a lumberman from Michigan. The American market was becoming increasingly important to Canadian lumbermen and it is probable that one thing they feared was the loss of their business opportunities to well-financed American investors ready to set up steam-powered mills and to buy timber lands at a cost per acre no higher than the timber dues on two good pine trees. The Canadian lumbermen had no difficulty in showing that while an immediate increase in the revenue might result from the "Michigan system," in the long run the prevailing practice of renting timber berths and collecting timber dues would be more profitable to the government.

Methods of dealing with land speculators which had been acceptable in the past were by 1854 coming to be recognized as not only inadequate but also harmful to settlers. The sovereign remedy advocated by the Colonial Office and by such men as Hincks and Merritt had always been taxation. But by 1854 some observers were astute enough to see that taxation as a remedy against the activities of speculators was a boomerang, hurting actual settlers and making their struggle more onerous, They also believed that some of those who had advocated this remedy had been interested primarily in using the credit and the taxing powers of the municipalities, enlarged by the Assessment Act of 1849 and the Municipal Loan Fund Act, to secure capital for railroads rather than in preventing speculators from garnering an unearned increment at the expense of the actual cultivators of the soil.

By 1854 also, questions of land policy were being considered not merely from the narrow standpoint of preventing one class in the community from profiting at the expense of another but from that of the national interest. The government of United Canada needed to be able to offer good land not only to immigrants but also to its native sons if it were to retain them in the country and conserve the "national strength." This argument, long recognized in Lower Canada, was beginning to be appreciated in Upper Canada also. The province could not afford to permit the limited quantity of land fit for settlement to be monopolized by men who would hold it for a rise and attempt to retail it at high prices that would drive settlers over the border. "We cannot be too strongly impressed with the importance of facilitating the extension of settlement with a view alike to the welfare of the settlers themselves and to the consolidation of the Province to secure our progress in prosperity and future national power," said Andrew Russell. But nature had set the limits of successful permanent farm settlement, as Russell fully realized. Canada could not build her national prosperity by flying in the face of nature, by destroying instead of husbanding her timber resources, and by drawing her expanding population of farmers into country in which they could not stay as farmers. What was the solution?

"We should," said Russell, overlooking for the moment all political and geographic obstacles, "... extend our settlements and political organization over the vast regime of the Red River and Saskatchewan before we begin to convert our valuable timber forests into worthless fields." The fundamental question of land policy had now been raised. From this date forward the basic issue was not what was to be done about the scraps of cultivable Crown land remaining in United Canada, and particularly in Upper Canada, but what was to be done about the Canadian West. Could Canada develop from the resources of that extensive area the national strength for which, it was clear, United Canada could never provide adequate support?

The inquiry of 1854-5 did not result in legislation for about six years. In the meantime, explorations were pushed north and west of the French River and Lake Nipissing in an effort to find additional land fit for settlement. Some 5,000,000 acres were added to the surveyed area of Upper Canada by 1862, when the unnecessary and expensive surveys were stopped. At that time, there were over 3,000,000 acres of surveyed land ungranted, much of it unfit for settlement.[63] Although the inquiry had brought forth divided opinions on the wisdom of encouraging settlement in the Ottawa–Huron region, the network of roads previously referred to was constructed and free grant lands offered along them. These free grants were advertised in Europe in a futile effort to draw immigrants to a province whose attractions had long ago paled before those of the American prairies. The unsuccessful assault on the Laurentian Barrier by way of these colonization roads is a topic already so ably treated by several writers that it is unnecessary for anything more to be added here.[64]

Between settlers and lumbermen, as between settlers and cattlemen in the United States, conflict over the public domain continued. The latter argued that settlers should be content to follow the lumbermen who provided roads and markets for them. The settler contended that cut-over lots had been deprived of half their value to settlers since not enough timber suitable for building was left upon them. Settlers wanted the timbered lands thrown open to settlement and the free grant policy extended beyond the front lots on the colonization roads; lumbermen fought to keep settlers from taking possession of lots which bore choice stands of pine or which were vital to their operations because of their location. Settlers complained of the regulation which forbade them to sell timber from their land until it was paid for in full; lumbermen accused them of being timber strippers. In 1861, the Crown Lands Department gave settlers the privilege they wanted. The Department stipulated, however, that the proceeds from the sale of timber were to be applied to the price of the land and the occupants were to show proof that they were genuine settlers who had land under crops. In an effort to minimize the disputes, the Department began, in 1859, to require more "detailed and discriminating" surveys with a view to classifying land as suitable for settlement or timber berths.[65]

New regulations were adopted in 1859 which remained in force until Confederation.[66] Land in new, subdivided townships was now offered at auction at an upset price of 70¢ an acre cash or $1.00 on five years' credit with a down-payment of one-fifth. Once offered land could be purchased at private sale at the upset price. All land, whether purchased with cash or on credit, was once again made subject to settlement duties consisting of buiding a house 16' by 20', two years' continuous residence, and the cultivation of 10 acres out of 100 within four years.[67] No limitation was placed on the amount of land that could be purchased in Upper Canada. A $6.00 patent fee for every 200 acres was imposed on those who had not completed their payments or performed their settlement duties within the allotted time. Squatters were notified that their pre-emption privileges would end on September 1, 1859, and delinquents were warned that their land would be resumed by the Crown if instalments in arrears were not paid within twelve months' time. This threat was not strictly carried out.[68]

Although the inquiry of 1854 had shown strong popular opposition to cash sale and sales in large quantities, the new regulations permitted townships to be purchased *en bloc* for cash at 50¢ an acre on condition that they be surveyed at the expense of the purchasers and that settlers be placed on every 200-acre lot fit for settlement within ten years. Philip Vankoughnet, Commissioner of Crown Lands in the Cartier-Macdonald ministry, favoured cash sales to get the country settled. He stated that he had been repeatedly informed that large numbers of Norwegians would settle in Canada if they could settle together in a block and that frequent similar applications had come from England. One such sale, of ten townships in the Ottawa-Huron region, was made in 1861 to the Canadian Land and Emigration Company on the terms given above. The contract had to be renegotiated in 1864 when the Company discovered that 92 square miles of its land had been included within timber berths. The Company made a beginning in the township of Dysart where it sold land to settlers at $1.00 an acre cash. Subsequently, its land was priced at $1.00 to $2.00 an acre and five years' credit was given. Land could also be rented from the Company at 10¢ to 15¢ an acre. The Company is said to have spent $100,000 on surveys, roads, mills, and other preparations for settlement. Its speculation was not a success but its later history belongs not to United Canada but to the province of Ontario after Confederation.[69] In 1862 the Crown Lands Department recommended the acceptance of Fred Widder's offer to purchase 21 townships in the Parry Sound area on terms similar to those granted the Canadian Land and Emigration Company, but this sale was never completed.[70]

In 1860 the Cartier-Macdonald government passed what proved to be the last land act of United Canada before Confederation.[71] This act, like its predecessors, did not prescribe the price of land or the terms of sale but left these details to the governor-in-council. Various regulations and penalties, designed to secure honest and impartial conduct from the district agents and *bona fide* bids at public auctions, were established. The act permitted claims to land under repealed regulations and orders-in-council to be entertained, although it did not allow U.E. loyalist, militia, or military claims to be brought forward, and entrusted the determination of claims to the Commisioner of Crown Lands alone. It provided for the issuing of scrip to satisfy these claims and extended the date for using scrip issued before January 14, 1853, which had run July 1, 1854, to January 1, 1862. Claims to deficiencies were by this act required to be made within five years of the date of patent and compensation was provided, in land or in scrip, on a scale commensurate with the original value of the grant.

The reports of the Commissioner of Crown Lands reveal the vigorous efforts that were made after 1860 to close out the business of the Crown Lands Department in the older townships and thereby to reduce the number of its agents and its expenses. Scattered lots in these townships, many of which were refuse lots, were sold at auction for cash; but when lots were occupied by squatters, time was allowed, provided the occupants made their bargain with the Department before the day of the sale. Partly in response to the popular criticism of speculators and partly out of a desire to reduce the large quantity of land on which payments were in arrears, the Department began to declare forfeit and to offer for sale land which had been sold on credit, had not been occupied or improved and on which only one instalment had been paid.

Although the regulations of 1851-9 had required the performance of settlement duties on all land before patent, whether a free grant or a cash or a credit sale, the Act of 1860 provided that failure to perform the duties did not invalidate a patent or affect the title of subsequent purchasers. It also permitted the Commissioner of Crown Lands to dispense with the conditions of a sale or grant. These wide powers, which seem to be another reversal of policy, appear to have been granted to enable the commissioner to dispense with conditions that were not being fulfilled and were preventing unoccupied land being brought to patent and taxed.[72]

It is obvious that as high a degree of executive discretion prevailed in the administration of the Crown lands after the establishment of responsible government as before, and that the opportunities for partiality, political patronage, and corruption were as numerous as they had been in the days of Lieutenant-Governors Gore and Maitland. Mackenzie's remedy had been to regulate the administration of the lands by statute. The Reformers had not wholly accomplished this, but they had made it possible for the province to "kick the rascals out"—and perhaps to let another set of rascals in. What Canada had to rely on in the administration of its natural resources for the general welfare was not the minutiae of legislation but, as before, the vigilance of the legislature and the character of its public men and civil servants.

Land fit for permanent agricultural settlement—the province's most important natural resource—was gone before 1860. Andrew Russell had realized that in 1854 and had called attention to the need for extending Canada's western boundaries to include the Saskatchewan and Red River country. In 1857, the Commissioner of Crown Lands, in his published report, had admitted that if Canada were to attract immigrants and to hold her own young men she must have easily cultivated prairie lands like those of the United States to offer them. "It is in the valley of the Red River, the Assiniboine, the Saskatchewan that such lands are to be found." [73] The time had come for ending the Hudson's Bay Company's control of the area Canada needed.

When those prairie lands should become available for settlement, what land disposal policies would be applied to them? Undoubtedly land grants would be made to railways. The legislature of United Canada had considered numerous petitions for railway land grants and had already accepted the policy and written it into six railway acts.[74] Since none of these grants was earned in the period to which this study is limited, it has seemed unnecessary to do more than merely refer to them.

On what terms would the settler receive his land? As a free grant, on credit, in restricted quantities, subject to settlement duties, or by cash purchase? Since 1841 these various solutions to the problems of land policy had been tried and debated back and forth. During the closing decade of United Canada's existence, the demand that land be made cheap or even free to actual settlers had grown stronger. The legislature and the Crown Lands Department had repeatedly been urged to reduce the price of land sold on credit during the boom years that preceded 1857 and to extend the free grant policy beyond the lines of the colonization roads.[75] From the lumber interests and the land companies, opposition to a more liberal land policy continued. On the other hand, an enlightened Commisioner of Crown Lands, who regarded settlers as more important than revenue, suggested that the whole of the really uncultivable land be set apart as a pine region and be carefully administered on a sustained yield basis.[76]

The demand in United Canada for free land was a compound of the convictions that a free land system would help create a democratic and stable society, that population was more important than revenue, that wild land was worthless until labour and capital had been applied to it, and that to charge the settler for his land was to deprive him of the capital he badly needed or to place him under a crushing debt that would take years to lift and that might have the effect of depriving him of the fruits of his labour in the end. The $6,500,000 still due on Crown, clergy, and school land in Upper Canada in 1862,[77] the 500,000 acres which settlers had leased, not purchased, from the Canada Company, the large quantity of Crown Reserves still unsold by the Company, and the 3,500,000 acres still in the hands of absentee owners documented this point. If any additional arguments for free land were needed, the Americans had just supplied one. In 1862 they had enacted their Homestead Law.

CHAPTER TWENTY-ONE

CONCLUSION

THE LAND OF UPPER CANADA was initially regarded in Great Britain and in Canada as Crown land to be managed under the direction of the Colonial Office by the Lieutenant-Governor and Executive Council of the province, assisted later by an official who bore an English title, Commissioner of Crown Lands. The Imperial government was at first disposed to give the land away to reward loyalty and services; later it wanted to make the land pay the expenses of its administration; finally it became eager to develop a revenue from the Crown lands to further emigration from the mother country. Gradually, the land came to be thought of as public domain subject to the legislature of the province, and this foreign concept came to be accepted by the Colonial Office.

Those who first devised and administered the land policies of Upper Canada were convinced that the American Revolution would not have occurred if there had been a loyal aristocracy and clergy of the established Church throughout the thirteen colonies, and if, in addition, the Crown had enjoyed a revenue independent of the legislature. They thought of Upper Canada as virgin soil on which political, social, and religious institutions of the right kind could be developed, and the specific land policies adopted reflected this belief. The Crown Reserves, the Clergy Reserves, the limited grants to "common" settlers, the larger grants to officers and gentlemen—all were intended to establish the social structure that prevailed in the mother country.

The early land policies of the province were a failure because in 1791 Upper Canada was not virgin soil. Between 1784 and 1791 the province had acquired a body of settlers who had brought with them from the thirteen colonies, along with their loyalty, a preference for democratic institutions and a belief in religious equality. They were not likely to be weaned away from these sentiments on the Canadian frontier. Moreover, the physical and economic environment of the province was not suited to the development of an aristocracy of country gentlemen and to the maintenance of an endowed clergy but to the creation of a democratic society. The immigration of settlers from the United States and the very existence of the successful republic to the south strengthened this tendency. In addition, the devices from which Simcoe had hoped so much, the reserves, failed of their purpose because they proved to be obnoxious to the settlers. A growing majority in Upper Canada came to the conclusion which Jefferson had earlier expressed—possession by the Crown of a revenue independent of the legislature is inconsistent with public liberty.

The land policies in force before 1826 failed to attain their economic, as well as their political, objectives. One difficulty was that the policy was not a consistent whole, and parts of it, particularly the settlement duty requirements, were sabotaged. The free grant policy became in effect an inconvenient sales system, and, although it was the declared policy of the Crown to prevent speculation, the Crown and Clergy Reserves made the government the largest speculator of all. Finally, the Colonial Office, by yielding to the demands of special interests, such as the children of loyalists, contributed to the very speculation it wished to avoid.

In theory, a free grant policy was in force in Upper Canada prior to 1826 and a sales policy subsequently. In practice, there was neither. Paradoxically, the free grant policy became practically a sales policy, and, after a sales policy was officially adopted, free grants, free even of patent fees, continued to be made to such an extent that from 1826 to 1838 the Crown disposed of forty times as much land by grant as by sale, exclusive of the sale to the Canada Company.[1] By 1838 the Crown had granted or appropriated 16,506,525 acres in Upper Canada. If 450,000 acres are deducted for roads, 500,000 for school reserves, 715,740 for Indian reserves, 1,521,561 for unsold Canada Company land,[2] 1,928,945 for unsold Clergy Reserves, and 755,400 for located but unpatented land, this leaves 10,505,279 acres in the possession of individuals.[3] In 1838 the provincial assessors reported that there was 6,060,332 acres of occupied farm land, of which 2,064,903 acres were under cultivation and 4,853,890 were uncultivated.[4] About 4,500,000 acres must therefore have been in the possession of speculators—a drag on the resources of the genuine settlers.

Speculation might have been minimized if Portland had not yielded to the demand for free land for the children of loyalists and if an effective land tax had been imposed in the early days of the colony, as Peter Russell had suggested. Contemporary critics, however, advocated the adoption of the American system. This would have meant that no more scattered reserves would be created and that land would be offered for sale at what was practically a fixed price, for cash. It was recognized that this system played into the hands of speculators, but it was argued that this was an advantage. "In proportion to the extent to which speculation is carried in the States of the Union, the growth and prosperity of the district are stimulated," wrote Wakefield.[5] This belief was founded on divergent views of the nature of the American and the Canadian speculator. The Canadian speculator, it was asserted, let his property lie idle because the scattered reserves deterred him from expending capital on its improvement and because there was no adequate wild land tax to oblige him to make his property productive. The American speculator, on the other hand, was assumed to be a capitalist who, unhindered by reserves, was prompt to open up his property and to attract settlers to it by building roads, bridges, and mills. Baldwin and Wakefield probably were not aware of such New York State speculators as the Pierponts and Nicholas Devereaux, who let their land lie idle for years, nor did these critics of Canadian land policy refer to the unsatisfactory relations which developed between American speculators and their purchasers or tenants. The troubles of the Holland Land Company in western Pennsylvania, of Timothy Pickering in eastern Pennsylvania, of John Cleves Symmes in Ohio, of William Cooper at Otsego, New York, of Edward Ellice himself at Little Falls were an unknown story. All, it was assumed, would be well if the simple, cheap, and quick American method of transferring the public domain into the hands of individuals was adopted. Baldwin was hostile enough to the Canada Company and he believed that the results of its speculation would be "accumulating debt, broken contracts, lost labour, dissatisfied children. The Company will become if it is not so already a stimulus to Democratic longings."[6] But it seems not to have occurred to him that these same results might have been produced in a dozen other instances, although on a smaller scale, by the American system which he favoured, or by the township system which he had so strongly advocated.

In fact, the effects of the land policies pursued on either side of the border were similar. On the American side, first the credit system then the cash sale systems favoured speculation; on the Canadian side, the free grant system in force until 1826 produced the same result, and so did both the credit and the cash sale system when they were adopted. What would have worked? One is tempted to conclude that the opening up of a new country is not an orderly process. Without efficient law enforcement, it is something like opening the strings of a gigantic grab bag. Those whom the late Professor Edwin F. Gay once described as "the men with a hard cutting edge" grab what they can and find their way through whatever maze of regulations may be created in an effort to restrict them. The less fortunate pick up the bits and pieces of the good things that are left and hang on to them—if they can.

In Upper Canada, however, it was not the system of free grants to immigrants that had failed, as Wakefield was fair enough to point out,[7] but the practice of using the land to reward U.E. loyalists, militia men, and officials already resident in the colony. Not one-sixth as much land was granted to later immigrants as to these classes of privileged persons. Yet in 1826 it was made to appear that the free grant system had failed and it was abolished while the real evil was permitted to continue until 1837 and, in an altered form, until 1851, when scrip ceased to be issued. James Stephen also realized where the real trouble lay. "I have very little doubt that while too much cannot be said against the practice of making large grants of land as a matter of favour to the rich, great exaggeration has prevailed as to the evil of making small allotments to the poor.... I cannot but believe that the unqualified doctrine of never giving away land has done much mischief in British North America...."[8] What did settle the country—apart from the assisted settlement—was squatting. Clergy Reserves, Crown Reserves, Crown land, Indian land, and private land were occupied by squatters both before and after 1841, and pre-emption privileges had subsequently to be allowed them.

No major questions of land policy had been set at rest by 1841. In Upper Canada, the Crown lands had been managed by the lieutenant-governor-in-council subject to such restrictions as the Colonial Office imposed; in United Canada, the Crown lands were managed by the governor-in-council subject to such restrictions as the colonial legislature imposed. The Reformers had contended for the regulation of the Crown lands by statute, but they did not achieve it. Administrative details relating to price, and to the terms and the conditions of sale, were left to the governor-in-council. This system remained in force until 1867. Between 1841 and 1867 the Executive Council resorted to many of the expedients which had been tried before and rejected: cash sale at fixed prices, local valuations, graduated prices, credit policies, auction sales, settlement duty requirements, sales of townships or blocks of land to capitalists, and free grants in certain areas. Upper Canada began with a policy of free grants which was gradually restricted and ended with a policy of strict cash sale. United Canada began with a policy of strict cash sale and turned to the credit system; later, it gradually eased the conditions of sale and extended the use of free grants.

Legislative criticism of the way in which the Crown lands were managed was no less under responsible government than it had been prior to the Rebellion, both on questions of policy and details of administration. The malcontents continued to argue that population was wealth and that therefore the province would gain more by placing the land in the hands of settlers as quickly as possible than by administering it for the purposes of revenue. They pressed for lower prices, the credit system, free grants on colonization roads, and wound up advocating a homestead policy. In this they were supported by the Minister of Agriculture and Immigration, Thomas D'Arcy McGee.[9]

There was no more certainty, honesty, impartiality, and efficiency in the administration of the Crown lands after they came under provincial control than there had been before. It is true that United Canada inherited many tagends of unfinished business from Upper Canada but it created many additional problems of its own by insisting on re-introducing the credit system and its supposed safeguard, settlement duties. The members of the legislature made matters worse by using their influence to bring about a re-examination of land disputes supposedly settled and by pressing the legislature to extend the time for the exercise of squatters' pre-emption privileges, for the receipt of land scrip, or for the postponement of forfeiture provisions. The Crown Lands Department in the period of the Union was not for many years a revenue-producing department, partly because it was receiving scrip in payment for land and partly because the investigation of many individual grievances made it an expensive department to administer. In addition, the system of district agents was unsatisfactory. The officials of the old Land Department of Upper Canada had been accused of feathering their own nests and of showing favouritism to insiders. The district agents appointed under the Union were accused of exactly the same practices and, if Peter Robinson had failed to turn over his collections promptly to the Receiver General, so also did the district agents, and several of them became defaulters in the end.[10]

After responsible government was achieved, order was gradually brought out of chaos,[11] but not until United Canada had made many of the same errors that had been made by the lieutenant-governors-in-council and the Colonial Office. Nor was the task accomplished before all the land fit for permanent agricultural settlement had been disposed of. To the last, the debate continued among those who thought the government should be concerned primarily with getting revenue out of the land quickly and with as little trouble and expense as possible by disposing of the land in large blocks to capitalists, those who thought there should be no profit-taking intermediary between the government and the settler, and those who thought the government should be content to give the land away in small allotments to get it settled.

It must be admitted that those who opposed free grants or cheap land for immigrants and settlers with limited resources were often justified by the results. To entrust land to the unco-ordinated efforts of such settlers was not to ensure the rapid development of prosperous agricultural communities or the most efficient use of the resources of the province. But these persons were not merely "instruments of production"—labor—they were human beings. The steam-boats and wagons that carried them to their destination were freighted not only with their pitiful possessions but with their high hopes as well. A paternalistic government might advise such settlers in all sincerity that it would be better for them to work as labourers for some years before going on the land; otherwise, debts might deprive them of their hard-won equities in the end. On the other hand, a government indifferent to their wishes might prefer to risk entrusting the land to township promoters or land companies instead; this *was* a risk, as the experience of Upper Canada proved. But, given the values of the societies out of which most of the settlers came, what they wanted, what they had taken the risk of uprooting themselves for, was a chance at land and independence in the New World, or, in the case of native sons, on the newest frontier. Some of them made it—some didn't. For government, imperial or provincial, the ultimate question was the one posed by Robert Baldwin: What kind of society would the resources of Canada be used to create?

APPENDIX

SALES OF CROWN LAND IN UPPER CANADA, 1828–1865*

Year	Crown	Clergy	Grammar school	Common school	Total acres
1828					
1829	3883	18014			21847g
1830	6135	24705			30840
1831	4365	28563			32918
1832	10352	48484			58800
1833	26417	62282			88699
1834	8891	59326			68217
1835	22707	59003			81710
1836	7923	63440			71363
1837	7003	81549			88552
1838	3556	21475			25031
1839	12110	24949			37059
1840	26342	23586			49928
1841	14701	2665			17366
1842	19780a	1486			21266
1843	42501a	613			43114
1844	40510a	569	54862b		41079
1845	32256	40602			72858
1846	67879	179271			247150
1847	25933	196568			222501
1848	6583	81373			87956
1849	14265	70726			84911
1850	36536	93245			129781
1851	81949	91706		52611	226266
1852	50837	94942		61243	207022
1853	235228	150809	36471c	177483	563520
1854	529180	127638	3369	304985	965172
1855	461368	129087	1097	312393	903945
1856	140520	81086	2340	47715	271661
1857	122129	59937	76301	9978	268345
1858	121603	25812	5644	3571	155630
1859	167196	75698	5247	5852	253993
1860	126413	62522	6900	3221	199056
1861	157953	74366	5729	4498	242546
1862	101511	29711	2969	2249	136500
1863	91069	11912	1580	3370f	107931
1864	79145d	22265d	924d	3640d	105974
1864–5	59310e	119160	2061	4194	84725
1865	33340d	10941d	226d	2483d	46990

The figures in this table have been taken from the following sources. Where the authorities differed, they were taken from the return bearing the later date, on the assumption that the earlier return had been corrected. Totals have been compiled.

* a The figures for 1842–4 include Lower Canada sales. During these years, 2,235, 4,600, and 1,700 additional acres were sold on credit. b This figure represents the total sales of Grammar School lands to date. c This figure represents the total sales during the years 1845–53. d Represents sales for a half year. e In addition, 362,125 acres were purchased by the Canada Land and Emigration Company. f In addition, 25,765 acres were resumed and resold. g Fractions, town lots, and water lots have been disregarded. Totals prior to 1854 do not include Grammar School lands. Prior to 1851, they do not include Common School lands.

Crown Land: 1828-30—Great Britain, *Sessional Papers,* 1835, XXXIX, 280; 1831-7—Great Britain, *Sessional Papers,* 1840, XXXIII, 3; 1834-8—*J.L.A./C.,* 1846, App. E.E.; 1845-55—*J.L.A./C.,* 1856, XIV, App. 35; 1856-65, the appendices for those years (annual reports of the Commissioner of Crown Lands).

Clergy Land: 1828-55—*J.L.A./C.,* 1856, XIV, App. 35; 1856-65—annual reports of the Commissioner of Crown lands.

Grammar School Land: 1828-44—*J.L.A./C.,* 1844-5, IV, App. N.N.; 1844-53—*J.L.A./C.,* 1858, XVI, App. 15; 1854-5—*J.L.A./C.,* 1857, XV, App. 25; 1856-65—annual reports of the Commissioner of Crown Lands.

Common School Land: 1851-5—*J.L.A./C.,* 1858, XVI, App. 15; 1856-65—annual reports of the Commissioner of Crown Lands.

It has been stated that sales of Crown land are a good indication of agricultural prosperity, public confidence, and available capital (Gilbert Norman Tucker, *The Canadian Commercial Revolution, 1845-1851* [New Haven, 1936], 216-17). No doubt they are, but it should be borne in mind that sales were affected by other factors: the existence of a credit system prior to 1837 and subsequent to 1852; the availability and acceptability of land rights or scrip from 1837 to 1854; limitations on the quantity of other land available for sale or its complete withdrawal from sale, as was true of the Clergy Reserves; the announced termination of pre-emption privileges in 1859; reductions in price; the throwing open of new areas and new classes of land to sale and settlement, as was true of the Grammar and Common School lands; and even the availability of free grants, restricted in size and undesirable in location.

NOTES

Abbreviations used in these notes are as follows: *C.H.R.* — *Candian Historical Review*; C.L.P. — Crown Land Papers; *E.H.R.* — *English Historical Review*; ev. — evidence; *J.H.A./U.C.* — *Journal of the Legislative Assembly of Upper Canada*; — *J.L.A./C.* — *Journals of the Legislative Assembly of the Province of Canada*; *J.L.C./U.C.* — *Journal of the Legislative Council of Upper Canada*; *M.V.H.R.* — *Mississippi Valley Historical Review*; N.Y.H.S. — New York Historical Society; P.A.O. — Public Archives of Ontario; P.A.C. — Public Archives of Canada; s.p. — sessional paper; T.P.L. — Toronto Public Library.

CHAPTER ONE

1. Chester Martin, *Empire and Commonwealth* (Oxford, 1929), p. 95.
2. Philip Yorke, ed., *The Life and Correspondence of the Philip Yorke, Earl of Hardwicke* (Cambridge, 1913), III, 314; William James Smith, *The Grenville Papers, being the Correspondence of Richard Grenville, Earl Temple* (London, 1852), I, 342; Albert von Ruville, *William Pitt, Earl of Chatham* (London, 1907), II, 382.
3. *The Cambridge History of the British Empire* (Cambridge, 1929-40), I, 501-2; Jack M. Sosin, *Whitehall and the Wilderness* (Lincoln, Neb., 1961), p. 10.
4. Lewis Bernstein Namier, *England in the Age of the American Revolution* (London, 1930), pp. 321-2.
5. *A letter addressed to Two great men on the Prospect of peace* (London, 1760).
6. Theodore Calvin Pease, "Anglo-French Boundary Disputes in the West, 1749-1763," Illinos State Historical Library, *Collections*, XXVII (1936), lxxxi.
7. William Stewart Wallace, "The Beginnings of British Rule in Canada," *Canadian Historical Review (C.H.R.)*, VI (1925), 208-21.
8. Adam Shortt and Arthur G. Doughty, eds., *Documents relating to the Constitutional History of Canada* (2d ed., rev., Ottawa, 1918), I, 133-8.
9. Martin, *Empire and Commonwealth*, p. 96.
10. In meeting the objection that Canada in French hands had kept the colonies in awe and dependence on Great Britain, Lord Morton had written, "If ... care [be] taken that the new settlements ... be formed into new governments of small extent, the mutual jealousies amongst several Colonys would always keep them in a state of dependence ..."; Namier, *Age of the American Revolution*, p. 323. This policy was actually carried out in Nova Scotia. See Marion Gilroy, "The Partition of Nova Scotia, 1784," *C.H.R.*, XVI (1935), 91-3.
11. Verner W. Crane, ed., "Hints relative to the Division of the Conquered and Newly Acquired Countries in America," *Mississippi Valley Historical Review (M.V.H.R.)*, VIII (1921-2), 367-73.
12. R. A. Humphreys, "Lord Shelburne and the Proclamation of 1763," *English Historical Review (E.H.R.)*, XLIX (1934), 241-64.
13. Shortt and Doughty, eds., *Documents*, I, 142, 150.
14. *Ibid.*, I, 151-3.
15. *Ibid.*, I, 148, 152.
16. Great Britain, Privy Council, *Acts of the Privy Council of England, Colonial Series* (London, 1908-12), IV, 408, 580-99; Clarence W. Alvord, *The Mississippi Valley in British Politics* (Cleveland, 1919), I, 174, n. 311, and p. 213.
17. Martin, *Empire and Commonwealth*, p. 101.
18. Alfred LeRoy Burt, *The Old Province of Quebec* (Toronto, 1933), p. 82.
19. Alvord, *Mississippi Valley*, I, 207.
20. Shortt and Doughty, eds., *Documents*, I, 140-1.
21. Burt, *Province of Quebec*, p. 86; Humphreys, "Shelburne and the Proclamation"; R. Coupland, *The Quebec Act* (Oxford, 1925), p. 26, n. 2, and p. 34, n. 1.
22. Had this been done, it would have been no novelty. The Catholic population of Minorca had been allowed to retain its elected council of jurats which presented grievances and could petition the King; *The Importance of the Island Of Minorca ... in a Letter from a*

Merchant to a Noble Lord (London, 1756), p. 35.

23. C. S. Higham, "The General Assembly of the Leeward Islands," *E.H.R.*, XLI (1926), 190-209, 366-88.

24. Shortt and Doughty, eds., *Documents*, I, 142, 145.

25. Martin, *Empire and Commonwealth*, chap. II.

26. Shortt and Doughty, eds., *Documents*, I, 142, 156.

27. *Ibid.*, I, 380-1.

28. *Ibid.*, I, 247-8; *Acts of the Privy Council, Colonial Series*, V, 28.

29. Hillsborough had previously been back at the Board, from Aug. 18, 1766, to Dec. 18, 1766. There were no reports on Canada during this period; Arthur Herbert Basye, *The Lords Commissioners of Trade and Plantations* (New Haven, 1925), App. C.

30. Shortt and Doughty, eds., *Documents*, I, 377-93, 490. In 1768 Maseres had been ready to concede that if an assembly had to be established, Catholics should be admitted to it. The members were to be restricted to the seigneur and a representative of the inhabitants of each seigneury; William Stewart Wallace, ed., *The Maseres Letters, 1766-1758* (Toronto, 1919), p. 101.

31. Shortt and Doughty, eds., *Documents*, I, 194-9.

32. L. W. Larabee, *Royal Instructions to British Colonial Governors* (New York, 1935), II, 565, 577-9.

33. Shortt and Doughty, eds., *Documents*, I, 166.

34. P.A.C., C.O. 42/24/27-32, Murray to Egremont, Sept. 7, 1762; *Acts of the Privy Council, Colonial Series*, IV, 820-1, V, 600-1.

35. Francis Maseres, *An Account of the proceedings of the British and other protestant inhabitants of the province of Quebec to obtain an House of Assembly* (London, 1775), p. 270.

36. Burt, *Old Province of Quebec*, p. 93.

37. William Bennet Munro, ed., *Documents relating to the seigneurial tenure in Canada 1598-1854* (Toronto, 1908), pp. 197, 322-4.

38. Except for judicial powers; Shortt and Doughty, eds., *Documents*, I, 423.

39. Beverley Waugh Bond, *The Quit Rent System in the American Colonies* (New Haven, 1919), pp. 375-6; A. L. Burt, in a review of Graham's *British Policy in Canada*, *C.H.R.*, XII (1931), 203.

40. Burt, *Old Province of Quebec*, pp. 154, 163.

41. Shortt and Doughty, eds., *Documents*, II, 947, n. 1. Page references in their n. should be to pp. 288 and 292.

42. *Ibid.*, I, 284, 300, italics added.

43. *Journal of the Commissioners for Trade and Plantations*, p. 243.

44. *Acts of the Privy Council, Colonial Series*, V, 293.

45. *Ibid.*, V, 341; C.O. 42/31/115-16, Cramahe to Hillsborough, May 5, 1772.

46. Burt, *Old Province of Quebec*, p. 38.

47. Gerald Sanford Graham, *British Policy and Canada, 1774-1791* (London, 1933), p. 28; cf. Munro, *Seigneurial Tenure*, p. 204.

48. Burt, *Old Province of Quebec*, p. 178.

49. P. G. Roy, "Les Concessions en fief et seigneurie sous le régime anglais," *Le Bulletin des recherches historiques*, XXXIV (1928), 323-5.

50. Gustavus Myers, *History of Canadian Wealth* (Chicago, 1914), p. 63.

51. Only six seigneuries were conceded between 1775 and 1824; Roy, "Les Concessions en fief et seigneurie," pp. 323-5.

52. Burt, *Old Province of Quebec*, pp. 154, 163.

53. William Knox, *Extra Official State Papers* (London, 1789), II, 172-4; Sir Henry Cavendish, *Debates of the House of Commons in the Year 1774 on the Bill for making more Effectual provision for the Government of the Province of Quebec* (London, 1839), p. 195.

54. Shortt and Doughty, eds., *Documents*, I, 552; *Observations and Reflections on the Quebec Act, passed in the year 1774 for the settlement of the Province of Quebec. By a Country Gentleman* (London, 1782).

55. Thomas Perkins Abernethy, *Western Lands and the American Revolution* (New York, 1937), p. 30, quoting Franklin's statement that Hillsborough was "terribly afraid of dispeopling Ireland. . . ." Shortt and Doughty, eds., *Documents*, I, 552, n. 1, quoting William Knox to the same effect.

56. *Acts of the Privy Council, Colonial Series*, IV, 758; VI, 201; *Journal of the Commissioners for Trade and Plantations, 1759-1763*, p. 28; Labaree, *Royal Instructions*, II, 640.

57. Shortt and Doughty, eds., *Documents*, I, 552 (italics added).

58. Knox, *Extra Official State Papers*, II, 172-4.

59. Shortt and Doughty, eds., *Documents*, I, 554.

60. Cavendish, *Debates*, p. 195.

CHAPTER TWO

1. Shortt and Doughty, eds., *Documents*, II, 607, sec. 31.
2. P.A.C., B series, Vol. 122, pp. 26-32, 108-14, Governor Haldimand to Lt.-Gov. Hamilton, Aug. 6, 1778. This series hereinafter cited simply B with volume number.
3. Ernest Alexander Cruikshank, ed., "Records of Niagara 1778-1783," Niagara Historical Society, *Publications*, no. 38 (Niagara-on-the-Lake, 1927), 9-10; B 122, p. 215, Haldimand to Hamilton, Sorel, Oct. 7, 1778.
4. Ernest Alexander Cruikshank, *The Story of Butler's Rangers* (Welland, Ont., 1893), p. 59.
5. Cruikshank, "Records of Niagara," pp. 9-10.
6. B 96, part I, p. 248, Lt.-Col. Bolton to Haldimand, Niagara, Mar. 4, 1779.
7. B 54, pp. 185-91, Haldimand to Lord George Germaine, Sept. 25, 1779; B 44, pp. 8-19, 72-80, Germaine to Haldimand, Mar. 17, April 12, 1780; Cruikshank, *Butler's Rangers*, pp. 88-90.
8. Cruikshank, "Records of Niagara," p. 31. In 1764 the Six Nations had ceded a tract on the west side of the river two miles deep under the same restrictions as the tract on the east side. The Missisaugas and Chippewas had claimed this tract and its cession was not completed until 1781 when a four-mile strip was obtained without restrictions and apparently with the consent of the Six Nations; Canada, *Indian Treaties and Surrenders from 1680 to 1890* (Ottawa, 1891), III, 196.
9. B 96, part II, pp. 145, 147, Haldimand to Bolton, July 7, 13, 1780; B 105, p. 408, a return, not dated, of progress of loyalists at Niagara.
10. Burt, *Old Province of Quebec*, pp. 365-7; B 50, p. 136-47, Lord North to Haldimand, Aug. 8, 1783; B 56, pp. 21-4, Haldimand to Townshend (private), Oct. 25, 1782; B 57, pp. 602-6, Haldimand to North, Nov. 27, 1783; B 64, pp. 318-20, Haldimand to Desbarres, Oct. 10, 1784.
11. B 162, pp. 187-9, W. Marsh to Capt. Mathews, Vermont, Feb. 29, 1784; B 162, pp. 212-15, J. Sherwood to Mathews, St. Johns, Mar. 18, 1784; B 162, pp. 272-3, Sherwood to Mathews, May 1, 1784.
12. Graham, *British Policy*, p. 49; B 56, pp. 199-202, Haldimand to North, Nov. 27, 1783.
13. B 57, part II, pp. 602-6, Haldimand to North, Nov. 27, 1783; B 63, pp. 42, Mathews to Meyer, Jan. 15, 1784; B 63, p. 118, Mathews to Wear, Quebec, Mar. 8, 1784; B 63, p. 119-22, Mathews to J. Sherwood, Quebec, Mar. 8, 1784.
14. B 162, p. 180, J. Cass to J. Sherwood, Machiche, Feb. 23, 1784.
15. B 63, pp. 76-7, Mathews to Sir J. Johnson, Quebec, Feb. 5, 1784; B 63, p. 253, Mathews to Capt. Reuter, Quebec, April 29, 1784.
16. C.O. 42/47/133-4, Hamilton to Lord Sydney, Feb. 14, 1785; C.O. 42/17/212-18, Hope to Nepean, Nov. 5, 1785.
17. Great Britain, Historical Manuscripts Commission, *Reports on Manuscripts in Various Collections* (London, 1909), VI, 146, North to W. Knox, Aug. 8, 1778.
18. Great Britain, Historical Manuscripts Commission, *Reports on American Manuscripts in the Royal Institution* (London, 1904-9), III, 417.
19. Gilroy, "The Partition of Nova Scotia," *Canadian Historical Review (C.H.R.)*, XIV (1933), 375-91.
20. Graham, *British Policy*, chaps. IV, VI.
21. B 148, pp. 147-8, 155-9, 165-6, Carleton to Haldimand, New York, June 4, July 5, Aug. 8, 1783, with returns of loyalists and troops.
22. P.A.C., *Report, 1884* (Ottawa, 1884), xli.
23. Shortt and Doughty, eds., *Documents*, I, 142.
24. John Bartlett Brebner, *The Neutral Yankees of Nova Scotia* (New York, 1937), pp. 5-6, 110-17.
25. P.A.C., Upper Canada Sundries, "Memo of W. D. Powell on the Rise, Progress and Present Situation of the Colony of Upper Canada," May 27, 1801.
26. William Canniff, *History of the Settlement of Upper Canada* (Toronto, 1869), pp. 421-5.
27. Egerton Ryerson, *The Loyalists of America and Their Times* (Toronto, 1880), II, 197.
28. B 56, pp. 65-9, Haldimand to North, June 2, 1783.
29. B 125, p. 107, Haldimand to Major Ross (private), April 26, 1783; B 124, pp. 19-21, Ross to Haldimand, Oswego, April 29, May 14, 1783; B 115, p. 106, Haldimand to Johnson, May 22, 1783; B 115, p. 113, Haldimand to Johnson, May 26, 1783; B 56, pp. 65-9, Haldimand to North, June 2, 1783.
30. Burt, *Old Province of Quebec*, p. 371. The northwest boundary of this surrender was later re-drawn, and the grant to the Six Nations, being limited by this line, did not extend as far as the source of the Grand River; Canada, *Indian Treaties*, I, 5-6, 9; P.A.O., *Report*, 1905, p. 410.

31. B 115, pp. 159-63, Haldimand to Johnson, Oct. 2, 1783.

32. B 56, pp. 23-4, Haldimand to Townshend, Quebec, Oct. 25, 1783.

33. B 122, p. 152, Hamilton to Haldimand, Detroit, Sept. 9, 1778; B 123, p. 466, Lt.-Gov. Hay to Haldimand, Detroit, July 22, 1784; B 76, pp. 286-9, Mathews to Haldimand, Detroit, Aug. 3, 1784; P.A.O., *Report*, 1905, pp. 80-291; 1928, pp. 173-96, 211-23.

34. B 115, p. 105, Johnson to Haldimand, Montreal, May 19, 1783; B 126, part I, p. 1, Haldimand to Surv. Gen. Holland, Quebec, May 26, 1783; C.O. 42/46/6, Haldimand to North, Nov. 6, 1783; B 162, pp. 99-102, "Maj. Jessup's plan for the settlement of Sir John Johnson's Regiment and the Loyal Rangers."

35. Burt, *Old Province of Quebec*, p. 370; B 158, p. 339, Johnson to Haldimand, Montreal, Dec. 1, 1783.

36. B 103, pp. 441-3, De Peyster to Haldimand, Niagara, June 28, 1784.

37. Shortt and Doughty, eds., *Documents*, II, 730, 830-1, sec. 40, 42; P.A.O., *Report*, 1929, p. 133.

38. P.A.C., Supplementary Documents, II, instructions, Quebec and Lower Canada, 1774-1811, instruction of Aug. 7, 1783.

39. Shortt and Doughty, eds., *Documents*, II, 830, 831, sec. 42.

40. Ernest Alexander Cruikshank, ed., *The Settlement of the United Empire Loyalists on the Upper St. Lawrence and Bay of Quinte in 1784* (Toronto, 1934), pp. 35, 103, 114, 117, 121, 137.

41. B 63, p. 365, Mathews to Maj. Campbell, Quebec, May 3, 1784; B 63, p. 413, Mathews to Maj. Campbell, June 17, 1784; B 64, p. 145, Mathews to Capt. Robertson, Quebec, Aug. 12, 1784.

42. C.O. 42/47/362-3, Hamilton to Sydney, July 8, 1785; C.O. 42/47/195-6, Hamilton to Sydney, April 5, 1785.

43. C.O. 42/48/36-9, Sydney to Hope, Aug. 22, 1785; but see C.O. 42/17/136-7, Hope to Nepean, Nov. 5, 1785.

44. Shortt and Doughty, eds., *Documents*, II, 813.

45. P.A.O., *Report*, 1905, p. 308; B 77, pp. 203-5, Mabane to Haldimand, Quebec, July 27, 1789.

46. Shortt and Doughty, eds., *Documents*, II, 829-33 (italics added).

47. B 77, p. 2, A. Mabane to Haldimand, Woodfield, Jan. 6, 1788; P.A.C., minutes of the Council of the old province of Quebec, Minute Book D, 321-2; P.A.O., *Report*, 1928, p. 147.

48. P.A.C., Upper Canada State Records of the Executive Council, Upper Canada Minute Books, Vol. B, p. 12. These records are hereinafter cited as U.C. State Book plus appropriate letter and page.

49. P.A.O., *Report*, 1905, p. 379; P.A.C., S series, Vol. 24, report of Collins to Dorchester, Dec. 19, 1787; Vol. 28, statement of William Empey, 1788.

50. The Rev. E. C. Cartwright, *Life and Letters of the late Hon. Richard Cartwright* (Toronto, 1876), p. 94.

51. Shortt and Doughty, eds., *Documents*, II, 941-4.

52. P.A.O., *Report*, 1928, p. 10 *et passim*.

53. Shortt and Doughty, eds., *Documents*, II, 881.

54. *Ibid.*, II, 930-41.

55. P.A.C., State Records of the Executive Council, Quebec, Minute Book E, 165-7.

56 P.A.O., *Report*, 1928, p. 11.

57. Sutro Library, San Francisco, Sir Joseph Banks Papers, Henry Robinson to Banks, Glasgow, Nov. 28, 1789, June 17, 1802.

58. Louis B. Wright and Marion Tinling, eds., *Quebec to Carolina in 1785-1786: The Travel Diary and Observations of Robert Hunter Jr., A Young Merchant of London* (San Marino, Calif., 1943), 75.

59. C.O. 42/59/103-5, Dorchester to Sydney, May 17, 1788.

60. P.A.O., *Report*, 1905, pp. 309-10, 382.

61. P.A.O., *Report*, 1928, pp. 43-4, 50-2, 56.

62. B 77, pp. 192, 205, A. Mabane to Haldimand, Woodfield, June 27, July 27, 1789.

63. B 39, p. 495, Carleton to Col. Butler, Quebec, May 18, 1777.

64. It was subsequently decided that 100 acres should be added to the first grants of soldiers to put them on a par with new settlers; P.A.O., *Report*, 1928, p. 151.

65. P.A.O., *Report*, 1905, p. 296.

66. P.A.O., *Report*, 1928, p. 68.

67. Enclosure in C.O. 42/67/205, Dorchester to Grenville, May 27, 1790.

68. See *infra*, pp. 131-41.

69. "Journals of the House of Assembly of Upper Canada" (J.H.A./U.C.), Feb. 22, 1812, in P.A.O., *Report*, 1912, p. 47.

70. P.A.O., *Report*, 1928, p. 68.
71. *Ibid.*, pp. 149-50.
72. Shortt and Doughty, eds., *Documents*, II, 831.
73. *Ibid.*, II, 731; B 45, pp. 111-12, North to Haldimand, July 2, 1783.
74. P.A.O., *Report*, 1928, p. 79.
75. William Stewart Wallace, *The United Empire Loyalists* (Toronto, 1914), p. 110. In October, 1786, the Commissary General's statement of the provisions issued to loyalists showed 5,960 loyalists in Upper Canada; Ernest Alexander Cruikshank, ed., *Records of Niagara*, p. 95.
76. Shortt and Doughty, eds., *Documents*, II, 731.
77. William Knox, *Extra Official State Papers* (London, 1789), II, App. pp. 50-1.
78. Bond, *The Quit Rent System;* St. George Louis Sioussat, "The Breakdown of the Royal Management of Lands in the Southern Provinces, 1773-1775," *Agricultural History*, III (1929), 67-98.
79. B 103, pp. 441-3, De Peyster to Haldimand, Niagara, June 28, 1784; B 162, p. 430, E. Jessup to Haldimand, River du Chene, Dec. 11, 1783; B 162, p. 227, J. Hawley to Haldimand, Machiche, April 24, 1784.
80. C.O. 42/17/201, Finlay to Nepean, Jan. 14, 1785; C.O. 42/17/183, memo by Jessup, Oct. 31, 1784; C.O. 42/61/199-200, Finlay to Nepean, July 30, 1788; C.O. 42/47/211-14, memo. of Sir J. Johnson, Dec., 1784; Shortt and Doughty, eds., *Documents*, II, 773.
81. Burt, *Old Province of Quebec*, 388-90; Shortt and Doughty, eds., *Documents*, 942-9; C.O. 42/50/5-13, Dorchester to Sydney, Quebec, Jan. 3, 1786.
82. The loyalists asked no more than that they should hold their land on the same terms as lands were granted in New Brunswick or Nova Scotia, which were subject to quit rents. One of their petitions expressly stated that they did not ask to be exempted from quit rents; Shortt and Doughty, eds., *Documents*, II, 941, 942, 945.
83. C.O. 42/51/203-6, Dorchester to Sydney, Nov. 8, 1787; C.O. 42/62/24-5, Dorchester to Sydney, Nov. 6, 1788; C.O. 42/49/53-4, memo of Carleton, Feb. 20, 1786; Shortt and Doughty, eds., *Documents*, II, 947, 1004.
84. P.A.C. G1 Series, Vol. 1, 144-52, Sydney to Dorchester, Sept. 14, 1787. No "compromise" was offered. Cf. Bond, *Quit Rent System*, p. 377.
85. Burt, *Old Province of Quebec*, p. 391; C.O. 42/51/309-17, draft instructions and Chalmers' observations thereon; G1, Vol. 1, 167-70, Sydney to Dorchester, Nov. 8, 1787.
86. William Renwick Riddell, *The Life of John Graves Simcoe* (Toronto, 1926), p. 78; Shortt and Doughty, eds., *Documents*, I, 957; C.O. 42/61/122-7, Dorchester to Sydney, Oct. 14, 1788.
87. When patents began to be issued in 1795 in exchange for certificates they contained no stipulation for the payment of quit rents.

CHAPTER THREE

1. Shortt and Doughty, eds., *Documents*, II, 1044, sec. 36.
2. Arthur G. Doughty and Duncan A. McArthur, eds., *Documents Relating to the Constitutional History of Canada* (Ottawa, 1914), pp. 59, 3, n. 4.
3. Shortt and Doughty, eds., *Documents*, II, 1047, sec. 42.
4. Doughty and McArthur, eds., *Documents*, p. 55.
5. *Ibid.*, p. 38, sec. 17; p. 51, sec. 13.
6. Labaree, *Royal Instructions*, I, 154, II, 780.
7. Duke de La Rochefoucauld-Liancourt, *Travels through the United States of North America*, trans. H. Neuman (London, 1800), I, 408.
8. P.A.O., *Report*, 1916, p. 125. W. R. Riddell, commenting on Neuman's translation, says, "The Articles of the constitution of the two Canadas as given by the translator are not at all those in the text . . ."; *ibid.*, p. 28, n. Cf. Neuman's translation of [François Alexandre Frédéric, duc de] La Rochefoucauld-Liancourt, *Voyages dans Les États-Unis d'Amérique* . . . (Paris, 1799), II, 38. Neuman strayed from the language of La Rochefoucauld and enabled Smith to contradict him by using the word *allotment*, which was certainly the function of the lieutenant-governor-in-council. But neither he nor La Rochefoucauld was wrong in implying that the provincial legislature had power to legislate respecting the Crown lands.
9. Ernest Alexander Cruikshank, ed., *The Correspondence of Lieutenant-Governor John Graves Simcoe* (Toronto, 1923-1931), I, 17-18, 28; II, 57; Graham, *British Policy*, chaps. IV and VIII.
10. "Canadian Letters. Description of a Tour through the Provinces of Lower and Upper Canada in the course of the years 1792 and 1793," *Canadian Antiquarian and Numismatic Journal*, IX, series 3, nos. 3 and 4 (July-Oct., 1912).

11. *Simcoe Correspondence*, I, 245, 251-2, 264; IV, 115-8; V, 247; Shortt and Doughty, eds., *Documents*, II, 978.
12. *Simcoe Correspondence* I, 18, 51-3; III, 265.
13. Huntington Library, San Marino, Calif., Simcoe Letter Book, Simcoe to A. McKee, June 27, 1793; Thomas Perkins Abernethy, *Western Lands and the American Revolution* (New York, 1937), pp. 357-9.
14. Dale Van Avery, *Men of the Western Waters* (Cambridge, Mass., 1956), p. 3.
15. *Simcoe Correspondence*, I, 20, 50.
16. P.A.O., Russell Papers, Russell to Simcoe, Aug. 26, 1791.
17. *Ibid.*, P. Russell to E. Russell, Aug. 15, 1791.
18. *Simcoe Correspondence*, I, 411-13.
19. Huntingdon Library, Clinton to Simcoe, Aug. 10, 1791.
20. *Simcoe Correspondence*, II, 81.
21. Oscar Zeichner, "William Smith's 'Observations on America'," New York State Historical Association, *Proceedings*, XL (1941), 328-40.
22. Graham, *British Policy*, chaps. IV and VIII.
23. P.A.O., *Report*, 1905, pp. 368-9.
24. The lines running parallel to the base lines of a township were known as concession lines and the area between two such lines as a concession.
25. P.A.O., *Report*, 1928, pp. 54-5, 62-5, 175, 194, 211, 222.
26. *Ibid.*, 1929, pp. 1-7. For the various methods of subdividing a township in use in Upper Canada, see Griffiths Taylor, "Towns and Townships in Southern Ontario," *Economic Geography*, XXI (1945) 88-96, and also Andrew F. Hunter, *A History of Simcoe County* (Barrie, Ont.: Barrie County Council, 1909), I, 40-1.
27. Simcoe was mistaken in thinking no reserves were set aside under the American system. Both the Land Ordinance of 1795 and the Act of 1796 provided for reserves, but not scattered reserves; Payson Jackson Treat, *The National Land System 1795-1820* (New York, 1910), pp. 85, 385. Reserves were also made by the State of New York; Ruth Higgins, *Expansion in New York* (Columbia, Ohio, 1931) p. 142.
28. *Simcoe Correspondence*, I, 264; III, 265-7.
29. *Ibid.*, I, 29, 33, 44, 54, 59, 145. Reserves for the Rangers were made in the township of Etobicoke; P.A.O., *Report*, 1929, p. 162.
30. William Smith, *A Historical Account of the Expedition against the Ohio Indians … under Henry Bouquet* (Cincinnati, 1868), pp. 110-20; Brebner, *Neutral Yankees*, p. 145; Higgins, *Expansion in New York*, p. 38.
31. *Simcoe Correspondence*, I, 27; La Rochefoucauld, *Travels*, I, 425.
32. *Simcoe Correspondence*, I, 142, 108-9; Doughty and McArthur, eds., *Documents*, p. 60, n. 1.
33. *Simcoe Correspondence*, I, 151, 178-9.
34. For the counties and districts of Upper Canada, see George W. Spragge, "The Districts of Upper Canada," *Ontario History*, XXIX (1947), 91-100.
35. P.A.O., *Report*, 1929, pp. 18-19, 27-28, 187-92.
36. Cartwright, *Life*, pp. 93-6.
37. P.A.O., *Report*, 1929, p. 95.
38. *Simcoe Correspondence*, I, pp. 245, 251, 254; IV, 340.
39. Cartwright, *Life*, p. 95; P.A.O., *Report*, 1916, 125, 151; La Rochefoucauld, *Travels*, I, 416-7.
40. P.A.O., *Report*, 1929, 96; P.A.O., Crown Land Papers (C.L.P.), collection labelled, "Surveyor-General's Dep't., Miscell., 1789."
41. P.A.O., *Report*, 1905, p. cxiii.
42. Milo Milton Quaife, ed., *The John Askin Papers* (Detroit, 1928-31), II, 146, 223, 241, 325-6.
43. Roy Hidemachi Akagi, *The Town Proprietors of New England* (Philadelphia, 1924).
44. *Simcoe Correspondence*, I, 33.
45. Ernest Alexander Cruikshank, "An Experiment in Colonization," Ontario Historical Society, *Papers and Records*, XXV (1920) 32-77.
46. P.A.O., *Report*, 1928, *passim*.
47. Harriet Taylor Upton, *History of the Western Reserve* (Chicago, 1910), I, 9-10; *Simcoe Correspondence*, I, 53.
48. *Simcoe Corespondence*, I, 131-3; New York Historical Society (N.Y.H.S.), Peters Papers, V, 70, Simcoe to Peters, Aug. 21, 1792.
49. Peters Papers, V, 107, Peters to Marquis of Buckingham, June 20, 1793.
50. P.A.O., *Report*, 1929, pp. 11-50.
51. *Simcoe Correspondence*, I, 339.

52. Upper Canada State Book, B, 78; Cartwright, *Life*, pp. 94-6.
53. Adam Shortt and Arthur G. Doughty, *Canada and Its Provinces* (Toronto, 1917), XVII, 43-4.
54. Cartwright, *Life*, p. 94; La Rochefoucauld, *Travels*, I, 425-6.
55. La Rochefoucauld, *Travels*, I, 413.
56. Toronto Public Libraries (T.P.L.), Elmsley Papers, Elmsley to Hunter, Mar. 5, 1801.
57. P.A.O., *Report*, 1929, pp. 29, 30, 32, 103, 108; *Simcoe Correspondence*, II, 191.
58. *Simcoe Correspondence*, IV, 109; V, 145.
59. *Ibid.*, V, 82.
60. Ernest Alexander Cruikshank, ed., *The Correspondence of the Honourable Peter Russell* (Toronto, 1932-36), III, 195; T.P.L., Russell Papers, Letter Book, D. W. Smith to Russell, Aug. 25, 1796.
61. *Simcoe Correspondence*, I, 311; T.P.L., William Jarvis Papers, B 45, p. 51, R. Eyre to Jarvis, Sept. 17, 1795.
62. P.A.O., *Report*, 1929, *passim.*
63. *Ibid.*, 1929, p. 57.
64. *Ibid.*, 1929, pp. 149, 167.
65. *Simcoe Correspondence*, I, 44, 53; II, 161; IV, 54.
66. *Ibid*, II, 57, 112, 160-61.
67. P.A.O., *Report*, 1928, pp. 15, 21.
68. *Simcoe Correspondence*, I, 293; II, 62-3; III, 57-61; IV, 165.
69. *Ibid.*, II, 84, 136, 203, 186-7; III, 58-61; IV, 230; Samuel Flagg Bemis, *Jay's Treaty* (New York, 1923), p. 237; Beverley Waugh Bond, *The Civilization of the Old Northwest* (New York, 1934), pp. 285-6.
70. Joseph Bouchette, *The British Dominions in North America* (London, 1832), I, 88-9.
71. *Simcoe Correspondence*, I, 343-4, 367.
72. *Ibid.*, II, 136.
73. *Ibid.*, II, 197, 203.
74. *Ibid.*, II, 102; IV, 66.
75. Except those at Kingston; *ibid.*, IV, 124.
76. *Ibid.*, IV, 155-8, 271-2; IV, 296.
77. *Ibid.*, IV, 296, 344.
78. *Russell Correspondence*, I, 33; *Simcoe Correspondence*, IV, 344; T.P.L., Russell Papers, Letter Book, Russell to W. Osgoode, Niagara, Sept. 7, 1796.
79. *Simcoe Correspondence*, IV, 102; V, 121; P.A.O., *Report*, 1929, p. 151; *Simcoe Correspondence*, V, 111.
80. *Simcoe Correspondence*, II, 112-13, 122, 157-63; IV, 303, 341.
81. Cartwright, *Life*, pp. 48-9; *Simcoe Correspondence*, I, 144.
82. La Rochefoucauld, *Travels*, I, 494-5; *Simcoe Correspondence*, III, 37.
83. Cartwright, *Life*, p. 55; P.A.O., *Report*, 1928, 8, 15.
84. *Simcoe Correspondence*, II, 91, 120.
85. "Canadian Letters," p. 38; *Simcoe Correspondence*, V, 76.
86. T.P.L., Russell Papers, Russell to Clinton (draft), Niagara, Dec. 27, 1794.
87. *Simcoe Correspondence*, II, 136; IV, 158.
88. The author of "Canadian Letters" states that Simcoe claimed a dispensing power and exercised it to permit the master of an American vessel, to whom he was under some obligation, to sell his cargo in Upper Canada duty free. The merchants were naturally irritated; "Canadian Letters," p. 67.
89. T.P.L., W. D. Powell Papers, B 83, p. 27.
90. "Canadian Letters," pp. 67, 161-2; William Renwick Riddell, "An Official Record of Slavery in Upper Canada," Ontario Historical Society, *Papers and Records*, XXV (1929), 393-7.
91. *Simcoe Correspondence*, I, 272-5, II, 150-2, III, 210; Richard A. Preston, *Kingston before the War of 1812* (Toronto, Champlain Soc., 1959), pp. 189-94.
92. P.A.O., Russell Papers, Russell to J. Williams, May 1, 1793.
93. *Simcoe Correspondence*, II, 124.
94. *Ibid.*, III, 136-8, 205-17.
95. T.P.L., Scadding-McGill Papers, Treasury to McGill, April 10, 1794.
96. *Simcoe Correspondence*, III, 205-17, 256-8.
97. *Ibid.*, IV, 37, 119, 136; T.P.L., Scadding-McGill Papers, Treasury to McGill, July 7, 1795.
98. Milo Milton Quaife, ed., *The John Askin Papers* (Detroit, 1928-31), I, 500.
99. *Simcoe Correspondence*, III, 152-3.
100. *Ibid.*, II, 90-1.
101. P.A.O., Russell Papers, Simcoe to Russell, July 17, 1791.

102.　*Simcoe Corespondence*, III, 153.
103.　*Ibid.*, III, 65-8.
104.　Cartwright, *Life*, pp. 54-5; T.P.L., Russell Papers, J. White to Russell, Niagara, June 30, 1796.
105.　*Russell Correspondence*, I, 52.
106.　Adam Shortt, "Founders of Canadian Banking: The Hon. John McGill . . . ," *Journal of the Canadian Bankers' Association*, XXIX (April, 1922), p. 277-90.
107.　Cartwright, *Life*, p. 55.
108.　La Rochefoucauld, *Travels*, I, 422.
109.　Duncan Campbell Scott, *John Graves Simcoe* (Toronto, 1905), p. 208.
110.　William Renwick Riddell, *The Life of John Graves Simcoe* (Toronto, 1926), pp. 283-4; La Rochefoucauld, *Travels*, I, 478; *Russell Correspondence*, I, 150; *Simcoe Correspondence*, II, 104; IV, 232, 344; V, 199.
111.　Samuel F. Bemis, *Pinckney's Treaty*, p. 322.
112.　*Simcoe Correspondence*, IV, 152, 240.
113.　T.P.L., Russell Papers, Russell to Clinton (draft), Niagara, May, 1795.
114.　S. R. Mealing, "The Enthusiasms of John Graves Simcoe," Canadian Historical Association (C.H.A.), *Report*, 1958, pp. 50-62.

CHAPTER FOUR

1.　T.P.L., Russell Letter Book, Russell to D. W. Smith, Aug. 26, 1796.
2.　Cruikshank, ed., *Russell Correspondence*, I, 22, 36, 79.
3.　P.A.O., *Report*, 1929, pp. 166-7.
4.　*Russell Correspondence*, III, 257; Higgins, *Expansion in New York*, p. 29.
5.　P.A.O., *Report*, 1929, p. 170.
6.　Doughty and McArthur, eds., *Documents*, p. 60; Cruikshank, ed., *Simcoe Correspondence*, IV, 338-9. The proclamation was reprinted at Newark in 1795, probably by disgruntled township promoters, after townships had ceased to be granted. A copy is in Upper Canada State Papers, Vol. 87.
7.　William Colgate, "Letters from the Honourable Chief Justice William Osgoode," *Ontario History*, XLVI (1954), 79-95, 141-68.
8.　*Russell Correspondence*, III, 95; T.P.L., Smith Papers, B 9, pp. 73-4, Littlehales to Phelps, Oct. 18, 1795.
9.　*Simcoe Correspondence*, IV, 233; Cruikshank, "Experiment in Colonization," p. 59; *Canada Constellation*, Sept. 13, 1799; Patrick T. C. White, ed., *Lord Selkirk's Diary 1803-1804: A Journal of His Travels in British North America and the Northeastern United States* (Champ. Soc., XXVII, Toronto, 1958), pp. 173-4; 305; James J. Talman, ed., *Loyalist Narratives from Upper Canada* (Champ. Soc., XXVII, Toronto, 1946), pp. 87-8; *Russell Correspondence*, I, 246-8.
10.　A. J. H. Richardson and Helen I. Cowan, "William Berczy's Williamsburg Documents," Rochester Historical Society, *Publications*, XX (1942) pp. 141-265; P.A.O., *Report*, 1929, p. 56.
11.　[J. C. Ogden], *A Letter from a Gentleman to his friend in England* (Philadelphia, 1795), pp. 102-3.
12.　*Russell Correspondence*, I, 167, 246-8.
13.　Colgate, "Letters from . . . Osgoode," p. 98.
14.　P.A.O., *Report*, 1929, pp. 29, 45-6.
15.　P.A.O., Richard Duncan to D. W. Smith, Dundas, July 2, Rapid Plat, July 10, 1796, and copy Smith to Duncan, n.d.; C.O. 42/324/444, Simcoe to Portland, Dec. 7, 1799.
16.　P.A.O., *Report*, 1930, pp. 2-3; 1931, p. 44.
17.　*Russell Correspondence*, II, 282; T.P.L., Russell Papers, Letter Book, Russell to Osgoode, Feb. 14, 1797; Lower Canada, Executive Council, *Extract from the minutes of Council, with a preface signed by Charles Berczy* (Quebec, 1798).
18.　T.P.L., Russell Papers, Letter Book, Russell to Liston, Jan., 18, 1788, Russell to Simcoe, June 6, 1798; P.A.O., Russell Papers, Liston to Russell, Oct. 30, 1797.
19.　P.A.O., *Report*, 1931, pp. 18, 139; *Russell Correspondence*, I, 79; C.O. 42/322/96-9, report of the Council, printed.
20.　P.A.C., Land Records of the Executive Council of Upper Canada, Minute Book D, pp. 240-2. These records are hereafter referred to as U.C. Land Book with appropriate letter and page.
21.　T.P.L., Russell Papers, Letter Book, Russell to Smith, Dec. 14, 1796; White, ed., *Selkirk*

Diary, p. 146; John Grew, *Journal of a Tour from Boston to Niagara Falls and Quebec, 1803* (privately printed, n.p., n.d.), 80.

22. T.P.L., Powell Papers, B 83, paper entitled "Notice of the pamphlet addressed to the Pres. Russell by the Executive Council—revision of the Minutes respecting Townships". For the pamphlet, see *supra* n. 19.

23. T.P.L., W. W. Baldwin Papers. These papers include a rough draft of the statements Baldwin was preparing to make to Charles Buller in answer to his request for information on the land systems that had been successively pursued. It is a more extensive commentary than is printed as Baldwin's evidence in Durham's *Report* and includes a condemnation of the way in which the system of township planting had been summarily terminated.

24. *Russell Correspondence*, I, 163-4.

25. B 76, pp. 287-9, Mathews to Haldimand, Detroit, Aug. 3, 1787. See *infra*, p. 125 and S. D. Clark, *Movements of Political Protest in Canada* (Toronto, 1959), pp. 225-6.

26. See records of land transactions in Macaulay, Cartwright, and Street Papers in P.A.O., and in William Allan papers in T.P.L. The Macaulay papers show the shifting financial interests of this and other prominent Upper Canada families during the nineteenth century.

27. T.P.L., Elmsley Papers, Elmsley to Hunter, Dec. 24, 1802.

28. P.A.O., Russel-Powell Papers, Russell to Osgoode, July 22, 1802.

29. T.P.L., Powell Papers, M 762, memo of May 5, 1802; Elmsley Papers, Elmsley to Hunter, Feb. 1, 1802.

30. N.Y.H.S., Asa Danforth to T. Green, Feb. 17, 1801; Mathew L. Davis, ed., *Memoirs of Aaron Burr with Miscellaneous Selections from his Correspondence* (New York, 1837), II, 151, 152, 155.

31. T.P.L., Powell Papers, M 762, memo of May 5, 1802; Elmsley Papers, Elmsley to Hunter, Feb. 1, 1802; P.A.O., Russell Papers, Russell to Osgoode, July 22, 1802; Richardson and Cowan, "Berczy's Williamsburg Documents," p. 146, n. 20.

32. *Simcoe Correspondence*, IV, 169.

33. P.A.O., *Report*, 1929, p. 175. T. D. Regher, in his "Land Ownership in Upper Canada, 1783-1796: A Background to the First Table of Fees," *Ontario History*, LV (1963), 35-48, has traced the history of this table of fees. See *infra*, p. 62.

34. *Simcoe Correspondence*, IV, 301-2.

35. P.A.O., *Report*, 1906, p. 186. The survey fee was £1 6s. 8½d. on every 200-acre grant and 20s. on lesser quantities. Later it became £1 7s. 6d.; U.C. Land Book C, 291-3, 296; U.C. State Book B, 150.

36. *Simcoe Correspondence*, IV, 339; U.C. State Book B, 152.

37. T.P.L., Russell Papers, Letter Book, Elmsley to Russell, Dec. 5, 1797.

38. U.C. Land Book C, 294.

39. *Simcoe Correspondence*, IV, 340-2.

40. *Russell Correspondence*, I, 210, II, 172, 210, 216, 292; C.O. 42/322/23-4, Russell to Portland, Nov. 19, 1797; C.O. 42/322/31, Russell to Portland, Dec. 21, 1797; C.O. 42/322/80-99, Russell to Portland, Feb. 20, 1798, with encl.; C.O. 42/322/169-91, Russell to Portland, July 7, 1798, with encl.; C.O. 42/108/264-77, Portland to Prescott, July 13, 1797; C.O. 42/108/168-72, Prescott to Portland, Dec. 24, 1796.

41. *Russell Correspondence*, I, 210; U.C. State Book B, 130-5; C.O. 42/322/80-96, Russell to Portland, Feb. 20, 1798.

42. T.P.L., Elmsley Papers, Elmsley to Hunter, Mar. 5, 1801.

43. *Russell Correspondence*, II, 120.

44. U.C. State Book B, 130-5.

45. P.A.O., *Report*, 1929, p. 173.

46. *Russell Correspondence*, II, 292-4; C.O. 42/324/19-24, Russell to Portland, Nov. 3, 1798.

47. G1, Vol. 53, part I, p. 85, Portland to Russell, Sept. 11, 1797.

48. U.C. State Book C, pp. A and 280; *Russell Correspondence*, II, 60; III, 62; G1, Vol. 53, part I, p. 85, Portland to Russell, Sept. 11, 1797.

49. Certain minor alterations were authorized for Upper Canada which reduced the unit of sale to 1,000 acres or less.

50. U.C. State Book B, 172-3, 179-80, 210-14.

51. *Russell Correspondence*, II, 292; C.O. 42/324/27-8, Russell to Elmsley, Oct. 26, 1798; C.O. 42/324/291, Russell to Prescott, Nov. 3, 1798.

52. Doughty and McArthur, eds., *Documents*, p. 189; P.A.C., *Preliminary Inventory, Record Group 10, Indian Affairs* (Ottawa, 1951), pp. 1-2.

53. U.C. State Papers, Vol. 60, Russell to Brant, June 10, 1799; Huntington Library, R[ichard] V[arick] to General Knox, June 19, 1792; N.Y.H.S., "O'Reilly's Western Mementos," XII, no. 57, Brant to . . . July 7, 1797; VIII, no. 272, Brant to Chapin, Dec. 11, 1792; XII, no.

10, I. Chapin to J. Brant, April 30, 1796.

54. *Simcoe Correspondence*, II, 59, 292; *Russell Correspondence*, I, 92-3.

55. Canada, *Indian Treaties*, II, 9-10.

56. N.Y.H.S., "O'Reilly's Western Mementos," XII, no. 3, Brant to Chapin, Jan. 12, 1796; IX, p. 26, Brant to Chapin, Mar. 26, 1793; XII, no. 10, Chapin to Brant, April 30, 1796.

57. *Russell Correspondence*, II, 21.

58. N.Y.H.S., "O'Reilly's Western Mementos," XII, no. 22, Brant to Chapin, July 11, 1796.

59. *Russell Correspondence*, I, 223.

60. *Ibid.*, II, 19-22; N.Y.H.S., "Records of Councils and Speeches to and from the Indian Nations in the province of Upper Canada," July 24, 1797; T.P.L., Russell Papers, Letter Book, Russell to Simcoe, Sept., 1797.

61. See *supra* chap. IV.

62. *Russell Correspondence*, I, 48-9, 84, 131-6. Charles M. Johnston's article "The Grand River Lands and the Northwest Crisis," *Ontario History*, LV (1963) 267-282, which has appeared since this book was submitted to the press, gives a more extended discussion of the "war of nerves" to which Brant subjected Russell.

63. *Russell Correspondence*, II, 186.

64. *Ibid.*, II, 123, 135, 185. The Indians wanted to reserve land on either side of all the creeks and two or three chains along the shore; letters of Brant to W. Claus and reports of Claus in P.A.C., Record Group 10, A1, Vol. 1.

65. *Russell Correspondence*, II, 138, 247, 271.

66. The French Royalists were a group of *émigré* nobles and their followers whom the British government permitted to settle as colonists in Upper Canada and to whom it granted land, and other forms of assistance, in proportion to their rank. The project failed, however; see Lucy Elizabeth Textor, *A Colony of Émigrés in Canada*, University of Toronto Studies in History and Economics, III, no. 1 (Toronto, 1905); John Weatherford, "The Vicomte de Vaux: Would-Be Canadian," *Ontario History*, XLVII (1954), 49-57; Janet Carnochan, "The Comte de Puisaye: A forgotten page of Canadian History," Ontario Historical Society, *Papers and Records*, V (1910), 36-52.

67. U.C. State Papers, Vol. 60, Russell to Brant, June 10, 1799.

68. Canada, *Indian Treaties*, I, 35-6.

69. U.C. State Book, I, pp. 265-8.

70. *Russell Correspondence*, III, 172; Canniff, *Settlement of Upper Canada*, p. 226.

71. John Mills Jackson, *A view of the political situation of the province of Upper Canada in North America* (London, 1809), p. 24.

72. T.P.L., Smith Papers, B 6, p. 47; G1, Vol. 53, 161-9 (extract), Portland to Prescott, June 8, 1798.

73. T.P.L., Elmsley Papers, Elmsley to Hunter, Nov. 12, 1799.

74. U.C. Land Book D, 478-9, 483-4.

75. *Russell Correspondence*, III, 12, 173.

76. C.O. 42/325/329-33, Hunter to Portland, Sept. 1, 1800; U.C. State Book B, 363; Land Book F, 44.

77. Shortt and Doughty, eds., *Documents*, II, 1044.

78. Doughty and McArthur, eds., *Documents*, p. 59, n. 3.

79. L.C. State Book A, 212, 214; C.O. 42/90/102-7, Grenville to Clarke, Nov. 8, 1792; C.O. 42/94/190-2, Report of Land Committee, May 18, 1793; C.O. 42/108/169-72, Prescott to Portland, Dec. 24, 1796.

80. P.A.O., *Report*, 1929, p. 13.

81. *Simcoe Correspondence*, II, 52; P.A.O., *Report* 1929, p. 28.

82. *Simcoe Correspondence*, II, 185; Colgate, "Letters from ... Osgoode," p. 151; C.O. 42/108/264-77, Portland to Prescott, July 13, 1797.

83. C.O. 42/320/62-87, report of D. W. Smith, Nov. 9, 1795.

84. *Simcoe Correspondence*, II, 51-2, 184-5.

85. T.P.L., Smith Papers, B 9, pp. 379-83; Sir Charles Prestwood Lucas, ed., *Lord Durham's Report on the Affairs of British North America* (Oxford, 1912), III, 1-4.

86. Regher, "Land Ownership in Upper Canada," p. 46.

87. P.A.O., *Report*, 1929, pp. 23, 146; *Simcoe Correspondence*, IV, 149.

88. P.A.O., *Report*, 1929, p. 146.

89. P.A.C., Upper Canada Sundries, memo of W. D. Powell to Lt.-Gov. Hunter, May 27, 1801.

90. *Simcoe Correspondence*, IV, 185-6.

91. *Ibid.*, IV, 146-50.

92. P.A.O., *Report*, 1906, pp. lxxxvi, 32.

93. *Simcoe Correspondence*, IV, 149.

94. Cartwright, *Life*, p. 87.
95. *Ibid.*, p. 89.
96. *Simcoe Correspondence*, I, 141, III, 57.
97. *Ibid.*, IV, 162.
96. *Simcoe Correspondence*, I, 141, III, 57.
97. *Ibid.*, IV, 162.
98. La Rochefoucauld wrote, ". . . ils [les titres] ne leur sont remis qu'après un tems [*sic*] plus ou moins prolongé par la volonté du Conseil; . . . La Protection, la Conaissance des bons colons fait sans doute délivrer quelquefois ces titres et facilite ainsi les secondes ventes, mais ces faveurs sont partielles et toujours arbitraires"; *Voyages*, II, 53-4.
Neuman wrote, "The lands are indeed given away gratis; a certificate . . . gives the new settler a right to the usufruct of these lands; but the property thereof is sooner or later transferred, according to the will of the Council. To the best of my knowledge, none of these free grants includes a transfer of the right of property . . . The Canadian planter has to look for the permanency of his possession merely to the will and pleasure of the governor. Interest and an acquaintance with substantial and respectable settlers may, no doubt, procure him sooner the right of property and thus facilitate a second sale. But favours of this kind are always confined to a part of the estate, and depend on the arbitrary will of the Council"; La Rochefoucauld, *Travels*, L, 423-4.
99. *Simcoe Correspondence*, IV, 76, 162.
100. C.O. 42/320/45-109, Simcoe to Portland, Dec. 22, 1795, with encl.
101. *Simcoe Correspondence*, IV, 141-3.
102. *Ibid.*, IV, 141.
103. *Ibid.*, IV, 186-7; T.P.L., Powell Papers, n.d., B 83, p. 29.
104. *Simcoe Correspondence*, IV, 136-8, 147-9.
105. *Ibid.*, IV, 146-50, 162-3, 178, 188-90.
106. P.A.C., Upper Canada Sundries, memo of Powell to Hunter, May 27, 1801.
107. P.A.O., *Report*, 1930, p. 21.
108. *Ibid.*, pp. 8-9.
109. *Simcoe Correspondence*, IV, 149-50.
110. G1, Vol. 53, part I, pp. 11-19, Portland to Simcoe, April 22, 1796; U.C. Sundries, April 18, 1796.
111. T.P.L., Russell Papers, W. Osgoode to Russell, Jan. 20, 1797.
112. *Russell Correspondence*, II, 22-7.
113. *Simcoe Correspondence*, IV, 248.
114. P.A.O., Russell Papers, "Diary of P. Russell," July 1 to Aug. 10, 1797.
115. P.A.O., Russell Papers, Russell to Hunter, Aug. 25, 1800.
116. C.O. 42/320/369-73, Powell to Portland, Upper Canada, July 21, 1796; C.O. 42/284/61, Powell to King, Upper Canada, Nov. 20, 1797.
117. Quaife, ed., *Askin Papers*, II, 241, 315, 447.
118. The Heir and Devisee Act of 1805 was silent on the subject of majority decisions and restricted the issuing of commissions to the Justices and the members of the Executive Council.
119. C.O. 42/328/1, Hunter to Portland, Aug. 27, 1801, with encl.
120. Quaife, ed., *Askin Papers*, II, 260.
121. P.A.O., *Report*, 1929, p. 105; U.C. State Book B, p. 10; Quaife, ed., *Askin Papers*, II, 232-4, 466; T.P.L., Smith Papers, B 5, p. 265.
122. U.C. Land Book D, p. 239; *Russell Correspondence*, II, 279, 246.
123. Quaife, ed., *Askin Papers*, II, 146; White, ed.,*Selkirk Diary*, p. 146.
124. G1, Vol. 60, p. 90, Bathurst to Maitland, Dec. 6, 1822.
125. P.A.O., Crown Land Paper (C.L.P.), "Surveyor-General's Dept., Miscellaneous, 1789," Proclamation, Nov. 6, 1794.
126. Quaife, ed., *Askin Papers*, II, 232-3, 241.
127. U.C. Land Book D, pp. 421, 437.
128. Quaife, ed., *Askin Papers*, II, 300-301.
129. *Ibid.*, II, 238.
130. The Act of 1797 had been extended by U.C. Stat. 39 Geo. III, c. 2.
131. Canniff, *Settlement of Upper Canada*, p. 170.
132. U.C. Stat. 45 Geo. III, c. 2, and 48 Geo. III, c. 10.
133. The records of the Heir and Devisee Commission for the years 1797-1805 included at one time ten report books in which the awards were reported in summary form. I found in P.A.O. and used numbers 5, 6, 7, 9, and 10.
134. *Simcoe Correspondence*, IV, 185-6; P.A.C., Askin Papers, Askin to W. Robertson, Sept. 18, 1800.

135. The last meeting of the commissioners occurred in January, 1796, but the Commission was not abolished until 1911; William Renwick Riddell, *The Life of William Dummer Powell* (Lansing, Mich., 1924), 215, n. 14.

CHAPTER FIVE

1. T.P.L., Russell Papers, White to Russell, July 5, 1796; Cruikshank, ed., *Simcoe Correspondence*, I, 142-3, II, 36-7; Burt, *Old Province of Quebec*, p. 148.
2. Ontario Historical Society, *Papers and Records*, XLVI (1954), 88, Osgoode to Simcoe, Jan. 30, 1795.
3. *Simcoe Correspondence*, II, 307; P.A.O., *Report*, 1929, p. 83; Shortt and Doughty, eds., *Documents*, II, 732, 831.
4. P.A.O., *Report*, 1906, pp. 184-5; U.C. State Book B, 113-16.
5. C.O. 42/320/369-97, Powell to Portland, July 21, 1796; T.P.L., Powell Papers, B 83, pp. 27-34 (vindication of a letter to Lieutenant-Governor Simcoe of July 2).
6. Shortt and Doughty, eds., *Documents*, II, 831, sec. 42.
7. P.A.O., *Report*, 1930, p. 26.
8. U.C. State Book B, 87.
9. U.C. State Book B, 12; P.A.O., *Report*, 1931, p. 169.
10. See *infra*, p. 66; *Simcoe Correspondence*, IV, 339.
11. C.O. 42/108/169-72, Prescott to Portland, Dec. 24, 1796; C.O. 42/110/29-35, Prescott to Portland, Dec. 16, 1797; C.O. 42/322/180-91, Russell to Portland, July 17, 1798.
12. C.O. 42/322/23-4, Russell to Portland, Nov. 19, 1797.
13. U.C. State Book B, 122, 130-8.
14. C.O. 42/322/80-95, Russell to Portland, Feb. 20, 1798.
15. C.O. 42/322/128-216, Russell to Portland, Feb. 20, 1798, with encl.
16. Cf. S. R. Mealing, "D. W. Smith's Plan for Granting Land to Loyalists' Children," *Ontario History*, XLVIII (1954), 133-7.
17. G1, Vol. 53, 161, Portland to Prescott, June 8, 1798; Cruikshank, ed., *Russell Correspondence*, II, 172.
18. P.A.O., *Report*, 1906, p. 194.
19. *Russell Correspondence*, II, 222-4.
20. P.A.O., *Report*, 1906, p. 196.
21. C.O. 42/324/349, Hunter to King, Oct. 27, 1799; G1, Vol. 53, part II, 444, Portland to Hunter, Jan. 6, 1801.
22. Gilbert C. Paterson, *Land Settlement in Upper Canada:* The Sixteenth Report of the Ontario Public Archives (Toronto, 1921) prints the returns in App. A., from which these averages have been computed.
23. *Russell Correspondence*, II, 159.
24. P.A.O., *Report*, 1930, 1931, *passim.*
25. P.A.O., C.L.P., "Letters Received, Surveyor-General's Office", no. 7, p. 12; P.A.O., *Report*, 1930, pp. 93, 111, 154, 173.
26. T.P.L., Smith Papers, Elmsley to Smith, Feb. 28, 1798.
27. P.A.O., *Report*, 1930, p. 85, 1931, *passim*; P.A.O., C.L.P. "Letters Received, Surveyor-General's Office", no. 7, p. 205.
28. *Russell Correspondence*, I, 163-4; C.O. 42/322/143, Portland to Russell, Nov. 5, 1798.
29. *Simcoe Correspondence*, V, 191-2; P.A.O., *Report*, 1929, p. 147; *Letter from an American Loyalist in Upper Canada to his friend in England on a pamphlet published by John Mills Jackson*, Esquire (York, 1810), p. 20. Jackson's criticisms on this point were fully justified. Down to 1807, about 163,400 acres of land had been conferred on the civil officials of Upper Canada, not including members of the legislature of which 19,000 acres were granted under standing instructions, 44,400 by special instructions, 38,150 by Simcoe, and 55,700 by Russell; C.O. 42/350/31-2, encl. in Gore to Castlereagh, Jan. 9, 1810.
30. *Russell Correspondence*, II, 60; U.C. State Book B, 199.
31. Quaife, ed., *Askin Papers*, II, 241.
32. P.A.C., *Report*, 1892, note D, pp. 39, 51.
33. Macaulay was the supposed author of *A Letter on Canada in 1806 and 1817, during the Administration of Governor Gore* (privately printed, 1853).
34. Riddell, *Life of Powell*, pp. 92-3.
35. U.C. State Book B, 427-8; White, ed., *Selkirk's Diary*, p. 156.
36. U.C. State Book B, 459-62.
37. U.C. State Book B, 461.

38. U.C. Sundries, James Green to D. W. Smith, Aug. 12, 1801.
39. *Russell Correspondence*, III, 78.
40. T.P.L., Smith Papers, B 9, 229-30.
41. P.A.C., *Report*, 1892, note D, p. 72; U.C. Land Books D, 794-803; F, p. 161.
42. P.A.C., *Report*, 1892, note D, pp. 70, 91.
43. *Ibid.*, note D, p. 62.
44. *Ibid.*, note D, pp. 72, 91.
45. U.C. Land Book F, pp. 60,383.
46. William Kingsford, *The History of Canada* (Toronto, 1889-1898), VIII, 100.
47. U.C. State Book B, 150-2; U.C. Land Book E, 362.
48. Kingsford, *Canada*, VIII, 100.
49. Jackson, *A View*, App. no. 5.
50. T.P.L., Upper Canada Land Papers, "List of Free Grants Remaining in the Secretary's Office."
51. U.C. State Book B, 150, 410-14.
52. *Russell Correspondence*, III, 290; U.C. Land Book D, 252.
53. U.C. State Papers, Vol. 40, pp. 105-17, Memo of Jarvis; S. R. Mealing, "D. W. Smith's Plan."
54. U.C. Land Book D, 252, 566-7, Land Book E, 181-5, 289; State Book C, 270, 281, 406-7.
55. U.C. Land Book F, 61.
56. P.A.C., *Report*, 1892, note D, p. 91.
57. Quaife, ed., *Askin Papers*, II, 493. This regulation is probably the basis of Thorpe's charge that "the loyalist that was entitled to land without fees, could not get any, but the alien that could pay was sure of succeeding . . ."; note D, p. 39.
58. P.A.C., *Report*, 1892, note D, p. 47.
59. *A Letter on Canada in 1806 and 1817*, p. 15.
60. *Russell Correspondence*, III, 20.
61. On every grant subject to fees the Lieutenant-Governor received, under the regulations of 1796, £1 and sums varying from 13*s.* 7*d.* to £1 1*s.*, according to the size of the grant under the regulations of 1804; P.A.O., *Report*, 1929, p. 174; U.C. State Book C, 409.
62. U.C. Land Book F, 79.
63. *Ibid.*, 139; P.A.O., orders and regulations I, 92.
64. Riddell, *Life of Powell*, p. 92.
65. U.C. Land Book F, p. 139.
66. *Lord Durham's Report on the Affairs of British North America*, App. B., p. 99. The Report, with appendices, is to be found in Great Britain, House of Commons, *Sessional Papers*, 1839, XVII, 1-690. This source is hereafter cited as *Durham's Report*. W. A. Langton, ed., *Early Days in Upper Canada: Letters of John Langton from the Backwoods of Upper Canada and the Audit Office of the Province of Canada* (Toronto, 1926), p. 14.
67. P.A.C., Manuscript Division, *Preliminary Inventory, Record Group 1, Executive Council Records, 1764-1867* (Ottawa, 1953), pp. 27-8.
68. T.P.L., Powell Papers, M, 762.
69. U.C. State Papers, Vol. 34, Jarvis to Clerk of the Council, Oct. 21, 1800; T.P.L., Russell Papers, Thomas Welch to Russell, Charlotteville, Oct. 12, Dec. 20, 1803, July 9, Dec. 21, 1804.
70. U.C. Land Book D, p. 701; Land Book E, 152, 155, 309. Figures have been compiled from Abstracts of Auditor's Docket Books of Grants which had passed the Great Seal. These are printed in calendars of the Q series. As Hunter died in August, 1805, and Grant was not sworn in until September, three-fourths of the total number of grants for 1805 have been included in this estimate.
71. T.P.L., Powell Papers, M, 762; T.P.L., Smith Papers, B 10, p. 327.
72. From the London district, patents were returned to the Secretary; T.P.L., Russell Papers, Welch to Russell, May 18, 1805.
73. T.P.L., Powell Papers, A 30.
74. Riddell, *Life of Powell*, p. 93.
75. C.O. 42/350/301-5, Gore to Liverpool, Sept. 10, 1810.
76. T.P.L., Smith Papers, B 8, pp. 51-2.
77. Riddell, "Mr. Justice Thorpe," *Canadian Law Times*, XL (1920), 907-24.
78. Paterson, *Land Settlement*, p. 103.
79. S. R. Mealing, "D. W. Smith's Plan."
80. C.O. 42/340/92, Allcock to Adam Gordon, Worcester, April 21, 1805.
81. U.C. State Papers, Vol. 40, 105-17, memo of Jarvis; U.C. State Book E, 176-82.
82. Quaife, ed., *Askin Papers*, II, 399; Cartwright, *Life*, pp. 89-90.

83. P.A.C.,*Report*, 1892, note D, p. 51.
84. Quaife, ed., *Askin Papers*, II, 493.
85. P.A.C., *Report*, 1921, App. 3, pp. 79-80.
86. Kingsford, *Canada*, VII, 519-20. The following lines, taken from a lengthy piece of doggerel copied down inaccurately by Powell and found among his papers in T.P.L., illustrate the spirit that prevailed after Hunter's departure:

Seballon Long on Genl. Hunter's Administration

We sacrificed our living our laws for to maintain
Thro wars our blood was given our honour to retain
Like heathen we suffered, for loyalty did bleed
And now ye bloody subjects come pay for your deeds.

. . . in spite of old H. we'll not pay for our Deeds.
The man that has the money he need not fear commands
He Loyalty can purchase besides our noble lands
And if he be a rebel too who against the King did bleed
It's money, Boys, it's money will fetch the ready Deed.

CHAPTER SIX

1. Matilda Edgar, *Ten Years of Upper Canada in Peace and War, 1800-1815; being the Ridout Letters with Annotations* (Toronto, 1890), p. 21.
2. Hunter died at Quebec, Aug. 21, 1805. Grant was sworn in as Administrator on Sept. 11, 1805, and Gore on Aug. 25, 1806.
3. William Renwick Riddell in his "*Scandalum Magnatum* in Upper Canada," *Journal of the American Institute of Criminal Law and Criminology*, IV (1913-14), 12-19, expresses the opinion that much of Thorpe's radicalism was due to spite and disappointment at not being made Chief Justice.
4. Quaife, ed., *Askin Papers*, II, 506.
5. J.H.A./U.C., Feb. 10, 1806, in P.A.O., *Report*, 1911, pp. 64, 68-70, 81. As Grant reminded the Assembly, it was only the sons of loyalists who were obliged to come to York.
6. U.C. State Book D, 220, 235-6.
7. J.H.A./U.C., Feb. 21, 1806 in P.A.O., *Report*, 1911, p. 81.
8. U.C. State Book C, 275-80.
9. U.C. State Book D, 103; see *supra*, p. 70.
10. U.C. Sundries, Russell to Gore, Sept. 6, 1806.
11. U.C. State, Book E, 130.
12. P.A.C., *Report*, 1892, note D, p. 36.
13. J.H.A./U.C., Feb. 12, Mar. 1, 1806, in P.A.O., *Report*, 1911, pp. 79, 107.
14. P.A.C., *Report*, 1892, note D, pp. 32, 36.
15. *Ibid.*, note D, p. 36.
16. J.H.A./U.C., Mar. 3, 1806, in P.A.O., *Report*, 1911, p. 113.
17. *Ibid.*, p. 114; Jackson, *A View*, p. 27.
18. Kingsford, *Canada*, VIII, chap. V; P.A.C., *Report*, 1892, note D, pp. 85-6; William Stewart Wallace, *The Family Compact*, Chronicles of Canada, XXIV (Toronto, 1915), p. 9.
19. J.H.A./U.C., Feb. 19, 1805, in P.A.O., *Report*, 1911, p. 32.
20. *Ibid.*, p. 48.
21. P.A.C., *Report*, 1892, note D, pp. 53-5, 61, 65, 81, 113; T.P.L., Powell Papers, A 28, Gore to Powell, Mar. 8, 1819.
22. Jackson, *A View*, App. p. 9.
23. *Letters from an American Loyalist*, p. 89.
24. P.A.C., *Report*, 1892, note D, pp. 69-71.
25. *Ibid.*, note D, pp. 74, 98.
26. C.O. 42/347/211-13, Thorpe to . . . , Sept. 18, 1807.
27. Jackson, *A View*, App., p. 9.
28. *Ibid.*, *A View*, App., p. 101; see *supra*, p. 70.
29. *Letters from an American Loyalist*, p. 23, 43, 91; T.P.L., Powell Papers, Gore to Powell, Jan. 26, 1811; G1, Vol. 56, p. 30, Gore to Liverpool, Aug. 15, 1811; G1, Vol. 56, p. 251, Peel to Brock, Aug. 14, 1812.
30. P.A.C., *Report*, 1892, note D, p. 90.
31. C.O. 42/350/20, Gore to Castlereagh, Jan. 9, 1810; Jackson, *A View*, p. 11.

32. U.C. State Book D, 291-2.
33. P.A.C., *Report*, 1892, note D, p. 56.
34. *Ibid.*, note D, pp. 97-100.
35. J.H.A./UC, Mar. 4, 1807, in P.A.O., *Report*, 1911, p. 168.
36. *Ibid.*, p. 255.
37. J.H.A./U.C., Mar. 4, 1812, in P.A.O., *Report*, 1912, p. 84.
38. J.H.A./U.C., Feb. 2, 1807, in P.A.O., *Report*, 1911, p. 122.
39. Except Washburn and Thorpe; *ibid.*, p. 175.
40. P.A.O., *Report*, 1892, note D, p. 62.
41. *Ibid.*, p. 75.
42. W. P. M. Kennedy, *Documents of the Canadian Constitution* (Toronto, 1918), p. 165.
43. Shortt and Doughty, eds., *Documents*, II, 1004.
44. P.A.C., *Report*, 1892, note D, p. 71.
45. J.H.A./U.C., Mar. 3, 1806, in P.A.O., *Report*, 1911, p. 114.
46. P.A.C., *Report*, 1892, note D, p. 92; see *infra*, p. 128.
47. J.H.A./U.C., Feb. 12, 1807, in P.A.O., *Report*, 1911, pp. 137, 148, 159.
48. P.A.C., *Report*, 1892, note D, pp. 73, 114.
49. *Ibid.*, note D, p. 63.
50. J.H.A./U.C., Mar. 4, 1807, in P.A.O., *Report*, 1911, p. 168.
51. P.A.C., *Report*, note D, p. 115.
52. *Letters from an American Loyalist*, p. 57.
53. Jackson, *A View*, p. 7.
54. *Letters from an American Loyalist*, pp. 30-1.
55. G1, Vol. 55, p. 115, Castlereagh to Gore, June 19, 1807, with encl.
56. *Letters from an American Loyalist*, p. 26.
57. See *infra*, pp. 156, 157, n. 39.
58. J.H.A./U.C., Mar. 10, 1810, Mar. 4, 1811, in P.A.O., *Report*, 1911, pp. 372, 452, and Mar. 2, 1812, in P.A.O., *Report*, 1912, p. 73.
59. U.C. Stat. 1 & 2 Will. IV, c. 23.
60. William Renwick Riddell, "William Firth," *Canadian Bar Review* I (1923), 326-37, 404-17.
61. J.H.A./U.C., Feb. 21, 1808, in P.A.O., *Report*, 1911, p. 228. The *Upper Canada Guardian* of Sept. 3, 1807, hints that one-time critics have been bribed into silence. This issue, and extracts from other issues were included in C.O. 42/350/231-51, Gore to Liverpool, Aug. 9, 1810, contain many paragraphs of vague accusations.
62. J.H.A./U.C., Jan. 30, Feb. 18, 1808, in P.A.O., *Report*, 1911, pp. 199, 225.
63. C.O. 42/350/5-126, Gore to Castlereagh, Feb. 1, 1810.
64. J.H.A./U.C., Mar. 10, 1808, in P.A.O., *Report*, 1911, p. 369; T.P.L., Powell Papers, A 27, Gore to Powell, Mar. 6, 1808.
65. Edgar, *Ridout Letters*, p. 31.
66. J.H.A./U.C., Mar. 10, 1810, in P.A.O., *Report*, 1911, pp. 368-77.
67. *Ibid.*, pp. 360-65.
68. *Ibid.*, p. 376.
69. T.P.L., W. W. Baldwin Papers, Baldwin to Firth, June 12, 1812.

CHAPTER SEVEN

1. C.O. 42/355/18-20, Drummond to Bathurst, Kingston, Mar. 20, 1813; C.O. 42/156/131-2, Drummond to Prevost, Quebec, Feb. 19, 1814.
2. G1, Vol. 6, pp. 27, 47, Bathurst to Prevost, Oct. 29, 1813, Sept. 8, 1814.
3. U.C. State Book E, p. 217; U.C. Sundries, Nov. 27, 1809.
4. George W. Spragge, ed., *The John Strachan Letter Book*, 1812-34 (Toronto, 1946), p. 166. Strachan's statement is not borne out by the return of deserters to be found in Vol. 5 of the Civil Secretary's Letter Books. This source shows 83 deserters in both the Leeds and the London districts, of whom 11 and 5 respectively were not born in the United States. This may be the return Gourlay says he was promised but did not receive; Robert Fleming Gourlay, *The Banished Briton and Neptunian* (Boston, 1843), p. 209.
5. C.O. 42/356/69, Robinson to Bathurst, July 29, 1815.
6. G1, Vol. 6, 43, 47, Bathurst to Prevost, July 12, Sept. 8, 1814; C 622, p. 135, General Order of Dec. 6, 1814, signed "E. Baynes, Adjutant General". Subsequently, this privilege was extended to soldiers discharged elsewhere.
7. P.A.C., E series, "Minutes of the Land Committee of the Executive Council of the Province of Canada," Land Book A, p. 351. These records are hereinafter referred to as Prov.

Can. Land Book with appropriate letter and page.

8. G1, Vol. 62, p. 407, Bathurst to Maitland, Nov. 30, 1826; G1, Vol. 17, 432, Hay to Dalhousie, July 25, 1828; G1, Vol. 58, p. 172, Bathurst to Gore, July 30, 1817.

9. C.O. 42/165/122, Campbell to Bathurst with encl., Edinburgh, Mar. 28, 1815.

10. Helen I. Cowan, *British Emigration to British North America*, 1783-1837 (Toronto, 1929), p. 68.

11. C.O.42/354/185-6, Gore to Goulburn, April 3, 1813; see *supra*, chap. v. n. 17.

12. G1, Vol. 58, p. 4, Bathurst to Gore, Jan. 8, 1816.

13. U.C. State Book F, 228-9.

14. G1, Vol.7, pp. 10-23, Bathurst to Drummond, June 13, 1814.

15. G1, Vol. 6, p. 47, Bathurst to Prevost, Sept. 8, 1814.

16. See *infra*, p. 128.

17. U.C. Sundries, Mar. 8, 1815.

18. U.C. Sundries, Ridout's report of Feb. 23, 1816; U.C. State Book F, 228-9.

19. U.C. Sundries, Beckwith to Gore, Feb. 3, 1816.

20. C.O. 42/357/10, 20, 41, Drummond to Gore, Nov. 25, 1815; Gore to Drummond, Dec. 11, 1815, Feb. 23, 1816.

21. C 621, p. 103, Beckwith to Drummond, Quebec, Nov. 21, 1815; Robert Fleming Gourlay, *A Statistical Account of Upper Canada* (London, 1822), I, 540.

22. U.C. Sundries, Beckwith to Gore, Feb. 3, 1816.

23. *Ibid.*, Rogers' report, May 23, 1816.

24. *Ibid.*, Rogers to Ridout, April 22, 1816.

25. T.P.L., Powell Papers, A 29, Gore to Powell, n.d.

26. U.C. Sundries, Rogers to the Surveyor General, Dec. 16, 1816.

27. C.O. 42/357/41, Gore to Drummond, Feb. 23, 1816.

28. U.C. Sundries, Drummond to Gore, Mar. 15, 1816.

29. T.P.L., Powell Papers, A 29, Gore to Powell, n.d.

30. C.O. 42/357/35, Gore to Bathurst, Feb. 23, 1816.

31. Report and map by Beckwith in U.C. Sundries, Mar. 16, 1818.

32. Gourlay, *Statistical Account*, I, 540.

33. *Ibid.*, I, 542.

34. C 623, p. 137, Bathurst to Administrator of Upper Canada, Sept. 8, 1817; C 624, p. 80, Cockburn to Sherbrooke, Quebec, July 13, 1818.

35. The Rev. William Bell, *Hints to emigrants; in a series of letters from Upper Canada* (Edinburgh, 1824), pp. 73, 80; Cowan, *British Immigration*, p. 74; C 623, p. 22, dupl., Bathurst to Sherbrooke, April 14, 1817.

36. C.O. 42/175/126-9, Sherbrooke to Bathurst, Nov. 26, 1817; C.O. 42/167/277-9, Sherbrooke to Bathurst, Nov. 20, 1816; C.O. 42/174,, 202-5, Sherbrooke to Bathurst, Aug. 20, 1817.

37. C.O. 42/175/132-5, Sherbrooke to Administrator of Upper Canada, Aug. 27, 1817.

38. C.O. 42/357/41, Gore to Drummond, Feb. 23, 1816; T.P.L., Powell Papers, A 29, Gore to Powell, n.d.

39. C 623, pp. 113-20, Captain Fowler to Deputy Quarter-Master General Myers, Aug. 7, 1817; U. C. Sundries, Ridout to Gore, April 10, 1817.

40. C.O. 42/359/15-84, copies of correspondence between Gore and Sherbrooke and reports of the Executive Council; U.C. Land Book J, 38-40.

41. T.P.L., Powell Papers, A 27, Gore to Powell, Aug. 19, 1817.

42. C.O. 42/173/56-9, Sherbrooke to Bathurst, Jan. 13, 1815; C.O. 42/167/336-41, Sherbrooke to Bathurst, Dec. 19, 1816; C 623, pp. 122-3, Ridout to Superintendant Fowler, July 29, 1817.

43. C 623, pp. 113, 122-3, Fowler to Myers, Aug. 7, 1817, and Ridout to Fowler, July 29, 1817; C.O. 42/175/132-5, Sherbrooke to Administrator of Upper Canada, Nov. 25, 1817.

44. C.O. 42/175/130-3, Sherbrooke to Administrator of Upper Canada, Aug. 27, Nov. 25, 1817; U.C. Sundries, Fowler to Ridout, July 8, Sept. 29, 1817.

45. C.O. 42/175/136-7, Smith to Sherbrooke, Oct. 20, 1817, with encl.

46. After 1816 civilian immigrants did not receive rations; C.O. 42/175/130-31, Sherbrooke to Bathurst, Nov. 10, 1817.

47. C 623, pp. 162-5, Bathurst to Sherbrooke, Nov. 10, 1817.

48. G1, Vol. 10, pp. 42-51, Bathurst to Sherbrooke, May 16, 1818.

49. Cowan, *British Immigration*, pp. 77-82; Bell, *Hints to emigrants*, p. 80.

50. G1, Vol. 60, pp. 114-7, Bathurst to Maitland, May 6, 1820.

51. C.O. 42/187/166-76, reports on settlement by the Deputy Quarter-Master General, May 20, 1821; U.C. Land Book M, 578-83; C 623, pp. 54-72, Cockburn to Dalhousie, with encl., Quebec, May 22, 1821; C 631, p. 42, Marshall's report on advances to settlers, Mar. 8, 1829.

52. Robert Lamond, *A Narrative of the Rise and Progress of Emigration to the New Settlements in Upper Canada on Government Grant* (Reprint: San Francisco, 1940), pp. 70, 84.

53. C 627, pp. 68-9, Dalhousie to Maitland, Mar. 15, 1822.

54. P.A.C., Upper Canada Land Petitions P, nos. 47, 77.

55. U.C. Sundries, May 23, 1816.

56. C 627, p. 141, return of persons in military Settlements of Upper Canada, April 22, 1824.

57. G1, Vol. 58, p. 131, Bathurst to Gore, Jan. 10, 1817; C.O. 42/177/35-6, Buchanan to Goulburn, New York, April 10, 1817; C.O. 42/177/45, Buchanan to Bathurst, New York, June 3, 1817. On the verso is a draft of the countermanding instructions.

58. C.O. 42/357/318-9, Gore to Buchanan, July 31, 1816; C.O. 42/359/145-6, Gore to Bathurst, April 28, 1817; G1, Vol. 58, p. 72, Bathurst to Gore, July 30, 1817.

59. C 627, p. 20, return showing the appropriation of land; Q 179A, p. 16, Cockburn to Dalhousie, May 22, 1818. For Maitland's views, see *infra*, chap. xii.

60. Lamond, *A Narrative*, p. 68; Bell, *Hints to emigrants*, p. 80.

61. C 628, pp. 39-42, Bathurst to Maitland, Dec. 7, 1822.

62. U.C. Sundries, May 14, 1821, location ticket for military settlers.

63. U.C. Land Books K, L, and M, *passim*.

64. See the deed records in the registry office at Perth.

65. Lamond, *A Narrative*, pp. 36-8, 75.

66. C.O. 42/425/3-7, report of Rankin on the District of Bathurst.

67. Ontario Agricultural Commission (O.A.C.), *Report* (Toronto, 1881), 11, 271-81.

68. C 631, pp. 114-9, Captain Marshall's report.

69. U.C. Land Book O, 65.

70. G1, Vol. 15, p. 61, Bathurst to Dalhousie, Mar. 11, 1821; C.O. 42/393/225-7, Colborne to Goderich, April 17, 1831; C.O. 42/419/2-16, Colborne to Goderich, May 2, 1833, with encl.

71. C.O. 42/425/1-7, Colborne to Spring-Rice, Jan. 3, 1835, with Rankin's report encl.

72. U.C. Land Books S, 206-16, T, 538-9; G1, Vol. 76, pp. 96-8, Glenelg to Head, Feb. 4, 1836.

73. Cowan, *British Emigration*, pp. 96-101.

74. *Ibid.*, p. 105; Basil Hall, *Travels in North America in the Years 1827 and 1828* (Edinburgh, 1829), I, 282-3.

75. Cowan, *British Emigration*, pp. 153, 162.

76. U.C. Sundries, Robinson to Hillier, Dec. 18, 1822.

77. C.O. 42/377/244-52, Maitland to Bathurst, May 1, 1826, return encl.; Great Britain, House of Commons, *Sess. Papers*, 1826-7, V, 655.

78. They had, however, settled Irish settlers themselves in Beckwith, Huntley, and Goulburn, but whether Catholic or Protestant cannot be stated; C 626, p. 132.

79. Cowan, *British Emigration*, pp. 105-6; C.O. 42/373/66-78, Maitland to Bathurst, July 27, 1824, with encl.

80. Cowan, p. 106.

81. C 628, pp. 83-8; U.C. Land Book L, pp. 449-50; U.C. Land Book M, p. 1; P.A.O., C.L.P., "Orders and Letters Received, Surveyor General's Department," p. 62.

82. P. A. O., Strachan Papers, Wilmot-Horton to Strachan, May 26, 1826.

83. G1, Vol. 67, p. 89, Goderich to Colborne, Mar. 7, 1831.

84. C.O. 42/377/168-75, Maitland to Bathurst, Mar. 31, 1826.

85. At Perth and Lanark, the Military Settling Department settled virgin townships not selected by it, whereas Peter Robinson's settlers went to townships chosen by the government of Upper Canada, three of which (Emily, Otonabee, and Smith) had been open to settlement since 1819 and in which a considerable number of emigrants had already received 50-acre free grants; P.A.O., return of the Land Board of the District of Newcastle.

86. C.O. 42/377/241-52, Maitland to Bathurst, May 1, 1826, with encl.; C.O. 42/380/ Strachan to Horton, July 5, 1826.

87. U.C. Land Book R, 207-8.

88. U.C. Land Books, M, 1, Q, 385-90, S, 491, U, 390.

89. Great Britain, *Sess. Papers*, 1848, XLVII, 714-15.

90. P.A.O., fiats for settlers under Peter Robinson.

91. P.A.O., microfilm abstract of Emily township.

92. Great Britain, *Sess. Papers*, 1826-7, V, 571.

93. P.A.O., Robinson to Arthur, Mar. 9, 1841, in Box "Irish Emigration, 1823-5: Accounts."

94. This would include the cost to the Navy for passage of the immigrants as well as the sums spent by Robinson.

95. Great Britain, *Sess. Papers*, 1848, XLVII, 708, 714-15.

96. When these townships were inspected in 1840 it was found that there were many lots with large improvements which were not claimed by their occupants; P.A.O., report of the Surveyor General's Office of lands inspected under the order-in-council of April 4, 1839.

CHAPTER EIGHT

1. G1, Vol 57, p. 82, Bathurst to Drummond, Jan. 10, 1815.
2. U.C. Stat. 35 Geo. III, c. 2; Doughty and McArthur, eds., *Documents*, 194-6.
3. T.P.L., Powell Papers, B 83, p. 291.
4. U.C. Stat. 40 Geo. III, c. 3.
5. *Niagara Herald*, June 13, 1801.
6. Michigan Pioneer and Historical Society, *Historical Collections*, XV (1890), 19-20.
7. *Niagara Herald*, Feb. 21, 1801, quoting *Upper Canada Gazette and Oracle*.
8. Ernest Alexander Cruikshank, "A Study of Disaffection in Upper Canada, 1812-1815," Royal Society of Canada, *Proceedings and Transactions*, series 3, VI (1912), 11-65. See *infra*, p. 85.
9. *Niagara Herald*, June 13, 1801, quoting *Upper Canada Gazette and Oracle*.
10. P.A.O., *Report*, 1909, p. 185; 1911, pp. 45, 79, 300.
11. Quaife, ed., *Askin Papers*, I, 437.
12. U.C. Stat. 33 Geo. III, c. 2.
13. U.C. Stat. 54 Geo. III, c. 4; *J.H.A./U.C.*, 1812, 1814, in P.A.O., *Report*, 1912, pp. 12, 14, 114, 120, 128, 129, 133.
14. W. H. Higgins, *The Life and Times of Joseph Gould* (Toronto, 1887), pp. 100-1; *The Caroline Almanack* (Rochester, 1840), p. 29.
15. C.O. 42/355/8, Drummond to Bathurst, Mar. 20, 1814.
16. U.C. State Book G, 490.
17. C.O. 42/356/121-4, Gore to Bathurst, Oct. 17, 1815; Robert Fleming Gourlay, *A Statistical Account of Upper Canada* (London, 1822), II, 427.
18. In Upper Canada the patents contained a clause obliging anyone who subsequently obtained the land by inheritance, devise, or purchase to take the oath of allegiance. Mr. H. E. Turner of the Ontario Archives, who kindly inspected the patents on file in the Provincial Secretary's office, informs me that after 1835 this requirement was no longer inserted. The Act 23 Vic., c. 2, validated the titles of those holding under the earlier style of patent if the requirement had not been fulfilled.
19. U.C. Sundries, Oct. 20, 1817, W. Claus to S. Smith, enclosing a statement by Dickson.
20. Gourlay, *Statistical Account*, II, 438-40, 468; U.C. State Book F, 306-7.
21. Riddell, *Life of Powell*, pp. 228-9, n. 20; P.A.O., Macaulay Papers, Hagerman to J. Macaulay, Feb. 25, 1821.
22. *J.H.A./U.C.*, April 13, 1817, in P.A.O., *Report*, 1912, p. 419.
23. Gourlay, *Neptunian*, pp. 202-3.
24. Arthur G Doughty, and Norah Story, eds., *Documents Relating to the Constitutional History of Canada, 1819-1828* (Ottawa, 1935), pp. 3-5.
25. Gourlay, *Neptunian*, pp. 348-50.
26. *J.H.A./U.C.*, April 17, 1817, in P.A.O., *Report*, 1912, pp. 419-42; Gourlay, *Neptunian*, pp. 202-3.
27. *J.H.A./U.C.*, April 7, 1817, in P.A.O., *Report*, 1912, pp. 422-4.
28. Doughty and Story, eds., *Documents*, pp. 5-6, 9; see also *infra*, pp. 119-20.
29. U.S. Stat. 58 Geo. III, c. 9; *J.H.A./U.C.*, Mar. 6, 1818, in P.A.O., *Report*, 1912, p. 498.
30. Spragge, ed., *Strachan Letter Book*, p. 139.
31. C.O. 42/361/27, Smith to Bathurst, Feb. 23, 1818.
32. Gourlay, *Neptunian*, p. 180.
33. *Ibid.*, 105-6; Robert Fleming Gourlay, *Appeal to the Common Sense, Mind and Manhood of the British Nation* (London, 1826), p. 76.
34. Gourlay, *Appeal*, p. 47.
35. Gourlay, *Neptunian*, p. 237.
36. John Melish, *Travels Through the United States of America* (Belfast, 1818), p. 502.
37. Gourlay, *Neptunian*, p. 180.
38. Gourlay, *Appeal to Common Sense*, pp. 76-7.
39. U.C. State Papers, Vol. 32, pp. 142-5.
40. Gourlay, *Neptunian*, p. 310.
41. Gourlay, *Statistical Account*, pp. 270-4; Robert Fleming Gourlay, *General Introduction to Statistical Account of Upper Canada* (London, 1822), pp. clxxxvi-cxcvi.

42. Spragge, ed., *Strachan Letter Book,* pp. 62-5; C.O. 42/374/427-9, Strachan to Bathurst, June 8, 1824.

43. Gourlay, *Neptunian,* pp. 180, 220-2.

44. *Ibid.,* 179; Spragge, ed., *Strachan Letter Book,* p. 163.

45. Gourlay, *Statistical Account,* I, 554-5; Doughty and Story, eds., *Documents,* p. 4.

46. Gourlay, *Neptunian,* p. 177. Gourlay states that the resolution he particularly referred to related to the taxation of wild land. No such resolution was proposed (Doughty and Story, eds., *Documents,* pp. 3-5), although the Assembly did pass a wild land tax bill.

47. Spragge, ed., *Strachan Letter Book,* p. 163. See *infra,* p. 145.

48. G1, Vol. 57, 36; C.O. 42/356/121-4, Gore to Bathurst, Oct. 17, 1815.

49. G1, Vol. 59, 35, Bathurst to Maitland, Dec. 9, 1818; U.C. Land Book K, 429.

50. J.H.A./U.C., April 3, 1817, Mar. 9, 13, 1818, in P.A.O., *Report,* 1912, pp. 419, 509, 526, 541; C.O 42/363/257, Maitland to Goulburn, July 22, 1819.

51. Gourlay, *Statistical Account,* II, 469-70.

52. Gourlay, *Neptunian,* pp. 186-91, 199.

53. Gourlay, *Statistical Account,* II, 554; J.H.A./U.C., Feb. 5, 1818, in P.A.O., *Report,* 1912, p. 432.

54. Gourlay, *Statistical Account,* II, 413, 565.

55. Gourlay, *Neptunian,* pp. 191, 193.

56 *Ibid.,* p. 252.

57. *Ibid.,* p. 250.

58. *Ibid.,* pp. 195, 213.

59. U.C. Land Book J, 273, 436-7.

60. Gourlay, *Neptunian,* pp. 205-14, 217.

61. *Ibid.,* p. 241.

62. Gourlay, *Statistical Account,* II, 492.

63. Doughty and Story, eds., *Documents,* pp. 3-4.

64. Gourlay, *Appeal to Common Sense,* p. 19.

65. J.H.A./U.C., Mar. 30, 1818, in P.A.O., *Report,* 1912, p. 262; Kingsford, *History of Canada,* IX, 219.

66. Doughty and Story, eds., *Documents, pp. 10-13.*

67. Robert Fleming Gourlay, *Chronicles of Canada* (St. Catharines, Ontario, 1842), pp. 4, 6; Gourlay, *Statistical Account,* II, 370-80, 488-94, 571; U.C. State Papers, Vol. 32, pp. 142-5, gives the text of Clark's statement as read to a meeting in the township of Stamford.

68. This was a reference to the Treaty of 1818 with the United States.

69. Gourlay, *Chronicles,* pp. 12-14, 25-6.

70. *Principles and Proceedings of the Inhabitants of the District of Niagara for addressing H.R.H. the Prince Regent respecting the claims of sufferers in the war, lands to militia men, and the general benefit of Upper Canada* (*Niagara Spectator* office, 1818).

71. C.O.42/178/299, Sherbrooke to Goulburn, June 20, 1818 with encl.

72. Gourlay, *Chronicles, passim.*

73. *Ibid.,* 14, 17, 21; *The Centennial of the Settlement of Upper Canada by the United Empire Loyalists* (Toronto, 1885), App. A and B.

74. Gourlay, *Chronicles,* pp. 15-23; Gourlay, *Neptunian,* pp. 321.

75. Gourlay, *Introduction,* p. ccxxiv; *Transactions of the Upper Canadian Convention and Friends to Enquiry with addresses to His Royal Highness the Prince Rupert, Sir Peregrine Maitland, etc. etc.* (*Niagara Spectator* office, 1818). Encl. in C.O. 42/377/50-66, Maitland to Bathurst, Mar. 7, 1826.

76. U.C. Sundries, Dec. 16, 1818.

77. U.C. Sundries, Robinson to Smith, July 4, 1818, and Powell to Smith, July 7, 1818.

78. J.H.A./U.C., Oct. 12, 17, 22, 31, 1818 in P.A.O., *Report,* 1913, pp. 3, 8, 16-17, 38; U.C. Stat. 58 Geo III, c. 11.

79. T.P.L., Powell Papers, Gore to Powell, May 6, 1819.

80. Gourlay, *Neptunian,* pp. 135-42.

81. *Ibid.,* pp. 149-50.

82. U.C. Sundries, Hagerman to Hillier, Jan. 12, 1819.

83. Gourlay, *Neptunian,* pp. 136-8; U.C. Sundries, replies from various persons to Maitland of Nov. 28, 1818, Jan. 22, Nov. 19, 1819.

84. U.C. Sundries, Robinson to Jarvis, June 13, 1818.

85. Gourlay, *Neptunian,* p. 410.

86. T.P.L., Powell Papers, A 30, Powell to Gore, Jan. 18, 1818.

87. Riddell, *Life of Powell,* pp. 28, 35; Spragge, *Strachan Letter Book,* p. xxii.

88. Gourlay, *Chronicles,* p. 20; Gourlay, *Neptunian,* pp. 147-8.

89. C.O. 42/362/251-3, Maitland to Bathurst, July 19, 1819. See *infra,* p. 158.

90. Gourlay, *Neptunian,* p. 154.

91. U.C. Stat. 44 Geo. III, c. 1.

92. Gourlay, *Appeal to Common Sense,* p. 14.

93. Gourlay, *Neptunian,* pp. 165-8; Gourlay, *Chronicles,* p. 28; Gourlay, *Appeal to Common Sense,* p. 17.

94. William Renwick Riddell, "Robert Fleming Gourlay," Ontario Historical Society, *Papers and Records* XIV (1916), 61-3, n. 107.

95. Riddell, *Life of Powell,* pp. 119, 223.

96. *Ibid.,* p. 234, n. 7.

97. Gourlay, *Chronicles,* p. 28, Gourlay, *Neptunian,* p. 164. The oath was required by 1 Geo. I, c. 13.

98. Riddell, *Life of Powell,* p. 234, n. 8.

99. The opinion of the judges is in U.C. Sundries of Nov. 10, 1818.

100. Gourlay, *Neptunian,* pp. 120, 121 *passim.*

101. Kingsford, *History of Canada,* VIII, 232. Maitland intimates that Gourlay's arrest was a surprise to him and that he would have preferred a different course of action; C.O. 42/362/257, Maitland to Goulburn, July 22, 1819. Yet the fact is that Maitland had fortified himself with the judges' opinion six weeks earlier and that Isaac Swayzie had written to his secretary on Dec. 16, 1818, that Gourlay's arrest was imminent; U.C. Sundries, Swayzie to Hillier, Dec. 16, 1818.

102. Jedediah Prendergast Merritt, *Biography of the Hon. W. H. Merritt* (St. Catharines, Ontario, 1875), p. 49; C.O. 42/365/28, Maitland to Bathurst, Mar. 4, 1820; Edward Allen Talbot, *Five Years' Residence in the Canadas* (London, 1824), I, 418; U.C. Sundries, Dec. 21, 1818.

103. J.H.A./U.C., Mar. 7, July 5, 1820 in P.A.O., *Report,* 1913, pp. 171, 255.

104. J.H.A./U.C., June 7, 1819, P.A.O., *Report,* 1913, p. 99; C.O. 42/377/71, Bathurst to Maitland, Aug. 8, 1821.

105. See p. 118 and p. 119, n. 138.

106. Gourlay, *Statistical Account,* II, 629.

107. Ernest A. Cruikshank, "Post War Discontent in Niagara in 1818," Ontario Historical Society, *Papers and Records,* XXIX (1933), 14-46.

108. Andrew Picken, *The Canadas as they at present commend themselves to the enterprize of emigrants, colonists, and capitalists* (London, 1832), App. XXXI; Merritt, *Biography,* p. 44.

109. Great Britain, House of Commons, *Sess. Papers,* 1828, VII, no. 569.

110. Cartwright, *Life,* pp. 49-50.

111. Merritt, *Biography,* p. 51.

112. Exports from Great Britain to British America amounted to £4,093,062 in 1814, to £3,098,817 in 1815, to £2,208,041 in 1816. From 1808 to 1812 they had averaged roughly £1,610,000 annually and from 1817-27 £1,921,786. From 1808-12 imports into Great Britain from British America averaged £782,448. In 1814 these imports amounted to £322,897, in 1815 to £368,873 and in 1816 to £493,025. They did not exceed the pre-war average until 1820. (John Marshall, *A Digest of all the Accounts diffused through more than 600 volumes of Journals, Reports and Papers presented to Parliament since 1799* (London, 1833), part III, p. 74.

113. John Howison, *Sketches of Upper Canada* (Edinburgh, 1822), pp. 94-7.

114. Gourlay, *Introduction,* p. cccxxxi; see *infra,* chap. xv, n. 71.

115. Exports from the United States to British North America, excluding Newfoundland, amounted to $1,345,965 in 1814-15, $3,345,965 in 1815-16, and $3,918,819 in 1816-17. Ninety-nine per cent of these exports were the produce of the United States; Adam Seybert, *Statistical Annals: Embracing Views of the Population, Commerce ... of the United States of America* (Philadelphia, 1818) pp. 133-41. There does not seem to be much basis for the statement that large amounts of high-priced foreign luxuries were imported into Canada via the United States; Adam Shortt, "The Economic Effect of War upon Canada," Royal Society of Canada, *Proceedings and Transactions,* series 3, X (1917), 65-74.

116. Robert Kay Gordon, *John Galt* (Toronto, 1920), p. 50; Merritt, *Biography,* p. 55; Gourlay, *Introduction,* p. ccxxvi.

117. William Freeman Galpin, *The Grain Supply of England during the Napoleonic Period* (London, 1925), p. 211; The Right Hon. Lord Ernle, *English Farming, Past and Present* (4th ed., London, 1927), p. 44.

118. Gourlay, *Introduction,* p. cccxxix; J.H.A./U.C., April 13, 1821, in P.A.O., *Report,* 1913, p. 495; H. A. Innis, and A. R. M. Lower, eds., *Select Documents in Canadian Economic History, 1783-1895* (Toronto, 1933), pp. 235-7.

119. 8 Geo. IV, c. 12; 11, Geo. III, c. 41; 19 Geo. III, c. 22; 33 Geo. III, c. 40.

120. 5 Geo. III, c. 45; 26 Geo. III, c. 53.

121. 27 Geo. III, c. 13.
122. 35 Geo. III, c. 20; 41 Geo. III, c. 28; 49 Geo. III, c. 98; 52 Geo. III, c. 17.
123. 46 Geo. III, c. 127; 48 Geo. III, c. 19; 50 Geo. III, c. 12.
124. J.H. Clapham, *An Economic History of Modern Britain; The Early Railway Age, 1820-1850* (London, 1926), pp. 237-8.
125. Gourlay, *Neptunian*, p. 136.
126. Gourlay, *Introduction*, pp. ccxlv-cccxlvii, quoting *Edinburgh Review* of Aug. 1817 and *Bell's Weekly Messenger* of Feb., 1818.
127. Gourlay, *Chronicles*, p. 13.
128. J.H.A./U.C., Mar. 5, 1817 in P.A.O., *Report*, 1912, pp. 350-1.
129. G1, Vol. 58, p. 113, Bathurst to Gore, Oct. 3, 1816.
130. Frances Wright D'Arusmont, *Views of Society and Manners in America in a Series of Letters, During the Years 1818, 1819, and 1820* (London, 1821), pp. 269, 276.
131. Although reports were received from a number of townships which had been surveyed before 1791 and in which no reserves had been made, 45 per cent of the total replies condemned the clergy reserves.
132. Gourlay, *Appeal to Common Sense*, p. 151; Gourlay, *Introduction*, pp. ccclxxxi-ccclxxxv.
133. Gourlay, *Introduction*, pp. ccclxxxvii-cccci.
134. *Ibid.*, pp. lxxxiii-cvii, clxxxii, cxxxxviii-cxlvi, cclxxiii-cclxxvi.
135. *Ibid.*, pp. cccxl, cccxxxix.
136. *Ibid.*, cccxxxv-cccxxxvi; C.O. 42/381/468, Maitland to Hutchinson, enclosing Gourlay to Thos. Coleman, Cold Bath Fields, Oct. 10, 1825; Gourlay, *Appeal to Common Sense*, p. 27.
137. C.O. 42/377/69-71, Maitland to ... Mar. 7, 1826, with encl.
138. J.H.A./U.C., 1825-6, pp. 96-7, 117.
139. Gourlay, *Neptunian*, p. 27.
140. See *infra*, pp. 227-8.
141. Gourlay, *Statistical Account*, II, 528-38.
142. *Simcoe Correspondence*, I, 113, 163; C.O. 42/91/13-14, Clarke to Dundas, Aug. 11, 1792; C.O. 42/91/102-7, Grenville to Clarke, Nov. 8, 1792.
143. Doughty and Story, eds., *Documents*, pp. 6-9.
144. Doughty and McArthur, eds., *Documents*, p. 38.
145. Doughty and Story, eds., *Documents*, p. 234.
146. *A Tour through parts of the United States and Canada. By a British Subject* (London, 1828), p. 114, stresses the feeling on this point; see also the *Niagara Gleaner*, Mar. 3, 1827.
147. U.C. Stat. 9 Geo. IV, c. 20.
148. G1, Vol. 72, 398-40, Aberdeen to Colborne, Dec. 26, 1834.
149. See *infra*, p. 124.
150. Doughty and Story, eds., *Documents*, pp. 298-9.
151. *Colonial Advocate*, Mar. 2, 1826.
152. Doughty and Story, eds., *Documents*, p. 303.
153. J.H.A./U.C., 1826-7, p. 10.
154. G1, Vol. 69, pp. 1-9, Goderich to Colborne, Jan. 10, 1832.
155. C.O. 42/411/248-53, Colborne to Hay, May 7, 1832.
156. *Constitution*, Jan. 25, 1837; J.H.A./U.C., 1836-7, p. 459.
157. *Patriot*, Feb. 24, 1837.
158. *Constitution*, Aug. 3, 1836; *Patriot*, Feb. 24, 1837.
159. J.H.A./U.C., 1836-7, p. 459; 1837, p. 51.
160. Prov. Can. Stat. 12 Vic., c. 197.

CHAPTER NINE

1. Talbot, *Five Years' Residence*, I, 415.
2. C.O. 42/170/54-5, Buchanan to Bathurst, Dec. 24, 1816; C.O. 42/170/56-9, Buchanan to Sherbrooke, Dec. 10, 1816.
3. U.C. Sundries, Buchanan to Maitland, Sept. 12, 1818.
4. U.C. Land Book I, 262.
5. J.H.A./U.C., 1833-4, App. p. 41; P.A.O., "Military Settlements, Soldiers and Emigrants, 1816-1828"; James Buchanan, *Project for the Formation of a Depot in Upper Canada with a view to receive the whole Pauper Population of England* (New York, 1834), p. 9.
6. U.C. Sundries, D. M. Rogers to Hillier, Mar. 17, 1822; *Durham's Report*, App. B, p. 115; P.A.O., C.L.P., original returns of the land boards.

7. U.C. Sundries, D. M. Rogers to Hillier, June 9, 1819.
8. C.O. 42/361/115 Maitland to Bathurst, Aug. 19, 1818; Gourlay, *Statistical Account*, II, 42.
9. C.O. 42/365/216, Maitland to Dalhousie, Oct. 2, 1820.
10. Shortt and Doughty, eds., *Documents*, I, 195-6.
11. Labaree, ed., *Royal Instructions*, II, 530-1.
12. Shortt and Doughty, eds., *Documents*, I, 315-16.
13. Munro, *Seigneurial Tenure*, p. 43.
14. P.A.O., *Report*, 1928, p. 51.
15. *Ibid.*, p. 151; U.C. Land Book D, 321-2.
16. P.A.O., *Report*, 1905, p. lxxvii, 1928, pp. 68, 204.
17. P.A.O., *Report*, 1929, pp. 4-5.
18. *Ibid.*, 1905, pp. cvii, 217, 239, 242; 1917, pp. 262-3; 1928, p. 51.
19. Cruikshank, ed., *Russell Correspondence*, III, 71, 135; P.A.O., *Report*, 1929, p. 28; 1930, pp. 11, 13, 18, 22, 29, 30.
20. Paterson, *Land Settlement*, p. 89.
21. Cruikshank, ed., *Simcoe Correspondence*, II, 323.
22. *Ibid.*, II, 107; P.A.O., *Report*, 1929, p. 150.
23. *Russell Correspondence*, III, 25.
24. P.A.O., *Report*, 1929, p. 155; 1930, pp. 149-50.
25. *Russell Correspondence*, III, 98-9; P.A.O., Crown Lands Department, Report Book 6, pp. 769-70.
26. U.C. Land Book D, 555.
27. *Russell Correspondence*, III, 257.
28. P.A.O., *Report*, 1930, p. 149; 1931, p. 170; P.A.O., Crown Lands Department, Report Book 7, p. 1466.
29. C.O. 42/342/63, Gore to Windham, Oct. 1, 1806; U.C. Land Book G, 84, 87, 88.
30. U.C. Sundries, Mar. 18, 1812.
31. C 1210, p. 70, Hunter to Smith, July 10, 1802.
32. T.P.L., Smith Papers, Book 9, p. 369, Elmsley to Smith, May 9, 1800.
33. U.C. Land Book E, 181-5.
34. C.O. 42/365/216, Maitland to Dalhousie, Oct. 2, 1820.
35. U.C. Land Book F, 79. Five volumes of settlement duty papers remain in the Public Archives of Ontario, dating from Oct. 3, 1800 to June 16, 1818, but only a few of them bear a date subsequent to August, 1803.
36. U.C. Land Book G, 206, 318.
37. U.C. Land Book H, 187; C.O. 42/350/301-5, Gore to Liverpool, Sept. 10, 1810.
38. Gourlay, *Statistical Account*, II, 310-11.
39. Talbot, *Five Years' Residence*, II, 268.
40. U.C. Land Book D, 462.
41. *J.H.A./U.C.*, 1836, App. no. 22, Talbot to Maitland, Jan. 24, 1820.
42. James H. Coyne, "The Talbot Papers," Royal Society of Canada, *Proceedings and Transactions*, series 3, I (1907-8), sec. 2, 15-210; III (1909-10), sec. 2, 67-196.
43. See Fred Coyne Hamil, *Lake Erie Baron* (Toronto, 1955), for an excellent map of the Talbot Settlement and an account of Talbot's relations with his settlers and with the government of Upper Canada.
44. T.P.L., Powell Papers, A 30, Powell to Gore, Sept. 8, 1823.
45. Coyne, "The Talbot Papers," series 3, I, sec. 2, 38; Lamond, *Narrative*, pp. 59-60.
46. *J.H.A./U.C.*, 1836, App. no. 22, Talbot to Hillier, Oct. 6, 1820.
47. T.P.L., Powell Papers, Powell to Gore, June 16, 1817.
48. *J.H.A./U.C.*, 1836, App. no. 22, Talbot to Colborne, July 29, 1831.
49. G1, Vol. 59, p. 3, Bathurst to Smith, Feb. 26, 1818.
50. C.O. 42/389/236, Colborne to Murray, Nov. 10, 1829.
51. *J.H.A./U.C.*, 1836, App. no. 22.
52. William Henry Smith, *Canada: Past, Present and Future* (Toronto, 1851), I, cxxii.
53. New York State, *Census of the State of New York for 1835* (Albany, N.Y., 1836).
54. Hamil, *Lake Erie Baron*, 116.
55. See *infra*, p. 238.
56. Library of the University of Western Ontario, leases and agreements of sale by Talbot and his nephew, J. Airey. On wild land taxes, see *infra*, p. 238.
57. G1, Vol. 58, p. 103; Gourlay, *Neptunian*, p. 155-6.
58. *J.H.A./U.C.*, 133-4, App. p. 41.
59. U.C. State Book G, 75; Paterson, *Land Settlement*, p. 125-7, is incorrect in stating that all settlement duties were waived in 1819. The reference given refers only to the land given

to surveyors in payment for their services.
60. U.C. Land Book K, 223; J. H.A./U.C., Feb. 2, 1821, in P.A.O., *Report, 1913,* p. 268.
61. U.C. Land Books K, 368; M, 427, 576.
62. Samuel Strickland, *Twenty-Seven Years in Canada West* (London, 1853), I, 88.
63. U.C. State Book G, 75; Land Books K, 223, 377; L, 18; O, 351.
64. U.C. Sundries, Talbot to Hillier, May 7, 1824; *J.H.A./U.C.,* 1836, App. no. 22, Talbot to Colborne, July 29, 1831.
65. U.C. State Book F, 296.
66. U.C. State Book G, 40-2; C.O. 42/362/126, Maitland to Bathurst, Feb. 18, 1819.
67. U.C. Land Book K, 223, 229; U.C. State Book G, 76.
68. P.A.O., C.L.P., "Orders- in Council and Regulations," I, Mar. 5, 1829; U.C. Land Book E, 160, 188.
69. P.A.O., Macaulay Papers, Hillier to J. Macaulay, Feb. 12, 1822.
70. P.A.O., C.L.P., Surveyor General's locations, 1803-7, 1807-11. Those who located sizeable quantities of U.E. rights prior to 1818 were:

J. Chrysler	60,200 acres	Mr. (R?) Hamilton	9,400
J. H. Campbell	36,800	Mr. Hamilton as attorney	6,000
Allan and T. McLean	36,100	T. Hamilton	8,000
D'Arcy and H. Boulton	31,000	The Rev. A. McDonnell	8,400
J. R. Small	17,400	J. Beikie	8,600
T. Baynes	10,600	S. Jackson	8,500
S. & R. Sherwood	10,800	R. Cartwright	8,500
G. H. Detlor	20,400	A. Mercer	8,800
		T. Bell	7,374

71. *J.H.A./U.C.,* Nov. 16, 1818 in P.A.O., *Report,* 1913, pp. 68, 74, 133, 180.
72. U.C. State Book G, 193-4; U.C. Land Book N, 482.
73. William Lyon Mackenzie, in his *Sketches of Canada and the United States* (London, 1833), p. 281, states that in 1825 settlement duties cost $50 to $60 on a 200-acre lot. In 1831, Samuel Street paid £9 for settlement duties on 600 acres plus £2 15s. for agency on the duties and patent, but by this time it was no longer necessary to erect a house; P.A.O., Street Papers, A. Mercer to Street, Oct. 8, 1831.
74. *J.H.A./U.C.,* 1828, p. 50; *Colonial Advocate,* Feb. 2, 1828.
75. *J.H.A./U.C.,* 1829, pp. 42, 46, 48.
76. Strickland, *Twenty-Seven Years,* I, 89.
77. U.C. Land Book O, 96-7.
78. *Ibid.,* p. 351.
79. *J.H.A./U.C.,* 1831-2, pp. 115-16.
80. *Durham's Report,* App. B, p. 17.
81. U.C. Land Book P, 181-2.
82. U.C. Land Book Q, 336, 346; C.O. 42/418/49, Colborne to Stanley, Jan. 10, 1834.
83. *J.H.A./U.C.,* 1833-4, App. p. 48; U.C. Land Book Q, 381-3.
84. C.O. 42/418/286-8, Colborne to Stanley, April 18, 1834.
85. U.C. Land Book Q, 312-13.
86. *Ibid.,* p. 336.
87. P.A.O., Macaulay Papers, Stanton to Macaulay, April 16, 1834.
88. U.C. Land Book Q, 337-8.
89. P.A.O., Macaulay Papers, Stanton to Macaulay, April 16, 1834.
90. *J.H.A./U.C.,* 1833-4, pp. 13, 17, 42, 43, 138, App. p. 213.
91. *Ibid.,* pp. 147-50.
92. See *supra,* pp. 20-21.
93. P.A.O., *Report,* 1905, pp. lxxiv-lxxvii.
94. Benjamin Horace Hibbard, *A History of the Public Land Policies* (New York, 1924), pp. 125, 126.
95. *Correspondent,* Nov. 30, 1833; *Niagara Gleaner,* Nov. 30, 1833.
96. U.C. Land Book Q, 339-47.
97. C.O. 42/418/286, Colborne to Stanley, April 8, 1834; U.C. Land Book Q, 339-47.
98. *Correspondent,* April 26, 1834.
99. P.A.O., C.L.P., orders and letters received, Surveyor General's Department, 1818-41, April 2, 1835.
100. U.C. Land Book M, 56; Land Book R, 202-4.
101. P.A.O., C.L.P., orders and letters received, Surveyor General's Department, Nov. 18, 1835; U.C. Land Book R, 202-4.
102. *J.H.A./U.C.,* 1839-40, App. II, 233-6.

103. C.O. 42/471/355, report of an investigation into the Crown Lands Department, encl. in Arthur to Russell, Sept. 24, 1840.

104. Innis and Lower, eds., *Documents in Canadian Economic History*, pp. 127-30.

105. C.O. 42/429/243-82, Head to Glenelg, Feb. 29, 1836.

106. *Correspondent and Advocate*, Mar. 3, 1836; *Constitution*, Nov. 9, 1836.

107. *J.H.A./U.C.*, 1839-40, App. 233-4. They included:

F. Caldwell	2,600 acres	W. Morris	1,400 acres
A. McLean	1,600	A. N. McNabb	3,500
G. McMicking	1,900	M. Cameron	1,900
A. McDonnell	1,600	P. Perry	5,800
E. Malloch	5,100	J. P. Roblin	1,400
E. Murney	1,000	D. Thorburn	1,600
		F. Walsh	1,200

P.A.O., C.L.P., general entry of locations, April, 1835, to Nov. 1837.

108. In 1833 the upset price of government land was 10*s*. but John Langton found that U.E. rights could be purchased for 3*s*. 9*d*. to 5*s*. an acre; Langton, *Letters*, 14.

109. G1, Vol. 73, pp. 104-8, Aberdeen to Colborne, Feb. 18, 1835.

110. G1, Vol. 74, pp. 326-8, Glenelg to Colborne, Aug. 18, 1835.

111. U.C. Land Book R, 76.

112. *J.H.A./U.C.*, 1835, pp. 47, 311, 352-3, 360, 364, 396-7, 409.

113. C.O. 42/427/341, Colborne to Glenelg, Nov. 21, 1835, with encl.; U.C. Land Book R, 152-3.

114. P.A.O., C.L.P., general entry of locations, April, 1835, to Nov., 1837 (the 1838 figures are included in this volume); *Durham's Report*, App. B, p. 192. The figures for patented land include a small quantity of Crown land sold and patented and also free grants made prior to 1825 to other than privileged claimants, and patented by them. The effect of the removal of the restrictions is nevertheless plain.

115. P.A.O., Macaulay Papers, Stanton to Macaulay, Nov. 27, 1835.

116. D. M'Leod, *A Brief Review of the Settlement of Upper Canada by the U.E. Loyalists* (Cleveland, 1841) p. 21.

117. Those who located sizeable quantities of U.E. rights in the period 1835-7, in addition to the members of the legislature mentioned *supra* in n. 107, were:

J. B. Spragge	52,662 acres	Philip Ham	6,000 acres
J. Henderson	34,892	Alex. Grant	8,000
L. Phillips	14,400	Mathew Elliott	7,600
A. Hamilton	7,000	A. MacDonnell	4,000
T. Fraser	6,800		

118. P.A.O., Box marked "U.C. Militia, 1812-14, Prince Regent's Bounty," contains this report.

119. U.C. Land Book R, 189. Until 1803, the practice was for the Surveyor General to give an applicant for land a location upon receiving from him a warrant of survey, issued to him by the Clerk of the Council in conformity with an order-in-council. After July, 1803, the order-in-council served as a warrant of survey without a separate document being necessary and the applicant for land took it first to the Attorney General who issued his fiat to the Surveyor General to locate. After Nov. 10, 1835, fiats were dispensed with and the order-in-council became a sufficient authority to the Surveyor General for granting a location.

120. The figures for 1823-33 were taken from C.O. 42/422/. But in Great Britain, House of Commons, *Sess. Papers*, 1835, XXXIX, 277, the total acreage granted to U.E. loyalists during these years is given as 433,400 acres. The figures for 1791-1835 were taken from the rough return referred to in n. 118. The located land is included in the figure for land described. Figures for 1791-1838 were taken from *Durham's Report*, App. B, 192.

121. C.O. 42/427/341, Colborne to Glenelg Nov. 2, 1835.

122. See *infra*, p. 193; *Durham's Report*, App. B, 106-7.

123. U.C. Stat. 7 Will. IV, c. 118.

124. *J.H.A./U.C.*, 1836-7, pp. 288-9.

125. P.A.O., C.L.P., land rights, n.d. Those who presented large quantities of land rights in payment for land were G. S. Boulton, 12,700 acres, William Proudfoot, 9,300, James Henderson, 11,540, and James Henderson and James McDonald, 41,000 acres. It will be noted that the total number of rights applied is not a correct total of the column, in which there is a figure missing. It corresponds, however, to the total value.

126. U.C. Stat. 2 Vic., c. 41.

127. Prov. Can. Stat., 4 & 5 Vic., c. 100.

128.   *J.H.A./U.C.*, 1839-40, p. 184.
129.   *J.L.A./C.*, 1846, V, App. E.E.

CHAPTER TEN

1.   P.A.O., Russell Papers, Russell to Pitt (draft), Feb. 7, 1792.
2.   Quaife, ed., *Askin Papers*, I, 435-6.
3.   Cruikshank, ed., *Simcoe Correspondence*, I, 250.
4.   Doughty and McArthur, eds., *Documents*, pp. 91-8.
5.   Cruikshank, ed., *Russell Correspondence*, II, 221; C.O. 42/325/211-15, report of the Solicitor General.
6.   U.C. Stat. 43 Geo. III, c. 12.
7.   *Russell Correspondence*, II, 222.
8.   The bill neglected to grant the fines it imposed for the use of the Crown, as required by article sixteen of the instructions. C.O. 42/323/1-3, Russell to Portland, Aug. 11, 1798; G1, Vol. 53, part II, 278, 284-5, J. King to Russell, Feb. 8, 1799, and encl.
9.   Doughty and McArthur, eds., *Documents*, p. 38.
10.   U.C. Stat. 35 Geo. III, c. 4.   No method of enforcing payment was provided, however. The act taxing non-residents for roads was repealed by the road act of 1810, 50 Geo. III, c. 1.
11.   C.O. 42/331/3-5, Hunter to Hobart, June 3, 1803.
12.   *Niagara Herald*, Mar. 13, 1802.
13.   J.H.A./U.C., July 3, 5, 1802, in P.A.O., *Report*, 1909, pp. 307, 310.
14.   *Ibid.*, p. 377; C 120, p. 343, Hunter to Hobart, Mar. 20, 1803.
15.   J.H.A./U.C., Feb. 24, 1803 in P.A.O., *Report*, 1909, pp. 394-6.
16.   *Selkirk Diary*, p. 184.
17.   Doughty and McArthur, eds., *Documents*, p. 98.
18.   J.H.A./U.C., Feb. 23, 24, 1803, in P.A.O., *Report*, 1909, pp. 374, 376-7.
19.   J.H.A./U.C., Mar. 3, 1803, in P.A.O., *Report*, 1909, p. 395; *Simcoe Corespondence* II, 184.
20.   *Niagara Herald*, June 29, 1801.
21.   U.C. Stat. 43 Geo. III, c. 9.
22.   J.H.A./U.C., Mar. 3, 1803, in P.A.O., *Report*, 1909, p. 395.
23.   J.H.A./U.C., Feb. 18, 1808, in P.A.O., *Report*, 1911, p. 222.   The petition refers to the Act of 1808 but the same provision was in the Act of 1803.
24.   U.C. Stat. 47 Geo. III, c. 7; U.C. Stat. 51 Geo. III, c. 8.
25.   U.C. Stat. 55 Geo. III, c. 5.
26.   U.C. Stat. 59 Geo. III, c. 7.
27.   J.H.A./U.C., Mar. 17, 1817, in P.A.O., *Report*, 1912, p. 375; P.A.O., Oct. 16, Nov. 14, 1818, in P.A.O., *Report*, 1913, pp. 7, 67.
28.   J.H.A./U.C., June 7, 1819, in P.A.O., *Report*, 1913, p. 99; C.O. 42/361/165, Maitland to Bathurst, Dec. 8, 1818; G1, Vol. 59, p. 95, Bathurst to Maitland, May 11, 1819.
29.   J.H.A./U.C., June 23, 1819 in P.A.O., *Report*, 1913, p. 134.
30.   U.C. Stat. 59 Geo. III, c. 7.
31.   Paterson, *Land Settlement*, p. 128.
32.   U.C. Stat. 59 Geo. III, c. 8.
33.   *Russell Corespondence*, III, 46; J.H.A./U.C., Feb. 20, 1817, in P.A.O., *Report*, 1912, p. 320.
34.   U.C. Stat. 4 Geo. IV, c. 9.
35.   U.C. Stat. 6 Geo. IV, c. 7.
36.   J.H.A./U.C., Dec. 19, 30, 1823, in P.A.O., *Report*, 1914, pp. 565, 593.
37.   C.O. 42/372/49-82, Maitland to Bathurst, with encl., Feb. 6, 1824.
38.   J.H.A./U.C., Jan. 2, 1824, in P.A.O., *Report*, 1914, p. 599.
39.   C.O. 42/372/126-9, Powell to Bathurst, York, Jan. 22, 1824.
40.   C.O. 42/372/119-25, Maitland to Bathurst, Feb. 25, 1824.
41.   U.C. State Book G, 348-56.
42.   *J.H.A./U.C.*, 1828, App., report on petitions for alterations in the Wild Land Assessment Law.
43.   C.O. 42/372/49-82, Maitland to Bathurst, Feb. 6, 1824; C.O. 42/383/382, Maitland to Huskisson, Mar. 31, 1828.
44.   *J.H.A./U.C.*, 1828, pp. 39, 40-63, 92 and App., report on petitions for alterations in the Wild Land Assessment Law.
45.   C.O. 42/383/405, petitions encl. in Maitland to Huskisson, Mar. 31, 1828.

46. J.L.C./U.C., Jan. 14, 1824, in P.A.O., *Report*, 1915-16, pp. 260-61.
47. *J.H.A./U.C.*, 1828, App., report on petitions, etc.
48. *Ibid.*
49. Clements Library, Ann Arbor, Simcoe Papers, Smith to Mrs. Simcoe, May 3, 1824.
50. Province of Canada, *Journals of the Legislative Assembly*, 1841-67 (*J.L.A.C.* hereafter), 1850, IX, App. B. B., ev. Price.
51. *J. H. A./U.C.*, 1828, App., report on petitions, etc.
52. U.C. Stat. 9 Geo. IV, c. 3.
53. Estimated from the acreages actually sold and the percentages of the land exposed for sale; *J.H.A./U.C.*, 1831, App. p. 144.
54. *J.H.A./U.C.*, 1828, App., report on petitions, etc.
55. *Ibid.*, 1831, App. p. 144.
56. U.C. Stat. 7 Will. IV, c. 19.
57. John Galt, *The Autobiography of John Galt* (London, 1833), I, 308.
58. Innis and Lower, eds., *Documents in Canadian Economic History*, p. 79.
59. P.A.O., Macaulay Papers, John Macaulay to Ann Macaulay, Aug. 10, 1839.
60. J.H.A./U.C., Dec. 14, 1823, in P.A.O., *Report*, 1914, p. 565.
61. *J.H.A./U.C.*, 1835, App. part I, no. 21, pp. 20, 32-3.
62. D. M'Leod, *A Brief Review*, pp. 79-80.
63. Mackenzie, *Sketches*, pp. 162, 245-6, 393.
64. U.C. Stat. 4 Geo. IV, c. 10.
65. U.C. Stat. 6 Geo. IV, c. 7.
66. Mackenzie, *Sketches*, pp. 46, 372-3, 346. The district treasurers were appointed and dismissed by the Justices and paid out money on their order and laid their accounts before them. A sworn copy of each district treasurer's account was sent via the Lieutenant-Governor to the legislature.
67. *Colonial Advocate*, Oct. 30, 1828.
68. *J.H.A./U.C.*, 1828, App., report on petitions, etc.
69. See *infra* chap. XVI.

CHAPTER ELEVEN

1. Canada, *Indian Treaties and Surrenders*, I, 42-3, 47, 58, 63, 71, 117. Bruce and Grey Counties were not secured until 1836.
2. C.O. 42/354/187, memo of Gore on sale of land, n.d.
3. C.O. 42/342/63, Gore to Windham, Oct. 1, 1806.
4. T.P.L., Powell Papers, A 30, Powell to Gore, Oct. 18, 1817.
5. C.O. 42/372/210-14, Maitland to Wilmot-Horton, Sept. 30, 1823.
6. See *supra*, pp. 47-8.
7. C.O. 42/336/95-8, report of the Executive Council on fees.
8. U.C. State Book G, 29, 34-5.
9. *Ibid.*, pp. 75-6, 360, 378-80.
10. C.O. 42/362/408-11, Maitland to Bathurst, Dec. 20, 1819; C.O. 42/372/210-14, Maitland to Bathurst, May 15, 1824; C.O. 42/374/267-8, memorial and memo to Bathurst, Jan. 2, 1824.
11. G1, Vol. 60, p. 200, Bathurst to Maitland, Jan. 31, 1823.
12. C.O. 42/372/210-14, Maitland to Bathurst, May 15, 1824; U.C. State Book G, 34-5, 496-501.
13. G1, Vol. 60, 266, Bathurst to Maitland, Aug. 13, 1824.
14. U.C. State Book G, 387-97.
15. See *supra* n. 12.
16. U.C. Land Book M, 8-9; U.C. State Book H, 208.
17. U.C. Sundries, Mahlon Burwell to Hillier, Nov. 16, 1818; C.O. 42/354/185, Gore to Goulburn, April 13, 1813.
18. J.H.A./U.C., Mar. 8, 1823, in P.A.O., *Report*, 1914, p. 389.
19. U.C. Sundries, report of Ridout, April, 18, 1819.
20. U.C. Land Book K, 285, 368; *Durham'sReport*, App. B, p. 115.
21. Gourlay, *Statistical Account*, I, 378-81; Talbot, *Five Years' Residence*, II, 169-81; Mackenzie, *Sketches*, 469; Adam Hodgson, *A Letter from North America written during a tour in the United States and Canada* (London, 1844), II, 43-8.
22. U.C. Land Book K, 450; *J.H.A./U.C.*, 1833-4, App. pp. 4-5; U.C. Land Book G, 86; Andrew F. Hunter, *History of Simcoe County* (Barrie, Ont., 1909), II, chaps. VIII and IX.

23. U.C. Land Book L, 141.
24. C.O. 42/368/11, Maitland to Bathurst, Jan. 23, 1822; Q 331, pp. 13-14, Maitland to Bathurst, Jan. 23, 1822.
25. *J.H.A./U.C.*, 1830, App. pp. 61-135, a return of the lands located and granted in each township, 1816-1828.
26. P.A.C., Colborne Papers, Mackenzie to Colborne, Mar. 8, 1829.
27. *J.H.A./U.C.*, Mar. 8, 1823, Jan. 2, 1824, in P.A.O., Report, 1914, pp. 388-9, 600.
28. G1, Vol. 58, 113-14, Bathurst to Gore, Oct. 3, 1816.
29. See *supra*, p. 82.
30. J.H.A./UC., Mar. 5, 7, 1817, in P.A.O., *Report*, 1912, pp. 350-1, 357-8, 394.
31. U.C. State. 56 Geo. III, c. 26.
32. *J.H.A./U.C.*, Mar. 24, 31, April 1, 1817, in P.A.O., *Report*, 1912, pp. 390, 406, 411, 417; *ibid*, Mar. 28, 1818, in P.A.O., *Report*, 1912, p. 559.
33. *Ibid.*, 1819, in P.A.O., *Report*, 1913, pp. 7, 10-13, 15.
34. *Ibid.*, Oct. 31, 1818 in P.A.O., *Report*, 1913, pp. 41-2.
35. Doughty and Story, eds., *Documents*, p. 24.
36. J.H.A./U.C., Oct. 31, 1818, in P.A.O., *Report*, 1913, pp. 41-2.
37. C.O. 42/381/399-420, Maitland to Huskisson, Dec. 15, 1827.
38. [Barnabas Bidwell] *The Honourable Mr. Sedgwick's Political Last Will and Testament with an Inventory and Appraisal of the Legacies therein Bequeathed* (Houghton Library, Harvard, n.p., 1800).
39. See *supra*, p. 82, and Doughty and Story, eds., *Documents*, pp. 24-5, 233.
40. J.H.A./U.C., Mar. 28, 1818 in P.A.O., *Report*, 1912, pp. 539-60.
41. *Ibid.*, June 11, 1818, in P.A.O., *Report*, 1913, 105-7.
42. P.A.O., C.L.P., records surveys in Upper Canada, 1819-1829, 1856-62.
43. U.C. Land Books J, 523-4, L, 279.
44. Hodgson, *Letters*, II, 47.
45. *Upper Canada Gazette*, April 1, 1819.
46. *J.L.A.C.*, 1850, IX, App. B.B., ev. Price.
47. Canada, *Indian Treaties*, I, 47-57.
48. U.C. State Book G, 58; C.O. 42/362/199, Maitland to Bathurst, May 15, 1819; G1, Vol. 59, 256, Bathurst to Maitland, Dec. 7, 1820.
49. C.O. 42/365/76, memo in Maitland to Bathurst, May 8, 1820; Canada, *Indian Treaties*, I, 47-57.
50. C.O. 42/365/123, 182, Maitland to Bathurst, Quebec, June 11, 1820, and Maitland to Bathurst, York, Nov. 18, 1820; C.O. 42/365/294, Harrison to Goulburn, Treasury, Nov. 11, 1820.
51. *J.H.A./U.C.*, 1825-6, p. 21.

CHAPTER TWELVE

1. Shortt and Doughty, eds., *Documents*, II 947-8.
2. P.A.O., *Report*, 1928, pp. 63-6.
3. Shortt and Doughty, eds.,*Documents*, II, 970-87.
4. 18 Geo. III, c. 12.
5. Durham's *Report*, App. B, p. 5; Hilda Neatby, "Chief Justice William Smith: An Eighteenth Century Whig Imperialist," *C.H.R.*, XXVIII (1947), 44-67.
6. C.O. 42/67/184-7, Dorchester to Grenville, May 27, 1790.
7. Doughty and McArthur, eds., *Documents*, 59, n. 3.
8. P.A.O., *Report*, 1905, p. 179.
9. P.A.C., Askin Papers, V, Askin to Smith, Nov. 4, 1795.
10. C.O. 42/322/11, Russell to Portland, Aug. 20, 1797.
11. P.A.O., *Report*, 1905, p. 179; Doughty and McArthur, eds., *Documents*, p. 200; C.O. 42/322/14-15, Simcoe to Portland, Nov. 8, 1795.
12. Cruikshank, ed., *Simcoe Correspondence*, IV, 13.
13. *Ibid.*, II, 51-2; C.O. 42/349/241, Gore to Castlereagh, Dec. 23, 1809; G1, Vol. 60, p. 78; U.C. Land Book K, 340.
14. Cruikshank, ed., *Russell Correspondence*, II, 117; U.C. Land Book D, 257.
15. C 623, 156-7, Smith to Sherbrooke, Oct. 20, 1819; U.C. Sundries, Oct. 30, 1820, return of locations on the reserves.
16. T.P.L., Powell Papers, "Notice of some late acts of Lt. Gov. Gore for himself," 1817.
17. Doughty and Story, eds., *Documents*, p. 4.

18. T.P.L., Powell Papers, Gore to Powell, Oct. 30, 1817.
19. G1, Vol. 59, p. 162, Bathurst to Maitland, Aug. 26, 1819.
20. C.O. 42/361/61, Maitland to Bathurst, Dec. 7, 1818.
21. C.O. 42/365/213-4, Maitland to Dalhousie, Oct. 2, 1820.
22. Talbot, *Five Years' Residence*, II, 210.
23. Doughty and McArthur, eds., *Documents*, p. 205, n. 4.
24. *Simcoe Correspondence*, IV, 113.
25. U.C. State Book B, 83.
26. C.O. 42/323/207-11, W. D. Powell to Portland, Oct. 20, 1797.
27. C.O. 42/322/195-221, Russell to Portland, Aug. 11, 1797, enclosing Smith's plan for the Clergy Reserves.
28. *Russell Correspondence*, II, 143; U.C. State Book B, 142-8.
29. *Russell Correspondence*, II, 179-80.
30. *Ibid.*, II, 300-1; III, 63.
31. U.C. State Book C, 69-80.
32. C.O. 42/329/55-66, Hunter to Hobart, July 17, 1802; P.A.O., *Report*, 1906, pp. 218-9.
33. *Simcoe Correspondence*, IV, 134; T.P.L., Smith Papers, B 15, Simcoe to Portland, Nov. 20, 1799; U.C. State Book C, p. 222.
34. U.C. State Book B, 147.
35. U.C. State Book B, 142, 147.
36. U.C. State Book C, 70.
37. Picken, *The Canadas*, p. 172.
38. U.C. State Book C, 223.
39. U.C. Land Book E, 127-9.
40. U.C. State Book C, 312-13.
41. C.O. 42/370/321, Ridout's report on the reserves, encl. in Maitland to Wilmot-Horton, Sept. 30, 1823.
42. U.C. State Book E, 347-8; State Book G, 55.
43. U.C. Land Book N, 186; P.A.O., "Leased Crown Reserves," in Box "Crown Reserves."
44. U.C. State Book H, 109. One hundred and sixty-four lots were reserved for lease by a group of Amish settlers in Wilmot, and there were apparently 184 leases uncompleted at the time the report was made.
45. U.C. State Book E, 175, 245; Land Book M, 667.
46. P.A.O., Robinson Papers, Robinson to Wilmot-Horton, Jan. 10, 1823.
47. U.C. Sundries, Aug. 18, 1815, opinion of Robinson; G1, Vol. 63, 408, opinion of the law officers of the Crown.
48. P.A.O., Robinson Papers, Robinson to Wilmot-Horton, Jan. 10, 1823.
49. C.O. 42/371/49, W. Ash to Wilmot-Horton, Treasury, Feb. 11, 1823.
50. C.O. 42/370/197-221, Maitland to Wilmot-Horton, with encl., Sept. 30, 1823.
51. *Ibid.*
52. *Ibid.*
53. *Ibid.*
54. Gourlay, "Introduction," p. cccxxxiii; Gourlay, *Statistical Account*, I, 425.
55. Gourlay, *Neptunian*, p. 102.
56. C.O. 42/367/198, Gourlay to Bathurst, Margate, Oct. 2, 1821.
57. G1, Vol. 60, p. 176; Galt, *Autobiography*, I, 280-2, 294; Jennie W. Aberdien, *John Galt* (London, 1936), p. 134.
58. Galt, *Autobiography*, I, 297-8, 300; Aberdien, *Galt*, p. 134.
59. P.A.O., Robinson Papers, Robinson to Wilmot-Horton, Jan. 10, 1823, endorsed, "Copy of the Paper given to Mr. Horton re the Reserves which led to the formation of the Canada Co. —as it seems, by Mr. Galt." Appended is a note of Mar., 1853, in which Robinson says he has just copied his rough draft of these papers into readable form. The papers include also a copy of Robinson's reply to Powell's criticisms of his plan and to those of an official of the Treasury.
60. Galt, *Autobiography*, I, 300-1; Aberdien, *Galt*, p. 136.
61. Aberdien, *Galt*, pp. 137-8.
62. Gourlay, *Appeal to Common Sense*, pp. 67, 108-9, 194-6.
63. C.O. 42/381-419, Maitland to Huskisson, with encl. Dec. 15, 1827.
64. C.O. 42/396/459-77, Wilmot-Horton to Cockburn, Sept. 4, 15, 23, 1824 and Cockburn to Wilmot-Horton, Sept. 16 and 19, 1824; G1, Vol. 62, p. 312, Wilmot-Horton to Maitland, Oct. 3, 1826.
65. See *supra* n. 59.
66. *J.H.A./U.C.*, 1835, App., part II, no. 39, Agreement of May 23, 1826.
67. P.A.C., Prov. Can., Proceedings in Council, 1841, Widder to Harrison, Oct. 30, 1841;

P.A.O., C.L.P., Surveyor-General, Letters to the Canada Co., Aug. 5, 1847.
68. G1, Vol. 63, p. 29, Bathurst to Maitland, Mar. 31, 1827.
69. *Durham's Report*, App. B., p. 100.
70. G1, Vol. 183, pp. 218-20, 269-72, 386.
71. T.P.L., Baldwin Papers, rough draft of Baldwin's reply to Hanson.
72. Galt, *Autobiography*, II, 346.
73. John McTaggart, *Three Years in Canada: an Account of the actual state of the country in 1826-7-8* (London, 1829), II, 283.
74. *Montreal Daily Advertiser*, March 24, 1834.
75. P.A.C., E series, report, "Settlers placed on Crown Lands by the Canada Co.," 1829-40.
76. U.C. Sundries, Widder to Murdoch, Feb. 3, 1840; *Correspondent and Advocate*, May 22, 1835.
77. Returns of the Crown Reserves sold by the Canada Co. for 1829-43 are given in "Surveyor-General to the Government re the Canada Co.," in P.A.O.
78. *Kingston Herald*, May 2, 1843.
79. This statement rests only on a pencilled note by an unknown person in the Canada company's "Register of Lands Undisposed of, Dec. 31, 1876," in P.A.O.
80. P.A.O., Canada Co's "Register of Lands Undisposed of Dec. 31, 1854."
81. Adam Lillie, *Canada: physical, economic and social* (Toronto, 1855), p. 14, quoting a Canada Company pamphlet: "Information for Intending Emigrants of all Classes to Upper Canada."
82. P.A.O., Canada Company's "Register of Lands Undisposed of," Dec. 31, 1876.
83. Robina and Catherine McFarlane Lizars, *In the Days of the Canada Company*, 1825-50 (Toronto, 1896), p. 295.
84. Patrick Shirreff, *A tour through North America; together with a comprehensive view of the Canadas and United States* (Edinburgh, 1835), pp. 175-6.
85. U.C. Land Book K, 23.
86. U.C. Sundries, reports of Ridout, Oct. 25, 1811 and Oct. 7, 1818. The lands could not be sold and were thrown open to location again in 1824; U.C. Land Book M, 56.
87. *J.H.A./U.C.*, 1829, p. 13; 1831-2, p. 63, App. p. 195.
88. *J.H.A./U.C.*, 1836, App. 22; Hamil, *Lake Erie Baron*, chaps. ix and x; C.O. 42/378/14-30, Maitland to Bathurst, July 25, 1825.
89. G1, Vol. 61, p. 245, Bathurst to Maitland, July 28, 1825.
90. U.C. Land Book P, 65-6; Prov. Can. Land Book A, 351-57; G1, Vol. 70, p. 30, Spring-Rice to Colborne, Aug. 14, 1834.
91. U.C. Land Book M, 422-4.
92. U.C. Land Book M, 456-9, 501, 607.
93. U.C. Land Book M, 641-2.
94. U.C. State Book H, 425-9.
95. P.A.O., Strachan Papers Wilmot-Horton to Strachan, May 26, 1826.
96. See *supra* n. 93.
97. G1, Vol. 67, p. 89, Goderich to Colborne, Mar. 7, 1831; U.C. Land Book O., 472.
98. C.O. 42/378/51-7, Maitland to Wilmot-Horton, Aug. 14, 1826.
99. An error on Galt's part. Twelve hundred acres was the most that could be obtained under the quit rent system as first devised.
100. G1, Vol. 62, pp. 130-50, Galt to Wilmot-Horton, St. Helen's place, Mar. 9, 1826.
101. *Durham's Report*, App. B, pp. 191, 193.
102. Shirreff, *Tour*, p. 362.
103. U.C. Sundries, "Petition, Township of Moore," Jan. 11, 1836; J. Burns to J. Joseph, Feb. 14, 1836, A. B. Hawke to J. Joseph, July 30, 1836.
104. *Correspondent and Advocate*, Jan. 11, 1837.
105. *J.H.A./U.C.*, 1831-2, p. 63 *et seq.*
106. *Ibid.*, Feb. 27, 1835.

CHAPTER THIRTEEN

1. C.O. 42/387/101, Maitland to Wilmot-Horton, Mar. 7, 1827.
2. C 628, pp. 39-43, Cockburn to Dalhousie, Mar. 13, 1823.
3. C.O. 42/366/208-14, Maitland to Bathurst, July 21, 1821.
4. *J.H.A./U.C.*, Feb. 26, Mar. 5, 1821, in P.A.O., *Report*, 1913, pp. 358, 374.
5. U.C. Sundries, Sept. 9, 1826.
6. C.O. 42/394/177, Colborne to Hay, Nov. 28, 1831.

7. C.O. 42/411/248-53, Colborne to Hay, May 7, 1832.
8. Mackenzie, *Sketches*, p. xx; *Constitution*, Jan. 29, 1835, Dec. 21, 1836; *Correspondent*, Aug. 16, 1834.
9. C.O. 42/414/264, Colborne to Goderich, April 16, 1833.
10. C.O. 42/388/327-30, Colborne to Goderich, May 23, 1829. The township promotion plans had been tried in Dover under Lord Selkirk, in Dunwich and Aldborough under Col. Talbot, in Thorah and Eldon under Donald Cameron, and in McNab under Archibald McNab; see Paterson, *Land Settlement*, chap. VIII; Norman MacDonald, *Canada, 1763-1841; Immigration and Settlement* (London, 1939), pp. 151-202.
11. C.O. 42/391/524, Colborne to Hay, Oct. 4, 1829; P.A.C., Colborne Papers, H. Jones to Colborne, Plympton, Aug. 14, 1828.
12. P.A.O., C.L.P., "Orders and Letters Rec'd., Surveyor-General's Dep't., 1818-1841," p. 182 See *supra*, pp. 132-3.
13. G1, Vol. 65, p. 299, Murray to Colborne, Sept. 1, 1829; C.O. 42/389/244-51, Colborne to Hay, Nov. 25, 1829; P.A.C., Colborne Papers, Hay to Colborne (private), July 28, 1829; G1, Vol. 66, p. 17, Murray to Colborne, Feb. 3, 1830.
14. G1, Vol. 66, p. 122, Murray to Colborne, April 7, 1830.
15. Great Britain, House of Commons, *Sess. Papers*, 1831-2, XXXII, pp. 23-46.
16. G1, Vol. 72, pp. 423-72, Spring-Rice to Colborne, Aug. 30, 1834; G1, Vol. 73, pp. 113-14, Aberdeen to Colborne, Feb. 19, 1835.
17. P.A.C., *Report*, 1935, pp. 278-84.
18. G1, Vol. 22, pp. 259-68, Goderich to Aylmer, Mar. 7, 1831.
19. P.A.C., *Report*, 1935, p. 317.
20. U.C. Sundries, J. Burns to J. Joseph, Feb. 24, 1836.
21. Great Britain, *Sess. Papers*, 1831-32, XXXII, p. 4.
22. P.A.C., *Report*, 1935, pp. 281, 292, 318-19.
23. C.O. 42/411/28-32, Colborne to Goderich, Feb. 8, 1832.
24. C.O. 42/414/3-10, Colborne to Goderich, Jan. 10, 1833.
25. C.O. 42/389/244-51, Colborne to Hay, Nov. 25, 1829; Samuel Delbert Clark, *Movements of Political Protest in Canada* (Toronto, 1959), pp. 482-7.
26. C.O. 42/394/71, 135-73, Colborne to Goderich, Sept. 5, Nov. 24, 1831.
27. G1, Vol. 67, p. 245, Goderich to Colborne, July 7, 1831; G1, Vol. 69, pp. 37-47, Goderich to Colborne, Feb. 1, 1832.
28. *Correspondent*, Jan. 5, 1833; *J.H.A./U.C.*, 1835, App., part I, no. 21, p. 73.
29. C.O. 42/414/1-10, Colborne to Goderich, Jan. 10, 1833; C.O. 42/418/187-200, Colborne to Stanley, Mar. 21, 1835; *Correspondent and Advocate*, Nov. 9, 1833; Hunter, *History of Simcoe County*, II, 229, 232-3.
30. *J.H.A./U.C.*, 1836, pp. 176-86, App., p. 110; Aileen Dunham, *Political Unrest in Upper Canada, 1815-1836* (London, 1927), p. 157.
31. *J.H.A./U.C.*, 1835, App., part I, no. 21.
32. C.O. 42/427/201-28, Colborne to Glenelg, Sept. 22, 1835.
33. C.O. 42/411/28-32, Colborne to Goderich, Feb. 8, 1832.
34. [John Galt] "Colonial Discontent, part II, Upper Canada," *Blackwood's Magazine*, XXVI (Sept., 1829), 334-7; C.O. 42/388/86-91, Colborne to Hay, April 2, 1829.
35. P.A.C., Colborne Papers, A. McDonald to Colborne, Cobourg, Dec. 8, 1828.
36. C.O. 42/411/474, Colborne to Hay, Sept. 21, 1832.
37. Colborne Papers, W. L. Mackenzie to Colborne, York, Mar. 8, 1929.
38. C.O. 42/427/89, Goderich to Colborne, Sept. 6, 1835; P.A.O., Macaulay Papers, W. Allan to J. Macaulay, Dec. 12, 1835.
39. T.P.L., Powell Papers, B 83, pp. 53-4, Jarvis to Powell, n.d., P.A.O., Macaulay Papers, C. Hagerman to J. Macaulay, April 17, 1832.
40. P.A.O., Macaulay Papers, R. Stanton to J. Macaulay, June 10, 1829.
41. C.O. 42/356/121-4, Gore to Bathurst, Oct. 17, 1815.
42. P.A.O., Macaulay Papers, R. Stanton to J. Macaulay, Jan. 18, 1830; Kingsford, *History of Canada*, X, 319-21; Macaulay Papers, Strachan to Macaulay, May 3, 1831.
43. P.A.O., Allan Papers, Macaulay to W. Allan, May 3, 1831.
44. P.A.O., Strachan Letter Book, 1827-39, Strachan to J. Stephen, Jan. 18, 1831, pp. 109-11.
45. P.A.O., Macaulay Papers, Strachan to J. Macaulay, Mar. 12, 1832.
46. Dunham, *Political Unrest*, p. 157.
47. Kingsford, *History of Canada*, X, 338-9, gives an account of the personal esteem in which Colborne was held.
48. G1, Vol. 75, p. 151, Glenelg to Colborne, Oct. 28, 1835.
49. *J.H.A./U.C.*, 1835, App. 110, pp. 46, 49.

50. *Ibid.*, 1839-40, App. 11, p. 323.
51. C.O. 42/471/268, Arthur to Russell, July 28, 1840.
52. Great Britain, *Sess. Papers*, 1840, XXXI, 9-11.
53. George Julien Poulett Scrope, *Memoir of the Life of the Right Honourable Charles, Lord Sydenham* (London, 1844), pp. 199-201.

CHAPTER FOURTEEN

1. P.A.C., *Report*, 1935, pp. 381-97.
2. *J.H.A./U.C.*, 1836, p. 473.
3. C.O. 42/429/158-60, Head to Glenelg, April 6, 1836.
4. *Durham's Report*, p. 58.
5. *J.H.A./U.C.*, 1836-7, App. 5.
6. U.C. State Book I, 426, May 26, 1836.
7. U.C. Sundries, J. R. Askin to J. Joseph, June 6, 1836.
8. U.C. State Book J, 426-7, April 28, 1836.
9. U.C. Sundries, Lloyd Richardson to J. Joseph, May 16, 1836.
10. *Constitution*, Dec. 7, 1836.
11. Great Britain, House of Commons, *Sess. Papers*, 1837, XLII, 765.
12. *J.H.A./U.C.*, 1839-40, App. II, p. 223.
13. Doughty and Story, eds., *Documents*, pp. 422-7.
14. U.C. Sundries, Jameson to J. Joseph, June 13, 1836.
15. *Constitution*, July 29, 1836, Jan. 4, 1837.
16. *Ibid.*, July 2, 1836.
17. *Ibid.*, Aug. 10, 1836, Jan. 25, 1837.
18. Samuel Thomson, *Reminiscences of a Canadian Pioneer for the Last Fifty Years* (Toronto, 1884), p. 19.
19. They put it differently, however. "Mackenzie is like a monkey on the floor and incessantly chattering..."; P.A.O., Macaulay Papers, Stanton to J. Macaulay, Jan. 12, 1829.
20. *J.H.A./U.C.*, 1836-7, Nov. 11, p. 29.
21. *Constitution*, Dec. 4, 1836.
22. C.O. 42/440/325, Baldwin to Glenelg, July 26, 1836.
23. Kingsford, *History of Canada*, X, 356.
24. Langton, *Letters*, pp. 160-1, 171-2; C. B. Sissons, *Egerton Ryerson: His Life and Letters* (Toronto, 1937), I, 314-15. The Assembly's failure to vote supplies caused Head to refuse assent to other supply bills for internal improvements which had been expected to provide employment and a market for farmers' produce.
25. C.O. 42/431/6-10, Head to Glenelg, Aug. 20, 1836.
26. G1, Vol. 78, p. 313, Glenelg to Head, Oct. 4, 1836.
27. P.A.C., *Report*, 1931, 376-87, Glenelg to Campbell, Aug. 31, Sept. 5, Sept. 10, 1836.
28. *Ibid.*, 1931, pp. 375-6, Glenelg to Gosford, Sept. 30, 1836.
29. *Ibid.*, 1936, pp. 446-9, Glenelg to Head, Sept. 8, 1836.
30. G1, Vol. 78, p. 313, Glenelg to Head, Oct. 4, 1836.
31. C.O. 42/431/6-10, Head to Glenelg, Aug. 20, 1836.
32. C.O. 42/430/412, Head to Glenelg, July 23, 1836.
33. This occurred when Head communicated to the legislature his own instructions and also those of the Commissioners of Inquiry in Lower Canada.
34. P.A.C., *Report*, 1936, pp. 446-9, Glenelg to Head, Sept. 8, 1836.
35. *J.H.A./U.C.*, 1836-7, p. 80.
36. U.C. Sundries, A. B. Hawke to J. Joseph, July 20, 1836.
37. *Durham's Report*, App. B, pp. 109-10.
38. C.O. 42/431/344, Head to Glenelg, Dec. 30, 1836.
39. James Daniel Richardson, ed., *A Compilation of the Messages and Papers of the Presidents, 1789-1897* (Washington, 1895-99), I, 250.
40. G1, Vol. 79, pp. 321-33, Glenelg to Head, Mar. 2, 1837.
41. *Ibid.*, p. 265, Glenelg to Head, Feb. 24, 1837.
42. Sir Francis B. Head, *A Narrative* (Third ed., London, 1839), p. 490.
43. U.C. Stat. 7 Will. IV, c. 118.
44. This had been one of Hawke's suggestions.
45. C.O. 42/438/455-8, Head to Glenelg, Aug. 22, 1837.
46. *J.H.A./U.C.*, 1837, pp. 288-9.
47. *Correspondent and Advocate*, Feb. 1, 1837; *Toronto Patriot*, Jan. 20, 1837.

48. T.P.L., Baldwin Papers, rough draft of reply to enquiries of the Durham Commission.
49. *Durham's Report*, App. B, pp. 106-7.
50. C.O. 42/437/344-9, Head to Glenelg, April 4, 1837.
51. *Toronto Patriot*, Jan. 20, 1837.
52. *J.H.A./U.C.*, 1836-7, pp. 88-9, 372; 1837, p. 42; 1837-8, p. 20.
53. *Ibid.*, 1837, pp. 43-5.
54. *Ibid.*, 1836-7, p. 287.
55. *Ibid.*, 1836-7, pp. 558-9.
56. Wisconsin Historical Society, Perrault Papers, O'Callaghan to Louis Perrault, May 29, 1839.
57. Head, *Narrative*, pp. 491-2.
58. T.P.L., Baldwin Papers, rough draft of reply to enquiries of Durham Commission.
59. P.A.O., Macaulay Papers, J. Macaulay to A. Macaulay, Mar. 5, 1837.

CHAPTER FIFTEEN

1. See *supra*, pp. 90-91.
2. Shortt and Doughty, eds., *Documents*, I, 191-2.
3. *Ibid.*, II, 1030.
4. Great Britain, House of Commons, *Sess. Papers*, 1828, VII, 554.
5. See *supra*, p. 160.
6. Knox, *Extra Official State Papers*, I, App. pp. 8-18; Margaret Marion Spector, *The American Department of the British Government, 1768-1782* (New York, 1940), pp. 145, 151.
7. Cruikshank, ed., *Simcoe Correspondence*, V, 247.
8. William Cobbett, ed., *The Parliamentary History of England from the Earliest Period to the Year 1803* (London, 1806-20), XXIX, 107, 114, 429.
9. C.O. 42/98/75-82, Dundas to Dorchester, May. 11, 1794. No reservation for the Crown was expressed in the patents.
10. This is also the conclusion at which the Canada Committee arrived; Doughty and Story, eds., *Documents*, p. 474.
11. *Parliamentary History of England*, XXIX, 114, XXVIII, 1271.
12. The quantity of Clergy Reserves has been derived by doubling the acreage of Clergy Reserves which the Canada Company consented to forgo in return for the Huron Tract. A report of the Surveyor General of 1826 shows that 8,000,000 acres had been granted by the Crown by 1824. The census returns of 1825 show that 3,035,516 acres were occupied, of which 535,212 were cultivated. This means that almost 5,000,000 acres were in the hands of speculators, large and small; C.O. 42/377/16-18, Maitland to Wilmot-Horton, April 10, 1826 with encl.; W. H. Smith, *Canada: Past, Present and Future* (Toronto, 1851), I, cxxii.
13. Shortt and Doughty, eds., *Documents*, II, 1030; *Simcoe Correspondence*, II, 80; C. A. Hagerman states that the Constitutional Act, as it left the Commons, provided that the endowment of a rectory with Clergy Reserves was to be taken in lieu of tithes but that the Lords struck out these words; C.A. Hagerman, *Speech on the Clergy Reserve Question*, Dec. 16, 1836 (Toronto, 1837).
14. Doughty and McArthur, eds., *Documents*, 191-2, 211-2; C.O. 42/102/150-1, Dorchester to Portland, July 11, 1795; C.O. 42/319/22, Simcoe to Portland, Nov. 10, 1794.
15. C.O. 42/357/206, Gore to Bathurst, April 30, 1816.
16. See *supra*, p. 164.
17. Doughty and Story, eds., *Documents*, pp. 3-5; *J.H.A./U.C.*, 1817, in P.A.O. *Report*, 1912, pp. 419, 420, 424.
18. *Constitution*, Dec. 21, 1836; Spragge, ed., *Strachan Letter Book*, Strachan to Mountain, July 10, 1818, p. 188.
19. *Strachan Letter Book*, Strachan to Mountain, May 12, 1817, pp. 129-32.
20. Thomas R. Millman, *Jacob Mountain: First Lord Bishop of Quebec* (Toronto, 1947), pp. 153-6.
21. P.A.O., Strachan Papers, memo to Maitland on the reserves, 1818; U.C. State Book G, p. 165.
22. U.C. State Book G, 57.
23. U.C. Land Book K, 539.
24. P.A.O., "Minutes of the Clergy Corporation of Upper Canada, 1819-35," p. 20.
25. *Ibid.*, 36.
26. G1, Vol. 60, p. 347. Bathurst to Maitland, Dec. 11, 1824.
27. P.A.O., "Minutes of the Clergy Corporation of Upper Canada," p. 16; see also *Infra* p. 165.

28. G1, Vol. 68, pp. 241-2, Goderich to Colborne, Nov. 21, 1831.
29. Great Britain, *Sess. Papers*, 1840, XXXII, 80-9, 168-9.
30. P.A.O., "Minutes of the Clergy Corporation of Upper Canada," p. 108.
31. He had taken over this duty in 1833; *ibid.*, p. 125.
32. U.C. Land Books S, T, U, *passim*.
33. U.C. Land Book S, p. 584.
34. P.A.C., Durham Papers, Report of R. B. Sullivan to J. Joseph on the Clergy Reserves, Mar. 28, 1838.
35. Great Britain, *Sess. Papers*, 1840, XXXII, 80-89.
36. *J.L.A./C.*, 1849, App. I.I.I.I.
37. P.A.O., C.L.P., "Receipts of Crown Lands, 1868-79," Shelf 33, no. 2; "Annual Reports, Commissioner of Crown Lands," in appendices to *J.L.A./C.* 1857-66.
38. Great Britain, *Sess. Papers*, 1828, VII, 565.
39. Doughty and Story, eds., *Documents*, pp. 27-8, 203-4.
40. *J.H.A./U.C.*, Dec. 12, 1823 in P.A.O., *Report*, 1914, pp. 547, 561, 592, 606-7.
41. Gourlay, *Appeal to Common Sense*, 152.
42. G1, Vol. 12, p. 181, Wilmot-Horton to Dalhousie, Mar. 19, 1823.
43. C.O. 42/372/31-41, Maitland to Bathurst, Mar. 9, 1824, with encl.
44. P.A.O., "Canada Company, Minutes of the Provisional Court of Directors," May 15, 1824, p. 17.
45. C.O. 42/396/50, Galt to Wilmot-Horton, April 27, 1824.
46. P.A.O., Canada Company, "Minutes of the Provisional Court of Directors," May 15, 1824, p. 17.
47. *Ibid.*, June 2, 1824, p. 31; C.O. 42/396/112.
48. C.O. 42/374/423, Strachan to Wilmot-Horton, May 31, 1824.
49. P.A.O., Canada Company, "Minutes of the Provisional Court of Directors," June 26, p. 31.
50. C.O. 42/396/46, Galt to Wilmot-Horton, April 23, 1824.
51. P.A.O., Canada Company, "Minutes of the Provisional Court of Directors," Sept. 13, 1824, p. 65.
52. C.O. 42/396/543-50, Strachan and Robinson to Wilmot-Horton, June 30, 1824.
53. C.O. 42/396/157-66, Galt to Bathurst, July 8, 1824.
54. C.O. 42/396/198, 466-77; P.A.O., Canada Company, "Minutes of the Provisional Court of Directors," Sept. 13, p. 65; Doughty and Story, eds., *Documents*, pp. 253-63.
55. G1, Vol. 61, p. 77, Wilmot-Horton to G. J. Mountain, June 14, 1825; U.C. Sundries, Robinson to Hillier, June 6, 1825.
56. It was subsequently modified in some particulars; C.O. 42/396/217, 265, 269.
57. U.C. Sundries, Mountain to Maitland, Mar. 1, 1825, quoting Strachan to Mountain of Feb. 17, 1825.
58. C.O. 42/375/5-7, Maitland to Bathurst, Jan. 19, 1825, Strachan's comments encl.
59. C.O. 42/399/140-4, Strachan to Wilmot-Horton, Aug. 9, 1825.
60. C.O. 42/375/5-7, Maitland to Bathurst, Jan. 19, 1825.
61. U.C. Sundries, Mountain to Maitland, Mar. 1, 1825.
62. C.O. 42/375/5-7, Maitland to Bathurst, Jan. 19, 1825.
63. U.C. Sundries, Strachan to Hillier, Mar. 16, 1825.
64. Millman, *Mountain*, p. 165; T. P. L., Scadding Collection (extract), Strachan to Mountain, Feb. 17, 1825.
65. See Strachan to Hillier, Mar. 16, 1825, and Mountain to Maitland, Mar. 1, 1825, in U.C. Sundries.
66. C.O. 42/399/390-401, Maitland to . . . May 7, 1825.
67. Roughly the size of a purchase from the Chippewas that had just been made.
68. U.C. Sundries, Strachan to Hillier, May 16, 1825; C.O. 42/399/140-4, Strachan to Wilmot-Horton, Aug. 9, 1825.
69. See *supra* n. 66.
70. The *Correspondent and Advocate* of Jan. 22, 1835, complained that the magistrates and commissioners appointed by Colborne for the Huron Tract were all "low subservients" to the Canada Company.
71. P.A.O., Strachan Papers, memo to Maitland, June 14, 1825.
72. Millman, *Mountain*, p. 167.
73. C.O. 42/399/138, G. Mountain to Wilmot-Horton, London, June 14, 1825.
74. C.O. 42/399/26-9, Robinson to Wilmot-Horton, July 6, 1825.
75. U.C. Sundries, Robinson to Maitland, July 6, 1825.
76. C.O. 42/399/147-66, Society for the Propagation of the Gospel to Wilmot-Horton, May 2, 1825.

77. G1, Vol. 61, p. 177, Wilmot-Horton to G. J. Mountain, June 14, 1825.
78. U.C. Sundries, G. J. Mountain to Hillier, July 6, 1825; C.O. 42/399/147, Robinson to Wilmot-Horton, Sept. 28, 1825.
79. Galt, *Autobiography*, I, 327-8; C.O. 42/406/73, [Wilmot-Horton] to Bosanquet, May, 1826; C.O. 42/436/99, Galt to Wilmot-Horton, May 13, 1826; C.O. 42/436/262-4, Strachan to Bathurst, May 22, 1826.
80. *J.H.A./U.C.*, 1835, App., part II, no. 39, Agreement of May 23, 1826.
81. C.O. 42/406/262-6, Strachan to Bathurst, May 22, 1826.
82. Galt, *Autobiography*, I, 327-8; *J.H.A./U.C.*, 1836-7, App. 13.
83. Charles Lindsey, *The Clergy Reserves* (Toronto, 1851), pp. 14-15.
84. Doughty and Story, eds., *Documents*, pp. 282-3; *Colonial Advocate*, Dec. 22, 1825.
85. G1, Vol. 61, p. 177, Wilmot-Horton to G. J. Mountain, June 14, 1825.
86. G1, Vol. 62, pp. 130-50, Galt to Wilmot-Horton, Mar. 9, 1826; C.O. 42/380/101-15, Galt to Wilmot-Horton, Mar. 1, 1826.
87. U.C. Sundries, Robinson to Maitland, July 6, 1825; P.A.O., Macaulay Papers, Stanton to J. Macaulay, July 15, 1826.
88. C.O. 42/375/311-30, memo from Strachan in Maitland to Wilmot-Horton, Nov. 5, 1825.
89. Lindsey, *Clergy Reserves*, p. 32, quoting Bathurst to Smith, April 2, 1818.
90. U.C. Land Book L, 492; 2 Geo. IV, c. 32.
91. G1, Vol. 61, p. 230, Bathurst to Maitland, July 22, 1825.
92. Doughty and Story, eds., *Documents*, p. 28.
93. *Ibid.*, p. 274; P.A.O., Macaulay Papers, Stanton to Macaulay, June 29, 1826.
94. P.A.O., Macaulay Papers, Robinson to Macaulay, July 25, 1826.
95. *J.H.A./U.C.*, 1825-6, pp. 53, 107-8.
96. *J.H.A./U.C.*, 1826-7, p. 12.
97. Spragge, *Strachan Letter Book*, p. 221.
98. *J.H.A./U.C.*, 1826-7, pp. 12, 16, 23-5.
99. C.O. 42/381/399-417, Maitland to Bathurst, Dec. 15, 1827.
100. *J.H.A./U.C.*, 1826-7, pp. 48, 86.
101. *The Parliamentary Debates*, new series, XVI, 587.
102. *Ibid.*
103. John Strachan, *A Speech of the Venerable John Strachan, D.D., Archdeacon of York, in the Legislative Council, Thursday, Sixth March, 1828* (York, 1828).
104. Doughty and Story, eds., *Documents*, p. 386-7.
105. *The Parliamentary Debates*, new series, XVI, 587-8.
106. Doughty and Story, eds., *Documents*, pp. 271-6.
107. P.A.O., Macaulay Papers, Stanton to Macaulay, Aug. 28, 1827.
108. *Colonial Advocate*, Mar. 8, Oct. 11, Nov. 18, 1827, Jan. 10, 1828.
109. P.A.O., Macaulay Papers, Stanton to J. Macaulay, July 15, 1826.
110. Strachan, *A Speech*, p. 27; Sissons, *Ryerson*, II, 8.
111. P.A.O., Macaulay Papers, George Moffat to J. Macaulay, Dec. 15, 1827.
112. Great Britain, *Sess. Papers*, 1828, VII, 592.
113. P.A.O., Strachan Letter Book, 1827-1839, Strachan to Archdeacon of Kingston, Feb. 18, 1828, p. 148.
114. Great Britain, *Sess. Papers*, 1828, VII, 569.
115. *J.H.A./U.C.*, 1829, p. 14.
116. C.O. 42/388/76, Colborne to Hay, Mar. 31, 1829.
117. P.A.O., Robinson Papers, Robinson to Wilmot-Horton, Dec. 24, 1828.
118. U.C. State Book H, 435-40, Huskisson to Maitland, Nov. 20, 1827.
119. U.C. State Book H, 441; P.A.O., "Schedules of Applications for Clergy Reserves," 1828.
120. U.C. State Book J, 269-70.
121. *Correspondent*, May 17, July 19, Aug. 9, 1834; *Correspondent and Advocate*, July 16, 1835.
122. U.C. State Book H, 441; P.A.C., Durham Papers, Sullivan to Joseph, Mar. 28, 1837.
123. P.A.O., Box, "Clergy Reserves," Sullivan to Arthur, Sept. 14, 1839.
124. *J.L.A./C.*, 1849, App. I.I.I.I.
125. Charles Walker Robinson, *Life of Sir John Beverley Robinson* (Toronto, 1904), p. 171.
126. *J.L.A./C.*, 1849, App. I.I.I.I.
127. *Niagara Gleaner*, Aug. 3, 1833; C.O. 42/389/244-51, Colborne to Hay, Nov. 25, 1829.
128. C.O. 42/411/20-25, Colborne to Goderich, Feb. 3, 1832.
129. C.O. 42/388/257-64, Colborne to Murray, April 11, 1829.
130. G1, Vol. 68, pp. 217-50, Goderich to Colborne, Nov. 21, 1831.
191. G1, Vol. 68, pp. 277-92, Goderich to Colborne, Nov. 21, 1831.
132. *J.H.A./U.C.*, 1831, pp. 94-5.

133. C.O. 42/411/20-25, Colborne to Goderich, Feb. 3, 1832; P.A.C., Colborne Papers, *Papers,* 1840, XXXII, 138-41.
134. Lindsey, *Clergy Reserves,* p. 21.
135. P.A.O., Macaulay Papers, Strachan to Macaulay, Feb. 16, 1832.
136. *J.H.A./U.C.,* 1832-3, p. 22.
137. *Ibid.,* 1833-4, p. 41.
138. This bill was practically the same as the bill passed by the Assembly in 1835, according to the report of the Legislative Council. The latter bill is printed in Great Britain, *Sess.* Papers, 1840, XXXII, 138-41.
139. *J.H.A./U.C.,* 1833-4, p. 41.
140. Great Britain, *Sess. Papers,* 1840, XXXII, 254-5.
141. *J.H.A./U.C.,* 1835, p. 203; *Correspondent and Advocate,* Mar. 15, 1835.
142. *J.H.A./U.C.,* 1835, pp. 297, 365-6.
143. *J.H.A./U.C.,* 1836, Jan. 29, Feb. 24.
144. Lindsey, *Clergy Reserves,* p. 30.
145. *Ibid.,* p. 31; Sissons, *Ryerson,* 348; C.O. 42/437/478-80, Head to Glenelg, May 2, 1837.
146. *Constitution,* Oct. 2, 1836.
147. Lindsey, *Clergy Reserves,* p. 35.
148. Sissons, *Ryerson,* p. 338.
149. *J.H.A./U.C.,* Feb. 9, 1837; *Constitution,* Feb. 15, 1837.
150. G1, Vol. 81, pp. 228-63, Glenelg to Head, July 6, 1837; C.O. 42/439/392, Head to the Synod, Sept. 1, 1837; G1, Vol. 84, pp. 114-40, Glenelg to Arthur, Feb. 9, 1838.
151. G1, 69, pp. 526-34, 542, Goderich to Colborne, April 5, Nov. 22, 1832.
152. *Correspondent and Advocate,* Sept. 20, 1834; *Constitution,* Mar. 15, 1837; *J.H.A./U.C.,* 1837, App. 13.
153. Lindsey, *Clergy Reserves,* p. 32; italics added.
154. Bathurst to Smith, April 2, 1818, quoted in Lindsey, *Clergy Reserves,* p. 32; G1, Vol. 61, p. 230, Bathurst to Maitland, July 22, 1825. See *supra,* p. 207.
155. C.O. 42/425/56, Colborne to Glenelg, Feb. 28, 1835; G1, Vol. 73, p. 309, Glenelg to Colborne, May 20, 1835. Actually, the Assembly had rejected the re-investment bill when it came up as an amendment to Perry's bill during the session of 1834.
156. P.A.C., *Report,* 1935, p. 389.
157. Three times during 1835 Goderich had replied to memorials on the subject of using the Clergy Reserves, declining to interfere on the ground that the subject was in the hands of the provincial legislature; G1, Vol. 74, pp. 262, 277, 284.
158. P.A.O., Macaulay Papers, J. Macaulay to A Macaulay, Jan. 9, 1837.
159. Great Britain, *Sess. Papers,* 1840, XXXII, 154, 292; *Constitution,* Mar. 5, 15, 1837.
160. James Buchanan had made a similar appeal in 1818; *New York Albion,* Feb. 4, 1837.
161. Donald Grant Creighton, *The Commercial Empire of the St. Lawrence, 1760-1850* Toronto, 1937), p. 322.
162. *Constitution,* July 5, 1837; C.O. 42/437/437-53, report of Sullivan, Mar. 28, 1837.
163. C.O. 42/437/435, Head to Glenelg, April 24, 1837, enclosing a report of R. B. Sullivan.
164. P.A.O., Macaulay Papers, J. Macaulay to A. Macaulay, Mar. 5, 1837.
165. Sissons, *Ryerson,* 404.
166. Great Britain, *Sess. Papers,* 1840, XXXII, 191-2; James Fenton, *A History of Tasmania* (London, 1884), 150.
167. Charles R. Sanderson, ed., *The Arthur Papers* (Toronto, 1957), I, 103-9; *New South Wales: Its Present State and Future Prospects, being a Statement with Documentary Evidence* (London, 1837).
168. *The Arthur Papers,* I, 116-7.
169. P.A.O., Macaulay Papers, J. Macaulay to S. Macaulay, April 7, 1839.
170. *J.H.A./U.C.,* May 9, 1839.
171. Great Britain, *Sess. Papers,* 1840, XXXII, 151.
172. Sissons, *Ryerson,* 505.
173. *J.H.A./U.C.,* April and May, 1839.
174. Langton, ed., *Letters,* 160-1; Kingsford, *Canada,* X, 357.
175. P.A.O., Macaulay Papers, Strachan to Macaulay, May. 21, 1839.
176. G1, Vol. 43, p. 85, Russell to Thomson, Sept. 7, 1839.

CHAPTER SIXTEEN

1. Chester Martin, "Lord Durham's Report and Its Consequences," *C.H.R.*, XX (1939), 178-94.
2. *Durham's Report*, p. 7.
3. *Ibid.*, App. B, p. 3.
4. *The Parliamentary Debates*, series 3, LXXI, 768-69.
5. *Durham's Report*, App. B, p. 3.
6. *Ibid.*, App. B, "Minutes of Evidence: Questions," 729, 755, 782, 783, 784.
7. *Ibid.*, App. B, pp. 2-3.
8. P.A.O., Macaulay Papers, Hagerman to Macaulay, April 17, 1832.
9. P.A.C., Durham Papers, Vol. 32, R. B. Sullivan to Sir G. Arthur, June 1, 1838.
10. See *supra*, p. 123.
11. U.C. Sundries, John Burns to J. Joseph, Feb. 24, 1836. Neither the Constitutional Act nor the laws of Upper Canada required those who voted for township officers to be British subjects.
12. *J.L.C./U.C.*, 1838, App. p. 45.
13. *Durham's Report*, App. B, p. 119.
14. *Ibid.*, App. B., pp. 54, 62, 63, 78.
15. Knaplund, ed., *Letters from Sydenham*, p. 42.
16. Sanderson, ed., *Arthur Papers*, I, 237; P.A.C., Colborne Papers, W. L. Mackenzie to Colborne, York, Mar. 8, 1829.
17. *Constitution*, Aug. 16, Sept. 7, Nov. 22, 29, 1837.
18. *Durham's Report*, App. B, p. 118; P.A.C., Durham Papers, Vol. 24, W. W. Baldwin to Durham, Aug. 1, 1838.
19. *Durham's Report*, App. B, p. 111.
20. Mackenzie, *Sketches*, 489-90.
21. U.C. Sundries, Mackenzie to J. Joseph, Mar. 17, 1836.
22. *Correspondent and Advocate*, May 22, 1835.
23. *Ibid.*, Mar. 12, 1835.
24. *J.H.A./U.C.*, 1837-8, App. pp. 52-5.
25. Doughty and Story, eds., *Documents*, p. 261.
26. *J.H.A./U.C.*, 1835, App., part I, no. 21.
27. *Durham's Report*, App. B, p. 10. The acreage actually received by the Company in the Huron Tract made the price less than 3s. 6d.
28. *Correspondent and Advocate*, May 22, June 18, 1835; *Constitution*, Mar. 15, 1837.
29. T.P.L., Baldwin Papers, rough draft of W. W. Baldwin's reply to the inquiries of C. Hanson on behalf of the Durham commissioners of inquiry into the waste lands.
30. *J.L.C./U.C.*, 1838, App. p. 45.
31. *Durham's Report*, App. B, p. 10.
32. *J.H.A./U.C.*, 1825-6, p. 58; 1829, p. 9, 1830, p. 19; 1831-2, pp. 64-5, 73.
33. *Ibid.*, 1831-2, pp. 64-5.
34. *Durham's Report*, App. B, p. 104.
35. *Constitution*, Sept. 29, 1837.
36. U.C. Sundries, Mackenzie to J. Joseph, Mar. 17, 1836.
37. *J.H.A./U.C.*, 1825, p. 89; 1825-6, p. 21.
38. *Ibid.*, 1829, p. 67.
39. *J.H.A./U.C.*, 1935, App. part. I, no. 21.
40. G1, Vol. 67, p. 20, Goderich to Colborne, May 23, 1831.
41. *Correspondent*, Sept. 6, 1834.
42. Mackenzie, *Sketches*, p. 369.
43. *J.H.A./U.C.*, 1830, p. 17; G1, Vol. 69, p. 308.
44. G1, Vol. 70, p. 17, Goderich to Colborne, Jan. 1, 1833.
45. *J.H.A./U.C.*, 1830, App. p. 194; 1833-4, App. pp. 106-9.
46. U.C. State Book K, 112-13.
47. *J.H.A./U.C.*, 1836-7, pp. 107, 109.
48. *Ibid.*, 1836-7, pp. 148-9.
49. *Ibid.*, 1839-40, pp. 360-1, App. part I, p. 54.
50. C.O. 42/311/398-402, Sydenham to Russell, Montreal, Oct. 12, 1840; G1, Vol. 50, p. 27, Russell to Sydenham, Nov. 11, 1840; G1, Vol. 51, p. 454, Russell to Sydenham, Feb. 21, 1841.
51. *J.H.A./U.C.*, 1831, pp. 15, 63-5, 196; 1833-4, pp. 147-8; 1829, p. 13.
52. *Constitution*, July 5, 1837.
53. U.C. Sundries, Mackenzie to J. Joseph, Mar. 17, 1836.

54. *Durham's Report*, pp. 9, 17-8, App. B, pp. 95, 190.
55. *Ibid.*, App. B, p. 11.
56. *J.H.A./U.C.*, 1839-40, App. 11, pp. 224-7, 242.
57. *Arthur Papers*, II, 365, 432; C.O. 42/471/344-67, Arthur to Russell, with enclosures.
58. *The Report and Despatches of the Earl of Durham* (London, 1839), p. 278.
59. *Durham's Report*, p. 74.
60. *Ibid.*, App. B, p. 8.
61. *The Parliamentary Debates*, series 3, LXXXI, 767. Cf. Lucas, *Lord Durham's Report*, I, 156.
62. C.O. 42/476/233-6, report of J. Macaulay on immigration.
63. C.O. 42/468/53-7, Robinson to Normanby, Feb. 23, 1839.
64. *The Parliamentary Debates*, series 3, LXXI, p. 767.
65. Fred. B. Hitchins, *The Colonial Land and Emigration Commission* (Philadelphia, 1931), pp. 40, 309.
66. *Durham's Report*, App. B, p. 32.
67. *Ibid.*, App. B, p. 32.
68. *Ibid.*, App. B, p. 32.
69. *The Parliamentary Debates*, series 3, LXXI, 776.
70. *Durham's Report*, p. 74.
71. See *infra* chap. XVIII, n. 2.
72. G1, Vol. 43, p. 40, Russell to Thomson, Sept. 7, 1839.
73. Knaplund, ed., *Letters from Sydenham*, 45, 49.
74. Scrope, *Sydenham*, pp. 207-9.
75. *Ibid.*, p. 210.
76. *Durham's Report*, pp. 103, 116.
77. Scrope, *Sydenham*, p. 202.
78. Knaplund, ed., *Letters from Sydenham*, p. 172, n. 45.
79. Great Britain, House of Commons, *Sess. Papers*, 1840, XXXI, 661.
80. Sanderson, ed., *Arthur Papers*, II, 238-63, describes the Tory reaction to the first of these bills.
81. P.A.O., Macaulay Papers, J. Macaulay to A. Macaulay, July 22, 1840; P.A.O., Strachan Letter Book, Strachan to J. S. Cartwright, April 12, 1841.
82. *The Parliamentary Debates*, series 3, LIV, 1146, 1149, 1150, 1153; Knaplund, ed., *Letters from Sydenham*, p. 84; Kennedy, *Documents*, p. 535.
83. *The Parliamentary Debates*, series 3, LIV, 1143; Great Britain, *Sess. Papers*, 1841, Sess. 2, III, 21.
84. L. C. Ordinance 3 & 4 Vic., c. 4; Prov. Can. Stat. 4 & 5 Vic., c. 10.
85. Kennedy, ed., *Documents*, p. 563.
86. The *Western Herald*, Aug. 25, 1841.
87. Stephen Leacock, *Baldwin, LaFontaine, Hincks* (Makers of Canada Series, VIII, Toronto, 1912), pp. 101-2, is incorrect in saying that in Lower Canada the councils consisted of the nominees of the Crown. Leacock has missed the sarcasm of Viger's protest which, moreover, so far as it is quoted in Louis Turcotte, *Canada Sous L'Union, 1841-1867* (Quebec, 1882), 98-9, does not include the word *alone*.
88. *Western Herald*, Sept. 8, 1841; *Kingston Chronicle*, Aug. 11, 14, 18, 21, 1841.
89. *Ibid.*, Sept. 8, 1841.
90. P.A.O., Macaulay Papers, J. Macaulay to A. Macaulay, Aug. 7, 1841.
91. *Western Herald*, Aug. 11, 1841.
92. *Ibid.*, Sept. 8, 1841; George Metcalfe, "Samuel Bealy Harrison: A Forgotten Reformer," *Ontario History*, L (1958), 117-131.
93. William Morris pointed this out at the time, *Kingston Chronicle*, Aug. 28, 1841; *J.L.A./C.*, 1852-3, XI, App. B.B.B.
94. Prov. Can. Stat. 16 Vic., c. 183.
95. *The Parliamentary Debates*, series 3, LXXI, 776.
96. George E. Wilson, *The Life of Robert Baldwin* (Toronto, 1933), 198-9.
97. Until the passage of Prov. Can. Stat. 13 & 14 Vic., c. 67. See *infra*, p. 276.

CHAPTER SEVENTEEN

1. Knaplund, ed., *Letters from Sydenham*, pp. 25, 43.
2. Great Britain, House of Commons, *Sess. Papers*, 1840, XXXII, 27-34.
3. *J.H.A./U.C.*, 1839-40, pp. 173-4.

4. Knaplund, ed., *Letters from Sydenham*, pp. 44, 47-8.
5. John Richardson, *Eight Years in Canada* (Montreal, 1847), pp. 186-7.
6. P.A.O., Macaulay Papers, S. Harrison to J. Macaulay, Mar. 10, 1840, enclosing a list of newspapers to receive advertising and a list of those *not* to receive it.
7. Knaplund, ed., *Letters from Sydenham*, p. 48.
8. P.A.O., Macaulay Papers, Robinson to Macaulay, Mar. 23, July 6, 1843.
9. Knaplund, ed., *Letters from Sydenham*, pp. 62, 65; C.O. 42/308/214-38, Thomson to Russell, Jan. 22, 1840.
10. C.O. 42/308/267-71, Thomson to Russell, Feb. 5, 1840.
11. Kingsford, *Canada* X, 515; Kennedy, ed., *Documents*, p. 524.
12. P.A.O., Macaulay Papers, J.Macaulay to A. Macaulay, Dec. 12, 1839.
13. P.A.O., Macaulay Papers, Strachan to Macaulay, Dec. 28, 1839.
14. C.O. 42/308/267-71, Thomson to Russell, Feb. 5, 1840.
15. Knaplund, ed., *Letters from Sydenham*, p. 42.
16. Lindsey, *Clergy Reserves*, p. 44; G1, Vol. 47, p. 79, Russell to Thomson, April 14, 1840.
17. Knaplund, ed., *Letters from Sydenham*, p. 71.
18. *Ibid.*, p. 91.
19. *The Parliamentary Debates*, series 3, LIV, 1190, LV, 463.
20. P.A.O., report to Sir George Arthur, Jan. 5, 1841, in Box "Clergy Reserves"; on excess specification, see *Durham's Report*, App. A, pp. 1-3; Paul Knaplund, "Notes and Documents," *C.H.R.* XX (1939), 198.
21. MacDonald, *Canada*, pp. 435-6.
22. *The Parliamentary Debates*, series 3, LV, 465.
23. Knaplund, ed., *Letters from Sydenham*, p. 91.
24. C.O. 42/314/363, memorial of the Committee of the General Assembly of the Church of Scotland, 1840; C.O. 42/314/368-72, James Grant to Russell, July 20, 1840, and draft of Russell's reply encl.
25. *Minutes of Annual conferences of the Wesleyan Methodist Church in Canada 1824 to 1845* (Toronto, 1846), pp. 270-1.
26. C.O. 42/449/322-54, Arthur to Glenelg, Aug. 11, 1838.
27. Francis Hincks, *Reminiscences* (Montreal, 1884), pp. 76-7.
28. Lindsey, *Clergy Reserves*, pp. 48-9.
29. G1, Vol. 458, no. 44, Bagot to Stanley, Feb. 23, 1842.
30. C.O. 42/471/216, Arthur to Russell, July 17, 1840.
31. P.A.O., Box, "Clergy Reserves," Sullivan to Arthur, Sept. 14, 1839.
32. G1, Vol. 454, no. 89, Sydenham to Russell, July 13, 1841.
33. G1, Vol. 458, no. 44, Bagot to Stanley, Feb. 23, 1842.
34. G1, Vol. 458, no. 69, Bagot to Stanley; P.A.O., "Orders-in-Council, General, 1840-42, pp. 165-6.
35. G1, Vol. 447, no. 159, Stanley to Bagot, June 2, 1842.
36. *Canada Gazette*, July 15, 1843.
37. Prov. Can. State Book C, 228, 463.
38. Forty per cent of the expenses of the Crown Lands Department were charged to the Clergy Reserves by Sydenham's orders, or 20 per cent of the value of the reserves sold, according to Lord Cathcart. In addition, the collector of clergy rents received a commission of 10 per cent and the Crown land agents 5 per cent of their collections; *J.L.A./C.*, 1849, VIII App. N.N.N.
39. *J.L.A./C.*, 1846, V, App. E.E., regulations of Nov. 1, 1845.
40. P.A.O., "Returns of Inspections of Clergy Reserves."
41. *J.L.A./C.*, 1846, V, App. E.E.
42. *Ibid.*, 1847, VI, App. X.X.
43. The restrictive dates in these regulations subsequently proved meaningless. In practice, great leniency was shown to squatters by the Crown Lands Department.
44. *J.L.A./C.*, 1849, VIII, App. N.N.N.
45. *Ibid.*, App. N.N.N.
46. *Mirror of Parliament*, April 8, 1846, p. 56.
47. *J.L.A./C.*, 1846, V, 177; *Mirror of Parliament*, May 12, 1846, p. 75.
48. *J.L.A./C.*, 1849, VIII, App. N.N.N.
49. *Ibid.*, 1846, V, 108, 165, 262.
50. *Ibid.*, 1849, VIII, App. N.N.N.
51. *Ibid.*, 1847, VI, 124-5 .
52. John MacMullen, *The History of Canada* (Brockville, Ont., 1868), p. 514.
53. Robert Baldwin, *Election Speech to the 4th Riding of York, 1847.* (Broadside, Widener Library, Cambridge, Mass).

54. [Aliquis], *Observations on the history and recent proceedings of the Canada Company addressed in four letters to Frederick Widder esq., one of the commissioners* (Hamilton, Ont., 1845), p. 40.

55. See *infra* chap. XIX, n. 57.

56. Hincks, *Reminiscences*, p. 278.

57. Great Britain, *Sess. Papers*, 1852, XXXIII, 35.

58. *J.L.A./C.*, 1850, IX, pp. 103-5, 115.

59. Prov. Can. Stat. 18 Vic., c. 2.

60. *Leader*, Nov. 15, 1854.

61. *The Parliamentary Debates*, series 3, LII, 1348.

62. Great Britain, *Sess. Papers*, 1851, XXXVI, 227.

63. Disputes continued, however, over the stipends charged on the fund and also over the legality of the rectory patents; see John Moir, *Church and State in Canada West* (Toronto, 1959), 76-81, App. VI.

64. *J.L.A./C.*, 1854-5, XIII, App. L.L.

65. P.A.O., "Extracts from Minutes of Council, 1799-1871," regulations of Jan. 13, 1859; *J.L.A./C.*, 1854-5, XIII, App. M.M.

66. The statistics in his table have been taken or computed from *J.L.A./C.*, 1849, VIII, App. I.I.I.I., 1856, XIV, App. 35, from the annual reports of the Commissioner of Crown Lands (to be found in the appendices to the *Journals*, after 1856), and from P.A.O., "Returns of Clergy Lands leased as of Jan. 25, 1859," in Clergy Reserves, Package 33, no. 11. Only part of the 21,638 acres used for rectory endowments was taken out of the Clergy Reserves.

67. P.A.O., Box, "Clergy Reserves," Sullivan to Arthur, Sept. 14, 1839.

68. *J.L.A./C.*, 1844-5. App. N.N.

69. P.A.O., "Clergy Reserves," Shelf 77, Box. 1.

70. P.A.O., "Return of Clergy Lands under Lease as of Jan. 25, 1859," in Clergy Reserves, Package 33, no. 11.

71. P.A.O., Return, "Amounts still due on Clergy Land in Upper Canada, Dec. 31, 1868."

72. See *supra*, p. 170.

73. P.A.O., Street Papers; *J.L.A./C.*, 1852, XIII, App. L.L.

74. *Leader*, Oct. 16, 1854.

75. John Moir, "The Settlement of the Clergy Reserves," *C.H.R.*, XXXVIII (1956), 46-62.

76. R. Flenley, ed., *Essays in Canadian History presented to George MacKinnon Wrong* (Toronto, 1939), 316-17.

CHAPTER EIGHTEEN

1. *The Parliamentary Debates*, series 3, Vol. 54, pp. 1126-7, 1147-8.

2. G1, Vol. 183, pp. 218-20, 268-72, 386.

3. William G. Ormsby, "The Civil List Question in the Province of Upper Canada," *C.H.R.*, XXXV (1954), pp. 93-118.

4. U.C. Stat. 2 Vic., c. 14, Sir Richard Jackson, the Administrator of Upper Canada after Sydenham's death, and the Executive Council were under the impression that this act was *ultra vires* and that therefore the Act of 1837 had expired. In 1843 Robert Baldwin, then Attorney General, pointed out that the Act of 1839 had been in force and had continued the provisions of the Act of 1837. Both acts were repealed by the Act of 1841; P.A.O., C.L.P., "Opinions of Law Officers of the Crown on O.C.'s & Regulations," Vol. 3.

5. *J.L.A./C.*, 1841, I, 7-8.

6. Hugh Mackenzie Morrison, "The Principle of Free Grants in the Land Act of 1841," *C.H.R.*, XIV (1933), 392-407.

7. Knaplund, ed., *Letters from Sydenham*, p. 97; Morrison, "The Principle of Free Grants," p. 399.

8. Scrope, *Sydenham*, pp. 199-201.

9. Great Britain, House of Commons, *Sess. Papers*, 1840, XXXI, 505, Thomson to Russell, Jan. 18, 1840. *Ibid.*, p. 566, Hawke to Secretary Murdoch, Dec. 31, 1840.

10. *Ibid.*, p. 3, Thomson to Russell, May 26, 1840.

11. *J.H.A./U.C.*, 1839-40, App. 234-6, 247.

12. U.C. State Book M, 375, 395, 405, 413-19.

13. Great Britain, *Sess. Papers*, 1841, XV, 432, Sullivan to Arthur, Dec. 17, 1840; E. W. Banting and A. F. Hunter, "Surveyor Charles Rankin's Exploration for the Pioneer Road, Garrafraxa to Owen Sound, 1837," *O.H.S.*, *Papers and Records*, XXVII (1931), 497-510; P.A.O., "Report on the Southern Division of the Owen Sound Settlement," in Box "Owen Sound

Settlement."

14. *J.H.A./U.C.*, 1839-40, App. 234-6.
15. U.C. State Book M, 448-51.
16. U.C. Sundries, Thomson to Arthur, July 1, 1840.
17. U.C. State Book M, p. 460. About half of the immigrants who landed at Quebec in 1840 got as far as Kingston. Very few reached the London and Western Districts; Great Britain, *Sess. Papers*, 1841, XV, 439-64, Sydenham to Russell, Jan. 26, 1841.
18. U.C. State Book M, 535; U.C. Sundries, Hawke to Thomson, Aug. 27, 1840; G1, Vol. 48, p. 84, Russell to Thomson, June 19, 1840.
19. U.C. Sundries, Hawke to Harrison, Dec. 17, 1840; Sydenham to Arthur, Dec. 4, 1840; Great Britain, *Sess. Papers*, 1841, XV, 437-8, memo of Harrison; 402, Sullivan to Arthur, Dec. 17, 1840.
20. Scrope, *Sydenham*, p. 199.
21. U.C. Sundries, Hawke to Harrison, Dec. 17, 1840.
22. Prov. Can. Land Book A, 307.
23. Prov. Can. Land Book B, 98-190.
24. G1, Vol. 50, p. 155, Russell to Sydenham, Dec. 12, 1840.
25. *J.H.A./U.C.*, 1836-7, pp. 196-9; 1839-40, App., p. 870.
26. Morrison, "The Principle of Free Grants," p. 403.
27. *J.H.A./U.C.*, 1839-40, App., 870; *Patriot*, Mar. 17, 1837.
28. P.A.C., series G 7, Arthur to Sydenham, Dec. 26, 1840.
29. *J.H.A./U.C.*, 1839-40, pp. 163, 359.
30. Great Britain, *Sess. Papers*, 1841, XV, 399-402.
31. *Ibid.*, 403, Sydenham to Russell, Oct. 12, 1840.
32. C.O. 42/492/15, Bagot to Stanley, April 19, 1842.
33. *Niagara Chronicle*, Sept. 4, 1841; U.C. Stat., 4 & 5 Vic., c. 7.
34. Great Britain, *Sess. Papers*, XV, 414; *J.L.A./C.*, 1860, XVIII, App. 4; P.A.O., "Journal of the Crown Lands Department, 1850-1860," p. 16.
35. Doughty and McArthur, eds., *Documents*, pp.. 42-3, and 205, n. 2; Cruikshank, ed., *Simcoe Correspondence*, III, 312-13; T.P.L., Russell Papers, Russell to D. W. Smith, Aug. 26, 1797.
36. *J.L.A./C.*, 1841, p. 409; *Toronto Examiner*, Sept. 1, 1841.
37. P.A.C., G 446, Dispatch 90, Stanley to Bagot, Mar. 3, 1842; C.O. 42/492/50, Bagot to Stanley, April 11, 1842.
39. P.A.O., C.L.P., "Orders and Letters Rec'd," p. 376; *Durham's Report*, App. B, p. 198.
39. U.C. StateBook T, 561.
40. *Upper Canada Gazette*, April 4, 1839. The quantities have been computed from the number of lots reported.
41. U.C. State Book U, 233, 235.
42. Prov. Can Land Book A, 154, order-in-council of Jan. 31, 1842.
43. P.A.O., C.L.P., "Extracts, Minutes of Council, 1799-1871," July 11, 1854.
44. P.A.O., C.L.P., "Crown Land regulations, 1829-84," order-in-council of Mar. 5, 1857.
45. *J.L.A./C.*, 1846, V, App. E.E.; P.A.O., C.L.P., "Report of the Surveyor-General's Office on Lands Inspected Under the O.C. of April 4, 1837." Summary of returns computed.
46. *J.L.A./C.*, 1846, V, App. E.E.; P.A.O., C.L.P., "Orders and Regulations," p. 99.
47. P.A.O., C.L.P., "Schedule of Forfeited Lands," Box F.
48. *Upper Canada Gazette*, Mar. 14, 1846.
49. *J.L.A./C.*, 1846, V, App. F.F.
50. Prov. Can. Land Book A, 24, 25, 35, 41, 55-7, 68, 74, 231.
51. U.C. Land Book U, 76-7.
52. *J.L.A./C.*, 1847, VI, 113-15, Grey to Elgin, April 1, 1847; Stanley to Bagot, Oct. 8, 1841; quoted in G. P. de T. Glazebrook, *Sir Charles Bagot in Canada* (London, 1929), App., p. 128.
53. Scrope, *Sydenham*, p. 200.
54. John Robert Godley, *Letters From America* (London, 1844), I, 185.
55. Great Britain, *Sess. Papers*, 1841, XV, 403, Sydenham to Russell, Oct. 12, 1840.
56. Prov. Can. Land Book A., 307.
57. *Ibid.*, 309.
58. *J.L.A./C.*, 1846, V, App. E.E.
59. Sir Richard Bonnycastle, *Canada as it was, is and may be* (London, 1852), I, 164.
60. *J.L.A./C.*, 1846, V, App. E.E.
61. *Ibid.*
62. *Ibid.*
63. Prov. Can. Land Book D, 432; E, 158.

64. P.A.O., C.L.P., "Owen Sound Settlement Report, Southern Division," July 30, 1845.
65. Prov. Can. Land Book C, 234-6.
66. Prov. Can. Land Book D, 89.
67. C.O. 42/541/253, Elgin to Grey, Mar. 26, 1847.
68. George W. Spragge, "Colonization Roads in Canada West," *Ontario History,* XLIX (1957), 1-17; Prov. Can. Land Book G, 469.

CHAPTER NINETEEN

1. *J.L.A./C.,* 1844-5, IV, 15, 59, 167, 237, 377, 482; 1846, V, 187, 213, 339; 1847-8, VI, 99, 121, 133, 140; *Mirror of Parliament,* June 3, 1846.
2. *J.L.A./C.,* 1841, I, 417-18.
3. *Ibid.,* 1844-5, IV, 33, 65, 109; 1847, VI, 49; 1850, IX, App. B.B.
4. *Ibid.,* 1846, V, 343; 1847, VI, 123.
5. J. Carruthers, *Retrospect of Thirty-Six Years' Residence in Canada West: Being a Christian Journal and Narrative* (Hamilton, 1861), pp. 199, 305-6.
6. Sir Arthur G. Doughty, ed., *The Elgin-Grey Papers 1846-1852* (Ottawa, 1937), I, 252.
7. *Ibid.,* I, 183.
8. *Ibid.,* 1, 10-12; *J.L.A./C.,* 1847, VI, 113-5, Grey to Elgin, April 1, 1847.
9. *Elgin-Grey Papers,* III, 1088-9.
10. Grey to Elgin, Jan. 29, 1847, quoted in Kenneth N. Bell, and F. P. Morrell, *Select Documents on British Colonial Policy, 1830-60* (Oxford, 1928), pp. 249-53.
11. *Elgin-Grey Papers,* III, 1110-13; Great Britain, House of Commons, *Sess. Papers,* 1847, XXXIX, 65-70, Elgin to Grey, Feb. 25, 1847.
12. *Elgin-Grey Papers.,* I, 10-12.
13. Great Britain, *Sess. Papers,* 1847, VI, 776-91.
14. *J.L.A./C.,* 1847, VI, 113-5, Grey to Elgin, April 1, 1847, *Elgin-Grey Papers,* I, 117, 126-7, 147, 207, 251-4.
15. *Elgin-Grey Papers,* I, 135, 203.
16. *Ibid.,* I, 236; IV, 1448.
17. *Ibid.,* I, 203, III, 1134; Brinley Thomas, *Migration and Economic Growth* (Cambridge [Eng.], 1954), p. 203.
18. *Ibid.,* I, 367.
19. *Ibid.,* IV, 1450.
20. *Ibid.,* IV, 1450.
21. *Ibid.,* I, 36.
22. Godley, *Letters from America,* I, 185.
23. J. E. Hodgetts, *Pioneer Public Service* (Toronto, 1955), p. 258.
24. The Toronto and Sydenham Road ran from the southeast corner of the township of Melanchton to the Owen Sound Road and was subsequently extended to the Saugeen River. The Durham Road ran from Nottawsage township, crossed the Owen Sound Road at the village of Durham, and continued on to the mouth of the Penetang River.
25. Prov. Can. Land Book E, 9; the Rev. Henry Christmas, ed., *The Emigrant Churchman in Canada* (London, 1849), I, 206.
26. John Charles Dent, *The Last Forty Years: Canada Since the Union of 1841* (Toronto, 1881), II, 128. Prov. Can. Land Book L, p. 94.
27. *Elgin-Grey Papers,* I, 255-9; IV, 1425-7.
28. *Ibid.,* I, 276.
29. Francis Hincks, *Canada: its financial position and resources* (London, 1849), 192; *Elgin-Grey Papers,* IV, 527.
30. Leacock, *Baldwin, LaFontaine, Hincks,* 301.
31. *Elgin-Grey Papers,* IV, 1435.
32. *Ibid.,* II, 870; IV, 1427-36.
33. *Niagara Chronicle,* Nov. 27, 1846.
34. *Mirror of Parliament,* Mar. 27, 1846.
35. *J.L.A./C.,* 1846, V, p. 95.
36. Prov. Can. Stat. 12 Vic., c. 81; 13 & 14 Vic., c. 67.
37. *J.L.A./C.,* 1860, XVIII, App. 4.
38. *J.H.A./U.C.,* June 18, 1798 in P.A.O., *Report,* 1909, pp. 66-7; C.O. 42/321/169-76, Portland to Russell, Nov. 4, 1797; Cruikshank, ed., *Russell Correspondence,* III, 28; U.C. State Book G, 36-7; John George Hodgins, *Documentary History of Education in Upper Canada* (Toronto, 1894-1910), I, 23, 26, 151.

39. *Russell Correspondence*, III, 174.
40. U.C. State Book I, 514.
41. James H. Coyne, "The Talbot Papers, Part I, *Transactions of the Royal Society of Canada*, series 3, 1907-8, I, section 2, p. 134.
42. *Ibid.*, 100-1; Hamil, *Lake Erie Baron*, pp. 62, 139.
43. U.C. Sundries, July 1, 1819.
44. U.C. Stat. 47 Geo. III, c. 6; 48 Geo. III, c. 16.
45. Hodgins, *Documentary History*, I, 77, 95, 98; *J.H.A./U.C.*, Mar. 11. 14, 15, 22, 1816, in P.A.O., *Report*, 1912, 233-48, 252, 261.
46. U.C. Stat. 56 Geo. III, c. 36.
47. U.C. State Book G, 259-61; C.O. 42/368/158-67, Maitland to Bathurst, June 29, 1822; Hodgins, Documentary History, I, 179.
48. Hamil, *Lake Erie Baron*, p. 131.
49. U.C. Stat. I Geo. IV, c. 7; Hodgins, *Documentary History* I, 172.
50. Great Britain, *Sess. Papers*, 1840, XXXI, 490-540; P.A.O., "Strachan Letter Book, 1827-39", pp. 139-40, Strachan to Colborne, May 26, 1830; see *infra*, p. 401; *J.L.A./C.*, 1841, I, App. K.K.
51. *J.H.A./U.C.*, 1831, pp. 55-7.
52. G1, Vol. 69, p. 219, Goderich to Colborne, July 5, 1832; G1, Vol. 73, p. 1, Aberdeen to Colborne, Jan. 7, 1835.
53. Prov. Can. State Book A, 163-8. In 1841 the district schools were made grammar schools.
54. Prov. Can. Stat. 4 & 5 Vic., c. 18.
55. Merritt, *Biography*, p. 272; *J.L.A./C.*, 1850, App. B.B.
56. *J.L.A./C.*, 1844-5, IV, 105, 257, 337, 409, App. N.N.; 1846, V, App. E.E.
57. P.A.O., Merritt Papers, F. Widder to Merritt, Nov. 21, 1844, Jan. 10, 1850.
58. *J.L.A./C.*, 1846, V, App. E.E.
59. Merritt, *Biography*, p. 336.
60. *Elgin-Grey Papers*, I, 250, 286-7.
61. P.A.O., "Miscellaneous Land Papers," Merritt to Secretary, Commissioners of Inquiry, Dec. 18, 1845.
62. *Durham's Report*, App. A, p. 4.
63. *J.L.A./C.*, 1844-5, IV, 148-51.
64. P.A.O., C.L.P. "Registered Land Rights," p. 146.
65. *J.L.A./C.*, 1844-5, IV, 39, 149-51, App. N.N.; *Toronto Globe*, July 10, 1847.
66. *J.L.A./C.*, 1846, V, App. E.E., p. 146.
67. Merritt, *Biography*, pp. 348, 354, 361.
68. Prov. Can. Stat. 12 Vic., c. 31; *J.L.A./C.*, 1849, VIII, 239, 336, 346, 356.
69. Prov. Can. Stat. 13 & 14 Vic., c. 56; 14 & 15 Vic., c. 56; Prov. Can. Land Book F, 679.
70. Prov. Can. Stat. 13 & 14 Vic., c. 16.
71. Prov. Can. Stat. 12 Vic., c. 200.
72. *J.L.A./C.*, 1847, VI, 102, 169.
73. *Ibid.*, 189-90.
74. The townships selected in whole or in part were Arran, Bruce, Elderslie, Huron, Saugeen, Brant, and Kinloss in Bruce County; Morris, Turnberry, Ashfield, Wawanosh, Grey and Howick in Huron County; Darling, Holland, Sydenham, Bentinck, Egremont, Glenelg, Normanby, Arthur, Durham, Elora and Wallace in Grey County. See P.A.O., Box "School Lands."
75. *J.L.A./C.*, 1856, XIV, 100, App. 35.
76. *Ibid.*, 1854-5, XIII, App. M.M.
77. "Annual Reports of the Commissioner of Crown Lands," in appendices to *J.L.A./C.*, 1857-66.
78. *Elgin-Grey Papers*, II, 762-4, 776, 781.
79. *J.L.A./C.*, 1850, IX, 176; 1851, X, 50.
80. *Niagara Chronicle*, June 12, July 6, 1851.
81. *J.L.A./C.*, 1851, X, 58.
82. Two small issues of compensatory scrip were later authorized; see *infra*, pp. 284, 301. They had amounted to some $41,000 by 1863; *Sess. Papers, Canada*, 1863, XXI, s. p. 11.
83. David Roblin, James Henderson, E. Murray, S. Chrysler, Charles Clarke, Alexander Fraser, J. B. Spragge, J. K. Kerr, and Edward Murney acquired large amounts of scrip; P.A.O., C.L.P., "Register of Land Rights."
84. Christmas, *The Emigrant Churchman*, I, 230.
85. *J.L.A./C.*, 1846, V, App. E.E.
86. *J.L.A./C.*, *Sess. Papers, Canada*, 1863, XXI, s.p. 11.
87. Langton, ed., *Letters*, p. 243.

CHAPTER TWENTY

1. *J.L.A./C.*, 1857, XV, App. 25; *Sess. Papers, Canada*, 1863, Prov. Can. Stat., 16 Vic., c. 19; XXI, s.p. 11.
2. *Canada Gazette*, Aug. 7, 1852.
3. *J.L.A./C.*, 1854-5, XIII, App. M.M.
4. *Ibid.*, 1856, XIV, App. 35; 1857, XVI, App. 15.
5. *Ibid.*, 1854-5, XIII, App. M.M.
6. Hunter, *Simcoe County*, I, 59; *U.C. Common Pleas*, II, 255; Prov. Can. Stat. 23 Vic., c. 2.
7. *J.L.A./C.*, 1854-5, XIII, App. M.M.; *Sess. Papers, Canada*, 1863, XX, s.p. 11, ev. Tarbutt and Kirkwood.
8. P.A.O., C.L.P., "Registers of Assignments."
9. Prov. Can. Land Book G, 48.
10. *Sess. Papers, Canada*, 1863, XXI, s.p. 5; 1866, XXVI, s.p. 3.
11. Prov. Can. State Book N, 429, O, p. 165; *J.L.A./C*, 1854-5. XIII, App. M.M.
12. See *supra*, p. 269.
13. P.A.O., C.L.P., "Orders-in-Council, II," contains Burke's letter of June 1, 1849.
14. Prov. Can. State Book N, 429. The Pembroke and Mattawan Road was to go from Pembroke on the Ottawa to the mouth of the Mattawan, along that river to Lake Nippissing and ultimately along the French River to Lake Huron. The Ottawa and Opeongo was to go from Farrell's Point on the Ottawa to Great Opeongo Lake and from there to Georgian Bay. The Hastings and Mattawan was to go from Madoc in Hastings County north to the Pembroke and Mattawan, and the Addington Road was to run from Sheffield in Addington north to the Madawaska River.
15. Jones, *History of Agriculture*, pp. 291-2; P.A.O., C.L.P., Journals of the Crown Lands Department, 1856-66.
16. P.A.O., *Report*, 1905, p. 6; 1929, p. 58; T.P.L., *A Proclamation Against Pitchers* (1799, n.p.); U.C. State Book D, 121-2.
17. C.O. 42/396/211-16, Heads of Agreement of Sept. 22, 1824.
18. C.O. 42/396/241, Galt to Bathurst, Oct. 20, 1824.
19. C.O. 42/396/299, minute of the intended arrangements.
20. C.O. 42/396/569, Markland to W. Horton, May 16, 1825.
21. P.A.O., C.L.P., "Collection of Orders, Instructions and Pamphlets, Vol. V," Agreement of Mar. 28, 1828.
22. Merritt, *Biography*, 113-4.
23. It is true that a negotiated price was arranged by Galt for the first few sales made to squatters; P.A.O., "Canada Company, Commissioners' Letters and Reports," Sept. 20, Oct. 17, 1827.
24. *J.L.A./C.*, 1846, V, App. E.E.
25. P.A.O., *Report*, 1905, pp. 63-4, 164-6.
26. *Durham's Report*, App. B, p. 117.
27. Great Britain, House of Commons, *Sess. Papers*, 1841, XV, 6-7.
28. *Ibid.*, 1839, XXXII, 166-78.
29. *Ibid.*, 1841, XV, 6-7.
30. *Ibid.*, 1841, XV, 30.
31. C.O. 42/461/307-9, Arthur to Normanby, July 27, 1839.
32. *J.L.A./C.*, 1846, V, App. E.E.
33. U.C. Land Book S, 267-8; P.A.O., C.L.P., "Orders-in-Council, General," order-in-council of Oct. 17, 1841.
34. P.A.O., C.L.P., Box "Squatters," circulars to agents dated Dec., 1842, Jan. 25, 1844, Jan. 29, 1851.
35. P.A.O., C.L.P., Box "Squatters," order-in-council of July 1, 1848.
36. Elora *Backwoodsman*, Dec. 15, 1844.
37. P.A.O., C.L.P., "Journal of the Crown Lands Department," A. Geddes to the Commissioner, Oct. 14, 1847, Oct. 10, 1848, Sept. 30, 1850.
38. Prov. Can. Land Book G, 481; *J.L.A./C.*, 1857, XV, 32.
39. Elora *Backwoodsman*, Sept. 7, 1851; clipping in Box "Squatters."
40. *J.L.A./C.*, 1857, App. 32.
41. P.A.O., Robinson Papers, J. Luke Robinson's petition to the Executive Council, Feb. 14, 1857.
42. P.A.O., CL.P., "Report of the Squatter Commission," E. Leach to the commissioners, p. 48.
43. *J.L.A./C.*, 1858, App. 22.
44. *J.L.A./C.*, 1858, XVI, App. 22, order-in-council of Mar. 22, 1858.

45. Sess. Papers, Canada, 1863, XXI, s.p. 11.
46. Prov. Can. Land Book H, 601; *J.L.A./C.*, 1857, XV, App. 25; Prov. Can. Land Book I, 350-1; *J.L.A./C.*, 1858, X, App. 22; P.A.O., C.L.P., "Crown Land Regulations, 1829-84," Regulation of Nov. 2, 1861.
47. P.A.O., *Report*, 1905, pp. 164-6.
48. P.A.O., Samuel Jarvis Papers, B 66, pp. 127-88, 132-3.
49. *J.L.A./C.*, 1851, X, App. V.
50. Prov. Can. Land Book L, 206.
51. *J.L.A./C.*, 1854-5, XIII, App. M.M.
52. P.A.O., C.L.P., "Crown Land Regulations, 1829-84," Regulation of Jan. 7, 1859.
53. Sess. Papers, Canada, 1862, XX, s.p. 11.
54. Prov. Can. Stat. 16 Vic., c. 205.
55. *J.L.A./C.*, 1854-5, XIII, 109, 308, 1110, 1115, 1162.
56. *J.L.A./C.*, 1856, XIV, 72, 131, 682-3, 689, 694.
57. Prov. Can. Stat. 27 & 28 Vic., c. 29.
58. P.A.O., Macaulay Papers, J. B. Robinson to J. Macaulay, July 20, 1852.
59. *J.L.A./C.*, 1854-5, XIII, 138.
60. *Ibid.*, App. M.M.
61. Theodore Walrond, ed., *Letters and Journals of James, eighth Earl of Elgin* (London, 1872), pp. 150-1.
62. A. R. M. Lower and Harold R. Innis, *Settlement and the Forest and Mining Frontier* (Canadian Frontiers of Settlement, IX, Toronto, 1936), p. 48; Michael S. Cross, "The Lumber Community of Upper Canada," *Ontario History*, LXII (1960), 213-33.
63. P.A.O., C.L.P., "Records of Surveys, Upper Canada, 1819-29," 1856-66, p. 149; "Reports of the Commissioner of Crown Lands" for 1861 and 1862 in *Sess. Papers, Canada*, 1862, XX, s.p. 11, and XXI, s.p. 5.
64. See A. R. M. Lower, "The Assault on the Laurentian Barrier," *C.H.R.*, X (1929), 294-307; Paul W. Gates, "Official Encouragement to Immigration by the Province of Canada," *C.H.R.*, XV (1934), 24-38; Hugh M. Morrison, "The Background of the Free Land Homestead Law of 1872," C.H.A., *Report*, 1935, pp. 58-66; Jones, *History of Agriculture in Ontario*; George W. Spragge, "Colonization Roads in Canada West," *Ontario History*, XLIX (1957), 1-17.
65. Sess. Papers, Canada, 1861, XIX, s.p. 15; 1864, XXIII, s.p. 5.
66. P.A.O., C.L.P., "Crown Land Regulations, 1829-84," Regulation of Jan. 7, 1859.
67. Land in some new townships had been sold after 1854 at cash sale and not subject to settlement duties; *J.L.A./C.*, 1857, XV, App. 25.
68. Sess. Papers, Canada, 1864, XXIII, s.p. 5; P.A.O., C.L.P. (Extracts), minutes of Council, 1799-1871.
69. *Canada Farmer*, I, 323; II, 35; *Sess. Papers, Canada*, 1866, XXVI, s.p. 3, App. 33; P.A.O., C.L.P., "Journals of the Crown Lands Department, 1856-66, pp. 97, 155; Ontario Department of Agriculture, *Emigration to Canada* (Toronto, 1869), p. 26.
70. P.A.O., C.L.P., "Journals of the Crown Lands Department, 1856-66."
71. Prov. Can. Stat. 23 Vic., c. 2.
72. See *supra*, p. 293.
73. *J.L.A./C.*, 1857, XV, App. 25.
74. Prov. Can. Stat. 12 Vic., c. 197; 16 Vic., c. 38; 20 Vic., c. 149; 19 & 20 Vic., c. 112; 22 Vic., c. 56; 24 Vic., c. 80.
75. *J.L.A./C.*, 1860, XVIII, App. 4 & 5; *Sess. Papers, Canada*, 1862, XX, App. 1; 1864, XXIII, s.p. 5, 1865, XXV, s.p. 157.
76. Sess. Papers, Canada, 1866, XXVI, s.p. 3.
77. Sess. Papers, Canada, 1863, XXI, s.p. 11.

CHAPTER TWENTY-ONE: CONCLUSION

1. *Durham's Report*, App. B., p. 99.
2. J.H.A./U.C., 1837-8, App. pp. 52-5.
3. *Durham's Report*, App. B., pp. 190, 191, 198.
4. Great Britain, House of Commons, Sess. Papers, 1849, XXXII, 63.
5. *Durham's Report*, App. B., p. 29.
6. P.A.C., Durham Papers, W. W. Baldwin to Durham, Aug. 1, 1838.
7. *Durham's Report*, App. B., p. 17.
8. Morrell, *British Colonial Policy*, 221.
9. Canada, Sess. Papers, 1866, XXVI, s.p. 5.
10. Canada, Sess. Papers, 1863, XXII, s.p. 11, ev. Russell.
11. Innis and Lower, eds., *Select Documents*, 68.

BIBLIOGRAPHY

MANUSCRIPT SOURCES

Public Archives of Canada (P.A.C.)

G series. G1, Dispatches from the Colonial Office to the Governors of Quebec, Lower Canada, and United Canada, and to the Lieutenant-Governor of Upper Canada. G7, Dispatches from the Lieutenant-Governors to the Governor General, vols. 1-3. G16, Internal Letter Books of Lieutenant-Governor of Upper Canada; Civil Secretary's Letter Books.

B series. The volumes of the B series are transcripts of the Haldimand papers in the British Museum.

C series. The correspondence of the Commander of the Forces. Used for Lieutenant-Governor Hunter's administration and for the activities of the Military Settling Department.

E series. The volumes of the E series are the state records of the Executive Council. They are lettered alphabetically. The minute books of the Executive Council of Upper Canada have been cited as U.C. State, plus appropriate letter, and those of the Province of United Canada have been cited as Prov. Can. State, plus appropriate letter.

L series. The volumes of the L series are the records of the Executive Council relating to land. They are lettered alphabetically. They have been cited as U.C. Land plus appropriate letter or Prov. Can. Land plus appropriate letter.

S series. The Upper Canada Sundries (correspondence received by the Civil Secretary).

C.O.42 (microfilm). Correspondence of the Governors, Lieutenant-Governors and Administrators of the old province of Quebec, Lower Canada, and Upper Canada with the Colonial Office.

Record Group 10. A1 (correspondence received in the Lieutenant-Governor's office respecting Indian Affairs), vol. 1.

Mss. Group 11/2, Supplementary II, 8, Instructions, Quebec and Lower Canada, 1774-1811.

John Askin Papers
Colborne Papers (xeroxed copies)
Dalhousie Papers
Durham Papers
Upper Canada Land Petitions, P

Public Archives of Ontario (P.A.O.)

Crown Lands Papers. A series of orders, instructions, regulations in pamphlets, and circulars issued, as collected by the Crown Lands Department 1793-1872
    Assignment Book, 1839-48 (assignment of claims to land, distinguishes between U.E. loyalist claims and Crown sales)
    Colonial Office Regulations, Land Grants, 1831-41
    Collection or orders, instructions, and pamphlets regarding the Crown lands, vol. 5
    Crown Lands Department, Letter Book 10
    Crown and Clergy Reserve Reports, 1794-1856
    Crown Lands Regulations, 1829-84
    Extracts from Minutes of Council, 1799-1871 (contains some printed notices)
    Fiat and Warrant Books, U.E. loyalist and military claimants, 5 vols., 1798-1837 (show acreage issued to these classes of claimants)
    Fiats for settlers under the Hon. Peter Robinson
    General Entry of Locations, April, 1835, to Nov., 1837
    Irish Emigration, 1823-5, Accounts
    Journal, Letters Written, 1802-3
    Journals of the Crown Lands Department, 1856-66
    Lanark Settlement, Rankin's Report, 1834
    Letters Received, Crown Lands Department, 1789-1877
    Letters Received, Surveyor General's Office, No. 7

Minutes, Land Board of Nassau
Opinions of law officers on the Regulations
Orders and Letters Received, Surveyor General's Department, 1818-41
Orders and Regulations, 2 vols.
Orders-in-Council, Military Settlements
Orders-in-Council, General, 1840-42
Orders-in-Council under Regulations commencing Oct. 29, 1825, to Nov. 21, 1826
Orders-in-Council, II
Owen Sound Settlement Report
Quarter-Master General's Department, Discharged Soldiers, 1815-22
Quarter-Master General's Department, Emigrants, 1815-22
Records of Surveys, 1819-29, 1856-62
Register of Asignments, 1839-1859
Register of Assignments, 1860-4
Register of Descriptions issued as free grants under Land Act of 1838
Registers of Land Board of Hesse, 4 vols.
Register of Land Rights, n.d. (a register of land rights received in the purchase of Crown
    and Clergy Reserves, showing the name of original nominee, the purchaser of right, the
    acreage on which applied, and the price)
Report Books, Crown Lands Department, Nos. 5, 6, 7
Reports of Inspectors, Located Lands, 1839-41
Reports on Petitions for Land by Purchase
Report of the Squatter Commission
Report of the Surveyor General's Office on Lands Inspected under Notice of April 4, 1839
Reports to Council on Published Schedule of Lands Liable to Forfeiture, April 4, 1839
Schedule of Forfeited Lands
Settlement Duty Papers, 5 vols.
Surveyor General's Department, Miscellaneous, 1789 (contains the early proclamations, plans
    of survey, the chequered plans)
Surveyors' Letters, 2 vols.
Surveyor General's Locations, 3 vols., 1803-7, 1807-11, 1811 (show location of U.E. loyalist
    grants)
Return of Warrants of Survey to U.E. Loyalists and Their Children, 1800-1803 (shows loca-
    tion of U.E. loyalist grants)
The Surveyor General to the Canada Company
The Surveyor General to the Government regarding the Canada Company
Three boxes labelled as follows: U.[pper] C.[anada] Militia, 1812-13, Prince Regent's Bounty;
    Leased Crown Reserves Squatters

Clergy Reserves Papers
    Minutes of the Clergy Corporation of Upper Canada
    Returns of Inspections of Clergy Reserves
    Schedules of Applications for Clergy Reserves
    Box labelled Clergy Reserves

Heir and Devisee Commission
    Report Books, 5, 6, 7, 8, 8, 10

Canada Company Papers
    Commissioners' Letters and Reports
    Minutes of the Provisional Court of Directors
    Register of Lands Undisposed of to Dec. 31, 1854
    Register of Lands Undisposed of to Dec. 31, 1876
Cartwright Papers
Macaulay Papers
Robinson Papers
Russell Papers
Strachan Papers
Street Papers
Toronto Public Library
    Allan Papers
    Baldwin Papers
    Elmsley Papers
    Jarvis Papers

Powell Papers
Russell Papers
Scadding-McGill Papers
D. W. Smith Papers
Huntington Library, San Marino, California
    Simcoe Letter Book
Samuel Clements Library, Ann Arbor, Michigan
    Simcoe Papers
Wisconsin Historical Society
The Perrault Papers
Diary of a Journey from Trois Riviers to Detroit, July 17, 1796, to Jan. 8, 1797, with extracts
    from several works on North America

B. PRINTED SOURCES

1. Documents

BELL, KENNETH N., and MORRELL, W. P., eds. *Select Documents in British Colonial Policy,
    1830-1860*, Oxford, 1928.
CANADA, PUBLIC ARCHIVES. *Reports*, 1882-1945. Ottawa, Canada.
CANADA. *Indian Treaties and Surrenders from 1680 to 1890*. 3 vols. Ottawa, 1891.
CANADA, BUREAU OF STATISTICS. *Census of Canada*, 1870-71. 5 vols. Ottawa, 1876.
COBBETT, WILLIAM, ed. *Parliamentary History of England from the Earliest Period to the Year
    1803*. 36 vols. London, 1806-1820.
DOUGHTY, ARTHUR G., and McARTHUR, DUNCAN A., eds. *Documents relating to the Constitu-
    tional History of Canada*. Ottawa, 1914.
DOUGHTY, ARTHUR G., and STORY, NORAH, eds. *Documents relating to the Constitutional
    History of Canada, 1819-1828*. Ottawa, 1935.
DOUGHTY, ARTHUR G., ed. *The Elgin Grey Papers, 1846-1852*. 4 vols. Ottawa, 1937.
DURHAM, JOHN GEORGE LAMBTON. *Report on the Affairs of British North America, from the
    Earl of Durham, Her Majesty's High Commissioner* (&c, &c, &c., Parl. Paper, 1839, No.
    13). London, 1839.
——. *The Report and Despatches of the Earl of Durham*. Ridgways, London, 1839.
GREAT BRITAIN, BOARD OF TRADE. *Journal of the Commissioners for Trade and Plantations,
    1759-1763*. London, 1935.
——. ROYAL COMMISSION ON HISTORICAL MANUSCRIPTS. *Report on Manuscripts in Various
    Collections*. 8 vols. London, 1901-14.
——. *Report on American Manuscripts in the Royal Institute of Great Britain*. 4 vols. London,
    1904-9.
——. HOUSE OF COMMONS. *Sessional Papers*.
INNIS, H. A., and LOWER, A. R. M., eds. *Select Documents in Canadian Economic History,
    1783-1885*. Toronto, 1933.
KENNEDY, W. P. M. *Documents of the Canadian Constitution*, Toronto, 1918.
LABAREE, LEONARD WOODS, ed. *Royal Instructions to British Colonial Governors*. 2 vols. New
    York, 1935.
LOWER CANADA. EXECUTIVE COUNCIL. *Extract from the Minutes of Council containing His
    Majesty's late regulations relative to the waste lands of the Crown, with His Excellency's,
    the Governor-General's order of reference respecting the same, to a Committee of the
    whole Council of the Province of Lower-Canada, the Said Committee's report thereon, and
    His Excellency's speech in reply*. (With a preface signed by Charles Berczy.) Quebec, 1798.
MARSHALL, JOHN. *A Digest of All the Accounts diffused through more than 600 volumes of
    journals, reports and papers presented to Parliament since 1799*. London, 1833.
MUNRO, WILLIAM BENNETT, ed. *Documents Relating to the Seigneurial Tenure in Canada,
    1598-1854*. Toronto, 1908.
NEW YORK STATE. *Census of the State of New York for 1835*. Albany, N.Y., 1836.
ONTARIO AGRICULTURAL COMMISSION. *Report*. 5 vols. Toronto, 1881.
ONTARIO PUBLIC ARCHIVES. *Reports*, 1905-1933. Toronto.
ONTARIO DEPARTMENT OF AGRICULTURE. *Emigration to Canada*. Toronto, 1869.
Parliamentary Debates.
RICHARDSON, JAMES DANIEL. *A Compilation of the messages and papers of the presidents, 1789-
    1897*. 10 vols. **Washington, 1895-9.**
SEYBERT, ADAM. *Statistical Annals of the United States of America, 1789-1818*. Philadelphia,
    1818.
SHORTT, ADAM, and DOUGHTY, ARTHUR G., eds. *Documents Relating to the Constitutional
    History of Canada*. 2 vols. Ottawa, 1918.

UPPER CANADA, "Journals of the House of Assembly," 1792-4, 1798-1808, 1810-12, 1814, 1816-24. Printed in Public Archives of Ontario. *Reports,* 1909, 1911-14, from the manuscript journals.

——. "Journals of the Legislative Council," 1792-4, 1798-1808, 1810-12, 1814, 1819, 1821-24. Public Archives of Ontario. *Reports,* 1810, 1915-16.

——. *Journals of the House of Assembly,* 1825-40.

——. *Journals of the Legislative Council,* 1825-40.

——. *Statutes,* 1792-1840.

PROVINCE OF CANADA. *Journals of the Legislative Assembly,* 1841-67.

——. *Statutes,* 1841-67.

2. *Contemporary Material*

[ALIQUIS] *Observations on the history and recent proceedings of the Canada Company addressed in four letters to Frederick Widder esq. one of the commissioners.* Hamilton, Ont., 1845.

BALDWIN, ROBERT. *Election Speech to the 4th Riding of York,* 1847 (Broadside) Widener Library, Cambridge, Mass.

BELL, WILLIAM. *Hints to emigrants; in a series of letters from Upper Canada.* Edinburgh, 1824.

[BIDWELL, BARNABAS] *The Honourable Mr. Sidgewick's Political Last Will and Testament with an Inventory and Appraisal of the Legacies therein Bequeathed.* n.p., 1800. Harvard: Houghton Library.

BONNYCASTLE, SIR RICHARD HENRY. *Canada as it was, is and may be. With considerable additions and an account of recent transactions.* Ed. Sir James Edward Alexander. London, 1852.

BOUCHETTE, JOSEPH. *The British Dominions in North America.* 3 vols. London, 1832.

——. *A Topographical Description of the Province of Lower Canada, with Remarks upon Upper Canada, and on the Relative Connexion of both Provinces with the United States of America.* London, 1815.

BUCKINGHAM, JAMES SILK. *Canada, Nova Scotia, New Brunswick, and the other British Provinces in North America with a Plan of National Colonization.* London, 1843.

CAMPBELL, P. *Travels in the interior inhabited parts of North America in the years 1791 and 1792.* Ed. H. H. Langton, for the Champlain Society. Toronto, 1937.

"CANADIAN LETTERS. Descriptive of a Tour through the Provinces of Lower and Upper Canada in the Course of the Years 1792 and '93." *Canadian Antiquarian and Numismatical Journal,* series 3, IX (July, Oct., 1912.)

CARRUTHERS, J. *Retrospect of Thirty-Six Years' Residence in Canada West: Being a Christian Journal and Narrative.* Hamilton, 1861.

CAVENDISH, SIR HENRY. *Debates … in the year 1774 on the bill … for the government of the province of Quebec.* London, 1839.

CHRISTMAS, the Rev. Henry, ed. *The Emigrant Churchman in Canada.* 2 vols. London, 1849.

CRUIKSHANK, ERNEST ALEXANDER, ed. *The Correspondence of the Honourable Peter Russell.* 3 vols. Ontario Historical Society. Toronto, 1932-6.

——. *The Correspondence of Lieutenant-Governor John Graves Simcoe.* 5 vols. Ontario Historical Society. Toronto, 1922-31.

DARBY, WILLIAM. *A Tour from the City of New York to Detroit.* New York, 1819.

D'ARUSMONT, FRANCES WRIGHT. *View of Society and Manners in America; in a Series of Letters from that country to a friend in England during the Years 1818, 1819 and 1820. By an Englishwoman.* London, 1821.

DAVIS, MATHEW L., ed. *Memoirs of Aaron Burr with Miscellaneous Selections from his Correspondence.* 2 vols. New York, 1837.

DUNCAN, JOHN MORISON. *Travels through a part of the United States and Canada in 1818 and 1819.* 2 vols. Glasgow, 1823.

EDGAR, MATILDA. *Ten Years of Upper Canada in Peace and War, 1805-1815; being the Ridout Letters with Annotations.* Toronto, 1890.

FAIRLEY, MARGARET, ed. *The Selected Writings of William Lyon Mackenzie.* Toronto, 1960.

FERGUSSON, ADAM. *Practical Notes made during a Tour of Canada and a Portion of the United States, in MDCCCXXXI.* Edinburgh, 1833.

FIRTH, EDITH G., ed. *The Town of York, 1793-1815.* The Champlain Society. Toronto, 1962.

GALT, JOHN. *The Autobiography of John Galt,* 2 vols. London, 1833.

GODLEY, JOHN R. *Letters from America.* 2 vols. London, 1844.

GOURLAY, ROBERT FLEMING. *Appeal to the Common Sense, Mind and Manhood of the British Nation.* London, 1826.

——. *The Banished Briton and Neptunian.* Boston, 1843.

——. *Chronicles of Canada.* St. Catharines, Ontario, 1842.

——. *General Introduction to Statistical Account of Upper Canada.* London, 1822.

——. *A Statistical Account of Upper Canada.* 2 vols. London, 1822.

GRAY, HUGH. *Letters from Canada, written During a Residence There in the Years 1806, 1807, and 1808.* London, 1809.

GRECE, CHARLES FREDERICK. *Facts and observations respecting Canada and the United States of America: affording a comparative view of the inducements to emigration presented in those countries.* London, 1819.

GREW, JOHN. *Journal of a Tour from Boston to Niagara Falls and Quebec.* 1803 (Privately printed. n.d.).

HAGERMAN, C. A. *Speech on the Clergy Reserve Question, December 16, 1837.* Toronto, 1837.

HALL, BASIL. *Travels in North America in the Years 1827 and 1828.* 3 vols. Edinburgh, 1829.

HODGSON, ADAM. *Letters from North America written during a Tour in the United States and Canada.* 2 vols. London, 1824.

HOWISON, JOHN. *Sketches of Upper Canada.* 2nd. ed., Edinburgh, 1822.

HINCKS, FRANCIS. *Canada: its financial position and resources.* London, 1849.

Importance of the Island of Minorca and Harbor of Port Mahon ... with a History and Description of both in a letter from a Merchant to a Noble Lord. London, 1756.

INNIS, H. A. and LOWER A. R. M., eds. *Select Documents in Canadian Economic History, 1783-1835.* Toronto, 1933.

JACKSON, JOHN MILLS. *A view of the political situation of the province of Upper Canada in North America.* London, 1809.

JAMESON, MRS. ANNA. *Winter Studies and Summer Rambles in Canada.* 2 vols. New York, 1839.

KNAPLUND, PAUL, ed. *Letters from Lord Sydeham, Governor General of Canada, 1839-41.* London, 1931.

KNOX, WILLIAM. *The Justice and Policy of the Late Act of Parliament for Making more Effectual provision for the Province of Quebec.* London, 1774.

KNOX, WILLIAM, ed. *Extra Official State Papers.* 2 vols. London, 1789.

LAMOND, ROBERT. *A Narrative of the Rise and Progress of Emigration from the Counties of Lanark and Renfrew to the New Settlements in Upper Canada on Government Grant.* Glasgow, 1821. (Mimeographed reprint, California Library, Sutro Branch, San Francisco, 1940.)

LANGTON, W. A., ed. *Early Days in Upper Canada: Letters of John Langton from the Backwoods of Upper Canada and the Audit Office of the Province of Canada.* Toronto ,1926.

LA ROCHEFOUCAULD-LIANCOURT, François Alexandre Frédéric, duc de. *Voyages dans Les Etat-Unis d'Amérique fait en 1795, 1796 et 1797.* Paris, 1799.

——. *Travels through the United States of North America, the country of the Iroquois and Upper Canada, in Years 1795, 1796, and 1797 by the Duke de La Rochefoucauld-Liancourt.* Trans. H. Neuman. 2nd ed., 3 vols. London, 1800.

Letter addressed to two great men on the prospect of peace. London, 1760.

Letter from an American Loyalist in Upper Canada to his friend in England on a pamphlet published by John Mills Jackson, Esquire. York, 1810.

Letter on Canada in 1806 and 1817, during the administration of Governor Gore. Privately printed, 1853.

LILLIE, the REV. ADAM. *Canada, physical, economic, and social.* Toronto, 1855.

MACKENZIE, WILLIAM LYON. *Sketches of Canada and the United States.* London, 1833.

M'LEOD, D. *A brief Review of the Settlement of Upper Canada by the U.E. Loyalists and the Scotch Highlanders in 1783; and of the Grievances which compelled the Canadas to have recourse in defence of their Rights and Liberties, in the Years 1837 and 1838.* Cleveland, 1841.

MACTAGGART, JOHN. *Three years in Canada; an account of the actual state of the country in 1826-7-8.* 2 vols. London, 1829.

MAGRATH, T. W. *Authentic Letters from Upper Canada; With an Account of Canadian Field Sports.* Dublin, 1833.

MARRYAT, FREDERICK. *Second series of a diary in America with remarks on its institutions.* Philadelphia, 1840.

MASERES, FRANCIS. *An account of the proceedings of the British and other protestant inhabitants of the province of Quebec to obtain an House of Assembly.* London, 1775.

MELISH, JOHN. *Travels Through the United States of America.* Belfast, 1818.

Michigan Pioneer and Historical Society. *Historical Collections*, XV (1890), Lansing, 1890.

Minutes of Annual Conferences of the Wesleyan Methodist Church in Canada 1824 to 1845. Toronto, 1846.

MOODIE, SUSANNA. *Roughing it in the Bush.* New York, 1852.

Observations and Reflections on the Quebec Act, passed in the year 1774 for the Settlement of the Province of Quebec. By a Country Gentleman. London, 1782.

Observations upon the Report made by the Board of Trade against the Grenada Laws. London, 1770.

[OGDEN, J. C.] *A Letter from a Gentleman to his friend in England.* Philadelphia, 1795.

OGDEN, J. C. *A Tour through Upper and Lower Canada by a Citizen of the United States.* Litchfield, 1799.

PICKEN, ANDREW. *The Canadas, as they at present commend themselves to the enterprize of emigrants, colonists and capitalists.* London, 1832.

PICKERING, JOSEPH. *Inquiries of An Emigrant; being the Narrative of an English Farmer from the year 1824 to 1830.* 4th ed. London, 1832.

PRESTON, RICHARD A. *Kingston Before the War of 1812: A Collection of Documents.* The Champlain Society. Toronto, 1959.

Principles and Proceedings of the Inhabitants of the District of Niagara for addressing H.R.H. the Prince Regent respecting the claims of sufferers in the war, lands to militiamen, and the general benefit of Upper Canada. Printed at the *Niagara Spectator* office, 1818.

QUAIFE, MILO MILTON, ed. The *John Askin Papers*, 2 vols. Detroit, 1928-31.

RICHARDSON, JOHN. *Eight Years in Canada.* Montreal, 1847.

ROBERTSON, JOHN ROSS, ed. *The Diary of Mrs. John Graves Simcoe, Wife of the First Lieutenant-Governor of the Province of Upper Canada, 1792-6.* Toronto, 1911.

SANDERSON, CHARLES R., ed. The *Arthur Papers*, 3 vols. Toronto, 1957.

SCOTT, DUNCAN CAMPBELL. *John Graves Simcoe.* Toronto, 1905.

SCROPE, GEORGE JULIUS POULETT. *Memoir of the life of the Right Honourable Charles Lord Sydenham.* London, 1844. 2nd ed.

SHIRREFF, PATRICK. *A tour through North America; together with a comprehensive view of the Canadas and United States* (as adapted for agricultural emigration). Edinburgh, 1835.

SMITH, MICHAEL. *Geographical View of the British Provinces in North America.* Baltimore, 1814.

SMITH, WILLIAM. *Historical Account of the Expedition against the Ohio Indians, in 1764.* Ohio Valley Historical Series. Cincinnati, 1868.

SMITH, WILLIAM JAMES, ed. *The Grenville Papers, being the Correspondence of Richard Grenville, Earl Temple.* 4 vols. London, 1852.

SMYTH, DAVID WILLIAM. *A Short Topographical Description of His Majesty's Province of Upper Canada in North America.* London, 1799.

SOCKETT, T. *Emigration Letters from Sussex Emigrants, who sailed from Portsmouth, in April, 1832 ... for Upper Canada.* London, 1831.

———. *Continuation of Letters from Sussex Emigrants.* London, 1833.

———. *A Letter to a member of Parliament containing a statement of the method pursued by the Petworth Committee in sending out Emigrants to Upper Canada.* London, 1833.

SPRAGGF, GEORGE W., ed. The *John Strachan Letter Book, 1812-34.* Toronto, 1946.

STRACHAN, JAMES. *A Visit to the Province of Upper Canada in 1819.* Aberdeen, 1820.

STRACHAN, JOHN. *A Speech of the Venerable John Strachan, D.D., Archdeacon of York, in the Legislative Council, Thursday, Sixth March, 1828.* York, 1828.

STRICKLAND, SAMUEL. *Twenty-Seven Years in Canada West.* 2 vols. London, 1853.

TALBOT, EDWARD ALLEN. *Five Years' Residence in the Canadas.* 2 vols. London, 1824.

TALMAN, JAMES J., ed. *Loyalist Narratives from Upper Canada.* Publications of the Champlain Society, XXVII. Toronto, 1946.

THOMSON, SAMUEL. *Reminiscences of a Canadian Pioneer for the Last Fifty Years.* Toronto, 1884.

Thoughts on the Canada Bill. London, 1791.

A Tour through parts of the United States and Canada. By a British Subject. London, 1828.

[TRAILL, CATHERINE PARR.] *The Backwoods of Canada.* London, 1836.

———. *The backwoods of Canada; being letters from the wife on an emigrant officer illustrative of the Domestic economy of British America.* 2d. ed., London, 1846.

Transactions of the Upper Canadian Convention and Friends to Enquiry with addresses to His Royal Highness the Prince Rupert, Sir Peregrine Maitland, etc. etc. (Niagara Spectator Office, 1818).

WRIGHT, LOUIS B., and TINLING, MARION, eds., *Quebec to Carolina in 1785-1786: The Travels, Diary and Observations of Robert Hunter, Jr., A Young Merchant of London.* San Marino, California, 1943.

YORKE, PHILIP C., ed. *The Life and Correspondence of Philip Yorke, Earl of Hardwicke.* 3 vols. Cambridge, England, 1913.

WALLACE, WILLIAM STEWART, ed. *The Maseres Letters, 1766-1768* (University of Toronto Studies in History and Economics, III, no. 2). Toronto, 1919.

WALROND, THEODORE. *Letters and Journal of James, eighth Earl of Elgin.* London, 1872.

WHITE, PATRICK T. C., ed. *Lord Selkirk's Diary 1803-1804: A Journal of His Travels in British*

North America and the Northeastern United States. Publications of the Champlain Society, XXXVIII. Toronto, 1958.

3. *Newspapers and Almanacks*

Backwoodsman (Elora)
Canada Constellation (Niagara)
Canada Farmer
Canada Gazette
Caroline Almanack (Rochester)
Colonial Advocate and *The Advocate* (Queenstown, York, Toronto)
Constitution (Toronto)
Correspondent and Advocate (Toronto)
Kingston Chronicle
Kingston Herald
Leader (Toronto)
Mirror of Parliament (various)
Montreal Courier
Daily Advertiser (Montreal)
Niagara Chronicle
Niagara Herald
Gleaner (Niagara)
Niagara Spectator
Examiner (Toronto)
Globe (Toronto)
Upper Canada Gazette (York, Toronto)
Upper Canada Guardian
Western Herald (Sandwich)
Patriot (York, Toronto)

C. SECONDARY MATERIAL

1. *General Histories*

The Cambridge History of the British Empire, by eds. J. H. Rose, A. P. Newton, E. A. Benians. 6 vols. Cambridge, England, 1929-40.
Kingsford, William, *The History of Canada.* 10 vols. Toronto, 1889-98.
MacMullen, John, *The History of Canada.* Brockville, Ont., 1868.
Shortt, Adam and Doughty, Arthur G., eds., *Canada and its Provinces.* 23 vols. Toronto, 1917.
Winsor, Justin, *Narrative and Critical History of America.* 8 vols. Boston, 1889.

2. *Monographs*

ABERDEEN, JENNIE W. *John Galt.* Oxford, 1937.
ABERNETHY, THOMAS PERKINS. *Western Lands and the American Revolution.* New York, 1937.
AKAGI, ROY HIDEMACHI. *The Town Proprietors of New England.* Philadelphia, 1924.
ALVORD, CLARENCE WADSWORTH. *The Mississippi Valley in British Politics.* 2 vols. Cleveland, 1917.
BASYE, ARTHUR HERBERT. *The Lords Commissioners of Trade and Plantations.* New Haven, 1925.
BEMIS, SAMUEL FLAGG. *Pinckney's Treaty.* Baltimore, 1926.
———. *Jay's Treaty.* New York, 1923.
BOND, BEVERLEY WAUGH. *The Quit Rent System in the American Colonies.* New Haven, 1919.
———. *The Civilization of the Old Northwest.* New York, 1934.
BREBNER, JOHN BARTLETT. *The Neutral Yankees of Nova Scotia.* New York, 1937.
BURT, ALFRED LEROY. *The Old Province of Quebec.* Toronto, 1923.
CANNIF, WILLIAM A. *History of the Settlement of Upper Canada.* Toronto, 1869.
CARROTHERS, WILLIAM. *Emigration from the British Isles.* London, 1929.
CARTWRIGHT, the REV. C. E. *Life and Letters of the late Hon. Richard Cartwright.* Toronto, 1876.
Centennial of the Settlement of Upper Canada by the United Empire Loyalists, 1784-1884, published by the Centennial Committee. Toronto, 1885.
CLAPHAM, JOHN HAROLD. *An Economic History of Modern Britain: The Early Railway Age, 1820-1850.* London, 1926.
CLARK, S. D. *Movements of Political Protest in Canada, 1640-1840.* Toronto, 1959.

COUPLAND, REGINALD. *The Quebec Act.* Oxford, 1925.

COWAN, HELEN I. *British Emigration to British North America, 1783-1837* (University of Toronto Studies in History and Economics, IV, no. 2). Toronto, 1928.

CREIGHTON, D. G. *The Commercial Empire of the St. Lawrence, 1760-1850.* Toronto, 1937.

CRUIKSHANK, ERNEST ALEXANDER. *The Settlement of the United Empire Loyalists on the Upper St. Lawrence and Bay of Quinte in 1784.* Toronto, 1934.

——. *The Story of Butler's Rangers.* Welland, Ontario, 1893.

——. *Records of Niagara, 1778-1783* (Niagara Historical Society Publications, No. 38). Niagara-on-the-Lake, 1927.

——. *Records of Niagara, 1794-7* (Niagara Historical Society Publications, No. 39). Niagara-on-the-Lake, 1928.

DENT, JOHN CHARLES. *Canada Since the Union of 1841: The Last Forty Years.* 2 vols. Toronto, 1849.

DONALDSON, THOMAS. *The Public Domain.* Washington, 1884.

DUNHAM, AILEEN. *Political Unrest in Upper Canada, 1815-1836* (Published for the Royal Colonial Institute, Imperial Studies No. 1). London, 1927.

EDWARDS, BRYAN. *The history, civil and commercial, of the British colonies in the West Indies.* 4 vols. Philadelphia, 1806.

ERMATINGER, C. O. *The Talbot Regime, 1791-1840.* St. Thomas, Ont., 1904.

ERMATINGER, EDWARD. *Life of Colonel Talbot and the Talbot Settlement, Its Rise and Progress.* St. Thomas, Ont., 1859.

ERNLE, the RT. HON. LORD. *English Farming, Past and Present.* 4th ed., London, 1927.

FENTON, JAMES. *A History of Tasmania.* London, 1884.

FITZMAURICE, LORD EDWARD, *Life of William, Earl of Shelburne,* 3 vols. London, 1875-76.

FLENLEY, R., ed. *Essays in Canadian History presented to George MacKinnon Wrong.* Toronto, Toronto, 1939.

GALPIN, WILLIAM FREEMAN. *The Grain Supply of England during the Napoleonic Period.* New York, 1925.

GARNETT, RICHARD. *Edward Gibbon Wakefield.* New York, 1898.

GLAZEBROOK, G. P. de T. *Sir Charles Bagot in Canada.* London, 1929.

GORDON, ROBERT KAY. *John Galt.* Toronto, 1920.

GRAHAM, GERALD SANFORD. *British Policy and Canada, 1774-1791.* London, 1930.

GREY, EARL. *The Colonial Policy of Lord John Russell's Administration.* 2 vols. 2nd ed., London, 1853.

GUILLET, EDWIN CLARENCE. *The lives and times of the patriots; an account of the rebellion in Upper Canada, 1837-38 and the patriot agitation in the United States, 1837-1842.* Toronto, 1938.

——. *The Valley of the Trent.* The Champlain Society. Toronto, 1957.

HAMIL, FRED COYNE. *Lake Erie Baron.* Toronto, 1955.

——. *The Valley of the Lower Thames, 1640 to 1850.* Toronto, 1951.

HANSEN, MARCUS LEE, and BREBNER, J. BARTLETT. *The Mingling of the Canadian and American Peoples.* New Haven, 1940.

HIBBARD, BENJAMIN HORACE. *A History of the Public Land Policies.* New York, 1924.

HIGGINS, RUTH. *Expansion in New York.* Columbus, Ohio, 1931.

HIGGINS, W. H. *The Life and Times of Joseph Gould.* Toronto, 1887.

HINCKS, FRANCIS. *Reminiscenses.* Montreal, 1884.

HITCHENS, FRED B. *The Colonial Land and Emigration Commission.* Philadelphia, 1931.

HODGETTS, J. E. *Pioneer Public Service: An Administrative History of the United Canada 1841-1867.* Toronto, 1955.

HODGINS, JOHN GEORGE, ed. *Documentary History of Education in Upper Canada.* 28 vols., Toronto, 1894-1910.

HUNTER, ANDREW F. *A History of Simcoe County.* 2 vols. Barrie, Ontario, 1909.

JONES, ROBERT LESLIE. *History of Agriculture in Ontario 1613-1880.* Toronto, 1946.

KENNEDY, W. M. P. *Documents, of the Canadian Constitution.* Toronto, 1918.

KNAPLUND, PAUL. *James Stephen and the British Colonial System 1813-1847.* Madison, Wis., 1953.

LAJEUNESSE, ERNEST J. *The Windsor Border Region, Canada's Southernmost Frontier; A Collection of Documents.* The Champlain Society, Toronto, 1960.

LANDON, FRED. *Western Ontario and the American Frontier.* Toronto, 1941.

LEACOCK, STEPHEN. *Baldwin, LaFontaine, Hincks.* Makers of Canada Series, VIII. Toronto, 1912.

LINDSEY, CHARLES. *The Clergy Reserves.* Toronto, 1851.

LIZARS, ROBINA, and MCFARLANE, CATHERINE. *In the Days of the Canada Company.* Toronto, 1896.

LOWER, A. R. M., and INNIS, HAROLD A. *Settlement and the Forest and Mining Frontier.* Canadian Frontiers of Settlement, IX. Toronto, 1936.

LUCAS, SIR CHARLES PRESTWOOD, ed. *Lord Durham's Report on the Affairs of British North America.* 3 vols. Oxford, 1912.

MACDONALD, NORMAN. *Canada, 1763-1841: Immigration and Settlement,* London, 1939.

MARTIN, CHESTER. *Empire and Commonwealth.* Oxford, 1929.

——. *Lord Selkirk's Work in Canada.* Oxford, 1916.

MERRITT, JEDEDIAH PRENDERGAST. *Biography of the Hon. William Hamilton Merritt, M.P.* St. Catharines, Ont., 1875.

MILLMAN, THOMAS R. *Jacob Mountain, First Lord Bishop of Quebec.* Toronto, 1947.

MOIR, JOHN. *Church and State in Canada West.* Toronto, 1959.

MYERS, GUSTAVUS. *History of Canadian Wealth.* Chicago, 1914.

NAMIER, LEWIS BERNSTEIN. *England in the Age of the American Revolution.* London, 1930.

——. *The Structure of Politics at the Accession of George III.* London, 1929.

NEW, CHESTER. *Lord Durham.* Oxford, 1929.

PATERSON, GILBERT C. *Land Settlement in Upper Canada* (Sixteenth Report of the Ontario Public Archives). Toronto, 1921.

PEASE, THEODORE CALVIN. "Anglo-French Boundary Disputes in the West, 1749-1763." Illinois State *Historical* Library, Collections, XXVII. Springfield, 1936.

READ, DAVID BREAKENRIDGE. *The Lieutenant-Governors of Upper Canada and Ontario, 1792-1899.* Toronto, 1900.

REID, STUART J. *Life and Letters of the First Earl of Durham.* 2 vols., London, 1906.

RIDDELL, WILLIAM RENWICK. *The Life of John Graves Simcoe.* Toronto, 1926.

——. *The Life of William Dummer Powell.* Lansing, Michigan, 1924.

ROBINSON, CHARLES WALKER. *Life of Sir John Beverley Robinson.* Toronto, 1904.

RYERSON, EGERTON. *The Loyalists of America and Their Times.* 2 vols. Toronto, 1880.

SCOTT, DUNCAN CAMPBELL. *John Graves Simcoe.* Toronto, 1905.

SCROPE, GEORGE JULIUS POULETT. *Memoir of the life of the Right Honourable Charles Lord Sydenham.* London, 1844. 2nd ed.

SISSONS, C. B. *Egerton Ryerson, His Life and Letters.* 2 vols. Toronto, 1937, 1947.

SMITH, W. H. *Canada: Past, Present and Future.* 2 vols. Toronto, 1851.

SOSIN, JACK M. *Whitehall and Wilderness.* Lincoln, Neb., 1961.

SPECTOR, MARION MARGARET. *The American Department of the British Government.* New York, 1940.

TEXTOR, LUCY ELIZABETH. *A Colony of Émigrés in Canada, 1798-1816* (University of Toronto Studies in History and Economics, III, no. 1). Toronto, 1905.

THOMAS, BRINLEY. *Migration and Economic Growth.* Cambridge University Press, 1954.

TREAT, PAYSON JACKSON. *The National Land System, 1795-1820.* New York, 1910.

TUCKER, GILBERT NORMAN. *The Canadian Commercial Revolution, 1845-1851.* New Haven, 1936.

TURCOTTE, LOUIS. *Canada sous l'Union, 1841-1867.* Quebec, 1882.

UPTON, HARRIET TAYLOR. *History of the Western Reserve.* 3 vols. Chicago, 1910.

VAN AVERY, DALE. *Men of the Western Waters.* Cambridge, 1956.

VON RUVILLE, ALBERT. *William Pitt, Earl of Chatham.* 3 vols. London, 1907.

WALLACE, WILLIAM STEWART. *The United Empire Loyalists.* Toronto, 1914.

WILSON, GEORGE E. *The Life of Robert Baldwin.* Toronto, 1933.

YOUNG, D. M. *The Colonial Office in the Early Nineteenth Century.* London, 1961.

3. *Articles*

AITCHISON, J. H. "The Municipal Corporations Act of 1849," *Canadian Historical Review,* XXX (1949), 107-22.

BANTING, E. W., and HUNTER, A. F. "Surveyor Charles Rankin's Exploration for the Pioneer Road, Garrafraxa to Owen Sound, 1837," *Ontario Historical Society, Papers and Records,* XXVII (1931), 497-510.

BOND, C. C. J. "The British Base at Carleton Island," *Ontario History,* LII (1960), 1-16.

BREITHAUPT, W. H. "Dundas Street and other early Upper Canada roads," *Ontario Historical Society, Papers and Records,* XXI (1934), 5-10.

BURPEE, LAWRENCE J. "Influence of the War of 1812 upon the settlement of the Canadian West," *Ontario Historical Society, Papers and Records,* XII (1914), 114-20.

CARNOCHAN, JANET. "The Comte de Puisaye—A Forgotten Page of Canadian History," *Ontario Historical Society, Papers and Records,* V (1904), 36-52.

COLGATE, WILLIAM. "Letters from the Honourable Chief Justice William Osgoode," *Ontario History,* XLVI (1954), 79-95, 141-168.

COYNE, JAMES, H. "The Talbot Papers," Royal Society of Canada, *Proceedings and Transactions*, series 3, I (1907-8), Sec. 2, 15-210, III (1909-10), Sec. 2, 67-196.

CRAIG, GERALD M. "Comments on Upper Canada in 1836," *Ontario History*, XLVII (1955), 163-81.

CRANE, VERNER W., ed. "Hints relative to the division and government of the conquered and newly acquired countries in America," *Mississippi Valley Historical Review*, VIII (1921-22), 367-73.

CREIGHTON, D. G. "The Economic Background of the Rebellions of Eighteen Thirty-Seven," *Canadian Journal of Economics and Political Science*, III (1937), 322-34.

CROSS, MICHAEL S. "The Lumber Community of Upper Canada," *Ontario History*, LXII (1960), 213-33.

CRUIKSHANK, ERNEST ALEXANDER. "The Genesis of the Canada Act," Ontario Historical Society, *Papers and Records*, XXVIII (1932), 155-322.

———. "A Sketch of the Public Life and Services of Robert Nichol," Ontario Historical Society, *Papers and Records*, XIX (1921), 6-81.

———. "Post-War Discontent at Niagara in 1818," Ontario Historical Society, *Papers and Records*, XXIX (1933), 14-46.

———. "The Chesapeake Crisis as it affected Upper Canada," Ontario Historical Society, *Papers and Records*, XXIV (1927), 281-322.

———. "The Early History of the London District," Ontario Historical Society, *Papers and Records*, XXIV (1927), 145-280.

———. "The Founding of Three Military Settlements in Eastern Ontario—Perth, Lanark and Richmond, 1815-20," Ontario Historical Society, *Papers and Records*, XX (1923), 98-104.

———. "A Study of Disaffection in Upper Canada 1812-1815," Royal Society of Canada, *Proceedings and Transactions*, series 3, VI (1912) 11-65.

———. "An Experiment in Colonization in Upper Canada," Ontario Historical Society, *Papers and Records*, XXV (1929), 32-77.

FIRTH, EDITH G. "The Administration of Peter Russell," *Ontario History*, XLVII (1955), 163-81.

[JOHN GALT]. "Colonial Discontent." Part II: "Upper Canada," *Blackwood's Magazine*, XXVI September, 1829), 334-7.

GARLAND, the REV. M. A. "Some Frontier and American Influences in Upper Canada Prior to 1837," London and Middlesex Historical Society, *Transactions*, XIII (1920), 5-33.

GATES, PAUL W. "Official Encouragement to Immigration by the Province of Canada," *Canadian Historical Review*, XV (1934), 24-38.

GILROY, MARION. "The Partition of Nova Scotia," *Canadian Historical Review*, XIV (1933), 375-91.

GUEST, HENRY M. "Upper Canada's First Political Party," *Ontario History*, LIV (1962), 275-96.

HAMIL, FRED COYNE. "Lord Selkirk's Work in Upper Canada," Ontario Historical Society, *Papers and Records*, XXXVII (1945), 35-48.

HIGHAM, C. S. S. "The General Assembly of the Leeward Islands," *English Historical Review*, XLI (1926), 190-209, 366-88.

HUMPHREYS, R. A. "Lord Shelburne and the Proclamation of 1763," *English Historical Review*, XLIX (1934), 241-64.

HUNTER, A. F. "The Probated Wills Of Men Prominent In the Affairs Of Early Upper Canada," Ontario Historical Society, *Papers and Records*, XXIII (1926), 328-59, XXIV (1927), 381-409.

JOHNSTON, CHARLES M. "An Outline Of Early Settlement In The Grand River Valley," *Ontario History*, LIV (1962), 43-67.

———. "Joseph Brant, the Grand River Lands and the Northwest Crisis," *Ontario History*, LV (1963), 267-82.

KNAPLUND, PAUL. "Extract from Gladstone's Private Political Diary Touching Canadian Questions in 1840," *Canadian Historical Review*, XX (1939), 197-8.

———. "Notes and Documents," *Canadian Historical Review*, XX (1939), 198.

LANDON, FRED. "The Common Man in the Era of the Rebellion." Canadian Historical Association, *Report*, 1937, 76-91.

LONGLEY, R. S. "Emigration and the Crisis of 1837 in Upper Canada," *Canadian Historical Review*, XVII (1936), 29-40.

LOWER, A. R. M. "Immigration and Settlement in Canada, 1812-1820," *Canadian Historical Review*, III (1922), 37-47.

———. "The Assault on the Laurentian Barrier," *Canadian Historical Review*, X (1929), 294-307.

MACKAY, R. A. "The Political Ideas of William Lyon Mackenzie," *Canadian Journal of Economics and Political Science*, III (1937), 1-22.

MALTBY, PETER L., and MONICA. "A New Look at the Peter Robinson Emigration of 1823," *Ontario History*, LV (1963), 15-21.

MARTIN, CHESTER. "Lord Durham's Report and Its Consequences," *Canadian Historical Review*, XX (1939), 178-94.

MEALING, STANLEY R. "The Enthusiasm of John Graves Simcoe," Canadian Historical Association, *Report*, (1958), pp. 50-62.

——. "D. W. Smith's Plan for Granting Land to Loyalists' Children," *Ontario History*, XLVIII (1956), 133-37.

METCALFE, GEORGE. "Samuel Bealy Harrison: A Forgotten Reformer," *Ontario History*, L (1958), 117-31.

MOIR, JOHN. "The Settlement of the Clergy Reserves," *Canadian Historical Review*, XXXVIII (1956), 46-62.

MORRISON, HUGH MACKENZIE. "The Principle of Free Grants in the Land Act of 1841," *Canadian Historical Review*, XIV (1933), 392-407.

——. "The Background of the Free Land Homestead Law of 1872," Canadian Historical Association, *Report* (1935), 38-66.

NEATBY, HILDA. "Chief Justice William Smith: An Eighteenth Century Whig Imperialist," *Canadian Historical Review*, XXVIII (1947), 44-67.

NELSON, W. H. "The Last Hope of the American Loyalists," *The Canadian Historical Review*, XXXII (1951), 22-42.

NEW, CHESTER. "The Rebellion of 1837 in its Larger Setting," Canadian Historical Association, *Report* (1937), 5-17.

ORMSBY, WILLIAM G. "The Civil List Question in the Province of Upper Canada," *Canadian Historical Review*, XXXV (1954), 93-118.

PLAUNT, DOROTHY. "The Honourable Peter Russell, Administrator of Upper Canada," *Canadian Historical Review*, XX (1939), 258-74.

REGEHR, THEODORE D. "Land Ownership in Upper Canada, 1783-1796: A Background to the First Table of Fees," *Ontario History*, LV (1963), 35-48.

RICHARDS, J. HOWARD. "Lands and Policies: Attitudes and Controls in the Alienation of Lands in Ontario During the First Century of Settlement," *Ontario History*, L (1958), 193-209.

RICHARDSON, A. J. H., and COWAN, HELEN, I. "William Berczy's Williamsburg Documents," Rochester Historical Society, *Publications*, XX (1942), 141-265.

RIDDELL, R. G. "A Study in the Land Policy of the Colonial Office," *Canadian Historical Review*, XVIII (1937), 385-405.

RIDDELL, WILLIAM RENWICK. "*Scandalum Magnatum* in Upper Canada," *Journal of the American Institute of Criminal Law and Criminology*, IV (1913-14), 12-19.

——. "Robert Fleming Gourlay," Ontario Historical Association, *Papers and Records*, XIV (1916), 5-133.

——. "William Firth," *Canadian Bar Review*, I (1923), 326-37, 404-17.

——. "The Bidwell Elections," Ontario Historical Society, *Papers and Records*, XXI (1924), 236-44.

——. "An Official Record of Slavery in Upper Canada," Ontario Historical Society, *Papers and Records*, XXV (1929), 393-7.

——. "Mr. Justice Thorpe," *Canadian Law Times*, XL (1920), 907-24.

——. "Retention of Canada at the Peace of 1763," Ontario Historical Association, *Papers and Records*, XXV (1929), 388-92.

ROY, P. G. "Les Concessions en fief et seigneurie sous le régime anglais," *Le Bulletin des Recherches Historiques*, XXXIV (1928), 323-5.

SAUNDERS, ROBERT E. "What was the Family Compact?" *Ontario History*, XLIX (1957), 165-70.

SHORTT, ADAM. "The Economic Effect of the War Upon Canada," Royal Society of Canada, *Proceedings and Transactions*, series 3, X (1917), 65-74.

——. "The Honourable John McGill and the first problems of domestic exchange in Upper Canada," *Journal of the Canadian Bankers' Association*, XXIX (1922), 277-90.

——. "Founders of Canadian Banking: The Hon. John McGill," *Journal of the Canadian Bankers' Association*, XXIX (1922), 288.

SIOUSSAT, ST. GEORGE LOUIS. "The Breakdown of the Royal Management of Lands in Southern Provinces, 1773-1775," *Agricultural History*, III (1929), 67-98.

SOWARD, FREDERICK HUBERT. "The Laws of Canada, 1783-1791," *Canadian Historical Review*, V (1924), 314-35.

SPRAGGE, GEORGE W. "Colonization Roads In Canada West," *Ontario History*, XLIX (1957), 1-17.

——. "The Districts of Upper Canada," *Ontario History*, XXXIX (1947), 91-100.

TAYLOR, GRIFFITHS. "Towns and Townships in Southern Ontario," *Economic Geography*, XXI (1945), 88-96.

WALLACE, WILLIAM STEWART. "The Beginnings of British Rule in Canada," *Canadian Historical Review*, VI (1925), 208-21.

WEATHERFORD, JOHN. "The Vicomte de Vaux: Would-Be Canadian," *Ontario History*, XLVIII (1957), 49-57.

WILSON, G. A. "The Clergy Reserves: 'Economical Mischiefs' or Sectarian Issue?" *Canadian Historical Review*, XLII (1961), 281-99.

ZEICHNER, OTTO. "William Smith's 'Observations on America'," New York State Historical Association, *Proceedings*, XL (1941), 328-40.

ABERDEEN, Lord, 133, 136, 139
Addison, Rev. Robert, 50, 147
Aliens: unable to hold land, 92, 119–20; bills for naturalizing and validating titles of, 120–2, 188, 263. See also Americans.
Alien and Sedition Act, 112–3, 184
Allan, William, 183, 187, 259
Allcock, Henry, 58, 71, 75, 126
Allen Ebener, 40
Alvord, Clarence W., 5
Americans: admitted as late loyalists, 19; Simcoe promotes immigration of, 28–9; Dundas disapproves of, 29, 37; attitude of Land Boards to, 29; attitude of Russell to, 39; as speculators in township grants, 40, 46; intrigues of, 44–5, 49; during War of 1812, 85, 325, n. 4; plans to offset influence of, 85–6, 152; political disabilities of, 98–100; exclusion policy towards, 98, 100–7, 109, 120–1, 124; Buchanan on, 123; Mackenzie supported by, 121; located by Talbot, 128; votes of, refused, 188; political issues related to, 222–3
American Revolution, 9, 22, 25
Annexation crisis, 270, 274
Arthur, Sir George, 218, 220, 228, 230, 259, 260, 262, 265
Askin, J. H., 187
Askin, John, 30, 35, 44, 57, 75, 161
Assessment acts: early attempts at general land tax, 142–4; Act of 1803, defects of, 143–5; re-enactments of, 145; assessment and road acts of 1819, 145–6; opposition to Act of 1824, 147–9; results of tax sales under, 149–50; penalties of, modified, 149; reformers opinion of land tax, 150–1; powers of District Councils to tax, 239; efforts to amend assessment laws, 275–6
Assignments: register of provided by law, 284; restrictions evaded by means of, 286; quantity of, 286–7

BABY, James, 147
Bagot, Sir Charles, 246, 264
Baldwin, Augustus, 187, 259
Baldwin Robert: on secularization of reserves, 250, 307; on district councils, 237
Baldwin, William Warren: on township grants, 42-3, 319, n. 23; on Gore, 84; leads radicals, 101; opposes Assessment Act of 1824, 147; on sales of land for taxes, 149; on Canada Co., 169, 226, 304; on election

of 1836, 188; on voting on location tickets, 189; evidence for Durham's Report, 234; on Buller's ideas, 239
Baldwin–LaFontaine administrations, 270, 272–6, 280–2, 287
Ball, H. & Co., 51
Bathurst, Lord: and emigration from Scotland, 86; on Crown Reserves, 92; on exclusion of American immigrants, 98, 102, 119, 121; reduces size of free grants, 124; directs that collection of fees be postponed, 130–1; approves taxation of non-residents, 147; on rectories, 207; on Canada Company's Act, 207
Baynes, Colonel Edward, 87
Beasley, Richard, 44, 99, 110, 143
Berczy, William, 40, 41, 45, 49
Bidwell, Barnabas, 120, 157
Bidwell, Marshall Spring, 111, 188, 189
Board of Trade: and settlement of Canada, 3–5; and proclamation of 1763, 4, 5; and question of an Assembly, 5–6; and seigneurial tenure, 8; and Ireland, 10
Bolton, Colonel, 11
Bond, Phineas, 28
Bonnycastle, Sir Richard, 136
Boulton, George Strange, 177
Brant, Joseph, 14, 45, 49, 50
British-American Land Co., 271
Brock, Sir Isaac, 85
Buchanan, James, 92, 123, 130
Buller, Charles: share of Durham's Report, 221; on Wakefield's proposals, 232; proposes compensation for surrender of wild land, 238
Burr, Aaron, 41, 45, 77
Burt, A. L., 8, 9
Burton, Colonel Ralph, 9
Burwell, Mahlon, 219
Butler's Rangers, 14

CAMERON, Malcolm, 249
Canada Committee of 1828, 224
Canada Company: formation of, 168–9; purchases by, 169, 201–4; disposition of Crown Reserves by, 169–70, 254; criticisms of, 170; complaints by, 173; Reformers objections to, 174–5; benefitted from increased price of Crown land, 178, 190, 227, 233; valuation of reserves for, 201–2; Strachan's opposes sale to, 202–4; takes Huron Tract, 204–5; payments of, how used, 205–6; Act for, mis-

understood, 205; ignored by Durham, 225–6; wanted to manage Clergy Reserves and Crown lands, 250, 279; unwilling to aid emigration scheme 271. See also Clergy Reserves, Crown Reserves, Galt, Squatters, Strachan

Canadian Land and Emigration Co., 300–1

Canadian Letters, 34, 35

Canals: Rideau, 85–6, 87, 93; St. Lawrence, 35, 114, 117; Welland, 118

Canniff, William, 14, 59

Carleton, Sir Guy: opposed to grant of an Assembly, 6; recommendations on seigneurial tenure, 8; on Quebec Act, 9; instructions to, 10; sends loyalists to Canada, 14–5. See also Dorchester

Carolina, 7

Cartier–Macdonald administration, 300, 301

Cartwright, Richard: on magistrates' certificates, 29; on flour contract, 35; criticizes Simcoe, 39; on exchange of certificates for patents, 53; member Heir and Devisee Commission, 57; author of *Letters from an American Loyalist*, 78; on the economic future of province, 114; on settlement duties, 135; on clergy reserves, 219

Casey, Samuel, 150

Casey, Willett, 99, 111

Castlereagh, Lord, 82

Casual and Territorial Revenue: Assembly demands control of, 84, 155–8, 227, 229; Lieutenant-Governor instructed not to relinquish, 157, 158; Maitland fails to develop, 158, 159, 165–6; inadequate accounting for and information about, 186, 228–9; surrender of offered on conditions, 189; Head opposes offer of surrender of, 190; offer not accepted, 192; surrendered by Act of Union, 256

Cathcart, Lord, 249

Caveats, 42, 55, 142

Certificates of occupation, 23

Chalmers, George, 23

Chapin, Israel, 49

Chequered plan: devised and adopted, 51–2; deviations from, 51, 64; specifications for clergy reserves under, 52; effect of plan, 52; becomes unnecessary, 169; not applied to Huron Tract, 205

Chewett, William, 135

Chippewa Indians, 11, 313, n. 8

Church Society, 246

Clark, Thomas, 102, 103, 104, 108, 109, 117, 147, 150

Clarke, Lieutenant-Governor Alured, 33

Claus, William, 112

Clear Grits, 251, 284

Clench, Ralph, 44, 77, 99, 101

Clergy Corporation: created to lease reserves, 198–9; arouses opposition of dissenters, 199; work of terminated, 199; criticized by Colborne, 212; proposal to sell reserves through, 201, 207; legality of charter questioned, 212

Clergy Reserves: origin of, 24; location of, 27, 51–2; complicate issue of patents, 54–6; opposition to, 100, 101, 104, 116, 155; Gourlay on, 105, 116, 117, 331, n. 131; leasing system for, 198–9; as a hindrance to settlement, 198, 201, 202, 210, 212; Canada Co. proposes to buy, 201–2, 204; Church of England's claim to, 196–7, 200, 205; sectarian conflict over, 207, 209; Imperial Clergy Reserves Sales Act of 1827, 207–8, 210–11; sales under, suspended, 213; re-investment proposals, 213, 218, 220; Assembly's addresses and bills for utilization of, 207, 209, 214–5, 218–20; reserves as cause of rebellion, 224; attempts to settle clergy reserves question by Head, 217–8; by Arthur, 218–9; by Sydenham, 240–2; Strachan's attitude, 242; Imperial Clergy Reserves Act of 1840, 242–4; sales by Crown Lands Department under, 245–50; discontent with the clergy reserves act, 243–4; inspections of reserves, 247; management by ecclesiastical corporations proposed, 248–9; leads to Secularization Act of 1854, 250–1; opposition to clergy reserves analyzed, 252; total sales and average prices of, 253–4, 309; compared with sales Crown Reserves, 254; allocation of funds to municipalities, 254–5; general effect of reserves and chequered plan, 255. See also Strachan, Canada Co.

Clinton, Sir Henry, 26, 35

Cockburn, Lieutenant-Colonel 92, 176

Colborne, Sir John: remodels Legislative Council, 100; alarmed by influx of Americans, 121; struggles to control speculation, 133; settlement duty policies sabotaged, 132, 135; colonization policies of, 177–185; on control of revenues, 182; on nature of colonial society, 182–3; tries to build a third force, 183–4; Strachan's criticisms of, 183–4; dissatisfaction of Colonial Office with, 184; criticizes Canada Committee of 1828, 210; proposes re-investment of Clergy Reserves, 212–3; endows rectories, 215, disagrees with Wakefield and Goderich, 176, 180

Collins, John, 17, 18

Colonial Advocate, 177, 208

Colonial Land and Emigration Commission: powers did not extend to British North America, 232; attempts to instruct Sydenham fail, 256; suggestions for Land Act of 1841, 257, 263; advocated pre-emption, 262; object to 50-acre free grants, 264; on price for land, 262, 267

Colonial Tax Repeal Act, 22, 80, 82, 157, 232

Colonization Roads: Sydenham initiates policy; 259–61; attitude Draper–Sherwood ministries to, 268–9; D. B. Papineau's plan for additional roads, 269; limitations of policy, 273; new roads begun in 1848, 273–4, location of, 351, n. 24, 353, n. 14;

definition of, 287; source of funds for, 287; J. H. Burke on, 287, 298; new roads and lumber industry, 287–8

Concessions, 27, 408, n. 24

Connecticut, 30

Constitution, 224

Constitutional Act: provisions of, 23, 24; powers of provincial legislature under, 24–5, 81, 137, 226, 242; and Crown Reserves, 160; meaning of a Protestant Clergy in, 197, 208; repeal of clause 41 of proposed, 201; bills for repeal of Clergy Reserves clauses, 225, 244

Convention of 1818: organized by Gourlay, 108–9; delegates to, 110; petitions of, 110; complaints of Gourlay about, 110; anti-Convention bill, 110–11, 112, 114; members denied militia grants, 113, 118

Cooper, William, 305

Corn Laws, 114

Correspondent and Advocate, 193, 226

Counties: Bathurst, 89; Bruce, 276, 286, 292, 296; Dundas, 99; Durham, 77, 83, 99; Essex 99, 121; Frontenac, 276; Grey, 286, 296; Hastings, 17, 99; Huron, 190, 276, 286, 291, 295, 296; Lambton, 276; Leeds, 77, 85; Lennox and Addington, 99, 111, 121, 276; Lincoln, 77, 99, 114; Middlesex, 77, 99, 187, 188; Northumberland, 77, 83, 99; Oxford, 77, 99, 188; Peel, 296; Perth, 296; Peterboro, 276; Prince Edward, 77; Simcoe, 276; Stormont, 85, 109; Waterloo, 296; Wellington, 291, 293, 295, 296; York, 77, 99

County Rates, 142, 143

Cramahe, Lieutenant-Governor H. T., 9

Credit System: institutued, 284–5; tax problems created by, 286; restrictions of evaded 286, delinquents' land forfeited, 301; Crown Reserves: origin, 24, 160; purpose of, 28, 80, 160; chequered plan for 51; Simcoe on, 161; used by Military Settling Department, 92, 161; unpopularity of, 99, 101, 105, 155, 163, 164; grants of by Gore, 105, 109, 162; effect of free grants on value of, 152; leasing system of fails, 163–5; Robinson's plan for sale of, 166–8; Gourlay proposes sale of, 107, 117, 167; sold to Canada Co., 168; Maitland's objections to sale, 168–9; continuous creation of till 1840, 169. See also Canada Co.

Crysler, John, 131

Customs Duties: provincial, 82, 142; imperial, 81–3, 156–7, 227

DALHOUSIE, Lord, 92, 95, 123, 124, 157, 176

Danforth, Asa, 45, 50

Danforth Road, 51

Dartmouth, Lord, 10

Devereaux, Nicholas, 305

Dickson, William, 101, 102, 104, 105, 109, 112

Districts: Bathurst, 172, 265; Brock, 265; Col-borne, 265, 269; Dalhousie, 265; Eastern, 68, 87, 104, 107, 265; Gore, 104, 170, 172, 266; Home 68, 76, 78, 83, 87, 104, 107, 165, 170, 172, 266; Johnstown, 85, 87, 104, 107, 110; London, 69, 70, 77, 78, 79, 87, 104, 110, 116, 170, 172, 266; Midland, 68, 85, 87, 104, 110, 117, 123, 170, 172, 266, 269; Newcastle, 110, 165, 172, 265, 266; Niagara, 68, 77, 104, 110, 112, 116, 117, 123, 170; Ottawa, 104, 110, 265; Simcoe, 265; Talbot, 266; Victoria, 266, 269; Wellington, 265; Western, 75, 77, 104, 110, 172

District Councils: Durham and Sydenham's proposals for, 236; clauses of Union bill for, 236–7; Lower Canada ordinance creating, 237; Act of 1841 creating for Upper Canada, 237–8; tax problems arising from, 238; of Eastern Townships, 238; reorganized with elective officials, 276. See also wild land tax

Dorchester, Lord: Carleton returns as, 16; instructions to, 17, 22, 23; bounty of, 17, 20, 21; creates District Land Boards, 19; creates distinction U.E.L., 20–21; advocates free and common socage tenure, 22–3; land regulations of, 29, 63, 65, 69, 125, 134; on trans-Appalachian country, 26; opposes Simcoe's schemes, 32–7; renounces his land fees, 62; makes reserves for Crown, 160–1. See also Carleton.

Dorland, Thomas, 77, 83

Draper, William Henry, 193, 259

Draper administration, 279, 284, 289

Drummond, Sir Gordon, 85, 87, 88, 89, 100

Duncan, Richard, 40–1

Duncombe, Charles, 188

Dundas, Henry, 26, 29, 32, 119, 197

Dunlop, R. G., 189

Dunn, John Henry, 147

Durham's Report: on wild land tax, 151, on election of 1836, 187; on land as imperial capital, 221; imperfections of report on land system, 221, 230–1, 234–5; overemphasizes Clergy Reserves, 223–4; recommendations not implemented, 224–5; ignores discontent over Canada Co., 225; fails to do Colonial Office justice, 229–30; proposes local government bodies with taxing powers, 236; on squatters, 263, 289-90. See also Buller, Wakefield

EASTERN TOWNSHIPS, 12, 238

Economic conditions: 1818-20, 114–6, 222; 1836, 189; 1846-9, 270; 1848-52, 285

Egremont, Lord, 4

Elections: of 1808, 83; of 1812, 84; of 1820, 114; of 1834, 182, 183, 174; of 1836, 186–8, 189

Elgin, Lord, 97, 272, 297

Ellice Edward, 236, 305

Elliott, Mathew, 44

Ellis, Henry, 4

Elmsley, John: on Smith, 44; on the Assembly,

44; on American speculators, 46; on land fees, 47, 63; ideas compared with Wakefield's, 48; on auction system, 50; on land certificates, 56; on Heir and Devisee Commission, 57–8; on S. Jarvis, 70; on settlement duties, 126–7; and leasing system, 163–4

Elmsley, John Jr., 133, 187

Elora Backwoodsman, 291

Executive Council: on township grants, 40–2, 44, 45, 46; on a sales policy, 46, 50, 67; on fees, 47, 63; and confirmation of transferred certificates, 53, 55; advises suspension of land-granting, 67–8; and claims of U.E. loyalists, 65, 76; and American settlers, 66, 121; petitions for land for members of, 66; dominated by Elmsley, 70; disputes with Military Settling Department, 88, 90; membership of overlaps Legislative Council, 108; criticized by Gourlay, 114; criticizes Talbot, 127; on collection of fees, 130, 131; and speculation, 133; and U.E. rights, 134–5; and settlement duties, 137; and election of 1836, 187

FAMILY COMPACT, 157

Family Lands, 15, 19, 20

Fees: early grants free of, 15, 21, 52, 62; table of patent fees adopted, 27–8, 45, 52, 62; survey fee imposed, 45–6, 70; land officers' share of, 27–8, 48, 323, n. 61; half fees, 52, 62–6, 70, 71, 73; on certificates exchanged for patents, 53, 54, 57, 58; additional fees, 45–8, 70, 73, 76, 80, 153–4; unpaid fees, 70, 128, 130–1, 171; attempts to expedite collection of, 70, 76, 126, 130–1; protests against, 75, 76, 78, 83; regulation by statute demanded, 80, 81; reduced in special locations, 155; land forfeited for non-payment of, 265; time for payment of extended, 281

Fiats, 138, 334, n. 119

Finlay, Hugh, 17, 18, 22, 125

Fisheries, 1, 2, 3, 7, 13

Florida, 4, 5, 6, 13

Flour: contract for, 35–6; as a staple, 36; export of, 114

Forfeited lands, 265–6, 270

Fowler, Captain George, 90

Fox, Charles James, 197

France, 3, 50

French Canadians and proclamation of 1763, 5; and proposed Assembly, 6; dislike of free and common socage, 7–8; expanding population of, 12

French royalists, 50, 87, 320, n. 66

Friends of Civil and Religious Liberty, 215

Frontier: effects of, 78, 180, 229

GAGE, General Thomas, 9

Galt, Alexander Tilloch, 296

Galt, John: arranges sale of Crown Reserves to Canada Co., 167–8; attitude of Mait-

land to, 168; view on social structure of Upper Canada, 182; arranges sale of Clergy Reserves to Canada Co., 201–3; misinterprets amendment to Canada Co. bill, 205–6; reaches agreement on Huron Tract, 205; criticizes sales system, 173

Gaspé, peninsula of, 7, 8, 12

Gay, Edwin F., 305

Geddes, Andrew, 293

George, Henry, 117

Georgia, 7, 124

Gibson, David, 297

Gladstone, William Ewart, 249

Glebes: Haldimand makes reserves for, 27; Bathurst wishes to retain reserves for, 201; to be leased like Clergy Reserves, 206–7; Huskisson orders retention of land for, 210

Glenelg, Lord: delays decision on land rights, 136, 139; plans revision of land system, 139; on seventh report on grievances, 186; on casual and territorial revenues, 189–90; promises province shall determine land policy; 189–91, 245

Goderich, Lord: condemns land-granting system, 179; changes in land-granting system made by, 179; on assistance to indigent immigrants, 179–80; assents to five-acre allotments, 181

Godley, J. R., 271–2

Gore, Sir Francis: arrival of, 75, 77, 324, n. 2; policies of, 78, 79, 80, 81; attempts to allay discontent, 79; and control of provincial revenues, 79, 80–3, 156; has Thorpe and Wyatt removed, 83; goes on leave, 84; grants Crown Reserves, 87; 161; is censured, 162; opposed to assisted immigrants, 87; disputes with Military Settling Department, 87–90; opposed to receiving British immigrants via the U.S., 92; issues circular on oath of allegiance, 100; prorogues legislature, 101; goes home, 90, 102; on militia grants, 105; criticized by Gourlay, 105, 106, 107, 114; rescinds settlement duties for favoured persons, 126; advice to Powell, 147; criticizes land system, 152

Goulburn, Henry, 88

Gourlay, Robert: discontent previous to arrival of, 101, 103; plans *Statistical Account*, 103; queries and answers to his questionnaire, 104, 107, 116, 117, 167; opposition of Strachan to, 104–5; *First Address* of, 103–5; on exclusion policy, 105, 106, 107; on militia grants, 105, 107; *Second Address* of, 105–7; attacks Land Board and Executive Council, 107–8; on war losses, 106, 107; advocates sale of Crown Reserves, 107, 117, 167; *Third Address* of, 108; Convention organized by, 109–10; township meetings of, 109, 110, 112; arrested and acquitted, 111; arrested and convicted under Alien and Sedition Act, 112, 330, n. 101; leaves province disillusioned, 112–5; analyzes troubles of province, 114–9; compared with Henry George, 117; proposes creation of emigration fund from sale of Crown land, 117–8; and Wakefield, 119, 179; views on alien question, 119; compared with Richards, 178; advocates wild land tax, 107, 117–8, 144, 150

Gowan, Ogle R., 249, 292

Graham, Gerald S., 13

Grant, Alexander: on magistrates' certificates, 59; on Hunter, 74; becomes Administrator, 324, n. 2; troubles of, 75, 76, 77

Grant, William, 54

Grass, Michael, 14

Great Britain: colonizing policies of, 4–6, 9–10, 11, 13, 16–18, 152; and Canada–Guadeloupe controversy, 3; attitude in towards Upper Canada, 115–18, 121; view of Crown lands, 152, 221, 303

Greely, Aaron, 40, 44

Grenada, 5

Grenville, W. W., 26, 119, 160

Grey, Earl, 97

Grey, Sir George, 271–4

Guadeloupe, 3

HAGERMAN, C. K., 193, 217, 223, 241

Hagerman, Daniel, 150

Haldimand, Frederick: on locating loyalists, 11–16; on late loyalists, 16; instructions to, 15, 21–2; renounces land fees, 62

Halifax, Lord, 5, 6

Halifax currency, 70

Hall, Basil, 95

Hamilton, Henry, 11, 12, 14, 16

Hamilton, Dr. Morgan, 292

Hamilton, Robert: land acquisitions of, 50; and exchange of certificates, 54, 59; and Heir and Devisee Act, 58; and flour contract, 36

Hanson, R. Davies, 69

Hawke A. B.: Assembly asks dismissal of, 181; testifies on Colborne's policies, 184–5; advice on land act of 1837, 190–1; on land policy, 258, 262

Hay, Henry, 16

Head, Sir Francis: arrival of, 186; and election of 1836, 186–8; asks for free hand in land policy, 189; cautioned by Glenelg, 190; denounces Assembly's report on land policies, 191; *Narrative* of 192; and land act of 1837, 193; calls Reformers republicans, 186, 194; on rectory patents, 215; efforts to settle clergy reserves question, 217

Heir and Devisee Commission: created by act of 1797, 56; Powell dislikes, 57–8; functioning of, 60–1; and Act of 1802, 59, 74; and act of 1805, 59–60; work of anticipated, 72; proof of settlement duties evaded under, 135

Hemp, 7, 78, 127

Higham C. S., 5

Hillsborough, Lord, 5, 6, 8, 9, 10, 312, n. 29 and 55

Hincks, Francis: on Clergy Reserves, 244, 250, 254–5; on district councils, 237, 275; on land act of 1841, 270; on financing railways, 274; programme of financial reform of, 275; advocates American land system, 275

Hincks–Morin administration, 284, 287, 288, 295

Hodgetts, J. E., on Wakefield, 273

Holland, Samuel, 16, 18

Holland Land Co., 169, 305

Homesteads, 15, 302, 307

Howard, Peter, 77, 83

Hunter, General Peter: arrival of, 67, unpopular policies of, 67–71, 73–4, 78–9; historians on, 67, 71; has U.E. lists revised, 68; and U.E. rights, 71; forced issue of patents under, 72–3; fees of overestimated, 72; attempts to hasten payment of fees, 76; unauthorized use of revenue by, 76–7; sabotaged settlement duty requirements, 126; death of, 75, 324, n. 2; doggerel on, 324, n. 86

Hurd, S. P., 135–6

Huron Tract, 205, 269, 279, 281

Huskisson, William, 207

IMMIGRATION
imperial policies, 85–6, 91–2, 94–5. See also Military settlements and Irish immigration
provincial policies, 92, 120–1, 123, 124. See also Americans, exclusion policy

Ingersoll, Thomas, 40

Indians; uprisings feared, 9, 14, 15, 33, 34, 46; complaints of, 49; purchases from, 49–50, 87, 88, 89, 149, 152, 158, 259; payments from Military Chest for, 157, 159

Indian Department, 14, 48–9

Irish immigrants: the pilot project, 95; the Robinsons share in, 95; location and terms of settlement of, 95–6; location compared with Perth and Lanark settlements, 327, n. 85; degree of success, 96–7; cost of settlement, 97–8; Grey's proposals for, 271–2

Islands: Bois Blanc, 14; Cape Breton, 3, 12; Carleton, 11: Hog, 11

JACKSON, John Mills, 83, 322, n. 29

Jackson, President Andrew, 171

Jameson, Robert S., 188

Jarvis, William, 68, 70, 73, 187

Jefferson, Thomas, 303

Johnson, Sir John, 15, 16, 18, 22

Joseph, John, 187

Justices of the Peace: issue land certificates, 29; hear claims to the distinction U.E., 62, 76; name district treasurers, 336, n. 66; impose special assessments, 143; impose county rates, 144; proceeds of tax sales paid to, 151; appointed justices a grievance, 100, 151; election provided for, 184; in Huron Tract, 343, n. 70

KEEFER, Thomas Coltrin, 298
Kepler, James, 147
Kentucky, 25, 26
King's College, 169, 208, 209
Kingsford, William, 74, 113
Kirby, William, 188
Knox, William, 9, 10, 13, 22, 196

LABOUR: effect of free grant policy on supply of, 18; use of Queen's Rangers in lieu of, 28; Elmsley on land policy and supply of, 47; Gourlay on same, 117–18; Goderich on, 179–80; Colborne's views on supply of and market for, 180; Hawke on, 191; Wakefield on, 233; Sydenham, on market for, 257–8
Lanark: see military settlements
Land boards: created by Dorchester, 19; duties of, 19, 22, 125; of Hesse, 35, 61; of Mecklenburg, 21, 125; of Nassau, 20, 21; Simcoe's land boards, 29, abolished, 30; and late loyalists, 29; re-established by Maitland, 124; issue settlement duty certificates, 130; abolished, 130
Land certificates: unlocated, 48, 58; an obstacle to issue of patents, 51–2, 222; Cartwright's proposals for exchange of, 53; La Rochefoucauld on, 54; legal questions involved in, 55–7; transferred certificates, 53, 55–6, 58–9. See also, Heir and Devisee Commission, Magistrates' certificates
Land classification: need of realized, 298, 300, 302
Land Committee of Council
    Upper Canada: criticized by Convention, 109, by Gourlay, 107–8, by Maitland, 124
    Quebec: 17, 18, 19, 20, 22, 125
Land grievances, 109, 112, 116, 123, 206–10
Land Officers, 136, 153–4
Land policies
    under imperial regulations
        Free grant system: initial policies and purpose of, 25, 28; imperial instructions on, 15, 27, 28; maximum grants, 27, 46, 48; compared with U.S. policies, 28; additional fees on, 46–7; under regulations of 1763, 6–7; of 1771, 8–9; of 1783, 15–16, 22; of 1791, 27–8; of 1815, 124; of 1820, 153–4; favouritism and inefficiency under the system, 78–9, 80, 83, 84, 109, 123, 124, 226, 230; criticisms of the system, 152–5; actual cost of "free" grants, 154; limited application of system, 154, 170–1; objections to termination of, 170–1; forbidden by Act of 1837, 257; illegally instituted by Sydenham on colonization roads, 257–60; authorized by Act of 1841, 262. See also Colonization roads, Fee system, Settlement duties, U.E. U.E. rights

sales system: revenue policy proposed, 45–7, 62–3, 67; sales at auction proposed, 48; postponed, 50; trial of, 50–1; sales system adopted in 1826, 152, 170–1, 173; Talbot's objections to, 171; exceptions to the system, 171; valuations, prices, and terms of sale, 172; auction and credit system, 172; defects of, 174; compared to American system, 173; Glenelg abolishes credit system, 192
    under provincial legislation
        Land Act of 1837: Committee report on, 191; Head's objections to, 191–2; provisions of, 192–3, 257; compared with New Brunswick Act, 193; further speculation, 193; votes on, 192, 193; criticisms of, 193–5; Head's share in framing act, 192, 193; method of citation, 194; life of extended, 235, 349, n. 4; ignored by Durham and Wakefield, 234
        Land Act of 1841: provisions of, 257, 263–4, 266; cash sale regulations under, 264–7; provincial criticisms of, 368, 370; amended by Act of 1849, 281; credit system restored, 285; act repealed, 284
        Land Act of 1853, 284, 294
        Land Act of 1860, 301
    See also, Colonial Land and Emigration Commission, Colonization roads, Scrip, Sydenham, Legislative Assembly
Land Policies: estimate of, 303–7
Land Warrants, 68, 139, 334, n. 119
La Rochefoucauld, 24, 28, 29, 31, 37, 54, 315, n. 8, 413, n. 98
Leaders and associates
    in Lower Canada, 39, 40, 47; in New York State, 39
    in Upper Canada, 48; use of assignments by, 286. See also Township grants
Legislative Assembly of Upper Canada: restricted powers regarding Crown lands, 24; attempts to legislate on Crown Lands, 24–5, 81; executive control of Crown lands, 36; members bribed, 78, 109; payment of members, 143–4; hostile to assisted immigration, 176–7, 182; seventh report on grievances, of, 182, 186; role of ignored by Durham, 230
Letter addressed to Two great men, 3
Letters from an American Loyalist, 78, 81
Lieutenants of Counties, 29
Lindsey, Charles, 205, 244
Liston, Robert, 41
Locations: difficulty of obtaining, 68; special, 170–1; process of obtaining, 334, n. 119
Location Tickets: form of, 125, 134; voting on, 176, 177, 188, 189
Lount, Samuel, 136, 181, 182, 187, 188
Lower Canada: and Proclamation of 1792, 28, 31; township grants in, 31, 39, 40, 43, 46, 47; land fees in, 47; reserves in, 51
Loyalists
    Original: at military posts, 11; in seigneuries, 12; in the Maritimes, 13; Haldi-

mand's plans for, 12; and Quebec Act, 13; in Cataraqui township, 14, 15; on the St. Lawrence, 15; size of grants to, 15, 19; and seigneurial tenure, 22–3, 53; and episcopacy, 30; attitude to late loyalists, 29, 31, 154; to French royalists, 87, 154; and township grants 42, 46; attitude to British immigrants, 154; to Americans, 38, 85, 98–9

Late: 16-20, 47, 119

U.E.: origin of distinction, 20–1; scrutiny of lists of, 66, 68, 79; grievances of, 62, 65, 68, 69, 78–80, 82, 83, 222, 323, n. 57

Lumbermen: conflicting interests of settlers and, 297–300; opposed to cash sale, 298–9

MABANE, Adam, 16, 18, 19

Macaulay, John: on tax sales of land, 150; on Parish Officers Act, 184; on legislature of 1836, 194–5; on use of revenues, 232; on district councils, 236

Macaulay, Sir James Buchanan, 71

MacDonald, Archibald, 183

Macdonald–Sicotte administration, 293

McDonnell, Alexander, 147

McDonnell, Angus, 44, 99

McDougall, William, 293

McGill, John: and flour contract, 36; revises U.E. lists, 68; unpopularity of, 82; and Assessment Act, 147; advice to Mrs. Simcoe, 149

McGregor, Colin, 40

Mackenzie William Lyon: criticizes Canada Co., 226, 289; on election of 1836, 187, 188; on executive's control of revenues, 228; on voting on location tickets, 176–7; on pauper immigration, 177–8; obtains grievance committee, 182; on wild land tax and tax sales, 151; supported by American settlers, 121; and Thorpe, 78; on validity of official reports, 232

McLeod, Donald, 137–8, 151

MacNab, Allan Napier, 193

MacNab–Morin administration, 296

Magistrates' certificates, 29-30, 41, 58–9, 66

Maitland, Sir Peregrine: on Crown Reserves, 92, 162, 167; on Irish immigrants, 96–7; and Convention of 1818, 110–11, 118; and Gourlay, 112, 113, 118; characteristics of, 123; on settlement duties, 131, 142; and taxation of wild land, 142, 146, 147; dislikes Powell, 147; on free grant system, 124, 153; makes grants to paupers, 153; explains increased fees, 153–5; and assembly's efforts to control revenues, 156–7, 162; favours sales policy, 167; on sale to Canada Co., 168

Mallory, Benajah, 77, 78, 93, 99

Markle, Henry, 99

Marshall, Captain, 95

Martin, Alexander, 131

Martin, Chester, 3, 221

Maseres, Francis, 7

Mathews, Major Robert, 43

Melish, John, Travels, 193

Merchants: relations with Simcoe, 34, 35, 51, 53; influence of, 35, 78; on slavery, 35; acquire wealth in land, 43–4, 148; on exchange of certificates, 53–5; and Heir and Devisee Commission, 56–7, 60

Merritt, William Hamilton: wants aliens to be allowed to hold land, 121–2; objects to Act of 1837, 193; regards land as provincial capital, 276; opposed to free grants and to scrip, 279; becomes President of Council, 280; wants land managed on contract, 279, 282; obtains common school endowment, 281; leaves government, 282; opposes credit system, 284

Methodists, 208, 209, 243

Military Chest, 52, 64, 73, 89, 116, 130, 155, 157, 158, 227

Military grants: as of 1763, 7; as of 1783, 15–16, 314, n. 64; limited in 1797, 62; unlocated, 62; grievances of claimants to, 69, 75, 79; in military settlements, 86; value of, 152; and sales system 171–2, 193; value to commuted pensioners, 187. See also Military settlements.

Military settlements (Perth and Lanark): grants and assistance to soldiers and immigrants to, 86, 89; delays in locating, 86–8; Gore's disputes with governor-in-chief over, 86–91; arrival of unassisted Scottish immigrants in, 89, 91; use of Crown Reserves for, 88–9; Scottish hand weavers assisted to emigrate to, 91; degree of success of settlements, 92–4; conflict of Scots with later Irish immigrants, 95

Militia grants: not promptly made, 98, 101, 109, 116; Gore's recommendations on, 105; denied to members of Convention, 113; location of, 124, 131; factors affecting value of, 131; acquired by speculators, 132; restrictions imposed on by Colborne, 133; cash compensation proposed for, 133; Assembly's complaints regarding, 134; compared to U.S. military bounties, 134; failure of Colborne's regulations on, 135; abolition of settlement duties on, 137; sales system not to interfere with, 171; provisions of Act of 1837 on, 193. See scrip Minorca, 403, n. 22

Missisaugas, 11, 14, 50, 126, 127

Moneylenders, 268

Morin, Augustin Norbert, 284, 296

Morris, William, 200

Morton, Lord, 311, n. 10

Mountain, Bishop J. G., 163, 198, 200, 204

Murray, Sir George, 178

Murray, Governor James, 5, 7, 8, 124

NATURALIZATION ACT: see Aliens

New Brunswick, 3, 13, 190, 192

New England: township system, 6, 30, 100;

town meetings of, 178
New Hampshire, 7
New South Wales: land system of, 171; government assistance to religious denominations in, 219
New York Association, 40
New York State: colonial land regulations of, 7; common school fund in, 278; Genessee country in 43, 103, 129
Niagara Gleaner, 134
Niagara Spectator, 104, 107, 108, 112
Nichol, Robert, 101, 117, 147
Non-residents: taxation of, see Assessment and Road Acts
North, Lord, 10, 12
North American Colonial Association, 271
Nova Scotia, 4, 5, 6, 10, 13, 14, 18

O'CALLAGHAN, Edmund Bailey, 188, 194
Oath of allegiance, 21, 22, 28, 98, 100, 101, 112, 119, 120, 124, 328, n. 18
Orders-in-council (for land): unlocated, 70, 78, 87, 139
Osgoode, William, 40, 56
Overseers of highways: elected, 100; abolished, 151

PAPINEAU, Denis-Benjamin, 287
Papineau, Louis Joseph, 189
Parish Officers Act, 184
Park Lots, 27
Parliament, imperial: declaration of supremacy of, 21–2, 28. Patents: delays in issuing, 52, 71; omission of clergy specifications in, 54–5; exchange of certificates for, 52; fees on, 54; compared with American system, 72; issuance of and elections, 72, 176; attempts to expedite issue of, 72; privileged, 73; removal of restrictions in, 263
Pennsylvania, 96
Pensacola, 26
Pensioners: commuted, 187
Perry, Peter, 111, 136, 188, 214
Peters, Rev. Samuel, 30
Pickering, Timothy, 305
Pierpont family, 305
Pitt, William, 142, 196
Pontiac: uprising of, 4, 14
Portland, Duke of, 45, 48, 50, 63, 64, 67, 71, 161, 163
Posts, military: Niagara, 11, 32, 34; Carleton Island, 11, 15; Cataraqui, 14; Detroit, 11, 12, 32, 34, 35; surrender of western, 33, 34; expenses of, 33, provisioning of, 35–6
Powell, William Dummer: and Quebec Act, 13; member commission of Inquiry, 17; Judge of Court of Common Pleas, 17; and township grants, 42, 44; and exchange of certificates, 53, 54; and Heir and Devisee Commission, 57–8; on claims of loyalists, 62; on Hunter, 71; on unauthorized use of revenue, 76; frames

Act of 1795, 98; and Gourlay, 104, 111, 112; and anti-Convention Bill, 111; and Alien and Sedition Act, 113; on Talbot, 128; opposes Assessment Act, 147; on free grant system, 153; on leasing reserves, 163; on poll tax, 166–7
Pownall, John, 4
Prairies, 260, 302
Pre-emption: and Talbot's system, 171; effect on land sales, 402. See also squatters
Presbyterians: and claim to a share of clergy reserves, 196–7, 200, 208–12; glebes for, 207; and rectory patents, 216; and "settlement" of 1840, 240
Prescott, Governor Robert, 41, 47, 48, 50, 67
Prevost, Sir George, 85, 87
Prince, John, 121, 122, 268
Pringle, J. W., 236
Privileged grants, 52. See also U.E., military, and militia grants.
Proclamation of 1763, 4–7, 11
Public domain: regarded as a source for royal bounties, 45; as imperial capital, 152, 221, 303; as provincial capital, 270, 277; as security for railway loans, 277; as endowment for schools, 270, 277
Puisaye, Comte de, 50. See also French royalists

QUAKERS, 28, 31
Quebec, old province of, British government's plans for colonizing, 3–5; suggested division of, 3; assembly proposed for, 3, 5–6; addition of Indian reserve to, 10, 11; land policies for, 6–10; loyalist question in, 18; petitions for land in, 30
Quebec Act, 9, 10, 13, 22
Queen's Rangers, 28, 30, 33–5, 316, n. 29
Quit rents, 7, 8, 9, 22, 23, 46, 80, 96, 142, 161, 172, 173, 315, n. 82 and n. 87

RADENHURST, John, 135, 136, 230
Radicals: demands of, 75, 78, 82, 99–100; led by Willcocks, 77; and United Irishmen, 77; on Colonial Tax Repeal Act, 82; and elections of 1808, 83; discredited by War of 1812, 84, 100; objectives after 1815, 98, 100; leaders of, 101. See also Reformers
Railways: proposals for building with immigrant labour, 272–4; proposed change in timber duties to help finance, 274; Balwin–LaFontaine government offers land in aid of, 274; Hincks Guarantee Act, 274; land grants for, 302
Randal, Robert, 150
Rankin, Charles, 94
Rebellion of 1837: reveals influence of American ideas, 121; discredits pro-American party, 122; Colborne warned of possibility of, 180; precipitating causes of, 224; declaration of Toronto Reformers, 224; rebels promise clergy lots to squatters, 224; and Canada Co. lots free to

settlers, 226; and grievances related to, 227

Rectories: and clause 36 and 38, of Constitutional Act, 197, 200; creation and endowment of authorized, 215, 256–7; effect on election of 1836, 215–16; legality of disputed, 216–17, 345, n. 157; as precipitating cause of Rebellion, 224

Reformers: favour admission of Americans, 122; on U.E. rights, 137; detest Canada Co., 174, 175; want provincial control of Crown lands, 174; want elective institutions and religious equality, 183; regarded as republicans by Head, 186; criticize Land Department, 186; and election of 1836, 189; attitude to immigrants from Great Britain, 223; democratic faith of, 229

Reserves: for military purposes, 6, 27; as townsites, 7, 27; for clergy, 7; for schoolmasters, 7; for public purposes, 27, 160; of masting timber, 6, 263; of base metals, 263. See also School lands, Clergy Reserves, Crown Reserves

Revenues of Upper Canada: sources of, 82; Assembly demands to control all, 75–80, 82–3, 111–12, 119, 156, 157; reduced Imperial assistance to, 155, 165–6, 200, 227; sale to Canada Co. assists, 169. See also Casual and Territorial Revenue, Customs duties, Military Chest Richards, John: investigates land system, 178–80

Richardson, John, 241

Richey, Wellesley, 187

Riddell, William Renwick, 112, 113

Ridout, George, 83

Ridout, Thomas, 87

Roads: allowances for, 27; Dundas St., 32, 37, 126; Yonge St., 32, 37, 127; proposed sale of Crown lands for, 81; Talbot Roads, 128–9; Kempenfeldt Rd., 155; Long Woods Rd., 155; in Mohawk Tract, 155; Lake Simcoe to Ottawa Rd., 155

Road Acts: of 1793, 111, 143; of 1810, 145, 335, n. 10; of 1819, 145–6; of 1824, 151. See also statute Labour

Robertson, William, 35

Robinson, John Beverley: proposes assisted Irish emigration, 95; advises Gourlay's arrest, 111; denounces Gourlay in Assembly, 118; on alien question, 119; on American immigration, 120; opposes speculators in U.E. rights, 133; plan for sale of Crown Reserves, 166, 200; on Canada Co., 168, 169, 206; and proposed sale of clergy reserves, 204; on clergy reserves as obstacle to settlement, 210; and proposed district Councils, 236; on Sydenham's methods, 241; on squatters, 295

Robinson, J. Luke, 292

Robinson, Peter: in charge of Irish immigrants, 95–7; appointed Commissioner of Crown Lands, 172; manages sale of Clergy Reserves, 210; unsettled accounts of, 228

Roblin, David, 296

Rocheblave, Pierre de, 32

Rogers, David McGregor, 77, 82, 83, 84, 88, 98, 99

Russell, Andrew: on American land system, 297; on land classification, 298; on need to acquire Canadian West, 299

Russell, Peter: appointed receiver-general, 26; opinion of Simcoe, 26, 35, 39; temperament of, 39; views on settlement, 39; and forfeited townships, 39–45; and problem of patents, 51, 55–7; and problem of land revenue, 45, 47–8; and Six Nations, 49–50; on U.E. rights, 63, 65; Hunter's estimate of, 65; grants made by, 65, 66–7; attitude on fees, 67, 70; suggested general land tax, 142

Ryerson, Egerton, 14

St. Ours, Paul Roch de, 18

Sandon, Viscount, 196

School Lands
    common: no endowment prior to Union, 277, 279; repeated Assembly requests for, 277; legislative appropriation for, 277–8; one million acres reserved for, 281–2; Crown land revenues appropriated to, 282; sales of school land, 282, 401
    grammar: townships reserved for, 277; early cash sales of suspended, 277; endowment reduced, losses compensated for, 278; sales of, on credit, 278; after Union, 279, 282, 401

Scrip: issued for U.E. and militia rights, 140–1; diminishes land revenues, 280, 283; the Lower Canada militia scrip "job", 280; extension of restrictive dates on issue and utilization of, 266, 280, 281, 282, 301; quantity issued, 283; fraudulent issues, 283; usable on credit purchases, 285; not usable in purchase of common school land, 281; compensatory scrip, 284, 301

Secord, David, 99

Selkirk, Lord: observation of, 42; conditions of grant to, 127; Strachan's criticisms of, 127; and Assessment Act of 1803, 143; and township of Dover, 339, n. 10

Settlement duties: required, 7, 21; indefinitely expressed, 27; on magistrates' certificates, 59; delay patenting of land, 71; certificates of duty done, 72; in military settlements 93; advocated by Buchanan, 123; early requirements ineffective, 125; Yonge St. conditions, 125–6; enforced on Talbot roads, 127–9; Maitland impose on all grants, 130; requirements reduced, 130; false certificates for, 130, 265; delay payment of fees, 130–1; effect on U.E. and militia rights, 131–2; value of questioned, 132; Colborne's efforts to enforce, 132–9; policy of sabotaged, 136–7; surveyors' land free of, 158; U.E. and militia claims freed of, 193; required on Elergy Reserves, 211–14; required on 50-acre free grants, 264; time extended for, 281; required under credit system, 285; modified, 287; dispensed with, 293, reimposed, 294, 300; enforcement left to executive discretion, 301

Simcoe, John Graves: advises free and common socage tenure, 23; and American Revolution, 25–7; his five-year plan, 25–6, 37–8; instructions to, 27–8, 125; views on land policy, 28; and late loyalists, 28–9; land regulations of, 29–30; makes township grants, 30–2; settlement policies of, 32, 35; plans Yonge and Dundas St., 32; criticized by merchants, 34; and by Council, 35; and dispensing power, 317, n. 88; and slavery, 35; and legislature, 35, 36, 53, 55, 62; plans for a staple, 35–6; circumstances of departure, 38; his proclamation of 1792, 39–40; and free grant system, 45; on fees, 39–40, 62; opposes sales system, 46; suggests quit rents, 46–7; and Six Nations, 49; and patent problems, 51–2; and U.E. rights, 63; large grants made by, 66–7; favours general land tax, 142–3; and Crown Reserves, 161, 163, 164; and Clergy Reserves, 196

Six Nations: cession by at Niagara, 11; effects Treaty of 1783 on, 12, 14; settled on Bay of Quinte, 14; and Grand River, 14; disputes with government, 49; nature of title granted, 50; sales by, 50; 313, n. 8

Shade, Absalom, 279
Shelburne, Lord, 5, 22
Sherbrooke, Sir John, 89, 90–1
Sherriff, Patrick, 170
Sherwood, Henry, 244, 249
Slavery, 35
Smith, David William: disputes La Rochefoucauld, 25, 29; on magistrates' certificates, 30; and township promotors, 40, 44; on value of land, 51; devises chequered plan, 51; plans for children of loyalists, 64, 73; on American precedents, 100; rebuked by Russell, 116; on settlement duties, 126; on a general land tax, 142; plan for leasing reserves, 163

Smith, Colonel Samuel, 90, 98, 102, 105, 106
Smith, Sir William, 16, 26, 39, 40, 52, 161
Smith, Thomas, 35
Society for the Propagation of the Gospel, 155, 196, 204, 246, 248, 249
Sovereign, Philip, 99
Spain, 25, 26, 37, 49
Speculation: attempts to prevent, 7, 28, 124–5, 142; in township grants, 31, 40–1, 45, 52; Elmsley on, 46; in Indian lands, 46; in land board certificates, 54, 57–8, 60; in U.E. rights, 71, 131–3, 324, n. 117 and 125; in magistrates certificates, 116; Hawke on, 191

Speculators: and exclusion policy, 100, 101, 114, 116, 122; and settlement duties,

132–6, 294;· and assessment acts, 146, 239; prominent, 147, 150; and reformers, 190; abuse auction system, 174; quantity of land held by, 197, 276, 342, n. 11; and land act of 1837, 140, 239, 259; and district councils, 239; in 1861, 293

Spragge, J. B., 135–6
Spragge, William, 293, 296
Squatters: on Detroit frontier, 14; in loyalist settlements, 17; Dorchester's attempts to prevent, 19; on Indian land, 49; on Crown Reserves, 88, 161; abuse auction system, 174; on Clergy Reserves, 199, 211, 247; pre-emption privileges under Clergy Reserves Sales Act of 1827, 211; in Lower Canada under Durham's proclamation, 290; under Sydenham's regulations for sale of clergy reserves, 245; persistence and growth of practice, 253, 288, 290; Canada Co.'s treament of, 288–9; pre-emption rights recommended for, 263, 290; opposed by Sydenham, 263; protected at executive discretion, 264, 290; lenient treatment of, 291; squatter problems in Bruce, Huron, and Wellington counties, 291–3; report of Squatter Commission, 292; changing public attitude towards, 294; pre-emption privilege ended, 294, 300; effect on land sales, 310; failure of bills to protect squatter's improvements in Lower Canada, 294–5; Upper Canada opposition to such bills, 295; J. B. Robinson on squatters, 295; usefulness of, 305

Stanton, Robert, 183, 207, 208
Statute labour, 111, 118, 125, 146, 335, n. 10
Stephen, James, 200, 209, 210
Stevenson, Charles, 26
Strachan, Dr. John: on deserters, 85; and Irish immigrants, 96; opposes Gourlay, 101, 104–5, 107–8, 111, 198; wants appointment to Legislative Council, 102; criticized by Gourlay, 107–8; letter to Selkirk, 127; on sale of Crown Reserves, 166; criticizes Colborne, 184; propose creation Clergy Corporation, 198; suggests sale Clergy Reserves through, 200–1; opposes sale of Clergy Reserves to Canada Co., 201–5; opinion of Canada Co., 206; ecclesiastical chart of, 208, 209; on democracy, 209; fights re-investment, 213; on district councils, 236; appointed President of the General Board of Education, 278

Street, Timothy C., 286
Sullivan, Robert Baldwin: on land policy, 191, 245, 272–3; on investment of clergy funds, 218; appointed Commissioner of Crown Lands, 228; concern for poor immigrants, 259; opposed importation of Irish contract labour, 272; views compared with Wakefield's, 272-3; advocates settlement duties, 273; becomes a judge, 274

Surveys: methods of 27, 51, 316, n. 26; suspended under Hunter, 68; under Gore, 90; shortage of surveyed land, 68, 87, 89–90, 92, 154; paid for in land, 130, 157–8; cessation of in 1836, 244; American system for suggested and later adopted, 263; cessation of in 1862, 299

Surveyor General's Department: reports on township grants, 39; dilatoriness complained of, 88; sabotages Colborne's policies, 135–6; investigated, 230

Swayzie, Isaac, 99, 330, n. 101

Sydenham, Lord: on Wakefield, 235, 257–8; on wild land tax, 236; on control of casual and territorial revenues, 235; his Clergy Reserves bill, 240–2; political pressure used by, 241; anxious to retain immigrants, 258; on land policy, 262–4

Sydney, Lord, 22, 23

Symes, John C., 305

TALBOT, Edward Allen, 127, 162

Talbot Thomas: personal grant to, 127; criticized, 127; entrusted with supervising settlement in large area, 128–9; estimate of his work, 128–9; his pension, 129; unpaid fees of his settlers, 128, 131, 171; sales system not applied to Talbot settlement, 171; Richards' comment on, 171; and American pre-emption, 171

Tenures: free and common socage, 9, 10, 18, 22–3, 222; seigneurial, 7–9, 22, 125

Test Act, 6

Thomas v. Acklam, case of, 120

Thorpe, Robert: opinion of Hunter, 67, 323, n. 57, 324, n. 3; champions popular grievances, 75, 77–8; criticizes Gore, 79; supporters of, 81–2; dismissed, 83

Timber: stealing of, 85, 247, 294

Timber duties: imperial, 114, 115, 279

Tithes, 197, 206–7, 342, n. 13

Todd, Isaac, 73–4

Tories, 183, 188, 189, 190, 229

Towns and villages: Assumption, 27; Brockville, 89; Buffalo, 103; Chatham, 32, 34, 37; Cornwall, 85; Detroit, 32; Kingston, 32, 33, 34, 50, 85, 111, 122; Lanark, 93; Long Point, 32, 37; Niagara, 32, 112, 122; Newark, 37, 66; Perth, 89, 93, 103; Quenston, 33, 103, 105, 109, 112; Sandwich, 27; York (Toronto), 29, 32, 33, 34, 37, 50, 67, 104, 111, 122; London 25, 26, 32, 34, 37, 122

Town lots, 27

Town site, 27

Township: sales of, 300–1

Townships: Adelaide, 181, 187; Albion, 299; Alborough, 127; Alfred, 88; Ancaster, 126; Asphodel, 95; Augusta, 107; Bathurst, 89, 93; Beckwith, 89, 93, 126; Beverley, 126; Brock, 188; Burford, 128; Burgess, 93; Carradoc, 181; Cavan, 177; Cramahe, 44, 126; Dalhousie, 91, 94; Dereham, 50; Drummond, 89, 92; Douro, 95, 181; Dumfries, 101; Dummer, 181;

Dunwich, 187; Elmsley, 93; Emily, 95; Ennismore, 95; Glengarry, 85, 88, 122; Gosfield, 27; Goulburn, 93; Haldimand, 40, 45, 99, 126; Hamilton, 111; Hope, 44, 111, 126; Houghton, 277; Kingston, 269; Kitley, 89; Lanark, 91; Mara, 269; Markham 40, 126; Medonte, 181, 187; Minto, 291; Murray, 126; Niagara, 27; Nichol, 117; North Oxford, 126; North Sherbrooke, 91, 94; Norwich, 50, 51; Nottawasaga, 181; Ops, 95, 178, 181; Orillia, 181, 187; Oro, 181, 187; Otonabee, 95; Oxford, 40; Pembroke, 181; Percy 44, 126; Pickering, 126; Plantagenet, 88; Ramsay, 91, 93, 95, 96; Ross, 181; Scarborough, 126; Seymour, 88; Smith, 95; Southwold, 277; Stamford, 27; Stormont, 122; Sunnidale, 181; Warwick, 181; Westmeath, 181; Whitechurch, 126; Winchester, 126; Whitby, 65, 88; Yarmouth, 277

Township grants: and proclamation of 1792, 28, 39; by Simcoe to promoters, 30–1; monopoly of accessible land, 30; offends loyalists, 31; forefeiture of, 32, 39; terms misunderstood, 39–41; and attempted fraud and bribery, 39, 41; Russell makes settlement with nominees, 41–2, 66; Liston's suspicions of American promoters, 41; estimate of township method of settlement, 43; W. W. Baldwin on, 43; resentment of dispossessed promoters of, 44; Lower Canada's experience with, 41, 46; later government township promotion schemes, 178; later private schemes, 339, n. 10

Trade: exports and imports, 1808–20, 330, n. 112, 115

Trade and Navigation: instructions, 24

Treaties: of Paris (1763), 3, 14; Jay's (1795), 33; of San Lorenzo (1795), 38; of Paris (1783), 12, 14, 15, 16, 26, 119; Convention of 1818, 329, 68

Troops: Canadian Volunteers, 34; King's Royal Regiment of New York, 16; Eighty-fourth Regiment of Foot, 16, 69; Royal Artillery, 34. See also Queen's Rangers.

Tucker, R. G., 259

Turner, Frederick Jackson, 180

UNION, act of, 232, 256

U.E. rights: origin of, 20–1, 63–5; half fees on, 63–4; value of, 71–2; speculators in, 132–3, 333, n. 70, 334, n. 107; effect of settlement duty requirement on, 131–5; Colborne's policies on sabotaged, 134–6; Assembly requests removal of requirement, 131, 132, 134; Goderich's answer, 136; the Assembly's U.E. rights bill, 137; abolition of settlement duties on located rights, 137; results of, 137–9; clauses in Act of 1837 on U.E. rights, 140, 193; in Act of 1839, 141; in Act of 1841, 141, 266; land rights issued for, 140–1, 193;

scrip issued for, 266. See also Scrip

United Irishmen, 77, 83

United States: attractions of, 22; land system of, 22, 48; 167; 190–1; 207, 282, 298, 316, n. 27; Goderich on, 179; Head's criticism of, 192; Hawke on, 190–1; compared with Upper Canada system, 173, 231; not understood by Durham and Wakefield, 231; influence of democratic institutions of, 100, 121; Wakefield on economic influence of, 233; speculators in, 305, school reserves in, 277; annexation to discussed, 99, 100, 116; Upper Canada's attitude to, 116; plans to offset influence of, 85–6, 92–3

Upper Canada Gazette, 68, 83

Upper Canada Guardian, 83

VAN DIEMAN'S LAND: land system of, 171; government assistance to religious denominations, 218–19

Vankoughnet, P. M. M. S., 293, 300

Vermont, 30

Viger, Denis Benjamin, 280

Virginia, 36

WAKEFIELD, Edward Gibbon: author of Buller's Report, 221; imperfections of, 221, 222, 226, 229, 230; three-fold reform programme of, 229, 231–2; legal barriers to, 232; difficulties of implementing, 233–5; Russell's opinion of, 235; ideas of compared to Gourlay's, 119, 179; influence on Colonial Office, 267, 270; ideas unacceptable to Canadians, 239, 272–3

Wallace, William Stewart, 3

War of 1812; deserteurs during, 335, n. 4; effect on radicals, 84, 98, 100; leads to exclusion of American immigrants, 85,

100; promises to British troops serving in, 86; militia claims to land, 101, 109; losses during, 105, 106, 107, 109, 115, 117; economic effects of, 114–5; 330, n. 112 and n. 115

Warrants of survey: 68, 139, 334, n. 119

Washburn, Ebenezer, 77

Washington, President George, 25

Watson, George, 82

Wayne, Anthony, 33

Weekes, William, 75-6, 77, 79, 99

Whiskey Rebellion, 28

Wild Land Tax: Assembly attempts to impose, 145; Durham's proposal, 236; Pringle and Sydenham's proposal, 236. See also Assessment acts, Road acts, Buller, Gourlay, Maitland, Wakefield, District Councils, Speculators

Wilmot-Horton, Sir Robert John: and Irish emigration of 1823 and 1825, 95–6; and sale of Crown Reserves, 168; and quit rents, 172; and Clergy Reserves Sales Act of 1827, 207, 209; parish-assisted emigration scheme of, 176, 178

West, the Canadian: need of recognized, 299, 302; demand for homesteads in develops, 302

Withe, John, 53, 54, 55, 56

White, Johnathan N., 298

Widder, Charles, 292

Widder, Fred, 279, 301

Willcocks, Joseph, 77, 83, 84, 99

Willcocks, William, 50, 65

Williamson, Charles, 40

Willson, John, 83, 99

Wilmot, Samuel Street, 177

Wyatt, Charles, B., 83

YOUNG, H., 182